MUSCLEMAG INTERNATIONAL'S

ANABOLIC PRIMER

An Information-Packed Reference Guide To Ergogenic Aids For Hardcore Bodybuilders

By Phil Embleton and Gerard Thorne

Published by MuscleMag International
5775 McLaughlin Road
Mississauga, ON
Canada L5R 3P7

Designed by Jackie Kydyk
Edited by Mandy Morgan

10 9 8 7 6 5 4 3 2 Pbk.

Canadian Cataloguing in Publication Data

Embleton, Phil J., 1963-
    Musclemag International's anabolic primer: an
information-packed reference guide to ergogenic aids for
hardcore bodybuilders

Includes bibliographical references and index.

ISBN 1-55210-010-3

    1. Bodybuilding-- Physiological aspects. 2. Metabolism--
Effect of drugs on. 3. Dietary Supplements. I. Thorne,
Gerard J., 1963- II. Title. III. Title: Anabolic primer.

RC1220.W44E42 1998   646.7'5   C98-900213-6

Distributed in Canada by
CANBOOK Distribution Services
1220 Nicholson Road
Newmarket, ON
L3Y 7V1
800-399-6858

Distributed in the States by
BookWorld Services
1933 Whitfield Park Loop
Sarasota, FL 34243

Printed in Canada

WARNING

This book is not intended as medical
advice, nor is it offered for use in the
diagnosis of any health condition or
as a substitute for medical treatment
and/or counsel. Its purpose is to
explore advanced topics on sports
nutrition and exercise. All data are for
information only. Use of any of the
programs within this book is at the
sole risk and choice of the reader.

MUSCLEMAG INTERNATIONAL'S

ANABOLIC PRIMER

An Information-Packed Reference Guide To Ergogenic Aids For Hardcore Bodybuilders

Dedicated to the World's Greatest Fitness Trainer – Vince Gironda

He was called everything from the "Iron Guru" to "the world's greatest trainer." When Vince Gironda died on October 18, 1997 bodybuilding lost more than just another personality; it lost an enduring icon. We thought it appropriate to dedicate this book to Vince as he was endorsing supplements long before anyone heard of EAS, TwinLab, or MuscleTech.

Vince's death hit the MuscleMag family hard as his column "Wild Physique" was a regular staple of the magazine. In addition, he co-wrote the best-selling book Unleashing the Wild Physique *with* MuscleMag International *founder Robert Kennedy.*

Whether you thought of Vince as a contrary old sod, or trainer par excellence, few can argue the sport of bodybuilding lost one of its founding pillars.

So long Vince. We'll see you in heaven's version of Muscle Beach.

Robert Kennedy, editor
MuscleMag International

Acknowledgments

Few books are solely the work of the authors and this one is no exception. At the risk of omitting someone, the authors would like to thank the following people for their help in making this book possible.

To Jackie Kydyk and the staff at MuscleMag International, thanks for your expertise over the past few years. Your talents have brought our words to life.

Thanks to Robert Kennedy for giving us another opportunity to add to MuscleMag's growing library of publications. From its early beginnings in 1974, MuscleMag is now one of the premier bodybuilding and fitness publications in the world, and we're happy to be able to contribute in our own small way.

Our thanks to you all!
Phil Embleton and Gerard Thorne

About the Authors

Phil Embleton BSc, BA, BEd, was born in Sunderland, England and emigrated to Canada in the early 1960s. In 1980 he enrolled at Memorial University of Newfoundland, majoring in biology and psychology. While attending university he met his future writing partner, Gerard Thorne. They have written two books together, *Steroid Myths* and *MuscleMag International's Encyclopedia of Bodybuilding*. Phil currently resides in Cornwall, Prince Edward Island, with his wife and three children. Phil is currently employed with Haliburton Oil Industries.

Gerard Thorne, BSc, BEd, was born in St. John's, Newfoundland. Gerard has written for numerous publications including *MuscleMag International, Sharkhunters International* and *The Titanic Historical Society*. Along with Phil Embleton, Gerard has authored two previous books, *Steroid Myths* and *MuscleMag International's Encyclopedia of Bodybuilding*. An avid weight trainer for 15 years, he is currently the strength and conditioning consultant at the St. John's YM/YWCA.

Table of Contents

Foreword

Long before I became interested in bodybuilding, I had already begun a lifelong affair with books. My favorites were historical romances, particularly the Arthurian legends. I would rise early on a Saturday morning (though on school days my dad would have to roar several times), and sit by the banks of a nearby lake. While the morning mist rolled off the water I would visualize the Lady of the Lake arising out of every ripple. Like all young boys, I wanted to be magically transformed from a small lad to a massive hero! Invariably, I would return home to a delicious breakfast of fresh baked scones, and my mum would say, "Robert, the only thing that will change you is time; and God will let you decide if it's for the better."

Of course that simple piece of wisdom went in one ear and out the other. A few years later, as an avid reader of bodybuilding magazines, I came across an advertisement that claimed a certain breakfast cereal would turn me into a monument of muscle. Becoming bigger was an obsession at that point. No, schoolyard bullies generally left me alone, and I never did get sand kicked in my face. (Mind you, there was a friend of the family who used to come over to watch soccer and he would eat all of the sausage rolls that mum had made. For a growing teenager, there was no greater provocation! I just wanted to thump him so he'd lay off the sausages, a crime of passion if you will).

After saving my pennies, I made the discovery that despite the ingestion of several boxes of cereal, I was the same Bob (except I was far more regular and had two cavities from all the sugar I'd dumped on the stuff). The Lady of the Lake obviously did not work for Kelloggs!

As a bodybuilder and journalist, I have encountered articles on hundreds of potions, powders, and snake oils which claim to metamorphosize skinny nerds into walking pillars of muscle. Most are hype, but some have partial merit. There are also side effects, serious or benign, and possible legal consequences. I often feel I have somehow stumbled onto Merlin's fabled laboratory.

The staff at MuscleMag does not include a pharmacist, but with the way things are going that might change. More supplements hit the market every day, and our journalists are left to struggle through the information and come up with a balanced report for our readers. Would I print an article condemning a product advertised in *MuscleMag*? Yes! I've lost money before (for years it was a familiar feeling). When a magazine pushes it's own supplements there is no question that a conflict of interest arises. Advertising is a big part of our revenue, but without integrity we'd lose readers and be out of business.

But we're not out of business. Things are great! After we experienced the phenomenal success of *MuscleMag International's Encyclopedia of Bodybuilding*, we received some amazing letters. They were all constructive criticism, and many pointed out that while the book was comprehensive, ergogenic aids deserved a chapter of its own. I totally disagreed. I felt that it deserved a book of its own! Hence the volume you now hold in you hands, *MuscleMag International's Anabolic Primer*.

From preparations made in ancient times to creatine and MET-Rx – it's all here. For our politically sensitive readers, please remember that *MuscleMag International* is read throughout the world. Thus laws and culture vary accordingly. Obviously it would be foolish to have a beer in Saudi Arabia, or use anabolic steroids in Texas. If it is against the law to use a drug mentioned in this guide, obey the law! The freedom of information must be balanced by the wisdom to use it responsibly.

I hope you will be as entertained as I was, and find a supplement that is right for you.

Robert Kennedy,
publisher,
MuscleMag International

▶ Preface

This book can be considered a response to many of the comments we received concerning our previous work – *MuscleMag International's Encyclopedia of Bodybuilding*. Although the nutrition chapter was praised for its thoroughness, many readers felt the issue of ergogenic aids needed expanding. This is not surprising given the multitude of supplements that invade the market on a monthly basis. It seems a book is out of date almost as soon as it hits the store shelves!

Like most issues, supplement use has a broad grey area. This can range from legal issues and effectiveness to cost and safety concerns. Throughout the text we will, where applicable, address all four areas. For example, the chapter on hormonal manipulation contains, for the most part, drugs that are illegal in many countries. On the other hand, the chapter on vitamins is important as research indicates that these are perhaps the most widely used food supplements.

We have divided the text into "books," each containing three to four related chapters which cover the main categories of ergogenic aids. Unlike many books which simply list the supplement and what it does, we cover the whole spectrum, looking at everything from biochemistry and source, to mechanisms of action and legal issues. We also dive into an often-neglected area – health issues. We feel this is warranted, given the dosages that some bodybuilders are taking these days.

True to MuscleMag's philosophy of being unbiased, we attempt to evaluate the various supplements based on effectiveness. This may seem a contradiction given the amount of revenue generated by supplement advertising; however, we feel our readers must come first. If we believe that a given supplement is dangerous or a waste of money, we will say so. Conversely, if something looks promising than we will be the first to recommend it. This text is a guide to ergogenic aids, not a paid advertisement for supplement manufacturers.

Although some texts define ergogenic aids as substances other than drugs taken by athletes, we are going to include the whole spectrum of ergogenesis – both legal and illegal. We feel this is necessary given the array of substances out there. In addition, we look at a few techniques that, while not substances to be swallowed or injected, are nevertheless used by athletes to stay one step ahead of the competition. For example, most wouldn't consider hair care an ergogenic issue, but with the number of bodybuilders suffering steroid-induced hair loss, we feel it necessary to explore the various treatment options.

As a final word we must stress something mentioned earlier. Many of the supplements mentioned in this book are illegal. Anabolic steroid possession will get you hard jail time in the United States. Also, most sports organizations, such as the International Olympic Committee (IOC), have banned many of the substances described in the following pages. The onus is left to you, the reader: Be aware of the laws set down by your country and sports federation. If a drug is illegal avoid it like the plague. And while we question the policy of grouping steroid users with rapists and murderers, suffice to say, if you decide to use any of the supplements described in this book, check your country's laws beforehand. It's much more fun to pump iron at the local gym than in the prison courtyard.

Phil Embleton and Gerard Thorne

Bruce Patterson

Introduction

Τhis book, for the most part, is about nostrums, particularly where modern supplements are concerned; and few bodybuilding topics receive as much attention these days. It seems no iron pumper's gym bag is complete without the latest pill or powder. A trip to the local health-food store can mimic an African safari, and a flip through a recent issue of *MuscleMag International* often produces what could be termed "supplement sensory overload"!

While supplement advertisers are big on claims, many are particularly elusive on manufacturing processes and the data to support their positions. Ever since bodybuilding magazines first hit the market in the 1930s and early 1940s, products have been overhyped. One product advertised in *Ironman* magazine (March/April 1950) was a vitamin supplement that contained "compressed sunshine."

> **"The medical community's ignorance about steroids has also contributed to the steroid problem. Doctors tend to generalize about steroid side effects. That's like comparing the effects of codeine and heroine simply because they are both derivatives of opium."**
>
> – Sergio Oliveira, former steroid dealer and bodybuilder.

Lee Apperson

FILING A FALSE CLAIM!

Many false claims have been made about what food supplements can and cannot do, but, as P.T. Barnum said, "There's a sucker born every minute." By now bodybuilders are used to advertisers that claim their supplements can turn an average person into a Nasser El Sonbaty. Often the reader is left scratching his head, wondering, 'could it be true?' Many advertisers follow a practice that was perfected by Dr. Joseph Goebels (Nazi Minister of Propaganda) – if you tell a lie often enough, people begin to believe it. American supplement manufacturers have long used this form of manipulation.

Nasser El Sonbaty

Incredible tales (big fibs) of fantastic adventures, rivaling those of Indiana Jones, were part of the sales pitch right into the early decades of this century. One of the best was the one used by the sellers of the aphrodisiac, "Vital Sparks." The story went something like this: The Chinese nation was in serious peril. A mysterious ailment had rendered the men impotent! The most numerous race, the creators of a culture that had surpassed all others, the inventors of advanced technology and priceless works of art, were faced with immediate extinction. The Emperor responded to this crisis by offering a pricely fortune to anyone who could find a cure. Countless doctors and scientists tried, without success. All seemed lost, until the incredible discovery of He Tuck Chaw, wise man and explorer. During an expedition into a volcanic region, Chaw stumbled upon a rare variety of turtle, the Kup Ki See. This species was unusual because the females outnumbered the golden-striped males 1000:1. What could possibly be the source of the male turtle's stamina? Chaw worked relentlessly, until he found that the males alone possessed a small pouch, the Quali Quah, at the base of the brain. Chaw (who did not seem concerned how the remaining males would find the time to take up the slack) removed the Quali Quah pouches, dried and powdered them, and gave tiny portions to the Chinese people. The reaction was swift and effective. The nation was saved!

"Every medium prepared by a secret process and sold for the private advantage of an individual is a nostrum."

– Dr. John Ayerton Paris, British physician and author of the most comprehensive pharmacology text in his day, Pharmacologia, in 1820.[1]

Ronnie Coleman

An actress dressed in Oriental robes, presenting herself as "Princess Lotus Blossom," would conclude her mesmerizing story with this sales pitch: "There is, gentlemen, a sufficient quantity of this same substance in these Vital Sparks I am going to offer tonight to restore you to health, virility, and happiness."

Alas, as far as we know, Vital Sparks is no longer sold. But you can still make your own, using the original recipe. Using a desk drawer, fill it with buckshot candy. Add enough water to dampen, and mix in powdered aloes (yes, the stuff you sometimes find in soap and hand creams).[2] Better still, bottle the contents and sell it at an outrageous price. Why not? There are few regulations for dietary supplements. If you can't beat 'em, join 'em.

NO PRESCRIPTION THEREFORE . . .

Perhaps the most sobering aspect to supplement effectiveness is their ease of availability. In short, supplements would require a prescription if they were as effective as claimed. After all, a substance with strong biological properties, used in an unsupervised manner, can produce serious life-threatening effects. Does this mean if something is easily obtainable, it is useless? No, but you must exercise caution before ingesting something made from ingredients you are not familiar with and made under conditions you know little about. Always ask yourself, why am I taking this? What do I really know about it? Is this the answer to my prayers, or the beginning of my problems? Remember, if someone does something in secret, it is usually because they have something to hide.

WHY BODYBUILDERS?

Why do supplement manufacturers need bodybuilders? Simply because bodybuilding is a huge and growing market – the primary source of revenue for the supplement industry. Bodybuilding has become a cash cow, worth hundreds of millions annually. Gym equipment is generally a once in a lifetime purchase, clothing and memberships are purchased annually. The lion's share of money is provided via the daily consumption of supplements. The need for these supplements is created through advertising in bodybuilding magazines, which often depend on advertising revenue as much (if not more) than that generated by circulation. How much money is involved? A full-colour, multipage ad in *MuscleMag International* will set you back thousands of dollars, yet just look at the TwinLab and MET-Rx ads, and count the pages! Of course many of these manufacturers have been just as good to bodybuilding. They sponsor contests, pay bodybuilders for endorsements, and keep most of the bodybuilding magazines financially afloat. Bodybuilding is growing because the supplement industry helps finance it.

Roland Cziurlok

A FAMILIAR PRECEDENT

The next question becomes, why are bodybuilders such a lucrative market? After all, the medical community has been quite loud in dismissing the claims put forward by supplement manufacturers. Most doctors would say eat your wheaties and you'll be fine. The problem is that the medical associations lost credibility with bodybuilders years ago. Until the mid '80s, medical journals were carrying articles that dismissed muscle gains from anabolic steroid use. After 1988, articles began to appear claiming that steroids caused, among other false statements, liver cancer. Enough bodybuilders had either used steroids, or known people who had, who were still healthy to realize that the doctors didn't know what they were talking about.[3]

"MuscleMag has always taken a responsible and sensible approach to our coverage of steroid use among athletes. Rather than take a 'head in the sand' or 'this never happens' attitude, MuscleMag has always tried to give honest and factual information about steroids without actually advocating their use. To pretend that bodybuilders and athletes do not ever use steroids would be not only dishonest but also rather silly. Talking openly and honestly about steroid use does not mean we encourage bodybuilders to take steroids, any more than talking about birth control encourages sex. The way to get people to understand steroids – and to prevent abuse of steroids and other drugs – is through education, not through lies and fear tactics."

– Greg Zulak, former *MuscleMag* editor outlining MuscleMag's philosophy with regards to the complicated drug issue in modern bodybuilding.

Now that steroids are illegal substances in the United States and Canada, bodybuilders are looking for alternatives. And they're not looking to the medical community for answers.

Until the early '80s, supplement advertising was an experience in boredom. Weight-gain powders were sold in boxes, with block lettering and simple color schemes. As steroids became a media scandal, supplements changed in their packaging. They stopped looking like food and began to mimic pharmaceuticals. To further promote their cause, supplement manufacturers often advertise their products as "steroid replacers," and make frequent use of such eye-catching terminology as ANABOLIC, STEROID, HORMONAL, TESTOSTERONE, and METABOLIC.

The simple descriptions found on old labels were replaced with detailed biochemical assays. Advertisements now leave the reader befuddled with scientific terms. Plain English has been replaced by biochemical hyperbole. Even the articles appearing in bodybuilding magazines have become more technical in nature, and often appear with references. The

"The readers all want to look like me so they'll take anything. Listen, in the gym, if I start drinking Nestle's Quick, everyone will start drinking Nestle's Quick. If I started drinking Woolite, everyone would start drinking Woolite before long."

– Unknown IFBB Pro commenting on the "take anything available" mentality of many amateur bodybuilders.

Joe DeAngeles and Deborah Lynn Hunter

Gerard Dente

evolution of bodybuilding has been shaped by this experience. From the days of "all you can eat, all you can lift," we have now found ourselves carefully balancing the amino acids in our daily diets, and supplementing our creatine reserves. Has it all been necessary, or is it all a passing fad? Time will tell. Until then, bodybuilders continue to look for magic supplements that will make their muscles burst out; and the manufacturers will continue to sell any nostrum they can.

CATEGORIES OF ERGOGENIC AIDS

In the broadest sense, ergogenic aids are substances taken by athletes to improve athletic performance. The term ergogenic comes from the Greek *ergo* – to work, and *genesis* – the beginning.

Ergogenic aids may be in tablet, capsule, powder, liquid, or solid form. Most are taken orally with meals, but a few like growth hormone and insulin are injected using a hypodermic needle. Others, like anabolic steroids and amphetamines, are illegal in some countries, but bodybuilders take them anyway to do such things as speed recovery time between workouts, increase energy levels during workouts, and increase the oxidation rate of fat.

Besides illegal aids, a typical bodybuilder's diet will include such supplements as amino acids, multivitamins, protein powders, and often an assortment of herbs and glandular tablets. And while the scientific evidence is sketchy at best, bodybuilders continue to consume megadoses of such concoctions in the belief that it keeps them on par with other athletes.

EVOLUTION OF SUPPLEMENTS

The most popular supplements until the 1960s were proteins. In most cases these were powders made from such sources as: beef, fish, milk, egg, and soybean. One message frequently hammered home was the more protein the better. Also popular were liver tablets, vitamins, and minerals, becoming part of the supplement hit parade. Then things began to change.

> **"Unfortunately, the average bodybuilder still lives under the delusion that some supplements are 'steroid replacements' or work like drugs. Supplements can produce certain results, but they cannot make a genetically inferior bodybuilder into a Mr. Olympia champion. Not even steroids can do that."**
>
> – Greg Zulak, former *MuscleMag* editor and well-known bodybuilding writer commenting on one of the biggest fallacies concerning natural supplements – that they are as effective as anabolic steroids.

With the rapid growth in the food supplement industry, the major players such as York and Weider found themselves being challenged by a multitude of upstarts. Suddenly the low-quality soybean products saturated with sugar to bring up caloric levels were no longer acceptable. Bodybuilders began to avoid protein powders that were mostly milk and very little egg. The competition benefited bodybuilders by causing a dramatic increase in product quality over what was previously available.

In such a competitive environment, the best way to get a jump on the rest is to introduce a new product. Literally hundreds of new products are now available for the bodybuilder to choose from.

THE ERGOGENIC-AID REVOLUTION

Although there are numerous reasons for the explosive growth of the supplement industry, none have contributed as much as the recent crackdown on performance-enhancing drugs – chiefly anabolic steroids. Thousands of athletes at the high-school and college level have turned to supplements in response to more stringent drug-testing policies. Supplement producers have responded to such demands in a number of ways –

Charles Clairmonte

with the primary strategy of fostering the belief that their product gives the same results as anabolic steroids without unsavoury side effects and the risk of failing a drug test.

Another favourite gimmick is to make it sound as if a given supplement can speed up a biological process. Pick up the latest bodybuilding magazine and you're immediately hit with such phrases as "burn fat faster," "increase your hormone levels," or "the greatest muscle builder ever." To the aspiring Dorian Yates, such vocabulary is music to the ears. Unfortunately, the melody centres around coins being deposited in supplement manufacturers' bank accounts. And judging by the rapid growth of the supplement industry, such strategies have paid off handsomely. For example, The Council for Responsible Nutrition, based in Washington, DC estimated that the sales for dietary supplements amounted to over 3.3 billion dollars in 1990.[4]

> **"Budweiser! It would definitely have to be the cure-all, mega multi-pak bodybuilding supplement extraordinaire. Budweiser! And if I got to pick a second choice to go with that, it would, of course, be aspirin, right?"**
>
> – Dave Fisher, regular *MuscleMag* columnist responding in his "unique way" to a reader's question about which is the best bodybuilding supplement.

A DANGEROUS AND COSTLY PRACTICE?

From the athletes point of view, the practice of megadosing has numerous considerations. First and foremost is cost. Many bodybuilders spend hundreds, and in some cases thousands of dollars a month on dietary aids. If an individual wanted to consume at least one tablet of the major supplement groups (vitamins, protein, minerals, carbohydrates, etc.), his or her monthly expenditure could easily exceed $1000.

Another consideration is legitimacy. Let us state here and now that no single dietary supplement has been shown to be as effective as any anabolic steroid. In fact, none come close. Put another way, if these supplements were as effective as claimed, they would have to be regulated by drug-enforcement agencies. The fact that they're not gives some indication of their usefulness.

Having said that we'll now partially contradict ourselves. Taken separately no one supplement comes close to producing the effects of anabolic steroids, but research over the last few years indicates that when numerous supplements are combined, they may produce moderate degrees of anabolism. The evidence also suggests that individual supplements combined together often produce what's called a synergistic effect. This means two or more substances taken together may produce an added effect that is much greater than the effects of the substances taken separately. And while the safety aspects of such "cocktailing" are not clear, the market, nevertheless, continues to be flooded with the latest in biochemical combinations.

THEN THERE'S SAFETY

The previous leads us to perhaps the most serious consideration – safety. The phenomenon of supplement megadosing is relatively new – say within

Eddie Moyzan and Mark Erpelding

"The part nutrition can play in maximizing your chance for complete recovery is not to be overlooked. As a rock-bottom minimum, you should have the recommended daily allowance of protein, vitamins, and minerals. If you feel that your post-workout recovery proceeds at a snail's pace, I suggest you take a multivitamin tablet as general insurance. In addition, you might also benefit from daily doses of a high-quality protein powder mix, C, E and B-complex vitamins, and some type of chelated mineral supplement."

– Robert Kennedy, *MuscleMag* publisher and executive editor commenting on the importance of supplementation to bodybuilding success.

Paul DeMayo

"The placebo effect has been known and recognized for ages. It's resulted in tens of thousands of folk remedies. If someone took something, anything, and felt better, it went down in the books as a cure."

– Brian Mangravite, *MuscleMag* contributor commenting on the placebo effect – the only way many modern supplements "work."

the last ten years. It's true that long-time members of bodybuilding remember ingesting copious amounts of protein powders back in the "good old days." But, for the most part, it's only in recent years that concentrated forms of such supplements have become available. In addition, many of today's high-tech supplements were not available twenty or thirty years ago.

There's little known about the long-term health effects of supplement megadosing. While consuming high doses of water-based vitamins may be relatively safe, can the same be said for chromium picolinate or gamma oryzanol? Most of the supplements advertised as steroid replacers have never been scientifically tested in healthy human subjects, and certainly not in the dosages consumed by bodybuilders.

THE LONG ARM OF THE LAW

A final consideration is legality. While vitamins and protein supplements are for over-the-counter sale, most countries have enacted legislation to make distribution of anabolic steroids illegal. The United States has gone further and made possession of steroids a criminal offence. In simple terms, that bottle of Winstrol in your gym bag could get you serious jail time.

BUYER BEWARE

The majority of dietary supplements are not illegal and as such can be bought and consumed in endless quantities. In most cases the limiting variable is money. This ease of access raises many important issues. Regulatory agencies usually only become interested in supplements when manufacturers start making false claims. Health-care professionals only take notice when a health problem can be traced back to one particular supplement. Unfortunately this can be taken the wrong way as illustrated by the amino acid L-tryptophan.

In the late 1980s over 1500 cases of the painful muscle disorder Eosinophil-myalgia syndrome (EMS) – including 38 deaths – were attributed to tryptophan. With a speed that is seldom seen in a government agency, the US FDA banned all sales of tryptophan, even before all the facts were in. This was tragic as it was later determined that the amino acid was not at fault but a contaminant that was produced along with the product at one Japanese manufacturing plant. As of this writing L-tryptophan has not been allowed back for over-the-counter sale. As Robert Kennedy stated in a follow-up article in *MuscleMag International,* "When a contaminant that was responsible for killing several children was found in hamburger meat, did they ban hamburger meat permanently? When a poison was found in Tylenol, was it banned? Of course not."

Paul Dillett and
Flex Wheeler

CATCH-22

If a given supplement has never been implicated in a health problem, and if its manufacturer is not claiming outlandish results, the odds are good to excellent that the FDA or other such regulatory agency has never evaluated it. In fact, given the vast array of supplements that hit the market every year, the supplement industry can be termed poorly regulated.

To address some of the concerns of health-care workers, the FDA has begun testing the claims of some of the supplement manufacturers – the outcome of which could put producers in a catch-22 situation. If the claims are true, the product has to be marketed as a drug, and this entails a whole new set of stringent standards. Conversely, if the claims are not true, the advertising must be toned down or curtailed – eliminating much of the product's appeal.

A FAMILIAR MIND SET

Another issue facing health-care professionals is the attitude of many athletes, particularly bodybuilders, toward supplements. In many cases bodybuilders hold the same beliefs about supplements as they do about performance-enhancing drugs. All too often the individual believes the manufacturers' claims about the effectiveness of a product. It is left to the scientific community to provide evidence to the contrary. And just as with steroids, little hard evidence is available. Few studies have been carried out to determine the effectiveness or safety of "steroid replacers." Compounding the issue is the practice of "stacking" or combining different supplement

Mark Erpelding

preparations (a familiar observation among steroid researchers). One supplement may be safe, but how about five or ten taken together? Little is known about the long-term effects of such a "supplement cocktail."

THE PLACEBO EFFECT

Although this term is very familiar to physicians and medical researchers, many readers may not have come across it before. In simple terms, a placebo is an inert substance that produces the same results as a potent drug. Physicians treating wounded soldiers have long known of the powers of suggestion and in times of medicine shortage many "painkillers" were nothing more than sugar or flour tablets, or saline injections. Even though the given substance had no known effect on pain, the patients "belief" that it is a painkiller causes the pain to disappear. Over-the-counter cold medications are heavily influenced by the placebo effect. Even though most contain very low dosages of active ingredients, many individuals swear by them and most have their favorites.

Perhaps the greatest role placebos play in modern society is in medical research – particularly pharmacology. Before a new drug is allowed to be marketed it must undergo an extensive battery of tests. Called "trials," they are divided into two groups – experimental and control. The experimental group consists of those test subjects (willing volunteers) taking the actual drug. The control group are those subjects taking a placebo pill but told that it is the actual drug. The purpose of such tests is to determine if a new drug does what the manufacturer claims, or whether most of the ecidence suggests a placebo effect.

By now you're wondering what all this has to do with ergogenic aids. Well let's apply the placebo effect to supplements. Flip through any copy of *MuscleMag International* or other such bodybuilding magazine, and you'll experience sensory overload in the form of supplement advertising. From 1/4-page black and white ads, to multipage color masterpieces; all do their best to convince you to buy their product. And given the worth of the supplement business – billions annually – they work. Nothing is as convincing as a full-page color ad featuring tables, charts, pictures, and graphs. For many inexperienced or unknowing bodybuilders, one glance at such impressiveness and they're hooked. They conclude that the product must "work," and chances are, when they use the product it does work. Of course it is probably the placebo effect that is working and not the supplement. Many argue that as long as the product is giving the desired results they don't care. This is fine if the bottom line is results, but who wants to be spending hard-earned cash on a product that is nothing more than a psychological bluff?

Paul DeMayo

DO THEY WORK?

Of all the questions raised about ergogenic aids, the issue of effectiveness is perhaps the most important. In their quest to make the fastest gains possible, young or inexperienced bodybuilders often neglect to look past the catchy labels of their favorite muscle-building supplement. And given that most acquire their knowledge from friends or magazines, is it any wonder that supplement manufacturers have seen such exponential growth in the past ten years?

How can you tell if these fantastic claims are true? The best answer we can give is to first and foremost keep things in perspective. The word supplement means just that – a supplement. It does not mean a replacement for meals

"**Not that all high-level athletes are unhealthy people, but health is certainly not the reason they are in sports. Modern sports is big money. When there are big bucks involved, health usually goes out the window. It is a sad but true aspect of life in our commercialized dehumanized 'win at all costs' society.**"

– Will Brink, author and regular *MuscleMag* columnist commenting on the real reason athletes aspire to greatness in their chosen sports.

(even the latest "meal replacers" are not complete in the nutritional sense). For all the wisdom gained by scientists and dieticians, there is still a heap of knowledge out there just waiting to be discovered. One sandwich and glass of milk contains far more "ergogenic aids," than an entire shelf of supplements. And as for a full-course meal consisting of all the major food groups – supplement manufacturers can't even come close to duplicating the nutrients provided – many of which are as yet to be discovered.

ON THE OTHER HAND . . .

Having said all that, the evidence does suggest that some amount of supplementation may be needed. If you are in the habit of skipping meals, or are a hard-training athlete, taking extra protein or vitamins may be necessary. Much of the food we eat has been processed for storage and transportation, destroying a large percentage of its nutrient value. Cooking vegetables may destroy up to 75 percent of the B vitamins they contain. As for canned goods – most have their contents cooked THREE times before they hit the sales shelf. Home cooking brings the total to four. Yes, it does kill any microorganisms present, but it also reduces the nutrient value by a considerable degree.

"Too many bodybuilders think there are wonder supplements which will give steroid-like growth. Too many bodybuilders think there are huge differences among the quality of the food supplements made by major food supplement manufacturers, that one brand will give them gains while another won't. It ain't so."

– Greg Zulak, former *MuscleMag* editor commenting on one of the common beliefs of many bodybuilders toward food supplements.

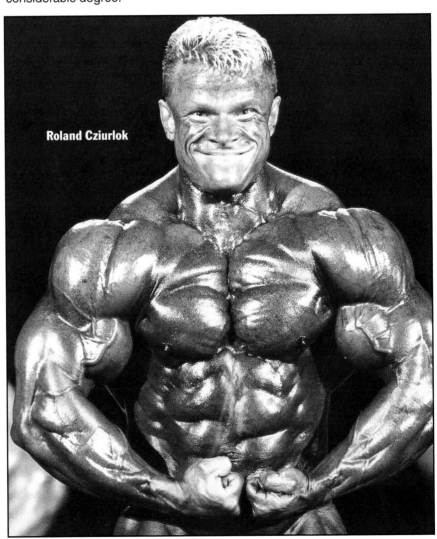

Roland Cziurlok

Fruits are not immune either. For example, that large orange you had for breakfast may in fact be missing 50 percent or more of its vitamin-C content. In this case taking extra vitamin C is recommended. Stored grapes can lose up to 40 percent of their vitamin B before being consumed.

Jay Cutler

Much the same argument can be made for protein supplementation. Although we will go into much more detail later, suffice to say, the evidence does suggest that hard-training athletes (particularly bodybuilders) do benefit from taking extra protein.

THE RDA – RECOMMENDED DAILY ALLOWANCE

Before we dive into the supplements and their relative merits, a brief discussion on the RDA is needed. It seems no nutrition article or TV show these days fails to make mention of this wonderful term. How often has a beaming TV image looked you straight in the eye and asked, "Have you consumed the correct amount of vitamin C today?" So powerful are the RDAs that they are often used to stifle the arguments of biochemists who promote food supplementation.

RDAs – Recommended Daily Allowances – are government limits or amounts set down for each of the major food nutrients. They were developed in response to the vast food-refining processes which came into being with the industrial revolution. While industry greatly increased the amount of food available, the refining processes often leached valuable nutrients from the food. As an example, white flour loses much of its nutrient value in the refining process. Similarly, oranges may have much of their vitamin C leached during their transit to a market.

Recognizing that the US population was at a risk for developing nutritional-related diseases, the US Government passed the Enrichment Act of 1942. This piece of legislation required manufacturers to replace the nutrients lost during processing. Today most foods are "fortified" with just about every nutrient known, and one look at a tin of juice or box of cereal provides such proof.

ARE THEY ALL THEY'RE CRACKED UP TO BE?

We would assume that given the Food and Nutrition Board's devotion to ensuring healthy diets, American consumers need look no further than the RDAs for practical advice. Unfortunately this is not the case. There are numerous reasons for not blindly following the RDAs.

"The RDA for protein is only 0.8 grams per 2.2 pounds of bodyweight, but the RDA was never intended for people who train hard or who are trying to put on pounds for a season of football. The Russian Olympic weightlifters were really the forerunners in taking ultrahigh quantities of protein. They did a great deal of research on the subject in the sixties. One study showed that a protein level 250 percent of the RDA still wasn't enough to prevent a negative nitrogen level in 40 percent of the weightlifters."

– Bill Starr, strength and conditioning coach, John Hopkins University.

For starters, RDA limits were based on studies involving individuals under the age of 50. Given the "aging" of world populations, we must ask ourselves whether or not the values derived from studies using young people are applicable to the elderly. It is generally accepted that as we age our biological systems slow down. Further, many elderly persons have chronic health problems – particularly those related to digestion and absorption. It doesn't take a leap of faith to see why such individuals would probably benefit by consuming nutrient levels above the RDAs.

A second issue, also related to the origins of the RDAs, concerns the physical health of individuals. The RDA values were calculated based not only on young individuals, but healthy young people. They don't take into account those with metabolic deficiencies or diseases. Further, RDAs have no respect for individuals on medication – many of which prevent nutrient absorption.

> "You cannot be a champion just by eating the best foods, you cannot be a champion just by training the most, and you cannot be a champion just by taking the most or the best steroids and drugs. The most important attribute you need to be a champion is attitude."
>
> – Franco Columbu, two-time Mr. Olympia winner commenting on what it really takes to be a champion bodybuilder.

A third reason goes back to the original goal of the RDAs. Initial designers of the RDAs were only concerned with preserving life. Given the times, death from malnutrition was a frequent occurrence. Today starving to death (at least in Western societies) has been virtually eliminated. People today are more concerned with eating for long-term health than base-line survival. Given this change in philosophy it is easy to see why the RDA values should reflect this – but in many cases they don't.

The final reason to question the merits of relying on RDAs – and this is the most applicable to athletics – is that the RDA values were calculated using sedentary individuals. In effect, people who engaged in little or no exercise. Can the RDA values calculated for a 40-year-old 1950s businessman be applied to a 1990s, 250-pound bodybuilder? Likewise, how much does a 1960s housewife have in common with her present day counterpart – a teenage college track star?

Franco Columbu

While the experts continue to argue back and forth, most in the bodybuilding community agree that hard-training bodybuilders need nutrients in amounts well above the RDA values. Even so, the megadosing engaged in by some may not be necessary (if not downright dangerous), but taking extra vitamins and protein is recommended.

Henderson Thorne

A FINAL WORD

For those bodybuilders intent on consuming vast quantities of supplements, a few words of caution are needed. First, remember that little research is available concerning the long-term health effects of long-term megadosing. By long term we mean five, ten, or even twenty years down the road. One multivitamin tablet may be fine but the synergistic effects of twenty supplements or more is a potential Pandora's box. This is not a trivial issue as most of the new supplements these days consist of a mixture of numerous substances.

Another point to highlight is legitimacy. If the claims of a supplement advertiser sound too good to be true, they probably are. If the advertisement starts with "studies have shown," check out these studies. Most university libraries contain the more popular medical and dietary journals and are open to the public. So don't be shy. If a given supplement is "based on new evidence," check the evidence out for yourself. Publications such as *The New England Journal of Medicine* and *The Journal of The American Medical Association (JAMA)* rarely, if ever, publish shoddy research. Chances are, if such a journal writes up a particular study, the odds are good to excellent that the study has been carried out using the proper scientific method. After verifying the existence of a study, check to see if its conclusions have been accurately portrayed. One example will suffice to emphasize our point.

"I think it's more important to eat lots of good food than to take supplements. You can buy several pounds of meat for the price of one supplement and it would do you more good than the supplement. Too many beginners waste money on supplements that would be better spent on food."

– Henderson Thorne, top Canadian pro bodybuilder giving his views on the high consumption of supplements by beginner bodybuilders.

In the early 1980s, supplement manufacturers made millions promoting the muscle-building properties of the amino acid arginine. The centerpiece to many of their ads was the "results" of a study carried out in Europe. On the surface the results seemed promising for bodybuilders, but closer inspection revealed a different story. The story put forward by supplement advertisers was that arginine increased the rate at which protein was turned into muscle tissue – chiefly by increasing levels of circulating growth hormone. Taken at face value, arginine seemed like a wondrous bodybuilding supplement, but soon sceptics uncovered the truth behind the European study. Instead of healthy subjects such as athletes, the study's experimental group consisted of individuals with a number of debilitating diseases. Upon being given high doses of arginine, there was a marked increase in muscular bodyweight. Supplement manufacturers emphasized this last point but conveniently omitted the subject group's backgrounds. Also omitted was the dosages involved – in the high gram range. Instead of citing the study in accurate terms, the bodybuilding public was left with the impression that a couple of 500-milligram tablets could turn 150-pound wannabes into 230-pound, rock-hard behemoths. The true story emerged only after the details of the study became mainstream.

Besides safety and legitimacy, a third point must be emphasized, and that is cost. Gone are the days of one-dollar vitamin bottles and two-dollar tins of protein powder. Most of the major supplement packages these days cost $100 to $200 or more for a one-month course. This is fine if you have the cash, but are the results really worth it? Often the athlete is left with nothing more than the most expensive urine in town! Why spend hundreds or thousands of dollars a month if much of it ends up down the drain?

Paul Dillett and Vince Taylor

Jason Arntz

A final suggestion concerns the acquisition of knowledge. Don't blindly consume hundreds of pills having little or no idea as to what you're taking. Before consuming any powder, pill, or potion, read as much literature as possible on the concoction. If there's any doubt – save your money. At the most you may be avoiding a serious health problem down the road. Every month *MuscleMag International* and other bodybuilding magazines bring you the latest in supplement research. Read everything you can get your hands on. The fact that you've purchased this book is a good start.

References

1) C. Wall, *The Curious Lore of Drugs and Medicines* (Gordon City, New York: Garden City Publishing, Inc., n.d.).
2) J. Young, *The Toadstool Millionaires – A Social History of Patent Medicine in America before Federal Regulation* (Princeton, New Jersey: Princeton University Press, n.d.).
3) P. Embleton and G. Thorne, *Steroids Myths – The Responsible Use of Anabolic Steroids* (St. John's Nfld: Thorton Publishing Ltd.,1991).
4) V. Cowart, "Dietary Supplements," *The Physician and Sports Medicine,* 20: 3 (March 1992).

BOOK ONE

Hormone Manipulation

O f all the methods employed by bodybuilders to increase muscular gains, by far the most effective is hormone manipulation. Realizing that there is only so much that can be achieved by increasing nutrient intake – protein, vitamins, minerals, etc. – many athletes get to the heart of the matter and boost the rate at which these nutrients are utilized by the body. Before we look at the various drugs which athletes use to modify their biochemistry, a brief introduction to basic endocrinology is needed.

HORMONE CONTROL

The human body contains two main control networks – the endocrine and nervous systems. Although both are important, it is the endocrine system that athletes tend to tinker around with.

The chief messengers of the endocrine system are hormones which may be either peptide or steroid in nature. Peptide hormones are manufactured from amino acid combinations. Steroid hormones are produced from cholesterol in the gonads and cerebral cortex. Hormones are released by glands into the surrounding extracellular fluid and travel by way of the bloodstream to target organs.

"Whether or not we gain or lose fat, or gain or lose muscle, or any combination in between is under hormonal control, which is regulated by your diet and genetic makeup. Therefore, recommendations regarding the diet should always be made with the knowledge of what effects a chosen food or combination of foods will have on the hormonal cascades that make us fat, huge, ripped, etc."

– Will Brink, regular *MuscleMag* columnist commenting on the interaction between diet and hormonal control.

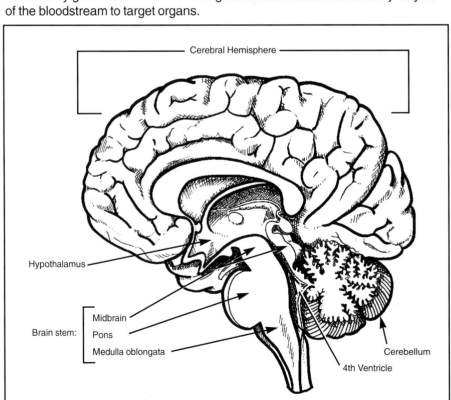

Cerebral Hemisphere

Hypothalamus

Brain stem:
Midbrain
Pons
Medulla oblongata

Cerebellum
4th Ventricle

The hypothalamus controls such behaviors as hunger, thirst, rage, sex and fear.
– Grant Henderson

Hormones are not believed to start chemical reactions but merely increase or decrease existing reactions. They do this in a number of ways. First, they can speed up the production of enzymes (substances that control the rate of chemical reactions). Second, hormones may increase or decrease the amount of reactants available for a chemical reaction. Or third, hormones may increase the rate at which substances cross cell membranes (called permeability).

Most endocrine glands are controlled by various structures in the brain – the most important of which is the hypothalamus. This small structure, located towards the front of the brain, is the body's chief control centre. The hypothalamus controls such behaviors as hunger, thirst, rage, sex, and fear. Closely associated with the hypothalamus is a structure known as the pituitary gland. The pituitary gland is subdivided into posterior and anterior sections – both of which have separate functions.

The posterior pituitary releases peptide hormones (protein in nature) which are produced in the hypothalamus. Included in this category of hormones are vasopressin (a water-conserving hormone) and oxytocin (a labor-inducing hormone).

From a bodybuilding perspective it's the anterior pituitary that has the greatest role as this gland controls the gonads (testes and ovaries). For these two structures to function properly they must be regularly stimulated by hormones produced by the anterior pituitary. Called luteinizing hormone (LH) and follicle-stimulating hormone (FSH), these two hormones "tell" either the testes or ovaries to produce testosterone or estrogen.

FEEDBACK CONTROL

Over the process of evolution, the human body has developed a mechanism whereby its hormone levels are constantly monitored and adjusted. Called feedback control, this system allows the body to maintain hormonal equilibrium by increasing or decreasing hormone production.

The best example we can think of to explain feedback control is the common household furnace and thermostat. If we set the thermostat to 20°C and the temperature falls below 20°C, the thermostat will signal the furnace to increase the output of heat. Once the temperature reaches 20°C the thermostat detects the increase and now tells the furnace to decrease its output. After a period of time the temperature once again falls below 20°C and the thermostat tells the furnace to rectify the situation. This interaction between the furnace, thermostat and heat is called feedback control.

"In general, hormones are responsible for the process of 'tissue remodeling' – that is, the process of laying down new muscle tissue. Although you can exert great control over some hormones by diet alone, exercise is required to generate the complete hormonal spectrum which will result in muscle gain and fat loss."

– John Parrillo, regular *MuscleMag* columnist and recognized expert on nutrition and exercise commenting on the interaction between exercise and hormonal control.

Art Dilkes and
John Simmonds

Analogous systems occur in the human body. In males, sperm production is controlled by the interaction of testosterone produced by the testes and LH produced by the anterior pituitary. When testosterone levels fall, the anterior pituitary picks up on this and begins producing more LH. Increased LH signals the testes to increase testosterone levels which in turn increases sperm production. Once testosterone levels reach a certain level, LH production shuts down. When testosterone levels decrease, the anterior pituitary once again increases LH output and the cycle repeats.

TESTOSTERONE

Of all the hormones circulating in the human body, none play a more active role than the sex hormones. They are the chief reason why males and females have physical differences. The primary "male" hormone is testosterone – produced by the testes. We stress the word "male" because females also have testosterone circulating in their bodies. Conversely, males have estrogen in their bodies, even though estrogen is referred to as a "female" hormone. One of the breakdown products of testosterone is estrogen. It is the relative concentrations of both that has given rise to the terms "male" and "female."

Testosterone has two main functions in males – sperm production, and the development of the secondary sex characteristics. With regards to sperm production, sperm cells are the male reproductive cells containing half the human chromosome number.

The second major function of testosterone is to start and maintain the male's secondary sex characteristics. These characteristics can be subdivided into anabolic and androgenic effects. The word anabolic comes from the word anabolism – one of the two subdivisions of metabolism. In brief, metabolism is the sum total of all the chemical reactions that take place in the human body. Reactions involving a synthesis of large molecules from smaller ones are called anabolic. Breakdown reactions where large molecules are broken down into smaller ones are called catabolic.

Testosterone is primarily anabolic in nature, and chief among its effects are increasing muscle size and strength. The main reason why males are, on average, bigger and stronger than females is because they have higher testosterone levels. Besides anabolic effects, testosterone produces androgenic effects. These include acne, increased facial and body hair, and a deepening of the voice. Testosterone produces it's greatest effects during puberty – the time period in early adolescence when males and females become sexually mature.

Having seen the importance of endocrinology to human physiology, we now turn our attention to the actual means by which athletes modify their biochemistry. We must stress that many of the substances and practices outlined in the following section are illegal in many countries. If there's any doubt as to your country's laws, play it safe and refrain from using any of these substances.

In addition, the medical evidence is not conclusive as to the health risks of many of the following drugs. For this reason we suggest that teenagers NEVER use any of the following drugs, and older individuals should only do so under medical supervision.

Samir Bannout and Mo Switzer

"As you may know, hormones do not work alone in the body. It is the combined inter-action of all hormones which generate the physiological adaptations to exercise. Hormones are released into the bloodstream to exert their effects on target tissues throughout the body, while sub-stances called 'growth factors' act mainly locally to stimulate growth."

– John Parrillo, regular *MuscleMag* columnist.

CHAPTER ONE

Anabolic Steroids

O f all the drugs associated with athletics, none have captured the public's attention like anabolic steroids. From Canadian sprinter Ben Johnson's debacle at the 1988 Olympics to revelations of use by WWF wrestlers, few sporting events have been left untouched by these muscle-building agents.

HISTORY

Contrary to popular belief, anabolic steroid use did not start with Ben Johnson in 1988. They are the result of over a century's research into hormonal control. Early researchers were not attempting to improve athletic performance, they were searching for the fountain of youth!

In 1889 Dr. Brown-Sequard developed an extract derived from dog testes. After injecting himself with the concoction he felt a rejuvenating effect – particularly in matters of sexual performance. His colleagues never took him seriously though, and within five years he died.

"So many people write such incredibly insane things about steroids that sometimes you wonder if these people aren't employed by Oscar Meyers. It's good baloney."

– Jeff Everson, former *Muscle & Fitness* editor commenting on the most misunderstood drugs in bodybuilding – anabolic steroids.

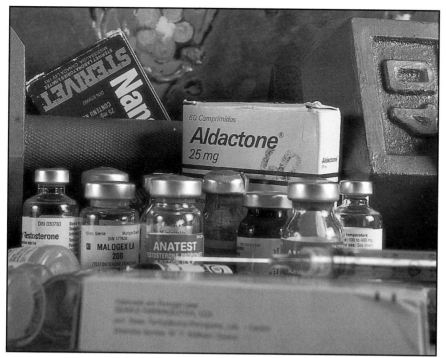

At the turn of the century other researchers went a step further and began carrying out transplants on humans using monkey testicles. Although there was a temporary "rejuvenating" effect, life spans were not increased and the only substantiated side effect was to give the recipients monkey syphilis.[1]

The first big break in anabolic steroid research came in the mid 1930s when German pharmacologist, Dr. Laqueur, isolated crystals from bull testicles. Dutch chemists gave the substance the name testosterone. Shortly there after, Swiss researchers succeeded in synthesizing testosterone and other closely related derivatives from cholesterol.

Research carried out over the next decade indicated that these newly synthesized drugs, which belonged chemically to a class of drugs called steroids, produced such anabolic effects as increased muscle size and strength. It wasn't long before the terms "anabolic" and "steroid" were mated together and a new age in pharmacology begun.

During the late 1930s and early 1940s, researchers realized that these new "anabolic steroids" had potential for use in sports. After all, any drug that increased muscle size and strength, and at the same time decreased bodyfat levels, was applicable to a wide range of athletic events. Once this news got around the athletic community, it wasn't long before the first syringes and vials started appearing in locker rooms.

DEBUT IN SPORTS

Trying to pinpoint the exact moment steroids became part of sports is difficult because most of the participants have since passed away. And given the harsh treatment experienced by modern athletes who fail drug tests, it's doubtful that any surviving athletes from the 1930s and 1940s would ever admit to their use. Another point to consider is that anabolic steroid classification did not take place overnight, but over a few decades. In all probability many athletes were using some form of steroid or testosterone derivative

"We all know steroids are used throughout bodybuilding. I have to admit that I like to see the freaky size of the steroid users. But I am quite bothered when a roid boy says he got his muscular development from his great genetics and hard training. OK, so maybe some of them do have above-average genetic potential and train hard, but so do a lot of naturals out there. There is a major difference in the size of the competitors in the nontested shows and the tested shows. You can't tell me that the difference is due to hard training or genetics. There is no doubt about it – steroids work."

– *MuscleMag* reader voicing his opinion on bodybuilders who blame their freaky size on hard training and good genetics rather than chemical assistance.

and not even aware of it. The first documented case of steroid use was in 1931 when four Swedish athletes admitted to using a product called Rejuven. Rejuven was a German drug that contained testosterone – albeit in small doses.[2]

THE WORKS OF DR. JOHN ZIEGLER

Bill Pearl

One of the most prominent steroid researchers during the 1950s was Dr. John Ziegler. In 1954, while accompanying the US weightlifting team to Vienna, Ziegler heard through the grapevine that Soviet athletes were using testosterone derivatives to boost their performance. And it wasn't just males as Ziegler noticed many female athletes who revealed a degree of masculinization that could only be attributed to steroid use.

After witnessing the effect the drugs had on Soviet athletes, Ziegler went back to the States and began to carry out his own research. His investigations carried out in the late 1950s were probably the first medically supervised studies ever conducted using athletes and steroids.[3]

Dr. Ziegler's research reached a climax in 1959 when he began examining the effects of the steroid Dianabol on California weightlifters. Ziegler's satisfaction of achieving hard data was quickly erased when he discovered that some of his research subjects were taking up to twenty times the recommended dose.[4] After Ziegler terminated his studies, he was heard commenting, "I lost interest in fooling with IQs of that calibre."

USE IN BODYBUILDING

The first reported use of anabolic steroids among bodybuilders was by former Mr. Universe, Bill Pearl. In an interview with *Muscle & Fitness* magazine in June of 1987, Pearl told of having his curiosity aroused by Dr. Arthur Jones (inventor of the Nautilus line of exercise machines) in 1958. Dr. Jones told Pearl of the "secret chemical" the Soviets were using. Not being one to blindly take anything he was unfamiliar with, Pearl headed to the library of the University of California to do his own research. After a veterinarian informed him about the effects the steroid Nilivar had on cattle, Pearl decided to settle his curiosity. A three-month trial period brought Pearl a twenty-five pound increase in muscle mass accompanied by a dramatic increase in strength.

"If I were to tell you just how many of the athletes are on the gear around the world, you would be a very surprised and yet sad man. Sorry but that is the way it is. I cannot change it, and the more you guys make the worst of it, the worse it will get. Finally, I would suggest you look at the fact that there are as many athletes on hard drugs as there are on steroids."

– Mick Hart, *MuscleMag* columnist responding to a British reader's accusations that "only" bodybuilders use steroids, and other forms of athletics are "steroid free."

Throughout the 1960s and 1970s the use of steroids among the world's bodybuilders grew at an alarming rate. The situation reached the point were virtually all contestants in a given show were believed to be using one or more anabolic steroid. The proof for such speculation began to surface in the 1980s as many of the sport's greatest stars admitted to steroid use. Among the bodybuilders who have admitted to using steroids during their competitive careers include: Arnold Schwarzenegger, Mike Matarazzo, Larry Scott, Mike Mentzer, and Tom Platz.

FIRST SYNTHESIS

After the isolation of testosterone crystals in the 1930s, scientists began to work on developing derivatives that would maximize the anabolic (growth promoting) effects and minimize the androgenic (masculinizing) effects. Since complete disassociation of anabolic to androgenic effect is not possible, most of the available anabolic steroids act in the same manner as testosterone.

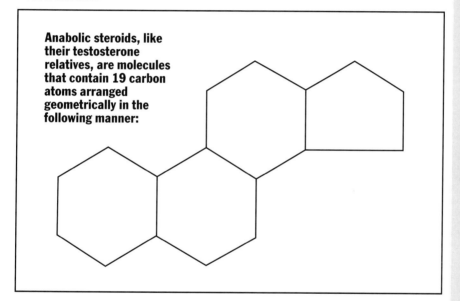

Anabolic steroids, like their testosterone relatives, are molecules that contain 19 carbon atoms arranged geometrically in the following manner:

The above molecule consists of three, six-sided rings joined to one, five-sided ring. Even though they are not written in, at each corner there is one carbon atom. In some respects, scientists are like secretaries in that they prefer to use shorthand to make things simpler. For classification purposes, each carbon is numbered from one to 19. This whole structure represents one molecule of the particular drug, and is called a steroid molecule. Although other side groups (attachments of atoms to one or more of the carbon atoms) may be present, all of the popularly used anabolic steroids contain this basic steroid molecule or nucleus.

Like most steroid hormones, testosterone is poorly absorbed by the gastrointestinal tract. And anything which does reach the bloodstream is quickly deactivated by the liver. To increase the effectiveness of anabolic steroids (for therapeutic purposes), scientists have added a side group to the carbon 17 position. Called an alkyl group, these forms of steroids are less susceptible to degradation by the liver. Other derivatives called 19-nortestosterones are among the most effective anabolic steroids known. They have great anabolic properties and small androgenic properties.

"There is an almost universal belief that the champions of the past were natural. Hardly a week goes by that someone doesn't remind me how the past Mr. America and Mr. Universe winners 'did it naturally.' Not so. Nearly all of the famous old-timers – 95 percent – were on gear."

– Robert Kennedy, *MuscleMag International* creator and best-selling author commenting on the misconception that the great bodybuilding champions of the past were all natural.

BIOSYNTHESIS

Given the horror stories circulating about the evils of cholesterol, it may surprise many readers that this molecule is the primary precursor for testosterone and most of its synthetic derivatives. Without going into too much detail, cholesterol is converted into the precursor pregnenolone, which in turn is converted to three additional intermediate molecules and eventually to testosterone. The entire process takes place in the male testes with the average daily secretion being about 2.5 to 10 milligrams.

PATHWAY FOR TESTOSTERONE SYNTHESIS

Cholesterol

↓

Pregnenolone

↓

17-hydroxypregnenolone

↓

Dehydroepiandrosterone

↓

Androstenediol

↓

Testosterone

"A lot of the women today are even using them. There's no excuse for women to use them. Any way you slice it, steroids are male hormones. In my book, a women using anabolic steroids is like a man taking estrogen. I know I'm a little outspoken about this, but it's really the way I feel.

– Lee Labrada, multititle winner offering his views on steroid use by female bodybuilders.

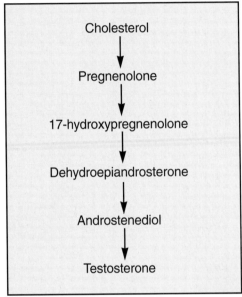

Shawn Ray, Gunter Schlierkamp, Porter Cottrell and Flex Wheeler

Mike Matarazzo

DEGRADATION AND ASSIMILATION

Once produced, testosterone follows a number of primary pathways. It may be absorbed by testosterone-dependant tissues like the prostate and seminal vesicles; it may act upon testosterone sensitive tissues like the kidneys and skeletal muscles; it may be immediately metabolized by the liver and excreted; or it may become bound to plasma proteins such as albumin and sex-hormone binding globulin (SHBG).

No matter what the metabolic pathway, testosterone has a half-life (the amount of time necessary for one half the original substance to degrade) of only ten to twenty minutes. This short life span means natural testosterone is of limited therapeutic use.

MECHANISM OF ACTION

Like most chemicals, testosterone and its anabolic derivatives produce their effects at the cellular level. The sites at which drugs combine with cells are termed drug receptors. Each drug is specific for a given receptor. Molecular biologists term this uniqueness of affinity the lock and key hypothesis. Just as a lock is shaped to receive one distinct key, so too are cell receptors designed to receive only one geometrically shaped molecule. Once the drug binds to it's specific receptor we have what is called a drug-receptor complex. This complex initiates a series of chemical reactions (much of which is still not fully understood); the ultimate result of which is called a biological response.

Research indicates that most anabolic steroid receptors are found in the nucleus of the cell. Upon activation, the drug-receptor complex increases the cells level of RNA and protein synthesis. There is also evidence to suggest that steroids increase the growth rate of steroid-sensitive cells.

The response to a given drug may vary considerably among individuals. For example, two individuals using the same anabolic steroid in the same dosages may experience vastly different results. One may gain twenty pounds of muscular bodyweight over a four-week period, while the other may notice no effects. In all probability the second individual has less receptors for that particular drug. By switching drugs the effects may change dramatically.

ROUTES OF ADMINISTRATION

There are two primary methods of introducing steroids into the human body – oral and injection. Oral steroids come in tablet or pill form and are taken in the same manner as other medications. Physicians and athletes both agree that oral steroids are more taxing on the liver than other forms of steroids. Because they have been modified to slow their breakdown and increase their life span, oral steroids are more likely to become concentrated in the

"I go off for long periods of time and stay off as long as I can. I know guys who spent $40,000 to $50,000 getting ready for the Arnold Classic. I stay off as long as possible and then I'm under the supervision of a very good doctor. I'm very cautious. It's not just bodybuilders. I know plenty of baseball and tennis players who are on drugs too."

– Mike Matarazzo, top IFBB Pro commenting on steroids at a seminar he gave in Toronto, Canada.

liver. Since an oral steroid must pass through the digestive tract, much of it will be deactivated before it enters the bloodstream. A pass through the liver will deactivate even more. This means that oral steroids need to be taken in higher dosages to get the same effect as injectables. Most athletes report more minor side effects when using oral steroids than other forms. These side effects include nausea, headaches, and a bloated feeling.[4]

Injectable steroids are introduced into the body by way of a long hypodermic needle. Although it sounds more dangerous, inject-able steroids are safer than orals. As the drug is injected intramuscular (into a muscle) and not intravenous (into a vein), most athletes prefer the thighs or glutes. The thighs offer the advantage of being easy to reach and provide a large area to work with. The glutes are harder to reach but offer the advantage of having fewer nerve endings. This means less pain when injecting. Most individuals who choose this site of administration have a friend inject for them.

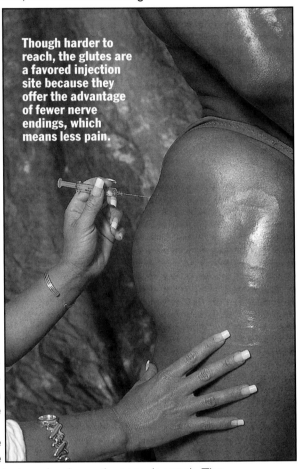

Though harder to reach, the glutes are a favored injection site because they offer the advantage of fewer nerve endings, which means less pain.

RISKS OF USING INJECTABLE STEROIDS

It would be irresponsible for us to avoid discussing some of the dangers of injectables – most of which are the result of poor technique and not the drugs themselves.

Anytime you break the body's outer skin layer, you are making the body more vulnerable to invasion by pathogens (germs). The skin is the body's first line of defence against invaders and works most efficiently when intact. A tear or break in the skin provides a route inside for such germs. Pushing a dirty needle into the body is asking for trouble. Needles are relatively cheap to buy and can be found at most drug stores. After using a needle (called a syringe) throw it away and use a new one next time. As for sharing needles – UNDER NO CIRCUMSTANCES SHOULD INDIVIDUALS SHARE NEEDLES. You may think you know your friend but down the road when you're diagnosed with AIDS or hepatitis, you'll regret ever having participated in needle sharing.

Closely related to the previous is the issue of particle poisoning. This is a reaction to a particle of fiber – such as cotton – or other foreign substance that gets injected into the bloodstream along with the drug. Within two to four hours the individual may be suffering from muscle cramps, chills, cold sweats, and nausea. If "lucky" these symptoms disappear after two to three hours. In a few cases, however, the reaction progresses to seizures, shock, and possibly coma.

"You are quite right that at your age your testosterone levels are probably lower than a snake's arse. By going on the gear you would only be adding to what you are already starting to miss, and with the right one I would certainly not worry about side effects. I would suggest a good Cypionate and/or Deca, one shot a week of each. No problem! But you have to get it legally through a doctor's prescription to aid your sagging libido.

– Mick Hart, colorful *MuscleMag* columnist commenting on one of the primary reasons why anabolic steroids were first synthesized – to supplement low testosterone levels.

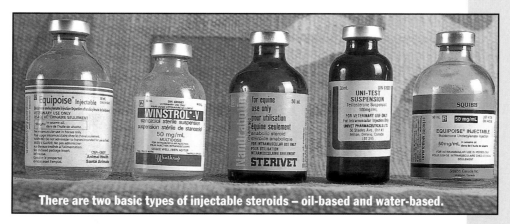

There are two basic types of injectable steroids – oil-based and water-based.

Another concern is the risk of puncturing a major blood vessel, particularly a vein or artery. If you inject into your thighs and accidentally strike the large femoral artery (the large pressurized blood vessel which provides blood to the whole leg region) you will probably bleed to death within a matter of minutes.

At the slightest indication of blood-vessel damage, apply pressure, elevate the limb, and most of all – seek medical attention. It's far better to be embarrassed than dead!

Besides blood vessels, the body has a system of nerves that interact with muscles to produce movement. If you hit one of these with a needle, at the least you'll experience intense pain, but more important, may suffer permanent nerve damage. Not only will your 28-inch thigh degenerate but you may actually paralyze your leg.

If you decide to use injectable anabolic steroids, first receive prior instruction from a medical professional such as a doctor or nurse. Properly injecting a needle into the body is an acquired skill that should only be attempted after much practice.

TYPES OF INJECTABLE DRUGS

There are two basic types of injectable steroids – oil-based and water-based. The terms imply the medium in which the steroid crystals are dissolved and injected into the body. The oil frequently used is sesame or cottonseed. Many water-based injectables are suspensions with the steroid crystals floating around. If left sitting for any period of time, the crystals fall to the bottom of the vile – necessitating the shaking of the vile before use to resuspend the crystals.

Although oil-based steroids carry their own risks, water-based drugs are especially risky. Author and regular *MuscleMag* columnist Will Brink estimates that nine out of ten infections associated with steroids are the result of water-based injectables (Winstrol or testosterone suspension). Many bodybuilders who repeatedly use these drugs develop abscesses which must be surgically removed. If this is not enough to grab your attention – an untreated infection may necessitate the amputation of the entire leg.

MAKING YOUR OWN INJECTABLE DRUGS!

We thought it necessary to conclude the topic of injectable drugs with a few words of wisdom concerning the follies of making your own steroids. You may think that all steroids are created in high-tech labs by highly trained individuals, but nothing could be further from the truth. Depending on the

"Most top body-builders stack at least three steroids along with human growth hormone and other contest prep drugs when getting ready for a show. This may mean a diuretic to lose water, a thyroid drug to speed up fat burning and L-Dopa to work with HGH."

– Greg Zulak, former *MuscleMag* editor commenting on the pharmacological aspect of competitive bodybuilding.

Milos Sarcev and Chris Cormier

"There are two main reasons. The first is that steroids drastically increase fluid retention, particularly in the muscles, which are 70 percent water. One will often notice large increases in muscle mass attributable to increased water retention alone . . . the second reason is that steroids exhibit their increased protein effect primarily by inhibiting other hormones from protein catabolism."

– Sergio Oliveira, former bodybuilding champion outlining the two primary ways anabolic steroids increase bodyweight among users.

steroid involved, it's possible most of the supply of a given steroid was created in a basement lab.

The reason we are making such a fuss out of this issue is because a few of the more popular bodybuilding writers occasionally offer "advice" on how to make anabolic steroids in your kitchen. A few go a step further and encourage readers to obtain a copy of the *Merc Index* – the "bible" of drug pharmacology outlining how most of the world's drugs – including steroids – are synthesized. This is pointless if you don't have the necessary skill (a minimum of a degree in organic chemistry) to follow such technical chemistry.

While offering suggestions on using steroids is itself debatable, providing information for the purposes of concocting designer steroids is dangerous and in our opinion downright unethical. For those not dissuaded yet, hopefully the following will change your mind about kitchen pharmacology.

DANGERS OF BASEMENT PHARMACOLOGY

The first problem with making your own steroids concerns the drug "recipe" itself. Although a few may have access to the *Merc Index*, most basement chemists are following a few scratches on a piece of paper. In many cases the proportions of the ingredients are off, resulting in byproducts that may be lethal.

Another concern is the preciseness with which the chemical reaction must be carried out. A variation in temperature, the quality of the ingredients, or the solvent used to dissolve the various substances can all shift the equilibrium of the reaction. Instead of a pure product, you may end up with a concoction containing who knows what. The suspension may contain a whole spectrum of products that may not only be dangerous them- selves, but may interact with one another to produce even more toxic effects.

Another problem for basement chemists lies with lack of proper lab equipment. Unless you have access to some very precise instruments and glassware, leave pharmacology to Dow Chemical and Upjohn. A few kitchen pots and pans are no substitute for laboratory beakers, test tubes, and centrifuges. And even if you had such equipment, do you know how to use it? Like any profession, laboratory pharmacology requires many years of training and experience.

A final concern involves the consequences of a chemical reaction getting out of control. Most university and industrial labs are designed in case of a large explosion. Thankfully such events rarely occur but the safeguards are in place nevertheless. As an example, the university chemistry building where we studied was designed with many key walls built on hinges. Such an arrangement would allow the walls to absorb most of the blast leaving the remainder of the building intact.

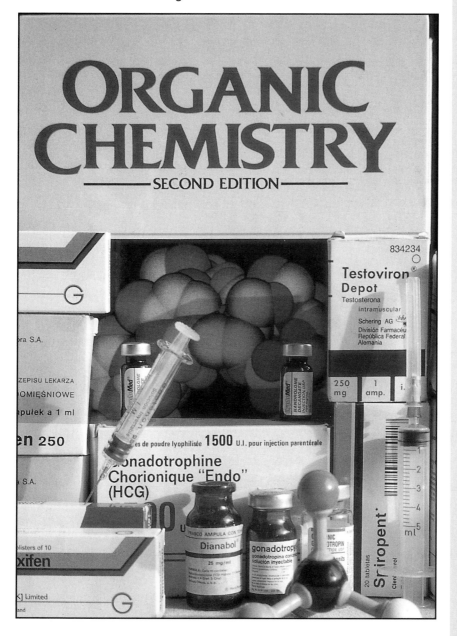

"They are actually safer than orals but they are not completely safe. The orals pass through the liver twice, the injectables but once. And you must be aware that individuals differ in how they react to any chemical introduced in their systems."

– Bill Starr, John Hopkins University strength and conditioning coach commenting on a common misconception among bodybuilders that injectable steroids are "completely" safe.

Even if you hold a degree in organic chemistry the dangers of basement pharmacology far exceed any possible benefits. Leave steroid synthesis to trained laboratory professionals.

Besides the structural safeguards, all industrial chemistry labs carry the latest in firefighting and first-aid equipment. Our question to you is this: If such safeguards are deemed necessary in large industrial complexes, what makes you think your basement or kitchen is safe if something goes wrong during steroid synthesis 101!

Given the previous concerns (and there are many more we assure you), we strongly suggest you avoid the temptation to manufacture your own drugs. A few "highly regarded" writers may make it sound easy and profitable, but they won't be the ones attending your funeral when you scatter your remains over the neighborhood.

ALTERNATIVE METHODS OF STEROID DELIVERY

Although injectable and oral steroids are by far the most common forms of anabolic steroids, there are lesser-known methods by which to introduce the drugs into the body.

Since the reunification of Germany, top athletes from the former East Germany have reported using a nasal spray, used like an over-the-counter decongestant. Further, the reports suggest the drug leaves the athlete's system in as little as three days. This made it ideal for athletes in such drug-tested sports as the Olympics and World Championships.[5]

Another less used method for taking steroids is skin patches. Long used for helping smokers fight the cigarette urge (the famous nicotine patch), in recent years, researchers have begun developing a similar patch to provide testosterone and its steroid cousins to those suffering from AIDS. Unlike previous patches that had to be applied to the scrotum, the new forms can be applied directly to the arm or leg. From here the drug is absorbed through the skin and into the bloodstream. One company, ALZA Pharmaceuticals, expects to have a Deca-Durabolin patch available for sale in September of 1998.[6]

A third method of taking steroids is by sublingual tablets. Although a popular method of administering other medications, it's only in recent years that researchers began looking at this technique as a means to deliver steroids. Although it sounds rather crude to place a tablet under the tongue, this method is one of the fastest ways to get medication into the body. If you don't believe us, think about how heart patients

Laura Binetti

> "Besides your losing all control of administered dosages, you can't simply use regular water in the solution with 100-percent confidence. Most water is tainted in some way and shouldn't be injected into the body in any fashion. And allowing the cycle to continue for a longer period of time if the drug is diluted? What's longer? Two, three, four months? I don't think you know enough to make an educated decision on whether you should experiment with such a powerful drug."
>
> – Robert Kennedy, *MuscleMag* publisher responding to a reader's question about diluting testosterone suspension with ordinary tap water to prolong the duration of use.

Kevin Levrone, Dorian Yates and Nasser El Sonbaty

immediately put a nitroglycerine tablet under the tongue to ward off a heart attack in times of stress. Within a matter of seconds the drug has crossed the thin membranes under the tongue and entered the bloodstream.

With the increased use of steroids to fight AIDS, and the new strategies being developed to reduce the loss of sex drive in older men, many pharmaceutical companies are developing sublingual tablets to deliver steroids.

If there is a disadvantage to sublingual routes of administration it's the relatively low amounts of active drug that can be supplied. For treating an AIDS patient, or helping an older male keep his sex drive high, a few tablets will provide more than enough medication. But for a 250-pound bodybuilder, taking 20 to 30 sublingual tablets a day might not be too attractive. With the increased crackdown on oral and injectable steroids, the most popular method of taking steroids might become sublingually (at least in terms of access). And the increased use of steroids for fighting AIDS will mean increased production of the drugs. This in turn means greater availability. It will be interesting to see what the future holds for sublingual delivery methods. Those working with teenagers will have to keep informed of the situation.

DRUG TERMINOLOGY

As with most practices, anabolic steroid use has its own vocabulary. The drugs themselves may be referred to by any number of names. Besides anabolic steroids or steroids, bodybuilders may use the terms "juice," "juicing," or "gear." Another popular name is "roids" (a name used frequently by the media, especially in terms of "roid rage").

The practice of alternating periods of use with nonuse is called "cycling." The purpose of such a practice is to allow the body's depressed natural hormones to return to normal. Of course there are other reasons, such as going off the drugs to pass a drug test. In recent years the practice of cycling tends to be based solely on economics. As long as individuals can afford to purchase steroids they will stay on them. This is dangerous as the risk of side effects is proportional to the duration of use – the longer the time period on steroids the greater the risk.

"I can tell you that various transdermal systems have been designed, all of them aimed at achieving a constant release rate of the molecules contained in their reservoir through intact skin. Transdermal testosterone patches are difficult to duplicate without the proper materials. Any application of testosterone on an absorbable medium and applied to the scrotum will not provide smooth serum testosterone levels as do commercial testosterone patches."

– Dr. Mauro DiPasquale, regular *MuscleMag* columnist and best-selling author commenting on transdermal testosterone patches.

The fat-burning properties of various drugs are much coveted given the emphasis on the "ripped look" these days.
– Hamdullah Aykutlu

When an individual uses more than one steroid at a time, the concoction is referred to as a "stack," with the practice being called "stacking." In the last ten years drug stacks have included more than steroids. Very frequently competitive bodybuilders will include such drugs as growth hormone, insulin, and diuretics in their stacks. Many go further and take just about every performance drug they can get their hands on. This is called "shotgunning" and like stacking, poses risks since the consequences of multiple-drug use is unknown.

PHYSIOLOGICAL EFFECTS

One of the most disputed areas concerning anabolic steroids is the issue of physiological effects. For bodybuilders, the desired physiological effects are to increase muscle size and strength, and at the same time lower bodyfat levels. While the medical literature is inconclusive in this regard, bodybuilders know different. All things being equal (training, diet, age), an individual using anabolic steroids will gain muscular bodyweight faster and to a greater degree than a nonuser. The primary reason why medical studies have difficulty confirming this concerns experimental dosages.

Because of the ethics and legalities of conducting experiments involving anabolic steroids, most laboratory test subjects are given a fraction of what a competitive bodybuilder uses. So while two or three times the recommended dosage may not produce dramatic results, ten or twenty times will. Many bodybuilders go further and inject hundreds of times the accepted therapeutic dosage.

Another problem is the number of steroids involved. For obvious reasons, researchers generally administer only one drug in small amounts. Competitive bodybuilders frequently combine four or five steroids into the previously described "stack." Such a concoction invariably produces great gains in muscle size and strength.

Besides increasing muscle size and strength, anabolic steroids have other effects. From a therapeutic aspect one of the most important is their effect on bone density. Steroids increase the retention of calcium – one of the building blocks of bone tissue. The more calcium retained and utilized, the thicker and stronger the bone. So effective are steroids in this regard that NASA has evaluated their use as a combatant to bone loss experienced during long space flights.[7]

Anabolic steroids also influence ion balance. Ions are electrically charged atoms that aid in the regulation of many metabolic reactions throughout the body. Studies consistently show that steroids increase the retention rate of such important ions as nitrogen, calcium, chloride, and potassium.

With regards to nitrogen, steroids produce what is called a "positive nitrogen balance." This means steroids improve the utilization of consumed protein and increase the rate of nitrogen retention – two physiological processes necessary for muscle-tissue synthesis.

Another physiological benefit of steroids is their role in counteracting catabolic hormones. Anabolic hormones cause muscles to use amino acids to form protein to build muscles. Catabolic hormones do the opposite, prompting amino acids to be released from muscles into the blood. Have you ever noticed how individuals, especially males, lose bodyweight when under stress. This is because their systems are being flooded with cortisol and other catabolic hormones. After a few months these individuals end up looking stringy and grossly underweight.

Normal individuals produce enough anabolic hormones to counteract these effects. There is a continuous war between anabolic and catabolic hormones taking place in the body – the result of which is the shifting of amino acids into and out of the body's muscles. Preventing the loss of amino acids from the muscles has the same effect as increasing amino acids and protein in your muscles. Anabolic steroids are believed to do this by competing with catabolic hormones for receptor sites. Since anabolic receptor sites are saturated (completely filled) on very low dosages of anabolic steroids, the surplus attaches to the available catabolic steroid receptor sites, preventing cortisol from initiating the loss of amino acids from the muscles. The anti-

"Relative to other classes of steroid hormones, particularly the estrogens and glucocorticoids, the androgens are seldom capable of producing serious toxic side effects."

– John A. Thomas and Edward J. Keenan, from their book *Principles of Endocrine Pharmacology.*

J.D. Dawodu

catabolic properties of anabolic steroids are so pronounced that some researchers suggest renaming the drugs from anabolic to anticatabolic steroids.

Another effect of steroids is to increase the kidneys' production of erythropoietin. This hormone stimulates the bone marrow to increase production of red blood cells. Increased red blood cells can then carry more oxygen to the body's cells. But there is an upper limit and too many blood cells can thicken the blood, reducing oxygen-carrying capacity.

SIDE EFFECTS

No area of the anabolic steroid phenomenon is as hotly debated as the issue of side effects. There seems to be an almost daily stream of horror stories emitted from the more popular media sources. Everything from brain cancer and liver disease to psychosis and roid rage is attributed to these drugs. Yet a close examination of the medical literature reveals a very different story. In the following section we shall look at the more common side effects credited to anabolic steroids. For convenience we have divided the segment into two broad categories – physiological and psychological side effects.

"Although the horror stories of cancer and liver failure aren't pervasive enough to make a real impact, I have yet to meet a steroid user who didn't suffer some form of painful or disfiguring side effect."

– Ron Harris, from a "Guest Editorial" in *MuscleMag* giving another viewpoint on the potential dangers of anabolic steroids.

Mauro Sarni and Bruce Patterson

Birgitta
Carlsson

PHYSIOLOGICAL SIDE EFFECTS

CANCER

One of the greatest media frenzies in history took place during 1991 and 1992, when former pro football player Lyle Alzado was diagnosed with brain cancer. After twenty years of continuous steroid use and no side effects, Lyle suddenly came forward preaching the evils of these drugs. Antisteroid advocates were quick to latch on to Lyle's story as it only served to further their cause.

Cancer ranks second only to heart disease as a primary cause of death of North Americans. It may surprise many to learn that cancer is not one disease but a combination of many physical abnormalities. The common denominator to most is an uncontrollable growth of body cells. Such a growth forms a tumor which if not treated often leads to the individual's death. In many cases death is the only outcome – treatment or otherwise.

As of yet scientists don't know what causes cancer. They have theories and hypothesises, but the actual mechanism of how body cells suddenly turn cancerous is not fully understood. Therefore when antisteroid advocates state that steroids cause cancer, they are either spreading propaganda or know something that the world's top cancer researchers only dream about.

There is no medical evidence to even suggest anabolic steroids cause cancer. To prove (or even suggest) that a substance causes cancer takes decades of research involving thousands of studies. And by studies we mean long-term comparison studies involving steroid-using and nonsteroid-using groups. If after carrying out such studies it was shown that steroid users had a higher incidence of cancer, only then could we state that the drugs may lead to cancer. As of yet, no such studies have been carried out. The only studies written up in medical journals are case studies.

Case studies are reports based on solitary individuals who have developed cancer. In short, subject A died of cancer and subject A used steroids, therefore subject A died of steroid-induced cancer. To the uneducated such an approach sounds convincing, but in reality it has no merit. The same logic can be applied to individuals who drive, say, blue cars. A researcher could easily track down 50 or 100 individuals who died of cancer and happened to drive blue-colored cars. A few paragraphs of convincing vocabulary and automobile manufactures would have to cease ordering blue paint.

"I'm a very, very strong fan of female bodybuilding. But you have to remember, it's female bodybuilding. I think that's what they should look like. I don't like our sport being given a bad rap through females up onstage looking like men."

– Lee Haney, eight-time Mr. Olympia commenting on the implications for bodybuilding given the extreme masculinization of many female bodybuilders.

Until more evidence is collected, no conclusions can be drawn to show a relationship between cancer and anabolic steroids. It is possible that down the road evidence will surface to tie the two together. But remember, anabolic steroids have been used by athletes for over 50 years. The first generation of such individuals are now in their 60s and 70s. If steroids caused cancer, we'd expect an epidemic of geriatric-aged athletes dying of cancer. But this hasn't happened and the odds are it never will.

Darrem Charles

LIVER DISEASE

It is true that steroids may produce unwanted liver abnormalities, but for the most part these are transitory and will disappear upon cessation of drug use.

The primary effect steroids have on the liver is to alter enzyme levels. This is not surprising as the liver is the body's main detoxifying organ. With every pass through the liver, the body's blood is filtered and substances such as drugs are deactivated. Obviously the more drugs in an individual's system the greater the workload placed on the liver. The best example to illustrate this is people who consume heavy amounts of alcohol for extended periods of time. Most heavy users of alcohol develop a condition called cirrhosis of the liver. In short, their livers have burned out because of overuse.

Anabolic steroids are no different than other drugs in that heavy use for extended periods of time may lead to liver abnormalities. This is not so much a case of the drugs themselves but the characteristics of their use. As with other forms of cancer, the only documented evidence to suggest that steroids cause liver abnormalities are case studies. Antisteroid advocates routinely cite studies showing that steroids cause peliosis hepatis, a form of hepatitis. But close inspection shows that the individuals involved in the study were not healthy athletes but individuals suffering from various diseases.[8] Little or no evidence exists to suggest a relationship between liver disease and steroid use.

We must add that most of the liver side effects appearing in literature involve the use of orally active C-17 alpha alkyl derivatives. There have rarely been case reports involving injectable anabolic steroids.

> **"The medical community is still reeling from their original position on these drugs because most doctors remain ignorant on the subject, both in terms of steroid side effects and their potential to be effective performance-enhancing drugs. The so-called experts have overstated the health risks in an effort to discourage use, and in doing so have abandoned accepted principles of research by drawing conclusions based on speculation and conjecture."**
> – Sergio Oliveira, former steroid dealer and bodybuilder.

HIGH BLOOD PRESSURE

This is one side effect that most steroid users experience. The condition, called hypertension, develops because anabolic steroids cause the body to retain fluids. It is, however, transitory and blood pressure returns to normal after steroid use is stopped. Hypertension can be controlled during a cycle by the removal of salt from the diet. Some bodybuilders go further and use a diuretic, but as we shall see later, these drugs have their own risks. It must be stressed that an individual with heart disease, kidney disease, or a history of stroke in his or her family should avoid anabolic steroids. Hypertension can aggravate all of the previous conditions with lethal consequences.

ELEVATED CHOLESTEROL LEVELS

Anabolic steroids have been shown to increase the ratio of low-density lipoprotein cholesterol (LDL-C) or "bad" cholesterol to high-density lipo-protein cholesterol (HDL-C) or "good" cholesterol. As elevated levels of LDL have been linked to heart disease, an individual with a history of heart disease in his or her family should be cautious of using steroids. It should be pointed out that cholesterol levels return to normal after cessation of use. One study carried out in the late 1980s serves to illustrate these points.

The study involved twenty-three power lifters, three who had used steroids previously, the other 19 who had never. Cholesterol levels were recorded before, during, and after steroid use. The results showed elevated cholesterol levels (specifically LDL) in all cases during the entire period of steroid use. Following termination of use, cholesterol levels returned to presteroid levels. [9]

Derrick Whitsett

An analysis of the data revealed that presteroid choles-terol levels were not indicative of levels during use. In addition, low levels before steroid use did not seem to offer any degree of protection – steroid use elevated cholesterol levels irregardless. Based on these findings the researchers concluded that the use of anabolic steroids may increase the risk of coronary heart disease, but as there were no reports of such in the medical literature, the situation was unclear. Research is needed to demonstrate a link between the two.

ACNE

Acne is probably one of the few side effects that virtually all steroid users experience. It may take the form of slight facial abrasions commonly called pimples or "whiteheads," or (as is more frequently the case) take

"It's apparent that many people don't understand the way drugs work. Once the steroid is out of the tissues and blood, you lose all the effects gained from the drugs. Any legitimate endocrinologist will confirm this. Ever see a person who has used steroids for a long time and then stopped? He shrinks right back to his original size."

– Professional body-builder commenting on the rapid weight loss experienced by all long-term users of steroids when they go off the "juice."

Many athletes are willing to trade the unsightly appearance of acne for the performance-enhancing effects of steroids.

the form of widespread scarring on the back. The former case usually clears after the athlete stops taking steroids, but the latter case is more serious as the blood-filled cysts produce scars which remain with the person for life, even after cessation of steroid use. Although the exact cause of steroid-induced acne is not fully understood, it is believed that steroids (particularly androgens) increase the activity of the skin's sebaceous glands. This over-stimulation increases glandular secretions, especially oils – a perfect medium for acne-causing bacteria to grow.

There seems to be a relationship between prior development of acne and increased amounts during steroid use. Those that suffered acne before steroid use will in all probability experience the most severe cases while using steroids.

We should add that most athletes are willing to trade the unpleasant cosmetic appearance for the performance-enhancing effects. Still for those bodybuilders intending to compete, a severe case of acne will have to be treated by a dermatologist. And as many forms of acne treatment involve the use of medication, the individual will have to be closely monitored for drug interactions.

TREATING ACNE

As just discussed, one of the least threatening but most unpleasant-looking side effects of steroids is acne. Even without steroids, many male bodybuilders have acne; the back being a particular problem area. For a bodybuilder preparing for a contest, this can be a great source of distress. For a teenager already suffering from poor self-esteem, the condition can create severe psychological problems.

Although acne is 95 percent hereditary, and most common in males, females can also suffer from the condition, especially those in their late teens and early twenties who use heavy amounts of cosmetics. Called acnea cosmetica, the condition is caused by the heavy use of cosmetics in adolescence. It is not caused by a lack of cleanliness, but by the pores working overtime. It may surprise you to learn the average pimple is three years old! It may have only swollen up recently, but it has been waiting a long time to surface. Diet has often been listed as the chief villain behind acne flare-ups, but the reality is that chocolate and soda pop do not have any effect. Until recently, bodybuilders depended on tanning beds to get rid of acne. The increased incidence in skin cancer has produced a situation in which the cure is worse than the disease. Tanning oils are now used to produce tans, and most responsible bodybuilders avoid tanning beds.

A dermatologist can prescribe Accutane (the most effective acne drug available), an agent similar to vitamin A, but it is expensive and can have numerous side effects including: skin dryness, itching, muscle soreness, joint pain, headaches, fatigue, nausea, and in some cases (estimated by some to be as high as one in four users) bone spurs. Pregnant women should not use Accutane, especially in the first few months of gestation. The drug has been linked to fetal deformities. Such effects have led to a movement to have Accutane limited to males.

One of the least known drugs for treating acne in females are birth control pills. These agents are very effective in all but the most severe cases of acne. The primary mechanism of action of such drugs is to decrease the effectiveness of any circulating male hormone. In many cases the physician will prescribe an antiandrogen drug as well.

Other treatments for deep-cysted acne involve antibiotics, such as tetracycline. Benzoyl peroxide is effective for mild cases of acne, but for severe conditions, more powerful techniques are needed. One of these, cryotherapy, involves the use of liquid nitrogen to freeze the inflammatory cysts. Another technique uses ultraviolet radiation (in the sunburn range) to dry out and clear up the skin. This form of treatment is not without risks as increased exposure to ultraviolet radiation increases the risk of skin cancer.

One of the best preventative treatments is increased water intake, coupled with frequent cleansing and the regular use of a sauna. Some dermatologists do not recommend the sauna, claiming that because the pores are clogged, the pimples will only get bigger. Others argue that by cleansing the pores to keep them open, and getting the pores to sweat by providing plenty of water in a hot environment, one can restore the complexion to natural health.

Another option, though somewhat more expensive, is to have regular facials (beginning with once a week, and progressing to once a month) at a local beauty salon. Many macho actors have facials, and both men and women can benefit from this procedure of professional skin care and cleansing.

"Accutane may produce several temporary side effects and its use requires careful medical supervision. Nearly all patients experience dryness and itching of the skin and chapped lips. Other side effects include muscle soreness, joint pain, head-aches, fatigue, irritated eyes and nausea."
– Dr. Mauro DiPasquale, regular *MuscleMag* columnist and world authority on drug use commenting on the potential side effects of the popular acne-fighting drug, Accutane.

One of the best preventative treatments for acne is increased water intake.

There are a variety of topical cleansing agents available. Very oily complexions can benefit from wiping with alcohol pads a few times a day. Another agent is hydrogen peroxide. It can be bought over the counter at any pharmacy, and is very effective at drying up pimples and removing black-heads. It can also bleach hair. Using hydrogen peroxide too liberally can result in blond facial hair, which near the forehead of a brunette can look somewhat odd.

Two oils which are very useful in treating acne are hazelnut oil and jojoba oil. Used topically, these oils dissolve the sebum which blocks pores, causing acne in the first place.

Whatever treatment you choose to use, please see a doctor first; keep your hands away from your acne, and do not break pimples unless you have discussed the technique with your doctor.

GYNECOMASTIA

One of the most unpleasant and potentially serious side effects of anabolic steroid use is a condition known as gynecomastia. By a peculiar twist of evolution, one of the breakdown products of testosterone and its steroid derivatives is the feminizing hormone estrogen. In some males excessive amounts of testosterone is converted (the pharmacological term is aroma-tized) to estrogen in the peripheral tissues. As the male breast region contains estrogen receptors, the individual's nipples may begin to swell and take on the appearance of female breasts. Bodybuilders call the condition "bitch tits," and in most cases the swelling disappears after steroid use is stopped. In a few cases treatment with anti-estrogen drugs is required, but even then a few individuals may not respond and the only alternative is surgery.

> **"I know one guy at school who still had severe gynecomastia two months after his last cycle. The guy's too embarrassed to take his shirt off in gym. He's got better breast development than half the girls. He won't see a doctor about it."**
> – Teenager commenting on his friend's gynecomastia.

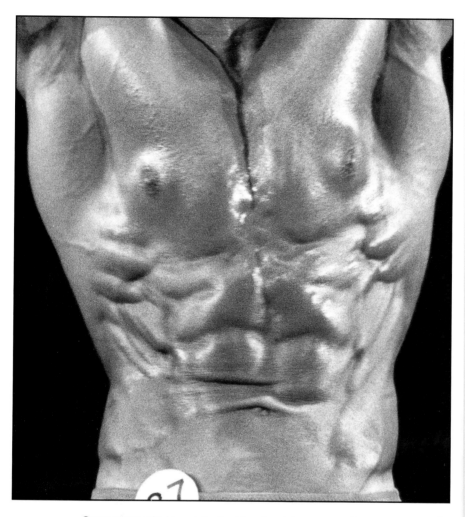

Gynecomastia is not limited to steroid users as it occurs naturally throughout the male population. Studies indicate that 60 to 90 percent of newborn babies show gynecomastia – the result of some estrogen leakage from the mother into the placenta.

The next age group which often exhibits the condition is adolescence. Endocrine researchers estimate that 65 percent of all teenage males will experience the condition in varying degrees.

The third stage of life where gynecomastia often occurs is the post 65 age group. As males age, their bodies produce less testosterone. In addition, a plasma protein called sex-hormone binding globulin increases and binds to circulating testosterone, lowering the amount of active hormone available for reactions. Coupled with this is the increase of bodyfat due to a slower metabolism and decreased exercise. This increase in fat boosts production of aromatase – the enzyme that converts testosterone into estrogen.

Although there is generally no way to predict if a steroid user will develop the condition, males who experienced the condition naturally as teenagers are at greater risk. This is one of the many reasons why teenagers should never use anabolic steroids. Older individuals should stop using the drugs at the first sign of swelling, and immediately see their physician.

Besides prior history, the type of drug being used is related to gynecomastia. Most steroids that are high in androgenic properties are likely candidates to produce the condition. Virtually all testosterone derivatives (propionate, cypionate, and enanthate) have been known to cause gynecomastia. Other drugs that may produce gynecomastia include: thyroid preparations, HGH (human growth hormone), marijuana and Valium.

No matter what you believe is the cause of your gynecomastia, seek immediate medical attention. This is because gynecomastia is one of the symptoms of testicular cancer. Odds are the condition was brought on by steroid (or other drug) use and not cancer, but it's still better to play it safe and go for a checkup.

EFFECTS ON THE GENITALIA

MALES
Contrary to popular belief, anabolic steroids do not cause an increase in penis size. There may be slight swelling because of fluid retention, but this is temporary and not indicative of true penile growth.

The previous myth may have developed because anabolic steroids do in fact cause a condition known as priapism in some males. Priapism is the medical term for a persistent and painful erection that is not relieved by intercourse or any other form of sexual release. Although on the surface this

Contrary to popular belief, anabolic steroids do not cause an increase in penis size, though they may cause testicular shrinkage during a cycle.

may sound desirable to the average male, those who suffer from the condition report otherwise. This is not surprising as penile tissue is not designed to remain engorged with blood for extended periods of time. In extreme cases of priapism there may be more blood forced into the penis than normal. Like most side effects, priapism is transitory and will disappear following cessation of drug use.

One area where there is a definite size change is the testicles. But the change is down not up! Most steroid users report some degree of testicular shrinkage during their cycle. This is to be expected given the body's hormonal control mechanism. Operating on the "use it or lose it" principle, once anabolic steroids are added to the system the body assumes its own testosterone levels are high and shuts down hormonal production. As the testes are the site of testosterone production, it is here that the effects are noticed in the form of shrinkage.

"I'm afraid that increasing your endogenous level of testosterone or even using exogenous testosterone, while possibly having an effect on libido, erection frequency and duration, will not increase penile size past puberty. Using exogenous testosterone will actually decrease testicular size while the testosterone is being used, and permanently in some cases of long-term abuse."

– Dr. Mauro DiPasquale, regular *MuscleMag* columnist, world authority on ergogenic drugs, and best-selling author "telling it like it is" with regards to steroids and sex-organ size change.

The degree of shrinkage and the duration depends on a number of factors. There are individual differences, but people using multiple steroids for extended periods of time will suffer the greatest degree of shrinkage. Furthermore, it usually takes these individuals longer for their natural testosterone levels to return to normal. In some instances medical intervention in the form of human chorionic gonadotropin (HCG) is needed to "kick start" the body's testosterone production.

As sperm production is greatly reduced during steroid use, some researchers have experimented with these drugs as a form of "male birth control." Unfortunately, even in the most extreme cases, there is still some sperm produced. And since only one is required for fertilization, relying on steroids as a form of contraception is very risky.

FEMALES

If the most noticeable genitalia side effect in men is testicular shrinkage, the most prominent in women is clitoral enlargement. In some cases the condition becomes so pronounced that the clitoris takes on the form of a small penis.

The biological basis for such a reaction lies with sexual differentiation. In the developing fetus, the presence of testosterone masculinizes the genital tissue into the testes, penis, and other male reproductive structures. The absence of testosterone causes the tissue to become female. The tissue, however, will always contain androgen receptors, and will masculinize if high levels of testosterone become present. As this rarely happens in healthy females, the reproductive structures remain female in appearance. Unfortunately, women using anabolic steroids face the risk of such masculinization. While most of the effects are transitory, a few women will need corrective surgery or drug therapy to "demasculinize" their genitalia.

Women who use anabolic steroids face the risk of masculinization – deepening of the voice, facial hair and clitoral enlargement to name only a few nasty side effects.

"I have had some success with trying to counter masculinizing side effects of anabolic steroids in women. The drug combination I have found most useful in treating hirsutism, clitoral enlargement and voice changes is the combination of an antiandrogen such as cyproterone acetate or flutamide along with an oral contraceptive, which has a progesterone component that is minimally androgenic."

– Dr. Mauro DiPasquale, regular *MuscleMag* columnist, best-selling author, and world authority on drug use in sports.

AIDS

Anabolic steroids (or any other drugs for that matter) do not cause AIDS. This disease is spread by a rhinovirus. Although there have been exceptions, the AIDS virus is transmitted during unprotected sex with an infected individual, or through sharing dirty needles among drug users. Once the virus enters the individual's body, it goes to work destroying the immune system. The virus itself does not cause death, but destroys the body's defence against other harmful organisms. Most AIDS-related deaths are the result of pneumonia or cancer.

Having said this, antisteroid advocates continuously spread the rumor that AIDS is caused by steroid use. "Bodybuilder dies of AIDS" scream the headlines. While tragic to the individual and his or her family and friends, the truth of the matter is far different. The incidence of AIDS among steroid users is no greater or less than among nonsteroid users. If steroid users practice unsafe sex, they are at the same risk for contracting AIDS as anyone else in our society.

The main focal point for associating steroids with AIDS lies with a few case studies where needle-sharing bodybuilders all developed AIDS. We must stress that what was in the needle (be it steroids or any other drug) had no influence on the presence or absence of the AIDS virus. If one of the users was infected with AIDS he or she was spreading infected blood to the others through shared needles. This is one of the main reasons why AIDS went rampant through the drug-using community in the early and mid 1980s. Steroid user or not, anyone who shares needles is putting themselves at great risk for contracting any number of deadly diseases including AIDS.

> **"Yet another fact that seems to elude the purveyors of 'steroid doom' is the use of steroids by the medical community for the treatment of various diseases. At this very moment there is research going on with AIDS patients to see if steroids can be used to stop the muscle-wasting and immune suppression of AIDS, and I know several researchers who are already achieving positive results in using steroids with AIDS patients."**
>
> – Will Brink, author and regular *MuscleMag* columnist commenting on a lesser-known side to the anabolic steroid issue.

Needle sharing among drug users is a foolish practice.

Lee Priest

Ironically, not only do steroids not cause AIDS, but they are currently being tested as a form of AIDS treatment (something that antisteroid advocates conveniently forget to mention). Such steroids as Oxandrolone, Deca-Durabolin, and Oxymetholone are being used to arrest many of the side effects of the AIDS virus including catabolism, anemia, and decreased immune response. And while the drugs are not a cure for the disease, they show great promise in prolonging the life of those afflicted with the virus.

Given the previous, you'd think it would be easy for medical professionals to start widespread treatment with steroids, but nothing could be further from the truth. The tough legislation concerning steroids has made them a taboo subject among the medical community. Physicians not only face banishment from their medical association but also run the risk of being prosecuted for a criminal offence. It's a sad state of affairs when a drug that could prolong the lives of hundreds of thousands of people is difficult to obtain simply because of the actions of a few "power seeking" politicians in Washington.

COSMETIC SIDE EFFECTS

Although the least significant in terms of health risks, the effects steroids have on physical appearance may be the most traumatic. Besides the previously mentioned acne, gynecomastia, and genitalia changes, steroids can produce other physical transformations.

In both men and women, there is usually a marked increase in facial and body hair. Many contestants in female bodybuilding contests reveal a "five o'clock shadow" that most males would be proud of.

Countering the increase in facial and body hair is the loss of scalp hair. For reasons not fully understood, high levels of circulating androgens cause scalp-hair follicles to degenerate. Many bodybuilders in their teens and early twenties show receding hairlines that belong on much older individuals. It is not uncommon for steroid users to be totally bald by the age of thirty. Although there are personal differences, those individuals with a history of male-patterned baldness in their family are at the greatest risk.

"That's not to say that steroids don't make a huge difference because they do, but again, if all it took to develop a champion physique was steroids, why aren't there more champions walking around? Millions of people take steroids, yet only a handful are good enough to make it to the pros each year. I'm just saying, wake up and smell the coffee. Use your common sense."

– Greg Zulak, former *MuscleMag* editor explaining how steroids are just one part of developing a contest-winning physique.

Another effect that can have social implications, particularly in females, is masculinization of the vocal chords. Many females who use steroids have voices deeper than most males. This is one of the few side effects that usually does not disappear after steroid use has stopped. A woman is permanently left with a deepened voice once the vocal chords have thickened and masculinized.

BONE CHANGES

James Hampton

In recent years the use of anabolic steroids by teenagers has increased dramatically. This practice is dangerous as most teens are not physically mature. Besides the negative effects on a teen's maturing endocrine system, steroids may have a detrimental effect on bones.

Normally a person's bones do not cease lengthening until the late teens or early twenties. Anabolic steroids have been shown to increase the rate at which the epiphyseal plates fuse. These growth areas at the ends of the body's long bones are responsible for giving the skeleton its full height. Once fused, further growth is impossible. A 14- or 15-year-old using steroids is putting him- or herself at risk for prematurely stunting his or her growth. This can have devastating psychological and social implications.

From a psychological perspective, most teens wish they were taller. For the teenage male, being bigger is often the shortcut to social acceptance and popularity at school. Not only will smaller bones mean shorter height, but smaller bones carry less muscle mass. If a teenager ends up shorter than his peers, when he could have been much taller, there may be severe mental stress and anguish.

Socially speaking, it's a fact that taller individuals have a greater chance of success than shorter individuals. A survey of corporate executives found that the average height was 6'2". Teenagers who choose to use anabolic steroids may be curtailing their long-term success just for a few extra pounds of bodyweight.

> "The ten-week cycle of cypionate will actually strengthen the tendons, ligaments, muscles and joints, making them better able to withstand the stress of heavy lifting. Thus the use of anabolic steroids gets rid of the pain by allowing the structures in and around your shoulder to take the heavy lifting without getting stressed out and inflamed."
> – Dr. Mauro DiPasquale, regular *MuscleMag* columnist and world authority on drug use in sports contradicting the view by antisteroid groups that steroids cause a weakening of tendon tissue.

TENDON CHANGES

Although steroids mainly affect muscle and not tendon tissue, there is some spill-over strengthening effects. This is, however, contrary to what many antisteroid advocates would have you believe. Over the past ten years bodybuilders have read countless magazine articles about some of their favorite stars tearing tendons. Antisteroid advocates are quick to seize these cases as further evidence of the evils of steroids. The basis of their argument is that they somehow weaken tendons. This is unfounded as no medical evidence exists to suggest steroids cause a breakdown of tendon tissue. But why the high incidence of tendon tears among bodybuilders? The answer is perhaps more basic than it seems.

Although not conclusive, the evidence suggests that steroids increase muscle size and strength proportionally faster than tendon strength. A nonuser's tendon strength keeps pace with muscle strength, but a steroid user's muscles vault way ahead. The result – muscles capable of producing much more power than the tendons can handle.

We should conclude that like most negative side effects, the incidence of tendon tears is often exaggerated to further the antisteroid cause. Nevertheless, bodybuilders (and other athletes using steroids) should be aware of the possible risks.

PSYCHOLOGICAL SIDE EFFECTS

ROID RAGE

It only makes sense to start this section with the most discussed behavioural side effect attributed to anabolic steroids. No topic related to steroids has received as much media coverage in recent years as "roid rage."

The term "roid" comes from steroid, and rage is a manifested form of intense anger. The theory behind roid rage is that anabolic steroids cause some individuals to become overly aggressive and hostile – in some cases to the point of criminal violence. Unfortunately, there is little credible evidence to support the theory of roid rage. In fact, roid rage was a "created" side effect put forward by a crafty defence attorney to get a client off.

AN INVENTED SIDE EFFECT?

It is difficult to pinpoint the exact moment roid rage entered the steroid vocabulary. It is believed to have originated in the mid to late 1980s when a number of attorneys tried using it as a novel defence strategy. One case involved a steroid-using construction worker who picked up a hitchhiker and beat him to death after an attempted robbery. Another was an angry motorist who, after being cut off at an intersection, forced the other driver off the road and beat the windows out of his car with a road sign! Despite a spirited effort on the part of defence attorneys the juries rejected the notion of roid rage and found their clients guilty.

Over the past ten years other criminal cases have featured roid rage as the star performer, and in most cases the jury doesn't buy the issue of roid rage. The media's approach, however, is another story.

No topic related to steroids has received as much media coverage in recent years as "roid rage."

> **"People will ask 'Well, aren't you afraid of getting roid rages?' I tell them that that's just an excuse for people who wanna go off and get angry. Look at all the guys who get drunk and drive cars and kill people. People get drunk at parties, stand around and spew, and everybody laughs and thinks it's hilarious."**
>
> – Lee Priest, top IFBB pro commenting on the hypocritical stance of antisteroid advocates who raise the "roid rage" issue.

Mark Costantini

AND THE MEDIA'S RESPONSE . . .

During the early 1990s viewers were treated to an almost endless parade of criminals who had supposedly "flipped out" after using steroids. In most cases the script was the same. A supposedly meek and mild individual was suddenly transformed into a psychotic criminal after "going on the juice." On the surface the stories seemed credible and convincing, but the truth is much different.

In virtually every case the individual had a history of violence before being charged with a criminal offence. The presence of alcohol was also common. Sounds familiar doesn't it? Alcohol user with a history of aggression goes too far and murders someone – in most cases a girlfriend or wife. This is sadly a far too common event in our society. Yet this gets little airplay during the media's presentation of each case. It's made to sound as if the steroids were the cause of the whole episode. The fact that the individual had a history of alcohol use and violence is all but ignored.

Valerie Gangi, Laura Binetti and Lynea Brehm

Milos
Sarcev

PSYCHOLOGICALLY SPEAKING

Besides defence attorneys and the media, a number of psychiatrists have developed reputations as being experts on roid rage. Taking the media's approach of ignoring the individual's history, many prominent medical journals have featured articles proclaiming the evils of anabolic steroids. The tragic part of this is that once a case study gets published in a reputable journal, the viewpoint is all but agreed to be true. It has reached the point where roid rage has become part of the psychiatric language – all because of a few "experts" who have carved out a niche for themselves by writing on roid rage.

All of this leaves us with the question, "Does roid rage actually exist?" In the minds of creative defence attorneys it does. After all, anything to diminish a clients responsibility for a crime is fair game.

The media regularly features roid rage because it's more "glamorous" than other criminal acts. Heroine and cocaine use have become so common in North American society that they've lost the viewer appeal. Anabolic steroids and "roid rage" offer many more exciting possibilities.

Finally, a few psychiatrists write about roid rage because it builds reputations and academic standing. In most cases (and we are only talking about a dozen or so) the individual had a history of violence, but this doesn't seem to matter.

In conclusion, it's safe to say that anabolic steroid users are no more or less likely to commit a criminal activity than nonusers. Yet as long as antisteroid advocates keep "inventing" side effects, the portrayal of these drugs will never reflect the realities of the situation.

AGGRESSION

While the evidence for roid rage is sketchy at best, most steroid users readily admit to becoming more agitated while on a cycle. This does not mean they become raving lunatics stalking the city late at night looking for victims. What it means is that for most users, aggression levels are elevated. The degree of elevation is usually related to presteroid aggression levels. If someone has a mild-mannered personality before using steroids, steroid use will in all probability not make much of a difference. If the person was "quick on the trigger" to begin with, steroid use may aggravate the condition. But to suggest that steroids cause an individual to become overly aggressive is doing the drugs an injustice. Yet, as with roid rage, antisteroid types continuously wave case studies about. They try to make it sound as if steroids are a shortcut to criminal activity (they can lead to jail time but for different reasons as we shall discuss later).

Chris Cormier and Pavol Jablonicky

"The first dosage feels good, and the second one feels even better. Pretty soon you are looking for higher and higher dosages, and the end point might not be as happy as you think it will be."

– "Doctor E" in an interview conducted by Will Brink for *MuscleMag*, commenting on how steroid addiction can creep up on unsuspecting bodybuilders.

In discussing steroid-related aggression we must be wary of situational factors. Many steroid users, especially the larger ones, take jobs in the security field – particularly as night-club bouncers. Such jobs continuously put individuals in potentially aggressive situations. As is often the case, by closing time some drunken patron calls the bouncer a "steroid head" or "juiced gorilla" and you can guess the rest – thrown punches and a bouncer being charged with "excessive violence." This is not to suggest that some steroid users with a chip on their shoulder don't initiate fights and then go too far. They often do. But steroid-related aggression can often be explained by circumstantial factors.

There is a benefit to the slightly elevated levels of aggression experienced by steroid users. Training day in day out at the local gym can sometimes be boring and monotonous. Steroid users report that while on a cycle they have elevated motivational levels, and the increased aggression allows them to attack the weights with a determination that is absent when they're off the "juice." Much of the extra intensity may be psychological rather than physical in nature; nevertheless, users value it just the same.

ANABOLIC ADDICTION

Although addiction to anabolic steroids has been suggested for some time, it is only in recent years that the medical community has taken serious notice. Addiction can be physical, psychological, or both in nature. Physical addiction can be defined as the condition whereby the body's chemical functioning has altered in such a way that its normal state is now the drug state. The body has become so dependent on the drug that it cannot function properly without it. Psychological addiction is often called "dependence," and involves the psychological craving for a drug. Although there may be no physical need, the individual feels that he or she must have the drug to survive.

Compounding the problem of addiction is the issue of tolerance. Tolerance is the condition whereby the body becomes accustomed to a given dosage of drug and the individual must consume ever increasing amounts of the drug to experience the same effect.

Closely associated with tolerance are withdrawal symptoms. Once the body becomes accustomed to using large quantities of a drug it will manifest a host of physical and psychological symptoms as it attempts to readjust to the predrug state. These symptoms include: depression, headaches, sweating, fatigue, and often psychomotor retardation (lack of control over muscles).

Although the evidence is limited, there is scientific data to suggest that steroids can be addictive. In one case study a 24-year-old male weightlifter was admitted to a psychiatric emergency room complaining of depression and increased outbursts of anger. The previous night he had experienced suicidal thoughts of crashing his car. He requested professional help because he felt "controlled" by the drugs and was unable to stop using them. The patient's history showed no symptoms of any kind for the first three months of anabolic steroid use. The symptoms started after he switched from using one drug in a cyclic manner to using five drugs in a noncyclic (continuous) manner.

In evaluating the patient, psychiatrists found that he met six of the criteria set down in the accepted diagnostic manual – DSM III. Among the symptoms of dependence exhibited by the individual were:

1) Continued use of the drug for a period longer than was intended.
2) Unsuccessful in his attempts to cut down on the drugs use.
3) Continued use of the drugs despite their effects on his social life.
4) Developed tolerance to the drugs.
5) Experienced withdrawal symptoms after cessation of drug use.
6) Continuation of drug use to avoid withdrawal symptoms.[10]

Zuzana Korinkova

The key word to many of the previous criteria is "continuous." Most bodybuilders who gain 20 to 30 pounds or more of muscular bodyweight become so accustomed to their new physique that any thoughts of losing it are out of the question. As soon as they go off the "juice" and begin losing weight, the immediate reaction is to reach for the steroid vile. In fact, as has become the practice these days, individuals no longer cycle the drugs but continue to use. Often the only limiting variable is money. And as long as the person's finances hold out, he or she will continue to stay on the juice. Of course this is where the problem lies. The longer a person stays on a drug and the higher the dosages become, the greater the chance of becoming addicted.

"**Short kids can get growth hormone. Heavy people can get drugs to take off weight. Bald people can get drugs to grow hair. People take stuff to pep up, calm down, elevate their mood, sleep better, etc. All these drugs have extremely bad reactions. Drugs such as female hormones can have potential dangers similar to anabolic steroids, yet thousands of women use them. If a thin person takes an anabolic drug to help build-up, he or she is a criminal. I'm very sorry but I don't understand this.**"

– *MuscleMag* reader commenting on the irrationality of current drug legislation which makes steroid use criminal and other drug use acceptable.

There are other cases in the medical literature to support the theory of steroid addiction. In all cases the individuals were using multiple steroids (four or five) for extended periods of time – often for years at a stretch.

DEPRESSION

Although rare, a few individuals have being diagnosed with depression following steroid use. In its broadest sense, depression is defined as the loss of interest in normal day-to-day activities. It includes such symptoms as low self-esteem, low libido, poor hygiene, insomnia, and loss of appetite.

Depression may be physiological or psychological in nature. Researchers suggest that physiological depression is caused by changes in the brain's neurotransmitter levels (chemicals that carry messages within the brain). Psychological depression is usually caused by external forces. Among these are the death of a loved one and job-related stress.

Depression related to anabolic steroid use may include one or both of the previous. If the individual was using heavy dosages of steroids for long periods of time, his or her system is altered in such a manner that when he or she comes off the drugs the body takes a couple of months to re-adjust. This "normalizing period" can include periods of physiological depression.

Coming off heavy steroid use may trigger depression as the body tries to re-adjust and normalize to its presteroid state.

The loss of muscular body-weight brings with it its own set of problems. Most bodybuilder's lives revolve around their physiques. If the daily comments of "you're looking ripped today" or "you're as big as a house," are suddenly replaced by "are you losing weight?" or "where's the rest of you?" the user often loses self-esteem and may slip into psychological depression.

The degree of depression depends on a number of factors, one of the most important being how drug use was terminated. If the user quits "cold turkey" (stops abruptly) the body is suddenly left in a shocked state. In these cases depression is usually more pronounced than in someone who gradually decreases the drugs over time. Gradually lowering the drug dosage allows the body's endocrine system to normalize back to pre-steroid levels.

Another indicator of the degree of depression is the pattern of steroid use. Individuals using multiple drugs in a noncyclic manner will in all probability suffer a more severe depression than someone who cycled one drug over a short period of time.

> "When you take in a synthetic type of testosterone your body stops manu-facturing it. Your body is always trying to remain in equilibrium. In this case, your hypo-thalamus sends signals to your testicles that there is plenty of testosterone available, so they can take a rest. When they rest for an extended period of time, they stop doing their job altogether. So it may take several months for your body to bring its testosterone level back to where it was before you started taking steroids."
>
> – Bill Starr, John Hopkins University strength and conditioning coach responding to a friend's comments about his struggle to re-adjust after coming off the "juice."

The thought of losing 20 to 30 pounds by coming off the juice is out of the question for many bodybuilders.

Whether physiological or psychological in nature, users who report feeling low or experience any of the previous symptoms should consult their physician. Depression is not something to be taken lightly and may even lead to suicide.

SUICIDE

From what is known about the behavioral effects of steroids, it is likely they have played a role in a few suicides. Untreated depression may lead to some individuals choosing death as a way to escape the feelings of despair. For others, the loss of muscular size may be enough to send them into a suicide spiral.

Teenagers may be at special risk for steroid-related suicide as there have been cases of adults selling steroids to teenagers in exchange for sexual services.[10] In such cases the loss of self-esteem, which often accompanies such practices, may lead to suicide. As some teenagers have committed suicide over acne or the breakup with a girlfriend or boyfriend, it is clear that steroids should never be used by anyone in this age group.

Although the incidence of steroid-related suicide is low, users should watch for any negative psychological symptoms. At the slightest indication of such, terminate steroid use and seek medical attention.

CONCLUSION

Like most drugs, anabolic steroids are not side effect free. In any population there will be individuals who experience adverse reactions to certain drugs. The common antibiotic penicillin is a perfect example. Most individuals can use the drug with out any side effects. Others can go into allergic shock and die. The same goes for the most used steroid in society – birth control pills. Yes, they're steroids (just not the anabolic type), and if you look them up in the *Physicians Desk Reference* (*PDR* or *CPS* – the manuals listing most of

"This seems a totally irresponsible position by the board. This means that no longer can a person go to his doctor to get off steroids, to ask which are mild and safe drugs, how to use them safely and how to avoid side effects. Presumably you can no longer even go to your doctor and ask for blood tests to find out if you are causing yourself harm while on the steroids, because then the doctor would be 'assisting' you."

– Greg Zulak, former *MuscleMag* editor commenting on the Ontario College of Physicians' governing body which threatened to take away physicians' licenses if they offered any type of advice or counseling to steroid users.

the world's commonly prescribed medications) you'll see a long list of horrendous side effects. But birth control pills are considered relatively safe because the vast majority of women who use them don't experience severe side effects. The side effects listed in the *PDR* are there for legal reasons to cover the drugs' manufacturers.

The same holds true for anabolic steroids. Despite what sports organizations and antisteroid advocates say, the vast majority of steroid users don't experience the horrendous side effects commonly cited in the popular media. This is not to say there is no risk. Any drug can be dangerous if abused. This goes for alcohol, Valium and anabolic steroids. But to say that steroids are cancer-causing, psychotic-inducing chemicals is a gross misrepresentation. And while teenagers and females should never use these drugs, individuals in their twenties or beyond, who do so under medical supervision, can use them in relative safety. Of course the legal aspects are another story.

LEGAL ISSUES

Recognizing that laws vary among countries with respect to anabolic steroid use, we thought it appropriate to include a brief discussion. As most readers are residents of Canada and the United States, the bulk of our analysis will center on these two countries.

The criminalization of anabolic steroids in the United States started in 1988 with the passing of the Anti-Drug Abuse Act. This piece of legislation made it illegal for physicians to prescribe anabolic steroids for nonmedical reasons. On the surface this may have seen justified but it only made things worse. Instead of going to their physicians for regular checkups, steroid users were left to their own devices.

The real bombshell was dropped in 1990 when Congress passed the Federal Anabolic Steroids Controls Act, which made steroids a controlled substance. This law put steroids in the same category as such hard street

> **"Part of the problem is due to the misconception by legislators and the general public that all steroids are essentially the same. This is in large part due to the fact that package inserts and the *Physician's Desk Reference* are written by drug company attorneys, who, to protect their clients, feel compelled to list all 70 or so side effects ever reported for anabolic steroids as a group. Such warnings tend to convince a medically uninformed public that all anabolic steroids are dangerous drugs. The reasons behind much of the other antisteroid propaganda which has become so fashionable in the last decade are less clear."**
>
> – Dr. Robert Price, well-known bodybuilding writer commenting on some of the reasons why the general public's perception of anabolic steroids is so negative.

Hamdullah Aykutlu and Willie Stalling

drugs as heroine, morphine, and crack cocaine. In short, the United States made steroid users part of the "drug war." Possession of so much as one bottle or vial of steroids will get an individual serious jail time. What was once a recreational practice among the bodybuilding fraternity now leads to lengthy prison sentences.

In Canada things are not as drastic, but they're slowly getting there. In the early 1990s steroids were reclassified under the Food and Drug Act. Instead of a $500 fine for possession, steroid dealers may face a $5000 fine and/or jail time. Possession of steroids is not a criminal offence in Canada, yet. But the law has a problem as it doesn't distinguish between quantity for personal use and quantity for trafficking. One bottle of Winstrol may be for personal use but two bottles could be considered quantity enough for selling. We must emphasize that Canadian drug agencies follow their American counterparts very closely (they often work together) and there is a determined effort in Canada to make possession of steroids a criminal offence. It's quite possible that by the time this book goes to print the legislation will have changed. Readers of this book living in Canada should pay particular attention to any new laws concerning steroids. In particular, *MuscleMag International* keeps its readers up to date on the steroid scene. If steroids become an illegal drug you may have to rethink your whole training strategy.

Gunter Schlierkamp

EASY TARGETS

When anabolic steroids began making front-page news in the late 1980s, following Canadian sprinter, Ben Johnson's debacle at the 1988 Olympics, it was more than just other athletes who took notice. Law-enforcement agencies saw an area where easy arrests could be made, and hence careers furthered. As most steroid users tend to be law-abiding citizens, the new legislation caught most off guard. Many were unaware of the new legislation making steroids illegal; others chose to ignore it assuming that the authorities had no interest in prosecuting "mere steroid users."

Both groups had much to learn as ambitious district attorneys made reputations and careers prosecuting steroid users. The late 1980s and early 1990s were a boom time for law-enforcement agents "hunting" steroid

> "When anabolic steroids were declared a controlled substance, availability decreased, black-market prices soared, and thousands of people who may have done themselves physical and emotional harm were spared the temptation. Though we don't realize it, on an individual basis, we're saved as a society."
>
> – Bryan Denham, regular *MuscleMag* contributor offering an entirely different opinion on the government's reclassification of anabolic steroids.

Flex Wheeler

"It was supposed to be some super drug from East Germany. And there were some real good pros who tried it. I was just sitting watching from far away. Then we find out that some guy was making it in his basement using ordinary steroids, and cashing cheques for $300 for five cents' worth of sesame seed oil. And this bunch of idiots were buying it."

– Samir Bannout, 1983 Mr. Olympia commenting on how anyone can be taken in by bogus steroids including top pros.

users. Success was found in every gym bag and locker room. The agents' jobs were made easier by the "inexperience" of their targets. As stated earlier most steroid users were not versed in the art of avoiding law-enforcement agents. This is because they followed the laws of society. It takes practice to become a successful criminal, and as most steroid users were not, arrests came quick and easy.

A PREDICTABLE BACKFIRE

The reclassification of steroids in the late 1980s accomplished two things – it gave steroids the greatest possible advertising and drove the practice underground. Let's look at both in more detail.

Up until the much publicized crackdown on steroid users, most people were unaware that the drugs even existed. Steroid use was one of the few "secrets" that athletes had known about since the 1950s. Both Ben Johnson and law-enforcement agencies changed all that. Now everyone was walking in to gyms wanting vials and syringes. Steroid dealers reported that the late 1980s and early 1990s were the greatest time ever for "business." Many reported having shipments sold before they even arrived at their door. It seemed all the attention steroid busts made had the opposite effect of what was planned. Instead of a decrease in use, the demand was greater than before.

Besides the increased business for dealers, the other major change brought about by the crackdown was to revamp the nature of the black market. Before the increased attention, typical steroid "dealers" were patrons at the local gym, who, with the exception of selling a few tablets, were law-abiding citizens. In most cases they sold steroids to pay for their own use. Making "big bucks" was not an issue as the profit margin was only small – say $5 to $10 a bottle. As soon as the legislation changed and steroids became illegal, however, most of these individuals got out of the business. The problem, however, was that the demand was greater than before.

THE BLACK MARKET

Anytime you have a drug that is illegal but in big demand, you'll find someone willing to take risks to sell it. Whether alcohol, as in the 1920s, or crack cocaine in the 1990s, selling illegal drugs is big business. As soon as the steroid crackdown started, many of the major supplier of the drugs were either shut down or stopped making the drugs. To meet the continued demand, steroid use went underground and became the attention of big-time drug dealers. Where before the $5 to $10 profit margins were ignored by street drug dealers, the increased risks associated with steroid dealing meant that a bottle or vial of steroids now sold for $80 to $100. Instead of a bodybuilder buying from someone he knew at the gym, in all probability he was having to deal with individuals directly or indirectly associated with organized crime. As these dealers have other "products" to sell, steroid users began to garner more and more attention from law-enforcement agencies. Hence the situation we've now reached.

BOGUS DRUGS

The days of walking into a sympathetic physician's office and obtaining steroids are over. So too are the days of trusting your contact at the local gym. With the involvement of so many "players" on the steroid scene, users have little or no idea as to where their supply is coming from.

Samir Bannout

The majority of body-builders these days obtain their steroids from illegal sources. In many cases the drugs are stolen from legitimate pharmaceutical labs. With the profits so high it doesn't take much coaxing on the part of a drug dealer to convince an employee to "divert" a few hundred steroid bottles before they're catalogued and recorded.

Another popular route is to send couriers to countries were steroids are legal and easy to obtain. Many of the steroids on the North American black market come from Mexico and Europe, and tales abound of high-speed pursuits across international borders.

In recent years, by far, the most popular form of anabolic steroids are bogus or counterfeit. There are two types of counterfeit steroids. If the buyer is lucky the drug is real but not manufactured in a legitimate pharmaceutical laboratory. Called semibogus, these drugs may or may not contain the steroid

"The best advice I can give you is, if you're not feeling well, if you don't feel right, get looked at by a doctor immediately. If you're cramping up and you're nauseous and ill, something is obviously wrong. Take it seriously. Don't wait. Don't say, 'I'll get looked at later; first I've got to do my show.' The heck with the show. Later may be too late. Go to the hospital. Get checked out. Get blood work done."

– Dr. Mauro DiPasquale, best-selling author and regular *MuscleMag* columnist offering good advice for those who decide to use steroids and other performance-enhancing drugs.

advertised on the label but a cheaper form instead. Users don't really care, however, as long as the drug works without any noticeable side effects.

The other category of bogus steroids are fake from bottom to cap top. In most cases the bottle or vial contains inert substances that have no anabolic properties whatsoever. Stories circulate of users injecting cooking oil into their thighs and consuming sugar or flour tablets. If the buyer is lucky the substance they are using has no detrimental health effects, and the only thing lost is money. But if individuals tamper with sealed Tylenol bottles (as occurred in the mid 1980s in a number of United States drugstore outlets) steroid users buying from unknown black-market sources are leaving themselves open to direr consequences.

COMING OFF STEROIDS

Given the recent crackdown on steroid use and the daily bombardment of potential side effects (many of which as we said are exaggerated) many steroid users reading this text may decide to "come off the juice." In many respects this is a smart decision as the black market is flooded with bogus steroids – many of which are more dangerous than the drugs they're supposed to imitate. If your particular country has made steroids illegal you have this to consider as well. As for the teenagers reading this text, you should not be using steroids period.

Whatever your personal reasons for coming clean, there are a few points to consider. You should be aware that like most other drugs, steroid use is often a difficult habit to quit. Your first priority should be to seek out

"I could feel a tremendous catabolic process taking place in my body and in the space of three weeks I weighed 182 pounds! I couldn't believe it. I looked and felt like a little boy. My gynecomastia was really starting to get bad. My nipples were very tender and sore. So, the bottom line was I weighed 182, had pulled muscles, sore joints, bad gynecomastia, and because my hypothalamus was so suppressed, my immune system was a joke. I had swollen glands, a sore throat, and a constantly elevated body temperature. It was at this point that I realized I could go no lower."

– J. Michael Fine, former steroid user.

Lee Priest

medical assistance. Granted you should have been doing so from the beginning, but it's now an absolute must. You may have to "shop around" because most medical doctors are wary of associating with steroid-using athletes, least they be prosecuted by their medical governing boards. The best approach may be the direct approach. March into his or her office and lay everything out – you were using this, that, and the other thing, but now wish to come clean. Most doctors will appreciate the honesty, and may agree to help you.

Besides medical support, the help of concerned friends and relatives is essential. Withdrawing from any drug is highly emotional and requires constant psychological support. Besides the depression and irritability produced by fluctuating hormone levels, the loss of muscular bodysize is a source for much emotional grief. Care and consideration by significant others is an absolute must.

Finally, the role of nutrition should not be overlooked. With your immunity system left in a precarious state, don't be surprised if you catch one flu on top of another. While nutrition can't prevent these ailments, it can lessen the chances of catching and speed recovery when you do.

Nutrition also plays a role in helping reduce the amount of muscle tissue lost. Yes, you will lose much of that hard-earned size, but you can hold on to some of it by making sure your dietary needs are met. Supplements play a big role as you'll discover your appetite is diminished after coming off steroids. Instead of force feeding, try one or two protein shakes a day to keep intake high. Also, vitamins and minerals should be consumed to keep the body's major systems functioning properly – particularly your much abused endocrine system.

How long it takes to fully recover from heavy steroid use depends on a number of factors. Generally speaking, the longer you have been using the more difficult the transition. Those who have been stacking four to five drugs will have a much more difficult time than those only taking one or two. Although it varies from individual to individual, steroid withdrawal can be broken down into three phases.

Paul DeMayo

PHASE I

Phase I is probably the hardest to initiate but the easiest to handle. After months or even years of steroid use, the user decides to quit. To a nonuser this doesn't seem to be a monumental decision, but to someone used to daily injections and popping pills, deciding to come off the juice can be very traumatic. Although there are good reasons for quitting "cold turkey" – chief of which are the legal aspects – a gradual tapering off of dosage will ensure an easier recovery period.

The first few weeks off steroids are not too physically demanding as there are still circulating drugs in the system. This enables workout poundages and energy levels to remain relatively unchanged. Psychologically, things may be tough as users realize it's only a matter of time before they begin to lose size. About six to eight weeks after terminating steroid use, most individuals start realizing the effects steroids have had on their system. Instead of being able to train for two to three hours at full intensity, most are lucky to go an hour without burning out. Waking up in the mornings becomes interesting as well. The once unheard of feelings off tiredness and soreness start to rear their ugly heads. Users may also notice that where before they had huge appetites and couldn't eat enough food, now finishing a meal is a chore. At times like this, protein and carbohydrate drinks play an important role in slowing the loss of valuable muscle tissue.

"Today, when steroid users buy their drugs, most times they don't even know if they're buying real drugs or fake imitations. Even if they're real, who knows if they're sterile? With so many risk factors how can people sink a loaded syringe full of this garbage into their butts?

– Ron Harris, *MuscleMag* guest editorialist commenting on the dangers of black-market steroids.

In terms of bodyweight, most individuals will lose an average of 15 to 20 pounds during the first 10 weeks. This is not a big deal if you weigh 245 to 250 to begin with, but for a smaller body-builder, a 15-pound weight loss can make a big difference in appearance.

PHASE II

Starting about 12 to 15 weeks out, individuals enter Phase II of steroid with-drawal. This is by far the most difficult phase to endure, but if individuals make it through, things are uphill from here on.

Andrulla Blanchette

If the individual had trouble cop-ing with the weight loss in the previous weeks, the radical changes experienced during Phase II can be psychologically devastating. Loses of 30 to 40 pounds are normal and are due to the almost total elimination of the steroid's anabolic and anticatabolic effects on the body. In addition, individuals who had been using steroids for extended periods of time will have had their own testosterone produc-tion virtually shut down. Not only have the steroid's effects wore off but the individ-ual's own hormone supply is nonexistent.

Besides the weight loss, strength levels decrease and workouts fail to produce a meaningful pump. It is at this stage that many users decide to go back on the juice. They just can't handle the repeated barbs from their "friends" and the loss of their once proudly displayed physique.

Another problem stems from a combination of attempting to use the same poundages as before, and a greatly reduced recovery ability between workouts, leading to an increased susceptibility to injuries.

Many users also report that during this phase of withdrawal they catch every virus going around. Sore throats and colds – something never experienced while on a cycle – are now the norm.

Rock bottom for many former steroid users is a loss of 50 pounds or more of muscular bodyweight, one or more painful injuries, and a chronic flu that just won't seem to go away. Most give up training at this point – either out of necessity or embarrassment. This is perhaps the most crucial time period in the entire steroid withdrawal phase. Those who resist the urge to resume taking steroids can take solace in the fact that by about 20 weeks natural recovery begins.

PHASE III

After having bottomed out, individuals can begin to climb out of the previous phase's rut. A few weeks off will do wonders for nagging injuries, and natural testosterone levels should begin to rise. By a process called overcompen-sation, natural levels may even rise above normal. After months or years of not producing testosterone the body may overcompensate and produce as

"My poundages dropped somewhat, my muscle had atrophied on some level, and my recu-perative abilities were not as before. While I was taking the anabolics my recuperation was remarkable. It seemed that I could train all day, and be able to train the same bodypart the very next morning. All of a sudden I was sore for sev-eral days after a training session and I realized my recuperative powers were now that of a mortal man."

– J. Michael Fine, former steroid user commenting on side effects experienced while coming off "the juice."

much as possible in a short time period. Bodybuilders can take advantage of this and regain much of their previously lost bodymass. After a period of time the body's hormone production will settle down and workouts will have to be adjusted accordingly.

Although it varies, most individuals will find that it takes six to eight months for their bodies to go through all three phases of steroid withdrawal. As the entire process can be called "endocrine shock," constant monitoring by a physician is an absolute must. In extreme cases, a short therapy of HCG (human chorionic gonadotrophin) is needed to kick start the testes into testosterone production.

EXERCISING – BACK TO BASICS

Former steroid users must realize that their bodies cannot handle the same intensity levels as when they were on the juice. Six-day-a-week split routines are out of the question. Ease back into training using a three-day-a-week routine and see what happens. You may be able to progress to a four-day routine, but be wary. Most natural trainers need far more rest than individuals using steroids.

Another thing, don't make the mistake of piling on the same number of plates as you did in your "steroid days." Not only are your muscles not used to this amount of weight after a layoff, but your reduced hormone levels mean your recovery system will be taxed to the limit trying to keep up with such stress. Those trying to "pick up where they left off" invariably injure themselves during the first few days back.

"Listen, I know this is not going to be the easiest thing you ever did, but it isn't going to be the hardest either. The first thing you have to do is forget how much you lifted back in your steroid days. Start with a clean slate on training. You need to start out slowly, using very basic movements. And you need to make haste slowly. The gains will come, but they will come more slowly."

– Bill Starr, explaining the realities of natural training to a friend who had resumed training after coming off anabolic steroids.

Ease into your workouts to prevent injuries after coming off the juice. Don't fool yourself into thinking your body can handle the same intensity levels.
– Dennis Newman

Your training during the first few months back will probably be the most difficult of your career. Strength levels are down, recovery takes much longer, and the rapid weight gains experienced during your steroid days will no longer be present. On the positive side, however, every little bit of success you achieve will be natural. No, it won't rival that of a steroid user, but it won't disappear either (unless you give up training). With time, patience, and dedication, you will build a physique you and others can be proud of.

THERAPEUTIC AND GYM DOSAGES

For many of the drugs listed in the Appendix we list therapeutic and "gym" dosages. Therapeutic dosages are self-explanatory and simply refer to the dosage administered for medical treatment. Gym dosage is the amount consumed by athletes during a steroid cycle. Unlike therapeutic dosages, gym dosages have not been calculated using any scientific method. For the most part it is "hand me down" knowledge and even this gets increased from generation to generation. The steroid users of thirty years ago would be aghast at what some bodybuilders are taking these days. For comparison purposes the gym dose will be expressed as a percentage of the therapeutic dose.

STEROID CYCLES

The training seasons of most athletes can be subdivided into two broad categories – the off-season and precontest season. For bodybuilders the off-season consists of focusing their attention on increased muscular size and bringing up lagging bodyparts. Workouts tend to be shorter and more intense in nature, with the greatest emphasis on maximum weight. During the precontest season most bodybuilders increase workout duration by adding more sets and reps, using less weight and concentrating on stricter style.

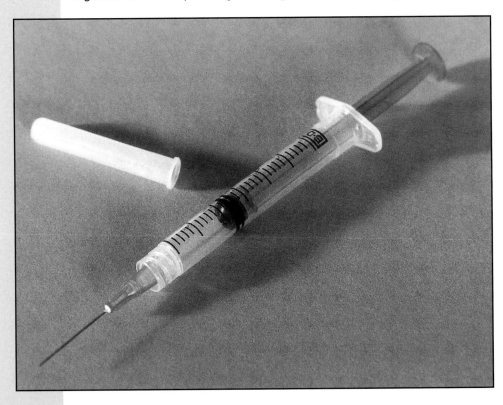

Athletes who use anabolic steroids usually plan their cycles around the season. If they're competing in a drug-tested event, drug use needs to be stopped to allow clearance from the system. Most bodybuilding contests are not drug tested but bodybuilders usually eliminate steroids from their systems in the weeks leading up to a contest for other reasons – the most important being water retention.

Among their many properties, steroids cause the user's body to conserve salts and other bodily fluids. During the off-season this is fine but on contest day the objective is to be as ripped as possible. Therefore most bodybuilders tailor their cycles to correspond with the competitive season.

Milos Sarcev

TYPES OF CYCLES

Although other books may use a different classification, we are going to describe the five types first put forward in our book *Steroid Myths*, first published in 1991. These cycles are not meant to be a guide for use, but to give readers an idea of the various patterns of steroid use.

STRAIGHT ARROW

The "straight arrow" pattern of use consists of a steroid stack in which the drug dosages remain consistent throughout the cycle. From start to finish the individual keeps the dosages the same.

CLIFF-HANGER PATTERN

This pattern involves a gradual increase in dosage during the cycle, and then the user abruptly stops. For most athletes this pattern is used during the off-season as the high concentrations of steroids in their system would otherwise not allow them to pass a drug test. The big disadvantage of this pattern is the sudden withdrawal, causing shock to the person's endocrine system. As a result the individual often experiences such symptoms as low sex drive, impotence, lack of motivation, and in some cases, depression.

Rozann Keyser

SKI-SLOPE PATTERN

This pattern can be considered the opposite of the previous. Instead of gradually increasing the dosages and stopping at the highest dosage, the individual starts the cycle at the highest dose and gradually decreases over time. This pattern is popular with competitive athletes as it leaves the lowest levels of steroids in their systems close to a contest. Another advantage is that the body's endocrine system is given a chance to "kick in" towards the end of the cycle.

PYRAMID PATTERN

This is perhaps the most complex of steroid cycles but is one of the more popular. The pattern can be broken down into three phases. Phase One consists of gradually increasing the dosage until the maximum is reached. Phase Two consists of maintaining this maximum dosage for a given period of time. Phase Three consists of gradually decreasing the dosage until the cycle terminates. As with the previous pattern, the pyramid pattern is popular with athletes who want to pass a drug test.

NON-CYCLIC PATTERN

Although it sounds like a contradiction, this is by far the most popular method of taking steroids these days. In simple terms, athletes take as many different steroids as possible, in the highest dosages possible, for the longest period of time. As long as both the supply and the cash to buy remains, the individual never terminates the cycle. This is a very dangerous practice as the likelihood of serious side effects increases with increased dosage and duration. Even the most diehard of steroid users will admit that using multiple steroids in high dosages for extended periods of time puts the user at great risk for serious health problems.

Perhaps the most frightening aspect of this cycle is that its most popular patrons are teenagers. They know many of their heroes are using the "juice." Therefore, they invest hundreds and in some cases thousands of dollars in purchasing the latest in pharmacological aids. Following the old adage "if some is good more is better," many teenagers use dosages and amounts which surpass many professional athletes.

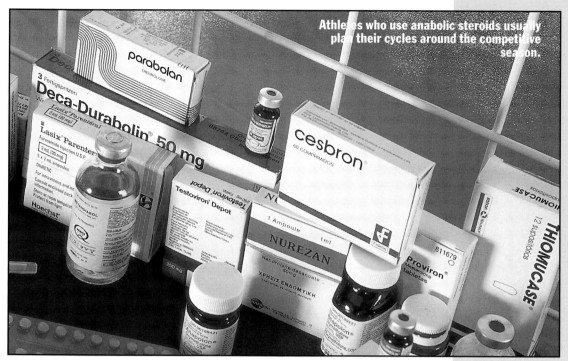

Athletes who use anabolic steroids usually plan their cycles around the competitive season.

TRADE AND GENERIC NAMES

There are two primary categories of names used to describe anabolic steroids (a third – called the chemical name – is usually reserved for chemical research only, and consists of naming the drug according to its atomic structure). The generic name is the name used by chemists and pharmacologists the world over. The trade name is a copyrighted name used by the manufacturer of a given steroid. For example, any manufacturer can market the common painkiller acetasalicylic acid (ASA), but only the Bayer corporation of Germany can call the drug "Aspirin." Most anabolic steroids have the same naming format. For example, the commonly used steroid Dianabol (no longer manufactured as such) has the generic name methandrostenolone.

References
1) P. Embleton and G. Thorne, *Steroids Myths – The Responsible Use of Anabolic Steroids* (St. John's Nfld: Thorton Publishing Ltd.,1991).
2) Reuters, "Nurmi Won With Drugs in Olympics, Swede says," *The Globe and Mail* (December 14, 1990), A-19.
3) "Anabolic Steroids: Doctors Denounce Them But Athletes Aren't Listening," *Science*, 176: 30 (June 1972), *News and Comments.*
4) J. Mathas, "Dan Duchaine: The Steroid Guru," *MuscleMag International* (July 1989), 58.
5) "Sports in Brief: An Anabolic Spray," *The Globe and Mail* (December 5, 1990), A-13.
6) *MuscleMedia* 2000 (April 1996).
7) P. Stepaniak, J. Furst, and D. Woodard, "Anabolic Steroids as a Countermeasure Against Bone Demineralization During Space Flight, Aviation," *Space and Environmental Medicine* (February 1986).
8) H.A. Haupt, and G.D. Rovere, "Anabolic Steroids: A Review of the Literature," *The American Journal of Sports Medicine*, 12 (1984) 469-484.
9) J.C. Cohen and others, "Hypercholesterolemia in Male Powerlifters Using Anabolic Androgenic Steroids," *The Physician and Sports Medicine*, 10: 8 (1988), 49-56.
10) V. Cowart, "Natural Institute on Drug Abuse May Join In Anabolic Steroid Research," *JAMA*, 261:13 (April 7, 1989).

CHAPTER TWO

Estrogens and Anti-Estrogens

It only makes sense to follow up the previous chapter on anabolic steroids – derivatives of testosterone – with estrogen, the equivalent female hormone.

Although testosterone is the primary steroid hormone responsible for increasing muscular size and strength, there is evidence to suggest estrogen also plays a role. Farmers have been aware of this for years, as giving cattle estrogen injections produces significant increases in body-weight. In recent years reports have surfaced of bodybuilders adding small amounts of estrogen to their steroid stacks. While the anecdotal reports are sketchy, studies with animals seem to suggest the practice may be supported by scientific theory.

Debbie Kruck

ESTROGEN

Estrogen can be considered the female counterpart to testosterone as it is the primary hormone secreted by the female ovaries. It regulates female reproduction, and develops and maintains female secondary sex characteristics. This hormone is also important for the proper functioning of the liver, bones, arteries and skin, and affects estrogen tissues in the hypothalamus and anterior pituitary gland.

Contrary to popular belief, males also produce estrogen – albeit in much smaller concentrations than females. Virtually all of the estrogen produced in males comes from the conversion of testosterone to estrogen by way of special enzymes called aromatases. The process is called aromatization.

HOW IT WORKS

Muscle tissue was once thought to be estrogen insensitive, yet recent studies with animals have shown estrogenic substances demonstrate an anabolic effect in beef cattle. The anabolic effect is believed to be caused by the indirect action on the pituitary which causes the release of bovine growth hormone and a direct action on skeletal muscle receptors.[1] There is evidence to show estrogens induce the production of testosterone receptors, which would result in an anabolic response without an increase in endogenous

There is some evidence to suggest birth control pills may increase amino acid utilization.

androgen levels.[2] Bovine skeletal muscle contains both free-androgen and estrogen receptors. Since only androgens appear to exert a direct growth effect on receptor sites, the combination of the two would explain the additive growth response observed in cattle given combinations of estrogenic and androgenic drugs.

When subcutaneous implants of estradiol benzoate were used alone, muscle growth (with a small increase in masculinity in steers) was observed. In the subjects in which this drug was combined with Trenbolone Acetate (in subcutaneous implants at a ratio of 1:10) increases in muscle and fat were produced, as well as increases in masculinity in both heifers and steers.[1]

APPLICATION TO BODYBUILDING

Given what is known from animal research, it is possible that estrogen use in humans might produce both an increase in endogenous growth hormone and the total number of testosterone receptors. There were at least two cases of bodybuilders using estrogen propionate in the province of Newfoundland, Canada, in 1991. Both reported gains above what they normally experienced while using steroids alone. While the effect may be placebo in nature, there may actually be a synergistic effect when combined with steroids. When asked why they used it, one bodybuilder responded, "Estrogen propionate, testosterone propionate; what's the difference?"

BIRTH CONTROL PILLS

While estrogen is often seen as a problem because of its feminizing actions (for example, gynecomastia), the right ratio of anabolic steroids to estrogen might be the key to massive muscle growth. There is some evidence to suggest birth control pills may increase amino acid utilization – although the exact procedure is not known. One theory has it that the estrogen-containing birth control pills may boost vitamin B6's ability to moderate amino acid metabolism. Vitamin B6 functions as a coenzyme in the decarboxylation, transamination and deamination of most amino acids.[3] As many female athletes use birth control pills for both birth control and timing their menstrual periods, it would be interesting to conduct a comparison study between users and nonusers.

RU 486 – ANOTHER GROUNDS FOR CONTROVERSY?

One of the most controversial drugs to become available in recent years is the European-manufactured abortion pill, RU 486. The pill works by inducing massive hormone fluctuations in the female body, thus causing any developing fetus to abort. The moral implications of such will be left to others. For our purposes, besides its abortion-inducing properties, the pill seems to have anticatabolic characteristics. Some studies have suggested the pill protects muscle tissue from the catabolic effects of cortisol. Before rushing for a prescription however, other research indicates the pill may decrease the sensitivity of testosterone receptors. So while the pill may be anticatabolic, it may also be antianabolic. Both effects cancel one another out, and reports from European bodybuilders seem to confirm this. Few, if any, report any significant benefits from taking RU 486 – certainly none that compare to an average cycle of anabolic steroids. So while the drug may not have any life-threatening side effects, it doesn't seem to offer any physiological benefits either. In short, it's a waste of money for bodybuilders and other athletes trying to gain muscle mass.

SIDE EFFECTS

We would be negligent if we left the impression that males should use estrogen for ergogenic purposes. Let's face it, if nature had meant males to have high levels of estrogen circulating in their bodies, there would have been an entirely different evolutionary plan. The fact that small amounts of estrogen can cause gynecomastia, and transsexuals (male to female) use estrogen to feminize the body after surgery, should give an indication of the risks associated with estrogen therapy.

Suzan Kaminga and Ericca Kern

Despite the limited evidence (and it is very limited) about estrogen inducing testosterone receptors, and estrogen-fed cattle increasing in bodyweight, we feel obligated to advise you not to use estrogen for athletic purposes. The risks far outweigh the benefits.

ANTI-ESTROGENS

It may seem ironic when a bodybuilder uses both estrogen and anti-estrogen drugs, but this gets back to what we were saying earlier about ratios. In small amounts estrogen may increase the number of testosterone receptors, and hence boost the effects of circulating testosterone. If excessive amounts of estrogen are present however, numerous unpleasant side effects may develop. The most well-known of these is gynecomastia – swelling of the breast region in males caused by testosterone being converted (aromatized) to estrogen. (see the section on gynecomastia in Chapter One)

Most steroid users are aware that anabolic steroids may produce gynecomastia and include anti-estrogenic drugs in their steroid stacks to minimize the condition. The following are three of the most common anti-estrogen drugs used by bodybuilders.

> Trade Name: Nolvadex
> Generic Name: tamoxifen citrate
> Tablet Size: 10 and 20 mg
> Therapeutic Dosage: 1 to 2 tablets daily
> Gym Dose: 5 to 100 percent

Although not an anabolic steroid, many bodybuilders include it in their stacks in the belief that its anti-estrogen properties will prevent the feminizing effects brought on by steroid aromatization. Others use it to treat existing cases of gynecomastia.

Nolvadex's primary mechanism of action is to compete with estrogen for estrogen receptors, thereby reducing estrogen's feminizing effects. For most this is a viable option, but for others it may be counterproductive because, as mentioned earlier, the evidence suggests estrogen may increase the quantity or quality of testosterone receptors. Other researchers have found Nolvadex may inhibit enzymes needed for testosterone production. Finally, Nolvadex has been found to act like an estrogen in some individuals.[4] If any of the previous is true, bodybuilders may be adding to their problems rather than eliminating them.

One of the least known effects of Nolvadex concerns its termination before a contest. Like most hormonal drugs, Nolvadex may produce a "rebound effect" when coming off the drug. In this case, estrogen levels may shoot skyhigh, causing the body to retain enormous amounts of water, leaving the individual looking like a water-soaked sponge on contest day.

Although not often considered, there is evidence to suggest Nolvadex may influence HGH levels. One study found that the increases in HGH brought about by testosterone enanthate administration could be blocked by Nolvadex.[5] The effect is probably due to testosterone acting on HGH release at the suprapituitary level – an action that is secondary to its aromatization to estrogen. Conversely, another study found that HGH levels rose after testosterone enanthate and Nolvadex administration.[6] For athletes, such studies are a mixed bag of results. While some will no doubt start stacking the two drugs in an attempt to increase HGH levels, they may in fact do the complete opposite. And since HGH release is tied to insulin and other hormones, the long-term implications of such drug interactions are unknown.

We should add that since the crackdown on anabolic steroids and related drugs, physicians have become very reluctant to prescribe Nolvadex

"Nolvadex cuts into the effectiveness of any steroid stack. Your health, muscle gains and wallet are best served by taking the smallest dose of steroid possible which gives you gains, and adding in 10 to 20 mg of Nolvadex if you have to. If 10 to 20 does not do the trick, you are taking too much damn stuff!"

– Will Brink, author and regular *MuscleMag* columnist commenting on the double-edge sword properties of the popular bodybuilding drug, Nolvadex.

products for nonmedical reasons. Even though a bodybuilder who is suffering from steroid-related side effects is, in our opinion, a legitimate medical patient, most physicians are afraid of backlash from their medical governing bodies. This is a sad state of affairs as it has forced bodybuilders to turn to the black market. In actuality, the antisteroid movement has made things more dangerous for steroid users, not safer.

Frank Sepe

Trade Name: Teslac
Generic Name: testolactone
Tablet Size: 50 and 250 mg
Therapeutic Dosage: 150 to 250 mg/day
Gym Dose: 25 to 100 percent

Teslac is made from fermented progesterone (the second primary female sex hormone). It works by combining with cytochrome P-450 (a cell pigment involved in electron transport within cells) and blocking the aromatase enzymes at receptor sites. One of the novel things about Teslac is that it also acts as an anabolic agent. It is believed to do this in two primary ways – elevating testosterone production, and increasing mineral retention.

With regards to testosterone, the evidence suggests testolactone indirectly stimulates the hypothalamus to increase production of GnRH – gonadotropin-releasing hormone. GnRH is secreted when hormone levels – particularly estrogen – decline. More GnRH indirectly leads to the production of more testosterone and hence increased anabolic activity. It's not surprising that once bodybuilders heard of this information many began adding Teslac to their cycles.

Testolactones's effects on mineral conservation are more straightforward. By increasing retention of nitrogen, potassium, and phosphorous, the body is kept in a more favorable state for protein anabolism. Conversely, protein catabolism is reduced. The net result is a limited anabolic effect (we say limited because testolactone is nowhere near as powerful as other anabolic steroids in this regard).

As a final comment, since it's considered an anabolic steroid by the FDA (erroneously we might add), it falls under Schedule III DEA controlled substance status. It's illegal and trafficking and/or possession will get you hard prison time.

Trade Name: Cytadren
Generic Name: aminoglutethimide
Tablet Size: 250 mg
Therapeutic Dose: 2000 mg/day for cortisol control
Gym Dose: 1 to 12 percent (250 mg/day)

This prescription drug is primarily used to treat Cushing's syndrome, a disease characterized by increased cortisol production. Cytadren works by blocking various enzymes which convert cholesterol into pregnenolone and ultimately into such hormones as aldosterone, cortisol, and estrogen. Although the recommended dose for treating Cushing's syndrome and related diseases is in the gram range, dosages as low as 250 milligrams

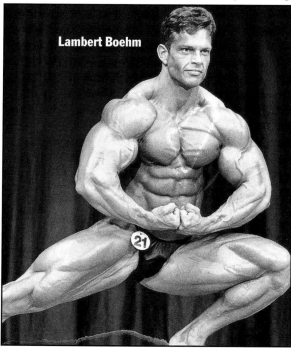

Lambert Boehm

have been found to be effective in controlling steroid-induced aromatization. Cytadren is relatively cheap ($40 to $50 per bottle), and is available by prescription. Of course, given its common usage by athletes, most physicians are reluctant to prescribe it for reasons other than "legitimate" medical conditions.

A SAFER ALTERNATIVE TO ANTI-ESTROGEN DRUGS?

Researchers are continuously looking for ways to provide safer alternatives to performance-enhancing drugs, and anti-estrogen drugs are no exception. Realizing that gynecomastia continues to be a problem among steroid users, and that the previous products have their limits, biochemists are taking a closer look at one of the members of the vitamin family – vitamin P – also known as bioflavonoids.

BIOFLAVONOIDS

Bioflavonoids are made up of the following: flavonals, flavones, citron, rutin and hesperidin.[7] This group consists of water-soluble, brightly coloured substances found in vegetables and fruits with vitamin C. A good source of bioflavonoids are the rind and pulp of citrus fruits, with buckwheat leaves being a good source of rutin.[8] Flavonoids are the most important pigments in floral coloration and are structural compounds in which two six-carbon rings are linked by a three-carbon segment. One major class of flavonoids are the anthocycanins: dephindin (blue), pelargonidin (red) and cyanidin (violet). Another class of flavonoids, the flavonals, are found in both leaves and flowers. While generally colorless, they contribute to the yellow or ivory hues of some flowers. The carotenoids are red, orange, or yellow. Betalins are red. Combinations of these pigments give flowers their characteristic colors (other factors such as pH also contribute to color). In the leaves, flavonoids block for ultraviolet radiation, which is highly destructive to nucleic acids and proteins. The flavonoids selectively admit the light of blue-green and red wavelengths, vital for photosynthesis.[9]

USE IN HUMANS

Can bioflavonoids exert a biologic effect in humans? In France they have been used to treat gynaecological problems and as a replacement for hormone-replacement therapy in cases of irregular or painful menstrual flow not caused by anatomical problems.[8] It is believed that bioflavonoids may act as antioxidants, preventing copper-containing enzymes from oxidizing adrenaline and vitamin C.[7] Finally, and this is what bodybuilders have been getting excited about, there is "talk" to suggest flavinoids can inhibit the aromatization of testosterone to estrogen. If true, we have an ideal supplement for steroid users. But before you rush out and buy mega-doses of the stuff, a few precautionary points are in order.

Laura Binetti

First, there is nothing in the medical literature to support this position. And even if it could, is it desirable? Estrogen significantly lowers the level of plasma cholesterol. Lowering the levels of endogenous estrogen might cause more harm than good, particularly among steroid users who normally experience a rise in plasma-cholesterol levels during a cycle. (Pure testosterone is high in androgenic effects, hence more acne and hair loss.) Estrogen also induces the production of testosterone receptors. More testosterone receptors means more sites for testosterone to bind and exert a biological effect. Blocking production would seem to be counterproductive.

We raise these last points because a new product by Dan Duchaine, Flavone X, is advertised as an aromatase inhibitor. By using his product most men experience an increase of at least 20 percent over normal testosterone levels. According to Mr. Duchaine, the production of testosterone is controlled by estrogen receptors in the hypothalamus. An increase in testosterone will cause an increase in estrogens produced from testosterone. Flavone X is claimed to prevent this conversion of testosterone to estrogen. Mr. Duchaine will not name the mystery compound in Flavone X because of a nondisclosure agreement.[10] This is rather interesting in itself given Mr. Duchaine's well-known legal history and in-your-face style of journalism. We find it puzzling that he legally agreed to a gag order. One might speculate that self-interest might be involved. But let's be fair, one cannot legally patent a naturally occurring compound, so why tell the competition? Mr. Duchaine has a history of being accurate, so the matter is certainly worth examination.

According to Dan Duchaine, the entire point of using Flavone X is to allow the user to stay on steroids indefinitely. The problem with this position is that the chance of side effects with any drug increases the longer it is used. Even the most diehard of steroid users will admit that long-term steroid use is risky. About all we can say concerning Flavone X is that, if used to combat excessive aromatization, the product may have its merits. But using the product so that steroid use can be extended is a foolhardy endeavor. We strongly advise against it.

Sandy Riddell, Lenda Murray and Shelley Beattie

References

1) R. Herschler and others, "Production Responses to Various Doses and Ratios of Estradiol Benzoate and Trembolone Acetate Implants in Steers and Heifers," *Journal of Animal Science*, 73 (October 1995).

2) P. Embleton and G. Thorne, *Steroids Myths – The Responsible Use of Anabolic Steroids*, (St. John's, Nfld: Thorton Publishing Ltd., 1991).

3) T. Basu, *Drug Nutrient Interactions*, (New York: Croom Helm Ltd., 1988).

4) *Flex*, 13: 5 (summer 1995).

5) L. Lima and others, "Growth Hormone Response to GHRH in Normal Adults is Not Affected by Short-Term Gonadal Blockade," *Acta Endocrinology*, 120:1 (January 1989).

6) J. Devesa and others, "The Role of Sexual Steroids in the Modulation of Growth Hormone Secretion in Humans," *Journal of Steroid Biochemistry and Molecular Biology*, 40:1-3 (1991).

7) H. Winter, *Complete Guide to Vitamins, Minerals and Supplements* (Tucson: Fischer Books, 1988).

8) L. Dunne, *Nutrition Almanac*, 3d ed. (New York: McGraw-Hill Publishing Co., 1990).

9) P. Raven and others, *Biology of Plants*, 3d ed. (New York: Worth Publishers Inc., 1981).

10) D. Duchaine, "Hang On! Flavon X: The Next Frontier In Drug-Free Muscle-Building," *MuscleMedia* (May 1996), 62-67.

CHAPTER THREE

Growth Hormone

I t was only a matter of time before bodybuilders engaged in the practice of using human growth hormone (HGH). As soon as the potential muscle-building properties of this "wonder drug" surfaced, bodybuilders the world over began adding it to their medicine chests. Other athletes began to use it when they found out that, unlike steroid tests which were becoming more and more sophisticated, HGH is undetectable. Perhaps the most amazing thing about HGH is that it's not so much a drug as a naturally occurring hormone.

> Trade Name: Humatrope, Protropin
> Generic Name: human growth hormone (HGH)
> Therapeutic Dose: 5 to 10 mg/day
> Gym Dose: 100 to 200 percent

"Incredible. But everyone is different. I knew one guy who spent $15,000 on it and only got pimples. I wake up pumped when I'm on it. Some guys refuse to come off HGH."

– Mike Matarazzo, top IFBB pro.

Growth hormone was first isolated about 30 years ago. It is a polypeptide hormone secreted by the pituitary gland. Its molecular structure contains 191 amino acids held together by peptide bonds. About 10 percent of the pituitary's weight is made up of HGH – averaging 5 to 10 milligrams in healthy individuals. Males secrete about 0.5 to 1.0 milligram a day and it has a plasma life of about 60 to 90 minutes. Although it varies, most individuals release the greatest amount of HGH during the first 90 minutes of sleep.

Secretion of HGH is controlled by two additional hormones called growth-hormone releasing hormone (GHRH) and growth-hormone inhibiting hormone (GHIH) – both of which are produced in the hypothalamus and moderated by such factors as low blood sugar, amino acids, sleep, stress, and yes, you guessed it – exercise. Research suggests that HGH is secreted in greater concentrations following short, high-intensity exercise rather than long, moderate exercise. Extremely long, high-repetition exercise may actually lower HGH levels.

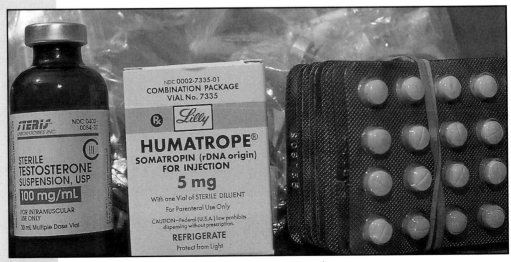

Mike Matarazzo

MECHANISM OF ACTION

HGH is by far the most important hormone for stimulating growth in children. Unlike anabolic steroids, HGH causes growth in almost all of the body's tissues, and HGH receptors have been found in the kidneys, liver, bone, and muscles. HGH's effects on the body's long bones are very apparent when something goes wrong. Excessive HGH early in life produces the condition known as "gigantism." Such individuals may reach eight feet or more with the tallest, Robert Wadlow, reaching an incredible height of 8' 11".

The reverse of gigantism is dwarfism, and is caused by insufficient HGH early in life. Individuals suffering from this condition may attain an adult height of only two to three feet.

Besides its effects early in development, HGH plays an important role throughout life, influencing such vital functions as protein, fat, and carbohydrate metabolism.

Although still the subject of debate, HGH is believed to exert its influence by increasing the transport of amino acids into tissues and speeding up their conversion into protein. HGH also increases protein synthesis by speeding up the cellular content of DNA and RNA. In these respects, HGH is similar to steroids in that it produces an "anabolic effect."

Another area of interest to bodybuilders is HGH's effects on fat storage. Unlike insulin which promotes the use of glucose as an energy source, HGH promotes the utilization of fat for energy supplies. It does this in a number of ways, chief of which are 1) reducing the rate of fat synthesis, 2) increasing the mobilization of fat from storage sites, and 3) increasing levels of fat-burning hormones like epinephrine and norepinephrine.[1]

In adipose tissue, HGH promotes the breakdown of stored triglyceride (bodyfat), increasing plasma levels of fatty acids. Since glucose uptake is suppressed by HGH, fat synthesis is also suppressed. These effects combined result in an overall loss of bodyfat. The important thing to remember is that HGH decreases glucose uptake and utilization, spares glycogen, and increases the use of fat for energy by mobilizing fat stores.

Perhaps HGH's greatest effects are felt in the body's immune system. In one study published in the December 1987 edition of the journal *Metabolism*, researchers found that the activity of cancer- and virus-fighting cells of the immune system were positively related to the levels of circulating HGH. Subjects with high HGH levels were found to have higher levels of activity of specific immune cells (natural killer cells). When some of the

"In the past, human growth hormone was thought to be essential only to the regulation of body growth and the attainment of adult height. Although growth hormone is critical to normal maturation, a clearly defined physiological role for growth hormone is just now coming to light in adults. A number of studies are now suggesting that the hormone is of importance after maturity to maintain a desirable body composition and for proper body functioning. Also, research is currently studying the role of growth hormone release during exercise and finding that the hormone is a factor in determining the lean body mass and bodyfat responses to exercise training."

– Dr. Douglas M. Crist, commenting on the new approach taken by researchers towards the physiological role played by growth hormone.

Dave Fisher

"What I don't like are guys and gals who do excessive growth-enhancing drugs. There are so many competitors on huge dosages of HGH, for example, that their muscles are popping and tearing left, right and center. Some people I know have a half-dozen tears. Drugs also make some bodybuilders goggle-eyed, and of course, there are the unsightly bitch tits (gynecomastia) on men and virilization in women. Now HGH is being linked with cancer."

– Robert Kennedy, *MuscleMag* publisher and chief editor commenting on the state of affairs in modern bodybuilding.

experimental group members were injected with small amounts of HGH (about the same amount as would be secreted by the body in a 24-hour period) the activity of their killer cells increased about 80 percent. In addition, the subjects gained about three pounds of muscle mass and lost an average of five pounds of fat.

Numerous doctors around the world are currently using HGH to treat AIDS patients. It is probably not as effective as anabolic steroids; nevertheless, it doesn't carry the same stigma developed by the FDA concerning steroids.

There is also research being conducted to examine the effects of HGH on treating multiple sclerosis (MS). The theory behind its use concerns HGH's effects on IGF-1 production. IGF-1 is a peptide growth factor, which has among its properties, the ability to promote nerve-tissue regeneration. As MS is caused by the degeneration of such tissue, it only follows that any drug that can directly or indirectly stimulate such tissue would be very useful.

WHERE IT COMES FROM

Just as scientists invented anabolic steroids as a synthetic version of testosterone, so too has HGH been synthetically produced. Up until 1985 individuals suffering from growth deficiencies had to rely on natural sources of HGH. In other words, HGH supplies were obtained from human cadavers. This procedure was terminated after several cases of viral Creutzfeldt-Jakob disease were reported in patients who had been administered pituitary-extracted HGH. As luck would have it, two synthetic versions were developed about the same time. Based on recombinant DNA research, synthetic HGH is now the primary source of HGH for treatment. Among the companies that market HGH, Genetech markets the brand name Protropin, and Eli Lilly and Company markets Humatrope. We should add that although Protropin mimics natural HGH, its slightly different structure – 192 amino acids instead of 191 (due to an extra methionine amino acid) – means that some individuals may have adverse reactions to the drug. The most common of these are the development of antibodies to the drug.

In recent years, Genetech has developed a successor to Protropin called Nutropin AQ (aqueous). Unlike Protropin, Nutropin does not come in a freeze-dried powder but is already liquefied. This means less preparation for users, and greatly reduces the risk of contamination from unsterile liquid sources. A third advantage is the stability of the drug, which is increased from 12 to 14 days to 28 to 30 days.

USE IN BODYBUILDING AND OTHER SPORTS

Unlike anabolic steroids, which have been associated with bodybuilding for over 40 years, HGH use is a relatively new phenomenon. A few enterprising individuals with the right cash and contacts probably used the cadaver extracts in the early 1980s, but for the most part, HGH use in athletics took off when the synthetic sources came on stream. It didn't take long for HGH to turn up on the black market, and by the early 1990s its use was widespread among bodybuilding's elite fraternity.

Gerard Dente

Reports from bodybuilders who have used HGH suggest that while many use the drug for its anabolic properties, by far, HGH's greatest asset is its ability to spare muscle tissue while on a strict precontest diet. During this period most bodybuilders report some degree of muscle catabolism, despite their best efforts at conservation. Many say that by taking HGH their muscle size is unchanged but fat deposits are eliminated.

A third less known but equally important reason for HGH use in athletics concerned its undetectablity in drug tests. As soon as anabolic steroids became easily detectable, athletes immediately began looking for a substance that provided the same benefits of steroids, but without the risks of detection. In HGH they appear to have found the ideal drug. And once word got around that HGH was untraceable in a standard athletic drug test, its use became widespread. While pro bodybuilders are not tested (it was tried back in the early 1990s without much success), athletes in most amateur sports are subject to

"I could have used growth hormone and nobody would've said a thing. Many female bodybuilders have disclosed their use of this drug to me, while at the same time sanctimoniously condemning other bodybuilders for drug use."

– Tonya Knight, Ms. International winner in an interview with *MuscleMag* commenting on the hypocrisy among female bodybuilders with regards to drug use.

very rigorous drug-testing procedures. HGH allowed many to maintain peak-performance levels right up to the week of the competition, without risk of detection.

We used the past tense to describe the previous as scientists believe they may have found a drug test that will detect HGH. Although reports are sketchy at the time of this writing, it's believed the test may make its debut in future Olympic games. Hopefully the test can differentiate between synthetic and natural HGH. If not, many athletes who have "boosted" their natural HGH levels will also end up in the penalty box. (see the related section on "Natural Ways to Increase HGH Levels," Chapter Three)

HOW EFFECTIVE?

HGH's short history has raised a number of issues – chief of which is its effectiveness. Forty years of steroid use has all but proven that these drugs do increase muscle size and strength. Many researchers remain unconvinced, but the athletic community has accepted that anabolic steroids do enhance physical performance. The evidence on HGH is unclear. The limited scientific or anecdotal evidence is the primary reason why drawing conclusions about HGH is so difficult. If we base opinions on theory, HGH should be a great benefit to bodybuilders. Certainly HGH's effects on protein synthesis and fat metabolism make it an ideal ergogenic aid. But, as of yet, few scientific studies have been carried out to examine the effectiveness of HGH in this regard. Even hearsay evidence is limited and consists of "so and so" used HGH and gained 25 pounds in two months. One study involving 18 young males given four times the naturally secreted amount of HGH found that HGH had no effect on muscle growth.[2] Another study, however, found different results.

> "If you know how to use it properly, it is a very effective anabolic substance. Trouble is, very few people know how to use it, and that's why many bodybuilders think it's a worthless investment."
>
> - From a *MuscleMag* interview with a dealer of anabolic drugs.

In a study carried out by Dr. Douglas M. Crist (*MuscleMag*, February 1991), subjects were given a low dosage (about twice the daily average) or a high dosage of HGH (about four times the weekly amount). Both groups showed marked increases in lean bodymass and decreased bodyfat over a six-week period. Surprisingly, both groups experienced the same increase in muscle mass (an average of five pounds). It appears the HGH dosage was not important in producing muscle growth. Low levels of HGH increased muscle mass to the same extent as high levels. This is something to dwell on given the huge dosages some pro bodybuilders are known to take. It appears that the same results can be obtained with much lower dosages. This means saving money and reducing

Bruce Patterson

Berry
DeMey

the risks of side effects all at the same time. A further application of these results is that if small amounts of HGH are just as effective as large amounts, then natural means of stimulating HGH release have great potential in bodybuilding. We will look at some of these techniques later in the chapter.

A theory put forward by regular *MuscleMag* columnist Dr. Mauro DiPasquale may offer the best insight into the effectiveness of HGH. He calls HGH a "plateau" drug. That is, once bodybuilders reach a maximum size with anabolic steroids, HGH will enable them to break the plateau and add another 20 to 25 pounds. Evidence for Dr. DiPasquale's theory can be seen in the pro bodybuilding ranks. How often have you seen competitors reaching 235 to 240 pounds, competing at this weight for a couple of years with no noticeable weight gains, and then within the space of 6 months show up onstage weighing 265 to 270 pounds of rock-hard muscle. There is no need to mention names here. Simply dig out the back issues of *MuscleMag International* or other bodybuilding magazines, and check out the vast differences. If your collection is complete you can almost nail down the month a certain pro started using HGH.

Why HGH enables bodybuilders to break plateaus is unclear. Most experts agree that the drug is probably producing a synergistic effect with steroids. In fact, HGH alone is not that great of an anabolic agent. Yet combine it with steroids (and as is the case nowadays, insulin and various thyroid drugs) and watch out – an extra 25 pounds of vein-popping muscle.

A SECRET WITHIN THE FAMILY

The problem in determining the athletic value of HGH is compounded by its pattern of use. Virtually all HGH users are also using anabolic steroids. So are the weight gains due to HGH, steroids, or both? Where do the steroid effects end and HGH effects begin?

Another problem facing researchers is secrecy. Over the years many bodybuilders have opened up about their steroid use, and there is a well-established network of information available to investigators. But not so with HGH. For the most part, HGH use is at the level steroids were at in the '50s and '60s. It's something that is kept quiet. The only thing we can definitely say is that many of the top pros use it. It's going to take many more years of research and evidence gathering before the true benefits and prevalence of HGH come to the surface.

"The nonmedical use of growth hormone can induce serious side effects (related to diabetes-like symptoms) brought about by a generalized resistance to the actions of insulin and acromegaly which, if uncontrolled for a prolonged period of time, could produce an overgrowth of soft tissue as well as an abnormal increase in bone mass. It is highly unlikely that pure growth hormone is available at any level of distribution other than that legally established to treat growth-hormone-deficient children or for FDA-approved experiments. For these and other reasons, one should never attempt to obtain and use injected growth hormone for athletic gain or for any reason in which the hormone is not presently indicated. The potential for adverse response from unprescribed use greatly outweighs any possible gain."

– Dr. Douglas Crist, *MuscleMag* contributor voicing his opinion on the dangers of HGH use.

Edgar Fletcher stands by as Nikki Fuller displays her awesome gun.

"When Arnold and I were competing, we did not have any growth hormones of any kind. Then in 1984 to 1985 bodybuilders started taking new hormone drugs and steroids. That's why a lot of them appear good and big, but their bodies look more like meat than the hard-trained muscle that we had. So to answer your question, we made a lot less money back then, we had more fun, and we did not have all the new hormones, drugs and steroids that today's bodybuilders have."

– Franco Columbu, former Mr. Olympia responding about how the sport of bodybuilding has changed since he and good friend Arnold Schwarzenegger retired from competition.

SYNERGISM WITH OTHER DRUGS

Given that most HGH users also use other "anabolic agents," a brief discussion on synergism is needed. As discussed earlier, synergism is the pharmacological term which refers to the increased effects of two drugs combined together, as opposed to their individual effects when not combined. Although sketchy, there is evidence of synergistic effects between HGH and certain hormone preparations.

Although testosterone doesn't seem to influence HGH release, HGH seems to improve the sensitivity of tissue receptors to androgens. How this mechanism works is not fully understood. Evidence suggests that some of the excessive testosterone, which has been converted to estrogen, may in fact be the cause. Studies indicate estrogen may in fact increase receptor sensitivity to testosterone and its anabolic derivatives. There is further evidence to suggest that estrogen may itself increase HGH production. For example, female bodybuilders with low bodyfat levels tend to have HGH secretions comparable to their male counterparts. Their low bodyfat levels increase estrogen production which in turn increases HGH release. Incidentally, the reason most females are not overly muscular is because estrogen also stimulates the production of fat which negates the effects of any extra HGH production.

Besides hormones, many bodybuilders stack HGH with thyroid and other fat-burning agents. One of the main reasons why today's bodybuilders are more "ripped" than their counterparts of ten or twenty years ago concerns the use of powerful thyroid medications such as Cytomel and Synthroid. Unfortunately, the long-term consequences of combining such agents with growth hormone and steroids is poorly understood. There is evidence to suggest excessive thyroid levels blunt or decrease the body's ability to use HGH. Other studies suggest HGH levels may be reduced due to an increase in somatostatin – a peptide hormone known to control HGH release. To add to the confusion, some researchers suggest HGH sensitivity can be increased by elevating levels of thyroid. We should add that few controlled studies have been carried out involving the combining of HGH with other ergogenic drugs. Current legislation tends to frighten most researchers away, and the potential side effects from such a "drug cocktail" don't help either. Until some hard credible evidence is collected, bodybuilders and other athletes should be wary of combining HGH with other pharmaceutical agents.

COST

Once it became possible to genetically manufacture unlimited supplies of HGH, it was assumed that the cost would drop accordingly, but this has not been the case. Although reliable estimates are hard to make, it is calculated that for a bodybuilder to achieve any ergogenic effect from HGH, he or she would have to spend $10,000 a year. This figure is probably an under-estimate as anecdotal reports circulate of top pros spending $50,000 a year on contest preparation.

One of the primary reasons for such an astronomical cost is the markup on the black market. Like steroids, HGH supplies are limited, but in big demand – two of the main variables controlling price. Estimates vary but reports of $500 to $1000 per vial are not uncommon.

Another reason for such a high cost is lack of knowledge by users. Unlike steroids which have a long history of "hand me down" knowledge, information on HGH use is very limited. Each new user is laying the foun-dation for the next generation. With such ignorance it's not surprising that many users take 10 to 20 times the needed dosage. As the weekly treat-ment of HGH-deficient children costs about $500, it is easily seen how a bodybuilder could spend thousands of dollars a month for HGH supplies.

Franco
Columbu

DANGERS OF THE BLACK MARKET

Like anabolic steroids, HGH takes many forms on the black market. If buyers are lucky, what they receive is real HGH, side-tracked (a polite way of saying stolen) from legitimate production lines. Unfor-tunately, the high demand has led to large amounts of bogus supplies being dumped on the black market. In these cases it's buyer beware!

In the late 1980s a potentially dangerous form of HGH began making its round on the black market. Advertised as "gorilla juice," this version of HGH was believed to be derived from South American rhesus monkeys. While the existence of the preparation is not in doubt, what it contained is open to debate. Rhesus monkeys are difficult to obtain and it's doubt-ful if the HGH preparation was made from the pituitaries of these animals. In all probability body-builders were duped into buying one of the cheaper versions of ana-

"Most of the stuff out there is fake, not worth bothering with. I am just glad I don't have to worry about it. I would rather be skinny with some money in the bank than blowing my cash on fake drugs with God knows what in them."

– Will Brink,
MuscleMag columnist.

bolic steroids. What's scary about this situation is that rhesus monkeys are well-known for harboring and originating many diseases fatal to humans – the most famous being the AIDS virus. Bodybuilders would be wise to keep this in mind if buying HGH on the black market.

Besides so-called monkey HGH, other versions of HGH turn up on the black market. Numerous bodybuilders tell of being sold saline (salt) solutions or even plain water. Other times, when real HGH is sold, the product is virtually useless because of handling inadequacies (as HGH must be kept refrigerated). And like its steroid counterparts, HGH sources may be smuggled in from Europe. This again brings up the issue of legitimacy. How safe is a product that was potentially manufactured in a basement lab in Eastern Europe, or derived from a wild Asian monkey? Quality control. Forget it! You'd be lucky if all you lost was your hard-earned cash.

Besides synthetic versions of HGH, cadaver HGH stills turns up on the black market. The chief source for this being the former Soviet Union where pituitary-derived HGH is still produced. Bodybuilders would be wise to avoid this form of HGH as analysis, carried out in the early 1990s by a team of Austrian endocrinologists, showed that samples contained impurities which indicated unsuitable precautions had been taken to eliminate virus contamination.[3]

Dennis Newman

Other bogus forms of HGH do not contain growth hormone but HCG. While HCG will stimulate the testes to produce testosterone, giving the physique a harder, more defined appearance, the agent can play chaos with the endocrine system (HCG is pharmacologically known as a gonadotropin – see Chapter Seven on HCG). Once again, you have bought a product that was advertised as one thing, but contains another. This leads to the obvious question of what else is in there?

SIDE EFFECTS

In patients who are deficient in HGH, the hormone has few side effects. Problems may arise, however, when excessive amounts (up to 20 times the recommended dosage by some bodybuilders) are taken by healthy individuals.

The most pronounced side effect of HGH use is acromegaly. Although usually produced by a pituitary tumor, the evidence seems to suggest HGH abuse can cause the disease. Acromegaly is a chronic disease characterized by enlargement of

Laura Creavalle

the bones of the head, the soft parts of the feet and hands, and sometimes other structures.[4] Children rarely experience the condition as their bone plates (the areas of long bones where growth in the form of lengthening occurs) are still soft and pliable. Once these plates fuse (a common side effect of anabolic steroids resulting in decreased adult height) HGH may cause the bones to become proportionally too thick as compared to their length. Besides the long limb bones, acromegaly sufferers may have a thickened and more pronounced forehead. They also exhibit a marked swelling of the hands and feet – all of which gives the individual what has been called the "Frankenstein look."

Another side effect of HGH is to throw off the body's delicate hormonal balance. Besides testosterone and HGH, the body's other primary "anabolic" hormone is insulin. If individuals take HGH in amounts over and above what is normally secreted, the body's insulin levels may be affected. As insulin is needed for maintaining proper blood-glucose levels, this delicate balance can easily be thrown off by high HGH levels. Excessively high levels of HGH may damage the body's insulin-producing pancreas, leading to the life-threatening disease of diabetes.

Besides insulin, HGH also seems to affect circulating levels of epinephrine and norepinephrine. Collectively known as catecholamines, these hormones are secreted by the body in response to stress. While elevated levels for short periods of time are not dangerous, the long-term effects of artificial elevation are not known. Certainly their effects on heart rate and blood pressure are grounds for concern.

A third hormone affected by HGH is insulin-like growth factor-1 (IGF-1). Most researchers believe that HGH's effects stimulate IGF-1 production in the liver, kidneys, and other tissues. If such is the case, boosting HGH levels may also increase IGF-1 production – the long-term consequences of which are unknown.

"Hard, brief exercise has been shown to result in higher growth hormone production. It is now known that athletes involved in vigorous training produce more growth hormone during sleep than do untrained people."

– Peter McGough, *MuscleMag* columnist commenting on one of the best natural ways to increase HGH levels.

> **"Successfully promoting HGH release is a complicated process, requiring critical knowledge about the coordination of a number of factors which all interrelate to influence the release of the hormone. If proper consideration is not given to all of the factors involved in stimulating HGH release, increased levels of hormone will probably not be achieved and the benefits of its physiological actions on lean body mass and bodyfat will be lost."**
>
> – Dr. M. Crist, *MuscleMag* contributor commenting on the importance of HGH stimulation for achieving ultimate performance.

Another side effect reported by bodybuilders using HGH is a unique form of acne consisting of large oil-filled cysts. Although not full understood, it is believed the cysts are the result of HGH's increased fat-burning ability. And while not life threatening, the horrendous appearance can be the source of severe emotional anguish – especially among those who suffer from low self-esteem to begin with.

One of the least understood side effects associated with HGH use in bodybuilders is the "inflated" stomach look. Numerous pro bodybuilders reveal midsections that would do a pregnant woman proud! Some experts suggest this is caused by a build-up of visceral fat. But this seems unlikely as HGH promotes fat loss, not fat gain. The most plausible explanation is that the excess HGH causes the internal organs to grow in size (remember, most organs contain

The distended stomach look coincides perfectly with the increased availability of synthetic HGH, starting in the early 1990s.

both HGH receptors and varying degrees of smooth muscle), with the end result being the distended stomach look. While it's possible other drugs in the bodybuilder's stack are causing the situation, the condition coincides perfectly with the increased availability of synthetic HGH, starting in the early 1990s.

One of the least known but potentially deadly side effects associated with HGH pertains to individuals using research-grade HGH. Unlike synthetic forms which are an exact copy of human HGH, research-grade HGH has been modified (it contains an extra amino acid) for cell-culture experiments. This form of HGH is not intended for human use, and for good reason – up to 40 percent of those using it develop autoimmune reactions. This means their immune system begins attacking their own bodies. In addition, there have been cases where people using research-grade HGH developed allergies to their own HGH! In effect, there is less HGH circulating in their bodies, not more. Not only does such a condition decrease athletic performance, but remember, if you throw off levels of one hormone, the odds are you've disrupted the balance of many of the body's other hormones. The end result could be fatal.

Rounding out the list of potential side effects associated with HGH use are: headaches, mood swings, excessive sweating, skin discoloration, visual interference, and even body odor. Finally, given HGH's ability to lower high-density lipoproteins (HDLs) and speed the conversion of low-density lipoproteins (LDLs) into artery lining "foam cells" (one of the first steps in atherosclerosis), those with a history of heart disease in their families should be cautious about using the hormone.[5]

NATURAL WAYS TO INCREASE HGH LEVELS

Not wanting to leave the impression that the only method for increasing HGH is by direct injection, we felt it necessary to discuss alternatives. While we will be the first to admit that the following alternatives are not as effective as directly administering HGH, they are nevertheless much safer and have the added bonus of being perfectly legal.

STIMULATION BY AMINO ACIDS

Research over the last ten years or so indicates that certain amino acids are vital for the proper release of HGH. Called the neurotransmitter group (because of their importance in brain-transmitter synthesis) they include arginine, leucine, lysine, phenylalanine, ornithine, histidine, valine, and methionine. Although the exact mechanism of action is not fully understood, it is believed that these amino acids cause the hypothalamus to increase its production of growth-releasing hormone. Other theories suggest that since amino acids are the precursors for HGH (it's a polypeptide chain remember), increasing their amounts in the body may lead to increased HGH production.

Among the more popular amino acid supplements for HGH release are arginine and orthinine. These two get the lion's share of research and, although the evidence is inconclusive, seem to suggest that large dosages (20 to 30 grams) may increase HGH release by a factor of 100. There are, however, problems with taking this at face value.

High dosages of arginine can lead to nausea. Also, scientists don't know in what proportions amino acids should be taken. Infusion of a high dose of one most certainly leads to a disruption of the body's natural balance of the others. Finally, most of the studies involving HGH release by amino

> "Scientists believe that growth hormone is released as a result of neuronal signals such as anxiety and stress of the type caused by exercise. Neural input to the hypothalamus causes a hormone-releasing factor to be secreted, which in turn causes growth hormone to be released. Of course, amino acids such as arginine, ornithine, glycine and others are known to have GH-releasing properties as well, but only after they're converted biochemically."
>
> – Dr. Frederick Hatfield, world powerlifting champion, and well-known bodybuilding writer commenting on two mechanisms that control HGH release – exercise and amino acids.

Lee Priest and Thierry Pastel

acid supplementation only involve medical patients. The effects of high doses on healthy individuals are poorly understood.

If you decide to make amino acid supplementation part of your daily routine, we offer a few helpful hints. From an economical point of view, it's far cheaper to buy the previous amino acids separately, than spending hundreds of dollars on the latest "HGH enhancer kit." It is also better if you take the amino acids just before bed because of the importance sleep plays in HGH release. Most important, always play close attention to any feedback signals your body gives you. Many individuals have negative reactions to amino acid preparations. If there's any doubt, discontinue or switch brands.

INTENSE EXERCISE

Perhaps the most profound change in training philosophy over the last ten years has been the duration of workouts. The old "twenty sets per bodypart" has been replaced by workouts lasting 45 to 60 minutes. Is it any coincidence that the most massive of today's bodybuilders (Yates, Francois, Baker) subscribe to this philosophy? Could these bodybuilders be on to something? As we shall see, this form of exercising may be just what your endocrine system ordered in terms of HGH production.

We should start by saying that most of the studies on natural HGH production have found that heavy resistance training is one of the best HGH stimulators. Your workouts must be short in duration, and high in intensity. This means that those two- or three-hour marathon training sessions must be reduced to no more than an hour – preferably 45 minutes. In addition, rest between sets should also be reduced. Sets consisting of 6 to 8 reps are more beneficial than those of 15+ reps. In one study, two different groups were analyzed to determine the best rep range for stimulating HGH release. One group performed 21 reps per set, using light weight (30 percent of a seven-rep maximum, or about 18 percent of a one-rep single), and the other group performed sets of seven reps using heavy weight (80 percent of a seven-rep maximum or about 60 percent of a one-rep single). The results: The heavy group had their HGH production increased by a factor of 2.5 over the pre-exercise level. The light group showed no appreciable change in HGH levels.[6]

Bruce Patterson and Joanne Lee exercise the right way – heavy resistance training is one of the best HGH stimulators.

Jean-Pierre Fux

Besides the length of your workouts, workout frequency plays an important role. Two or three 45-minute workouts a day are far more beneficial in boosting HGH production than one energy-draining three-hour session. HGH levels peak during the first 15 to 20 minutes of exercise and then decline.

One of the best pieces of evidence to back this up concerns the naturally occurring opiates – particularly the endorphins. The "high" experienced by marathon runners is due to the brain releasing these natural painkillers to null aching muscles. Studies have shown that high levels of endorphins decrease HGH output. And since it usually takes bodybuilders an hour or more to achieve the same "high," it follows that once this condition is reached, HGH production will be suppressed. A short 30- to 45-minute workout, however, will greatly reduce the amount of endorphins secreted – thus allowing for higher HGH production.

Workout design may also influence HGH production. High-intensity techniques such as "down the rack" and "forced reps" are more beneficial for boosting HGH than standard sets to positive failure. In addition, recent studies suggest that changing your workouts around to include new and innovative techniques may also increase HGH production. Finally, upper-body training seems to play a more important role than lower-body training. Therefore you may want to split your workouts up to take this into account.

We should not forget the value of experience either. Although the research is inconclusive, physiologists are leaning toward the view that trained individuals have a greater and more continuous output of HGH than untrained individuals.

BLOOD-GLUCOSE LEVEL

The level of circulating blood glucose has been shown to effect HGH production. When glucose levels drop to 50 percent of the norm, there is a dramatic increase (estimated by some researchers to be five fold) in HGH production. During fasting periods, when blood glucose tends to be low, the body increases production of HGH. This point has a practical application as athletes who consume sugar immediately before exercise have decreased HGH outputs.

CHOLESTEROL LEVEL

Besides glucose, cholesterol levels also influence HGH secretion. In a study published in the August 1988 edition of the *Journal of Applied Physiology*, researchers studied the relationship between HGH and blood-cholesterol levels. Healthy individuals with advanced levels of bodybuilding experience participated in the study.

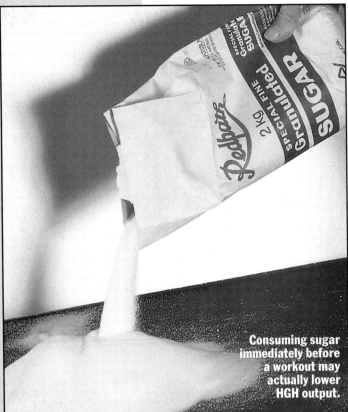

Consuming sugar immediately before a workout may actually lower HGH output.

The researchers found that there was considerable variation among the group with respect to HGH secretion. The one predictor, however, was cholesterol levels. Those individuals with high levels of circulating cholesterol had a diminished level of HGH secretion, whereas low levels of cholesterol were indicative of high HGH levels.

If the study had one drawback it was establishing cause and effect. Did high levels of HGH lower cholesterol, or did low levels of cholesterol increase HGH secretion? Further studies are being carried out to determine the direction of effect. Nevertheless, the results look promising for HGH, if used as a treatment in cholesterol-related heart disease.

SLEEP

Although not something that can be taken in tablet form, adequate sleep is vital for maximum HGH production. The biological basis is as follows. Growth hormone is secreted in maximum amounts during the first 90 minutes or so of deep sleep. Although not fully understood, it is believed that the process is moderated by the neurotransmitter serotonin. Evidence for this is found in trials using concentrations of the amino acid L-tryptophan – the primary building block for serotonin production. This amino acid is so effective that many individuals, including three-time Mr. Olympia Frank Zane, use it as a sleep aid.

Other evidence for sleep's effect on HGH production involves the elderly. Most individuals spend less time in deep sleep as they get older. Instead of one six- to eight-hour sleep episode, the period of sleep is typically spread over two to three shorter periods. This pattern of sleep usually means that an elderly person spends less time in deep sleep, and therefore one

"There are several things you can do to naturally increase your HGH levels. One is get a good night's sleep. Growth hormone is released maximally during deep sleep, normally about three hours after you fall asleep. Inadequate sleep impairs your ability to build muscle."

– John Parrillo, regular *MuscleMag* columnist commenting on the importance sleep plays in maximizing bodybuilding progress.

would expect less HGH production. Research backs this up. With few exceptions, those in the 65-plus age group produce much less HGH than younger age groups.

A final piece of evidence for the interaction between sleep and HGH involves "jet setters." Studies on individuals who have crossed several time zones show increased levels of HGH for several days. The theory is that the resetting of the human time clock (called the circadian or biological clock) somehow stimulates HGH production. When the "clock" becomes in phase with the new time zone, levels return to normal.

LEGAL IMPLICATIONS FOR HGH USE

Just as the "war" on drugs has expanded to include steroids, so too have legislators been working overtime to combat HGH misuse. Most of the legal pressure is directed at pharmacists and medical doctors who dispense the drug without valid medical reasons. But since most HGH is obtained from other sources it's doubtful the new legislation is having any effect. Black-market dealers are still selling HGH vials from gym bags everywhere. And given the swamping of police forces with more dangerous "street" drugs, prosecutions for HGH possession are few and far between.

References

1) "Drug World," *Flex*, 13:11 (December 1995), 185.
2) K. Yarasheski and others, "Effect of Growth Hormone and Resistance Exercise on Muscle Growth in Young Men," *American Journal of Physiology*, 262 (1992).
3) R. Deyssig and F. Herwig, "Self-Administration of Cadaveric Growth Hormone in Power Athletes," *The Lancet*, 341 (March 20, 1993).
4) *Webster's Encyclopedic Unabridged Dictionary of the English Language*, 1989.
5) "Drug World," *Flex* 13:10 (November 1995).
6) D. Crist, "Getting the Top GH For Your Rep!," *MuscleMag International*, 126 (December 1992).

Denise Paglia and
Paul DeMayo

CHAPTER FOUR

Insulin

W hen Dr.'s Banting and Best first isolated insulin back in the 1920s, it's doubtful that either could have envisioned its use by athletes seventy years later. But like many drugs developed exclusively for medical treatment, insulin has been added to the gym bags of many bodybuilders.

> Trade Name: Humulin
> Generic Name: insulin
> Concentration: 100 units/mL
> Duration of Action: 5 to 8 hours
> Average Therapeutic Dose: .5 units/kg

> Trade Name: Lletin II
> Generic Name: insulin
> Concentration: 100 units/mL
> Duration of Action: 24 to 28 hours
> Average Therapeutic Dose: .5 units/kg

Located between the stomach and small intestine is a small, five- to seven-inch organ called the pancreas. Unlike most glands, the pancreas is both exocrine (with ducts) and endocrine (without ducts) in nature. As an exocrine gland it aids in digestion by secreting enzymes and other substances into ducts which empty into the small intestine. As an endocrine gland it secretes hormones into the bloodstream. The endocrine section of the pancreas makes up only one percent of the total weight of the gland.

The cells that synthesize, store, and secrete pancreatic hormones are called the islets of Langerhans. These islets contain four types of cells called alpha, beta, delta, and F cells. For our purposes we shall focus primarily on beta cells, but as we will be discussing sugar and carbohydrate control later in the text, a brief discussion of alpha cells is presented.

ALPHA CELLS

Alpha cells produce the peptide hormone glucagon. When blood-glucose levels fall, glucagon stimulates glycogenolysis – the process by which the liver converts glycogen into glucose. Glucagon also stimulates

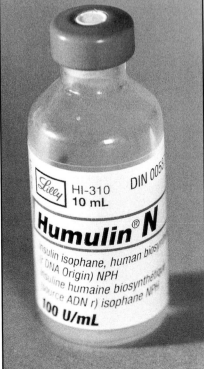

"Insulin plays an important role in your capacity for gaining muscle and losing fat, but only if insulin metabolism is working correctly. Problems with insulin metabolism, which occur commonly in people eating a typical high-carb/low-fat/low-fiber/low-vitamin-mineral diet, will lead to less muscle and more fat deposited."

– Will Brink, regular *MuscleMag* columnist commenting on the role insulin plays in moderating muscle gains and fat loss.

Joe Spinello

gluconeogenesis – the synthesis of glucose from noncarbohydrate sources such as amino acids and lactic acid. Although both pathways are essential, the former is the more important source of glucose.

In addition to the previous, glucagon increases the concentration of AMP from ATP in liver cells. It also stimulates the release of fatty acids and glycerol from adipose tissue.

INSULIN

Like its counterpart glucagon, insulin is a peptide hormone, and is secreted by beta cells when blood-glucose concentrations rise. The most important function of insulin is to speed up the rate of glucose transport across cell membranes. It also enhances the conversion of glucose to glycogen – called glycogenesis. Once synthesized, glycogen is stored in the liver as a fuel source. Finally, insulin increases muscle-cell glycogen storage by speeding up the membrane transport of glucose. If the muscle in question does not need glucose, it stores it as glycogen.

Of interest to bodybuilders is insulin's ability to facilitate the transport of amino acids through cell membranes where they are used for protein synthesis. There is also good evidence to suggest that insulin suppresses the breakdown of protein by catabolic hormones.[1] Other studies indicate that the anabolic effects of some amino acids may be increased when given in conjunction with insulin. For example, studies show that protein synthesis stimulated by the amino acid glutamine is increased by the presence of insulin.[2]

A BIASED HORMONE

One of the peculiar aspects about insulin is that it selectively performs the above actions depending on substrate availability and the demands placed upon the body. The evidence suggests that sedentary, obese individuals who overeat will gain fat if they take insulin, while athletes, especially bodybuilders, who train hard and take in extra calories, will have the nutrients converted to muscle tissue.

WHEN THINGS GO WRONG

If beta cells produce too much insulin, hypoglycemia occurs – the condition where blood sugar falls to excessively low levels. As is more often the case

"Glucagon is another hormone secreted by the pancreas. It opposes the effects of insulin. An increase in blood sugar triggers a release of insulin but inhibits glucagon release. Glucagon is released several hours after a meal when blood-sugar levels drop. It reduces the use of glucose for energy and stimulates the breakdown of bodyfat and the use of fat for energy. Glucagon also stimulates glycogen breakdown. The net result of glucagon is to raise glucose levels back to normal and to signal the body to begin using fat for energy since it's running low on carbs."

– John Parrillo, regular *MuscleMag* columnist.

Sonny Schmidt

however, the beta cells do not manufacture enough insulin, leading to the more popularly known condition of diabetes mellitus, or Type I diabetes. In some cases the problem is not insulin levels but insulin recognition. In Type II diabetes individuals produce enough insulin but their body cells have trouble recognizing it. The end result is the same – poor glucose regulation – although Type II diabetics often don't need to take insulin shots. They can live normal lives by closely watching their diets.

There are presently between 15- and 20-million North Americans who suffer from diabetes, and while Type II's can control the condition with weight loss and diet, Type I's must take regular injections of insulin.

Prior to insulin's discovery in the early 1920s, diabetes was almost always fatal. After insulin's isolation and commercial synthesis, a diagnosis of diabetes was no longer a death sentence, and today most diabetics can lead relatively normal lives. We must emphasize that insulin does not cure diabetes but merely controls it in the form of replacement therapy.

USE IN BODYBUILDING

Biochemists classify insulin as an anabolic hormone because of its ability to increase protein synthesis and fuel storage. Given the amount produced in North America for legitimate diabetic needs, it's not surprising that insulin is relatively easy to obtain on the black market. Many bodybuilders have taken advantage of this and made insulin injections a regular part of their weekly drug program.

Although the effects of insulin in deficient individuals are known, little research has been carried out on healthy subjects. This means, like HGH, most of the information available on insulin use in bodybuilding is anecdotal in nature.

HOW MUCH AND HOW EFFECTIVE

Most bodybuilders who open up about their insulin use say they take 20 to 50 IUs of the hormone every day. Personal preference plays a role and anecdotal reports suggest some top bodybuilders combine both types of insulin and take 10- to 15-IU shots, two or three times a day. If there is a preference it's for the short-acting type, as the long-acting version seems to be harder to control.

Timing is also an important consideration when using insulin. If the injection is taken first thing in the morning, and you only eat a small carbohydrate meal (or worse – nothing at all), there probably won't be enough sugar available by the time the insulin starts to work. The result is a deep state of hypoglycemia consisting of breathing difficulties, tremors, and extreme perspiration. If the condition is not treated, the end result can be death.

To combat the previous, "intelligent" bodybuilders take about 10 grams of glucose per IU of insulin, about 30 minutes after taking the hormone shot.[3] With many bodybuilders taking multiple shots throughout the day, it's easy to see how meticulous attention to diet is an absolute must for many of the sport's top pros.

There are three groups of bodybuilders when it comes to insulin use. Some bodybuilders swear by it, claiming it has outstanding muscle-building properties, allowing them to carb-load to a greater extent during contest time. Others try it and experience no beneficial effects, merely throwing their glucose levels off. A third group are not around to tell their story as their abuse of insulin lead to hypoglycemia and death.

> **"Most of us think of a diabetic relative or friend in connection with insulin usage, but insulin is rapidly becoming a drug of choice among bodybuilders in order to rapidly pack on muscle mass. And I am pretty sure that few if any of these bodybuilders are diabetics (yet!).**
>
> – Bruce Kneller, regular *MuscleMag* columnist commenting on the latest trend among competitive bodybuilders – the use of exogenous insulin to increase muscle size.

Top-ranking bodybuilders show their love for competition.

INTERACTION WITH OTHER DRUGS

Anecdotal reports suggest many top pro and amateur bodybuilders are adding insulin to their already laden drug stacks. Although the evidence is sketchy, it appears insulin has the ability to magnify the effects of other drugs – in particular, IGF-1 and HGH. One of the buzzwords in drug research over the past few years is "synergism." How often have you seen a bodybuilder plateau at 230 pounds, remain there for a few years, and then all of a sudden gain another 25 pounds in six months? Most experts believe that drugs such as insulin, IGF-1, and HGH produce only moderate results when taken separately, but produce a synergistic effect when combined. The end result is tremendous gains in muscle mass and strength, above what could be obtained with the drugs separately. In simple terms, if HGH produced a five-pound weight gain, and insulin produced a five-pound gain, you would expect both taken together to produce a ten-pound muscle gain. Instead, both drugs taken together produce weight gains of 25 to 30 pounds or more.

> **"High levels of insulin, if left unchecked, lead to insulin resistance, and can also cause a rise in cortisol levels (and vice versa)."**
>
> – Will Brink, regular *MuscleMag* columnist commenting on two of the lesser-known side effects of insulin.

Frank Sepe

FORMS AND RANDOM NOTES

Insulin is stable for six months at constant room temperature and up to 24 months when refrigerated. There are two primary forms of insulin available for human use – 1) semisynthetic forms made by converting animal (usually pork or beef) insulin to human insulin, and 2) biosynthetic forms made using recombinant DNA technology. In either case, preparations are usually in concentrations of 100 units per millilitre, and numerous studies indicate that both forms are equally effective in terms of controlling long-term diabetes. The only differences are the slightly faster absorption rates of biosynthetic forms, which mean a shorter duration of action in the body and the increased incidence of allergies and fat hypertrophy with animal forms.

Many bodybuilders who have tried both forms, animal and human, report that a simple switch from one to the other often produces dramatic results. Others report that by cycling both types over time, they can bypass the problems associated with tolerance. While there are many theories for explaining the previous, in all probability, receptor sensitivity is playing a role – although receptor types may also contribute.

Insulin can also be classified according to its rate of action. For example, rapidly acting insulin (called regular insulin) begins "working" a few minutes after being injected subcutaneously (under the skin). Peak effect is usually reached after two hours and lasts for six to eight hours. Such forms are primarily used for diabetic emergencies and in the long-term treatment of diabetes.

Intermediate forms of insulin have a longer onset of action – requiring, on average, two hours to take effect. They generally peak after eight to 10 hours and last up to 24 hours.

We should conclude by saying numerous pharmaceutical companies are working on new forms of insulin which work even faster than regular forms. One new version, Humalog, produced by Lilly, is designed to mimic the body's rapid insulin release in response to carbohydrate ingestion. The researchers at Lilly achieved this by modifying two amino acids in the human-insulin molecule. Although it only seems like a slight modification, it greatly enhances the new form's rate of reaction.

SIDE EFFECTS

A drug developed for medical treatment can be a health hazard in healthy individuals. Insulin is one of the few hormones used and abused by bodybuilders which can cause death.

Most of the side effects associated with insulin involve glucose regulation. Bodybuilders use the drug primarily for its effects on protein synthesis, but as we explained earlier, insulin also controls the level of glucose in the blood. When individuals with normal insulin production administer excessive insulin, not only are they throwing off their natural insulin levels, they are also interfering with glucagon levels. So sensitive is the interrelationship between the three (insulin/glucagon/glucose) that minor changes in one almost certainly lead to changes in the other two; the outcome often being confusion, loss of consciousness, convulsions, and even death.

Also important is the relationship between insulin and epinephrine release. Among epinephrine's functions is its ability to act as a backup

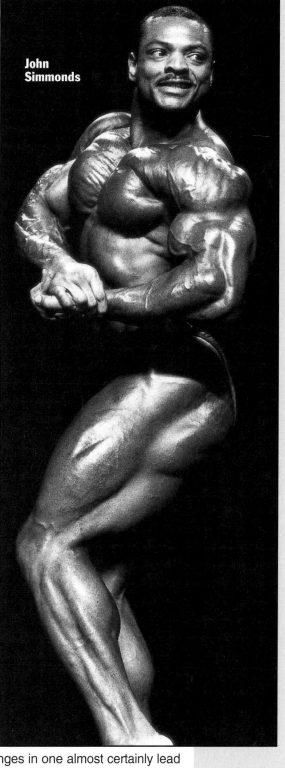

John Simmonds

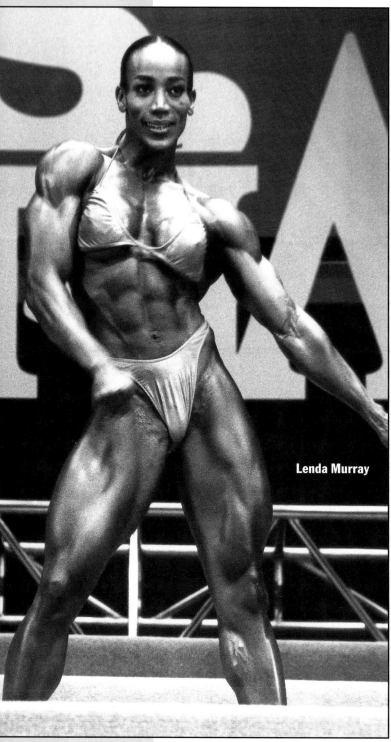

Lenda Murray

hormone to glucagon. When hypo-glycemia occurs and glucagon is not released to counteract the condition, epinephrine (and the closely related norepinephrine) steps in and carries out the job itself. Long-term use of insulin (both by diabetics and athletes) may interfere with this regulatory mechanism; the ultimate outcome being uncontrolled hypoglycemia. If the disruption is severe enough the body may not even recognize it is in a state of hypoglycemia (the condition is called hypo-glycemia unawareness), and hence no defensive strategies are employed.

A lesser-known property of insulin is its effects on heart disease. Researchers in France and Israel have discovered that, in some individuals, high levels of insulin often lead to elevated levels of fat in the blood. So promising are the studies that the researchers suggested using high-insulin levels to predict heart disease. We should add that determining cause and effect here is subject to debate. It may be that high-fat levels caused the increase in insulin levels and not the other way around as suggested by the studies. Since obese individuals often develop diabetes as a result of their condition, we should not rush to conclusions until more is known. Nevertheless, body-builders with a history of heart disease in their families should be cautious about using insulin for boosting athletic performance.

Given the potential dangers of taking insulin (unless for medically supervised diabetes), we strongly advise readers to avoid the drug. Sure it may be a current fad, and some 240-pound guy at the gym swears by it, but the risks far outweigh the benefits. Unlike steroids and growth hormone, insulin is one drug where one improper dosage could end your life within a matter of minutes. Unless you want to be remembered as the "good-looking" corpse with "low-blood-sugar levels," give insulin use a pass.

THE FUTURE OF INSULIN

Before leaving the topic of insulin, we thought it would be interesting to mention a new supplement that has recently gained attention in the body-building world. Called "insulin-potentiating factor" (IPF), the compound is being developed by the same people who introduced creatine monohydrate to bodybuilders. The compound will supposedly mimic the nutrient-transporting properties of insulin, but without the life-threatening effects on blood-glucose levels. In fact the supplement is not being designed for diabetics but for bodybuilders and other athletes. Although not currently available, it is believed the product will hit the supplement shelves within the next year.[3]

"Tests for insulin resistance could be an even earlier indicator of heart-disease risk than cholesterol evaluations."

– Dr. Micalea Modan, of the Tel Aviv University Medical School.

REFERENCES

1) Dr. Mauro DiPasquale, "Are You Insulin Ignorant?," *Flex*, 13:13, (February 1996).
2) K. Yarasheski and others, "Short-Term Growth Hormone Treatment Does Not Increase Muscle Protein Synthesis in Experienced Weightlifters," *Journal of Applied Physiology*, 74:6 (June 1993).
3) B. Phillips, "Uncensored Q and A," *MuscleMedia 2000* (May 1996).

Roland Kickinger

CHAPTER FIVE

Thyroid and Mineral-Conserving Drugs

THYROID DRUGS

"The max intake of thyroid would be something like 25 to 50 mcg a day. A dose of 10 to 20 is usually sufficient. This guy is really lucky he did not do serious harm to his body and totally screw up his thyroid. He had only been taking this dosage for a few days. After a few weeks it could have been game over!"

– Will Brink, *MuscleMag* columnist commenting on one bodybuilder's practice of taking 400 to 500 mcg of thyroid medication during his precontest stack.

Trade Name: Cytomel
Generic Name: liothyronine (T3)
Tablet Size: 5, 25, and 50 mcg
Therapeutic Dosage: 35 to 40 mcg/day
Gym Dose: 100 to 200 percent

Trade Name: Synthroid
Generic Name: levothyroxine
Tablet Size: 25 to 300 mcg (25 mcg jumps)
Therapeutic Dose: 60 mcg/day
Gym Dose: 100 to 200 percent

Trade Name: Proloid
Generic Name: thyroglobulin
Tablet Size: 16, 32, 65, 100, and 130 mg
Therapeutic Dosage: 65 mg/day
Gym Dose: 100 to 200 percent

Jean-Pierre Fux and Chris Cormier

Flex Wheeler, Roland Cziurlok, Jean-Pierre Fux and Kevin Levrone

Besides playing around with anabolic preparations, many bodybuilders modify their metabolisms to "define" and "cut up" the newly gained muscle tissue. It's great to gain thirty pounds of muscle, but it's useless if covered by a layer of fat. The soft look doesn't win contests these days. Only competitors with the lowest percentage of bodyfat find themselves in the winner's circle.

Since pharmacology has become such an integral part of modern contest preparation, it shouldn't surprise many that drugs may be used to increase metabolic activity. For many bodybuilders the drugs of choice are thyroid preparations, and they are frequently found at the top of precontest checklists.

The thyroid hormones are produced in the thyroid gland – a small two-lobed structure located on both sides of the trachea (windpipe). The thyroid gland has a well-developed circulatory system which enables such substances as amino acids, iodine, and glandular secretions to be transported. The bulk of the gland's volume is made up of hundreds of thousands of spherical sacs called follicles. These sacs are filled with a gelatinous substance used for storing the thyroid hormones.

There are two types of cells that make up the thyroid gland. The most numerous are the follicular cells, which secrete the thyroid hormones thyroxine and triiodothyronine. Because the thyroxine molecule contains four atoms of iodine it is often called T4. In a similar fashion, triiodothyronine is called T3 because it contains three iodine atoms.

The other type of thyroid cells are the parafollicular cells which produce the hormone calcitonin. As we are primarily concerned with T3 and T4, we'll just mention that calcitonin works in conjunction with other hormones to control the amount of calcium in the blood.

"Thyroid is a double-edged sword. Most bodybuilders take far too much. To use thyroid correctly, you really have to get regular blood tests, which 99.9 percent of all bodybuilders neglect. If you take just enough to keep you in the high-normal range, you will burn fat without eating up a lot of muscle. If you go far above the high-normal range on the blood tests, you deflate like a balloon – not to mention the potential health risks of having too much thyroid in the body."

– Will Brink, *MuscleMag* columnist commenting on the delicate balance that must be maintained when using thyroid medications.

Only competitors with the lowest percentage of bodyfat find themselves in the winner's circle. – Kim Chizevsky

Although T4 accounts for 90 percent of the thyroid's secretions, T3 is just as effective given its higher concentrations. Both hormones consist primarily of iodine and the amino acid tyrosine. The importance of iodine in the diet has been known for years. People who live in areas of low dietary iodine often develop a condition known as goiter. This disease is easily recognized by the extreme swelling in the neck region – a result of the thyroid gland enlarging to increase hormone production. In most industrialized countries the condition has all but disappeared as iodine has been added to water and salt supplies.

Although there are subtle differences, both hormones have the same functions – they accelerate cellular reactions in most body cells. They also increase overall body metabolism by increasing the rate at which cells use organic molecules and oxygen to produce heat and energy. Another function is to make the body more sensitive to the actions of sympathetic hormones – the effect of which is to increase cardiac out. Rounding out the list of functions include: controlling homeostasis, modulating the skeletal and central nervous systems, stimulating protein synthesis, and helping to maintain proper water balance.

With regards to potency, there are some differences between the two thyroid hormones. T3 is almost five times as active as T4, and T4 may be converted into T3 as the body needs it. This point should be kept in mind by bodybuilders using both drugs as many take large dosages of T4 and then forget to adjust their intake of T3. Anecdotal reports among bodybuilders seem to indicate T4 doesn't eat into muscle tissue like T3. Of course this could be a case of improper T3 dosing.

HOW IT'S CONTROLLED

The entire process of thyroid production and release is controlled by endocrine biofeedback and involves two hormones: TSH (thyroid-stimulating hormone) which is secreted by the anterior pituitary, and TRH (thyrotropin-releasing hormone), released by the hypothalamus. TSH is released when thyroxine levels in the blood fall. Other factors for release include stress, cold, or pregnancy. When blood concentrations of thyroxine rise, TSH production is reduced. TRH is inhibited as long as thyroxine levels are high in the blood. Once they fall, TRH output is increased, which in turn increases the pituitary's release of TSH – the end result of which is greater thyroid gland activity.

USE IN BODYBUILDING

Having seen the importance of thyroid hormones to metabolic functioning, it's not surprising that bodybuilders have added them to their list of pharmacologic agents. The less informed use them simply because they feel "everyone else is." Competitive bodybuilders, however, employ them in the weeks leading up to a contest to boost fat metabolism – in short, to get ripped.

There is a good biological reason for bodybuilders being tempted by thyroid use. One side effect of a rigorous precontest diet is the slowing down of the thyroid gland. Strict dieting produces a drastic decline in the body's BMR (basal metabolic rate). Although other factors are involved, it is mainly due to the fall in T3 production. Among the symptoms of reduced T3 are increased temperature sensitivity, sluggishness, and a seemingly unlimited need for sleep.

Another side effect of strict dieting is the slowing down of thermogenesis – the process by which excess calories are converted to heat rather than stored as fat. As soon as the body senses less calories in the diet it immediately cuts back thyroid functioning which in turn slows your metabolic rate and leads to the storage of fat. The strict diet, which is supposed to lead to a ripped appearance, may in fact be counterproductive. Besides strict dieting, another precontest strategy may lead to a slowing down of the thyroid gland. Most bodybuilders increase the duration and intensity of their workouts in the weeks leading up to the competition. For many the increased training and decreased eating leads to a state of overtraining. And as most readers of *MuscleMag* know, overtraining is one sure way to throw off the body's delicate hormonal balance.

"Be prepared to gain 30 pounds of blubber when you come off it, or be prepared to eat like a concentration-camp victim for eight weeks and have no energy. This is what Cytomel does. When you come off it, you need about eight weeks to get the TSH levels near normal. So for two months you can eat nothing and feel like shit or eat normally and gain a ton of fat."

– Dan Duchaine, best-selling author and well-known authority on ergogenic aids commenting on the drawbacks to thyroid medications.

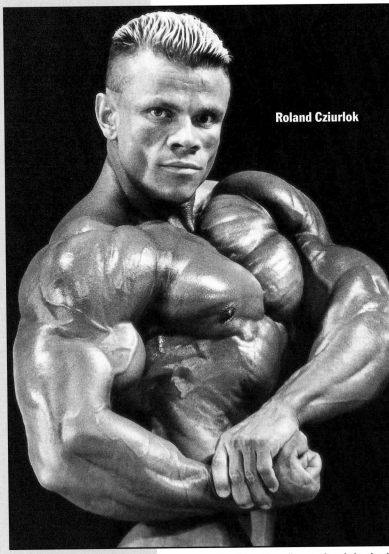

Roland Cziurlok

By an ironic twist of fate the two most popular strategies bodybuilders use for decreasing bodyfat may in some cases have the reverse effect. The solution for many is to turn to thyroid preparations in order to supplement hormone levels. If it was a case of just replacing the reduced hormone, it might be understandable, but as with most bodybuilding drugs, some individuals take as much as they can get their hands on.

SIDE EFFECTS

As with most drugs, the frequency and degree of side effects associated with thyroid hormones is usually proportional to the scale of use. Depending on the dosages taken, T3 and T4 preparations may cause muscle wasting or muscle growth. This is because there is an optimum level needed for proper metabolic functioning.

Excessive use of thyroid hormones may lead to a degradation of protein synthesis, which in turn leads to a loss of skeletal-muscle tissue. If this is not enough, extreme dosages of thyroid hormone may interfere with cardiac-muscle health.

"Thyroid hormones are like the bowls of porridge in *Goldilocks and the Three Bears*. There is a level that is just right. Too little or too much thyroid hormone causes havoc in the body."

Dr. Mauro DiPasquale, noted expert on performance-enhancing drugs and regular columnist in *MuscleMag*.

Besides the direct physiological side effects associated with thyroid hormones, there will most certainly be indirect effects due to the disruption of the thyroid biofeedback system.

Like most hormones, excessive amounts of T3 and T4 will shut down the body's natural hormone production. Not only will T3 and T4 synthesis be curtailed, but the pituitary and hypothalamus stop producing their respective hormones as well. Given the interaction between thyroid hormones and other hormones such as insulin and HGH, it should be easy to see how altering the balance of one could disrupt the body's entire endocrine system.

Besides interfering with the pituitary and hypothalamus, excessive thyroid activity can increase the adrenal gland's production of androstenedione – a weak hormone that is easily aromatized. And as explained earlier, this results in an excess of estrogen, which causes the unsightly condition of gynecomastia. Excessive thyroid activity can also increase the production of a blood protein called sex-hormone binding globulin. This circulating protein has a high affinity for testosterone and reduces the amount available for use. In effect, the body's ratio of testosterone to estrogen is thrown off – once again increasing the chance of developing gynecomastia.

Not to be overlooked is the effect of thyroid on IGF-1 levels. Recent studies show that individuals using high dosages of thyroid have increased levels of special proteins which bind to IGF-1 molecules. This is significant as only circulating unbound IGF-1 can influence cellular activity to any degree. Long-term thyroid usage may not only decrease bodyfat levels but muscle mass as well.

Another consideration concerns the effect of thyroid drugs on the liver. Any time the human body is flooded with extraneous substances – natural or synthetic – the liver has to work overtime to metabolize and remove the drugs. Just as an alcoholic's liver shows the ravages of abuse over time, so too can an athlete's liver incur damage if abused by thyroid drugs and other hormones.

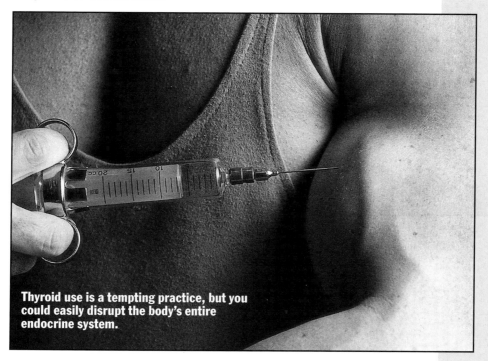

Thyroid use is a tempting practice, but you could easily disrupt the body's entire endocrine system.

THE VICIOUS CYCLE

Even though we discussed this in the chapter on anabolic steroids, it nevertheless needs repeating. Most drugs show the potential for addiction, and thyroid preparations are no different. As soon as a person gets used to the "new look" a drug produces, getting off it becomes so much more difficult. This is compounded by the fact that if someone somehow manages to quit, his or her system will take months or even years to return to predrug levels. And the longer on the drug, the longer it takes for natural levels to return to normal. If the degree of abuse is severe enough, the individual may require medical intervention to "kick start" his or her thyroid system.

Although it varies, the general symptoms seen during thyroid withdrawal include: water retention, excessively dry skin, chronic feelings of lethargy, brittle nails and hair, and perhaps the most devastating to bodybuilders – the gaining of bodyfat. Most individuals can't handle the previous so they go back on the thyroid preparations. This depresses the thyroid system further and makes it even harder to quit. In short, a vicious cycle has started which is extremely difficult to break.

Like steroid withdrawal, getting off thyroid drugs requires a multi-faceted approach. If you shunned medical attention while using the drugs, you definitely need it now. Yes, the physician in question will probably give you an earful on the folly of the practice, but the odds are he or she will also monitor your recovery – provided you seem sincere in your intentions.

Besides medical attention, you'll have to pay special attention to your diet. Your much-depleted thyroid levels will mean gaining fat at an almost unheard of rate. Make sure to keep dietary fat levels to a minimum, and take vitamin and mineral supplements.

Don't be afraid to talk things out with a sympathetic friend. Someone who went through the same ordeal would be the best source of council. Let's face it, he or she knows what you're going through. If the "guys at the gym" give you a hard time about your less than adequate appearance, either

Hamdullah
Aykutlu

Robby Robinson and Boyer Coe

ignore them or train at a different time of the day. You might even want to switch gyms. Don't let negative remarks put you back in the vicious cycle of thyroid abuse.

MINERAL CONSERVERS

One of the primary concerns of aging bodybuilders is that their skeletal systems won't be strong enough to support their larger, heavier muscles. Bone density decreases as we get older, usually due to declines in mineral-conserving hormones. Many individuals become more susceptible to fractures and breaks (the best example of this being osteoporosis). And while exercise can help prevent such injuries by strengthening bones, science has now joined in the fight with a new pharmacological agent.

A new drug recently approved for use in Canada and the United States is Fosomax, a bone builder. This nonhormonal drug, an alendronate of sodium, reduces bone breakage (particularly in elderly women) by stimulating the development of new bone material. Clinical trials found that Fosomax increased bone density by an average of 8.2 percent and in the hip by 7.2 percent. In addition, this drug does not have the side effects associated with hormone-replacement therapy.[1] Other tests carried out at Creighton University found it reduced spinal fractures by 50 percent. The same studies also showed that the women subjects who used Fosomax lost less height (a common occurrence in older individuals as the spinal vertebra shrink). Further, the effects of the drug could be potentiated by calcium supplements. This makes sense, as calcium is the primary mineral used in building bone tissue.

Although little research has been conducted on males, the results with women suggest the drug holds great promise, not only in treating osteoporosis, but for older bodybuilders who wish to reduce the risk of bone-related injuries.

Reference
1) "Bone Building Drug Wins Approval," *Globe and Mail* (January 1996), *Health*, A1.

CHAPTER SIX

Diuretics

The spectrum of athletic drugs is not limited to muscle-building agents. For bodybuilders the goal is to mount the stage on contest day sporting the greatest degree of defined muscularity. There are two approaches to achieving this condition. The first is to lower bodyfat levels to somewhere in the neighborhood of two to four percent. Most bodybuilders rely on diet to obtain the desired results, but as we explained earlier, many resort to using thyroid medications to speed up their metabolism.

The second approach for highlighting muscularity focuses on water removal. Like other mammals, humans are basically bags of water surrounded by a protective layer of skin. There's a few organs thrown in for good measure, but by and large humans are still dependant on the one substance from which our ancestors came. In fact, earth is the only planet in the solar system known to have water in any abundance. Water is so important that humans can go a week or more without food, but only a few days without water.

"We've seen the death of IFBB Pro Mohammed Benaziza and a few close calls in the last few years and I'm sure we'll see more. Bodybuilding standards have become so high that there are those who will risk death for a title. As long as freaky mass and unbelievable definition are in vogue, we will see further attempts by competitors to push the boundaries once thought impossible to surpass. I don't know the direction bodybuilding will take any more than the next guy. Let's hope it doesn't continue on its present course."

– Robert Kennedy, *MuscleMag* publisher and best-selling author responding to a reader's comments concerning the current state of bodybuilding with respect to judging standards.

Antidiuretic hormone (ADH) is a peptide-based hormone that helps regulate the body's fluid balance.
– Roland Cziurlok

Among its many functions, water serves as a medium for the transport of dissolved substances. Besides such important nutrients as amino acids and vitamins, water contains all-important ions which help regulate such systems as the cardiac and nervous systems.

It should come as no surprise that the mammalian body has evolved biological systems to conserve these precious life-giving substances. And as probably guessed by now, the body's primary conservation system is based on endocrinology.

Now all this talk of water and life may seem poetic, but it does in fact play a major role in preparing for a bodybuilding competition. Just as some athletes modify their testosterone and thyroid levels with drugs, so too have some competitors resorted to pharmacology to squeeze that extra ounce of water out of their bodies. The drugs in question are called diuretics and anti-diuretic blockers. As we shall see, they often remove more than just water – they may lower ion concentrations to potentially fatal levels.

Trade Name: Lasix
Generic Name: furosemide
Tablet Size: 5, 40 mg
Therapeutic Dose: 1 to 2 tablets daily
Gym Dose: 100 to 200 percent

Trade Name: Naturetin
Generic Name: bendroflumethiazide
Tablet Size: 5, 10 mg
Therapeutic Dose: 2.5 to 5 mg daily
Gym Dose: 100 to 200 percent

Trade Name: Anhydron
Generic Name: cyclothiazide
Tablet Size: 2 mg
Therapeutic Dose: 1 to 2 mg daily
Gym Dose: 100 to 200 percent

WATER AND MINERAL CONSERVATION IN THE HUMAN BODY

WATER CONSERVATION

Given the body's constant need for water, and its rapid loss by such bodily functions as sweating and urination, human evolution has put in place a mechanism by which water is conserved. Called antidiuretic hormone (ADH), this peptide-based hormone (composed of nine different amino acids) helps regulate the body's fluid balance.

ADH is produced by the posterior pituitary and released into the blood where it travels to the kidneys. Its main mechanism of action is to increase the permeability of the kidney tubules, thereby allowing water to be reabsorbed into the body rather than excreted in the urine. Such control is vital if the body begins to dehydrate for any reason. For example, haemorrhaging causes an increase in ADH secretion due to a decrease in blood pressure. The body compensates by conserving water to maintain fluid balance. Other factors such as physical and emotional stress, and exposure

"High levels of aldosterone cause sodium in the kidneys to be reabsorbed into the blood instead of being excreted with the urine. Low aldosterone, on the other hand, causes sodium to be excreted in large amounts through the urine. Thus, aldosterone is responsible for controlling the sodium balance in your body, and has a direct impact upon whether or not you're 'holding water.' "

– Dr. Frederick Hatfield, powerlifting champion and well-known bodybuilding writer commenting on the role played by aldosterone in controlling both mineral and water balance in the human body.

to intense dry heat (increased water loss due to evaporation from the skin), also raises ADH levels.

Paul Dillett, his index finger raised in conquest . . .

The opposite may also occur and numerous factors decrease ADH production. If you consume large amounts of fluid, the body compensates by decreasing ADH secretion, which in turn decreases water conservation by the kidneys. Individuals who drink large amounts of beer have an additional problem. Not only does the increased fluid lead to increased urine excretion, but alcohol is also an ADH blocker. Thus, the mechanism by which the kidneys reabsorb water is shut down. Further, many beer products contain lupulin from hops – a diuretic in its own right.

> "Then it happened. In an instant his world caved in all over him. From a vision of majesty, his index finger raised in conquest, he crumpled into a heap right before our eyes. What a shock! One moment Paul Dillett stood towering over us – huge, upright, ripped and confident, vying for top spot in a close battle with Vince Taylor and Kevin Levrone – and the next moment, all expectations he ever had of savouring his first major win were gone."
>
> – Johnny Fitness, *MuscleMag* editor commenting on pro bodybuilder Paul Dillett's collapse at the 1994 Arnold Classic.

MINERAL BALANCE

Besides conserving water, the body has a regulatory mechanism to control the amount of dissolved ions in the blood. As the control of ions is interrelated with water balance, bodybuilders end up modifying this system if they take drugs in an attempt to increase water excretion.

The body's chief mineral conservation mechanism is controlled by aldosterone – a hormone secreted by the adrenal glands. The two adrenal glands are located on top of the kidneys and consist of an inner medulla and an outer cortex. Not only do both structures produce different hormones but also have distinct target organs. For the purposes of this text we shall limit our discussion to the mineralocorticoids secreted by the adrenal cortex.

MINERALOCORTICOIDS

Although the adrenal cortex produces other hormones such as glucocorticoids and gonadocorticoids, it is the mineralocorticoids that are the most significant in bodybuilding contest preparation. Produced by the zona glomerulosa region of the adrenal cortex, mineralocorticoids are hormones which control the concentration of minerals. The primary mineralocorticoid is aldosterone, which regulates the retention of sodium and loss of potassium in urine.

The main target organ of aldosterone is the kidney, where the kidney tubules and collecting ducts are stimulated to reabsorb sodium into the blood. At the same time aldosterone stimulates the transport of potassium ions from the kidney tubules into the urine. Aldosterone acts on sweat glands in much the same manner, conserving sodium and secreting potassium to create a normal acid-base balance as well as a normal electrolyte balance in the body fluids.

MECHANISM OF ACTION

The primary action of diuretics is to decrease the kidney's efficiency for conserving electrolytes. Since such minerals as sodium, potassium, and zinc bind to water, they take the water with them when they are excreted. So even though most people use diuretics to "eliminate water," water is the secondary substance lost. In a manner of speaking, water loss is a side effect of diuretic use.

The primary site of action of most diuretics is the nephron – the kidney's main unit of activity. There are over a million nephrons in each kidney and such large numbers greatly increase the surface area available for absorption. Each nephron is made up of a renal capsule and a renal tubule. Both serve as the kidney's sites of absorption. Most of the diuretics used by bodybuilders work by interfering with the functioning of the renal tubule.

Although there are other classes of drugs, bodybuilders tend to use one of three types of diuretics. The most popular, Lasix, falls under the category of "loop diuretic" because it interferes with electrolyte absorption in the part of the renal tubule called the loop of Henle.

Loop diuretics are considered the most powerful type available, and cause an excretion of sodium, magnesium, and potassium. They are rapidly absorbed and begin to work in 30 to 45 minutes. If taken orally their influence peaks in one to two hours and lasts about six hours. In emergency situations (pulmonary edema) the drugs are injected and go to work in a manner of minutes.

Another commonly used "water drug" is Aldactone – an antidiuretic blocker or "potassium sparing diuretic." As discussed earlier the body's primary hormone for conserving electrolytes and water is ADH (antidiuretic hormone). Aldactone works by

... is suddenly caught off guard by excruciating muscle cramps at the 1994 Arnold Classic.

"**Momo was taking high dosages of diuretics to rid his body of excess fluid, as well as large amounts of other drugs. Several bodybuilders who personally witnessed Momo taking large amounts of diuretics confirmed this information. A source close to Momo said he was taking 40-mg Lasix tablets, as well as 70-mg Aldactone tablets. The consensus of those involved was that Momo died from taking too many diuretics, which stopped his heart. Lasix was probably the main culprit as it is notorious for flushing water and minerals out of the system and is not potassium-sparing like Aldactazide.**"

– Greg Zulak, former *MuscleMag* editor commenting on one of the theories behind the death of IFBB superstar, Mohammed "Momo" Benaziza.

blocking ADH receptors located in the kidney. Once blocked, ADH cannot exert its influence on the kidneys, and vital electrolytes such as sodium and zinc are excreted. Antidiuretic blockers are popular because they allow water loss without large amounts of potassium being lost.

A third group of popularly used diuretics are thiazides. These drugs are the most commonly prescribed diuretics in the medical field. Taken orally thiazides begin to work in an hour and their effects can last for up to 72 hours. Like most diuretics, thiazides work by preventing the reabsorption of sodium in the renal tubules. They also cause an excretion of zinc and magnesium. One of their biggest advantages is that they don't cause the same degree of calcium loss as other diuretics.

THERAPEUTIC APPLICATIONS

Like anabolic steroids and growth hormone, diuretics were developed for legitimate medical purposes. Their primary use is in the treatment of high blood pressure. They also play a role in treating edema (swelling) and excessive fluid retention caused by heart disease or kidney failure. Drugs such as Lasix are also used in the treatment of cancer patients to prevent the lungs from filling with fluid.

USE IN BODYBUILDING

Bodybuilders traditionally used diuretics for two main purposes – to shed excess extracellular water before a contest, and to dilute the urine before a drug test. While the former is still popular, the latter is no longer applicable as sports federations require urine to be of a specific concentration before it's accepted for testing. If the urine is too dilute some sports federations will ban you for using diuretics – regardless of the presence or absence of performance-enhancing drugs.

The late Mohammad Benaziza.

Losing water before a contest has two purposes. First, bodybuilders do everything in their power to bring out that extra vein or striation because of the emphasis on extreme muscularity these days. An excess of water can give the muscles a "soft" or "smooth" look. As water retention is pronounced in bodybuilders who use steroids, most bodybuilders stop steroid use a week or more before the contest. Even then, the lingering effects of the steroids may cause water retention.

Second, losing a few pounds of water can bring you from the bottom of one weight division to the top of another. For example, instead of being one of the smallest heavyweights, a competitor can lose two or three pounds and enter the show as one of the largest and most muscular light heavyweights.

For those that decide to use Lasix and other diuretics, a few points are in order (besides the health implications discussed next). Although it's tempting to start using a few days before the contest, try to leave it until the night before the prejudging. There are two primary reasons for doing so. First, as diuretics flush ions from the body, the transport of carbohydrates into the bloodstream is impeded. This is because some sodium is needed in the small intestine to facilitate the process. Second, there is good evidence to suggest diuretics reduce insulin's ability to transport glucose into the body's muscles to be stored as glycogen. If you start taking diuretics a few days before a contest, you run the risk of interfering with proper carbohydrate metabolism and therefore glycogen storage. By leaving diuretic use until the last minute, you still have time to flush excess water from the system, without interfering with the body's carb-loading ability. For those who abuse diuretics, hopefully the following section will make you think twice.

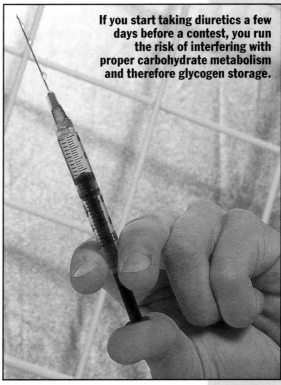

If you start taking diuretics a few days before a contest, you run the risk of interfering with proper carbohydrate metabolism and therefore glycogen storage.

DANGERS OF DIURETICS AND ANTIDIURETIC BLOCKERS

The main side effects of these drugs are related to dehydration. The human body is over 90 percent water by composition. Such a high percentage should give an indication of how vital water is for life. Even a minor decrease in water levels – such as on a hot summer's day – can lead to such life-threatening conditions as heat stroke and heat exhaustion.

Like most athletic drugs, diuretics and antidiuretic blockers tend to be taken in excessive amounts. Instead of sufficient amounts of water being lost to highlight muscularity, many bodybuilders end up dangerously dehydrated. Every year the number of amateur bodybuilders who faint on and offstage at competitions increases. Even the pro ranks are not immune to this. Mike Matarazzo, Albert Beckles, and Paul Dillett have had to be hospitalized for dehydration.

Diuretics may also have life-threatening effects on the kidneys. If taken in excessive amounts for long periods of time, they can deplete blood volume to such a low level that kidney functioning may be impeded. Besides interfering with the kidney's filtration mechanisms, low blood volume may lead to tissue damage. And unlike the liver, which has some regenerative powers, kidney degeneration is permanent.

With regards to specific side effects, the most common is muscle cramping. This is caused by a shortage of such ions as sodium, potassium, and especially calcium. Collectively called electrolytes, proper muscular functioning is heavily dependent on these ions. In addition, the nerves which stimulate the body's muscles also rely on these ions. When diuretics and blockers are used excessively, proper nerve and muscle functioning is impeded.

"Undoubtedly, there was an interaction between the various compounds Momo was on, whether it be diuretics, steroids, clenbuterol, growth hormone, or what ever. They all tend to affect electrolytes. They also all tend to cause various hormonal changes in the body and changes in the neuro-endocrine system."

– Dr. Mauro DiPasquale, best-selling author and regular *MuscleMag* columnist commenting on the death of IFBB pro bodybuilder, Mohammed Benaziza.

Yolanda Hughes

Besides skeletal muscle cramping, low electrolyte levels can interfere with the cardiovascular system – particularly the heart. Like skeletal muscles, the heart is composed of muscle tissue and proper contraction and relaxation depends to a large extent on ion concentrations. If this muscle "cramps" you are having a heart attack, and unlike a cramping calf or bicep, often leads to death.

Besides the heart, the level of ions floating in the blood may be thrown out of sequence. For example, thiazides block the reabsorption of potassium. This can lead to a condition known as hypokalemia – low blood potassium. Such a condition can cause muscular weakness, muscular degeneration, fatigue, and drowsiness.

Conversely, such ADH blockers as Aldactone cause an increase in potassium leading to a condition called hyperkalemia – high blood potassium. This condition can be fatal if the individual is consuming high-potassium foods or taking a potassium supplement. Potassium is such a powerful heart depressant that surgeons often use it to stop the heart before surgery.

Many bodybuilders try to keep potassium levels normal by taking thiazides and Aldactone together – as both have opposite effects on potassium levels. But this practice is dangerous as both drugs cause sodium excretion. By combining both drugs you are doubling the rate at which most electrolytes are excreted. Many individuals who follow such a practice trade in their posing suits for a hospital gown.

A DANGEROUS COCKTAIL

For those using thiazide diuretics, the issue of diabetes must not be overlooked. Research using these drugs to treat hypertension has shown some individuals may develop diabetes because thiazides increase blood-sugar levels. Many bodybuilders try to get around this by using antidiabetic drugs such as Metformin and Phenformin.[1] But once again we have a case of using one drug to treat the side effects of another drug. Such cocktailing can lead to a host of additional problems.

If not yet convinced of the dangers of diuretics, a number of bodybuilding's greatest stars have died of what were believed to be diuretic-induced heart attacks. In 1982, Austrian bodybuilder Hans Sallmeyer, winner of the lightweight class at the 1980 Mr. Universe, died of a heart attack brought on by excessive diuretic use. In October of 1992, Algerian super-star Mohammad Benaziza died after complications brought on by the use of multiple drugs including diuretics. Although in Benaziza's case there has never been an "official cause of death" most in the bodybuilding world agree that Benaziza had depleted his electrolytes to such an extent that it brought on a heart attack.

A few words also need to be said concerning Lasix – the most popular athletic diuretic. While Lasix is one of the most effective drugs available, it is not without side effects. The medical literature reports that many people who are allergic to sulpha drugs are also allergic to Lasix. In addition, combining Lasix with aspirin may lead to salicylate toxicity. Finally, Lasix has been implicated in a number of fetal deformities, so female athletes who are either pregnant or of child-bearing age should not use this drug unless it is an absolute emergency.

What makes Lasix so dangerous is how it works. Initially, a user will go to the bathroom every 10 to 15 minutes for an hour or two, but then the rate slows. This is the body's way of fighting back when water levels become too low. Unfortunately most bodybuilders assume the Lasix has worn off and take more. But the drug has not worn off and the additional amounts taken often push the individual "over the edge" – the result of which is severe dehydration, often leading to death.

Besides the serious health aspects, diuretics can have detrimental cosmetic effects for competitive bodybuilders. Like most body tissues, muscles are mainly composed of water. If an individual uses excessive

Kevin Levrone and Shawn Ray

amounts of diuretics, he or she runs the risk of flattening out the muscles and actually decreasing their size. Instead of appearing full the bodybuilder's muscles may appear drawn and stringy.

The risk of gynecomastia must not be overlooked either. Many ADH blockers, including Aldactone, are structurally similar to the feminizing hormone progesterone. For a few unlucky bodybuilders the result is an unsightly set of "bitch tits." Teenagers are especially at risk for developing this condition and should under no circumstances (except for medical reasons) use ADH blockers.

One of the pronounced effects of diuretic use is what happens after the drugs are discontinued. Like most drugs, diuretic use can lead to a "rebound effect" after cessation. Just as testosterone production may overshoot its presteroid levels after steroid use, so too may the body overcompensate following diuretic use. As soon as the synthetic diuretics are removed from the system, the body's homeostatic mechanisms go into overdrive to restore water and electrolyte levels. If a bodybuilder times things incorrectly, he or she may end up onstage looking like a water-soaked bag of sponges, rather than a highly defined bodybuilder.

Gunter Schlierkamp

We strongly suggest bodybuilders think twice about using drug-based diuretics and antidiuretic blockers. If you find you're still holding a little water under the skin a few days before the contest, try using a mild herbal diuretic. Not only will this leave the muscles full, but the health risks are minimal.

THE SEVEN COMMANDMENTS FOR DIURETIC USE

1) If at all possible only use diuretics under a physician's care.
2) Refrain from buying diuretics on the black market.
3) At the earliest sign of side effects seek immediate medical help.
4) Be cautious of combining diuretics as they may further complicate side effects.
5) Resist the urge to use potassium supplements as potassium is fatal in high dosages.
6) Try to lose water naturally.
7) Keep mineral levels adequate by eating proper foods.

Reference
1) The Harvard Health Letter, vol. 6, 1995.

**Sharon Bruneau and
Rich Gaspari**

CHAPTER SEVEN

Human Chorionic Gonadotrophin (HCG) and Related Compounds

L ike most bodybuilding pharmaceuticals, HCG was developed for purposes other than building competitive muscle tissue. But once athletes
heard of its potential, it wasn't long before HCG was added to "must
take" lists everywhere.

HCG is a protein hormone produced in the placentas of pregnant
women. It is collected from the urine about two months after the last menstrual period.

Trade Names: Pregnyl, Chorex, APL Secules
Generic Names: human chorionic gonadotrophin (HCG)
Preparations: 500, 1000, and 2000 units/mL
Gym Dose: 500 to 5000 units twice per week

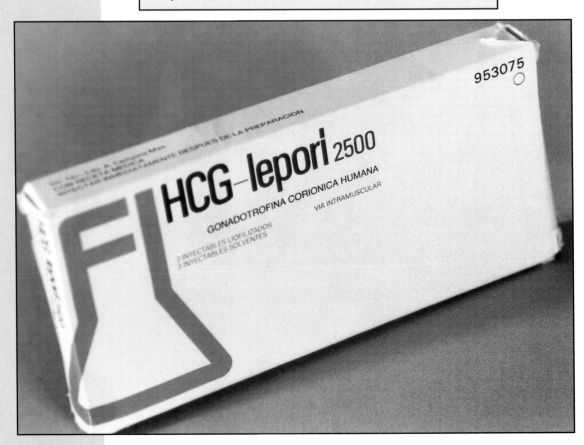

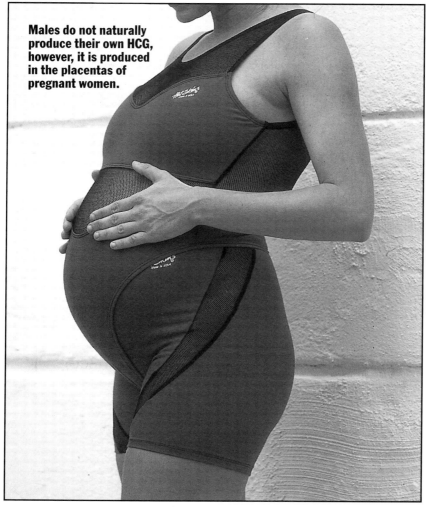

Males do not naturally produce their own HCG, however, it is produced in the placentas of pregnant women.

HOW IT WORKS

In females, HCG promotes the formation of cell tissue. It also helps develop the egg and promote ovulation (the release of the egg). After pregnancy, high levels of HCG prevent the menstrual cycle and boost the output of both estrogen and progesterone.

As males don't naturally produce their own, they must take it in injectable form. Since HCG is similar in structure and function to luteinizing hormone (LH), its primary action in males is to stimulate the testes to produce testosterone. Armed with this knowledge, it's easy to see why athletes take a special interest in HCG.

USE IN BODYBUILDING

Unlike anabolic steroids, which pretty much went from the research stage to the weight room, HCG use probably started as a legitimate form of medical treatment.

Until medical governing bodies started cracking down, many bodybuilders went to a sympathetic physician for their steroids. Such visits guaranteed that the drugs being taken were legitimate, and also gave the user access to medical supervision. And for many this was their first introduction to HCG.

"Human chorionic gonadotropin is slightly different from cow chorionic gonadotropin. However, they do cross-react and the cow CG is somewhat effective in humans. Because of the possible antibody response to cow CG I don't suggest you use it."

– Dr. Mauro DiPasquale, best-selling author and world authority on drug use in sports commenting on the dangers of using cow gonadotropin instead of the human variety.

Lenda Murray

Supervising physicians gave bodybuilders HCG shots both during and after a steroid cycle. HCG was given during a cycle to counteract the effects of high concentrations of estrogen – produced, as we explained earlier, from the aromatization of androgens. Once estrogen levels increase, the body shuts down production of LH. This in turn reduces testosterone output. Taking HCG during a steroid cycle helps keep testosterone levels high, and at the same time reduces the feminizing effects of estrogen.

Taking HCG after a cycle serves to boost the body's production of testosterone. While using steroids the body "thinks" natural testosterone levels are high and therefore shuts the testes down. Once the synthetic steroids leave the system, it takes the endocrine system a period of time to "get up to full production" as it were. If the individual was using high dosages of multiple steroids, it might take six to eight months for testosterone levels to return to normal. One way around this is by taking HCG, which stimulates the testes to begin testosterone production.

Once the legal authorities began to prosecute steroid dealers with a vengeance, the medical community was quick to disassociate itself from any involvement with the nonmedical use of anabolic steroids. Athletes who enjoyed the piece of mind of constant medical supervision were suddenly left high and dry. Many got off the "juice," but others took matters into their own hands.

With legitimate supplies cut off, many bodybuilders turned to the black market for their supply. Problems arose, however, when some individuals began to treat HCG as just another "anabolic steroid." Instead of using small dosages to help counteract the side effects of steroids, bodybuilders began to take megadoses to achieve the much coveted "anabolic effect."

"You could try using A, C, E, and folic acid, along with some zinc. This may be useful although in most cases like yours I've found the nutritional approach disappointing. HCG, in moderate dosages taken once a week for several weeks may increase the size of your testicles but may not help your sperm count."

– Dr. Mauro DiPasquale, regular *MuscleMag* columnist and best-selling author responding to a reader's question concerning his low sperm count and reduced testicle size following steroid use.

HOW EFFECTIVE?

Like growth hormone, the effectiveness of HCG is hotly debated. Many bodybuilders swear that taking the drug prior to a contest helps increase fat loss. And although the medical evidence is split, the anecdotal reports seem to support this. Other bodybuilders find that by using HCG alone, they get the same results of anabolic steroids without the side effects sometimes associated with the androgens.

With regards to dosage, the evidence seems to suggest that, like growth hormone, HCG effectiveness is not dose dependant. Studies involving trials with HCG administration have found that an injection of 1500 units produces significant increases in testosterone production for the following three or four days. Similar studies, using repeated injections, found no difference in testosterone production as compared to the one-injection study. Why this happens is not fully understood. Some researchers suggest that one dose stimulates the testes to the maximum and further doses are not needed. Others postulate that HCG receptors quickly desensitize after repeated doses. Whatever the cause, the evidence suggests that the megadoses taken by many bodybuilders are both a waste of money and potentially dangerous. Despite the previous, the most popular dosage among bodybuilders for HCG is 2000 to 4000 USPs taken three times per week.

SIDE EFFECTS

Like all drugs, HCG may produce side effects in some users. These effects can be reduced or eliminated by constant medical supervision, but here lies the problem, as most physicians are reluctant to become involved for fear of prosecution.

The most frequently reported side effects associated with HCG use are those that would normally be expected with any drug that increases testosterone production. These include irritability, acne, headaches, and increased libido.

Perhaps the most serious of these is the elevation of blood pressure due to increased water retention. For healthy individuals this is tolerable, but for those with a history of strokes in their family, elevating blood pressure is risky.

As with most drugs, the side effects associated with HCG are in most cases dose dependant. Given the research which suggests that megadoses are not needed to achieve the desired effects, why do bodybuilders continue to use such large quantities?

In all probability the reason lies with tradition. As most HCG users are also users of steroids and other anabolic agents, and the dosages for these drugs tend to be high, it only seems natural to use large dosages of HCG as well. But here lies the problem. For the most part, the dosages used by athletes for the popular performance-enhancing drugs is too high. The same results could be achieved with half or even one quarter of what's routinely taken by some bodybuilders. But as long as the "more

Charles Clairmonte

"By raising hormone levels, HCG causes pretty much the same problems as anabolics, except that the body's natural production doesn't decline in the same manner. The pituitary will generally shut down, however. Used in small and intermittent doses, HCG might be safe, but I wouldn't recommend it."

– Stephen Brooke, *MuscleMag* contributor commenting on the popular bodybuilding aid, HCG.

is better" attitude is held, no doubt the medical and popular literature will continue to report side effects associated with HCG abuse.

As a final comment, HCG must be mixed with sterile water before administering, and has a refrigerated shelf life of about four weeks. Like HGH, HCG quickly deteriorates if not properly stored. Not only does this reduce the effectiveness of the agent but increases the risk to the user.

BOVINE SOMATOTROPIN (BST) – BEEFING UP THE COMPETITION

As the name suggests, bovine somatotropin is a hormone derived from cows, used in the agriculture industry to increase production efficiency. In the past its use was limited because the only supplies available were those derived from slaughtered animals. In recent years recombinant DNA technology has led to cheap, mass production of the hormone. No doubt the cattle industry will see a marked increase of its use in the future.

Bovine somatotropin (BST) is a protein hormone produced naturally by the anterior pituitary gland of cows. When early researchers injected the abstract into rats they discovered it produced an increase in lean tissue mass. They gave it the name "somatotropin" because it could produce "tissue growth" – the original Greek definition for the word.[1] Modern endocrinologists usually refer to BST as bovine growth hormone (bGH), and it can be thought of as cattle's equivalent of human growth hormone. Once produced, the blood transports BST to various organs where it stimulates anabolic processes.

Sue Price and Dave Fisher

POTENTIAL USE IN BODYBUILDING

When injected into cows, BST boosts production of a peptide hormone called insulin-like growth factor-1 (IGF-1). Elevated levels of this hormone increase production of milk by increasing the flow of nutrients to the cows' udders. As would be expected, any drug that elevates IGF-1 levels is bound to receive attention from bodybuilders and others involved in strength sports. Further, like HGH, BST has the ability to stimulate various anabolic processes, while at the same time increasing the oxidation rate of fat.

Ronnie Coleman

In addition, the crackdown on anabolic steroids has forced many athletes to turn to "other drugs" in response to the reduced supply of steroids (one of the reasons put forward to explain the increase in HGH and clenbuterol use). In fact, thefts from veterinary drug suppliers has increased dramatically since steroid legislation has been stiffened.

The fact that BST is animal in origin in not unique as many of the most popular anabolic steroids (Winstrol, Nilivar, and Equipoise) were initially designed for animal use. Many bodybuilders actually prefer these drugs, alleging that they give a more pronounced "kick" than their human counterparts.

SIDE EFFECTS

As BST use has rarely been reported in humans, the nature of side effects is unknown. Given BST's similarity to HGH, we can extrapolate and expect much the same types of side effects. These include hypertension, acromegaly, and in rare cases, arthritis. BST's influence on IGF-1 levels might lead to side effects sometimes associated with this hormone.

The issue that the drugs were designed for animals is less important than would be expected. Although most assume that animal drugs are of lesser quality than human medications, this is not the case. Veterinary drugs are governed by the same set of quality standards as those intended for human usage. There are a number of reasons for this, chief of which is that most animals that receive widespread drug treatment (cows, pigs, poultry) are eventually consumed by humans. If a drug is toxic to these animals, it most certainly is toxic to humans, and therefore banned.

A secondary reason for high drug standards in animals is their financial worth. What stable is willing to jeopardize the health of a $2 million horse by using impure medications? What owner would willingly give his purebred dog a contaminated drug? So while the thoughts of injecting animal medications sound revolting, keep in mind that athletes have been doing it for over fifty years, and will no doubt continue to do so in the future.

"It has been tested and confirmed that BST does not cause malignant transformation of normal human cells."

– Bob Toth, director of animal science for Monsanto Canada Inc., Mississauga, ON, commenting on the safety of BST use in dairy cows.[2]

Like HGH, BST has the ability to stimulate various anabolic processes, while at the same time increasing the oxidation rate of fat.

BST is but one member of a class of drugs that bodybuilders and other athletes feel will give them the results they want. If it is reasonably priced, easily obtainable, and most important, does what it's supposed to do, we can be sure that the next wave of bodybuilding superstars might make BST an integral component of their contest preparations.

CYCLOFENIL

First marketed by an Arizona drug company, Cyclofenil is now only available by prescription. Like all gonadotropic drugs, Cyclofenil produces its effects by regulating the gonadal hormones. Cyclofenil shuts down the negative feedback loop, which controls LH levels in the blood. As increased LH stimulates the testes to increase testosterone production, it only follows that a drug preventing LH shutdown will lead to elevated levels of testosterone. As soon as bodybuilders heard about Cyclofenil's properties they began using it in droves. But like similar "ergogenic aids" the FDA quickly made the drug available by prescription only. Not to be deterred, the Arizona company set up shop across the border in Mexico and continued to sell the product. Other versions of the drug are also available in Mexico including the very popular Fertodur.[3]

In terms of dosage, most athletes take from 100 to 300 milligrams per day, but reports of 500 to 700 milligrams per day are not uncommon. Although it varies, most individuals quickly develop desensitivity to Cyclofenil, with the effects generally lasting for only six to eight weeks. This means the traditional practice of taking high dosages for extended periods of time is not only dangerous, but also a complete waste of money.

References
1) D. Hardin and others, "Recombinant Bovine Somatotropin: What's the Profit Potential?," *Veterinary Medicine*, 90:10 (October 1995).
2) M. Nichols, "Messing with Milk," *Macleans*, (July 31, 1995).
3) B. Phillips, *Natural Supplement Guide*, vol. 1 (Golden, Colorado: Mile High Publishing,

Franco Columbu

BOOK TWO

Thermogenesis – Beta Agonists – Fat Burners

Although not currently a prerequisite, it's probably only a matter of time before bodybuilders and other athletes need advanced degrees in pharmacology to successfully compete in the international sports arena. As it stands now, most have personal physicians to help guide them through the gauntlet of athletic pharmacology.

In recent years a class of drugs known as thermogenic agents have made substantial inroads into bodybuilding and other sports. And while most have their origins in legitimate medicine, many have become the drugs of choice for athletes affected by the crackdown on anabolic steroids and other fat-burning compounds.

Marjo Selin

WHAT IS THERMOGENESIS?

Thermogenesis is the biochemical term applied to the physiological state where the body converts excess calories into heat rather than storing them in the form of fat. Thermogenic drugs work in a number of manners. They increase the rate stored fat is burned for energy; they stimulate adipose tissue to release stored fat into the bloodstream where it is then available for oxidation; and they boost levels of other fat-burning compounds – usually hormones. The most popular thermogenic drugs are caffeine and ephedrine, but other more powerful agents like clenbuterol and epinephrine are also used.

The following chapters examine a few of the more popular thermogenic agents, paying particular attention to their fat-burning properties and potential side effects. Keep in mind that many thermogenic agents are also stimulants, but as they are primarily used for fat burning we have included them in this section.

Roland Cziurlok and Gunter Schlierkamp

"Imagine, if you will, a contest where all the athletes must test 10 percent or higher bodyfat. Goodbye diuretics, HGH, beta-agonists, pituitary drugs, thyroid medications and a whole wagonload of drugs best left out of bodybuilding. Would the athletes be sliced, diced, near-stasis cadavers that stumble onstage and have to be carried off? No. Instead they would be big and separated, cut and huge. Anyone less than the specified bodyfat level (whatever is deemed healthy) would be disqualified."

– Tony Monchinski, in an editorial featured in *MuscleMag*, offering an alternative to the dangerous practice of stacking numerous "cutting drugs" as followed by most pro bodybuilders.

CHAPTER EIGHT

Epinephrine

Although most medical studies use the name epinephrine, it's more popularly known as adrenaline. Adrenaline is a hormone secreted by the adrenal medulla of the adrenal glands – two small glands, one located just above each kidney. The interesting thing about adrenaline is that it acts both as a hormone and as a nervous-system transmitter. Although it may seem redundant, this allows the endocrine and nervous systems to work together as the body's primary control and communications network.

"Under normal conditions, epinephrine is delivered to fat cells mostly by direct innervation of the sympathetic nervous system, rather than systemic release from the whole body from the adrenal medulla. Its release is increased during exercise, and this is the primary mechanism whereby exercise serves as a stimulus for fat loss."

– John Parrillo, regular *MuscleMag* columnist commenting on the relationship between epinephrine, exercise, and fat loss.

MECHANISM OF ACTION

Although it has many biochemical actions, adrenaline is best known for its role in producing the "flight or fight" syndrome. This is the autonomic-nervous-system response which enables the body to deal with a potentially dangerous situation. Whether the individual decides to stay and confront the stress (fight) or avoid the situation (flight), the body's nervous system kicks into overdrive and stimulates the adrenal medulla to produce large amounts of adrenaline. As this gland has a proportionally high blood supply for its size, the newly released adrenaline is quickly carried throughout the body.

Melvin Anthony

High levels of adrenaline in turn produce such symptoms as increased heart rate, sweating, and general feelings of being on edge. It also readies your muscles for action. Besides the increased blood supply, adrenaline mobilizes fat stores from adipose tissue. This ensures an adequate supply of energy is available when needed. Research indicates that adrenaline release is increased during exercise, and this is believed to be the main mechanism of action of exercise-related fat loss.

There are two primary mechanisms of action for adrenaline to mobilize fat reserves. It can be a slow and controlled process involving systemic release to the whole body by the adrenal medulla or it can take the form of a direct innervation of the fat cells by the sympathetic nervous system.

At the cellular level it is known that adrenaline binds to receptors on fat cells and produces a product (a metabolite in biochemical terms) called cyclic AMP (cAMP). This in turn sets off a chain of intermediate steps ultimately resulting in the activation of a hormone called "hormone-sensitive lipase." Once activated, hormone sensitive lipase breaks down triglycerides into free fatty acids and glycerol. The free fatty acids are then carried by the bloodstream to the body's muscles where they are used as an energy source.

Sandy Riddell

USE IN BODYBUILDING

Like most hormones developed to treat endocrine problems, adrenaline has applications for bodybuilders. Although not as popular as steroids, growth hormone or clenbuterol, many bodybuilders make use of adrenaline in the weeks leading up to a contest.

Although it varies from individual to individual, most bodybuilders use the hormone for its fat-burning and energy-producing effects. The fat-burning properties are much coveted given the emphasis on the "ripped look" these days. While diet and exercise will enable most to shed excess fat, many are tempted to go for that extra degree of striation. This is where such hormones as adrenaline come in.

Besides its fat-burning properties, many bodybuilders find strict precontest diets leave them drained and lethargic. Just getting to the gym becomes a chore, not to mention putting in one to two gruelling hours at the weights. While caffeine provides the extra "kick" for some, others go one step further and boost their sympathetic nervous systems with adrenaline. Such a practice may be counterproductive. Like caffeine, the body quickly tries to normalize chemical levels, and in many cases the drug-induced burst of energy is followed by a "crash" into exhaustion. One minute you're blasting out set after set at the squat rack, and the next your only request is a blanket and pillow.

SIDE EFFECTS

Like most hormones, adrenaline has the potential to be abused. The human body did not evolve to have high levels of adrenaline circulating throughout it for extended periods of time. The "flight or fight" syndrome was designed for short-term consequences – not sustained activity. Bodybuilders who rely on adrenaline for that extra burst of energy are also boosting heart rate, blood pressure, and a host of physiological mechanisms that science is probably not even aware of yet. Even for those in excellent physical health, such side effects can be serious.

There is also the biofeedback operation of adrenaline to keep in mind. Like steroids, natural adrenaline levels will shut down if exogenous (outside) sources are taken. As long as you remain on the synthetic forms there should be no problem (we say this guardedly) but as soon as the outside source is stopped, the body is left with virtually no circulating adrenaline. Not only will adrenaline-dependant effects be curtailed, but given the interrelationship between adrenaline and many other hormones, it's conceivable that the individual could sabotage their entire endocrine system – the consequences of which are life threatening.

A final consideration is source. If you manage to find a sympathetic physician (the odds are you won't), you can get a prescription and be sure of the drug's authenticity. On the other hand, obtaining it on the black market brings with it the risks associated with all other black-market drugs. Buyer beware!

So although it sounds like a "glamorous" drug to try, our advice is to avoid it and use diet and exercise for your energy and fat-burning needs. Adrenaline is a powerful drug that should only be used under medical supervision and for the treatment of endocrine-related problems.

LEGAL ASPECTS

As of this writing, adrenaline falls under the category of a prescription drug. This means applicable laws relate to possession of a prescription drug without legitimate medical approval. Adrenaline possession is not as serious as steroid possession; nevertheless, given America's paranoia with the "drug war," possession of adrenaline with the intentions of trafficking could lead to serious jail time. And if you had a previous drug-related conviction, you may get the book thrown at you. While there have been few convictions for adrenaline trafficking (in most cases the individual had numerous drugs in their possession), the potential is there.

Finally, while not a strict legal aspect, adrenaline and related compounds are banned by the IOC and most other sports federations. So even if you use it without side effects and manage to avoid legal prosecution, you can't compete at intermediate or upper-level athletics which are tested.

**Gunter Schlierkamp
and Milos Sarcev**

Clenbuterol

I t seems every competition brings forth a new class of performance-enhancing drugs. Such was the case at the 1992 Summer Olympic Games, held in Barcelona, Spain, when two US athletes tested positive for clenbuterol – a common substance found in many asthma preparations. Its use appears to be on the increase given the crackdown on steroids, even though it isn't a member of the more familiar anabolic steroid class.

Trade Names: Clenasma, Monores, Prontovent
Generic Name: clenbuterol
Tablet Size: .01 (10 mcg) and .02 mg (20 mcg)
Solution: .001, .02, and .059 mg/ml
Therapeutic Dose: .02 to .03 mg/day
Gym Dose: 200 percent

Lorenze Matai

Clenbuterol is a member of a class of pharmacological agents which stimulate beta andrenoreceptors. These receptors are located in body tissues such as the heart, lungs, and skeletal muscles.

The drugs themselves can be subdivided into two groups – agonists and antagonists. Beta-2 agonists are used as bronchodilators in the treatment of asthma, while beta antagonists (blockers) are used as antihypertensive drugs. Both classes of drugs are chemical modifications of the more familiar hormones adrenaline (epinephrine) and noradrenaline (norepinephrine).

Clenbuterol has received little interest in the United States as other asthma medications are just as effective without the same degree of side effects. Although banned for both animal and human use in the United States, clenbuterol is frequently found in asthma preparations in other countries. Its most popular version is as a constituent in aerosol cans, the contents of which are inhaled for the treatment of bronchial ailments. Less popular forms include tablets and liquids. Clenbuterol is available by subscription in such countries as Germany, Austria, Mexico, Spain, and Italy. The US equivalent is a drug called albuterol.

MECHANISM OF ACTION

The primary action of clenbuterol is to stimulate the beta receptors found in such organs as the heart and lungs. It relaxes the smooth muscle surrounding the bronchioles – a blessing to asthma and allergy sufferers.

As clenbuterol is structurally similar to adrenaline, it mimics the actions of this hormone, producing the previously discussed "flight or fight" syndrome. Interestingly, athletes are not the only ones to suffer from such symptoms. There are numerous reports from Europe of individuals who had eaten clenbuterol-laced meat, suffering the same problems (one of the main reasons the drug is banned in the US). Most asthmatics don't experience these side effects because of the low dosages of clenbuterol available in medications.

Jackie
Paisley

The secondary effects of clenbuterol were discovered by accident. These effects could be termed "side effects" as they were unexpected. Researchers discovered that the animals given clenbuterol showed increases in skeletal-muscle, decreases in bodyfat, and greater energy levels.[1] Another study looked at the recuperative powers of rats following such negative physical stress as food deprivation, surgery, and bacterial injection. In all cases the experimental group (rats receiving clenbuterol) showed marked increases in skeletal muscle weight and decreases in bodyfat, as compared to the control groups (rats not receiving clenbuterol). The study also discovered that age has little bearing on the effects of clenbuterol as old rats showed the same degree of physical changes. There was also no weight change in the internal organs. This concurs with other studies that suggest clenbuterol's effects are limited primarily to skeletal muscle.[2]

Although the exact mechanism of action is not fully understood, it is believed that clenbuterol increases both protein utilization and RNA accretion. Animal studies seem to confirm this theory as dietary protein changes have a marked effect on clenbuterol's anabolic effects. Clenbuterol-fed rats deprived of protein showed little weight gain. Those receiving adequate amounts of protein showed the expected skeletal-muscle gains.[3]

With regards to bodyfat, it is believed clenbuterol increases the rate of lipolysis – the process by which fatty acids are converted first to acetyl CoA, and then later to ATP – the body's chief energy source. Other evidence suggests that clenbuterol increases the rate of brown-adipose-tissue thermogenesis.[3] In either case the body's fat reserves are depleted, and the individual loses weight.

Another important discovery is that clenbuterol's effects are time related. Rats being fed the drug showed weight gain and increased protein

Bodybuilders have become attached to clenbuterol because of both its ability to spare muscle tissue while on a strict diet, and decrease bodyfat – the two primary goals in the weeks leading up to a contest.

synthesis in as little as four days after administration. Conversely, clenbuterol's growth-promoting abilities seem to be time limited as the same rats showed reduced weight gain after 21 days.[4] It has been suggested that such factors as receptor desensitization and interaction with hormones may account for the drug's reduced effects over time.

USE IN BODYBUILDING

Once reports of the muscle-building and fat-losing properties of clenbuterol in animals began to surface in gyms, it was only a matter of time before athletes satisfied their own curiosities. Like other so-called performance-enhancing drugs, clenbuterol use can be broken down into many categories. At one end we have individuals who use the drug simply because it's there, and if other athletes are using it, "so must I." At the other end of the spectrum we have individuals who consider clenbuterol the greatest anabolic agent ever – even more so than steroids.

For the most part, however, athletes use clenbuterol simply because it's another drug that may increase performance. Bodybuilders have become attached to clenbuterol because of both its ability to spare muscle tissue while on a strict diet, and decrease bodyfat – the two primary goals in the weeks leading up to a contest. And since clenbuterol is much harder to detect than anabolic steroids, it's popular with bodybuilders in drug-tested events. This was especially true in the early 1990s when the drug first came into use. In many cases the drug tests were not even set up to search for clenbuterol because most sports federations were not aware of its widespread use.

Although it varies, clenbuterol should be able to be used up to 48 hours before a competition in order to pass a drug test (it has a half-life of about 50 hours).[3] With tests becoming more and more sophisticated every day (as the two US Olympic athletes found out in 1992), athletes in drug-tested events would be wise to give clenbuterol a pass for fear of being banned from their respective sports federation.

"To complicate the picture it appears from the literature that the many putative effects of clenbuterol rapidly diminish with time. For example, in one recent study the inhibitory effect that one dose of clenbuterol had on the sexual activity of normally sexually active male rats disappeared when the clenbuterol was given daily for a one-week period."

– Dr. Mauro DiPasquale, regular *MuscleMag* columnist commenting on the short metabolic action of clenbuterol.

Most anecdotal reports indicate that athletes prefer the tablet form of clenbuterol over the bronchial spray, and the "standard dosage" tends to be about twice the recommended therapeutic dose. This works out to about 50 to 100 micrograms per day. Other reports tell of clenbuterol being cycled on a three-week on/three-week off pattern, in doses up to 120 micrograms per day. During the three-week on period, the drug is taken for two days and discontinued for two.[5] Although the reasons for this are not fully understood, it appears athletes have paid close attention to the results of studies, which indicate that prolonged (chronic) use of clenbuterol may decrease its effectiveness. Researchers suggest that either receptor reduction or receptor desensitization may account for this.[6,7]

This last point depicts a paradoxical situation as most anecdotal reports suggest that the anabolic effects of clenbuterol are very short lived. That is, once a bodybuilder goes off clenbuterol, most, if not all muscle gains made while on the drug are quickly lost. This in turn leads many to promptly return to the drug. See the problem? Long-term use of clenbuterol also seems to reduce its effectiveness. It seems clenbuterol is an ideal drug for short-term, precompetition training, but has contradictory properties for long-term use as an anabolic agent.

HOW EFFECTIVE?

Assessing the effectiveness of clenbuterol in athletics is difficult to say the least. Like growth hormone, clenbuterol use is very clandestine in nature. This means researchers have a chore in trying to get athletes to open up about the practice. It's even more difficult if the athletes in question are participants in sports were the drug is banned. Even on conditions of anonymity, most athletes are fearful of having their use exposed.

Jeff Poulin

This issue of drug interactions must also be taken into account. Most individuals who use clenbuterol also take other "athletic drugs" such as anabolic steroids, growth hormone, and insulin. This makes it difficult to assess whether physical changes are due to clenbuterol, other drugs, or a drug combination. Many drugs when taken separately have little effect on human physiology, but when combined with others produce a synergistic effect that far surpasses each drug's individual effect.

Another problem concerns the lack of historical information – particularly anecdotal knowledge. Unlike steroids, which go back 40 years or more, clenbuterol use in athletics is a

'90s phenomenon. This means there are no "old timers" available to open up about clenbuterol use – either to researchers or other athletes. There is little "hand me down" knowledge available. Athletes presently taking clenbuterol are the first generation of users.

Researchers in ten or twenty years will no doubt have access to first-hand use, but this is of little benefit at present. This is especially frustrating to physicians and coaches trying to council athletes. Telling them to "come back and see me in ten years" just doesn't work with potential users.

Perhaps the most important reason for questioning the effectiveness of clenbuterol lies with the lack of scientific evidence as it relates to humans. There are volumes of data on clenbuterol use in animals. The effects of clenbuterol as a medical treatment for asthma and other lung conditions is also well-documented. But those all-important studies that look at the use of clenbuterol in healthy human athletes are sadly lacking.

It's possible to extrapolate data from animal studies – it's done all the time in medical research. But how relevant is data collected from a few rats to 250-pound bodybuilders? Comparing the anticonstriction effects of clenbuterol in monkeys to humans may be valid, but can the same be said for protein synthesis or fat lipolysis?

Closely related to the previous is the issue of dosages. Clinical trials with animals usually involve amounts that are "hundreds of times" what humans can tolerate. Even if scientists somehow received permission to conduct experiments on athletes, there is no way they could morally or legally use the same dosages.

Compounding the frustration of researchers is the fact that clenbuterol is not approved by the FDA for use in humans. This means that "Dr. Research" can't simply recruit 20 bodybuilders and go into the lab and carry out a controlled experiment to see what happens. He is lucky if he can get funding to experiment on animals. This is not a small point as funding size is proportional to the product's commercial potential in humans. If the drug is not expected to be used in humans, researchers are often left to their own devices.

**Sandy Riddell
pumps her bis.**

Paul Dillett

SIDE EFFECTS

Just as evaluating the effectiveness of clenbuterol poses problems, so too does classifying the associated health risks. Given the limited information available on side effects reported by athletes, we must rely once again on animal studies and human patients treated with clenbuterol and other beta agonists.

There are two primary groups of individuals who are exposed to beta agonists (excluding athletes): patients being treated with the drugs, and individuals who eat the meat of animals that have been treated with the drugs. Of the latter group, the most persistent side effects are associated with eating animal liver. This is to be expected given the liver's role in concentrating and metabolizing drugs.

In any case the most frequently reported side effects in humans are nausea, headaches, and insomnia – the three often being interrelated. The most serious side effect, and the one that shows the greatest potential for death is tachycardia, the medical term for excessively rapid heart beat. There have been a couple of deaths among athletes attributed to excessive clenbuterol use, over 1000 micrograms a day.[8]

Bodybuilders may be at special risk for developing this condition close to a contest as many use diuretics to flush water from their systems. Besides water, valuable electrolytes are lost, and since these electrically charged ions are integral parts of the cardiac and nervous systems, individuals may be compounding the situation by using clenbuterol – a drug which speeds up the excretion of such minerals, including potassium. Although not conclusive, it is believed that former IFBB pro bodybuilder Mohammad Benaziza died of complications brought on by excessive clenbuterol and diuretic use.

"I feel Mohammad screwed up his electrolytes. When you take clenbuterol in excessive amounts – you know, clenbuterol does block cortisol – you lower your cortisol and you tend to throw up when your cortisol is low. And then not drinking enough fluids, and taking aldosterone antagonists, estrogen antagonists, potassium, and taking this and that – that's a lot of different things and somehow they're going to interact."

– Samir Bannout, 1993 Mr. Olympia commenting on the death of fellow IFBB pro, Mohammad Benaziza.

The list of side effects associated with clenbuterol use in animals includes: tremors, seizures, cardiac arrest, haemorrhaging, and extreme nervousness. The effects on the heart are especially interesting as some studies show myocardial hypertrophy (enlarging of the heart) in animals – a condition that could cause vascular obstruction leading to death if it were to occur in humans.[5] It's not surprising that clenbuterol affects heart tissue as this organ contains large numbers of beta receptors. The common heart medication propranolol is a beta-receptor antagonist which helps stabilize heart rate.

Bill Davey

We should add that these side effects are usually associated with animals undergoing a great deal of stress. Further, many are being treated with other drugs besides beta agonists. Most animal researchers will admit that determining the exact cause of a given side effect is difficult. Everything from drug interactions to environmental variables must be taken into account.

By way of conclusion we must emphasize that the jury is still out concerning the health risks of clenbuterol use. Given the relative newness of this drug to athletics, it's probably going to take another five to 10 years for the first studies involving such subjects to appear. Until then, bodybuilders and other athletes intent on taking clenbuterol should pay close attention to signals given off by their bodies. If there's any doubt, play it safe and give clenbuterol a pass.

LEGAL IMPLICATIONS

Besides being banned by most sports organizations – including the International Olympic Committee (IOC) – clenbuterol is not approved for use as a medication in humans or animals in the US. This includes asthma preparations for humans and as a "fattening agent" in animals.

Although not a scheduled drug under the Federal Controlled Substance Act, distribution or possession of clenbuterol is punishable by law. In most states possession is classified as a misdemeanor and falls under the category of possession of a prescription drug without a valid prescription. We should add that a few states have taken the "drug war" to heart and made possession of clenbuterol a felony. Further, if you are caught importing clenbuterol from another country (the source of many clenbuterol preparations), you will face serious federal charges under the various drug-smuggling acts. This could mean serious jail time depending on the amount, prosecution tactics, and your criminal background.

It is in your best interests to be aware of your state's (and country's) laws with respect to clenbuterol possession. If unsure, avoid the drug like the plague.

A final consideration for potential clenbuterol users concerns the black market. With the recent crackdown on steroids and other performance-enhancing drugs, obtaining genuine clenbuterol on the black market has become difficult. Many individuals have reported buying fake clenbuterol tablets from dealers (at an average price of $100 to $200 a bottle). Other reports indicate that many preparations are not clenbuterol but anabolic steroids. As with growth hormone and steroids, the health risks associated with buying clenbuterol from unreliable sources increases as you go further away from legitimate sources. In short, that shadowy figure you regularly buy from is probably profiting at your expense. If you're lucky you'll only be out a few hundred dollars. Given the wrong set of circumstances, however, you may end up in the morgue.

References

1) M.N. Sillence and others, "Effects of Clenbuterol and Sotalol on the Growth of Cardiac and Skeletal Muscle and on B2 Adrenoreceptor Density in Female Rats," *Archives of Pharmacology*, 344 (1991).

2) W.J. Carter and others, "Effects of Clembuterol on Skeletal Muscle Mass, Body Composition, and Recovery From Surgical Stress in Senescent Rats," *Metabolism*, 40:8 (1991).

3) J.J. Choo and others, "Effects of the B2 Adrenoreceptor Agonist Clenbuterol on Muscle Atrophy Due to Food Deprivation in the Rat," *Metabolism*, 39:6 (1990).

4) P.J. Reeds and others, "Stimulation of Muscle Growth By Clenbuterol, Lack of Effect On Muscle Protein Biosynthesis," *British Journal of Nutrition*, 56 (1986).

5) I.D. Prather and others, "Clenbuterol: A Substitute For Anabolic Steroids?," *Medicine and Science in Sports and Exercise*, 27:8 (1995).

6) N.J. Rothwell and others, "Changes in Tissue Blood Flow and Beta Receptor Density of Skeletal Muscle in Rats Treated With the B2 Adrenorecptor Agonist Clenbuterol," *British Journal of Pharmacology*, 90 (1987).

7) J.R. Hadcock and C.C. Malban, "Down Regulation of B-adrenoreceptor, Agonist Induced Reduction in Receptor mRNA levels," Proc Natl Acad Scie, 88 (1988).

Be ready to face serious federal charges if caught importing clenbuterol from another country.

CHAPTER TEN

Ephedrine

Although considered a relatively new supplement, ephedrine has actually been used in Chinese medicine for thousands of years. It's gaining popularity among bodybuilders because of anecdotal reports stating it has great fat-burning abilities – especially when combined with aspirin and caffeine. Consuming these three agents has fast become one of the most widely used preworkout concoctions – despite the lack of hard scientific data to back up the various claims.

Ephedrine is a naturally occurring sympathomimetic amine found in plants of the genus Ephedra, including the familiar Chinese herb ma huang. Structurally, ephedrine is similar to adrenaline and amphetamines, and holds the same benefits and disadvantages of both.

HOW IT WORKS

Like clenbuterol and adrenaline, ephedrine produces most of its effects by stimulating beta adrenoreceptors – in short, it's a beta agonist. But unlike clenbuterol, ephedrine is nonselective in which beta receptors it stimulates. While clenbuterol produces its effects strictly at beta-2 receptors, ephedrine interacts with all three types of beta receptors (even this may be conservative as new evidence suggests the presence of additional beta receptors).

In low doses ephedrine produces effects similar to adrenaline and methamphetamines, including a greater sense of well-being and seemingly unlimited energy levels. Yet in high dosages, ephedrine can raise blood pressure, increase heart rate, and in extreme cases lead to stroke.

> "Ephedrine shares some of the properties of adrenaline and the amphetamines. Its use can make you jittery and give you heart palpitations like adrenaline, and it can give you some of the central nervous system effects of the amphetamines. Like the amphetamines, chronic use has unpleasant psychological and physical effects."
>
> – Dr. Mauro DiPasquale, regular *MuscleMag* columnist commenting on some of the side effects of the popular bodybuilding aid ephedrine.

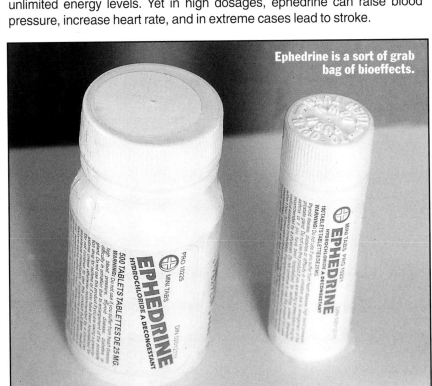

Ephedrine is a sort of grab bag of bioeffects.

BODYBUILDING APPLICATIONS

So far we have only discussed ephedrine's effects on the cardiovascular system. But bodybuilders and other athletes take the drug for two entirely different reasons – thermogenesis and elevation of strength levels.

Research over the last 10 years seems to confirm that ephedrine speeds up the rate at which stored fat is converted into heat energy. In one study performed at the University of Copenhagen in Denmark, obese women were given 20 milligrams of ephedrine with 200 milligrams of caffeine, three times a day. They were also kept on a low-calorie, low-fat diet. The results of the study were amazing! The "diet only" group lost 8.6 pounds of muscle and 9.9 pounds of fat. The ephedrine group only lost 2.4 pounds of muscle while losing 19.8 pounds of fat.

The exact mechanism is not fully understood, but the evidence suggests that ephedrine, when combined with caffeine and aspirin, increases the body's production of the hormone norepinephrine (noradrenaline). This hormone is very similar in structure and function to adrenaline, and among its actions are the stimulation of beta-3 receptors, which in turn increase the rate of thermogenesis. There is also evidence to suggest ephedrine stimulates the two thyroid hormones T3 and T4 – both of which increase the body's ability to burn fat.

So promising were the results of the studies that they led to the marketing of numerous over-the-counter supplements with ephedrine as the main ingredient for battling obesity. Bodybuilders first heard of ephedrine's thermogenic effects from these sources. True, many had been taking the drug in low doses for years as a stimulant, but once word got around about the fat-loss applications, the dosages were dramatically increased.

Besides its thermogenic effects, ephedrine is also reported to spare muscle tissue while the individual is dieting. When bodybuilders normally restrict calories, they lose a proportion of their bodyweight in the form of lean muscle tissue. As the amount of muscle tissue decreases, the person's metabolic rate slows down (metabolic rate is heavily dependant on the proportion of muscle tissue to adipose tissue). A point is eventually reached where losing additional bodyfat becomes almost impossible. If the anecdotal reports are correct (there are few if any research studies that look at the effects of ephedrine and bodybuilders), ephedrine could very well be the precontest supplement of the future.

Gunter Schlierkamp

"Taking 20 to 30 mg of ephedrine a few times a week before a workout will not do you any harm at all. The problem is, we have people taking handfuls of the stuff year-round (usually on top of clenbuterol, coffee, etc.) and occasionally getting cardiac arrhythmias, hypertension, and so forth. On rare occasions it can lead to serious complications, possibly even death."

- Will Brink, regular *MuscleMag* columnist offering his views on the potential side effects of ephedrine abuse.

The third reason for ephedrine's popularity among bodybuilders is its effects on strength. Anecdotal reports suggest that strength increases of 10 to 20 percent during a typical workout are common. The evidence is mounting to suggest ephedrine's effects on strength are more definite than effects on energy and thermogenesis (that is, more users report the former than the latter). Whether or not this can be confirmed scientifically is still unclear.

Shawn Ray

SOURCES AND SUPPLEMENTS

Ephedrine is one of the easiest supplements to find. There are also considerable differences between the various products. The most commercially used source for ephedrine is from the Chinese plant ma huang. This herbal source of ephedrine has been used in Chinese medicine for thousands of years, and surprisingly two of its most widely used applications were for the treatment of nasal congestion and low-energy levels. The ancient Chinese were probably not aware of beta receptors, but they selected the correct "medicine" for therapy.

It would be convenient if all ma huang sources were equal, but such is not the case. The ephedrine concentration varies between ma huang species, and the same species grown in different geographical areas. There may even be variation within the same plant.

Manufacturers try to select ma huang sources that contain the highest percentage of ephedrine, and also make sure to use only "L" sources of ephedrine. Like amino acids and many other substances with biochemical applications, ephedrine exists in various forms called isomers, which are labeled according to their structure or rotation around the central axis. When only two isomers exist they are usually mirror images of one another and rotate clockwise (L) or counter clockwise (D). In most cases humans have evolved to utilize the "L" forms, and such is the case with ephedrine.

Although products may be listed as "natural," many in fact have been "fortified" or "spiked" with additional ephedrine or norephedrine. Although found naturally in ma huang, norephedrine exists only in small amounts (concentrated forms appear in such diet supplements as Dexatrim).

Besides natural and modified forms, concentrated extracts of ma huang are also available. These products are far more powerful than natural ma huang, and often contain a mixed blend of different ephedrine isomers.

Perhaps the most widely used form of ephedrine – even though most don't realize it – is pseudoephedrine. Given the nature of many cold medications to cause drowsiness, manufacturers often add the substance to counteract these effects. The fact that it is itself an effective decongestant adds to its popularity.

> **"One word of warning: To take this energy cocktail occasionally when you need a special boost is one thing. To rely on such 'uppers' each and every day is another. You can't fool Mother Nature. If you stay on these energy boosters too long, there will come an inevitable crashing out for a month. So remember, moderation is the key word."**
>
> – Greg Zulak, former *MuscleMag* editor and well-known bodybuilding writer warning users of ephedrine, caffeine, and aspirin not to become dependant on the drugs for each and every workout.

In recent years ephedrine has taken on a new role – forming the basis for many over-the-counter stimulants. With the crackdown on powerful stimulants like amphetamines, manufacturers needed a substance that was both legal and capable of producing amphetamine-like effects. As ephedrine fit the bill, it was quickly adopted by most of the larger pharmaceutical companies.

As would be expected, the crackdown on amphetamines, and the huge profits to be made from selling stimulant drugs, has led to the establishment of underground basement labs. These clandestine operators have found a niche for themselves selling "pseudoamphetamines" to shift workers, athletes, and what is especially alarming – to teenagers. While shift workers and athletes use them for physiological effects (both groups use them as stimulants while athletes also covet the thermogenic effects), teens take them for recreational purposes to attain a cheap "high." This is a dangerous practice given the source of the drug (in most cases a lab not too concerned with hygiene) and the potential for side effects (discussed in the next section).

The most popular commercial brands of ephedrine supplements are TwinLab's Ripped Fuel and Diet Fuel, AST's Dymetadrine 25, and SportPharma's Thermagene. As an example, both TwinLab's products contain 20 milligrams of ephedrine, 200 milligrams of caffeine, chromium, and carnitine. In addition, Diet Fuel contains 250 milligrams of HCA.

Dymetadrine 25 supplies 25 milligrams of ephedrine but no caffeine or other fat-burning substances. This means you must purchase a caffeine source separately (either coffee, tea, or caffeine tablets). Dymetadrine 25 has the advantage of containing a buffered base, which means little or no stomach upset.

Although there will be individual differences, the recommended dosages for ephedrine and caffeine are 20 to 50 milligrams and 100 to 200 milligrams respectively (most bodybuilders add aspirin – about 300 milligrams – to the stack as well). Both the ephedrine and caffeine should be taken at the same time, two to three times daily (this only applies if you are using separate forms of the supplements. As we mentioned previously, the more popular brands contain both). For maximum effect take one of the servings about 30 to 45 minutes prior to your workout.

Dymetadrine 25 is another commercially available source of ephedrine.

SIDE EFFECTS

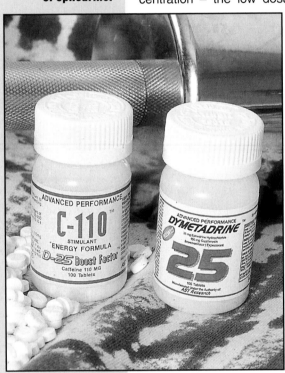

Like most drugs, side effects from ephedrine use are usually dose related. While a few individuals may be allergic to the drug – no matter what the concentration – the low dosages contained in herbs and over-the-counter medications pose little risk to the user. Even with ephedrine-based asthma medications – containing up to 25 milligrams of L-ephedrine – serious side effects are rarely seen. This is due to such factors as familiarity with the drug, constant medical supervision, and clearly marked bottles and inserts that list potential side effects and contraindications.

Most of the "horror" stories that occasionally surface are the result of individuals using high concentrations of ephedrine as a diet aid. In many cases the recommended dosage of 90 to 100 milligrams per day is ignored. Reports suggest that some bodybuilders are taking two to four times this amount.

Other people may develop side effects because of underlying cardiovascular disease, which interferes with ephedrine metabolism. For an individual with a weak or diseased heart, the stimulant effects of ephedrine could be life threatening. Others simply throw caution to the wind and take huge dosages (sound familiar?) using the old "if some is good, more is better" mentality.

Another concern is the interactive effects of ephedrine with other drugs. Even such common substances as aspirin and caffeine (ironically the two drugs taken with ephedrine by most bodybuilders) can produce a myriad of side effects when combined with ephedrine. The most common of these is increased blood pressure. But we must add that most studies suggest the increased blood pressure is only seen during the first few weeks of use and returns to normal with continued use. Still, this is one of the primary reasons why physicians and registered dieticians are reluctant to prescribe ephedrine-based compounds as a diet aid. For some people the risks surpass the benefits.

Without leaving the impression that ephedrine is free of side effects, we should add that some users report slight hand tremors when using the product. And while this would have little or no effect in the gym, those who use their hands for delicate work (electronic technicians, watch makers, etc.) might want to give the product a trial run before engaging in such work-related activity.

LEGAL IMPLICATIONS

This may seem a redundant topic given ephedrine's over-the-counter availability, but like most supplements, the US FDA wants to get in on the act and make ephedrine a controlled substance. There are numerous reasons for the increased attention by the FDA, chief of which are a few isolated cases blown out of proportion, and pressure from drug companies.

In 1994, Ohio restricted all ephedrine products after the death of a high-school student who'd taken an over-the-counter ephedrine product. In Texas a woman died after using an ephedra-caffeine herbal supplement. In August of 1995, a coalition of state drug regulators wrote to the FDA asking the agency to limit ma huang to prescription use only.[1]

Dave Fisher

TEENAGE ECSTASY!

In recent years a few cases of ephedrine-related side effects has prompted a movement by the FDA to ban most sources of ephedrine including cold medications, stimulant derivatives, and bulk forms of the drug. And while natural ma huang will probably remain safe, its concentrated relatives may be targeted.

No other class of ephedrine-containing products have done more to start the anti-ephedrine movement than recreational drugs like Herbal Ecstasy. Such concoctions are aimed mainly at teenagers for their alleged sexual-stimulant properties. Although little evidence exists to show such a relationship, this doesn't seem to matter to teens. Therefore, the drugs are frequently combined with other adolescent vices such as alcohol, marijuana, and tobacco. It's not surprising then that many teens tragically overdose and die. But while the alcohol and tobacco were probably as much to blame as the ephedrine, how many Congressman do you hear crusading to ban such drugs? None! And why? Because of the billions of dollars made each year by the tobacco and alcohol industry. Ephedrine has no corporate giants lobbying on its behalf and hence will probably be placed under much tighter controls.

"Most people have few side effects from using up to 30 mg of ephedrine at a time."

– Dr. Mauro DiPasquale, world-renowned expert on ergogenic aids in sports.

STRANGE BEDFELLOWS

The second reason for the anti-ephedrine movement is because of pressure from drug companies who manufacturer other fat-loss products. As bodybuilders are discovering, ephedrine is one of the best over-the-

Yolanda Hughes, Lenda Murray and Debbie Muggli compete for a big title win.

counter fat-burning substances available. Not only is it much more effective, but it's safer than many of the other reputed fat-burning compounds – including the much vaunted, yet now banned prescription drug, dexfenfluramine. Faced with such competition, numerous pharmaceutical companies which market such diet drugs, have begun lobbying the FDA to make ephedrine a banned substance. The fact that many pharmaceutical companies are owned by tobacco companies hasn't helped matters either. Such tobacco giants have the necessary money available to "influence" legislators.

The FDA has responded by resurrecting obscure and exaggerated toxic reports to promote their cause. The media then takes such information, and before you know it, a snowball effect has started. Relatively safe substances have been turned into "cancer-causing, heart attack-inducing agents." (The same approach was used to ban steroids and almost ban amino acids and other familiar food supplements.)

If such legislation is drafted and passed by Congress, the implications will be enormous (by the time you receive this book it may have already passed). Can you imagine a "major" drug bust involving cold medications? Or how about *Inside Edition* or *Hard Copy* featuring the latest bodybuilders to be busted for using their preworkout caffeine-aspirin-ephedrine mixture? It sounds far-fetched, but remember what nearly happened back in the early 1990s when Congress attempted to outlaw most forms of supplements. Only a concerted effort on the part of thousands of citizens prevented the arrest of hundreds of grandmothers for using Geritol mixtures.

It would make far more sense to simply force manufacturers to label ephedrine-containing products with the same warnings as other over-the-counter medications. After all, a bottle of aspirin could kill a person. Likewise, many cough syrups contain enough medication to seriously hurt or kill a child. If these products are freely available – albeit with well-labeled bottles and inserts – why not the same for ephedrine compounds? Banning a potentially valuable medication/diet aid because a few individuals abuse the drug makes little sense.

FINAL CONSIDERATIONS

Like clenbuterol and growth hormone, ephedrine use by bodybuilders is a relatively new phenomenon, and as such most of the available information concerning effectiveness and side effects is anecdotal. While studies with obese individuals suggest that the drug holds great promise for promoting fat loss, and is relatively safe, its effects in bodybuilders is poorly understood. It may be safe for a 400-pound person to use the drug to shed 50 to 100 pounds, but what about a bodybuilder whose fat levels are low to begin with? It is possible that side effects not seen in obese individuals will start surfacing in bodybuilders a few years down the road. And while we touched on this before, it deserves rementioning. The dosages used by bodybuilders ten or twenty years ago for stimulant purposes were much smaller than the dosages currently taken for thermogenesis. We are exploring new territory and only time will tell what the outcome will be.

Reference

1) J.C. Cohen and others, "Hypercholesterolemia in Male Power Lifters Using Anabolic Androgenic Steroids," *The Physician and Sports Medicine*, 16:8 (1988).

Terry Mitsos

CHAPTER ELEVEN

Miscellaneous Fat Burners

As long as sports have been organized into weight classes, athletes have paid attention to their bodyfat. With the possible exception of super-heavyweights, most competitors try to stay as lean as possible. The primary goal of most is to compete at the top of their weight class. A few extra pounds of fat can sabotage this plan by placing the athlete at the bottom of the next weight division.

The late Andreas Munzer.

For competitive bodybuilders a virtual absence of bodyfat is an absolute must. And although muscle-building drugs like steroids and growth hormone receive all the attention, there is more to competitive bodybuilding than just building muscle. It's no use to carry 240 pounds of muscle if it's covered by a layer of fat. A flip through a recent issue of *MuscleMag* shows the types of physiques winning contests these days – ones with cross-striations and eye-popping veins. And the only way to display such vascularity is to keep bodyfat levels to a minimum.

CHOOSING A FAT-BURNING SUPPLEMENT

Although personal preference plays a role, there are general recommendations for choosing a good fat-burning product. A well-designed fat-burning supplement should have ingredients to stimulate the adrenal and thyroid glands. It should also contain nutrients that increase the rate of fatty-acid usage. Finally, try to choose a supplement which helps regulate blood sugar and insulin – these two interrelated variables play a major role in fat loss.

In the following chapter we will look at some of the substances athletes use to keep adipose tissue on the run. Some of them have a basis in science; others have mechanisms of action not fully understood; and some are of questionable merit, but athletes use them anyway.

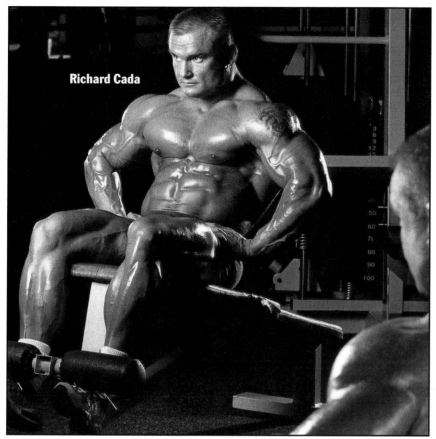

Richard Cada

HYDROXY CITRIC ACID (HCA)

First introduced as a diet aid to help treat obesity, HCA is fast gaining attention in the world's bodybuilding community. HCA is obtained from the rinds of the Garcinia fruit of South Asia. And although it can be used year-round, bodybuilders will find it most useful in the months leading up to a contest.

HCA is unlike such other appetite suppressants as caffeine and ephedrine in that it does not effect the central nervous system (CNS). In addition, it does not stimulate the body to cannibalize lean muscle tissue as a fuel source. Instead, it prevents the conversion of carbohydrates into fat.

HOW IT WORKS

For a full understanding of the effects of HCA we need to look briefly at how the body uses and stores both fat and carbohydrates.

When carbohydrates and sugars are consumed in the diet, the body reduces both to blood glucose. The glucose is then facilitated into cells by the hormone insulin. From here glucose may have a number of different destinies. Some is stored in the liver and muscles as glycogen. When needed, the body converts the stored glycogen back into glucose. The other primary metabolic route of glucose is to be broken down into smaller subunits by way of the citric-acid cycle (see Appendix 3).

If glucose is available in excess and not needed by the body, it is converted to fat by the process of lypogenesis. Although humans usually don't produce a great amount of fat from carbohydrates, any amount produced is significant as even small quantities can block the body's fat-burning processes.

"If you're currently overweight and the only change you make in your life is to add a lipotropic supplement, probably nothing will happen. I've said this a million times, but it's so central to my philosophy that I'm going to keep on saying it: Proper diet and training are the foundation of any successful fitness program. If you add the world's best supplements to a bad diet, you still have a bad diet. Nor are lipotropics a substitute for exercise. They will not 'melt the pounds off' as some companies would have you believe. They will, however, ensure that your body has everything it needs to burn fat at peak efficiency. Exercise is the ultimate stimulus for fat loss."

– John Parrillo, *MuscleMag* columnist explaining the limited potential of lipotropics in fat reduction.

The last step of glycolysis (the breakdown of glucose) takes place inside the mitochondria – the cell's little energy-storing organelles. The product produced is citrate, which is then sent outside the mitochondria to be broken down into subunits used in the production of fat. And here's where HCA comes into play.

In order for citrate to be broken down the enzyme "ATP citrate lyase" must be present. HCA blocks the activity of this enzyme and alters the body's fat and glucose metabolism in the following ways. First, the pathway for glycogen production becomes easier than continuing with glucose metabolism into fat. Second, with fat production slowed down the body begins to burn more stored fat as an energy source. Finally, pyruvate – the substance that enters the mitochondria to be converted into citrate – ends up either completely burned in the citric-acid cycle or is recycled to form lactate and phosphoenolpyruvate. These two substances can also be used for fuel during the production of glucose and ultimately glycogen. The increased glycogen supplies are then stored in the liver and muscles, and while liver storage is not noticeable, muscles full of glycogen appear larger and fuller.

Claude Groulx

Besides the direct effect on fat burning, HCA has the added benefit of indirectly suppressing appetite. After all, the body "thinks" it has plenty of fuel available so the brain decreases the sensation of hunger.

USE IN BODYBUILDING

HCA has great potential for bodybuilders who are trying to lose bodyfat without sacrificing hard-earned muscle tissue. Many athletes try to lose weight by cycling between low-carbohydrate and high-carbohydrate or low-calorie and high-calorie diets. Instead of losing just bodyfat they shed pounds of valuable muscle tissue. Supplementing with HCA prevents muscle lose and at the same time increases the rate of fat loss. Also, the increased glycogen storage will keep training intensity high and add to muscle fullness on contest day.

Although the evidence is inconclusive, anecdotal reports suggest that taking HCA with other "fat burning" products (ephedrine/caffeine mixtures and L-carnitine being the most popular) increases the effectiveness of the two. The sum total of the two taken together outweighs the effects of the two taken separately. Whether scientific evidence will confirm this is still unknown.

HOW TO TAKE HCA

As of this writing, HCA is the only substance available by over-the-counter sale that inhibits fat production by the body. Other products may increase the rate stored fat is burned (ephedrine), but none prevent fat synthesis. We should add that because of the relative newness of HCA, the effectiveness of the product for bodybuilders is still unclear.

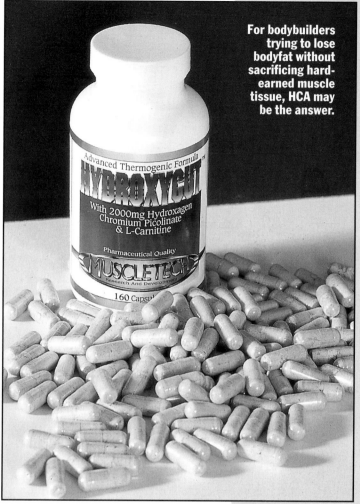

For bodybuilders trying to lose bodyfat without sacrificing hard-earned muscle tissue, HCA may be the answer.

Most HCA products are available as calcium salts and three of the most popular brands are CitriMax, Neway's Citrate, and MuscleTech's Hydroxycut, delivering 1000 milligrams per serving.

It is recommended that HCA be taken 30 to 60 minutes before meals, but individuals who are sensitive to other supplement preparations may want to avoid taking it on an empty stomach. The recommended dosage is 1000 milligrams, two or three times a day. This can be expensive, however, as most citrate products only contain 250-milligram tablets (although Newway's product contains 800-milligram tablets). With prices averaging $35 to $50 for 120 tablets, you could easily spend over a $100 a month on citrate supplementation.

SIDE EFFECTS

Few side effects have been reported by healthy subjects taking HCA. We must add, however, that given the product's short time on the market, it is remotely possible that side effects will surface years down the road. We say "remotely" because few individuals suffer side effects from natural food supplements.

In terms of specific side effects, some individuals may experience nausea when taking the product on an empty stomach. If you fall into this category, try taking with meals. A few weeks is recommended as a sort of breaking-in period. Like most supplements it generally takes a few weeks for the body to become accustomed to a new substance. Our advice is to play things by instinct.

Finally, the risk of side effects is often related to dosage. "Overdosing" on HCA is virtually impossible, though some individuals may be extremely sensitive to HCA's effects. Don't take the "more is better" approach and start ingesting hundreds of pills. The evidence seems to suggest that 2 or 3 tablets a day is just as effective as 15 to 20. It's also a lot cheaper.

Jay Cutler

INOSINE

Inosine hit the supplement shelves back in the mid 1980s. Like bee pollen and arginine before it, inosine was touted as the "next generation" of super supplements. While the advertising blitz paid off and millions of dollars was reaped, by all accounts inosine has become another supplement body-builders may want to add to their ergogenic kits.

Inosine is in the family of nucleotide molecules known as purines. Together with pyrimidines, purines make up the nitrogenous bases, which are the building blocks of DNA. Historically, it was one of the first organic substances to be isolated by the chemist Liebig back in the late 1840s. Despite being discovered almost 150 years ago, inosine was thought to be just another waste product of metabolism. The change came in the 1970s when Japanese researchers began looking at inosine and its role in fat metabolism.

MECHANISM OF ACTION

In their studies with vitamin-deficient rats, researchers discovered that inosine stimulated certain enzyme activities in the liver. Further studies suggest that inosine maintains ATP levels in bone marrow and also enhances cardiovascular functioning. Among its effects on the cardiovascular system are increased blood flow to the heart and promotion of strong heart contractions. And unlike some substances, which are only needed in adequate supply to produce these effects, supplementary inosine is shown to increase heart muscular contraction. Although the mechanism of action is not fully understood, it is believed that inosine can easily travel through cell walls triggering the release of factors essential for the release of oxygen from red blood cells. Such findings are of great benefit to physicians. Inosine has been used medically in the treatment of heart and kidney disease.

Besides its effects on the heart, inosine assists in carbohydrate metabolism. Under unique conditions (low ATP and oxygen levels) inosine can maintain normal metabolic reactions. Among these are the activation of enzymes, which contribute to the metabolism of carbohydrates.

USE IN BODYBUILDING

Given its effects on the cardiovascular system and its role in carbohydrate metabolism, it's not surprising that bodybuilders and other athletes would give inosine a try. Like many ergogenic substances, inosine was first used by Soviet athletes about ten years before their Western counterparts.

Most bodybuilders who use inosine report feeling a "kick" or energy boost about 30 minutes after taking. Whether this is a placebo effect or actual biochemistry, no one knows for sure. For the most part, those that use inosine swear by its effectiveness. Inosine's effects on the cardio-vascular system, especially as it relates to oxygen supply, could account for the positive effects reported by athletes. Inosine has been found to increase the oxygen-binding capacity of red blood cells. This means more oxygen is extracted at the lungs and available for cel-lular respiration. More oxygen means better muscle contrac-tions which means more pro-ductive workouts – one of the fundamentals to making the greatest gains possible.

Debbie Kruck

HOW IT'S TAKEN

When used for medical treat-ment, inosine is usually given in the form of an intramuscular injection. Although it varies, standard treatment is 250 milli-grams, one or two times a day. Anecdotal reports suggest that bodybuilders and other athletes will need more than this, the lower limit being about 8 to 10 milligrams per kilogram of body-weight. For a 100-kilogram bodybuilder (220 pounds) this works out to 800 to 1000 milli-grams per day. Soviet research indicates that even higher dosages are required and a typical Soviet athlete will take 2 to 4 grams (2000 to 4000 milli-grams) per day.

It was only a matter of time before inosine was made available to be taken orally. Most of the popular manufacturers market inosine in 500- to 600-milligram capsules. This is a very convenient size as you only need to take 1 or 2 capsules (or 6 to 8 if you follow the Soviet recommendations) daily to receive the recommended dosage. With regards to price, a 50- to 60-capsule bottle of inosine will cost somewhere in the $15 to $20 range. Therefore, an investment of $20 can get you about a month's supply of inosine. This is very reasonable for supplements. If you decide to use more than the recommended amount (as many bodybuilders do), it will cost more. Also, only use the pure nucleoside form of inosine. Other forms such as inosine-5-monophosphate have been found to be less active in medical studies. Finally, given the popularity of inosine, other versions of the product have turned up on the market – many of which are virtually useless.

WHEN TO TAKE

As with most supplements there are varying opinions on when to take inosine. Bodybuilders will probably obtain the most benefit by taking it about 30 minutes before a workout. Although it varies, inosine generally lasts anywhere from 2 to 4 hours. This is surprising as most research indicates that inosine is almost totally metabolized and degraded when it hits the bloodstream.

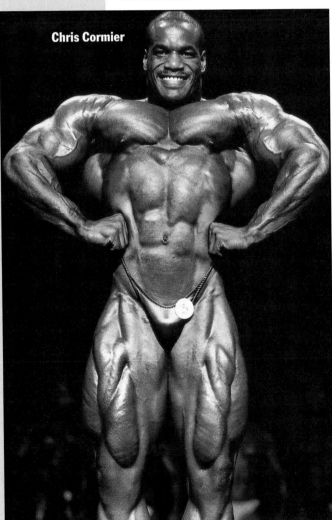

Chris Cormier

SIDE EFFECTS

In the ten years or so of inosine use by athletes, very few reports of side effects have surfaced. And this includes individuals who are using ten times the recommended dosage of the supplement. There is one group of people who should not use inosine and these are gout sufferers. Gout is a form of arthritis which develops when two much uric acid is produced, or when the kidneys do not remove enough of it. As uric acid is one of the metabolic products of purines – and as we said earlier, inosine is one such example – it only follows that taking supplementary inosine will only aggravate the condition. The ailment is the result of uric acid combining with sodium to form sharp needle-like crystals of sodium urate salt which settle in the body's soft tissues and cause intense pain and inflammation. Although it varies, the most common sites of gout are the big toe and the cartilage making up the rim of the ear.

Another side effect of high uric-acid levels are kidney stones. There is good evidence to

Edgar Fletcher

suggest those with kidney disease are at greater risk for developing kidney stones if uric acid levels are abnormally high. For this reason we strongly suggest those with any type of renal disease refrain from using inosine.

CHOLINE

Choline has long been familiar to bodybuilders as part of the choline/inositol fat-burning team. Like inosine, dibencozide, and carnitine, choline is supposedly a natural alternative to anabolic steroids and fat-burning drugs. While the scientific research is inconclusive, many bodybuilders swear by it as an effective, precontest fat-burning agent.

MECHANISM OF ACTION

Choline is a member of a class of biocompounds called phosphoglycerides, as well as a member of the B-complex group of vitamins. Among its functions include building cell membranes, mobilizing fat, decreasing cholesterol levels by increased utilization, and helping the liver metabolize fats and manufacture other fats called phospholipids. Choline also helps preserve the health of the liver and kidneys by combining with fatty acids and phosphoric acid to form lecithin – one of the body's primary fat-thinning agents.

Another role of choline is to boost the integrity of myelin sheaths – insulation which covers the body's nerves. Without such coverings, nerve impulses would short-circuit, leading to a host of physiological problems (one of the best examples being multiple sclerosis). Choline together with vitamin B5 produces the brain neurotransmitter acetylcholine – one of the body's primary neurotransmitters responsible for muscle contraction and such cognitive functions as alertness and memory. This last point has been latched on to in recent years and used to promote choline as a "brain food." According to Dr. Richard Passwater in his book *The New Supernutrition*, college students taking choline had significantly higher abilities to recall word sequences. Others have experienced similar results including *MuscleMag* columnist Greg Merritt, who found taking choline with vitamin

Milos Sarcev,
Chris Cormier and
Mike Matarazzo

B5 increased energy levels and made him feel more alert. Whether choline actually enhances memory or whether the increased alertness allows for better memorization is unclear at this point.

HOW TO TAKE

Limited amounts of choline are made by the body, but recent research suggests that many individuals don't manufacture enough. This means supplementing choline in the diet may be necessary (though determining a state of deficiency is another matter). Given it's positive effects on the liver and kidneys – two organs often damaged by heavy steroid use – bodybuilders using steroids may want to take supplementary choline. We should add that most bodybuilders who have used choline supplements have had only moderate success, and the "great claims" made by advertisers are rarely seen.

The general consensus regarding choline dosage is about 3 grams per day taken with 1 gram of vitamin B5 (this helps convert choline to acetylcholine). As vitamins go this is a large dosage but there have been no reported side effects among healthy individuals. There have been cases of manic-depressives having their depressive episodes intensified by choline, but it remains unclear whether the condition is caused by increased choline or other conditions.

INOSITOL

Inositol was one of the first fat-burning compounds discovered. Like choline, inositol deficiency leads to an accumulation of fat in the liver. Besides helping the liver metabolize fat, inositol acts as a messenger, transmitting various hormone signals within cells. When hormones bind to cell walls, inositol is involved in the messenger relay which tells the cell what to do. Without inositol, the hormone's message never gets delivered.

CARNITINE

Carnitine was first discovered back in the early 1900s by Russian scientists. Given 90 years of research you would think the substance would be classified by now, but such is not the case. Many biochemists consider carnitine a stable member of the B-complex family of vitamins. Others, however, classify it as an "accessory nutrient." A few even suggest it's an amino acid – although this view is fast falling out of favour.

Whatever the classification, carnitine is a water-soluble substance, synthesized by the liver, which requires the presence of other nutrients such as vitamin C, B6, B3, and iron to work most efficiently. Although how it works is a puzzle to most, carnitine is one of the most popular supplemental fat burners.

Mark Stone

MECHANISM OF ACTION

Carnitine's primary mechanism of action is to stimulate the transport of long-chain fatty acids across the inner membranes of mitochondria. It does this by the activation of an enzyme called carnitine acyltransferase (CAT1) which transfers one group of the fat molecule (called the fatty acyl group) to the hydroxyl group of the carnitine molecule. The resulting product, called an O-acyl carnitine ester, is then able to pass across the inner mitochondrial membrane. It is again cleaved by another carnitine acyltransferase enzyme (CAT2) once inside the complex. The end result is ATP, which can be burned as an immediate fuel source.

Besides its fat-burning properties, carnitine's greatest asset for athletes is its ability to speed up the intake of oxygen into the body's cells. The result is greater availability of oxygen for the cells in times of strenuous physical activity. Several studies have shown that carnitine supplementation increases oxygen consumption and fat utilization during exercise. Carnitine seems to increase the utilization of fats as fuel for exercise when exercise is intense – in the range of 60 percent maximum or greater.

Some of the best evidence to show the importance of carnitine involves studies focusing on genetic disorders in people who cannot manufacture carnitine. These individuals cannot use fat as a fuel source, have weak muscles and have a very low tolerance to exercise.

SOURCES

Carnitine is found naturally in animal meats (with beef and lamb being the best). It can also be synthesized by the body from the amino acids lysine and methionine. Like many biomolecules, carnitine exists in two basic forms, "L" and "D" (left- and right-hand isomers which rotate clockwise or counterclockwise). And like other molecules, the body has evolved to only use the L form. Not only is the D form not utilized, but it may be counter-productive to the effectiveness of the L version. (Think of them as positive and negative, with the ability to cancel one another out.) We mention this last point because at one time many supplement manufacturers combined the two together in one supplement. To the uninformed it sounds like a bargain – two for the price of one – but given the previous biochemistry, it's clearly not.

Carnitine supplements vary in price, but on average 60 to 100 tablets (average size – 250 milligrams) will set you back $15 to $25. As supplements go, this can be considered moderate. We should add that most carnitine supplements are about 67 percent carnitine and the rest is the tartate part of the compound. So don't be fooled into thinking the entire tablet is carnitine. With regards to dosage, try taking 500 milligrams twice daily. You might want to start with half this amount to see if there are any unwanted side effects. If not, double the dosage.

Given carnitine's legitimate background, backed by credible bio-chemical research (unlike some of the other well-hyped but totally worthless fat burners), we have no qualms about recommending carnitine as a dietary supplement. However, if you follow a lousy diet, you can take all the carnitine you want and still not lose any fat. The first step in fat loss is not to spend your hard-earned cash on dietary supplements but to reduce dietary fat intake. It's that simple.

DEXFENFLURAMINE (PONDERAL)

This fat-burning agent is a modified form of the drug fenfluramine – one of the best nonamphetamines available for weight-loss treatment. This amphet-amine derivative is unique in that it is not nearly as addictive as other amphetamines[5] and is devoid of a CNS effect.[1] Although used in Europe for

Frank Sepe

numerous years (under the brand name Redux), the drug was turned down by the FDA for use in the United States. It was also banned in Canada for a number of reasons, one of which concerned its connection to more than 24 cases of rare heart defects in American women.

MECHANISM OF ACTION

At the simplest level it's an appetite suppressant. That is, it kills your craving for food. It does this by reducing levels of the neurotransmitter serotonin – responsible for many basic drives including hunger.[1] By eat-ing less, you force the body to draw on fat reserves for energy, with the end result being weight loss. One of the nice things about dexfen-fluramine is that it's specific for carbohydrates and fat, not protein. So while you may have no inclination to eat fat or carbs, your desire for low-fat protein sources remains. For a bodybuilder on a precontest diet, such specificity is ideal.

Lee Priest

Besides suppressing appetite and hence not storing more fat, dexfenfluramine also has thermogenic properties – that is, it forces the body to convert excess fat into heat energy rather than store it as additional fat. In this regard the drug is similar to ephedrine and other beta agonists.

Closely related to the previous is dexfenfluramine's effects on blood lipids. A recent study found the drug lowers circu-lating cholesterol and fat levels.[2] A follow-up study found the mechanism of action was based on inhibiting such catecholamines as adrenalin and noradrenaline (epinephrine and norepinephrine). Blocking such fat mobi-lizers in turn reduces circulating levels of fat. Opposers to the drug argue that such effects reduce the amount of fat available for burn-ing during exercise. The end result, however, appears to be a stimulation of fat loss (some bodybuilders add that they don't care how it works as long as it does).

A final mechanism of action is dexfenfluramine's ability to reduce insulin resistance. Numerous studies have indicated dexfenfluramine supplementation can bring this about in as little as one week.[3] In animal studies fenfluramine has improved insulin sensitivity without weight loss. The end result is better metabolization of high-carb foods.

SIDE EFFECTS

Despite the FDA's paranoia, long-term European studies have been con-ducted without any serious health consequences (over ten years of use). The most frequently reported side effects are dry mouth, increased urination, occasional diarrhea, and slight drowsiness is some individuals. About 10 percent of users experience diarrhea and stomach cramps during the first week of use.[4] Tolerance also builds up rapidly, so it is only effective for a few weeks.[5]

Dexfenfluramine may potentiate the effects of antihypertensive and hypoglycemic drugs. Seek medical attention if you experience any decrease in exercise tolerance while on this drug. There have been cases of pul-monary hypertension from fenfluramine use. Bodybuilders who suffer from depression are also strongly advised to avoid this drug, since fenfluramine use or withdrawal can trigger episodes of depression.[5] As a final note we must point out that most of the side effects associated with fenfluramine concern the DL-fenfluramine derivatives – specifically the "L" section of the molecule, though most of the fat loss is attributed to the "D" section.

Sue Myers

BETA-3-ADRENERGIC AGONISTS – THE FUTURE FOR FAT LOSS?

In recent years there has been sort of a breakthrough in the war against obesity. Researchers have uncovered a type of receptor that promotes the oxidation of adipose deposits when stimulated by certain drugs. Applications are still in the preliminary stages, but these drugs – called Beta-3 agonists – may become as familiar as steroids and amino acids to the next generation of superstar bodybuilders.

WHAT THEY ARE

In mammals there are two types of adipose tissue, white (WAT) and brown (BAT) adipose tissue. WAT plays a major role in the storing of triglycerides as energy; BAT on the other hand is the major site of energy dissipation in the form of heat – thermogenesis. BAT is important, especially in rodents and newborns for the maintenance of body temperature during exposure to cold environments. For example, when rats are kept at four degrees Celsius, BAT thermogenesis is increased as a result of increased oxidation of fatty acids derived from triglyceride in this tissue and also from blood lipoprotein. There is also good evidence to suggest that glucose utilization and blood flow in BAT are enhanced.[6]

It has now been established that most of the previous changes are controlled through modulation of a series of receptors called Beta (ß) – adrenoreceptors. There are at least three types of ß receptors, and for convenience scientists have labeled them ß1, ß2, and ß3.

The first two (ß1 and ß2) were discussed earlier under the topic of clenbuterol use. Both ß1 and ß2 receptors are well known in pharmacology circles, being present in the heart, lung, and blood vessels. The presence of the third went unknown until 1984, when studies on BAT suggested that an atypical adrenoreceptor was present in brown adipose tissue. Since then numerous studies have indicated that long-term stimulation of such receptors may form the basis for future strategies in combating obesity.

THE RESEARCH

Once scientists had determined the presence of ß3 adrenoreceptors, the next step was to examine their role in fat metabolism. One of the most important studies was conducted by Japanese researchers in 1992.

The experiments consisted of giving rats various ß agonists, including those specific for ß3 adrenoreceptors, and then varying the temperature from four to 24 degrees Celsius. The drugs were administered for seven to 10 days by a pump implanted in the lumbar region.

Michael Poulsen

Data collected from the experiments indicated that chronic treatment with the ß3 agonist arotinolol increased BAT-tissue content of DNA and total protein – both of which strongly suggest that arotinolol increases the capacity of BAT thermogenesis and energy expenditure.[6] Of particular interest is that arotinolol is frequently used to treat hypertension, and since hypertension is often associated with obesity, chronic treatment with the drug could serve two purposes, reducing blood pressure and speeding up BAT thermogenesis.

APPLICATIONS TO BODYBUILDING

Although there are only scattered reports of arotinolol use by bodybuilders, present trends suggest that ß agonists are becoming more popular as time goes on. Five years ago the ß2 agonist, clenbuterol, was only known to asthmatics. Then came the 1992 Olympics and the positive testing of two US athletes for clenbuterol. Now bodybuilding gyms are rampant with clenbuterol use. Given the potential of ß3 agonists for increasing fat loss, how long will it take before the drug becomes part of bodybuilding pharmacology kits?

Besides the BAT-thermogenic properties of arotinolol, the drug has the previously mentioned ability to treat hypertension – the main medical application of the drug. Given that most top bodybuilders use steroids, and that one of the side effects of steroids is high blood pressure, use of arotinolol could serve numerous functions in the weeks leading up to a contest. With its thermogenic and anti-hypertensive properties, it's surprising that bodybuilders didn't discover the drug sooner.

THIOMUCASE

Unlike most fat burners, Thiomucase is not a drug to be injected or ingested, but applied as a cream (there are injectable and oral versions available but we are limiting our discussion to the form advertised in bodybuilding magazines).

Bodybuilders use Thiomucase to help speed the removal of fat from such stubborn areas as the lower back and obliques. This means the drug is generally used in the weeks leading up to a contest. Unlike exercising and dieting, which are nonselective in removing fat from the body (they take fat deposits from the whole body), Thiomucase is a "spot reducer." In short, apply it to the area you want to reduce and supposedly the product's active ingredient will shrink the fat deposit. The drug is not burning the fat away, but merely releasing some of the fat cells' fluid. This shrinks the fat cells, giving the area a tighter, leaner appearance.

Most bodybuilders who use Thiomucase report it does give the physique a more vascular look. Although some bodybuilders mix the drug with DMSO for added effect, we caution against this as DMSO will not only spread Thiomucase over the applied area, but also carry it throughout the bloodstream and to all parts of the body. For those wishing to try the drug, it can only be obtained through mail order, as the FDA has never approved the drug for use in the United States. It is freely available in Europe, however, with France being the biggest supplier. If you try to smuggle the drug into the United States and happen to get caught, you will face drug-smuggling charges. And given the harshness of such penalties, you could face a lengthy prison sentence. It doesn't seem worth it when exercise, diet, and other legal supplements can also do the job.

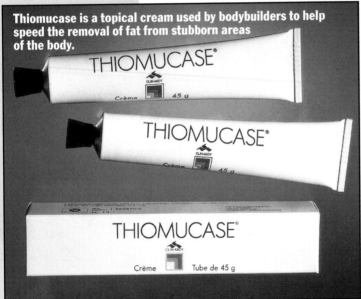

Thiomucase is a topical cream used by bodybuilders to help speed the removal of fat from stubborn areas of the body.

OTHER TECHNIQUES FOR WEIGHT LOSS

SURGERY

Gastric surgery or stomach stapling is an extreme method of controlling one's weight. While the technique is not really applicable to bodybuilders, we thought it interesting to show just how far some people will go to lose weight.

Stomach stapling involves decreasing the available stomach volume by stapling part of the stomach, preventing the person from overeating. Gastrectomy involves the partial or complete removal of the stomach. The basis to the theory is that a smaller stomach means less food and hence decreased calories. Unfortunately, the human body is very adaptable and there is good evidence to suggest it will compensate for lost stomach volume by increasing stomach digestion and absorption. The end result is a faster working stomach and hence more frequent feelings of hunger.

Another problem of stomach stapling is interference with nutrient absorption – particularly mineral and vitamin-B12 absorption. Many patients who have had the surgery require B12 injections, as well as other vitamin and mineral supplements added to the diet.

A final drawback, and this applies especially to bodybuilders, is the cosmetic disfiguration produced by the surgery. Any surgical incision made in the abdominal cavity will leave a permanent scar. And no matter how dark the skin, the scar will be noticeable. Judges don't deduct points for such scars (think of all the bodybuilders who have had appendectomies), but nevertheless, an ugly scar in the abdominal region does distract from an otherwise great physique.

PREFIL (HYDROPHILIC GRANULES)

A simpler technique for weight loss is the use of a dietary aid called Prefil. As the name suggests, you "trick" the stomach into thinking it's full. Much of the sensation of appetite is controlled by hormones, released in response to an absence or presence of food in the stomach. By using granules

Ericca Kern

made up of vegetable fiber, the sensation of fullness can be created without the consumption of large amounts of food. The product works when the granules are taken with copious amounts of water. Once in the stomach, the granules swell, causing a sensation of fullness which decreases appetite.[1]

References
1) A. Sullivan and others, *Nutrition and Drugs* (New York: John Wiley and Sons, 1983), Chapter 10.
2) "Drug World," *Flex* 14:2 (April 1996).
3) T.C Luoma, "The Fatburners," *MuscleMedia 2000*, (February 1996).
4) R. Sutherland, "More Than a Fat Chance," *Chatelaine*, 69:2 (February 1996).
5) Canadian CPS, *Compendium of Pharmaceuticals and Specialities*, 30 ed. (Toronto: Canadian Pharmaceutical Association, C.K. Productions, 1995).
6) I. Nagase, "Hyperplasia of Brown Adipose Tissue After Chronic Stimulation of ß-3 Receptors in Rats," *Japanese Journal of Vet Research*, 42:3-4 (December 1994).

BOOK THREE

Stimulants and Painkillers

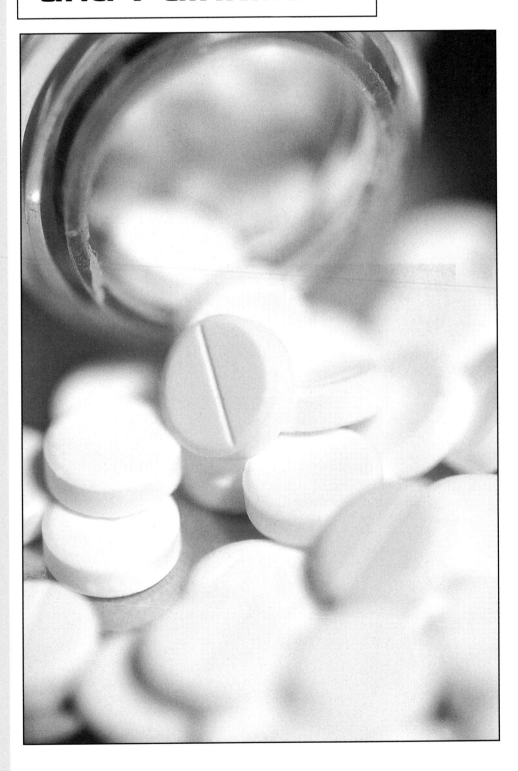

Monica Brant and
Jay Cutler

CHAPTER TWELVE

Stimulants

For many bodybuilders on a stringent precontest diet, just getting to the gym and completing a workout is a chore. It's fine if they have a willing training partner to give them a kick in the ass, but for many the logical solution is to turn to some sort of stimulant for that extra energy. The most commonly used stimulant is caffeine, taken in the form of coffee, tea, or soft drinks. Unfortunately, tolerance, desire or a combination of both leads many to use much stronger stimulants – usually amphetamines and cocaine. While caffeine is perfectly legal and has relatively minor side effects, amphetamine and cocaine can get you hard jail time or worse – put you in the ground. We will look at some of the most frequently used stimulants and their applications to bodybuilders. Where appropriate, legal implications will be discussed. If a given drug is illegal in your country, please refrain from using it.

NOTE: Before you read on, please pay close attention to the nine commandments of stimulant use; they could save your life.

Hard drugs are profoundly addictive and can ruin your life in short order.

THE NINE COMMANDMENTS OF STIMULANT USE

1) Discuss it with your doctor first
Because of individual responses and situations, a particular stimulant may agree with one person and not another. You can discuss potential side effects, and know what to do if there are adverse reactions. Medical monitoring is a sound way of protecting your health.

2) Find out if it is legal
As mentioned before, just because a drug is mentioned in this book, does not infer that it is legal in your country. Check your country's laws to find out the drug's status. Obey the law.

3) Only buy from your pharmacist over the counter
Remember, black-market suppliers are often liars. Legally sold drugs have to meet legal standards. The only sure way of knowing what you're getting is by buying from a regulated source.

4) Limit your frequency of use
The easiest way to become addicted is through frequent use of a drug. While stimulants can turn your workouts into euphoric bursts of power, their impact will decrease with frequent use. Never take a stimulant for longer than two days in a row.

5) Stick to low dosages
Bodybuilders have a well-deserved reputation for going overboard in their zeal to become the most massive living monuments in the history of humanity! The attitude of: "If one is good, two are better," reigns supreme. The lower the dosage, the easier it is for the body to adjust to its presence. For example, coffee and tea are naturally diluted drugs, and therefore easier for the body to tolerate than Benzedrine.

6) Take stimulants orally
Smoking, injecting, or snorting cause a rapid entry into the bloodstream. This in turns causes a greater rush, followed by a greater let down. This leads to more frequent use to ease the "crash." This can cause addiction. Such a vicious cycle can be harmful to the body if done regularly.

7) Use for a reason
A stimulant can help a bodybuilder get through a sticking point, work through a plateau, or prepare for a contest. It should not be used to help you wake up in the morning, or perform any other normal daily activity. If you begin to become dependant on stimulants to help get you through the most minuscule of tasks – you have other problems and need help.

Claude Groulx

"Any drug can be used successfully, no matter how bad its reputation, and any drug can be abused, no matter how accepted it is. There are no good or bad drugs; there are only good and bad relationships with drugs."

– A quote from the text *Chocolate to Morphine*, by Andrew Weil, MD and Winifred Rosen.[1]

Many people wouldn't dream of tackling their day without at least one cup of coffee.

8) Stimulants and depressants do not mix

Comedian John Belushi did this, and died. One drug counters the other. If you can't sleep because of the stimulants you're taking, reduce your dose or stop altogether. Don't start taking drugs to deal with another drug's side effects (one of the best examples of this being Elvis Presley). Pretty soon you're just taking drugs because you're taking other drugs and body-building is no longer part of the picture.

9) Be a bodybuilder, not an addict

Eat, sleep, and work out regularly. Stimulants drain your body of energy. The only way to replace that lost energy is through rest and a healthy diet. By maintaining top physical condition, your body will be able to do more with a lower dosage of stimulant.

CAFFEINE

Although the tea lovers of Great Britain might argue, coffee is probably the most widely used beverage (not counting water) in the world. For many, the day doesn't start until that first cup of freshly brewed coffee is trickling down the esophagus. So attached have North Americans become to their coffee that the workplace coffee break is part of most union collective agreements.

HISTORY

Legend has it that an Arabian goat herder named Kaldi was tending his flock when he noticed how lively they had become. Kaldi observed the goats eating berries, which he also tried. Soon he was merrily jumping along with his goats. Unfortunately for Kaldi, he kept dancing all through the night. A holy man also tried the berries, with the same effect. Legend has it that the Islamic prophet, Mohammed, gave instructions on how to brew a drink from the dried berries so that the faithful could stay awake to continue their prayers. Records indicate, however, that coffee was already being brewed and consumed in Arabia before Mohammed.

Coffee was so popular among Moslems that the authorities in the holy city of Mecca became concerned. The citizens were spending more time in the coffee houses than at work. Prohibition was brought in against coffee. Because almost everyone was addicted, illicit coffee houses multiplied, and the authorities gave up and let everyone drink coffee again.

Coffee reached Europe with returning crusaders. While the Catholic Church was originally opposed to the "heathen drink," the Pope had to try it. He loved it, and baptized it on the spot as a Christian drink, ". . . too good to leave to the pagans."

By the 17th century, coffee houses were popular meeting places for writers, scientists, philosophers, business people and politicians. King Charles II (his father, Charles I, had been beheaded by order of Parliament), understandably nervous given his background, closed the coffee houses after he was told that seditious talk was the rage. Eleven days later the English prohibition was repealed because of the threat of imminent rioting by caffeine-deprived mobs.

But it wasn't only the King who was against coffee. The wives of the coffee drinkers claimed that coffee use was destroying the very fabric of family life. Here is part of their blunt assessment from the Women's Petition Against Coffee (1674):

"Certainly our Countrymens pallets are become as Fanatical as their Brains; how else is it possible they should Apostatize from the good old primitive way of Ale-drinking to run a Whoring after such variety of destructive Foreign Liquors, to trifle away their time, scald their Chops, and spend their Money, all for a little base, black, thick, nasty bitter stinking, nauseous Puddle water: Yet (as all Witches have their Charms) so this ugly Turkish Enchantress by certain Invisible Wyres attracts both Rich and Poor . . ."

Today, most coffee is made from the beans of plants found mostly in South America. Coffee production is worth billions of dollars annually. Products such as Folgers, Maxwell House, and Nescafé have become household names. The main ingredient in coffee is caffeine, and although tea and soft drinks contain nearly as much, coffee is the number one "delivery method" for this much-craved drug.

> "Some of the most recent studies suggest that a couple of cups of coffee (or other caffeine-containing drinks) do not pose any real health risk for an average person. Caffeine remains a substance whose effects have not been conclusively determined, and yes, caffeine is supposedly able to stimulate not just one's energy level (temporarily) but also one's fat-burning functions."
>
> – Marjo Selin, former *MuscleMag* columnist commenting on recent evidence regarding caffeine and side effects.

Tolerance to caffeine develops quickly, making it unsuitable for long-term weight control.

SIMPLY STIMULATING

The effects of caffeine vary from one person to another. For some, 150 milligrams of caffeine (equal to one average cup of instant coffee) makes them nervous, jittery, and even produces insomnia. Other are so sensitive that one soft drink (about 45 milligrams of caffeine) leaves them anxious, nervous, and high-strung.[2]

At the other end of the spectrum we have the heavy coffee drinkers who need 150 to 300 milligrams of caffeine just to wake up. Full alertness usually doesn't arrive until the third or fourth cup. In these individuals such traits are explained by drug tolerance or low-caffeine sensitivity.

HOW IT WORKS

Although some individuals report being sedated and relaxed by caffeine, the primary pharmacological effect of the drug is to stimulate the central nervous system. In doing so caffeine produces a host of physiological effects. It speeds up heart rate, increases stomach acid, and works as a diuretic. Caffeine also dilates some blood vessels – making it suitable for many asthma sufferers. Over the last twenty years caffeine has become popular as a diet aid because it speeds up the rate at which the resting body burns energy. Unfortunately, what most manufacturers fail to mention is that tolerance to caffeine develops quickly, making it unsuitable for long-term weight control.

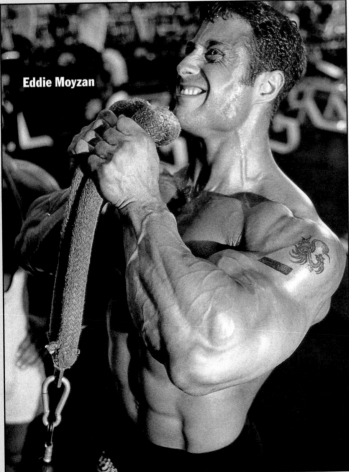

Eddie Moyzan

USE IN ATHLETICS

Of the previous effects, the two which athletes have focused on are the stimulant and fat-burning properties of caffeine. Endurance athletes have used coffee, tea, and cola beverages for years, for that extra burst of energy. And while the research is questionable as to caffeine's benefits in this regard, many athletes are lost without their caffeine "fix."

Bodybuilders have traditionally used caffeine for the same reasons – to get them through energy-draining workouts. The drug plays a very important role in the weeks leading up to a contest where strict dieting and increased exercising places enormous demands on the body's energy-supply systems.

Another role caffeine seems to fill is acting as a natural diuretic. Most coffee drinkers will admit that urine output is increased when additional coffee is consumed. Like many naturally occurring diuretics, caffeine interferes with the body's water-conservation systems. For an endurance athlete this is potentially

Darrem Charles

dangerous and can lead to dehydration, but for a competitive bodybuilder, caffeine is often the drug of choice to help shed those extra few pounds of water and bring out those contest-winning striations.

In recent years caffeine has taken on a new role – making up one third of the very popular caffeine/ephedrine/Aspirin combination. For years researchers have known that caffeine helps speed up the oxidation rate of fat. Although the mechanism of action is not fully understood, it is believed that caffeine stimulates the release of fats into the bloodstream, making them available for oxidation. Whether this is true or not, many athletes – especially those trying to make a weight class – rely on caffeine to get rid of those few extra pounds.

When ephedrine use became popular, many bodybuilders noticed that if combined with caffeine and Aspirin, the tri-concoction had dramatic fat-burning properties. While researchers have trouble duplicating the results in the lab, the accepted belief in the gym is that caffeine combined with Aspirin and ephedrine is one of bodybuilding's best dieting procedures. The normal dosages for the three substances are 25 milligrams of ephedrine, 250 milligrams of caffeine, and 1 or 2 Aspirin tablets.

A lesser-known effect of caffeine is to increase strength levels. Numerous studies involving bodybuilders and powerlifters have shown that caffeine boosts an athlete's strength levels during training. And while the exact mechanism of action is not fully understood (that is, whether caffeine's stimulant effects account for the strength increases or whether caffeine has a direct effect on strength), athletes the world over have taken advantage of this property.

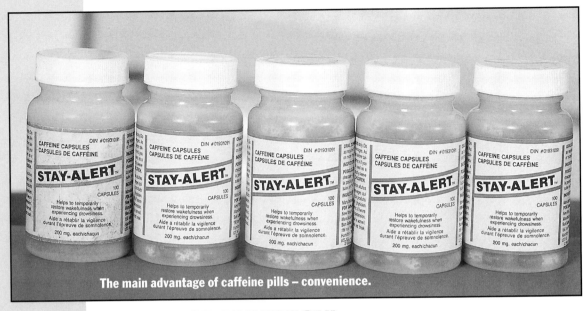

The main advantage of caffeine pills – convenience.

BEWARE OF ADDICTION!

Like all stimulants, chronic use of caffeine lessens the effect and increases the chance of developing an addiction. That one- or two-cup habit can quickly turn into an eight- to 10-cup daily addiction. Many caffeine "addicts" start out with good intentions, only to fall victim to the "more is good" philosophy. Bodybuilders are at special risk as they tend to overuse many supplements to begin with.

Besides tolerance and addiction, the issue of "increasing mental capacity" must be addressed. It's very common for many university students to resort to caffeine during exams. This allows them to stay awake longer and "cram," in some cases for up to three days. Unfortunately, while the extra time allows for increased study, the evidence suggests that retention is not increased. Therefore, in many cases, the students are no further ahead than if they received a good night's sleep before the exam. In many cases it's far worse as the dreaded "crash" arrives right in the middle of an exam.

Many individuals developed caffeine addictions in college or university. Our advice is to constantly be on guard for the misuse of caffeine. If you need eight to 10 cups of coffee just to make it through the day, we strongly suggest you restructure your daily routine.

OTHER CAFFEINE DELIVERY SYSTEMS

PILLS

Although coffee is the most popular method of consuming caffeine among the general public, it does have one big disadvantage – convenience. Unless the coffee is already brewed, taking caffeine in liquid form can be awkward. As most bodybuilders are used to consuming supplements in tablet form, it shouldn't surprise you that caffeine in tablet form is very popular among bodybuilders. Further, such brands as No-Doz and Vivarin are also very popular among long-distance truck drivers and shift workers.

If caffeine pills have a disadvantage it's their concentration – you get the equivalent of one large cup of coffee per tablet. Drinking three or four cups of coffee at one sitting may be difficult, but swallowing four or five tablets is relatively easy. Many individuals find such large doses of caffeine very irritating on the stomach, particularly the stomach lining. The feeling is very similar to the burning sensation felt by many Aspirin users. To address this manufacturers have produced caffeine tablets which have been specially designed not to irritate the stomach.

SOFT DRINKS

These are very powerful because they are loaded with added caffeine and sugar. Bodybuilders will drink a great amount of cola to quench their thirst, never realizing that they are really aggravating it because of caffeine's diuretic effect. A particularly popular soft drink among bodybuilders is called "Jolt." Marketed in response to all the diet, caffeine-free drinks being sold, Jolt's slogan is, "All the sugar, and twice the caffeine!"

TEA

Tea is believed to have first originated in China. Legend has it that a Buddhist holy man, Daruma, fell asleep while meditating. Vowing to never allow this to happen again, he cut off both his eyelids. When they touched the ground, plants arose, and their leaves could be brewed to make a drink that would fend off sleep. Tea reached Europe courtesy of Dutch traders, and found a permanent home in British culture. In fact, much of the British Empire during the reign of Queen Victoria in the 1800s was based on Far-East tea trade. From Britain, tea spread to various colonies, including Canada. And although use has declined in recent years, many prefer a cup of tea over a cup of harsh coffee.

The caffeine from soft drinks will only increase your thirst, so pick up a bottle of water instead.

Contrary to popular belief, a cup of tea contains about the same amount of caffeine as a cup of coffee. For some reason, tea doesn't produce the same "kick" as coffee. For those who find coffee keeps them awake at night, switching to tea often makes a world of difference. Conversely, athletes and shift workers prefer coffee specifically for this last reason – it gives them that extra spurt of energy and alertness.

COLA NUTS

These seeds are from the cola tree. They contain caffeine and are chewed for their stimulating effect. The nuts have a bitter and aromatic taste. They have not achieved great popularity in North America because spitting in public is considered both a cultural and legal no-no.

GUARANA

It is made from the ground-up seeds of an Amazonian Jungle shrub. This powder is brewed the same as coffee. Guarana contains more caffeine than coffee, and is often available in health- food stores.

YERBA MATE

This popular Argentinean drink is made from the leaves of the holly plant, and brewed as a tea.[1] These leaves contain a huge amount of mateina, a relative of caffeine, which does not produce the undesirable side effects of caffeine. This herbal tea is rich in vitamins C, B1 and B2, and is used as both a stimulant and a treatment for stress. It can be taken as a drink or in capsule form before a workout or competition.[2]

CHOCOLATE

Yes, Hershey's slogan could have been, "Hershey is the great American stimulant!" Chocolate is made by combining fat and sugar to the roasted, ground-up beans of the cocoa plant. These beans are rich sources of caffeine. Chocolate is a notoriously addictive stimulant and should be completely avoided during contest preparation. (Scoff-down those Almond Hersheys during the postcontest pig-out. They're great!)

Chocolate contains ground-up beans from the cocoa plant – one of the richest sources of caffeine.

SIDE EFFECTS

Being a stimulant – albeit a mild one – caffeine should not be used by individuals with heart conditions. Also, given its diuretic properties, those with kidney problems should be wary of excessive caffeine use. With regards to the horrendous side effects attributed to caffeine (heart disease, breast cancer, birth defects), we emphasize that the evidence is sketchy at best. There is some evidence to suggest that caffeine elevates cholesterol levels, increasing an individual's risk for developing heart disease, but other studies have failed to confirm this. All that can be said is that individuals with a history of such problems in their family might want to limit their usage of caffeine-containing products.

For those engaged in marathon sports – especially in hot weather – the diuretic effects of caffeine can lead to severe dehydration. And as for using caffeine beverages to quench your thirst after exercise, most studies suggest such products lead to more urine production than if plain water was consumed.[3]

One group of individuals who should limit their caffeine consumption are pregnant women. Numerous studies have indicated that pregnant women who consume more than 300 milligrams of caffeine per day have a higher risk of spontaneous abortions.[4] Further, there is evidence to suggest that heavy caffeine usage can retard fetal growth – especially early in the

Bodybuilders beware – most of the major sports organizations have made caffeine a banned substance.

gestation period.[5] This means that pregnant women should limit their coffee (or tea or cola) consumption to one to two cups a day. It might be a good idea to avoid caffeine products all together.

Finally, given its acidic nature, sufferers of ulcers or other stomach ailments should be wary of using caffeine (a few studies actually suggest caffeine may cause these conditions). Many individuals with no existing problems experience a burning sensation when using caffeine products.

LEGAL CONCERNS

Apart from being banned by many sports federations, caffeine has few legal issues. In other words, the only limiting factor concerning its use is an individual's pocket book. Whether purchased in beverage form (coffee, tea, or cola), or taken in tablet form as a supplement (often sold under such names as "wake-ups" and "stay-awakes"), caffeine has no legal restrictions.

For competitive athletes, however, caffeine use is more restraining in nature. Most of the major sports organizations, including the International Olympic Committee (IOC), have made caffeine a banned substance. Although nailing down the precise limit allowed is difficult, individuals with more than 900 to 1000 milligrams of caffeine in their systems would test positive. Theoretically, this works out to about four or five cups of coffee consumed over two or three hours. But since everyone is different in terms of metabolism, an individual who consumes only one or two cups of coffee might test positive, whereas another taking five or six cups might escape detection. What's ironic about this is that small amounts of caffeine may produce major stimulant effects, while large doses often produce a "crash" effect, impeding performance.

Mike Matarazzo

FINAL THOUGHTS

Given the absence of legal restrictions, insignificant costs, and low risk of side effects, many readers might want to experiment with caffeine supplements. Like any substance, caffeine may produce a broad spectrum of effects in different individuals. If you have not used significant amounts of caffeine in the past, we suggest easing into usage and gradually building up the dosage. The goal is to use enough for the desired effects (stimulant or in conjunction with ephedrine as a fat-burning agent) without developing side effects (upset stomach, heart racing, mid-workout "crashing"). And don't forget the tolerance effect either. The maximum effects of caffeine are seen in individuals who have not used caffeine for at least four or five days. As with any drug, desenitivity to caffeine can easily develop. Our advice is to only use the drug two or three times a week – say on heavy leg and chest days. Finally, beware of the regulations imposed by your sports organizations. If caffeine is banned, you have no choice but to abide by the rules.

AMPHETAMINES

Amphetamines were the drug of choice during WW II, with over 150-million doses being used by both sides. These stimulants kept troops alert and ready for battle. The Soviets experimented with them as work enhancers, but the side effects of chronic use ended that idea. They are presently popular with those involved in shift work and occupations requiring long periods without sleep. Their use among long-haul truck drivers is well-known.

It was inevitable that amphetamines would find a place in sports, and they were the drug of choice in the Olympics from the 1950s to the 1970s. Amphetamine use in sports continues, and has been reported among professional football players in the US and Canada.

Bodybuilders can benefit from these stimulants, provided they use them properly. Low doses of 5 milligrams a day may provide enough chemical motivation to improve a burned-out or exhausted bodybuilder's attitude towards working out.[6] One study demonstrated that a dose of 14 milligrams per 70 kilograms of bodyweight improved performance in 75 percent of the subjects: swimmers, runners and weight throwers.[7] It should be pointed out that improvements in performance are most often found in athletes who are already well-rested before taking the stimulant. The effectiveness of amphetamines is not related to their depression of the appetite center, but rather their stimulating action.[6]

TYPES OF AMPHETAMINES AND RELATED COMPOUNDS

Plain amphetamine (Benzedrine) was the first to become popular. Dextroamphetamine (Dexedrine) and methamphetamine (Methedrine) are effective in lower doses but are otherwise similar to the parent compound.[1] The following is a brief list of commonly available stimulants. Please note that the side effects mentioned are usually seen with chronic use, heavy dosages, or both.

DEXEDRINE

Trade Name: Dexedrine Spansule
Generic Name: dextroamphetamine
Dosage: 15 mg, 10 to 14 hours before bedtime.

Directions: Swallow the pill whole. If you miss a dose, take it as soon as possible. Never take two doses at once! Until you are familiar with the effects of this drug, do not drive, operate heavy machinery, or lift heavy weights. Even if you are familiar with the effects, make sure you have a spot when doing squats or lifting heavy. If there is a chance of pregnancy, or you are pregnant, do not take this drug.

Side Effects: The following side effects should disappear after a short period of use: dry mouth, bad taste in mouth, loss of appetite, constipation, tremors, weight loss, difficulty sleeping, nervousness and dizziness.[8]

RITALIN

Trade Name: Ritalin
Generic Name: methylphenidate
Dosage: 20-mg tablet

Milos Sarcev

Directions: Take 30 to 45 minutes before a meal, unless otherwise directed by a physician. To prevent this stimulant from disrupting your sleep, take it before 6:00 pm. If you miss a dose, and it is almost time for the next dose, just take one tablet. Never take two or more doses at once! Do not drive, operate heavy machinery, or lift heavy weights until you are aware of how the drug affects you. Even if everything appears okay, err on the side of caution and have a spot for any squats or heavy lifting.

Side Effects: Methylphenidate resembles amphetamines though it has a different chemical structure.[7] It can also have similar side effects (see Dexedrine). Rash or weight loss should be brought to your doctor's attention immediately.[8] Good monitoring is essential.

CYLERT

Trade Name: Cylert
GenericName: pemoline
Dosage: 37.5-mg tablet/day.

Directions: Take a daily dose in the morning. This CNS stimulant, while structurally different from the amphetamines and methyphenidate, has similar pharmacological effects. This stimulant should only be used while dieting for a contest as its chronic use has been associated with growth inhibition. Any bodybuilder with a history of psychiatric or behavioral problems is advised to stay clear of this stimulant. It can aggravate both conditions.

Side Effects: The same as those already mentioned for dextroamphetamine and methylphenidate. There is also the possibility of hallucinations.[9]

The occasional use of these drugs for competition or a heavy workout should not pose any danger, provided the bodybuilder is monitored by a physician, is not dehydrated, and gets plenty of rest afterwards.

Jean-Pierre Fux takes it to the extreme.

Craig Titus and Chris Cattlechak

NICOTINE

Nicotine is an unusual drug in that it first stimulates, and then depresses the central nervous system. Delivery systems for this drug include cigarettes, chewing tobacco, gum and skin patches. Smoking, while destroying much of the nicotine through burning, is the most rapid way of self-administeration. By controlling the amount inhaled, a smoker determines how much of a nicotine dosage, or bolus, will be delivered to the CNS. Within five minutes of smoking, blood nicotine levels are 16 to 35 nanograms per millilitre. Thanks to health education smoking is rapidly losing favor. The majority of bodybuilders spurn this harmful practice. Skin patches, which can deliver 14 milligrams per 24 hours, have recently been shown to deliver higher dosages during exercise. Blood nicotine levels rise from 9.8 nanograms per millilitre to 11 nanograms per millilitre. Researchers believe this is due to increased perfusion. Long periods of exercise, or heat excess (the sauna) might cause a cumulative increase, leading to side effects.[10] Nicorette, a nicotine-containing gum used as an aid to quit smoking raises blood nicotine levels to 25 nanograms per millilitre after 25 minutes. The user can self-administer by replacing the piece after 30 minutes and through increased chewing.[9] Nicotine is highly addictive, more so than heroin.[1] While a powerful stimulant, it has many harmful side effects including: headache, insomnia, gastric upset, vomiting, irregular heart beat, and chest pain. Tobacco-related diseases kill an estimated 400,000 Americans every year. Don't be a statistic. Avoid this stimulant.

"Although nicotine is a stimulant which some athletes use in their quest for better performance, it can have adverse effects if taken in higher dosages. At the higher doses nicotine affects several body systems and processes. The impact on performance is negative in most cases. Nicotine is an addictive drug – once you're hooked, it's extremely hard to kick the habit."

– Dr. Mauro DiPasquale, regular *MuscleMag* columnist commenting on the commonly used drug nicotine.

ALCOHOL

Of all the drugs currently used, alcohol is the most prevalent, lucrative and destructive. When used in moderation it can be beneficial; in excess, it can cause muscle disease and tremor. It does not make sense to build muscle, and then go to a club and get drunk. The effects of such abuse prevent the body from reaching its potential. Alcohol can be used as a supplement, but it must be used responsibly.

Art Dilkes

Alcohol depresses functions of the central nervous system. The effects have less to do with the amount consumed than with actual blood concentration. Provided blood-alcohol levels (BAL) are low (one or two drinks for a 200-pound bodybuilder will produce a BAL between 0.02 to 0.06 percent, depending on previous alcohol use and speed of consumption) the effect is usually mild sedation, relaxation, and release of inhibitions. Thus the bodybuilder becomes more talkative, active and aggressive. These are all positive things for a bodybuilder getting ready for a heavy workout. Since alcohol is a diuretic, it is necessary to drink an equal volume of water above what you normally consume during a workout. Problems arise if the bodybuilder uses alcohol with other drugs or drinks too much.

Roid rage, the popular media myth which journalists love to use, refers to uncontrollable outbursts of violence brought on by steroid use. Yet when these cases are investigated, alcohol use is the precipitating factor. Violent behavior brought on by excessive alcohol use is tragically common. This tendency towards violence is usually well-established. When alcohol is combined with other drugs this situation is triggered. A few individuals without a history of violence may become violent when they combine alcohol with certain drugs. The best advice for any bodybuilder is to refrain from alcohol use of any kind if he or she is taking anabolic steroids, or have a history of violence when consuming alcohol.

"Candy is dandy, but liquor is quicker."

– Old saying regarding alcohol and romance.

If bodybuilders are going to drink to excess, it is usually after the workout. But it may surprise the reader to hear that drinking sometimes goes on before a bodybuilding contest. At the regional level, it is not unusual for bodybuilding contestants to have a shot of sherry or brandy before going onstage. Unfortunately, in their dehydrated states, things can go wrong. One contestant was accidentally given two shots, and collapsed before he could get onstage. Another contestant decided to "self-medicate," and went on stage drunk out of his mind. He put on a routine that can only be described as a cross between lip-sync and lap-dancing. Despite falling during his routine, he still managed to place. He was the crowd favorite that night, but has since carried the label, "The Village People idiot."

Problems arise if the bodybuilder uses alcohol with other drugs or drinks too much.

"Although I don't consider your alcohol consumption excessive, there may be some adverse physiological effects from moderate to heavy alcohol intake. A recent study has shown that acute alcohol ingestion decreases growth hormone secretion as well as serum testosterone."

– Dr. Mauro DiPasquale, regular *MuscleMag* contributor commenting on the negative effects of alcohol on HGH and testosterone secretion.

". . . the boss would make us take three drinks each. Straight shots, no choice. Then he would ask each of us questions about business. It was real hard to keep from saying what you thought . . ."

– Mafia insider, describing how his "Godfather" used alcohol to control his subordinates.

References

1) A. Weil and W. Rosen, *Chocolate to Morphine: Understanding Mind-Active Drugs*, (Boston, Houghton Mifflin Co., 1983).

2) F. Hatfield, "Herbs: Plant Power for All Seasons," *Muscle and Fitness*, 51:9 (September 1990).

3) J. Gonzalez-Alonzo and others, "Rehydration After Exercise With Common Beverages and Water," *International Journal of Sports Medicine*, 13:5 (1992).

4) J.L. Mills and others, "Moderate Caffeine Use and the Risk of Spontaneous Abortion and Intrauterine Growth Retardation," *JAMA*, 269:5 (1993).

5) N. Clark, "What's Brewing With Caffeine?," *The Physician and Sports Medicine*, 22:9 (1994).

6) W. Witters and P. Venturi, *Drugs and Society*, 2d ed. (Boston: Jones and Bartlett Publishers, 1988).

7) G. Smith and H. Beecher, "Amphetamine Sulphate and Athletic Performance," *JAMA*, 170 (1959).

8) Patient Drug Education, Database (TM) Media Span INC. (1995).

9) Canadian CPS, *Compendium of Pharmaceuticals and Specialities*, 30 ed. (Toronto: Canadian Pharmaceutical Association, C.K. Productions, 1995).

10) T. Basu, *Drug Nutrient Interactions* (New York: Croom Helm Ltd. 1988).

CHAPTER THIRTEEN

Painkillers and Sedatives

PAINKILLERS

Of all the over-the-counter substances used, none play as central a role in North American society as painkillers. At the slightest twitch or twinge, our conditioned response is to reach for a bottle of Aspirin. Feel a cold coming on, break out the Tylenol. A tough day at the office – try two tablets of Anicin.

It seems everybody has his or her favorite pain reliever and body-builders are no different. The following chapter looks at a few of the more commonly used painkillers. While some were designed specifically for the job, others were discovered by accident.

> **"In separate studies scientists found just 30 mg of aspirin a day helped head off heart attacks and strokes while creating fewer stomach problems such as bleeding."**
>
> – The late Bruce Page, commenting on one of the lesser-known benefits of the common painkiller, aspirin.

Alq Gurley reps out on the leg-press machine.

DLPA

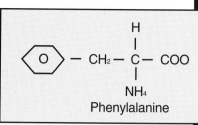

$$\langle O \rangle - CH_2 - \overset{\overset{\displaystyle H}{|}}{\underset{\underset{\displaystyle NH_4}{|}}{C}} - COO$$

Phenylalanine

The name DLPA is nothing more than an abbreviation for products containing both the "D" and "L" forms of the amino acid phenylalanine. DLPA is mild as painkillers go, but it does have the advantage of being natural and doesn't seem to cause the side effects often associated with stronger painkilling drugs.

Rod Ketchens

HOW IT WORKS

DLPA is believed to exert its effects by boosting circulating levels of endorphins and enkephlans – two of the body's primary natural painkillers. As soon as pain is detected, the brain releases these two opiate-like substances to produce an analgesic effect. As with most hormones, however, endorphins and enkephlans are rapidly metabolized by enzymes. Studies using DLPA suggest the amino acid compound reduces the effectiveness of the enzymes, giving the painkillers a longer life.

In addition to killing pain, the compound has a positive effect on mood, cognitive health, and appetite. This is because phenylalanine is a precursor to many of the brain's neurotransmitters, which control physiological processes. Although not as effective as other drugs, DLPA is used in the clinical treatment of depression and schizophrenia.

HOW MUCH FOR HOW LONG

For relief of muscle pain or soreness, take 600 to 800 milligrams of DLPA 15 to 30 minutes before each meal, for a total of 3.5 to 5 grams (3500 milligrams to 5000 milligrams) daily. As it takes time for the amino acid to build up in the body, and hence affect the degradation enzymes, it will probably take a week to ten days for the first reductions in pain to occur (for some it will take a couple of weeks). Some authorities recommend doubling the dosage if results are not obtained after two to three weeks. (Don't be surprised if you fall into this category – one in five users will receive little benefit from taking DLPA.) While overdosing on amino acids is virtually impossible, we recommend caution as high levels of phenylalanine might interfere with other metabolic processes, including the development of a severe allergic reaction. If the pain persists, consult a physician. Most minor muscle injuries heal after a few weeks but longer durations are often indicative of something more severe.

"Ibuprofen, a nonprescription painkiller has been found to have serious health effects, including kidney failure, in patients with pre-existing conditions such as kidney problems, high blood pressure and heart disease. Although occasional use seems to pose no problem, chronic users of the pills, such as arthritis sufferers and the elderly, risk kidney damage. The kidney failure is reversed in most cases as soon as the pills are stopped."

– The late Bruce Page, explaining how even common over-the-counter painkillers can have serious side effects in some people.

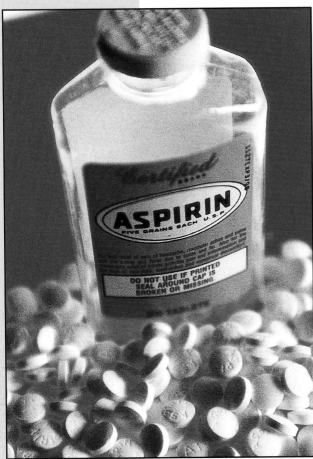

ASPIRIN

Perhaps the most familiar of all painkillers, Aspirin is found in almost every household medicine cabinet. The name Aspirin is a trademark of the Bayer corporation of Germany. Only Bayer can market acetylsalicylic acid (ASA) as Aspirin, even though numerous pharmaceutical companies can sell ASA. In fact, it's usually cheaper to buy the drug in this form.

Aspirin or ASA is taken for two primary reasons – pain relief and anti-inflammation. Bodybuilders find the drug very helpful in reducing swelling caused by such injuries as sprains, strains, and tears. Others use the drug to reduce the pain associated with intense exercise.

In recent years the drug has become popular in the treatment of heart disease. Numerous studies suggest taking one Aspirin tablet a day can greatly reduce the risk of heart attack or stroke. It does this by reducing the build-up of clotty deposits on arterial walls – the chief cause of blood restriction leading to cardiovascular disease. Aspirin is believed to reduce clotting by reducing platelet aggregation or clustering. For those with clotting problems to begin with, Aspirin would only compound the condition.

In terms of effectiveness, Aspirin is one of the most productive over-the-counter painkillers available. In many cases it surpasses the effects of more costly prescription painkillers. In addition, its anti-inflammatory properties make it a common staple of many athletic gym bags. For those who don't have problems with the drug's acidity, Aspirin is a valuable training aid.

> "Adding aspirin definitely increases the fat-burning potential of the ephedra/caffeine mix. This has been shown clinically. We recommend salix alba, an extract of white willow bark, which is related chemically and pharmacologically to aspirin, and can be taken in addition to aspirin or alone."
>
> – Dr. Dallas Clouatre, author of *Antifat Nutrients*.

SIDE EFFECTS

The only major side effect of Aspirin is its effects on the gastrointestinal tract. Many individuals find the drug causes intense stomach upset (described as a burning sensation) and, in rare cases, bleeding. Those with ulcers are strongly advised to avoid ASA products. Many of the acetaminophen painkillers were developed in response to Aspirin's unpleasant effects on the stomach. We should add that Bayer has introduced buffered versions of Aspirin (coated to reduce acidity) which most individuals can use.

DIMETHYLSULFOXIDE (DMSO)

Few substances took the bodybuilding world by storm back in the early 1980s like DMSO. Touted as a cure for everything from arthritis to overtraining, DMSO has – despite nearly 20 years of athletic use – failed to convince all of its potential merits.

DMSO was first discovered back in 1866 by Russian scientist Dr. Alexander Saytzeff. Despite his best efforts in promoting the substance – including a write-up in a German medical journal – Dr. Sayrzeff saw his discovery go the way of the dinosaur. It would be nearly 100 years before

DMSO reappeared, this time as an industrial solvent. Even then its origin was as a by-product of pulp and paper production.

> **DMSO is very simple in structure. It consists of two methyl groups (CH₃) joined to one central oxygen and sulphur group in the following manner:**
>
> $$CH_3$$
> $$|$$
> $$S = O$$
> $$|$$
> $$CH_3$$

Despite its relatively simplistic structure, DMSO has a unique affinity for water and many medicines. When added to water, DMSO does not freeze until minus 50 degrees Celsius – a property that makes it an excellent anti-freeze compound.

MECHANISM OF ACTION

If there is one property about DMSO that has endeared it to athletes and pharmacists alike, it's its ability to rapidly cross the skin and be absorbed by the bloodstream. The absorption is so fast that within a few minutes of rubbing on the arm, its characteristic taste – similar to garlic – is in the mouth. It is also smelt on the breath, a sure sign that DMSO has entered the bloodstream and traveled to the lungs.

The rapid absorption property of DMSO is not limited to itself. When combined with various medicines, DMSO can "piggyback" the medicine across the skin and into the bloodstream. From here it can travel to areas of the body not as reachable by other means.

THE WORKS OF DR. STANLEY JACOB

Much of our knowledge concerning DMSO is the result of one man – Dr. Stanley Jacob. In the 1960s Dr. Jacob was introduced to DMSO's unique properties by a chemist working for The Crown Zellerbach Corporation, America's largest producer of DMSO. Up to that time DMSO's characteristics were mainly limited to industrial applications, and even Dr. Jacob limited his research to using the compound as a freezing and pre-serving agent for organs meant for human transplant.

Monica Brant and Jay Cutler

> **"In previous studies it was thought that aspirin only protected men's hearts; however, it has been found that aspirin may prevent first heart attacks in women too."**
>
> – The late Bruce Page, commenting on the results of a Harvard Medical School study which showed women who took six aspirin a week had their incidence of heart attack reduced by 32 percent.

It wasn't long, however, before Dr. Jacob noticed that when applied to a small patch of skin, DMSO would cure a wide range of physical afflictions. Among his findings, DMSO could penetrate most body membranes, produce an additive effect when combined with other drugs, and even reduce such common inflammations as arthritis and bursitis. It appeared to Dr. Jacob that a new "wonder" drug had been discovered. But unfortunately he had not counted on the intervention of the US FDA (Food and Drug Administration).

PUT ON HOLD

Although a necessity given the number of drugs seeking patents these days, the FDA is not without its critics. Perhaps the biggest complaint concerning the FDA is its slowness in responding to new drug products. Much of this can be explained by sheer volume, but many insist that the organization's standards are not helping things. Before a drug is granted permission to be marketed it must undergo a rigorous, time-consuming, and very costly series of trials. And while this is no doubt necessary for public safety, it also means many potentially great drugs are either slow to receive approval or denied outright.

Such was the predicament that befell DMSO in the early 1960s. Also adding to the delay was the thalidomide scare of 1962. For those not familiar with the drug, thalidomide was a new tranquilizer with great potential. It was pulled from world distribution following a series of severe birth defects in newborn children in Europe. As the FDA was only months from granting thalidomide approval, there followed a reorganization of FDA standards for drug approval. And you guessed it, one of the first victims was DMSO; the FDA suspended human experimentation in 1965.

Pavol Jablonicky

Despite years of safe clinical trials and countless reports of medical applications, the FDA refused to soften its stand on DMSO research. It insisted the new drug-testing standards be applied to all drugs – irregardless of potential.

A TRUE BELIEVER

Despite the new regulations and public attack on his work by the FDA, Dr. Jacob remained convinced of DMSO's merits. Throughout the 1960s and 1970s he continued conducting trials with the drug and discovered a whole new spectrum of applications. Besides curing inflammation, DMSO increased the recovery rate from frostbite, improved healing after severe burns, and most surprisingly, helped spinal-cord patients recover partial use of their limbs.

It wasn't long before thousands of Dr. Jacob's patients began adding their own voices to the cry for DMSO

Milos Sarcev, Chris Cormier and Claude Groulx

approval. Among the most vocal proponents of DMSO use were Senator Ted Kennedy and former Alabama Governor George Wallace. In fact, Kennedy's committee on aging was successful in prompting the FDA to grant DMSO prescription status in the early 1980s.

AN ASSORTMENT OF CURES

Although many consider DMSO just another "placebo pill," the evidence seems to support the views that DMSO is a valuable aid in treating numerous ailments. DMSO's main application in athletics is its analgesic properties. Thousands of individuals report that DMSO alleviates pain like no other medication. Numerous bodybuilders swear by the product, and tout it as the ultimate treatment for sprains, strains, and tendonitis.

Among nonathletes, the most frequent use of DMSO is in the treatment of arthritis. There is an enormous amount of evidence to show that DMSO relieves the pain and stiffness associated with arthritis. In addition, there is a growing body of evidence to suggest that DMSO will actually slow down the spread and progression of some forms of arthritis. With the prescription availability of the drug, it's not surprising many physicians rely exclusively on DMSO for combating this painful condition (which affects tens of millions).

There are numerous theories as to how DMSO accomplishes the previous. One of the most popular concerns DMSO's affinity for water, which means it will be drawn to inflammation sites. All it takes is one topical treatment of DMSO and the swelling is greatly reduced.

Another theory focuses on DMSO's vasodilation properties. Time after time it has been clinically proven that DMSO can temporarily widen (dilate) blood vessels. Since a wider blood vessel can carry more blood, it's reasoned that the increased circulation causes a decrease in swelling and reduction in pain. As an example, Dr. Jacob has successfully used the drug to treat various forms of headaches.

Although not a physical reason, the placebo effect has not been ruled out for explaining DMSO's remarkable abilities. The medical literature is filled with stories (usually in war-time settings) of physicians running out of painkillers and having to resort to "sugar pills" as a cure for intense pain. As the patients "think" they are receiving a legitimate painkiller (with morphine being the most common), their pain miraculously disappears. Such is the power of the mind (not to mention providing evidence to suggest that "pain" has a psychological component). Many critics of DMSO suggest that this is the real theory behind its power. Whether this is the case or not, the bottom line is that DMSO does in fact have analgesic and anti-arthritic properties.

USE IN BODYBUILDING

Although not an anabolic steroid or the latest nutritional supplement, numerous bodybuilders over the years have become partial to DMSO. Former Mr. Universe and multi-Grand Prix winner, Boyer Coe, maintains that it cured him of a slow-healing shoulder injury back in 1981. He feels that without the drug, his competitive plans for that year would have been derailed.

DMSO may help decrease swelling and reduce pain after an injury.

Former Mr. USA and powerlifting champion, Pat Neve, has made extensive use of DMSO to deaden the pain from a torn triceps tendon suffered during his powerlifting days. Without the analgesic effects of DMSO, Pat said he wouldn't even be able to train arms.

The list of other bodybuilders who use DMSO is too long to record here. Suffice to say that many of the sport's top stars make use of the product when an injury crops up. And according to numerous football players, its use is widespread within football as well. This is not surprising given the nature of competitive college and pro football. When you have 275-pound behemoths slamming into one another, trying for the maximum amount of damage, it's only a matter of time before injuries occur. Added to this is the relatively short competitive season (as compared to other sports), which necessitates healing injuries as quick as possible.

POTENTIAL SIDE EFFECTS

Aside from the occasional allergic reaction, or accidental swallowing in high dosages by small children, there have been few serious side effects reported from DMSO use. Perhaps the most common side effect associated with DMSO is the strong breath odour produced. Although unpleasant to others (imagine carrying on a conversation with someone who just had a meal soaked in garlic) the condition is harmless and indicates the drug has completely entered the bloodstream.

Another side effect occasionally reported is a skin rash or burn. Although a few individuals may be susceptible to this – no matter what the dosage – such problems are usually the result of using very high concentrations of DMSO.

A few outspoken critics of DMSO (every drug has them) suggest that given its long duration in the body (five to seven days), it is possible that DMSO users may be at risk for liver damage. Further, the sulfide present in DMSO may reduce iodine levels, thus interfering with proper thyroid functioning. Other opponents add that DMSO may increase a person's sensitivity to other drugs such as alcohol, insulin, antibiotics, nitroglycerine and benzine.

We should add that research in the 1960s and 1970s suggested that DMSO may change the refractive index of the eyes (one of the reasons why research was terminated). Animal subjects from the same time period occasionally developed cataracts.

Although the debate continues, most pharmacists and physicians agree that DMSO appears safe for human use. That is to say, while a few users may experience unpleasantries, the vast majority of individuals can use DMSO without fear of harm. In over thirty years of human use there has been no evidence to suggest otherwise.

HOW TO USE AND WHAT TO BUY

Like most products, DMSO is available in many forms throughout North America, but keep in mind that medical sources are only available by prescription – usually under the trade name RIMSO-50. For most athletes the source of choice is industrial versions but this in itself may lead to problems as there are several grades and purities available. Whatever the brand, consumers should keep the following in mind when purchasing DMSO. The first point to consider concerns purity. As DMSO bonds with just about any substance (toxins and impurities included), it is imperative to acquire the purest form of DMSO and be sure that it has been handled as hygienically as possible. Make sure the dilution water is of laboratory grade and also check to see what the packaging material is made of. The reason we bring this up is because many sealing and packaging materials made of plastic or metal may themselves be broken down by DMSO. For example, polyvinyl chloride materials can become carcinogenic (cancer causing) when in touch with DMSO. Conversely, polyethylene materials are unaffected by DMSO and make the best packaging material.

Boyer Coe

What all the previous means is that most industrial forms of DMSO are potentially dangerous for human use. That's because they were not manufactured with purity in mind, and many are less than 50 percent pure. Some of the best sources of DMSO are veterinary derivatives. In most cases they are a mixture of 50 percent water and 50 percent DMSO. You may think veterinary products are unsafe for human use but remember, most veterinary drugs receive the same degree of scrutiny as drugs available for humans. We need only point you in the direction of many anabolic steroids to verify this point.

Besides purity, the concentration of the DMSO product is important. Anything above 75 percent is considered too harsh, and may lead to nasty skin burns and rashes. Most physicians recommend concentrations of about 65 to 70 percent DMSO.

When applying DMSO to an injured limb, make sure to clean the area with a clean, sterile, cotton pad or cloth. This will remove any residue which could otherwise be drawn inside the body by the DMSO. Also, don't wash using soap or other cleaning detergents. These too can be dissolved and transported into the body by DMSO. If the injured area happens to be covered by a layer of hair (calf, forearm, lower back, etc.), shave it off.

Apply the solution evenly with gauze or a cotton swab. Make sure to allow the chemical to dry (about 10 to 20 minutes) before putting clothes on over the area. This is because the dye in the material may react with the DMSO and be drawn inside the body.

Although it varies, most authorities recommend using DMSO two to three times a day for no more than seven to 10 consecutive days. If need be, stop treatment for two to three days and try another seven- to 10-day course. If this still has little effect, seek prompt medical assistance. (It wouldn't hurt to check with your doctor before the first treatment.)

"Realistically, DMSO is no wonder drug and for some, including myself, does very little. I often wonder how much of its effect is psychological instead of physiological, and whether it would in fact be used as just another liniment had there not been this long and bitter controversy, and the resulting fanaticism, over its use in humans."

– Dr. Mauro DiPasquale, best-selling author and regular *MuscleMag* columnist offering his views on DMSO.

Vince Taylor

IS DMSO THE WONDER DRUG OF THE FUTURE?

Like most "wonder" drugs, DMSO's effects are probably more down to earth than claimed. Nevertheless, the number of individuals who swear by its efficacy is growing by leaps and bounds. And with side effects rarely reported (something few drugs can claim) these numbers will take a quantum leap in the near future. Our advice is to approach DMSO use with what could be termed guarded caution. Sure, give it a try if you experience a mild injury, or have a pre-existing injury that doesn't seem to want to heal on its own. But don't let manufacturers' hype keep you from seeking perhaps the best cure of all – the doctor's office!

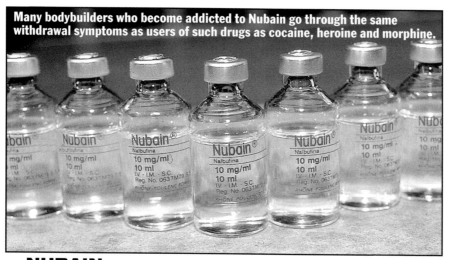

Many bodybuilders who become addicted to Nubain go through the same withdrawal symptoms as users of such drugs as cocaine, heroine and morphine.

NUBAIN

So far we have only looked at over-the-counter painkillers. If the pain is severe, or lingers for an extended period of time, many bodybuilders opt for something with a little more kick to it. And while a few go to extremes and use morphine, most play it safe and use a milder version of this powerful pain-killing narcotic. For many the drug of choice is Nubain, and anecdotal reports suggest it is becoming one of the most popular ergogenic aids used by bodybuilders. Unfortunately, if used improperly, the drug can have serious consequences.

Nubain is the trade name for nalbuphine hydrochloride – a synthetic narcotic prescribed by physicians for the relief of moderate to severe pain. Unlike most over-the-counter medications, Nubain is usually administered in injectable form (with 10 and 20 milligrams per millilitre being the most common concentrations), and starts working in 15 to 20 minutes. Depending on the individual, it usually lasts for four to six hours.

USE IN BODYBUILDING

Bodybuilders use Nubain (and similar painkillers) for two primary reasons – to null the pain associated with injuries, and to kill the pain acquired during superintense workouts. On the surface such reasons sound plausible, but in reality, can set the individual up for serious consequences.

Although training around injuries is very common with bodybuilders, it does have its drawbacks. First and foremost, it's virtually impossible to avoid stressing the injured muscle, tendon, or ligament. So even though

"Of all the drugs bodybuilders use, this one seems to be the most frivolous and useless to me. Maybe it sounds a tad macho, but to me, workout-induced pain is a badge of honor. It make bodybuilding a very unique activity, one which requires some level of courage, distinguishing it from Ping Pong or stamp collecting."

– T.C. Luoma, *Muscle Media* editor-in-chief commemnting on the popular painkiller Nubain, which seems to be used by bodybuilders more and more these days.

you may think you've given the injury a rest, it's still being stimulated. While in a few cases the increased blood flow may speed up the healing process, in most cases it only delays recovery. A second reason for avoiding pain-killers is that you may do further damage to the injury and not realize it.

Michael Poulsen

Although considered an annoyance by most, pain is the body's way of letting you know something is wrong. If you eliminate the sensation of pain you could literally break a bone or rip a muscle and not know it.

With regards to using Nubain to help your work-outs, this too can be foolhardy. Bodybuilders who are in tune with their bodies can differentiate pain caused by exercising muscles and pain produced by an injury. In fact, how a workout "felt'" is often the primary determiner of how effective it was. If you take Nubain to kill the pain associated with intense exercise, you have eliminated the primary safeguard of your body's moni-toring system. You may be able to blast out extra sets and reps at the squat rack, but how beneficial is this if you incur a spinal or knee injury in the process. Remem-ber, pain is a necessary aspect of life, and this includes during bodybuilding workouts.

SIDE EFFECTS

Like most prescription drugs, Nubain may produce a host of side effects. Most who use the drug never have any major problems, but the risks are there just the same.

Probably the most reported side effect is sedation. Like alcohol, Nubain eventually puts the user in a state of lethargy. This is because the drug does more than kill local pain, it also has profound effects on the central nervous system. Doctors often prescribe a stimulant with the drug to counteract these effects. For an indi-vidual who doesn't exercise or use heavy machinery, the sedative effects are acceptable, and in many cases welcome (there is nothing like sleep to speed up the healing process!). For a hard-training athlete, though, being knocked out is no way to improve one's performance.

A second side effect sometimes reported is a slowing down of the respiratory system. This is caused by the drug's depression of the central nervous system. Such effects have drastic consequences for athletes, as they have increased oxygen demands.

If the physiological effects were not bad enough, there is also good evidence to suggest Nubain is addictive. Tolerance to Nubain develops rapidly, and users need larger and larger dosages to achieve the same results. Many bodybuilders who become addicted to Nubain go through the same withdrawal symptoms as users of such drugs as cocaine, heroine, and morphine.

While the ultimate choice to use Nubain is yours, in our opinion it hardly seems worth it when the same results can be obtained with less dan-gerous drugs. Unless directed by your physician, we strongly suggest you avoid Nubain.

SEDATIVES

MELATONIN

It's safe to say no food supplement has grasped the public's attention in recent years like melatonin. Countless books have been written on the subject, all of which proclaim the wondrous merits of the supplement. From curing cancer to treating insomnia – it seems no ailment is safe from melatonin's clutches.

Melatonin is a naturally occurring hormone produced by the pineal gland – a small, pea-sized body located deep within the cerebral hemispheres of the brain. Like all hormones, melatonin is synthesized by the body. In this case, the neurotransmitter serotonin serves as the precursor.

HOW IT WORKS

Although other factors are involved, the stimulus for pineal production of melatonin is an absence of light. The greatest concentrations are produced at night when the individual is asleep. Conversely, increased light intensity decreases melatonin production. There is also an age-related aspect to melatonin as circulating levels decrease with age after puberty.

Hamdullah Aykutlu

The primary function of melatonin is to control sleep patterns – specifically by inducing drowsiness. Research has shown that melatonin is helpful in treating seasonal affective disorder, a condition caused by a lack of light during long winters, and characterized by lack of energy, mood swings, and in extreme cases, depression.

Other experiments (with mice) have shown a reversal of the aging process, and a lengthening of lifespans.[1] This is believed to be a result of melatonin's powerful antioxidant properties. It is also being used in Europe to treat epilepsy in humans.

IS IT AVAILABLE?

Melatonin is legally available in the US as a dietary supplement, but is classified as a drug in Canada. It's even illegal to advertise melatonin in Canada, and selling over the counter can net a $5,000 fine or three years in jail. It is legal, however, for Canadians to bring melatonin across the border, or to obtain it from abroad by mail order.[2]

Although it varies, the recommended dosage is 3 milligrams per night, taken one to two hours before bedtime. We should note that people have taken daily doses that are 600 to 3,000 times the normal level naturally present, without ill effect.[1]

In terms of cost, melatonin is one of the cheapest supplements to buy. Most distributors offer 60-capsule bottles for an average of $9.99 US. With each capsule supplying 3 milligrams of melatonin, for $10 you get a 60-day supply. If only creatine was sold in the same manner.

BODYBUILDING CONSIDERATIONS

Although not an anabolic agent or fat burner, melatonin may offer benefits for competitive bodybuilders. With the weeks leading up to a contest being perhaps the most stressful for competitors, the sleep-inducing effects of melatonin may be welcomed. There is nothing like anxiety and a precontest diet to throw off sleep cycles.

Closely related to the previous is the effects of melatonin on cortisol. A few studies have suggested melatonin may block the actions of this powerful catabolic hormone. If this is true, melatonin holds great promise for bodybuilders, especially in the weeks leading up to a contest (when increased training and decreased eating often lead to muscle loss due to catabolism).

An indirect benefit of melatonin is its effects on growth hormone. Since HGH is released in the greatest amounts during deep sleep, it only follows that a substance, which promotes such sleep, would indirectly increase HGH levels.

Gunter Schlierkamp, Porter Cottrell and Shawn Ray

Roland Cziurlok and
Porter Cottrell

Finally, the potential benefits of the hormone for treating depression and mood swings might be applicable to bodybuilders using or withdrawing from anabolic steroids and thyroid medications. Medical intervention is the best course of treatment for such; however, supplementation with melatonin could play a helpful role.

INTERACTION WITH OTHER DRUGS

Given the popularity of caffeine and aspirin with bodybuilders these days it only makes sense to relate them to melatonin. Recent studies suggest that taking excessive amounts of stimulants and painkillers may interfere with melatonin synthesis. Although the exact mechanism is unclear, researchers theorize that these drugs suppress various substances called prostaglandins, which are involved in the synthesis and release of melatonin. For those bodybuilders who regularly take the aspirin/ephedrine/caffeine mixture, you might want to start cycling the blend if you find your sleep patterns are disrupted.

BENZODIAZEPINES

Librium and Valium sales bring in hundreds of millions of dollars every year into the coffers of the international drug company Hoffman-LaRoche. Yet they owe their fortune to a bit of spring cleaning, and a chemist with an eye for beauty. In 1957, Dr. Leo Sternbach was a research chemist and group chief working for the company in New Jersey. Since 1955 he had been working on the heptoxdiazines, a group of substances he had first synthesized 20 years before as a graduate student. Sternbach had convinced the company to investigate this group of compounds, because, as Sternbach reasoned: 1) It is a fact that basic groups frequently impart biological activity; and 2) They had never been tested for biological activity.

After two years, the researchers had discovered that the substances were in fact quinazaline 3-oxides, they crystallized well, and that sadly, they were biologically inert. Deciding that two years was long enough, the company canceled the project and told Sternbach to get to work on some antibiotics.

Michelle Ralabate

"When you get up in the morning, I want you to take two Valium with breakfast. Now, when you get up for lunch. . ."

– Part of a comedy sketch by Newfoundland comedians Greg Malone and the late Tommy Sexton, poking fun at doctors and prescription drugs.

To quote Dr. Sternbach, "The lab was a real mess. There were dishes and beakers containing samples everywhere. We had no room to work." He decided it was time to clean up. He told his assistant Earl Reeder to throw out anything that did not look good, and bring to him anything that did. Reeder brought the base and chloride of RO-5-0690 to Sternbach's attention. Both were taken by the, "Prettiness and purity of the crystals." Sternbach disobeyed company orders and sent the samples for testing to Dr. Lowell Randell, head of the pharmacologist testing team. Sternbach's supervisor, Dr. Goldfarb, was not impressed. After some argument, Goldfarb told Sternbach, "Leo, you are dreaming."

For the company, it was a dream come true. This drug was one of the benzodiazepines. It was found to be a potent sedative, muscle relaxant, anticonvulsant, and in humans had antianxiety effects.

Naming the drug was another important step that Dr. Sternbach was involved in. During a lengthy meeting, several ideas were tossed out and rejected. According to Sternbach, one bright spark suddenly shouted out, "I know what to call it! This drug restores equilibrium to the body; we'll call it Librium!" Everyone liked that idea, and the name was approved. In 1959, Dr. Sternbach synthesized another benzodiazepine, given the name Diazepam. It's trade name was derived from the already successful Librium and the Latin word for health – valere – giving the name we all know, Valium.

Despite the billions that Hoffman-LaRoche made from Dr. Sternbach's dreaming about pretty crystals, he received only a few small bonuses. He is well-to-do, but not a millionaire. When asked if he was bitter, he replied, "No. They always treated me well and even though I am retired they still give me a nice office."[3]

Bodybuilders often use Valium for insomnia, muscle and back pain, nervousness produced by the popular caffeine/ephedra/aspirin stack, to counteract the anxiety of contest preparation and to deal with aggressive feelings from steroid use, or depression after completing a cycle. While Valium can be a beneficial drug, it can be addictive and should only be used for short periods of time. Bodybuilders and lay people alike often take more of the drug than necessary. It is known that 120 milligrams a day for two months will produce physical dependence,[4] yet 5 to 15 milligrams a day is often enough to treat and control depression.

The side effects of Valium and the other benzodiazepines include skin rashes, lethargy, nausea, decreased libido, menstrual irregularities, drowsiness, blood-cell abnormalities, and increased sensitivity to alcohol.[4] Even though these drugs are referred to as "minor tranquilizers," they are very potent drugs which should only be used under medical supervision. They should NEVER be used with alcohol as one bodybuilder related to the authors: ". . . I'm not stupid. I mean, I heard they can blunt emotion. Anyway, my girlfriend had dumped me for some pencil-neck engineering student, so my best friend got me tanked. His mother had this humungous prescription for Valium, so we each washed down 8 or 9 pills with a case of beer. I'm not a violent guy and I wasn't on the juice, but at one point I was ready to rip the shit out of the place! The next day was bizarre. I felt nothing. Absolutely nothing! Jokes weren't funny, nothing. My friend could have been lying dead in front of me and it wouldn't have mattered. I was like a robot all day. Scared the shit out of me! The next day I was back to normal. I won't do that again."

PROZAC (fluoxetine)

Although classified as an antidepressant, we thought it necessary to include the drug Prozac here given its sedative properties.

Prozac is the trade name for fluoxetine. It is an antidepressant which works by enhancing the effect of the mood-improving brain chemical serotonin, by blocking its reabsorption by neurons.[5] Prozac is a very effective drug for treating stress and mild depression. It had some bad press when it first came out, but that was because it was prescribed for cases of severe depression, where the drug was not as effective. Prozac is also prescribed for the treatment of gambling, obesity, premenstrual syndrome (PMS), fear of public speaking,[5] bulimia nervosa, and obsessive-compulsive disorder.[6]

While it normally takes two weeks for the drug to become effective, some users report an improvement within days, or even hours of first use. Common side effects include nausea, diarrhea, headache, poor appetite, and in some cases sexual dysfunction and a loss of libido. Most of

> **"When I'm on prozac, I'm more me."**
>
> – Prozac user on the internet, praising the drug.

Jean-Pierre Fux

Jeff Poulin

these side effects are transitory, and pass after the first week of use. Users often report a drastic improvement in mental skills, memory and problem solving. Life, in short, becomes more enjoyable and at the least, tolerable.

Why would bodybuilders use Prozac? Severe dieting and heavy training can exert a tremendous mental stress on any individual. Bodybuilders coming off a steroid cycle often experience depression,[7] therefore it would be prudent to begin this drug before a steroid cycle ends. While using steroids, some bodybuilders experience a dramatic increase in sex drive and aggression levels. Prozac could help control both of these symptoms.

Prozac also helps people improve their feelings of self-esteem. Surprisingly, a significant number of bodybuilders have low self-esteem. Many people get into bodybuilding to improve their physiques and raise their levels of self-esteem. Unfortunately, some individuals have such grandiose expectations that no matter how much they improve, physical reality can never match the mental fantasy. The image in the mirror is seen as thin and insignificant. This phenomenon is often referred to as megalomania, but we prefer the more descriptive title of "reverse anorexia." This drug could help some bodybuilders to accept themselves as they are: large, physically fit people.

Prozac is a prescribed drug in both the US and Canada. It is taken orally, in liquid or capsule form. Dosage varies between 20 milligrams to a maximum of 80 milligrams per day.[6] Even though it is a very safe drug, it should only be used under the supervision of a physician, and the use of alcohol and MAO inhibitors (a class of antidepressants)[6] should be avoided.

"Totally limp."

– Prozac user, commenting on a side effect he experienced at 2 pills (40 mg) per day. Once he cut back to one pill a day his erections returned.

References

1) S. Miller and others, "Melatonin Mania," *Newsweek* (November 1995), 63.
2) P. Kaihla, "The Ban Busters," *Macleans* (December 18, 1995), 74-75.
3) Authors' interview with Dr. Leo Sternbach, 1986.
4) W. Witters and P. Venturi, *Drugs and Society*, 2d ed. (Boston: Jones and Bartlett Publishers, 1988).
5) G. Cowley, "The Culture of Prozac," *Newsweek*, (February 7, 1994) 41-42.
6) Canadian CPS, Compendium of Pharmaceuticals and Specialties, 13 ed. (Toronto: Canadian Pharmaceutical Association, C.K. Productions, 1995).
7) P. Embleton and G. Thorne, "Anabolic Steroids in Atlantic Canada," Unpublished Survey, (Center for Newfoundland Studies, Queen Elizabeth II Library: Memorial University of Newfoundland and Labrador, January 1991).

Ahmo Height and Jean-Pierre Fux

BOOK FOUR

Ergogenic Nutrients

Ergogenic nutrients
are substances used
to enhance athletic
performance.

Jay Cutler

Protein and Amino Acids

O f all the natural supplements used by bodybuilders, none hold a position as close to the heart as protein. From the glory days of Muscle Beach to today's Olympia arena, few bodybuilders feel complete without the latest protein supplement.

Surveys consistently show that athletes not only believe that protein supplementation is needed, but virtually all include some form in their daily diet. So prodigious is this belief that the supplement business is worth billions of dollars annually with protein and amino acids comprising a large percentage.

We should add that diets high in protein are not a modern innovation. The ancient Roman and Greek athletes were fed copious amounts of red meat in the belief that the substances they contained would power them to Olympic and gladiator glory.

Robin Parker

PROTEIN

Although bodybuilders focus on muscle tissue (which is composed of over 50 percent protein), just about every form of tissue in the body contains protein, including blood hemoglobin, organs, tendons, ligaments, and bone. Many enzymes and hormones are also protein in nature. Anyone engaged in intense physical activity – especially bodybuilding – needs protein for growth and repair. And while biochemists may debate whether athletes need extra protein, bodybuilders are virtually unanimous in their belief that the RDA values for protein must be exceeded to keep the body's muscles growing.

Although there are hundreds of different types of protein, all contain one common element – nitrogen. Combined with such other elements as carbon, hydrogen, and oxygen, nitrogen gives protein a unique importance in human physiology.

Because protein cannot be stored as protein, it must be regularly consumed in the diet. If an excess is ingested, it will be used for energy, stored as fat, or excreted by the kidneys.

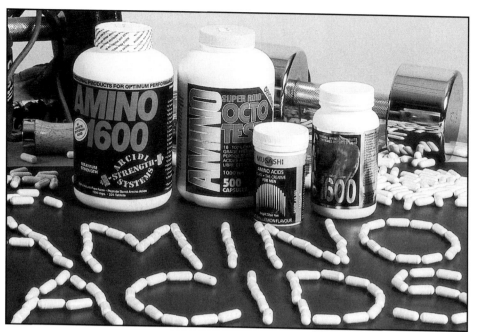

AMINO ACIDS

Protein that the body needs is digested and broken down into smaller sub-units called amino acids. Often called the "building blocks of life," each amino acid can be considered a link in a chain, and when joined together form protein strands (called polypeptide chains) hundreds or thousands of amino acids long.

If we look at a typical amino acid we see that it has a central carbon atom connected to four separate branches. At one end we have an amino group, at another we find the acid group (hence the name amino acid), and a third branch is just a hydrogen atom. All amino acids have these three branches in common. The fourth group is what gives each amino acid its uniqueness.

A typical amino acid is arranged as follows:

$$\text{AMINO GROUP} - NH_3 - \overset{\displaystyle \overset{H}{|}}{\underset{\displaystyle \underset{SIDE\ GROUP}{|}}{C}} - COOH - \text{ACID GROUP}$$

As most bodybuilders have probably seen the letters "L" and "D" placed in front of amino acids, we should briefly mention the reason here. The previous molecule, although written two-dimensionally (the limits of writing on a flat surface), exists in nature as a three-dimensional structure. The terms L and D stand for left and right, and denote the way the molecule is arranged three-dimensionally in space. For the purists among you, the two versions are mirror images of one another. That is, the atoms are arranged in the same order, but completely opposite. Although not con-clusive, it is believed that biological systems can only use the L version for metabolism. This is important as some cheap supplements may contain both or only the D version.

Animal products are far superior in terms of protein quality.

THE 22 BUILDING BLOCKS OF LIFE

For all the complexities of protein, and the tissues and chemicals it produces, protein strands are derived from just 22 amino acids (textbooks vary on this and some list 20, others go as high as 24 to 28. As 22 is the most commonly cited figure, this is the one we will use). The individual characteristics of each protein is determined by the unique way in which the amino acids are strung together. One arrangement may signal insulin, while another denotes growth hormone. Of the 22 amino acids, thirteen can be manufactured from raw materials by the body. The other nine, called "essential amino acids," cannot be manufactured by the body and must be consumed in the diet. These nine include leucine, isoleucine, histidine, lysine, methionine, pheny-lalanine, threonine, tryptophan and valine.

THE BEST SOURCES

The reason we emphasized this last point is because not all foods are alike when it comes to providing amino acids. For comparison purposes, bio-chemists use the terms complete and incomplete in describing protein sources. Complete proteins are those which contain all the essential amino acids in the right proportions. Such sources as ovalbumin, the main protein found in eggs, and casein, the primary protein in milk, are among the best examples of complete proteins.

Incomplete proteins are found in grains and vegetables. Grains, for example, are low in lysine, and legumes low in methionine. There are other examples too numerous to mention here, but the bottom line is that incomplete proteins must be combined to insure adequate amounts of amino acids are obtained in the diet.

Animal products are far superior in terms of protein quality. Of course, vegetarians counter that animal meat is high in fat (and they're right), but the fact remains that one good beef steak will supply all the essential amino acids while multiple plant sources would have to be consumed to achieve this. (The fact that plant sources contain nutrients that meat cannot supply is the main reason why a well-balanced diet should include both plant and animal sources).

The best sources of animal protein are also the highest in fat content. Such commonly consumed meats as beef and pork are loaded with protein, but contain whopping amounts of fat. A bodybuilder may get away with this in the off-season, but come contest time the extra fat must be eliminated from the diet. If your family has a history of heart disease, it may be a good idea to skip red meat altogether.

When it comes to high protein and low- to moderate-fat levels, most bodybuilders prefer fish and skinned chicken. The reason for skinning the chicken should be obvious as most of the fat is contained in or just under the skin. Besides chicken, other poultry products like ducks and geese are fine, but be wary of commercially fattened products. Although harder to get, wild geese and ducks (most wild game for that matter) have much less fat deposits than farm-fed birds.

Perhaps the most used source of protein by bodybuilders are eggs, but as with animal meats, they contain high levels of fat – in this case, cholesterol. Two whole eggs contain about 15 grams of protein but also contain similar amounts of fat. If there's a convenience about eggs it's their neat division into two equal halves – yolk and white. And as luck would have it all the fat is contained in the yolk. Many bodybuilders, including former Canadian great Roy Callender, remove the yolks in the months leading up to a contest. Consuming two to three dozen egg whites was not uncommon for Roy in his Grand Prix days. Another convenience is that they are already "packaged" for you. It's really simple to hard-boil a dozen eggs and carry them with you throughout the day, and then every hour or so you can eat one or two as a snack. Many of the sport's "old timers" made this a common practice in the days long before amino acid tablets.

TIMING AND PROPORTIONS

Essential amino acids must also be consumed in correct proportions. Studies suggest that for adequate repair, maintenance, and growth, the body prefers the same proportions of each amino acid. In building protein for growth or repair, the body needs all the amino acids to be present in the bloodstream at the same time in the correct amounts. If so much as one essential amino acid is proportionally deficient, protein synthesis is impeded.

Roy Callender

Although it varies, the amino acid which tends to be the limiting variable for most individuals is methionine. This is because many foods contain limited amounts. Besides methionine, most fruits and vegetables are deficient in one or more of the essential amino acids. For individuals who limit the amount of red meat they eat, there is a strong chance that their diet is inadequate in terms of available amino acids.

For practical purposes, let's assume your diet contains 100 percent of the daily requirements of all the amino acids except one – present at only 50 percent of its requirement. In this case your protein synthesis will be held back by this limiting amino acid. In short, your body will only carry out protein synthesis at 50 percent of its normal rate.

Having seen the previous it's easy to see why supplementing the diet with outside protein or amino acid sources makes good sense for bodybuilders. How much is needed will be discussed in the next section.

PROTEIN AND AMINO ACIDS – DO BODYBUILDERS NEED MORE?

Do athletes need extra protein? Few questions offer as many differing answers, and the issue of how much protein is needed daily by athletes has no doubt been debated since the 1940s and 1950s. There are two schools of thought on this issue. One is that if you eat the daily minimal amounts of animal meat or fish (1 gram for every kilogram of mass that you carry), protein supplements are not necessary. People have this attitude that more is better, and it's not. If one aspirin will kill your headache, will 100 aspirin make you better, faster? No, but they will end your headache problem permanently. Your body has been designed by evolution to remove the amino acids it needs from food, and process them accordingly. Jumping the first steps of digestion does not necessarily lead to an improvement in health. It may just overload your system and throw off your internal balance. There is a logical reason for our body breaking down food in the first place, to selectively remove what is needed, at a rate at which it can be safely absorbed. Putting in too much may cause the body to switch gears in an effort to remove the excess. For example, one prune a day will help regulate your bowel movements, while a large bag of prunes will result in a bowel movement that lasts all day. Your body needs fiber, but too much will give you severe diarrhea. It would appear that moderation is the key.

While a diet of high-protein mini meals every two or three hours should provide enough protein, amino acids can be used to ensure a positive nitrogen balance.

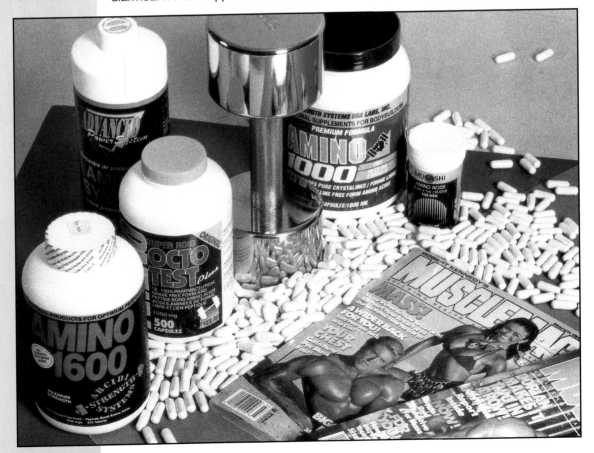

Another school of thought says that enough research has been done to show that it is possible to safely supplement using pure amino acids. Understand that amino acids are important in maintaining the body's nitrogen balance. The amount of nitrogen being taken in (from protein and amino acid sources) should be greater than the amount being excreted as nitrogenous wastes. This positive nitrogen balance means that muscle growth is occurring. To achieve such a balance, a hard-training bodybuilder must take in more protein to build up the components of growing muscle tissue. While a diet of high-protein mini meals every two or three hours should provide enough protein, supplements and amino acids can be used to ensure a positive nitrogen balance.

Other researchers, such as the people at L&S Research, believe that it is not the form of the amino acid that is crucial, but the proportions in which the amino acids reach the muscles. This compensation is claimed to be necessary because intensive resistance training creates specific metabolic demands. These needs result in the disproportionate consumption of certain amino acids for energy production and other nonanabolic needs. Our bodies use amino acids in precise proportions. By providing amino acids that are in the same proportions as they would be found in high-protein foods, the ability of the body to absorb and utilize amino acids can be exploited, to produce an anabolic effect.

Gunter Schlierkamp

THE DEBATE CONTINUES

As soon as word got around that the "boys from Muscle Beach" were consuming vast amounts of protein, many nutritionists felt obligated to step in and say "hold on a minute, you don't need all that protein and in fact too much may be dangerous" (the potential dangers will be discussed later). Adding to the confusion were opposing biochemists who agreed with the bodybuilders that extra protein was required by hard-training athletes. As for the bodybuilders themselves, virtually all agreed that their best gains came while taking protein supplements. Before we look at the available research, we need to understand the manner in which protein requirements are measured and calculated.

NITROGEN BALANCE

It may surprise you to learn that biochemists don't measure protein levels directly. Instead, they measure the individual's nitrogen balance because nitrogen is the common element to every amino acid.

By measuring how much nitrogen is lost against how much is consumed in the diet, researchers arrive at what's called nitrogen balance. When you lose less nitrogen through urine and sweat than you consume, you are said to be retaining nitrogen and scientists call this "positive nitrogen" balance. Although it signifies other things, the primary concern of bodybuilders is that positive nitrogen balance indicates increases in muscle tissue. Muscle growth can only take place during periods of positive nitrogen balance.

"Most bodybuilders were aware immediately that the high-carb, low-protein diet was not suitable for them, but it took sports nutrition several years to catch up. By 1983, experiments were documented that rebuked the low-protein theory. It was discovered that amino acids in protein increase the catabolic process, and act as hormone precursors as well. In fact, 15 percent of our energy is derived from protein."

– Greg Zulak, former *MuscleMag* editor and well-known bodybuilding writer commenting on the change in bodybuilding nutrition over the years.

Michael Francois

The opposite can also occur. If you are losing more nitrogen than you take in, you are in what's called a state of "negative nitrogen" balance. Such a state invariably leads to losses of muscle size and strength.

Laura Binetti

UNITED STATES AND WORLD STANDARDS

Like the RDAs discussed earlier in the book, protein requirements are set down by various health organizations. For convenience, biochemists measure protein requirements in grams per kilogram of bodyweight. In other words, the number of grams needed for every 2.2 pounds of bodyweight. The most used standard in medical studies is the US Food and Nutrition Board's value of 0.80 grams per kilogram (the corresponding Canadian value is .86 grams per kilogram). For a 200-pound male this works out to about 72 grams of protein daily. The World Health Organization is more conservative and puts the value at 0.75 grams of protein per kilogram.

You would think that with such precise numbers, the issue of protein requirements would be a dead issue. Lets face it, numbers, measurements, mathematics – the precise science, right? Wrong!

These values are not etched in stone and the people who cite them to denounce bodybuilders taking extra protein are forgetting one thing – the values were not calculated using hard-training athletes. These numbers – like the RDAs – were derived by measuring the requirements in sedentary individuals. If the word sedentary confuses you, it means lazy, not exercising, inactive – genuine couch potatoes.

There is no way that values obtained from such individuals can relate to a 250-pound bodybuilder squatting 600 pounds for 10 to 12 reps on a weekly basis. Such individuals are placing incredible stress on their muscles and they need extra protein. All that muscle tissue must be repaired and the only way this can take place is when sufficient quantities of building blocks – amino acids – are present. If the amino acids are not supplied in adequate amounts, negative nitrogen balance combined with catabolism takes place. And we all know what that leads to – muscle wasting or muscle loss.

"Muscle mass is determined by the balance of protein synthesis and protein degradation. When synthesis exceeds degradation, protein mass accumulates and the body is said to be in positive protein balance (or positive nitrogen balance). When degradation exceeds synthesis, the body is in negative protein balance and muscle mass is lost."

– John Parrillo, *MuscleMag* columnist.

Paul Dillett, Kevin Levrone and Vince Taylor battle it out.

CURRENT RESEARCH

Although there are still holdouts in the biochemistry field, the most recent studies indicate that athletes – particularly those engaged in strenuous exercise – do need additional protein. One study, involving sprinters and competitive bodybuilders, revealed that both groups required from 1.12 to 1.67 times more protein than sedentary controls.[1] Another study carried out using Romanian Olympic lifters showed that those given 4.4 times the RDA had much greater increases in size and strength.[2] There's more.

Researchers at Tuffs University found that men involved in such activities as running, swimming, and biking, need – are you ready for this – TWICE the protein requirements of sedentary controls.[3] We can only imagine what a 220-pound bodybuilder would need.

SEX-BASED DIFFERENCES?

One of the ongoing areas of research concerning protein requirements involves proposed differences between males and females. In one study, researchers measured nitrogen balance in male and female runners who were consuming .86 grams of protein daily. The first thing noticed was that this amount was inadequate for either sex during periods of intense training and both groups showed negative nitrogen balance. Additionally, it was found that males had a proportionately higher state of negative nitrogen balance.[4]

Further studies have found similar results and, although not conclusive, suggest that females need approximately 25 percent less protein than males, but still about 30 to 40 percent more than current RDA values.

YES – BODYBUILDERS NEED MORE!

Although it varies, hard-training athletes need anywhere from 1.2 to 1.6 grams of protein per pound of bodyweight per day to fully sustain the process of muscular growth and repair. For a 200-pound bodybuilder this works out to about 200 to 250 grams of protein per day. Now that we know body-

"Negative nitrogen balance can be caused by overly strict dieting, overtraining, physical trauma, and mistimed protein intake – that is, going too long between meals."

– The editors of *MuscleMag*, outlining some of the reasons why bodybuilders may put themselves in a state of negative nitrogen balance.

builders (and other athletes) need extra protein, it's time to look at some of the various sources of protein and how each may benefit the individual in his or her quest for ultimate size.

BIOLOGICAL VALUE (BV) AND DEGREE OF HYDROLYSIS (DH)

Given the number of references to "biological value (BV)" and "degree of hydrolysis (DH)" these days – especially as it refers to whey protein – we thought it necessary to take a closer look at these terms.

Although touted as the latest scientific breakthrough for measuring protein quality, BV is perhaps more important to advertisers than body-builders. The term was designed by biochemists to determine the quality of food protein, and is related to amino acid content – specifically essential amino acids. But as most well-read bodybuilders know, there is more to pro-tein metabolism than simply the amino acid content. Such factors as digestibility and utilization must also be taken into account.

Supposedly, the higher a protein's BV the more of it is used for protein synthesis. Starting with the reference number 100, protein utilization declines as the scale decreases. The problem, however, is that as protein intake increases, the BV of any protein consumed decreases. The research suggests that the decline starts at around 3 grams of protein per kilogram (2.2 pounds) of bodyweight per day. This means even the highest BV pro-teins may be utilized less efficiently when total protein intake is high.

Merle Ertunc

Another thing to keep in mind is the way most calculated BV values are obtained – prim-arily using animal subjects. This can be misleading as many animals have different protein-utilization rates than humans. As an example, studies using rats will give a BV value for egg protein of around 100, while the corresponding value for humans is 65.[5] While animal data can be extrapolated to humans, there are instances when such tech-niques are misleading, and BV calculations are one such example.

Despite all the previous, supplement manufacturers con-tinue to throw numbers at us in an attempt to sell more cans of protein powder. About the only way to accurately measure a protein's BV is in the lab using test subjects. Calculated BV values have their place, but don't think a few crunched numbers are all that matter in assessing protein quality.

Perhaps a better way of rating whey protein is to use what's called the degree of hydrolysis or DH. This term refers to the length of time allowed for enzymatic breakdown in the manufacturing process. The greater the DV, the greater the percentage of free amino acids, di- and tripeptides, and lower molecular-weight polypeptides.

For the bodybuilder this means the best products are unfortunately the more expensive (derived from a more extensive manufacturing process) and the worst tasting. With few exceptions, the better tasting the product the lower the percentage of amino acids and protein peptides. Although not conclusive, it's nearly a guarantee that such products have not undergone a lengthy enzymatic-hydrolysis duration.[6]

It would be convenient if there was a relationship between BV, DH, and other measuring variables, but this is not the case. Many low-DH products have high digestibility, and some high-BV supplements are poorly utilized. Our best advice is to try a few of the more reputable brands and make up your own mind. Remember, your instinct is the most accurate rating scale there is.

PROTEIN AND AMINO ACID SUPPLEMENTS

Note: Although protein and amino acids are really the same, they will be described separately as many manufacturers sell amino acids individually. Keep in mind that any product advertised as containing "all the amino acids" is nothing more than another protein source.

Hard-training athletes require anywhere from 1.2 to 1.6 grams of protein per pound of bodyweight per day to fully sustain the process of muscular growth and repair.

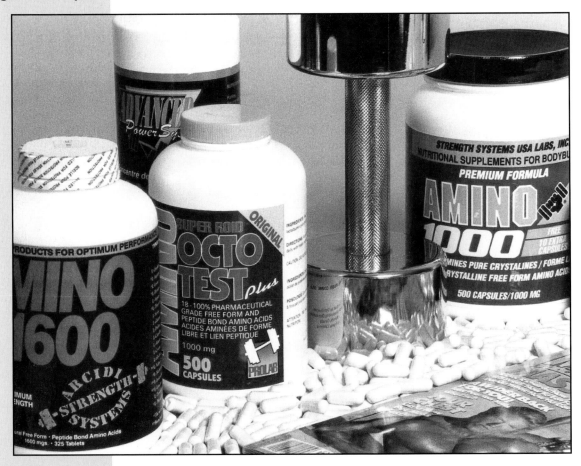

PROTEIN POWDERS

By far the most popular forms of protein supplements are protein powders. "Old timers" of the sport will remember the good old days when tins of protein powder were awarded as prizes in bodybuilding and weightlifting contests!

Although things have come a long way, the contents are much the same. Granted the tins have been replaced by plastic containers adorned with images of current stars, but the powder inside bears a distinct resemblance to its ancestors from the 1950s and 1960s. Protein powders are dried and processed protein sources, obtained from such products as milk, meat, egg, and soybean. Although plant proteins are popular with vegetarians, most bodybuilders prefer animal sources, with milk and egg forms being the most popular.

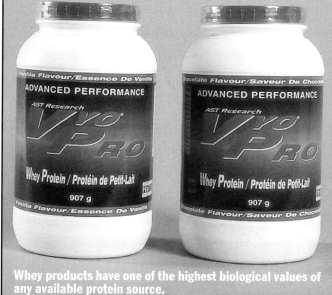

Whey products have one of the highest biological values of any available protein source.

WHEY PROTEIN

We thought it best to describe this protein source separately given its increased popularity in recent years. Up until four or five years ago the ultimate in protein supplements were those derived from whole milk and egg sources. Egg was thought to be the best because it had the highest protein efficiency ratio (PER) – a scale devised by biochemists to measure how well a protein source is utilized by the body.

In the past few years biochemists and nutritionists have improved on egg proteins by making available a new supplement called whey protein. Often called "ion-exchange" proteins, whey sources supposedly have the highest biological value of any available protein source.

Whey protein is derived from milk serum and is the soluble part of milk protein. It is different than the casein fraction of milk, not only in amino acid composition, but also in solubility. Whey protein is comprised of several different types of soluble proteins of which beta-lactalglobulin and alpha-lactalbumin make up 48 percent and 20 percent respectively.[5]

The two most popular purification techniques are ion-exchange and ultra-filtration. The main difference between the two is that ion-exchange isolates each protein fraction separately, producing a product that is composed of different percentages of protein fractions. Ultra-filtration purifies the protein fractions in the same ratios as the original raw source. While both can produce low levels of fat and lactose (a benefit to the large percentage of the population who are lactose intolerant), the ion-exchange process is superior in this regard.

ADVANTAGES

There are numerous reasons why whey sources are among the best forms of protein. First, they have higher amounts of branched-chain amino acids than other protein products. As will be seen later, these particular aminos are not only used to build muscle tissue, but are also used for oxidation during exercise.

"There are some really good gain-weight high-protein supplements out on the market which provide high calories for vigorous workouts, yet with enough protein for rebuilding purposes. These gain-weight high-protein powders can be thoroughly blended with milk or juices, to which any flavour can be added to suit your taste. One large glass of a 'gainer milk shake' with or between meals is enough for most active bodybuilders."

– John Grimek, bodybuilding legend.

Another of whey's benefits is to raise levels of glutathione. Arguably the most important antioxidant in the body, glutathione is a tripeptide composed of the amino acids cystine, glutamic acid, and glycine. Studies with elderly patients suggest glutathione decreases may lead to Parkinson's and Alzheimer's diseases. Although not conclusive, one theory suggests that such diseases are caused by free-radical damage brought on by low levels of glutathione. Studies with mice have shown that those animals fed whey protein lived an average of six months longer and had glutathione levels increased substantially.[7,8] We should add that only whey sources that are 90 percent or more undenatured have this ability to raise glutathione levels. Unfortunately, many products are manufactured using high-temperature techniques and this destroys much of the protein's unique characteristics. For maximum effect use whey sources that have been prepared using low-temperature methods.

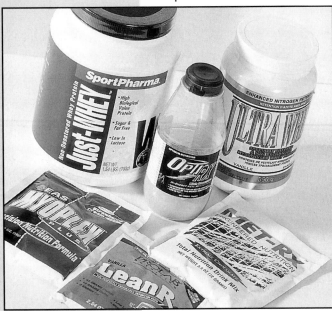

Read labels carefully when attempting to purchase the best protein source for your buck.

For bodybuilders, whey's greatest benefit is in promoting IGF-1 levels. Studies have shown that IGF-1 release is related to the quality of protein ingested, and topping the list are whey sources. In addition, there is limited evidence to suggest whey protein stimulates nitrogen retention – one of the conditions necessary for protein synthesis. We should add that this is a contentious issue, and other studies have not revealed any great nitrogen-retention abilities of whey protein.

Rounding out the list of whey's benefits include: fast absorption by the body, and a role in immune response. From a practical standpoint, whey protein doesn't seem to cause the painful bloating and gas problems experienced with other protein products.

THE BEST?

Despite the attempts of some supplement manufacturers to mislead, whey protein does not have drug-like qualities. A combination of number crunching and creative advertising may fool some, but hopefully by now most readers are informed enough to see through the guise. This is not to say whey protein is without merit. It is one of the best forms of protein available. But things must be kept in perspective. Don't let fancy terms such as "ion exchange" and "high biological value" make you think whey protein provides a pharmaceutical advantage. It doesn't. It's merely another great protein source.

WEIGHT-GAIN POWDERS

Besides being sold separately, protein can also be a major constituent of the very popular "weight gain" powders. These products are multi-ingredient powders which contain huge amounts of the basic food nutrients. As protein is one of the cheapest and easiest nutrients to produce, it's not surprising it comprises the bulk of these supplements. If you're underweight, and having trouble gaining muscular bodyweight, these high-calorie supplements may be what's needed to kick start your metabolism into new growth. But remember, these products are loaded with calories – over a thousand per serving in many cases. Chances are, after a couple of weeks you will gain more than just muscle tissue from such supplements. The dreaded "tire around the waist" might suddenly rear its ugly head!

Besides increasing fat levels, weight-gain powders have another, less celebrated side effect – gas. Many such products contain fructose as an ingredient, and since much of it doesn't get absorbed, the bacteria living in your lower intestine have a field day converting this simple sugar into methane gas. Many individuals bring back memories of the Hindenburg upon using such weight-gain products. The squat rack is often the site of such gas venting (a polite way of saying "fart," "breaking wind" etc.), and most gyms have members famous for their vapor discharges.

If you're underweight and having trouble gaining muscular bodyweight, high-calorie weight-gain supplements may kick start your metabolism into new growth.

Without jumping on the bandwagon too much, we suggest skipping the old-fashioned weight-gain powders, and purchasing one of the new, state-of-the-art optimizer supplements. Such products as MET-Rx, Phosphagain, or Metaform not only provide less calories, but are far easier to mix, and most important, do not produce noxious moments during your social life.

GOAT MILK – AN ALTERNATIVE?

As most individuals mix their protein powders with cow milk, we thought we should point out an alternative mixing medium. Aging bodybuilders, and bodybuilders from distinct ethnic backgrounds, often suffer from lactose intolerance. Some take lactose (an enzyme supplement), but another option might be goat milk. People with lactose intolerance can often drink goat milk because it forms lighter, smaller curds which are more easily digested than cow milk. Goat milk also lacks alpha S1, the major protein of cow milk, to which many people are allergic. Another consideration for bodybuilders is the fact that goat milk offers a high nutrition to caloric ratio, providing more phosphorus, niacin, potassium, calcium, and vitamin A than whole cow milk, and 15 percent less cholesterol.[9]

ADVANTAGES AND DISADVANTAGES OF PROTEIN POWDERS

If there is a disadvantage to protein powders it's their taste. Most taste awful and bodybuilders generally mix the powder with a favourite beverage such as milk or juice, although a few hardy individuals use plain water.

While it's possible to stir the powder into a glass and mix, you'll get the best results by using a blender. Using a spoon takes both time and effort, and even then much of the powder will be lumped together. A blender allows you to mix in a few seconds. Besides the powder and milk, most bodybuilders add a banana or two, and maybe a scoop of ice cream. Adding eggs is also popular, but beware. Even the freshest eggs may contain bacteria, including the ones that cause salmonella poisoning. Cooking destroys the bacteria but blending does not. Our advice is to leave raw egg eating to such movie characters as Rocky.

Perhaps the biggest advantage to protein powders is their cost. Compared to other supplements, powders are proportionately cheaper. A large container of powder that will last about a month will set you back between $20 and $30. This is relatively inexpensive compared to other products, which may cost that much for a week's serving.

TABLETS AND CAPSULES

While powders may be the most popular protein supplements, one of their disadvantages is inconvenience. Unless you have the drink premixed, you can't really use a protein powder "on the road." To address this, supplement manufacturers came up with protein sources available in tablet and capsule form.

Tablets tend to be larger, and in many cases are designed to be "chewable." That is, they can be chewed and swallowed like regular food. They don't taste as bad as their powder counterparts, but you still might want to drink a glass of water or milk to wash them down.

"I made my hands into fists and gave myself a good "punch" at the top of my stomach. Nothing. I did it again, this time even harder. Still nothing. One of the disadvantages of applying the Heimlich maneuvre to yourself is that you know when the blow is coming, so you instinctively contract your abs to resist. That makes it much more difficult to apply enough force to remove the blocked item. The third time I did it as hard as I could, and ping! The tablet flew out of my throat and hit the bathroom mirror hard."

– Greg Zulak, former *MuscleMag* editor and well-known bodybuilding writer commenting on his near-death experience at the hands of a supplement pill. Although a rare occurrence, the number of pills consumed by bodybuilders statistically increases the chances of choking to death. We advise learning the previously mentioned Heimlich maneuvre. It may save your life or someone else's.

Dorian Yates and Nasser El Sonbaty

Capsules are usually smaller and swallowed like a form of medication. This is one of the great advertising gimmicks of supplement manufacturers. The bottles tend to be "pill like" in appearance and many easily influenced individuals think that anything in a pill bottle must be doing something wonderful. Unfortunately, this creative sales technique also elevates the price. Even though tablets and capsules may contain equivalent amounts of protein, the capsules average $5 a bottle more in price.

Besides convenience, tablets and capsules offer another advantage – they're easily digested. Unlike a thick protein-powder mixture, which may take hours to digest and be absorbed, protein sources obtained in tablets and capsules require much less time in the gastrointestinal tract before being utilized by the body.

The chief disadvantage of tablets and capsules is their cost. Most are sold in bottles of 100 to 300 and cost anywhere from $15 to $30. This sounds comparable to powders but keep in mind that on average you will need to consume a couple of dozen each day (the normal practice is to consume eight to 10, three or four times a day). This means a bottle of 300 will only last you eight to 10 days – about a third as long as a container of protein powder. It's easy to see how an individual "hooked" on tablets could spend over a $100 a month on his "habit."

PROTEIN DRINKS

A third option for protein supplementation involves taking the product in liquid form. The simplest of these are protein drinks available in "pop-sized" bottles. Unlike tablets which have to be chewed or powders that need to mixed, drinks are easily consumed. Their moderate price ($1 to $3 per bottle) and convenient size make them ideal for drinking almost anywhere (on the way home from the gym being the most popular).

SIDE EFFECTS

Side effects from ingesting large quantities of protein are usually related to digestion. The most frequently reported problems are bloating and dehydration – in fact, the two are interrelated.

Bloating is the result of the digestive system taking above average lengths of time to move the food through the digestive tract. As protein digestion requires water, it is recommended that those on a high-protein diet drink eight to 10 glasses of water daily. Not only will this help facilitate digestion, but it prevents the dehydration often associated with high-protein diets.

"Notably, there is no evidence suggesting that strength athletes consuming a high-protein diet have an increased incidence of kidney disease. The data suggesting that a high-protein diet contributes to the progressive nature of kidney disease comes from people with pre-existing kidney problems."

– John Parrillo, regular *MuscleMag* columnist summarizing the data which suggests high-protein diets contribute to kidney disease.

Lambert Boehm

Many biochemists (usually those against supplementation) suggest that high-protein diets place undue stress on the kidneys and liver. While those who have existing kidney or liver problems should check with their physicians, healthy, hard-training athletes should have no problem consuming protein supplements. The extra protein is probably more of a help than hindrance.

If you experience any side effects after trying a particular protein supplement, often all it takes is a switch to another brand to solve the problem. If after trying a few different products you still have difficulties, consult your physician as you may have digestive problems. No need to be alarmed, but it's better to be safe than sorry.

> "I take more amino acids prior to a contest and I take more L-carnitine prior to a contest. I may increase my intake of B vitamins and also vitamin C."
>
> – Kathy Unger, world amateur champion.

Henderson Thorne

AMINO ACID SUPPLEMENTS

For those concerned about ingesting huge volumes of protein, biochemists have made available the individual amino acids, which can be absorbed and utilized without the negative consequences periodically associated with high-protein diets. There are generally three categories of amino acid supplements. The first are products containing all the amino acids. As we discussed earlier this is merely fancy advertising and any product containing "all" the amino acids is really nothing more than a protein source. Calling it "ultimate amino power" or some other such eye-catching name doesn't give it any special abilities over other protein sources.

The second group consists of individual amino acids sold separately. Some are touted as "growth hormone enhancers" and may boost natural productions of GH, but as we shall see this is a very controversial subject. Others, like tryptophan, are used to promote sleep and relaxation.

The third group of amino supplements lie somewhere in between and consist of two or three aminos sold together in a complex. Of these the most popular are branched-chain amino acids.

As the first group has been dealt with under the previous category of protein supplements, we will limit our discussion to the last two.

BUYER GUIDELINES

Before examining some of the aminos in more detail, a few guidelines for purchasing are in order. You may think it's only a matter of going to the health food store and plunking down $20 to $25 and that's it. Unfortunately, the major supplement manufacturers have produced a multitude of amino acid products in jockeying for the top-selling position. To the uninformed and inexperienced such a trip to the health-food store can be nothing short of a lesson in futility.

There are two basic types of free-form amino acid preparations – pure crystalline forms and peptide-bond versions. The former offer the greatest biological activity in the body and are the most effective when trying to obtain specific effects from individual amino acids. The latter are fine as a dietary supplement for increasing protein, but are not as effective for individual amino acid supplementation. Their main advantage is price, usually costing less than crystalline forms.

Another point worth mentioning is who the product was designed for. Although there are exceptions, most products designed for athletes – specifically strength athletes – are superior than cheaper versions designed for the average person.

Try to obtain products containing no added preservatives, sweeteners, or colouring agents. Not only will you be avoiding potential allergens, but many food preservatives can play havoc with your health down the road.

Without sounding too repetitive, only buy amino products designated as the "L" form. The body evolved to use this form most effectively and the "D" form is not only useless but may interfere with proper metabolism of the "L" forms.

Kathy Unger

Finally, for those living in areas where access to good-quality supplements is limited, most of the major manufacturers advertise in *MuscleMag International* and other bodybuilding magazines. For the cost of a few dollars shipping and handling (not forgetting the product's cost of course) you can buy just about any amino acid supplement out there.

AMINO ACIDS – GROWTH HORMONE RELEASERS?

No topic in bodybuilding has garnered as much attention over the past 10 to 15 years as the issue of amino acid-induced growth hormone release. In fact, the potential of specific amino acids to influence GH nearly led to many supplements being classified as drugs back in the early 1990s. Only a concentrated effort on the part of concerned citizens led to the scrapping of the proposed legislation.

The reason for the controversy was based on the results of numerous studies which found that when the amino acids arginine and orthinine were fed to individuals, levels of

"Arginine, an essential amino, is especially important to males since seminal fluids contain about 80 percent of this amino. It also helps detoxify poisonous wastes and filter out toxic substances. Arginine has a role in keeping the growth hormone healthy so an adequate supply promotes wound healing and general well-being. It has been suggested by several authorities that weight reduction and muscle building can be enhanced by its supplementation."

– Bill Starr, John Hopkin's University strength and conditioning coach and regular *MuscleMag* contributor, describing the importance of arginine to hard-training bodybuilders.

circulating GH increased dramatically. One of the first studies was carried out in the mid 1960s. The researchers gave arginine injections to healthy male and female subjects aged 17 to 35. To check the effect of arginine concentrations on HGH, the researchers divided the experiment into four subdivisions – 0, 1/12, 1/6, and 1/4 gram of arginine per pound of body-weight. After 75 studies were performed the results showed that at 1/12 gram per pound of bodyweight, females showed a rise in HGH levels but males did not. At 1/6 gram per pound of bodyweight, both groups exhibited a marked increase in plasma HGH, with females showing the largest

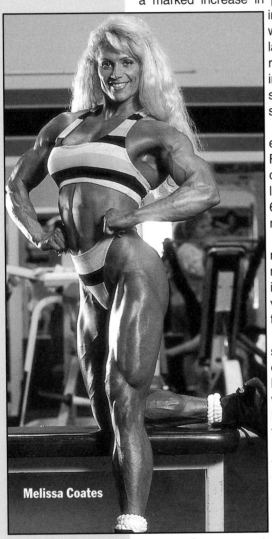

Melissa Coates

increase. Finally at 1/4 gram per pound of body-weight both groups showed similar but proportionally larger results compared to the 1/6 trial group. The researchers concluded that arginine infusion could increase HGH release and there appeared to be a sex-based variation with females being more sensitive to arginine than males.[10]

Another study, carried out in 1981, looked at the effect of arginine and lysine on HGH and insulin. Fifteen male subjects aged 15 to 20 were given one oral dose of 2400 milligrams each of arginine and lysine and blood tests were conducted after 0, 30, 60, 90, and 120 minutes. The experiment was then repeated after 10 and 20 days.

After collecting and analyzing the data, the researchers concluded that arginine/lysine treat-ment increases plasma levels of both HGH and insulin. What distinguished this study from the pre-vious is that the dosages were much lower, and taken orally rather than by injection.[11]

Another study carried out in 1982 looked at sleep-related HGH release after oral administration of arginine in concentrations of 250 milligrams per kilogram of bodyweight. Although the sample size was small (five subjects) all subjects showed a HGH peak that was 60 percent higher after arginine treatment.[12]

These last two studies are significant in that they formed the basis for much of the advertising frenzy which promoted the "anabolic effects" of arginine in the early to mid 1980s. These and similar studies helped initiate what could be called the "birth of HGH releasers."

A more recent study was carried out by Don Kelly, a regular contrib-utor to *MuscleMag International*. His experiment was part of a postgraduate honours degree, and like the previous studies, wanted to see if there was any evidence to suggest that amino acids may increase HGH release.

His subjects were nine bodybuilders who took the following "proposed HGH enhancers" on an empty stomach: 1.2 grams arginine and 1.2 grams lysine, 5 grams ornithine, 4 grams tyrosine, 3.5 grams arginine and 2.5 grams lysine, and a placebo (sugar pills). The substances were given on Saturdays and the subjects did not know which substance they were taking. Blood samples were analyzed after 0, 30, 60, 90, 120, and 150 minutes of taking the tablets. To avoid the possible interference of exercise-induced HGH release (short periods of intense exercise are known to increase HGH production), all the subjects remained sedentary throughout the experiment.

After collecting and analyzing the data, Kelly concluded that none of the amino acid preparations significantly increased HGH levels. He added that while other preparations on the market may elevate HGH levels, the odds make it highly unlikely.

GAMMA AMINO BUTYRIC ACID (GABA)

Given its popularity and alleged mechanism of action, we have decided to include GABA here, even though it is not universally accepted as an amino acid.

GABA use has increased tremendously since the early 1990s when its metabolite, GHB (see Chapter Twenty-Seven on "Natural Anabolics"), was pulled off the market. Bodybuilders use GABA in the belief that it increases plasma levels of HGH. The theory is based on the fact that GABA can act as a neurotransmitter in certain areas

Edgar Fletcher

of the brain, and one of these is the pituitary gland – the site of HGH production. Numerous medical studies indicate that when given in large doses – 5 grams or more – GABA may increase circulating levels of HGH. Other studies suggest GABA may suppress cortisol production, but the exact mechanism of action is poorly understood.

HOW EFFECTIVE?

Although not as convincing as GHB, most bodybuilders using GABA report that the supplement hardens their physiques and, in some cases, increases strength levels. Given GABA's ability to elevate mood levels, it's hard to determine if the increases in strength are genuine or placebo in nature. Reports from Sweden suggest GABA increases the effectiveness of clenbuterol, but as of yet no North American studies have confirmed this (the ban on clenbuterol makes such studies all but impossible to conduct).[104] Without sounding redundant, if GABA had the ability to significantly increase HGH levels, the odds are good to excellent the FDA would have stepped in and banned it. The fact that it's still available means GABA's effectiveness must be questioned. About all we can say is that GABA may offer a slight advantage to the user, but given the limited scientific data, we have to stop short of "highly recommending" it.

HOW MUCH?

The best results seem to be obtained when 2 grams of GABA are taken before bedtime, and another gram or two the next morning. Keep in mind these are anecdotal dosages and fall short of the megagrams used in the scientific studies. Finally, as of yet, few side effects have been reported from GABA use.

AMINO ACIDS AS GROWTH HORMONE RELEASERS – WHAT'S A BODYBUILDER TO BELIEVE?

The issue of amino acids as HGH releasers is one that will probably remain for years to come; more evidence is needed before a definite conclusion can be drawn. If you decide to try arginine, lysine, ornithine or GABA products, remember that most of the clinical trials involved injecting the amino acids in huge dosages of 15 to 30 grams. Taking a few 500-milligram tablets orally will probably not alter your HGH or insulin levels significantly. To put things in perspective, you would have to consume an average-sized bottle of amino pills to get the same dosage as used in the scientific studies. For those who like to plot numbers, a 3-ounce steak contains about 1700 milligrams of arginine and 2200 milligrams of lysine. You would have to consume eight to 10 average-size tablets to receive the same amount. And this omits the fact that steak provides all the other amino acids, plus additional nutrients.

> **"One problem with GHB is that the lethal dose is not known, and some feel that the margin between therapeutic and dangerous levels may not be acceptable. Also, if mixed in orange juice it is transformed into butyrolactone which is a very toxic compound."**
>
> – Dr. Mauro DiPasquale, regular *MuscleMag* columnist and best-selling author commenting on the potential dangers of GHB.

Josef Stefech

A final consideration concerns health. Although not conclusive, there is evidence to suggest arginine may produce replication of the herpes virus in those with the virus in the dormant stage. For those readers with such a condition, we strongly advise refraining from using arginine preparations. At the very least, check with your physician.

TRYPTOPHAN – A NATURAL CURE FOR INSOMNIA

For many, the hardest part of the day is that six- to eight-hour time period commonly termed "going to bed." For those who have never experienced insomnia, the idea of not being able to fall asleep is an alien concept. But for millions of individuals, spending hours twisting and turning between the bed sheets in an attempt to catch a few hours sleep is a traumatic experience. For such individuals, the only options are to either suffer through it, or take copious amounts of sleeping pills. The former is a poor alternative as humans need anywhere from six to eight hours of sleep each night. If you don't believe us, just notice how irritable and "cranky" you are the next time you stay up all night. Ingesting sleeping pills may knock you out, but many find they have trouble "waking up" the next day. It seems there's no happy medium.

For the average person, the previous is serious, but for a hard-training bodybuilder, not getting enough sleep ranks up there with skipping meals. Besides the restorative powers of sleep, humans need to enter the phase of sleep known as deep sleep for adequate amounts of growth hormone to be released.

In the late 1970s and early 1980s, when individual amino acid supplements first came into vogue, researchers discovered that one of the aminos, tryptophan, held great potential as a sleep inducer. And despite the bad press it received in the late 1980s, tryptophan is still regularly endorsed as a natural sleeping aid.

Tryptophan is a precursor of serotonin – a neurotransmitter found in the brain that induces sleep by decreasing blood pressure, alertness and appetite.

Tryptophan is found naturally in milk.

HOW IT WORKS

Being an essential amino acid, tryptophan cannot be synthesized by the body and must be consumed in the diet. Besides its importance as a major constituent of protein, tryptophan is a precursor of serotonin – a neurotransmitter found in the brain which influences both sleep and mental activity.

Serotonin induces sleep by decreasing blood pressure, alertness, and appetite. It was originally thought that neurotransmitters were distinct entities which could not be influenced by eating habits. The reason – the blood-brain barrier – a layer of specialized cells that line the walls of brain capillaries. These cells act as filters, only allowing oxygen to pass into the brain. Most toxic chemicals and wastes are stopped and transported back to the kidneys and liver where they are removed.

Over time researchers discovered that some substances do cross the blood-brain barrier, and amino acids are one of them. Once across the barrier, tryptophan combines with other molecule groups to produce serotonin.

MECHANISM OF ACTION

Experiments carried out in the mid 1980s (Spinweber, Korner, Carlson), have determined that tryptophan is one of nature's greatest sleep aids. Subjects who had taken 3 to 5 grams of tryptophan showed reduced difficulty falling asleep, increased total sleep period, and increased feelings of well-being.

Given its role in promoting sleep, tryptophan can be considered an indirect HGH releaser. It's generally accepted that HGH is secreted in the greatest concentration during the deepest stages of slow-wave sleep. Individuals who have trouble sleeping may never reach deep sleep, and hence their bodies are producing much less HGH. By increasing the amount of time spent in sleep, tryptophan is, in effect, fostering a more positive environment for the body to enter deep sleep; more deep sleep means more HGH release.

Besides its effects on sleep and consequentially HGH release, tryptophan has been found to be useful as a diet aid. Experiments have shown that individuals given tryptophan supplements after meals reduced the amount of carbohydrate snacking between meals. Although the exact mechanism is not fully understood, it is believed that tryptophan, serving as a serotonin agonist (stimulator), increases the brains sensitivity to certain food constituents. Experiments with animals have shown that tryptophan-fed animals reduced their intake of carbohydrate, but not protein. This suggests that serotonin production somehow increases the body's preference for protein. So promising were the experiments (Wurtman, 1978 and 1979) that it led to the suggestion of tryptophan being used as a treatment for obesity – particularly those who consume very large amounts of sweets and pastries.

"In our studies we found that a one-gram dose of tryptophan will cut down the time it takes to fall asleep from twenty to ten minutes. Its great advantage is that not only do you get to sleep sooner, but you do so without distortions in sleep patterns which are produced by most sleeping pills."

– Dr. E. Hartman, Boston State Hospital, commenting on the role of the amino acid tryptophan in promoting sleep.

Further roles of tryptophan include: reducing pain, treating depression and mania, improving sexual functioning, reducing cholesterol levels, and reducing high blood pressure.

HOW IT'S TAKEN

Tryptophan is found naturally in such foods as turkey, fish, and milk. (This is why a warm glass of milk before bedtime helps to induce sleep – increasing the temperature activates the amino acids, particularly tryptophan.) Taking

Ericca Kern

it in supplement form is best as you would have to consume a pound of turkey or fish to get the same amount provided by a couple of capsules. After all, we are talking gram ranges here. For those suffering from insomnia, 2 to 4 grams is recommended. Three-time Mr. Olympia Frank Zane finds 4 to 6 grams very beneficial.

As converting tryptophan to serotonin is dependant on many of the B vitamins (particularly vitamin B6), it is best to take both simultaneously to get the maximum benefit. In addition, many biochemists believe that vitamin C is also important in the conversion of tryptophan to serotonin, so taking extra vitamin C wouldn't hurt either.

Tryptophan also seems to be best absorbed on an empty stomach, followed by a carbohydrate meal. Carbohydrates stimulate the production of insulin, which reduces the competition from other amino acids, as it facilitates the absorption of these aminos into cells. This leaves tryptophan available for crossing the blood-brain barrier and converting into serotonin.

Like most supplements, the body can develop tolerance to tryptophan. After a while a few grams of tryptophan does not give the same results as originally obtained. For this reason it is recommended that you "go off" the aminos for a few weeks. This allows the body to normalize. When you resume taking tryptophan your body will be more sensitive to lower dosages.

SIDE EFFECTS

Although rare, some individuals may be at special risk for using high dosages of tryptophan. Research carried out by Pollack in 1986 found that high levels of serotonin may increase bronchial constriction. This means asthma sufferers should check with their physicians before taking tryptophan.

Animal experiments have found that high dosages of tryptophan may cause cataracts, but we should add that no such evidence exists for humans.

As with any substance taken in high dosages (alcohol, steroids, vitamins) some individuals may experience liver or kidney abnormalities. This usually takes long periods of time (20 plus years), but given that most bodybuilders who use tryptophan also use copious amounts of other substances, individuals should pay attention to any signs indicating liver or kidney problems.

One group of individuals who should definitely avoid tryptophan are those under treatment for depression. In such cases the medical treatment of choice are monoamine oxidase inhibitors (MAO). These drugs act by blocking the enzyme which prevents serotonin production. In short, they cause an increase in serotonin. As tryptophan does the same thing (increase serotonin production) the two substances could cause neurotransmitter levels to go through the roof. The end result of which could be dramatic mood swings.

THE GREAT TRYPTOPHAN SCARE!

Eric Alstrup

Although we touched on this one before, we feel it necessary to take a second look given its consequences to the supplement industry.

In the late 1980s, over 1500 cases of EMS (eosinophil-myalgia syndrome), including 40 deaths, were associated with tryptophan use. Included among the affected were National Hockey League goalie Mark Fitzpatrick of the New York Islanders.

EMS is a painful disorder of the white blood cells which affects both the muscle and nervous systems. In a fashion seldom seen by a government department, the US FDA banned all over-the-counter sales of tryptophan in the United States. This was jumping the gun on their part as it was later determined that the disease was not caused by the amino acid but by contamination in the manufacturing process at one Japanese plant. Antisupplement groups conveniently ignored this point and used the tryptophan incident to further their cause on the evils of "supplement drugs."

To address the growing "threat" of the dangers of supplements, the FDA proposed reclassifying most supplements as prescription drugs. Legislation was quickly drawn up and was to take effect on December 1, 1993. Only a determined effort by more rational minds (including *MuscleMag's* own Bob Kennedy) stopped the legislation from coming into being.

The implications of such laws would have been enormous. Individuals could buy unlimited amounts of tobacco and alcohol – two drugs that kill millions of people every year – but would need a doctors prescription to buy a bottle of vitamin C or amino acids!

Gordon Lavelle, Andrew Pace and Kevin Christie

To put readers at ease, let us say that tryptophan is no more dangerous than any other amino acid preparation. A few individuals may be sensitive to high dosages, but the chances of developing severe side effects from tryptophan are rare.

Having said that, free-form tryptophan is still banned in the United States for over-the-counter sale by the FDA. It is available in conjunction with other amino acid preparations, but if you want the individual form you'll have to buy it in other countries like Canada. Of course, then you run the risk of being charged with smuggling.

TYROSINE – A CURE FOR DEPRESSION?

In 1980, researchers at Harvard University's school of psychiatry wrote an article proclaiming the benefits of the amino acid tyrosine in treating depression. Led by Dr. Allen Gelenberg, the team tested tyrosine on a number of patients suffering from depression. They found that tyrosine was a more effective agent for treating depression than some of the more popularly prescribed antidepressive drugs.[13] Further research has determined that tyrosine is a precursor for many of the brain's neurotransmitters – many of which control mood swings.

As would be expected, the medical community is not unanimous on the issue of using tyrosine as an antidepressive replacement. Nevertheless, the amino is fast gaining acceptance as one of the best courses of treatment in cases of tyrosine deficiency.

L-GLUTAMINE

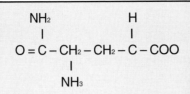

$$O = C - CH_2 - CH_2 - C - COO$$

with NH_2 on the first carbon, H on the fourth carbon, and NH_3 below.

Christa Bauch

Glutamine is another amino acid that has, in recent years, become voguish to take separately. Glutamine is the most abundant amino acid in the body and makes up over 50 percent of the intracellular and extracellular amino acids. Its functions include:

1) serving as a source of cellular fuel
2) helping to regulate protein synthesis
3) acting as a precursor to nucleotide and protein synthesis
4) boosting the immune system in times of stress
5) playing a role in anticatabolism and
6) increasing circulating levels of HGH

The role of glutamine in protein synthesis cannot be underestimated. When glutamine levels are low, other amino acids are converted into glutamine and become unavailable for protein synthesis. If, however, glutamine levels are high, other aminos won't be catabolized for conversion. Not only do high glutamine levels spare other amino acids but the evidence suggests that increased glutamine prevents the body from using muscle tissue as an amino acid source. Given such information it's easy to see why many biochemists refer to glutamine as an anticatabolic agent.

Besides its role in anabolism and anticatabolism, glutamine appears to boost the production of growth hormone. One study reported that 2000 milligrams of glutamine taken orally significantly raised plasma levels of HGH. Perhaps the study's most significant finding was that 2000 milligrams appeared to be an optimum dose. That is, anything above or below 2000 milligrams doesn't increase HGH levels any further. There appears to be an "all or nothing" mechanism of action, and 2000 milligrams is the trigger point. We should add that this is one of the few studies with these findings, and further research is needed before we can conclude glutamine is a decisive HGH releaser.

If there is a disadvantage to glutamine supplementation, it's cost. Most supplement manufacturers make the amino acid available in dosages of 50 to 200 milligrams per tablet or capsule (TwinLab's averages about 65 milligrams per capsule). To achieve the recommended amount of 2000 milligrams per day, you would need to consume 10 to 40 capsules! This means an average bottle (100 capsules) would only last about a week to ten days, depending on capsule size (less than three days if using the 50-milligram size).

There is one manufacturer producing a product with 2000 milligrams per serving and that is MuscleTech's Acetabolan. (see Chapter Thirty-Two on "Metabolic Optimizers")

OTHER AMINOS AND THEIR EFFECTS

Besides tyrosine, tryptophan, glutamine, GABA, and arginine, other amino acids are reputed to offer great benefits to the body.

In recent years it has become common practice to take any number of amino acids separately, so as to experience the benefits of each to a greater degree. Just be wary of the misguided hype by supplement manufacturers who only want your hard-earned money. Researching each amino acid is your best bet when it comes to supplementing your diet with the best products on the market.
– Paul Dillett

The following list shows a few amino acids and their potential effects:

AMINO ACID	EFFECTS
serine	Important for the production of energy and the formation of the neurotransmitter acetylcholine.
alanine	Helps regulate blood sugar and various energy pathways. Helps to prevent muscle wasting in times of stress.
arginine	Involved in the regulation of growth hormone release.
proline	Tissue repair
histidine	Aids growth hormone and other amino acids in tissue regeneration. Also involved in the production of red and white blood cells.
asparagine	Aids in the functioning of the nervous system.
aspartic acid	Helps convert carbohydrates into usable energy. Also aids the immune system by building antibodies and disease-fighting scavengers.
cystine	Plays a major role in fighting free radicals. Also promotes healing after inflammatory and tissue damage.
glutamine	Boosts production of such immune cells as lymphocytes and white blood cells. Used for fuel in long-distance sporting events. Also aids in memory, intelligence, and other cognitive functions.
lysine	Involved in muscle synthesis. Can be used for treating the herpes viruses. Combined with vitamin C forms carnitine – a fat-burning and oxygen-regulating compound.
phenylalanine	Aids the brain in such cognitive functions as memory, learning, and alertness. Is a major constituent in collagen – the body's main fibrous protein.

Lenda Murray, Shelley Beatie and Diana Dennis

CONCLUSION TO TAKING INDIVIDUAL AMINO ACIDS

Like all supplements, bodybuilders should enter into amino acid use with some degree of scepticism. If you have the cash, and are willing to experiment, give the various products a fair shake. For best evaluation, try to keep all of the variables the same for each product trial. Don't try different diets or training routines with different supplements. This way if you notice any increases in energy or muscle size you can conclude that the results are due to the supplement and not changes in other variables. If after trying most of the amino acid supplements you don't see any significant changes, re-evaluate your supplement philosophy. Why spend double or triple the money for a product that is really nothing more than another source of protein? For an equivalent amount of cash you could purchase greater quantities of complete protein.

BRANCHED-CHAIN AMINO ACIDS

The third popular form of amino acid supplements are those members of the branched-chain family. The three BCAAs consist of valine, leucine, and isoleucine. They are called BCAAs because of their unique molecular arrangement which consists of methyl side chains (CH_3) coming off the amino acid nucleus. They also come under the category of essential amino acids because they cannot be manufactured by the body and must be consumed in the diet. The importance of BCAAs to athletics was discovered from experiments carried out on monkeys. Researchers found that monkeys fed BCAAs did not experience the same degree of muscle wasting as monkeys using other amino acids. The experiments were so effective that they led to BCAAs being used in the treatment of such wasting diseases as cancer and Aids.

"Of all the supplements out there, BCAAs are certainly among the most high tech because they specifically target the metabolic problem at hand. When more BCAAs are supplied to the body, less muscle tissue is catabolized during exercise, helping to maintain positive nitrogen balance and a net gain of muscle tissue."

– John Parrillo, regular *MuscleMag* columnist and recognized authority on nutrition commenting on the importance of BCAAs to a hard-training bodybuilder.

If you decide to add BCAAs to your arsenal of supplements, start with small amounts and increase the dosage gradually. – Mike Matarazzo

A recent study published in the journal *Metabolism* compared the effectiveness of BCAAs and placebos (salt tablets) in their ability to spare muscle tissue. The results showed the experimental group (those taking BCAAs) had a sustained sparing of muscle tissue, but – and this is the part that should be emphasized – BCAAs did not appear to have any effect on protein synthesis.[14]

A more recent study adds further proof that BCAAs are very beneficial to athletes. The study, conducted at the University of Virginia, compared the time trials of cyclists covering 40 kilometers on a stationary bike. One group of cyclists used 16 grams daily of a BCAA mixture (50 percent leucine, 30 percent valine, 20 percent isoleucine) and another received a placebo. Both groups had standardized times set at the beginning of the experiment (both groups averaged 58 minutes) and were then measured two weeks later. While the placebo group improved by an average of one minute, the BCAA group lowered their time by an average of seven minutes.

Although some proponents (usually those who manufacture them) tout BCAAs as being as powerful as anabolic steroids, the truth is probably more conservative. Besides their tissue-sparing properties, BCAAs may boost anabolism. Further evidence suggests that branched-chain aminos may be oxidized during intense exercise, and contrary to popular belief, amino acids can be burned as a fuel source. Some experts suggest that anywhere from 5 to 15 percent of the body's energy requirements can be supplied by BCAAs. In fact, marathon runners probably burn more amino acids for fuel than fats or carbohydrates. This is why their physiques are thin and "stringy" in appearance. Their bodies are burning so many calories that their muscle tissue gets catabolized for fuel.

To fully understand the potential of BCAAs, a brief discussion on their mechanism of action is needed.

MECHANISM OF ACTION

When a high-protein meal is consumed, the fastest absorbed amino acids are the BCAAs. About 70 percent of all amino acids processed by the liver and released into the bloodstream are BCAAs. Once in the blood, BCAAs are rapidly absorbed by protein-craving muscles. Most studies suggest that 50 to 90 percent of the amino acids absorbed by muscles in the first three hours following a high-protein meal are BCAAs. In fact, the muscles absorb so many BCAAs that the aminos themselves begin assisting the muscles in manufacturing other amino acids. In effect, BCAAs are creating an anabolic effect in the muscles and this is why that they are lauded so highly in bodybuilding circles. The fact that BCAAs achieve this effect without the side effects associated with steroids doesn't hurt either.

In addition to assisting in the production of other amino acids, the evidence suggests that one of the BCAAs – leucine – may stimulate the production of insulin. From previous chapters we know that insulin has many important functions including increasing glucose and amino acid utilization by the muscles.

TAKING BCAAs

For maximum effect, the three BCAAs should be taken together as studies suggest taking them separately decreases the rate of absorption. In addition, high concentrations of one BCAA may actually impede utilization of other amino acids. This is not surprising as the body has evolved to strive for balance between its systems and substances utilized.

Hamdullah Aykutlu

If you decide to add BCAAs to your arsenal of supplements, you have two options open to you. First you can purchase the three aminos separately and combine them in the diet, or you can buy BCAA products that contain all three amino acids. Although most manufacturers sell BCAAs this way, it would be a good idea to shop around to see which method is cheaper.

Dr. Fred Hatfield, former powerlifting champion and regular contributor to *Muscle and Fitness* magazine, suggests that BCAAs should be taken 60 to 90 minutes after a workout. To ensure that BCAAs work effectively, take 50 to 100 milligrams of vitamin B6 daily. The only fly in the ointment is that the BCAAs actively compete with tryptophan and tyrosine. Therefore, if you are also consuming these amino acids, take them at different times. There is good evidence to suggest taking BCAAs with any high-protein meal will interfere with their absorption and effects.

With regards to dosage, take 500 to 3000 milligrams a day. John Parrillo, *MuscleMag International* columnist, and one of the world's leading authorities on bodybuilding nutrition, goes further and suggests a minimum of 10 grams per day; and going up to 20 grams per day is not out of the question. If your system is not used to amino acid supplements, start off by taking a few hundred milligrams and gradually increase over a period of a few weeks.

SIDE EFFECTS

Like most amino acid supplements, BCAAs have rarely been implicated in causing major side effects. A few individuals may have problems tolerating high concentrations, so start off slow. Don't suddenly start ingesting grams of the stuff without a trial period. It's better to find out that you're allergic to something after taking a small amount, rather than throwing your system into shock after consuming megadoses.

BCAAs are known to compete with two other amino acids – tyrosine and tryptophan – for absorption. Since the BCAAs are usually the victors, this may leave the body deficient in these two amino acids. In extreme cases this can be dangerous as both are precursors for neurotransmitters.

Another point to consider is BCAA's effects on insulin levels. Some individuals may be extremely sensitive to insulin's effects on blood-glucose levels. Instead of having energy sources available when needed, individuals may be left in a lethargic state.

FINAL THOUGHTS

As a final consideration, scientists are unsure as to the exact proportions that amino acids need to be consumed in the diet. After all, megadosing on amino acids is a relatively new phenomenon, and little data exists concerning amino acid imbalances in humans.

And since the human body evolved to utilize the balanced protein sources supplied in food, taking high concentrations of one or more amino acids may be producing biochemical states that are contraindicative to human biochemistry. It is possible that some individuals are very sensitive to high concentrations of amino acids, in which case the aminos may produce drug-like effects. This may seem extreme, but individuals should play close attention to any signals given off by the body after consuming amino acids.

> **"On the other hand, don't go overboard with a ton of various pills, capsules and tablets. Don't be one of those guys who blows his pay cheque downing 200 to 300 pills a day and who runs into various digestive problems. Extremes never work for long, especially when it comes to supplements."**
>
> – Greg Zulak, former *MuscleMag* editor offering good advice on keeping things in perspective with regards to consuming megadoses of supplements.

Ward off dehydration while training with adequate fluid intake.
– Debbie Kruck

Mike Matarazzo and
Milos Sarcev

Another issue is the effects of certain drugs on protein utilization. A number of drugs are known to adversely affect the metabolism of proteins and amino acids. Some include: glucocorticoids and the antibiotics chloramphenicol, penicillin, sulphonamides, and tetracyclines. The adrenal cortex is believed to play a central role in the development of protein-energy malnutrition, with increased blood-cortisol levels associated with malnourishment. Glucocorticoids appear to cause a depletion of muscle protein. Chloramphenicol, structurally similar to the essential amino acid phenylalanine, is believed to compete with it, causing an inhibition of protein synthesis. Chloramphenicol, penicillin and the sulfonamides may bind with serum albumin, thus interfering with the normal carrier function of serum proteins. Tetracyclines also have a profound effect by inhibiting protein synthesis, but only when used with diuretics.[15]

Since protein and amino acids may place extra stress on the body's digestive system, we suggest drinking copious amounts of water throughout the day. We suggest following the guidelines in the subsequent paragraphs.

FLUIDS

Adequate fluid replacement is important to bodybuilders because fluid in the blood carries oxygen to the muscles and takes away lactic acid. Water is also the medium in which all chemical reactions – particularly protein metabolism – occur. If you are training for a minimum of one to three hours, significant sweating is expected. Many bodybuilders become chronically dehydrated while training. Subsequently, their training sessions suffer and muscle gains are inhibited.

It is not possible to rely on thirst alone to tell you how much to drink. Your thirst mechanism may not reflect your actual fluid needs. The best way to monitor your fluid needs is by the colour of your urine. Clear-coloured urine in significant amounts indicates adequate hydration (note – amino

"Another point not to be overlooked is the simple fact that amino acids are in a balanced ratio in nature, and any time you start fooling around with nature, you usually end up on the short end of the stick. That doesn't mean that if you are trying to combat a rash of herpes with some additional lysine you're automatically going to have other problems. What it does mean is that if you start trying to take a number of aminos in high dosages, you will most likely create a deficiency in the others, and that does spell trouble."

– Bill Starr, John Hopkin's University strength and conditioning coach and regular *MuscleMag* columnist, outlining one of the disadvantages to taking individual amino acids in high dosages.

acid supplements can alter the colour and odor of your urine; therefore, adequate hydration would result in a decrease in the intensity of both odor and colour). Frequent trips to the washroom are another positive sign (note – frequent urination can be a symptom of diabetes, so be sure to have a doctor check you out, just to be on the safe side).

A professional bodybuilder weighing over 250 pounds, and lifting heavy for a two- to three-hour session may drink as much as three or four litres of water! If your workout lasts less than one hour, consuming 350 millilitres of water every 20 minutes will be fine. Weigh yourself before and after your workout. It is not unusual to lose between one or two pounds of sweat, and one pound equals 750 millilitres of water. Only use this as a guideline for fluid replacement. Some people sweat more than others. Any workout longer than an hour requires the addition of a carbohydrate (8 percent or less). The best choices are fruit juices. Even commercial soft drinks are fine, provided they are caffeine free. Caffeine is a diuretic, and thus defeats the purpose of consuming fluids. There is plenty of sodium and potassium in the average North American diet, but if you are training heavy, choose a fluid that contains 70 to 90 milligrams of sodium.[16] As a general guideline:

1) Fluids should be consumed throughout the day. A good rule of thumb is a glass of water an hour, and one or two glasses before bed (except children or those with bladder problems).
2) Drink at least 700 millilitres (or two glasses) of water fifteen minutes before you begin your workout. This immediate supply of water will enhance fat metabolism and thus spare muscle glycogen.

References

1) M. Tarnopsky and others, "Influence of Protein Intake and Training Status On Nitrogen Balance and Lean Body Mass," *Journal of Applied Physiology*, 64:1 (1988).
2) T. Galesloat and others, "Proceedings of the International Congress on Milk Proteins," Wageningen Netherlands, *PUDOC*, 1984.
3) "How Much Protein Do Athletes Really Need?," *Tufts University Diet and Nutrition Letter*, 5:8 (October 1987).
4) M.A. Tarnopsky, "Protein, Caffeine and Sports: Guidelines For Active People," *Physician and Sports Medicine*, 21:3 (March 1993).
5) "Drug World," *Flex* 12:9 (1994).
6) "Drug World," *Flex* 12:7 (1994).
7) Will Brink, "The Hidden Powers of Whey Protein Concentrate," *MuscleMag International* (November 1995).
8) G. Bounous and others, "The Influence of Dietary Whey Protein On Tissue Glutathione and Diseases of Aging," *Clin Invest Med*, 12 (1989).
9) "Try Goat Milk," *Active Canadian Journal of Health and Nutrition*, 153 (June 1995).
10) T.J. Merimee, "Arginine Initiated Release of Human Growth Hormone," *The New England Journal of Medicine*, 280:26 (June 1969).
11) A. Isidori, "A Study of Growth Hormone Release in Man After Oral Administration of Amino Acids," *Current Medical Research and Opinions*, 7:7 (1981).
12) A. Besset and others, "Increase in Sleep Related GH Secretion After Chronic Arginine Aspartate Administration in Man," *Acta Endo*, 99 (1982).
13) "Your Guide to Nutritional Supplementation," *Muscle and Fitness*, 5:7 (July 1990).
14) J. Brainum, "Advanced Nutrition," *Flex*, 14:2 (April 1996).
15) T. Basu, "Drug-Nutrient Interactions," (New York: Croom Helm Ltd., 1988).
16) N. Clark, "Fluid Facts, What, When, and How Much to Drink," *The Physician and Sports Medicine*, 20:11 (1992).

**Dave Hawk and
Laura Creavalle**

Vitamins

U ntil the early 1900s, it was believed that only carbohydrates, protein, some minerals, water and fat were needed to maintain health. It is now known that such a diet will not sustain life, and other nutritional components of food are essential.

Casimir Funk, a Polish biochemist working in London, studied the effects of beriberi, a disease caused by malnutrition. He prepared a potent antiberiberi substance from rice. Since, biochemically, it was an amine (a nitrogen-containing organic compound) and it was "vital" for life, he coined the name "vitamine." As other "vitamines" were discovered, only a few were found to be amine in nature, hence the final "e" was dropped, giving the present term vitamin.

Vitamins can be defined as chemical compounds, necessary for growth, health and normal metabolism. They may be essential parts of enzymes (organic compounds that control the rate of chemical reactions), or they may be essential parts of hormones (chemical messengers of the body). Traditionally, vitamins are divided into two categories: fat-soluble and water-soluble.

"Even though vitamin supplementation has been widely practiced by athletes, and continues to be, there are few research reports to support its effectiveness in the well-nourished athlete. A variety of studies have been conducted over the past 40 years involving vitamin supplementation and physical performance, particularly with vitamins C, E and the B-complex, and, with a few exceptions, have not revealed any beneficial effects.

– Dr. Melvin Williams, director of the Human Performance Laboratory, Old Dominion University, Virginia.

Supplementing your day-to-day diet with vitamin pills does not take the place of good nutrition.

Lee Priest knows he can't go wrong with natural food sources as they contain an abundance of vitamins.

FAT-SOLUBLE VITAMINS

These vitamins are called fat soluble because they can be stored in bodyfat. Excessive amounts of fat-soluble vitamins in the diet accumulate and are stored for use at a later time. If amounts become too excessive, they can become toxic (harmful) to such storage organs as the liver. Too much vitamin D, for example, can lead to heart disease, kidney stones, and other ailments.

"This is one hormone people should avoid consuming unless there is a clear medical reason for its use."

– Professor James Moon, commenting on vitamin D.

The principal fat-soluble vitamins are:

VITAMIN	NATURAL SOURCES
Vitamin A (retinol)	Carrots, yellow and green vegetables, fish, liver, milk and eggs
Vitamin D (cholecalciferol)*	Cod-liver oil, egg yolk, fortified milk
Vitamin E (alpha-tocopherol)	Vegetable oil, green leafy vegetables, fresh nuts, whole-grain cereals and wheat germ
Vitamin K (menadiol)	Green leafy vegetables and root vegetables, cheddar cheese, fruits, seeds, yogurt, cow milk and liver

* Vitamin D is also formed when ultraviolet rays from sunlight act on chemicals naturally present in the skin.

WATER-SOLUBLE VITAMINS

Water-soluble vitamins cannot be stored in the body to any great extent. The daily amount needed must be provided by the diet. Under some circumstances it may be difficult or impossible for an individual to obtain enough vitamins simply by eating his or her normal diet. The amount of vitamins an individual needs during illness or after surgery may be increased. A vitamin supplement may be necessary for these individuals.

The principal water-soluble vitamins are:

VITAMIN	NATURAL SOURCES
Vitamin B1 (thiamine)	Yeast, whole-grain cereals, nuts, eggs, pork and liver
Vitamin B2 (riboflavin)	Yeast, whole-wheat products, peanuts, peas, asparagus, beets, eggs, lamb, veal, beef and liver
Vitamin B3 (niacin)	Yeast, whole-grain breads and cereals, nuts, beans, peas, fish, meats and liver
Vitamin B5 (pantothenic acid)	Whole-grain products, yeast, green vegetables, cereal, eggs, kidney, liver and lobster
Vitamin B6 (pyridoxine)	Yeast, whole-grain cereals, spinach, tomatoes, yellow corn, yogurt and salmon
Vitamin B9 (folic acid)	Wheat, wheat germ, barley, fruits, rice, soybeans, green leafy vegetables and liver
Vitamin B12 (cyanocbalamin)	Clams, meat, chicken, fish, liver, kidney, cheese, eggs and milk
Vitamin H (biotin)	Chicken, yeast, liver, egg yolks, kidneys, tuna and walnuts
Vitamin C (ascorbic acid)	Citrus fruits, green leafy vegetables, potatoes and tomatoes

"Concerning the common cold, many new studies show that vitamin C can reduce its duration and relieve symptoms but cannot prevent the cold from occurring in the first place. My feeling, based on personal experience with vitamin C, is if it seems to work for you in combating your cold by all means indulge."

– Marla Duncan, regular *MuscleMag* columnist and women's fitness champion responding to a reader's question about vitamin C's effects on the common cold.

VITAMIN REQUIREMENTS AND EXERCISE

Taking vitamin supplements does not take the place of good nutrition. The body needs other substances such as carbohydrates, fats, proteins, and minerals for adequate nutrition. However, the North American diet has resulted in many individuals that are overfed yet undernourished.

Considerable misinformation and exaggeration regarding the relationship between vitamins and exercise exists. Vitamins are not a source of energy. Coaches, magazines, fitness journals and even the media send the message that high levels of vitamins are needed by hard-training athletes. This begs the question, "Does vitamin supplementation improve athletic performance?"

Numerous studies have examined the effect of large doses of vitamin supplements on endurance and performance. In virtually all cases the researchers concluded that no single vitamin or combination of vitamins had any effect on performance. After 40 years of research there is no conclusive evidence to suggest that vitamin supplementation improves performance in individuals whose diets are nutritionally adequate. Of course the key word here is "adequate," and common sense should tell you that a deficiency in any vitamin could lead to a decrease in performance or worse – health problems.

A NEW APPROACH

Researchers have recently focused their efforts on the role of specific vitamins and their effect on exercise, paying particular attention to vitamins B3, C and E. Once again, the researchers concluded that these vitamins, used as supplements, were of no benefit in improving athletic performance if the athlete receiving the supplement was following a balanced diet.

But we must point out that these researchers made one strategic error – they administered vitamins in a single large dose, or in more than one large dose daily. If a large dose is taken at one time, the result is decreased absorption and increased excretion. For example, if vitamin C is taken in doses of 100 milligrams or more, less will be absorbed than if a dosage of 50 milligrams is taken. Therefore, vitamin supplements should be taken in low dosages, several times a day.

If vitamins do not affect exercise (under certain conditions), does exercise affect vitamin requirements? There is evidence to suggest exercise or the use of certain performance-enhancing drugs may indeed increase the body's need for certain vitamins such as C, B2 and B6. As an example, anabolic steroids rapidly deplete the body of vitamin B6; therefore, bodybuilders using steroids should take extra B6 to replenish what's lost. Further, each of the principal vitamins required by our bodies performs a specific function that no other nutrient can. Vitamins trigger the release of energy in the body, and manage the way the body assembles tissues and uses food.

There is evidence to suggest exercise or the use of certain performance-enhancing drugs may increase the body's need for certain vitamins.

Citrus fruits – loaded with vitamin C!

Here is a partial list of some important vitamins and their functions:

VITAMIN	FUNCTIONS
Vitamin A (retinol)	Aids night vision and helps prevent eye disease, promotes bone growth in infants and children, and helps maintain the mucous membranes in the ears, nose, and intestinal lining.
Vitamin B1 (thiamine)	Helps regulate appetite, maintain a responsive nervous system (necessary for the synthesis of acetylcholine, a neurotransmitter), and releases energy from carbohydrates (acts as a coenzyme for 24 different enzymes involved in the carbohydrate metabolism of pyruvic acid to CO_2 and H_2O).
Vitamin B2 (riboflavin)	Aids food metabolism (component of certain coenzymes involved with carbohydrate and protein metabolism), promotes healthy skin, and helps the body use oxygen.
Vitamin B3 (niacin)	Involved in fat metabolism (during lipid metabolism it inhibits the production of cholesterol and aids in fat breakdown), tissue respiration, and the conversion of sugars to energy (essential coenzyme concerned with energy-releasing reactions).

VITAMIN	FUNCTIONS
Vitamin B5 (pantothenic acid)	Acid is a part of coenzyme A, which is essential for the transfer of pyruvic acid into the Kreb's cycle during protein metabolism. It is also involved in the transformation of amino acids and fats into glucose and the formation of cholesterol and steroid hormones.
Vitamin B6 (pyridoxine)	An essential coenzyme for amino acid metabolism and may function as a coenzyme in fat metabolism. It assists in the production of circulating antibodies.
Vitamin B9 (folic acid)	Part of the enzyme systems which synthesize the purines and pyrimidines built into RNA and DNA. This vitamin is necessary for normal production of red and white blood cells.
Vitamin B12 (cyanocbalamin)	A coenzyme necessary for red blood cell formation and to manufacture the amino acid methionine and the neurotransmitter precursor choline. It is also responsible for the entrance of some amino acids into the Kreb's cycle during the metabolism of proteins. This vitamin has a positive effect on the metabolism during exercise, particularly when oxygen levels are low. Certain drugs interfere with B12 and may limit its effectiveness: codeine, oral contraceptives, the antibiotic neomycin, chloramphenicol, aspirin and aspirin substitutes.

Flex Wheeler, Michael Francois and Charles Clairmonte

VITAMIN	FUNCTIONS
Vitamin B15	Aids metabolism in the myocardium (the thick inner layer of the heart wall) by increasing creatine levels in the layer while dilating the venous vessels. This vitamin also helps prevent the deposition of fat in the liver. A recommended dosage based on European standards is 100 mg daily.
Vitamin C (ascorbic acid)	Helps form collagen, the substance that binds body cells together. This acid promotes many metabolic reactions, particularly protein metabolism, and is essential to the growth and repair of teeth, gums, blood vessels, and specialized bone cells. This vitamin works with antibodies and, as a coenzyme, may bind with poisons, rendering them harmless.
Vitamin D (cholecalciferol)	Vital for absorption and utilization of the minerals calcium and phosphorus from the GI tract. There is also evidence to suggest the vitamin may work with the parathyroid hormone which regulates calcium metabolism.

"New studies have shown a vigorous workout can cause severe damage to the body's cells if vitamin E levels are low. Vitamin E helps bolster antioxidant defences and protects against cell damage from molecules known as free radicals, which increase during exercise and have been linked to cancer, heart disease, cataracts, arthritis and aging."

– The late Bruce Page, commenting on the role played by vitamin E in helping ward off free-radical damage.

Have you considered vitamin-E supplementation? The benefits to the hard-training athlete are well worth considering.

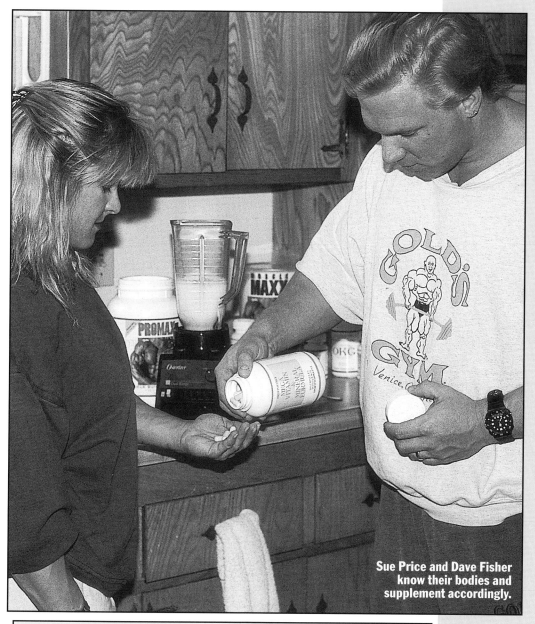

Sue Price and Dave Fisher
know their bodies and
supplement accordingly.

VITAMIN	FUNCTIONS
Vitamin E (alpha-tocopherol)	Involved in the manufacture of RNA, DNA, and red blood cells. It behaves as a cofactor in several enzyme systems. Vitamin E works as an anti-oxidant and prevents the enzyme action of peroxidase on the unsaturated bonds of cell membranes, and protects red blood cells from dissolving.
Vitamin H (biotin)	A vital coenzyme for the conversion of pyruvic acid to oxalocetic acid and in manufacturing purines and fatty acids.

VITAMIN MEASUREMENT

Water-based vitamins are measured in milligrams (mg). Fat-soluble vitamins are measured in International Units (IU), a standard of measurement used throughout the world. In the United States the system of measurement used that approximates IU is the United States Pharmacopoeia Units (USP). The IU and USP measure activity; thus, the weight varies with the vitamin.

VITAMIN	MEASUREMENT
A	1 IU = 1 USP = 0.6 mcg
B	1 IU = 1 USP = 0.003 mg
C	1 IU = 1 USP = 0.05 mg
D	1 IU = 1 US. = 0.000025 mg
E	Varies with the tocopherol:
dl-alpha tocopherol acetate	1.00 IU = 1 mg
dl-alpha tocopherol	1.10 IU = 1 mg
d-alpha tocopherol acetate	1.36 IU = 1 mg
d-alpha tocopherol	1.49 IU = 1 mg

Yolanda
Hughes

VITAMIN SUPPLEMENTS

Next to protein, vitamins are among the most popular bodybuilding supplements. There are generally three categories of vitamin supplements. The most commonly used in North America are multivitamin tablets which contain all the known vitamins in addition to other important nutrients like minerals. Prices range from $5 to $20. Given the importance of vitamins in the diet, manufacturers have made available children's versions shaped like cartoon characters (the "Flintstones" being one of the most popular brands). While we maintain that following a healthy diet should provide sufficient vitamins for just about everyone, giving growing children a one-a-day vitamin makes good sense.

A second category of vitamins are products containing two or three vitamins. The most common of these are sold as "B-complex + C." Other versions in this category may contain some of the B-complex vitamins and vitamin C, or combinations of some of the fat-based vitamins. Although it varies, prices range from $5 to $15.

The third category of vitamin supplements are single vitamin products. Go into any drug or health-food store and you will see shelves filled with the whole vitamin alphabet. There are advantages and disadvantages to taking vitamins in this manner. The primary advantage is the dosages involved. If you feel (or even better, have it verified by a physician or nutritionist) that you need extra amounts of a given vitamin, such products are the ideal solution. In most cases one tablet or capsule supplies more than enough for a day. As a word of advice, try to purchase products containing 50 to 250 milligrams of vitamin C. The 500- to 1000-milligrams versions sound better, but remember your body can only use 30 to 50 milligrams of vitamin C at one time. For every 1000-milligram tablet of vitamin C taken, about 950 milligrams is excreted. In short, you are wasting your money and producing the most expensive urine in town.

Before looking at the disadvantages of taking vitamins we should touch on the latest delivery method for taking vitamin C – transdermal skin patches. These patches allow the skin to directly absorb vitamin C, which results in a rejuvenation in the skin's appearance. Wrinkles and stretch marks are said to disappear, and skin takes on a youthful appearance. This would obviously have appeal for bodybuilders who overdo the sun-tanning beds, or are simply getting older. A three-month supply will cost about $125 in American currency. Be aware that there are no hard scientific studies to back these claims, and that once the patches are discontinued, skin returns to it's previous condition.

There are two primary disadvantages to taking individual vitamin supplements. Fat-based vitamins are not excreted like water-based vitamins, and as such are stored. Although rare, it is possible for these stores to reach toxic levels. We suggest taking fat-based vitamins no more than once a day, and for some individuals, every second day might be a better idea.

The second disadvantage could be called "playing with the unknown." No one knows for sure what the long-term effects are for taking high doses of one vitamin. Even though vitamins have been

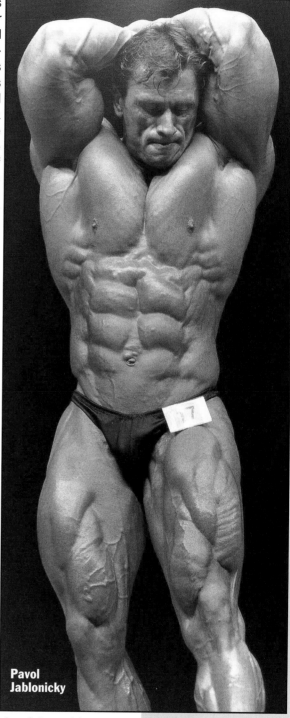

Pavol Jablonicky

around for over 50 years, the practice of megadosing followed by many bodybuilders (and other athletes we might add), is new territory. Given the body's habit of trying to maintain equilibrium, it is possible that high doses of one vitamin may interfere with levels of other vitamins. Or they might throw off other body systems. As an example, taking iron supplements with vitamin E reduces the amount of vitamin E absorbed by the body. Our advice is to use vitamins as just that – supplements, not drugs.

CHAPTER SIXTEEN

Minerals and Trace Elements

Besides protein and vitamins, most bodybuilders consume vast amounts of minerals and trace elements in their attempt to maximize performance, but as with vitamins, much of the information out there is misleading. Supplement manufacturers would have you believe that high doses of individual minerals will take the place of performance-enhancing drugs, but this is just not the case. Their rationale being if a mineral has a given effect in the body (that is, chromium stimulates insulin release, and iron helps blood cells carry oxygen), additional amounts of the mineral will magnify these effects. While a few studies suggest that this may be true (in isolated cases), the body has a set rate for given metabolic operations, and once sufficient mineral levels are present, additional amounts will make no difference.

We know this is not what many of you want to hear but it's a fact. The names of these nutrients should give you an indication of how much you need. Unless you have been diagnosed with a deficiency, or fall into a

> **"Manganese can strengthen connective tissues, prevent injuries, and decrease fatigue."**
>
> – The late Bruce Page, nutrition consultant.

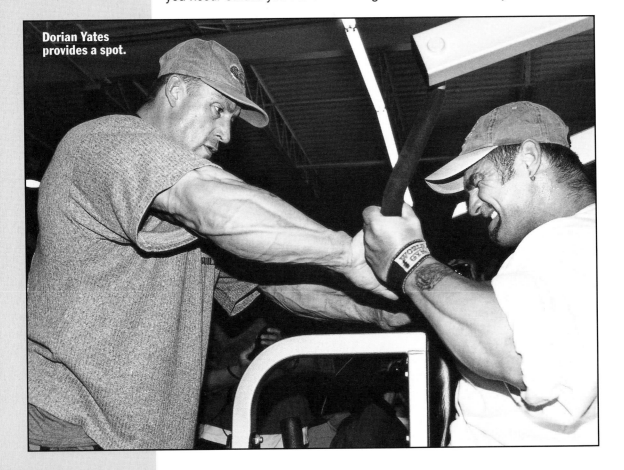

Dorian Yates provides a spot.

high-risk group (pregnant women, post-menopausal women, marathon athletes), there is probably no need to consume mineral supplements. A balanced diet can provide an ample supply of minerals and trace elements.

WHAT THEY ARE

There is a clear and important distinction between the terms "mineral" and "trace element." If the body requires more than 100 milligrams of an element each day the substance is called a "mineral"; if on the other hand the body requires less than that amount, the element is called a "trace element."

Minerals (elements such as iron or magnesium) can be defined as inorganic substances. They may appear in combination with each other, or in combination with organic compounds. Minerals constitute about four percent of the body's total weight, and they are concentrated most heavily in the skeleton. Some elements are known to be essential in the diet and must be consumed frequently, while others are only needed in trace amounts.

WHAT THEY DO

Minerals are element substances required for growth, maintenance and repair of the body. They help supply oxygen to cells, modify digestive processes, and help maintain osmotic pressure. In addition, minerals participate in the proper functioning of the nervous and muscular systems. Those "electrolytes" that you hear so much about are nothing more than electrically charged mineral atoms (called ions) involved in maintaining the body's various electrochemical systems. The main electrolytes in the extracellular fluid are sodium, calcium, and chloride, while in the intracellular fluid, potassium, magnesium, and phosphorus are the most common. For optimum functioning, electrolytes must be kept in proper balance.

Claude Groulx

Milos Sarcev, Chris Cormier and Claude Groulx

The following are examples of minerals and trace elements and their functions:

MINERAL	FUNCTIONS
Calcium	Essential for blood clotting, muscle and nerve activity, and bone and teeth formation.
Chlorine	Maintains water balance, pH balance of the blood, forms HCl in the stomach, and is involved in maintaining cellular osmotic pressure.
Magnesium	Part of many coenzymes, essential for muscle and nerve activity, involved in bone formation, and required for protein and carbohydrate metabolism.
Phosphorus	Involved in the transfer and storage of ATP. Part of the buffer system for the blood. Essential for muscle contraction and nerve activity, is a component of DNA and RNA, and is involved in bone and teeth formation.
Sodium	Part of the bicarbonate buffer system, and strongly affects distribution of water in the extracellular fluid.
Sulphur	Part of many proteins and hormones (including insulin) and some vitamins (including biotin and thiamine). It therefore helps regulate bodily activities.

TRACE ELEMENT FUNCTIONS

Cobalt
Component of B12, which is needed for the stimulation of erythropoiesis (the production of red blood cells).

Copper
Part of an enzyme required for melanin-pigment formation. Essential for the synthesis of haemoglobin.

Iodine
Needed by the thyroid gland to form two hormones which regulate metabolic rate: triiodothyronine and thyroxin.

Iron
Part of the coenzymes that form ATP from catabolism. Part of haemoglobin that carries oxygen to the cells.

Zinc
Part of enzymes involved in growth.

Chromium
Enhances the effect of insulin in glucose utilization. Helps transport amino acids to heart and liver cells.

Manganese
Necessary for growth, reproduction, lactation, haemoglobin synthesis, and essential for the activation of several enzymes.

Kevin Christie, and Andrew Pace watch as Gordon Lavelle blasts out one last rep.

DEFICIENCIES AND SOURCES

Because most minerals are widely distributed in foods, severe mineral deficiencies in the general population are unusual in developed countries, although it is seen in specific groups of individuals. If a deficiency occurs, it may be just as fatal as total starvation. This is because when the body excretes wastes, it must also excrete a certain amount of salt in the process. It is important to eat a well-balanced diet, so that the approximately 30 grams of mineral salts lost daily through excretion are replaced. The following is a list of the principal minerals and trace elements and some of their natural sources:

MINERAL	NATURAL SOURCES
Calcium	Green leafy vegetables, shellfish, egg yolks and milk
Chlorine	Meat, fish and table salt
Magnesium	Wheat germ, soybeans, green leafy vegetables, nuts, sunflower seeds and fish
Phosphorus	Nuts, dairy products, fish, poultry and meat
Sodium	Meat, fish and table salt
Sulphur	Beans, eggs, cheese, fish, poultry, lamb, beef and liver

If you're a competitive bodybuilder, keeping your sodium/potassium ratio in balance is imperative.

TRACE ELEMENT	NATURAL SOURCES
Cobalt	Clams, meat, liver, kidney, cheese, eggs and milk
Copper	Barley, mushrooms, oats, whole-wheat flour, beans, asparagus, spinach, beets, eggs, fish and liver
Iodine	Cod-liver oil, iodized table salt, seafoods and sunflower seeds
Iron	Whole-grain products, cashews, beans, dried fruits, cheddar cheese, egg yolks, shellfish, caviar, meat and liver
Zinc	Yeast, whole-grain products, soybeans, sunflower seeds, fish, poultry and meat
Chromium	Whole-grain products, fresh fruits, potato skins, seafoods, poultry and meat
Manganese	Barley, bran, buckwheat, ginger, coffee, spinach, peas and peanuts

IMPORTANCE TO ATHLETES

While mineral deficiencies are rare in the general population, athletes may be at special risk – especially if training outdoors. To a bodybuilder who trains all-out, hot summer weather is a time for concern as increased sweating often leads to a rapid loss of electrolytic minerals. Many cases of dehydration-related deaths are more often related to mineral loss than fluid loss.

One mineral athletes may become deficient in is iron. This is especially true for female athletes. One study investigating iron deficiency in Olympic athletes found that 5 percent of the female and 2 percent of the male athletes had iron deficiency anemia (a decrease in certain elements of the blood).[1] In another study, involving 18 adolescent female cross-country runners, it was found that 50 percent had either iron deficiency or iron deficiency anemia. It was suggested that irregular and unbalanced diets of the athletes may have contributed to the condition. An explanation suggested was that athletes lose more than a normal amount of iron through the feces, urine, sweat, and/or menses.[2] A further study, found that runners are likely to lose more iron through sweating than the average person.[3]

Another mineral, calcium, may be needed in greater amounts when individuals follow high-protein diets. Studies suggest that those who eat high-protein diets, but don't consume enough calcium, may force their bodies to draw on calcium reserves to neutralize the excess acid produced by protein metabolism. The loss of calcium from the bones (the body's chief calcium reserve) puts the individuals at greater risk for developing such degenerative conditions as osteoporosis. While most bodybuilders consume adequate amounts of calcium in the diet, older members of the sport, especially females, may want to take some sort of calcium supplement.

"Researchers think the kidneys work overtime to neutralize the acid by drawing on extra calcium and salts in the bloodstream. This greater demand for calcium due to high-protein diets puts such people at higher risk for osteoporosis, or accelerated bone loss."

– The late Bruce Page, commenting on the importance of calcium to those that consume high-protein diets.

Lenda Murray displaying awesome form once again.

Exercise may also cause large increases in excretion of chromium, zinc and copper. Without proper amounts of these trace elements, many metabolic processes are altered, possibly affecting athletic performance. There is, however, no evidence to indicate that taking large doses of these trace elements will improve health or athletic performance.[4]

FINER POINTS FOR COMPETITIVE BODYBUILDERS

Perhaps the most important time for paying attention to mineral levels is in the weeks leading up to a contest. Right before competition bodybuilders should become concerned about their sodium and potassium levels. Many contestants feel they must totally eliminate sodium from their diets. This is a fallacy as you need some sodium – between 500 and 1000 grams a day – to look hard and full. The goal is to obtain that amount from the food you eat, without going over.

The skill is keeping your sodium/potassium ratio in balance. By eating natural complex carbohydrates you take in high amounts of potassium. Once potassium levels increase, the delicate sodium/potassium ratio is changed, and the body compensates by increasing production of aldosterone – the body's primary hormone for regulating electrolyte levels. If sodium levels are low, you'll appear flat and smooth on contest day. Conversely, too much sodium will cause most bodybuilders to "hold" water and all that hard-won muscularity will be blurred by a layer of water under the skin (for a more in-depth discussion on water balance during the competitive season, see the section on carbohydrate loading).

Another way to disturb your electrolyte balance is to drink unpurified water sources. While most city water is filtered before distribution, it may contain high levels of sodium and calcium. If competing in an unfamiliar city with unknown water sources, bring your own water with you. If water in your own town or city has caused fluid retention in the past, buy distilled water (water with all the minerals removed). Of course, this is only applicable close to a contest. During the off-season you'll need regular water for the mineral content (one of the primary reasons humans need water to survive).

MINERAL CHELATES

Many mineral supplements are available in the form of chelates. Chelate is from the Latin word for "claw." A chelating agent is a substance that can engulf molecules of a metal. This process, called chelation, involves an amino acid donor atom bonding to a mineral ion through co-ordinate covalent bonds, forming a ring-like molecule. This mineral complex is defined as a mineral chelate. Mineral ions are not directly absorbed by the body. They must be chelated before they can be absorbed across the intestinal villi into the bloodstream. The digestive process does this, but mineral chelates are more readily absorbed than conventional mineral supplements because the chelation step can be skipped.

MINERAL AND TRACE ELEMENT SUPPLEMENTS

Mineral supplements are generally divided into three categories – those sold as part of a multivitamin, sold separately or sold as electrolyte drinks. The multivitamin forms are probably the best value for your dollar as most contain all the essential minerals and trace elements in the most appropriate amounts. One word of advice, since magnesium requires the presence of calcium for action, choose a mineral supplement that contains magnesium in an equal amount or at 70 percent of the amount of calcium.

Individual supplements are primarily designed for people who have specific deficiencies, although one, chromium, is very popular with many bodybuilders. (see Chapter Twenty-Seven on "Natural Anabolics, Anticatabolics and Hormone Boosters.) Other popular supplements are iron and calcium – iron for female athletes and pregnant women, and calcium for individuals with thyroid problems.

Electrolyte drinks, while high in most of the major mineral electrolytes, are poor sources of other minerals and trace elements. Most bodybuilders consume them for their designed purpose – replacing lost fluids and minerals during intense exercise. While marathon runners definitely benefit from such replacement, a typical bodybuilding workout should not deplete electrolyte levels to deficiency levels. If you are lucky enough to train outdoors, replacing fluid levels is an absolute must.

SHARK CARTILAGE

Although not thought of as a supplement, shark cartilage is one of the best sources of minerals available. Sharks belong to the class of fish known as Chondrichthyes. This class is made up of fish with cartilaginous skeletons. Cartilage is a connective tissue. It is found in the human body on the surfaces of skeletal joints, ends of ribs, the tip of the nose, the ears, the vertebral disks, the larynx

If you train outdoors consume fluids regularly so as not to dehydrate. You may even want to consider an electrolyte drink. – Paul DeMayo

"All of them, preferably in a multiple mineral tablet. It's a convenient way to get what you need and the multiple tablet ensures that you cover all the bases."

– Bill Starr, John Hopkins University, strength and conditioning coach responding to a question about which minerals are best to take.

and trachea. Cartilage cells secrete a hard rubbery matrix around themselves. This makes cartilage elastic, flexible and strong. Shark cartilage is made from the skeletons of freshly harvested sharks. This source of cartilage is low in fat and contains mucopolysaccharides, collagen, calcium, phosphorus and protein. It is believed that these components can restore and protect the joints.

CONCLUSION

We must stress that just because you consume a high-quality mineral supplement does not mean you will somehow boost the body's muscle-building abilities. Yes, if you have a deficiency in one or more minerals, supplementing makes sense, but the body has its own agenda, and those multivitamins and mineral supplements will have their fates decided at the cellular level. Further, megadosing on minerals may be dangerous for some individuals. The only thing we can say with any certainty is that the odds for developing greater muscle mass can be shifted by consuming high-quality foods, supplementing where necessary, and creating a metabolic demand through heavy exercise.

References

1) J. Dewijn and others, "Haemoglobin Packed Cell Volume, Serum Iron, and Iron Binding Capacity of Selected Athletes During Training," *Journal of Sports Medicine*, 11 (1971).
2) E. Haymes, "Nutritional Concerns - Need For Iron," *Medicine Science in Sports and Exercise*, 19:5 (1987).
3) P. Pulev and others, "Dermal Excretion of Iron in Intensely Training Athletes," *Clin. Chim. Acta*, 127 (1983).
4) W. Cambell and R. Anderson, "Effects of Aerobic Exercise and Training on the Trace Minerals Chromium, Zinc, and Copper," *Sports Medicine*, 4 (1987).

"According to new research from the University of Illinois, megadosing on calcium supplements can be detrimental to your health. The trace elements that are present in many calcium supplements can be poisonous, producing symptoms very similar to Parkinson's disease, researchers found. And trace metals were detected in nearly all the commercial supplements and antacids tested. While these trace elements are harmless if taken in normal doses by healthy people, they can be toxic if taken in huge doses by the elderly or by people with kidney problems."

– The late Bruce Page, commenting on the potential dangers of mineral and trace-element supplements.

Flex Wheeler

Melissa Coates

Carbohydrates – The Much Maligned Nutrient

N ext to protein, few other nutrients have received as much body-building press as carbohydrates. Unlike protein, however, where the general consensus is that hard-training bodybuilders need more than sedentary individuals, opinions vary on carbohydrate require-ments. Some experts suggest that it should comprise 75 to 80 percent of the diet, while others recommend no more than 25 to 30 percent. The debate still rages, yet most will agree that serious bodybuilders will hamper their progress if their diets are deficient in carbohydrates. Unfortunately, there are good and bad forms of carbohydrate. In the following chapter we shall examine some facts and myths about this all-important nutrient.

Your diet should provide you with an ample supply of complex carbohydrates.

Jean-Pierre Fux

Carbohydrates are the major source of energy for most cells because cells have the specific equipment to break down these compounds more easily than others. Carbohydrates contain carbon, hydrogen, and oxygen, with twice as much hydrogen as oxygen.

Carbohydrates are generally classified according to their molecular structure. The simplest are called monosaccharides, from the Greek words "mono" meaning one, and "saccharin" meaning sugar. Just as amino acids build larger structures, so too are monosaccharides used in the construction of more complex sugars. Unlike their larger sugar cousins, monosaccharides cannot be broken down by hydrolysis into smaller subunits. Examples of monosaccharides include glucose, fructose, and ribose.

Working up the ladder of carbohydrate complexity we find disaccharides – the combination of two monosaccharides. Such molecules are produced by a process called dehydration synthesis – the loss of water molecules to produce large organic molecules. Typical reactions that produce disaccharides from monosaccharides include:

$$\text{Glucose} + \text{fructose} \longrightarrow \text{sucrose} + \text{water}$$
$$\text{Glucose} + \text{galactose} \longrightarrow \text{lactose} + \text{water}$$

Note that in each case water is formed from the addition of two monosaccharides. The reverse can also occur – a disaccharide can be broken down into two monosaccharides by the addition of water. This process is called hydrolysis. One common example is:

$$\text{Maltose} + \text{water} \longrightarrow \text{glucose} + \text{glucose}$$

We should add that both hydrolysis and dehydration synthesis are reversible reactions which occur on a continuous basis in the human body.

> "I recommend that you include a maltodextrin-based supplement in your nutrition program. This is the ultimate carbohydrate formulation to add to the proper nutrition of lean proteins, starchy carbohydrates and fibrous carbohydrates. Maltodextrin is a complex carbohydrate derived from starch with a low-glycemic index (ranging from 22 to 29), meaning that it is released into the bloodstream more slowly than simple sugars."
>
> – John Parrillo, regular *MuscleMag* columnist commenting on maltodextrin, one of the best carbohydrate sources available for bodybuilders.

The most complex form of carbohydrates are polysaccharide chains (from the word "poly" meaning many). They are formed by dehydration synthesis and may be hundreds or thousands of monosaccharide molecules long. For bodybuilders and other athletes the most well-known polysaccharide is glycogen.

Sue Price

GLYCOGENESIS VERSUS GLYCOGENOLYSIS

Unlike many nutrients which are excreted if not used by the body (water-based vitamins being the best example), glucose that is not needed immediately is removed from the blood and stored in the skeletal muscles as glycogen. Glycogen is a macromolecule made up of highly branched chains of glucose molecules. This process of converting glucose into glycogen is called glycogenesis.

The process of glycogenesis involves a number of intermediate steps – all of which are assisted by specific enzymes. The whole process is stimulated by insulin produced in the pancreas. Excess glucose that cannot be stored in the liver or muscle cells is usually converted into fat and stored as dreaded adipose tissue. (see Appendix 4 for glycogenesis.)

When the body needs extra glucose, the above procedure is reversed and stored glycogen is reconverted into glucose by a process called glycogenolysis. Glycogen breakdown occurs in the liver cells under the control of two hormones – glucagon from the pancreas, and epinephrine from the adrenal medulla. Both hormones cause the activation of the enzyme phosphorylase to convert glycogen to glucose-1-phosphate. A couple of additional intermediary steps lead to the end product of glucose-6-phosphate, which can be used as an energy source or converted into free glucose to enter the bloodstream. (see Appendix 5 for glycogenolysis.)

HOW THEY ARE USED BY THE BODY

Although biochemists have their own system for classifying carbohydrates, nutritionists generally use two broad categories – simple and complex. Simple carbohydrates are more commonly known as sugars and are found in high concentrations in fruits and in such junk foods as candy and soft drinks (refined sugar). Simple sugars are released into the bloodstream immediately, causing a rapid increase in blood-sugar level and an insulin surge. Because simple carbs are released faster than the body can burn them for energy or store them as glycogen, insulin causes the excess to be converted to fat.

Complex carbohydrates may be subdivided into two categories – starches and fibrous carbs. Some of the best sources of starchy carbs include whole-grain breads, pasta, and beans. Examples of fibrous carbs include lettuce, spinach, and broccoli. One of the advantages of fibrous carbs is their high-cellulose content – the tough, plant material which gives plant cells their rigidity. Unlike herbivores, humans cannot digest cellulose and most of it passes through the intestines as bulk. Another role for fibrous carbs is to slow the digestion of starchy carbs, resulting in a more gradual release of insulin and a more sustained release of glucose into the bloodstream.

Starches, fiber, and sugars are grouped together under carbohydrates because of their similar chemistry. Such an association has given starch a bad name over the years, but all carbohydrates – irregardless of being complex or simple – are made up of simple monosaccharide molecules. For example, the combining of glucose and galactose produces lactose – the simple sugar found in milk. So even though we don't think of milk as being "sweet" it does contain a type of sugar.

Of all the carbohydrates used by the body, none play as vital a role as glucose. The brain and nervous systems are fueled almost exclusively by glucose. In addition, the muscular, digestive, immune, and respiratory systems all rely on glucose for energy. Any glucose not immediately used is stored by the body in the form of glycogen. Later, when energy stores are needed, the glycogen is transformed back into glucose and released into the bloodstream.

DOES ORIGIN MAKE A DIFFERENCE?

Given that glucose is the end product of both starches and sugars, it may seem that source is not an issue. But holding to such beliefs will only swell your waistline by many sizes.

If you make a habit of eating cake and pies – two foods loaded with simple sugar – your blood-sugar levels swing from one extreme to the next. Parents of small children know all about the perils of hot chocolate before bedtime. And elementary school teachers can add their own tales of recess candy.

Besides the swings in blood-sugar levels, simple sugars are one of the biggest

Flex Wheeler and Kevin Levrone

contributors to tooth decay. Junk foods high in simple sugars are almost always loaded with fat, and low in such nutrients as minerals and vitamins. So although it may taste better, a piece of strawberry shortcake can't compete nutritionally with a nice juicy grapefruit or slice of honeydew melon.

Although bashed repeatedly over the years, some of the best carbohydrate foods are bread and pasta. The old beliefs that such foods are "fattening" has given way to a more realistic appraisal of their benefits. Perhaps the biggest drawing card to whole-wheat breads and pasta is their lower fat levels than simple-sugar foods. In addition, not only do such starchy foods help satisfy the appetite, but it takes more calories to digest them than other carbohydrate sources.

All would be well and fine if you could eat a few chocolate bars and then hit the gym for an energized workout. But unfortunately it doesn't work that way. And while all carbohydrates produce varying degrees of energy, the time and type of carbohydrate eaten determines whether your workouts are lethargic or resemble Dorian Yates' on a good day!

Dorian Yates

Let's say you do load up on refined sugar just before your workout. In theory, this may make sense but here's what really happens. As soon as the body detects an increase of glucose in the bloodstream, the pancreas boosts the production of insulin to metabolize it. If only a given amount was removed there would be no problem, but as is usually the case, too much sugar is extracted from the bloodstream. And since removal generally peaks about an hour after eating, it typically falls right in the middle of a workout. Instead of energy to spare, you are left in a sluggish and slothful state.

For those planning on obtaining their carbohydrates from fruit, a few words of caution are needed. Although fruit is a much preferred substitute for cake and chocolate bars (it's high in fiber, low in fat and calories, and a great source of vitamins and minerals), there are two groups of individuals who may want to limit or avoid fruit altogether in their diets – competitive bodybuilders and those trying to maximize fat loss. This may seem like a contradiction of just about everything you've read. But as you shall see, fruit has one important property that makes it a poor source of carbohydrates – it gets stored as fat.

One of the leading authorities on nutritional needs of bodybuilders is regular *MuscleMag International* columnist, John Parrillo. He has studied carbohydrate metabolism extensively and concluded that fruit is not all that it's cut out to be. In working with some of bodybuilding's elite, Parrillo recommends they cut fruit from their diets. Although criticized by some, much of what he says is based on sound biochemistry.

Much of Parrillo's scepticism towards fruit originated from studies he conducted on competitive bodybuilders. He found that when fruit was substituted for rice in the diet, the bodybuilders got fat. The bodyfat was not due to an increase in calories because he paid meticulous attention to caloric totals throughout the studies. Instead it appeared to be due to some intrinsic property of the fruit itself.

As Parrillo adds, about 80 to 90 percent of the calories in fruit are supplied by the simple sugars fructose and glucose. And while some fruits like grapes and oranges contain a lot of glucose, most fruits provide the bulk of their calories in the form of fructose. And here's where the problem originates. Unlike other carbohydrate sources, which are usually stored as glycogen, fructose is rapidly converted to fat by the liver. The reason this happens is that fructose skips one of the regulatory steps in carbohydrate metabolism.

When carbohydrates are consumed in the diet, they are used by the body for many different purposes. Some are lost in the form of heat – one of the end products of basal metabolism. Other carbohydrate calories are used to perform work during day-to-day living. Any energy left over is then stored as glycogen in the muscles and liver. Once these storage areas are full (as every "container" has a set limit) the rest is converted to fat by the liver and transported by the bloodstream to adipose tissue. The enzyme responsible for this is called phosphofructokinase-1 (PFK-1), and is the determining factor in whether or not carbohydrates are stored as glycogen or fat.

Competitive bodybuilders and those trying to maximize fat loss should limit their intake of fruit and fruit juices.

> **"Notably, not all carbs are created equal. Complex carbohydrates that are broken down slowly are more effectively stored as glycogen than are simple sugars, which are released into the bloodstream faster than they can be converted to glycogen. This means some of the simple sugars will be converted into fat and "spill over" into bodyfat stores. Also, fructose is famous for its tendency to be converted to fat, and that's why I recommend limiting fruit and juice in your diet."**
>
> – John Parrillo, regular *MuscleMag* columnist commenting on the differences between simple and complex carbohydrates.

An average human can store anywhere from 300 to 600 grams of glycogen, depending on skeletal muscle mass. This sounds significant, but, in energy terms, is really only 1000 to 1600 calories – a modest amount that doesn't even meet the body's sedentary daily needs.

Given the body's relatively small storage capacity for glycogen, it's easy to see how excess carbohydrate can easily get stored as fat. Compounding the problem is the type of carbohydrate consumed. This brings us back to fructose. Unlike other sugars, fructose is not influenced by PFK-1, and instead of being directed towards glycogen storage, is converted by the liver into fat. Now you see why a competitive bodybuilder dieting for a contest should think twice about regularly including fruit in his or her diet. Such starchy foods as pasta and rice on the other hand are stored almost entirely as glycogen, which not only serves as an energy source for hard-working muscles, but also keeps bodyfat levels down.

NOT TO BE MISLED

Now before nutritionists and biochemists confront us, we must add that the previous recommendations are primarily aimed at elite competitive bodybuilders who are trying to bring their bodyfat levels down to the three to five percent range. For the aspiring bodybuilder trying to gain muscle mass, or the endurance athlete burning thousands of calories daily, regularly including fruit in the diet makes perfect sense. Fresh fruit is highly recommended by most nutritionists and dieticians. But as soon as maximizing fat loss becomes a priority, fruit consumption should be reduced or even eliminated.

APPLICATIONS TO BODYBUILDING AND OTHER SPORTS

On average, a hard-training bodybuilder can go "all out" for 60 to 90 minutes. A few hardy individuals may maintain energy levels for another 30 minutes, but for the most part, two hours is the maximum amount of time

Spaghetti – the ultimate starchy carb!

that energy levels can be maintained. In caloric terms this works out to about 1000 calories an hour or 2000 calories for an intense workout. This two-hour time limit is primarily determined by glycogen stores.

As we saw earlier, an average person can store about 400 grams of glycogen (about 1600 calories worth) in the skeletal muscles – most of which is burned up in 60 to 90 minutes. In theory, two minutes of isometric exercise could deplete a muscle's entire glycogen supply, but the build up of lactic acid and the accompanying pain forces the individual to terminate the set before this happens. Instead, it usually takes 10 to 15 minutes of 4 or 5 sets of intense exercise to deplete a given muscle's glycogen reserves. As most bodybuilders hit three or four major muscles per workout (even if they're only focusing on one or two) it's easy to see where the 60 to 90 minutes for total glycogen depletion comes from.

Once muscle-glycogen supplies are depleted, the body has one additional source of glycogen before drawing on fat reserves for energy. Biochemists now know that the liver can act as a glycogen storehouse and be called upon

Michael Francois

in times of intense exercise. When skeletal-muscle glycogen levels are depleted, the liver adds its own small supply. The liver actively synthesizes new glycogen from amino acids as the need requires.

Once all of the previous sources of glycogen are used up, general body tiredness sets in. The commencement of fatigue is generally quick, and in the space of a few minutes the individual's whole body has taken on a feeling of lethargy. Instead of energy to spare the person can only go through the motions, and even this becomes a chore after a few additional sets.

ENERGY SUPPLIED

Numerous experiments have determined that carbohydrates are the body's preferred fuel during exercise; and over 99 percent of the carbohydrates available are used by the body to produce ATP. ATP is not stored by the body so it serves as an immediate and direct source of fuel for muscle contraction. Elsewhere in the book we discussed the two primary pathways for ATP production – aerobic and anaerobic metabolism. Without repeating ourselves here, suffice to say aerobic respiration involves the use of oxygen and produces 36 ATP molecules, while anaerobic respiration does not use oxygen and only produces 2 ATP molecules. In addition, anaerobic respiration produces the by-product lactic acid, which in high concentrations interferes with muscle contraction (more on this later as well).

Laura Creavalle

POSTWORKOUT CONSIDERATIONS

Perhaps the most significant aspect of glycogen metabolism is that it's discriminating. In competitions were athletes compete more than once a day (judo, wrestling, track and field), glycogen stores in exercised muscles may not sustain energy levels in the next day's competition – even if total glycogen stores have not been drained. It generally takes the body 24 hours to restore glycogen levels to 85 to 90 percent of their maximum – at a rate of four to five percent per hour – provided adequate rest and carbohydrates are provided. For full recovery at least 48 hours are required. For bodybuilders this works out to two to four days rest between individual muscle groups. For many, even this is not enough and hitting the same muscle more than once every five to six days is too taxing.

What all of the previous means is that for maximum recovery and full glycogen repletion, bodybuilders should strive to consume a high percentage of complex carbohydrates in their diet. Why complex? Because as we said earlier, refined sugars (simple) can send your insulin levels through the roof. And if much of the carbohydrate is in the form of fructose, you have the issue of fat storage to consider.

Two hundred grams of simple sugar will have a much different effect on your body than 200 grams of a complex carbohydrate like starch, even though both contain 200 grams of carbohydrate.

Remember, our ancestors did not have candy bars and cake available to them, and hence the human body evolved to make use of naturally occurring carbohydrates.

There may be those among you who raise the results of studies which indicate that glycogen replenishment following exercise is the same no matter what the source (complex versus simple) of carbohydrate. This is true but only for the first 24 hours. During the second 24 hours athletes consuming complex carbohydrate have significantly more muscle-glycogen synthesis.

THE MOST EFFICIENT RATE OF CARBOHYDRATE CONSUMPTION

Given the complexity of carbohydrate metabolism and its importance to athletics, it's not surprising that numerous studies have been carried out to determine the optimal rate of carbohydrate ingestion.

These studies consisted of giving athletes varying concentrations of carbohydrate supplements every two hours following intense exercise. As a general summary the following table lists the amounts given and the rates of glycogen resynthesis as expressed in percentage form.

AMOUNT OF CARBOHYDRATE	RESYNTHESIS RATE PER HOUR
25 g every two hours	2 percent
50 g every two hours	5 percent
100 g every two hours	5 percent to 6 percent
225 g every two hours	5 percent to 6 percent

The researchers concluded that for optimum glycogen synthesis athletes should consume 50 grams of carbohydrate every two hours. It was possible to elevate resynthesis rates to nine percent by giving athletes 28 grams of carbohydrate every fifteen minutes, but the effect only lasted for short periods of time.

To test the theory as to whether or not intravenous glucose may boost resynthesis rate, researchers gave infusions containing 100 grams of glucose every two hours. They found that the rate could be elevated to seven to eight percent, but given the limitations of such a procedure, this was deemed an impractical procedure for athletes.

Bodybuilders should strive to consume a high percentage of complex carbohydrates in their diet for maximum recovery and full glycogen repletion after a strenuous workout. – Joanne Lee and Bruce Patterson

DAILY CARBOHYDRATE RECOMMENDATIONS

Before giving our recommendations for total carbohydrate needs, we should point out that biochemists and nutritionists have varied opinions on the issue. Even among bodybuilding experts there is widespread discontent. Finally, like most things in life, what works for one bodybuilder may not work for another. It takes many years of trial and error to determine the best nutrient ratio for achieving optimum competitive shape. So while we are going to give general recommendations, don't be surprised if your experience tells you to modify our values.

Generally speaking, bodybuilders and other hard-training athletes would be advised to consume 60 to 70 percent of their diet in the form of carbohydrate. To determine the amount of carbohydrate from total caloric intake, multiply total caloric values by .6 or .7. For example, if you are consuming 5000 calories a day, .6 X 5000 = 3000 or .7 X 5000 = 3500 calories which should be consumed in the form of carbohydrate. To convert this value to grams simply divide by 4 (there are four calories in one gram of carbohydrate). Using the previous example, 3000/4 = 750 grams.

Jay Cutler

Melissa Coates

As with protein consumption, individuals should try to consume carbohydrates in small, 50- to 100-gram portions rather than one or two large meals. Not only does this promote better utilization, but it greatly reduces the chance of it being stored as fat. The following table lists carbohydrate amounts for total caloric-intake values ranging from 1000 to 10,000 calories a day.

Total Caloric Intake	Calories of Carbohydrate	Grams of Carbohydrate
1000	700	175
2000	1400	350
3000	2100	525
4000	2800	700
5000	3500	750
6000	4200	1050
7000	4900	1225
8000	5600	1400
9000	6300	1575
10,000	7000	2500

WHEN TO EAT AND OTHER PRACTICAL CONSIDERATIONS

Biochemists and exercise physiologists have determined that during the two-hour period following exercise, muscle-glycogen synthesis takes place at a rate of seven to eight percent per hour. Although this is slightly higher than the normal rate of five percent per hour, it still isn't very rapid. Yet for an elite athlete engaging in intense exercise – such as a pro bodybuilder following a double-split routine – this two-hour time period allows quicker recovery before the next training session. To take advantage of this, bodybuilders should consume at least 50 grams of carbohydrate as soon after exercise as possible. Further, they should ingest at least 50 grams every two hours until they eat a larger meal.

Paul Dillett, Vince Taylor and Kevin Levrone

"As far as carb-loading and depletion are concerned, I'll deplete for three days, cutting my carb intake by about 50 percent, going from 400 down to 200 calories from carbs. To replace these calories, which is impor-tant, I'll increase the protein. Some people make the mistake of cutting the carbs but not replacing calories, so they burn muscle tissue. I never go to zero carbs."

– Dorian Yates, six-time Mr. Olympia.

With regards to type, researchers have not found any significant differences between liquid and solid carbohydrate sources. One consider-ation for intense-training athletes is that the source not be bulky and cause discomfort. It should be pliable, quickly ingested, and not interfere with training sessions. A large pasta meal before squats is definitely not recom-mended.

CARBOHYDRATE DEPLETION AND LOADING

We would be negligent if we left the topic of carbohydrates without some mention of depletion and loading. Those familiar to the sport have probably noticed how some competitors look small and flat one day, and full and vas-cular the next. In the space of 12 to 24 hours their bodies have taken on an entirely different appearance. Many pros will tell of "missing their peak" and while displaying mediocrity on contest day, show up for the post-contest photo shoot in outstanding shape. The difference is sometimes so remarkable that individuals placing out of the top five at the contest may be in better shape than the winner the following day. The biological mechanism behind this phenomenon involves glycogen levels and the amount of water that the muscles are holding. If the timing is exact, bodybuilders may step onstage as big as a house and have the hardness to go with it. Miss their peak and they look small, soft, and resemble the Pillsbury doughboy. Here's the bio-logical explanation for how it works.

As you should know by now the stored form of glucose is glycogen. What we didn't discuss earlier was that glycogen can hold four times its weight in water. For every gram of glycogen, the muscle contains four grams of water. Many bodybuilders take advantage of this and start depleting their glycogen stores to abnormally low levels, about a week before the contest.

The most common practice is to train for three days following a low-carbohydrate diet, completely depleting the muscles of glycogen. Then, for the next three days the bodybuilder rests and consumes a high-carbohydrate diet. This "loads" the muscles with as much glycogen as possible, increasing water storage and leading to the much-coveted increases in size and vascularity.

MuscleMag columnist John Parrillo cautions against totally depleting glycogen levels. If you drain the muscles of all glycogen reserves, the body may start catabolizing muscle tissue as a fuel source, with the result being losses of muscle size. As a general guideline Parrillo suggests reducing carbohydrate intake so that you lose the muscle pump about three quarters of the way through your workout. For most bodybuilders this works out to between 100 to 300 grams of carbs per day – an adequate amount to deplete glycogen reserves without going overboard leading to catabolism (another suggestion is to make liberal use of branched-chain amino acids).

With regards to training, it is recommended bodybuilders train all the major muscle groups to the point of depletion a few days before carb-loading. This is because glycogen depletion/loading is selective (that is, training legs will promote loading in the legs but not the arms, shoulders, etc. For maximum effect use high-rep sets until you lose the muscle pump).

THE BEST SOURCES

Complex carbs seem to be more effective in replenishing glycogen supplies than simple sugars. Such sources as brown rice, yams, and potatoes are loaded with complex carbs and as would be expected, do a better job promoting glycogen synthesis. They do this by being released slowly into the blood and maintaining elevated insulin levels, which in turn promotes glycogen synthesis. Simple sugars on the other hand are often stored as fat – the last thing a competitive bodybuilder wants.

ON THE REBOUND

What makes the practice of carbohydrate loading so effective is a phenomenon known as the "rebound effect." By a necessary property of evolution, following periods of low-carbohydrate ingestion, the body stores above normal levels of glycogen when carbohydrate supplies are once again available. This is a survival response left over from the early days of our evolution when periods of famine were common. As the body "thinks" it's in a state of starvation it

If you cut carbs out of your diet completely, and drain the muscles of all glycogen reserves, the body may start catabolizing muscle tissue as a fuel source.

stores carbohydrate in the form of glycogen as soon as it becomes available. Bodybuilders make use of this rebound period and try to time things so that they hit the stage carrying the fullest muscles possible.

PRACTICE MAKES PERFECT

The whole process of glycogen replenishment can take as little as 12 hours or as much as 72 hours. Such variation means that two bodybuilders may need different time periods to fully reglycogenerize their muscles. Few get it right the first time; therefore, it's quite common to see bodybuilders appear flat at the prejudging but arrive for the evening show looking like a totally different person. By then it's usually too late as the greater part of the competition took place at the prejudging. Unfortunately, many in the audience were not at the prejudging and have only the competitor's evening appearance to go by. They can't understand how such a huge and ripped physique could place so low. In many cases there's a chorus of boos following the low placings of some competitors. Those that witnessed the prejudging realize what has happened but the "evening crowd" is left in a state of bewilderment.

Perhaps the greatest change in appearance takes place overnight, but interestingly enough the reason is as much behaviour as physiology. With few exceptions, most bodybuilding competitions are concluded with what could be called the "post-show pigout." After months of paying meticulous attention to diet, it's only natural that bodybuilders will leave the stage and head for the nearest restaurant. In many cases the organizers have a formal banquet with unlimited amounts of food. What ever the source, most enjoy themselves and give themselves a long overdue food feast. For the winners of the contest such overindulging makes no difference. But to those who missed their peak and hadn't fully "topped up" their glycogen levels, waking up the next morning can be a frustrating experience. Instead of the

Kevin Christie, Andrew Pace and Gordon Lavelle

drawn, stringy appearance of the previous day, they look in the mirror and see the physique that probably would have given them the title, or at the least put them in the top three. But their only consolation is knowing they can file such knowledge away for next year.

Claude Groulx

Of course there is another side to carbohydrate loading. The desired goal is to carry the maximum amount of glycogen which will swell muscles to the fullest. If too much carbohydrate is consumed the extra sugar may be stored in the body's tissues. Besides the muscles and veins, excess water will accumulate under the skin, causing a bloated, fat appearance. All that hard-won muscularity will be blurred. This is the main reason why bodybuilders who look smooth at the prejudging often appear ripped at the evening show. All that posing and sweating under the lights drains the excess water, thus allowing the bodybuilder's true muscularity to show through.

We should add that many top pros no longer follow the depletion/load procedure. They find they achieve the best results by gradually shedding small amounts of water in the weeks leading up to the contest. For many, the drastic swings in glycogen levels would only hinder their contest preparations.

For those wanting to carb-load without ingesting huge amounts of carbohydrates, John Parrillo has an alternative solution. He bases his technique on gluconeogenesis – the synthesis of glucose from noncarbohydrate sources like protein and fat. As discussed earlier, this process occurs in the liver, the other primary glycogen-storage site besides the muscles.

John recommends eliminating high-rep sets and following a training routine based on heavy sets. He also recommends cutting aerobic activity by 50 percent. Added to the previous is a form of stretching known as fascial stretching. It involves stretching between exercise sets with special stretches, aggressive in their range of motion. This stretches the tissue surrounding the muscle allowing more room for the muscle to grow.

Parrillo's final suggestion is to use a slow-release carbohydrate supplement like maltodextrin. Maltodextrin is a complex carbohydrate derived from starch. It is released slowly into the bloodstream. This keeps energy levels high for your entire workout without the extra amounts being stored as fat.

While Parrillo's technique goes against the accepted practice in bodybuilding, many of his "pupils" are having great success with it. It's possible that in the years to come, carb-loading without "carb-loading" will become the norm.

Jay Cutler

> "Carbohydrate drinks can be a benefit to some, taken before, during, and after a hard workout. Sipping on a carb drink is an easy and effective way to get those carbs your body craves. Not only do carbohydrate drinks supply extra calories for those trying to gain weight, but they also enhance the amount of fuel available to your muscles during a workout by building glycogen stores."
>
> – Greg Zulak, former *MuscleMag* editor commenting on the benefits of carbohydrate supplementation.

IS IT FOR ME?

You will have to make up your own mind as to whether carb-loading is for you, and like most aspects to bodybuilding, the solution is experimentation. Only you can determine what's best for your individual physiology. It may take 12 hours to fully carb-load, or it may take close to a full week. Or you may prefer to give John Parrillo's method a try. Don't be surprised if it takes two or three contests to get it right, but the results will be worth it.

CARBOHYDRATE SUPPLEMENTS

Given the importance of carbohydrates to hard-training athletes it should come as no surprise that supplement manufacturers have developed a broad spectrum of carbohydrate products. Whether or not you decide to use them is a personal decision. The evidence suggests that as long as you receive adequate amounts of carbohydrate, it makes little difference as to whether or not the source is natural or in supplement form. Further, the evidence is inconclusive as to the effectiveness of consuming mega amounts of carbohydrate. Some studies suggest that athletes who take carbohydrate supplements hold a competitive advantage. Other studies are less specific and show little advantage to supplementation. About all we can say is that athletes involved in high-energy-burning, marathon sports (running, hockey, and cycling) would probably benefit from carbohydrate supplements. Athletes in sports lasting less than 60 to 90 minutes of intense exercise (bodybuilding, wrestling, judo) will have to decide for themselves. Don't be surprised if sipping carbohydrate drinks during your workouts makes little difference to your intensity level. As we discussed earlier, natural stores will last for 60 to 90 minutes. True, going beyond this time limit will necessitate additional energy stores, but this brings up the issue of overtraining. Given the trend these days of shorter but more intense workouts (followed by such superstars as Dorian Yates, Lee Labrada, Mike Francois, and Aaron Baker) it probably makes little sense to force additional hours of training out of the body by using carbohydrate supplements.

The bottom line – replace glycogen levels as soon as possible after a workout. If you can achieve this using natural sources (pasta, potatoes, oatmeal, etc.) so much the better. Not only are natural sources more likely to be complex in nature, but they also contain large amounts of vitamins and minerals.

Conversely, most carbohydrate supplements contain simple carbs and are low or absent in other essential nutrients. If they do have an advantage it's their convenience. Most can be eaten (sports bars) or swallowed (liquid forms) without any prior preparation. For a bodybuilder in the middle of a workout or driving to or from the gym, this holds a great advantage over cooking pasta or oatmeal; for this reason alone you may want to try them.

For those intent on taking carbohydrate supplements, they fall into three categories – powders, liquids, and sports bars.

Gayle Moher

POWDERS

The powdered forms are similar to protein products but are far easier to mix. Instead of a blender, you can mix one or two tablespoons of your favorite beverage into a glass with a spoon. While most contain simple and complex carbs, many of the more popular powders contain more than just carbohydrates. Besides the carbs, you get electrolytes and vitamins, and in some cases even 25 to 30 milligrams of inosine (claimed to increase ATP production).

To give an example of the complexity of modern carbohydrate powders, we'll take a closer look at one of the more popular – Weider's Carbo-Energizer. This product contains three types of carbohydrates – glucose for quick energy; fructose for longer lasting energy; and maltodextrin for slow release into the body. Such a combination of carbohydrates means that energy levels can be maintained over a prolonged period of time. Body-builders experiencing sluggishness during their workouts may want to take such a product about 30 minutes before their workouts, or immediately afterwards. The fructose content should be taken into account by those dieting for a contest.

LIQUIDS

Most liquid carbohydrate drinks are descendants of a product developed by Dr. Robert Cade in 1967. Through experiments conducted on university football players, Dr. Cade came up with a drink containing carbohydrates and electrolytes. To honour the university where most of the experiments were conducted – the University of Florida – Dr. Cade called the drink Gatorade after the university's nickname, the Gators. Within a short period of time the drink was commercialized and few sporting events are seen these days without the familiar green bottles nearby (it's even become a tradition to dump the container's remaining contents over the coach after a successful game). Even with competition from other major manufacturers, Gatorade is still the largest selling athletic drink in the United States.

For all the praise it receives, Gatorade has a few serious drawbacks – chief of which is its concentrated sweet taste. Many athletes find the product too syrupy to consume and there are frequent reports of stomach cramps and nausea. To address this, sports researchers have developed a whole spectrum of products that provide different degrees of electrolytes and carbohydrates. Modern energy drinks are absorbed rapidly and won't upset the stomach.

Liquid forms are usually available as ready-to-drink beverages or in concentrates which must be diluted with some other liquid. The ready to drink versions are usually sold under names containing such fancy terms as "carbo," "energize," and "fuel." Don't let the names mislead you. They all contain the same ingredients – varying degrees of sucrose, glucose, and fructose. The biggest advantage to these drinks is their convenience. No mixing, cooking, or dicing. Just take off the cover and drink away. The fact

The convenience of ready-to-drink carbohydrate supplements means quick and easy replenishment.

that these drinks contain an abundance of fresh water doesn't hurt either. Not only does sipping on such drinks provide a source of energy during a workout, but they also keep you from becoming dehydrated.

As would be expected, there are various types of liquid carbohydrate supplements on the market. The best forms for quick energy are those consisting of glucose polymers. Without going into the actual biochemistry, glucose polymers are absorbed faster because of their lower osmotic activity (osmosis is the process where water moves across a membrane from an area of high concentration to an area of low concentration). Carbohydrate products with high-osmotic activity tend to be absorbed much slower.

Although individual experimentation plays a role, you should start drinking the carb beverage 10 to 15 minutes into your workout. If you start too early your body will respond by increasing insulin levels, leading to the dreaded hypoglycemia-induced drowsiness. Exercise on the other hand slows down insulin release so it's all right to drink the carbs during your workout.

Don't drink the whole bottle in a few massive "chugs." This is not a fraternity house party. Sip the beverage slowly throughout the workout, and if you have any remaining afterwards, drink it on the way home. Not only will this increase utilization more effectively, but you won't run the risk of developing stomach cramps.

SPORTS BARS

Sports bars are fast becoming one of the most popular forms of carbohydrate, but keep the following in mind. Most contain fructose as the main ingredient. For example, John Parrillo examined 26 of the more popular sports bars on the market and found 25 of the 26 contained fructose. The reason for this is manufacturing cost. The two main sources of carbohydrate for sports bars are corn syrup and fruit juice. Both of these substances are plentiful, cheap, and from a selling point of view – very sweet. But as we discussed earlier, fructose is a poor carbohydrate source for serious bodybuilders. It makes far more sense to buy products that use rice dextrin (a short-chained glucose polymer made from rice) as the main ingredient. This gives you the energy you need without the potential conversion to fat.

SIDE EFFECTS

Like most essential nutrients, carbohydrate supplementation poses little risk to healthy individuals. Excess carbohydrate calories will lead to increases in bodyfat levels, and therefore all the

Albert Beckles

risks that are associated with such, but this applies equally to other main food nutrients (protein and fat).

Carbohydrate supplementation is only dangerous to individuals with pre-existing medical conditions, and chief among these are diabetics. Given the nature of diabetes, individuals who plan on using carbohydrate supplements, or even those contemplating a diet high in carbohydrates, should only do so after first consulting with their physicians. In most cases controlling diabetes is dependant on striking a balance between blood-sugar and insulin levels. Suddenly consuming a high-glucose supplement could throw this delicate balance off and lead to drowsiness, a diabetic coma, or even death.

Reference
1) M.J. Davis and others, "Carbohydrate-Electrolyte Drinks : Effects On Endurance Cycling In the Heat," *American Journal Of Clinical Nutrition,* 48 (1988).

"Be aware that many sports bars and carbohydrate supplements contain fructose. Why? Because corn syrup and fruit juice are quite cheap, and they're also very sweet."

– John Parrillo, regular *MuscleMag* columnist offering good advice to those intent on using sports bars as a source of carbohydrate.

CHAPTER EIGHTEEN

Desiccated Liver

I t only seems appropriate to begin this chapter with the one individual who has done more to promote desiccated liver than any other. Long-time readers of *MuscleMag* should be very familiar with the writing's of California's late Vince Gironda. Often called the "Iron Guru," Vince is regarded by most as one of the sport's most knowledgeable – although at times eccentric – experts. Unlike many in the sport, Vince has developed his vast pool of knowledge from over fifty years of practicing and teaching bodybuilding. Long before Gold's, World, or Powerhouse gyms, Vince's Gym in North Hollywood was regarded as the place to train, and it was quite common for the major studios to send their stars to Vince's for a crash course in "physique improvement."

The focal point to Vince's training philosophy was adequate nutrition. In fact Vince has gone down in history as saying bodybuilding is 80 percent nutrition! While many regard this figure as too high, few can argue with the results Vince achieved over the years. Long before pharmacology took hold in the sport, competitors from Vince's gym routinely took home the awards for "most muscular."

The late Vince Gironda

In many respects Vince was ahead of his time with regards to bodybuilding nutrition (he even "lost" a contest because the judges thought he was too muscular!). In the days before TwinLab, MET-Rx, and Cybergenics, Vince routinely advocated the copious use of supplements, and one of his favorites was desiccated liver. In the following chapter we will take a closer look at this long-time bodybuilding supplement, paying particular attention to the qualities that make it such a valuable training aid.

Desiccated liver is animal liver (usually beef) concentrated by vacuum drying at low temperatures. As most manufacturers use defatted liver, these supplements are very low in the fat that you would otherwise get from eating regular red meat. According to Vince, desiccated liver is four times as potent as whole liver, and "has more going for it than any other bodybuilding supplement."

WHAT IT CONTAINS

Because of the manufacturing process, desiccated-liver products contain all the nutrients and enzymes of the parent source – including large amounts of B-complex vitamins – without the high levels of fat. Perhaps desiccated liver's greatest assets are its high concentration of protein (up to 80 percent useable by some estimates), and its high levels of heme iron – something few other protein supplements provide.

The importance of iron in the diet is often overlooked by hard-training bodybuilders. Heme iron is important because it is the best absorbed of all iron sources. The primary function of iron is to help bind oxygen to red blood cells. It does this by forming a heme complex consisting of iron and porphyrin. The resulting structure forms an integral part of the binding protein hemoglobin. It is the heme complex that gives red blood cells their characteristic red color.

Besides hemoglobin, iron is a major component of myoglobin – the oxygen-binding protein found inside muscle cells. Without adequate supplies of iron, both oxygen transport systems (hemoglobin and myoglobin) would be seriously impaired. A third major role of iron is to facilitate enzymes involved in the electron transport chain – the series of biochemical reactions which allow cells to use oxygen. Iron also helps bring oxygen from the lungs to the muscle cells, transports it across cell membranes into the cells, and modulates the rate at which it is burned by the cells. A very important mineral indeed!

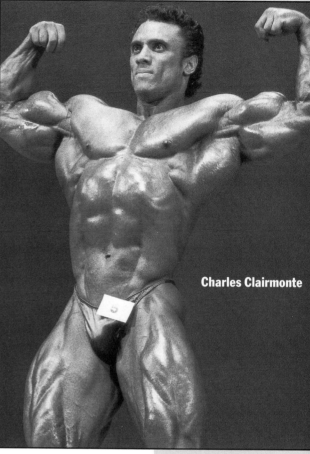

Charles Clairmonte

IRON DEFICIENCY – A HOST OF REASONS

According to many sources, including the prestigious journal, *Scientific American*, iron deficiency is the most common nutritional deficiency in the world. And this doesn't just apply to third-world countries. Some estimates suggest 20 to 22 percent of North American women are iron deficient. The reason women have higher needs for iron is because of the amounts lost during menstruation (the primary reason why many physicians recommend women take an iron supplement).

Besides normal physiology, athletes may be at special risk for developing iron deficiency (often called sports-related anemia). One of the few disadvantages to vegetarian diets is their inadequacies in supplying iron. Although many plant sources contain significant amounts of iron, it is poorly absorbed. Athletes who follow low-meat diets to lose weight or keep bodyfat levels low may not be receiving adequate amounts of iron.

A third reason for iron deficiency concerns the amounts lost during exercise. Hard-training athletes lose enormous quantities of fluid during exercise. Contained in the fluid are a wide range of substances, from harmful bacteria and respiratory wastes, to water and mineral salts. Numerous studies have confirmed that iron is one of the main constituents of sweat.

"Liver is one of the oldest known supplements and if you take enough combined with the BCAAs, I swear you'll notice a difference within three or four days of taking them. You'll have more energy, more strength, and a bigger pump. I've put a lot of people on a similar dosage, and they come back less than a week later and tell me how incredible they are feeling."

– Terry Mitsos, former Mr. Australia and Mr. World commenting on the powers of desiccated liver tablets.

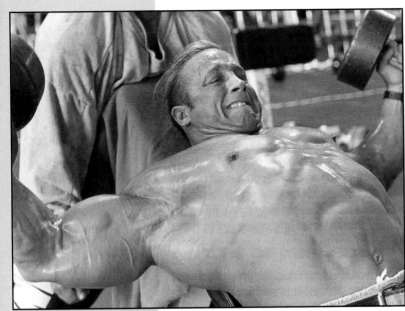

A final reason for deficiency involves the way we prepare our food. Most food is either cooked at home or super-heated in the manufacturing process. This one variable alone may reduce iron bioactivity by as much as 50 percent.[1] So even if the food you eat is high in iron, the preparation techniques may destroy much of its usefulness.

IMPLICATIONS FOR BODYBUILDERS

Given its biological importance, yet potential for deficiency, it's imperative that athletes receive adequate amounts of iron. Yet for all the reasons outlined, many are still deficient in this all-important mineral.[2] Female athletes are at increased risk, especially female bodybuilders in the weeks leading up to a contest.

> With the emphasis during the precontest season on training intensity and calorie reduction – especially of red-meat products – it's possible that many bodybuilders border on iron deficiency.
> – Craig Titus

Given the amount of red meat eaten by most bodybuilders, it's unlikely that many are suffering from iron deficiency – at least in the off-season. But the precontest season is another matter. With the emphasis during the precontest season on increasing training intensity but reducing calories – especially red meat – it's possible that many border on iron deficiency. Vegetarian bodybuilders and females should be concerned about iron levels.

With the best sources of iron (at least in terms of absorbable forms) also being the highest in fat, the natural alternative is to use an iron supplement. There are a wide range of iron sources out there, but iron alone does not appear to correct sports-related anemia. The condition is often related to both iron levels and protein amounts, and here's where desiccated liver comes in. Besides being loaded with heme iron, it contains protein that is in many respects superior to many of the commercially available protein sources. The fact that it also contains other important nutrients like vitamins is an added bonus.

HOW TO TAKE

The amount of desiccated liver taken depends on such factors as age, level of training, and energy requirements. The late Vince Gironda recommended beginners start with six tablets per day – spread over three main meals. Intermediates should take six tablets per meal, and add an extra tablet a week until they are taking double the starting dosage. On average Vince has his advanced bodybuilders take 50 to 100 tablets a day for a period of a couple of weeks. Like most supplements Vince recommended gradually building up to this amount. He also advised stopping the supplement for a few weeks to allow the body to normalize (a practice the Russians also follow).

Vince's suggestions for advanced bodybuilders may seem extreme but he swears by the results (with no reported side effects). The advantage of taking such large dosages of liver tablets is that you can consume huge amounts of protein and other nutrients without having to eat great quantities of food.

A FINAL WORD

Although desiccated liver tablets have been overshadowed in recent years by more modern high-tech supplements, they remain one of the most potent yet least expensive supplements available. A $20 investment in desiccated-liver tablets will give you the amount of protein that would normally cost $35 to $50 otherwise. And this doesn't include the other nutrients like vitamins and iron desiccated liver provides. In this age of creatine, HCA, and whey protein, it's nice to know there's a supplement out there that won't cost you an arm and a leg to buy, but does provide most everything a hard-training bodybuilder requires.

References
1) Wapnir, *Protein and Mineral Absorption*, CRC Press, 1990.
2) Sherman and Kramer, *Iron Nutrition and Exercise: Nutrition in Exercise and Sports*, CRC Press, 1989.

Terry Mitsos

Neurotransmitter and Hormonal Control of Appetite

THE ROLE OF NEUROTRANSMITTERS IN FAT LOSS

Although speculated for a long time, it's only in recent years that the role of neurotransmitters in fat loss has received widespread attention. And given North America's preoccupation with fat loss, we can be sure that many of the following compounds will play a major role in this regard in the future. Before we dive into the actual compounds, it only makes sense to lay a basic foundation of neurotransmitter biology.

A BRIEF INTRODUCTION TO NEUROTRANSMITTER BIOLOGY

Neurotransmitters are chemicals released into the clefts between nerve cells (neurons) in order to carry nerve signals within the brain. When a nerve is stimulated, the body (axon) of the nerve is progressively depolarized. Once the depolarization reaches the end of the axon, neurotransmitters are released into the cleft, called a synapse. These chemicals then diffuse across the synapse, binding to receptors on the membrane of the adjacent neuron. The briefly formed neurotransmitter-receptor complex, if formed in sufficient numbers, can trigger a depolarization of the neuron, thus repeating the process. A drug that facilitates this process is called an agonist; a drug that prevents or inhibits this process is called an antagonist.

This form of nerve transmission is the basis for classifying systems within the CNS. For example, if a particular set of nerves primarily depends on the neurotransmitter dopamine, the system is called dopaminergic. Though thermogenic drugs are the most popular among bodybuilders for dieting, other drugs exert their effect by acting on the following CNS systems:

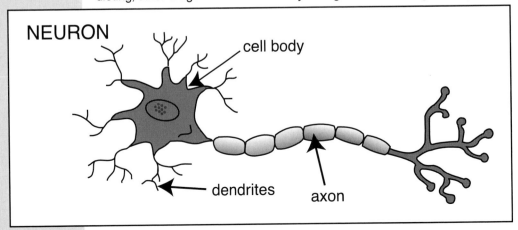

NEURON

cell body

dendrites   axon

Pavol Jablonicky

opiate control mechanisms, adrenergic, serotonergic, dopaminergic, peptidergic, gabanergic and purinergic systems. Other drugs exert their effects by modifying intestinal absorption, gastric emptying, lipid and carbohydrate metabolism, and peripheral cholinergic pathways.[1]

Many of the drugs that follow are experimental, or not yet commercially available. However, that could change, so we have them here for your edification. In many cases the compounds are also described in more detail elsewhere in the text (for example, inosine and GABA).

DRUGS THAT AFFECT THE CATECHOLAMINERGIC SYSTEM

Catecholamines are central monoamine neurotransmitters found in the CNS. With the exception of fenfluramine, amphetamine and its derivatives are structurally similar to catecholamines. The structurally similar amphetamines act as catecholamine agonists, producing an anorectic effect.[1]

DRUGS THAT AFFECT THE NORADRENERGIC SYSTEM

Both amphetamine and its derivative, diethylpropion, exert their effects on the noradrenergic system, though apparently not by mediating the role of norepinephrine. Salbutamol, a beta-adrenergic stimulant that affects this system, has been shown to be an effective appetite-suppressant drug in animal models.[1]

DRUGS THAT AFFECT THE DOPAMINERGIC SYSTEM

The ergot derivatives lisuride, lergotrile and bromocriptine are more potent than amphetamine and fenfluramine in this system. Other anorectic drugs are the catecholamine-reuptake inhibitor nomifensene and the dopamine-receptor agonist piribedil.[1]

DRUGS THAT AFFECT THE SEROTONERGIC SYSTEM

Fenfluramine is one of the best-studied drugs affecting this system, which derives its name from the neurotransmitter serotonin. Other drugs that exert an anorectic effect are quipazine, MK-212 (6-chloro-2-(1-piperzinyl)-purazine), meta-chlorophenylpiperazine and the antidepressant Zimelidine.[1]

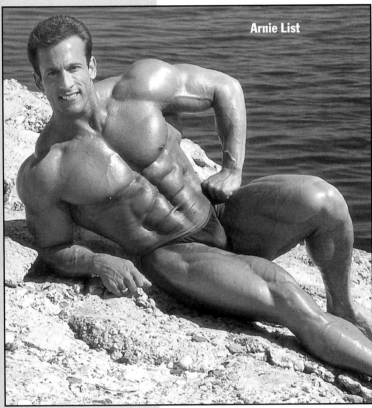

Arnie List

DRUGS THAT AFFECT THE GABANERGIC SYSTEM

This system is named for the neuro-transmitter gamma-amino butyric acid. (see Chapter Fourteen on "Protein and Amino Acids.") Among its properties, GABA has the ability to suppress appetite and food ingestion in animals, thereby reducing the animals overall bodyweight. Unfortunately, decreases in bodyweight in the animals were directly correlated with increases in brain GABA levels, and decreased appetite was directly correlated with a twofold increase in hypothalamus GABA levels. High levels of GABA have been shown to be toxic in animals, and this has made physicians hesitant to use GABA as a weight-loss drug (we should add that Muscimol, a GABA agonist, has been shown to be an appetite stimulant in animal models.[1]

DRUGS THAT AFFECT THE PURINERGIC SYSTEM

The purine inosine has been shown to suppress food intake in rats. Inosine and such related compounds as hypoxanthine, 2-deoxyguanosine and 2-deoxyinosine are believed to compete with the benzodiazepines (appetite stimulants) for receptor sites. Researchers theorize that the purines may have a role in the central regulation of appetite via interaction with the benzo-diazepine receptor.[1] (see Chapter Twenty-Seven on "Natural Anabolics, Anticatabolics and Hormone Boosters.")

HORMONAL CONTROL OF APPETITE

Many hormones, when injected, can be used to control appetite. Thyrotropin-releasing hormone (TRH) is a central neuropeptide that decreased food intake in rat studies. The hormone calcitonin also decreased food intake in animals and caused weight loss in human subjects. An anorexigenic glycopeptide (isolated from human serum) named Satietin has been shown to produce a dose-related decrease in feeding behaviour in animal models. The gastrointestinal hormone cholecystokinin (CCK) can suppress feeding behavior as well.[1]

THE ENDORPHINS AND THEIR ANTAGONISTS

Research shows that endogenous opiate peptides are involved in controlling food intake. Genetically obese rodents have higher levels of beta-endorphin in their pituitaries, and food intake can be increased in rodents with injections of this drug and another opiate peptide, dynorphin. This feeding behavior can be decreased by using the opiate antagonists naloxone and its long-acting derivative zinc tannate of naloxone. The glucocorticoid dexmethasone decreases feeding behavior by inhibiting both the synthesis and stress-release of beta-endorphin. Naloxone has been used successfully to treat obesity by reducing food intake.[1] There are a number of commercially available opiate antagonists. The first developed was nalorphine, but it has very unpleasant side effects and a short duration of action. The next antagonist produced was cyclazocine, which has a longer action time but produces psychomimteic side effects such as: racing thoughts, sedation and visual distortion. Tolerance to the side effects will develop if the dose is increased gradually over several weeks. Naloxone has a shorter time of action than nalorphine and cylazocine, but naloxone does not produce the already mentioned unpleasant side effects. This antagonist also differs in that it does not possess any analgesic properties.

It's derivative, naltrexone, has low toxicity, fewer side effects, and is a more effective antagonist. One dose of naltrexone will block the opiate receptors for approximately 72 hours; three doses a week are enough to maintain a high level of receptor blockade.[2] There is, as of yet, no recommended dosage for the purpose of dieting.

Laura Creavalle

While this would appear to be a panacea for bodybuilders who cannot diet down for a contest, there are other issues to consider. What effect might opiate blockade have, if any, on protein synthesis? Would there be synergistic effects with other drugs? And since heroin addicts report that they never get colds, and withdrawal symptoms resemble those of a respiratory flu,[3] opiate antagonists might best be avoided by bodybuilders with a history of respiratory disease.

METABOLIC AGENTS FOR WEIGHT CONTROL

Both Ascarbose (a complex polysaccharide which inhibits glucosidase activity) and Trestatin (Ro 9-0154, an alpha-amylase inhibitor) decrease bodyweight gain, either because they suppress food intake or inhibit the digestion of polysaccharides. These two drugs are of particular interest because they can lower insulin and glucose levels after a meal.

References
1) A. Sullivan and others, *Nutrition and Drugs*, (New York: John Wiley and Sons, 1983).
2) W. Witters and P. Venturi, *Drugs and Society*, 2d ed., (Boston: Jones and Bartlett Publishers,1988).
3) A. Weil and W. Rosen, *Chocolate to Morphine: Understanding Mind-Active Drugs*, (Boston: Houghton Mifflin Company, 1983).

BOOK FIVE

Energy Sources

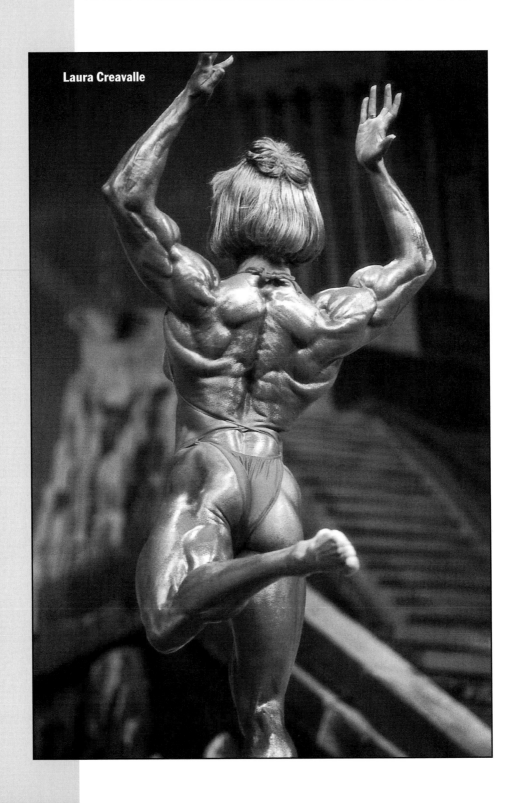

Laura Creavalle

Jean-Pierre Fux

Creatine

I n their never-ending quest to achieve the ultimate in muscular development, bodybuilders and other athletes have been willing to inject or ingest just about every concoction that hits the health-food stands. For the most part, their hard-earned money helps produce the most expensive urine in town, but occassionally a supplement comes along that may in fact do what the advertisers claim it does – increase athletic performance. One such substance is creatine, and while it was isolated over 160 years ago, it has fast become the hottest thing in bodybuilding since amino acids.

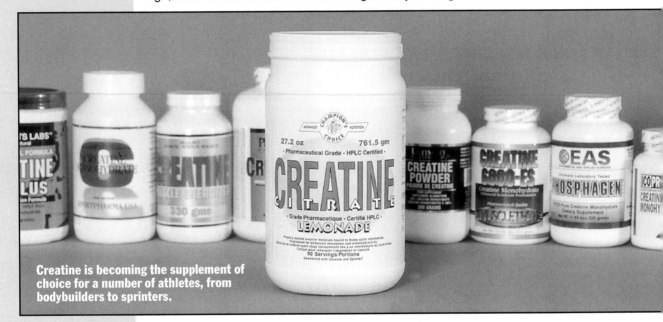

Creatine is becoming the supplement of choice for a number of athletes, from bodybuilders to sprinters.

HISTORICAL PERSPECTIVES

The name "creatine" was first coined in 1832 by French scientist Chevreul, who reported the discovery of a new component of meat. Unfortunately, the limited isolation techniques of the time prevented Chevreul from determining if creatine was a regular or intermittent part of meat. Another scientist discovered that wild fox meat had ten times the muscle-creatine content compared to farm-raised animals just 15 years later. He concluded that creatine levels were influenced by muscle exercise.

In the early 20th century, researchers began experiments with creatine feeding in animals. By comparing the amount given and the amount collected in the urine, they determined that much of the creatine was retained in the body. As an example, studies by Folin and Denis in 1912 determined that the muscle-creatine content of cats increased by 70 percent after creatine ingestion. Further studies by Hahn and Meyer in 1923 estimated the total creatine content of a 160-pound human male to be 140 grams – a figure which closely matches the present value.

One of the biggest breakthroughs in creatine research came in the late 1920s when researchers discovered that creatine exsists in two main forms – free creatine and phosphorylated creatine.

Over the next seventy years additional findings determined that creatine played a major role in ATP-ADP synthesis and breakdown.

WHAT IS CREATINE?

Creatine is one of eight naturally occurring guanidine-derived compounds synthesized from three amino acids – arginine, glycine, and methionine. Without going into too much biochemistry, starting with the precursors arginine and glycine, and by way of numerous enzymes and intermediate products, the end result is creatine. The following schematic shows the major steps in creatine synthesis:

GLYCINE + ARGININE ⟶ GUANIDINOACETATE ⟶ CREATINE
ENZYME (TRANSAMIDINASE)   ENZYME + METHYL (CH_3) GROUP

In humans over 95 percent of the total creatine content is located in skeletal muscle, with approximately one-third being free creatine (Cr-f) and the remainder being in the phosphorylated (Cr-phos) form. As the enzymes needed for creatine synthesis are located in the liver, pancreas, and kidneys, it means that creatine is produced outside the muscles and then carried to the muscles by way of the bloodstream, where it is absorbed.

TOTAL CREATINE LEVELS

Biochemists define total creatine (Cr-tot) as being the total amount of creatine in the body from a combination of free and phosphorylated forms. Studies have determined that creatine is used or "turned over" at a rate of about 1.6 percent per day. For a 160-pound male with a total creatine pool of 120 grams, this works out to about 2 grams per day. The creatine that is used is replaced by both internal synthesis (called endogenous sources) and by the diet (called exogenous sources). As synthesis is heavily dependant on external sources, dietary sources are considered the most important in determining creatine levels.

The best sources of creatine are meat, fish and other animal products. The average creatine intake from dietary sources is estimated to be 1 gram per day. As plants are very low in creatine, vegetarians rely solely on internal synthesis for creatine sources.

Both forms of creatine are subject to individual variations. Levels may be influenced by such factors as muscle-fiber type, age, and disease.

Kim Chizevsky

> "Scientific experimentation has shown, time after time, that dietary supplementation can increase the total creatine concentration in skeletal muscle. The result is a significant increase in energy, stamina, strength and muscle mass, which enhances athletic performance significantly."
>
> – Franco Cavaleri, IFBB Mr. North America.

MECHANISM OF ACTION

The intermediate energy source for skeletal-muscle contraction is adenosine triphosphate – ATP. During exercise ATP is hydrolyzed (broken down by water) to form adenosine diphosphate – ADP. As long as energy requirements are maintained, ATP must be continuously replaced. Once ATP is used up, the body must dip into creatine stores. If creatine stores are low, fatigue sets in much faster and exercise intensity is reduced.

As energy demands increase, creatine phosphorylate is broken down to produce free creatine and a liberated phosphate group. This high-energy phosphate is then added or "donated" to ADP to reform ATP. The remaining free creatine is not wasted as it is rephosphorylated back to the creatine-phosphorylate form during periods of recovery. The previous reaction can be summed up as follows:

$$Cr\text{-}phos + ADP + H \longleftrightarrow Cr\text{-}free + ATP$$

INTERELATIONSHIP BETWEEN CREATINE AND HIGH-INTENSITY EXERCISE

During brief periods of intense exercise ATP demands made by the muscles may increase by a factor of several hundred over resting values. Different studies put ATP turnover rates in the range of 6 millimoles per second to 15 millimoles per second. For those not familiar with these biochemical units, the values suggest that total creatine stores can be depleted by 10 seconds of high-intensity exercise. For bodybuilders this means one set of 10 to 12 reps on the leg press (about as intense as it gets) will deplete creatine supplies.

RESYNTHESIS

The resynthesis of creatine phosphate in humans is dependant on oxygen supplies. Although it varies, a muscle can restore 50 percent of its creatine levels in about one minute. Total creatine levels can be restored within five or six minutes. We should point out that individual genetics play a big role as different fiber types (fast versus slow twitch, or type I versus type II) respond differently. Studies have shown that type-I fibres restore creatine levels faster than type-II fibres. The reasons include type I's higher aerobic potential and more stable pH (the ratio of acid to base) levels.

Natural sources of creatine include meat, fish and other animal products, however, the average intake from dietary sources is only one gram per day.

BENEFITS TO BODYBUILDERS

Although the debate rages as to whether creatine supplementation is of any benefit to endurance athletes, the scientific community agrees that athletes engaged in sports requiring short bursts of power (weightlifting, wrestling, bodybuilding, sprinting, etc.) will benefit from taking creatine. Before we look at some of the research findings we must emphasize that creatine use by athletes is a relatively new occurrence. Further, as of this writing, less than a dozen analytical studies have been carried out to determine its effectiveness for athletes. So while the evidence looks promising, caution is warranted.

THE RESEARCH

One of the most recent studies to investigate the effects of creatine on high-intensity exercise was conducted in Sweden in 1994. Eight male subjects with an average age of 24 and weighing an average of 172 pounds, performed five, 6-second bouts and one, 10-second bout of high-intensity exercise on a specially designed cycle ergometer. The trials were carried out both before and after supplementation with 20 grams of creatine monohydrate per day. The researchers adjusted the tension on the bike so that the test subjects could maintain 140 revs per minute for the first five, 6-second exercise periods but not for the 10-second bout. To measure creatine levels muscle biopsies were taken after the fifth and sixth trial periods.

Craig Titus

The data collected showed a creatine increase of 24.6 millimoles per kilogram, accompanied by an average bodyweight increase of 1.5 kilograms (3.3 pounds). Additionally, all subjects were able to maintain the target speed towards the end of the 10-second trial periods. A third finding was that even though more work was performed following creatine supplementation, post-exercise lactate levels were much lower than before creatine supplementation.

The researchers concluded that increased fatigue resistance during high-intensity exercise may be explained by both high pre-exercise creatine levels and also by a possible decrease in total muscle lactate levels.[1]

Another study conducted in 1992 set out to determine if creatine given as a supplement was absorbed and if exercise increased uptake into the muscles. There were seventeen subjects in all – between the ages of 20 and 62 years. The five females and twelve males had varing degrees of fitness and all continued their normal pattern of life throughout the study. In effect, no restraints in terms of diet or exercise were placed on them.

All the subjects were given creatine monohydrate in different amounts for different periods of time to determine the best dose of creatine to use per trial period. It was found that 5 grams per serving was best and this was then given for 20 grams a day (4 X 5) for 4.5 days, 7 days, and 10 days; and 30 grams a day (6 X 5) for 7 days and on alternate days for 21 days.

To study the effects of exercise and creatine supplementation, five subjects were given creatine and performed one hour of one-leg cycle ergometer riding per day – with the resting leg serving as the "control." Although

> "Creatine has to combine with phosphate before it is of any value. Creatine phosphate is a potent chemical which can generate high-energy contractions for ten to fifteen seconds. Creatine phosphate rebuilds adenosine triphosphate, which is the ultimate energy source. The reaction is quite rapid, so it benefits the muscles but for a short period of time."
>
> – Bill Starr, John Hopkins University strength and conditioning coach commenting on perhaps bodybuilding's most popular supplement.

Besides increasing energy reserves there is good evidence to suggest creatine may indirectly promote muscle growth.

the subjects were allowed to adjust the intensity themselves, they were asked to perform as much as they could during the time period. As before, the dosages ranged from 20 to 30 grams.

The results obtained showed that regular supplementation with 5 grams of creatine monohydrate, four to six times a day for two or more days resulted in a significant increase in total muscle content (measured in the quadriceps femoris muscle). The greatest increases were in those subjects with the lowest pre-study creatine levels. In some cases the increase was as much as 50 percent.

The trials involving exercise showed that creatine levels increased dramatically in the exercised leg (by 25 percent in some subjects) but had no effect on the resting leg. Although numerous theories have been put forward to explain this, most researchers suggest that increased blood flow from exercise and changes in fibre-membrane permeability may be the reason for increased creatine uptake.[2]

Besides increasing energy reserves there is good evidence to suggest creatine may indirectly promote muscle growth. Research, carried out by Dr. Kenneth Baldwin at the University of California at Irvine, suggests that depleting phosphocreatine reserves may serve as a muscle-growth stimulus. In his experiments, Dr. Baldwin was able to artificially deplete creatine stores and trick the muscle into growing despite the absence of the normal stimulus of exercise.[3] Dr. Baldwin's research backs up earlier work by other scientists, suggesting creatine is involved in protein synthesis. The results are so promising that one application of such research is preventing muscle atrophy that normally affects astronauts on long space flights.

A study conducted in 1993 set out to determine the role creatine supplementation played in muscle-force production, and ammonia and lactate accumulation. The test group consisted of twelve subjects – nine males and three females, ranging in age from 20 to 28. Before the tests began the subjects were given two or three familiarization visits so that reproducible measurements could be taken. To establish base-line values, the subjects were told not to engage in any form of strenuous physical activity and fast for at least five hours. They then performed five trials of 30 reps each of one-leg extensions. After measurements were taken the subjects were divided into two groups – control and experimental. The control group received 6 grams of glucose while the experimental group recieved 5 grams of creatine plus 1 gram of glucose. Both groups were given the supplement four times daily for a period of five days. As before, the subjects engaged in one-leg extensions for five sets of 30 repetitions.

The major finding of the experiment was that six subjects were all able to sustain peak muscle contraction and movement at a higher level during repeated trials involving creatine supplementation. The changes in ammonia concentration were shown to be lower both during and after exercise, after creatine supplementation. Although other studies indicate that lactate levels decline with creatine use, this study did not show any difference in lactate levels before or after creatine ingestion.[4]

IS THE EVIDENCE CONCLUSIVE?

Although we have only looked at the results from three studies, eight to 10 others have drawn similar conclusions. Such studies document that creatine ingestion does lead to greater and more sustained bursts of power. Further, creatine can delay muscular fatigue by anywhere from 10 to 20 percent.

Most studies suggest that creatine serves its greatest role during the early to middle reps of an exercise set. Creatine benefits seem to decline after the first three or four sets of an exercise. Both of these points are important as most bodybuilders today tend to do fewer sets per bodypart than years gone by.

Although the effects on lactic-acid build-up are inconclusive, the evidence suggests that some individuals may have their lactic-acid levels reduced by as much as 70 percent. Anecdotal reports indicate that bodybuilders using creatine become less winded during intense training – one of the signs of decreased lactic-acid build-up and the associated oxygen debt.

Evidence suggests creatine could be the start of a new wave of "state of the art" supplements, which may replace performance-enhancing drugs down the road. We only say "may" because the evidence is still preliminary. If creatine and its high-tech cousins do replace steroids, the problem of defining the word "drug" arises once again. You may counter that creatine is found naturally in the body and therefore not a drug. The same

Most studies suggest that creatine serves its greatest role during the early to middle reps of an exercise set. – Aaron Maddron

rationale can be used for testosterone, yet try telling that to law-enforcement agents or sports federations. Their response is an unequivocal "yes, testosterone is a drug!"

INTERACTION WITH INSULIN

Although many bodybuilders using creatine are also using a wide spectrum of anabolic drugs, one in particular – insulin – deserves special consideration.

Studies consistently show that insulin forces creatine into muscle cells. Therefore the more insulin available, the more creatine that can be stored. Not only does this increase cell volumizing, leading to increased size, but it also leads to greater strength and performance. According to numerous reports, many athletes are stacking creatine and long- and short-acting injectable insulin in an attempt to maximize the previous. Everything would be all and well if insulin was a forgiving hormone, but it isn't. Take the wrong dose at the wrong time and you could die. Our advice is to stimulate insulin release naturally and leave insulin injections to diabetics.

Vince Taylor and Shawn Ray

"Glad to hear you have decided to give creatine a try. I would say that more than 90 percent of bodybuilders who use creatine correctly get a positive response."

– Will Brink, regular *MuscleMag* columnist adding his endorsement to the value of creatine supplements for bodybuilders.

HOW TO USE CREATINE SUPPLEMENTS

Taking creatine in supplement form is a relatively new phenomenon in bodybuilding, even though studies conducted in the early part of the century suggested that total creatine supplies can be increased by ingesting creatine in the diet. For example, in 1912 and 1913, two seperate studies concluded that rabbits and cats fed creatine had increased muscle creatine levels of up to 70 percent.

As supplements go, creatine monohydrate is one of the easiest substances to take. It comes in the form of creatine monohydrate – a white powder which is tasteless and odourless. Although cold water can be used, you'll find it disolves more easily in warm water. If excessive heat is used (boiling a kettle, or microwave) much of the creatine will be destroyed. For those who find water too bland, try using fruit juice.

For maximum absorption take the supplement on an empty stomach followed by a small, simple-carbohydrate meal, also containing the amino acids glycine, arginine, and methionine. Both the carbohydrate and amino acids are needed by the body to increase the synthesis and storage of creatine. Conversely, taking creatine with a high-protein meal reduces absorption and storage. This point should not be overlooked as some new creatine manufacturers have released protein powders containing creatine. It sounds great in theory – two for the price of one – but it makes little practical sense as consuming the two together contradicts human biochemistry. Some of the most popular creatine sources on the market include Twinlab's Creatine Fuel, AST Research's Creatine Complex – 5, SportPharma's Creatine, and EAS's Phosphagen and Phosphagen HP.

Perhaps the most powerful form of creatine monohydrate is Creatine 6000ES, manufactured by MuscleTech of Canada. Each teaspoon provides 6 grams (6000 milligrams – hence the name) of creatine monohydrate, therefore, it's easily the most potent creatine supplement produced. With this product bodybuilders have access to one of the most powerful, nondrug, muscle-building agents ever developed.

OTHER SOURCES

Besides creatine monohydrate, two other forms of creatine are available. The first is creatine phosphate. Manufacturers say it is "many times" better than creatine monohydrate. But there is one problem with their claims: None of the studies involving creatine phosphate have involved giving the compound orally to humans. All have used injections of creatine. This is because creatine phosphate is too unstable to be given orally.

The other form of creatine to hit supplement shelves is creatine citrate. With the ads claiming "five times more soluble" and "more absorbable" than creatine monohydrate, it would seem creatine citrate is by far a better product. Unfortunately, despite the claims, there are no human studies available using orally administered creatine citrate. It is possible by the time this book goes to print such data will have been collected. Who knows, maybe it will turn out to be a "far better" product.

Until legitimate scientific studies involving orally adminstered creatine phosphate or creatine citrate become available, we suggest you stick to the form with credible research behind its name – creatine monohydrate.

LOADING

Manufacturers of creatine products recommend a loading phase of 30 grams a day for one week, followed by 5 to 10 grams a day for maintenance. These are average numbers and the larger members of the sport might need 20 to 25 grams a day for maintenance.

Another important point is to spread the ingestion out over five to six small servings rather than one or two large servings. The body can absorb only so much at a given time (vitamin C is famous for this). In terms of actual amount, this works out to one teaspoon (approximately 5 grams) taken four times a day.

**Some individuals may have their lactic-acid levels reduced by as much as 70 percent after creatine supplementation.
– Debbie Kruck**

Although personal preferrence plays a role, anecdotal evidence suggests that one serving should be taken before and after working out. This increases creatine levels before exercise and speeds up recovery afterwards.

Finally, the issue of cost should be addressed. As would be expected, any supplement that is promising and hence highly popular, will not be cheap. Creatine is no exception. As supplements go, creatine is one of the more expensive single-substance products on the market.

Jay Cutler

Although prices vary from state to state and country to country, a one-week maintenance supply of creatine (about 100 grams) will set you back about $25 US. Even by switching to the maintenance schedule discussed earlier, regular creatine supplementation will cost over $100 a month. Therefore such factors as level of training, goals, and available finances will play a major role in determining if an athlete is going to include creatine in his or her arsenal of ergogenic aids.

SIDE EFFECTS

None of the studies carried out have shown creatine to be toxic. Some individuals may retain water (something to keep in mind during the precontest season as anecdotal evidence suggests that bodybuilders should discontinue creatine usage about two weeks before a contest), but for the most part, creatine has no known side effects. Having said that, a few words of caution are needed. Even though the studies conducted used relatively high doses of creatine the average trial period fell in the 5- to 10-gram-per-day range. Bodybuilders and other athletes will no doubt be taking creatine continuously for months if not years. Such a pattern of use has no analogy in the medical literature. Today's bodybuilders are breaking new ground with each week of creatine use. The effects of such long-term, high-dose use are unknown. While extrapolation suggests that there should be no problems, discretion is highly recommended.

Laura Bass

References

1) K. Soderland and others, "Creatine Supplementation and High-Intensity Exercise, Influence on Performance and Muscle Metabolism," *Clinical Science*, 87 (1994).
2) R.C. Harris and others, "Elevation of Creatine in Resting and Exercised Muscle of Normal Subjects By Creatine Supplementation," *Clinical Science*, 83 (1992).
3) "Drug World," *Flex*, 12:6 (1994).
4) P. Greehuff and others, "Influence of Oral Creatine Supplementation of Muscle Torque During Repeated Bouts of Maximal Voluntary Exercise In Man," *Clinical Science*, 84 (1993).

Oils

As long as the science of nutrition has been in existence, few nutrients have recieved as much negativity as fats. Carbohydrates – sure, eat your fill; protein – a minimum of 2 to 2.5 grams per pound of bodyweight, right? Even such nutrients as vitamins and minerals are recommended by some to be taken in high dosages. But fats – avoid at all costs!

The problem with such an attitude is that it groups all fats under one catagory – enemy. Medical experts routinely tell us that fats cause strokes, heart disease, and high blood presure. We are consistently told to rid our diets of all fats and do everything possible to refrain from eating them.

Before we provide evidence to contradict some of the previous we should say that, yes, too much of certain types of fats can be detrimental to long-term health. But the key words here are "too much" and "types." Not all fats are bad, and further, some are essential to good health.

WHY ARE THEY IMPORTANT?

In terms of energy supply, fats are the most concentrated sources of energy in the diet. As an example, carbohydrates and protein supply only four calories per gram, while fats provide nine calories per gram. Biochemists also

tell us that during sleep about 70 percent of our energy comes from fat stores. Not convinced yet? If the body contained no fat, absorbtion of the fat-soluble vitamins (A, D, E, K) would be almost impossible.

Not to be ignored are the synthesis properties of fats. Without adequate fat supplies the production of such important biochemicals as prostaglandins and essential fatty acids is impaired. And despite all the negative TV and magazine coverage, one form of fat – cholesterol – is needed for the manufacture of such life-giving substances as hormones, vitamin D, and bile.

Fats help insulate the internal organs from injury, help keep the whole body from cold, and from a cosmetic point of view, give the male and female forms their respective shapes. The substance you've been trying to avoid may not be as bad as you thought.

Kevin Christie, Gordon Lavelle and Andrew Pace enjoy the fruits of their labor.

TYPES OF FATS AND OILS

The types of fats found in foods are called triglycerides because they contain one glycerol molecule attached to three fatty acid groups. The length and molecular make-up of each fatty acid determines the characteristics of each fat.

The glycerol molecule contains three hydroxyl groups (OH) and the fatty acid molecule has a long hydrocarbon chain and a single carboxyl group (COOH), as shown in the following diagrams:

$$CH_2 - OH$$
$$|$$
$$CH_2 - OH$$
$$|$$
$$CH_2 - OH$$

Glycerol

$$O$$
$$||$$
$$HO - C - (CH_2)_{14} - CH_3$$

Fatty Acid

The double perpendicular lines joining the carbon (C) and oxygen (O), represent a double bond and a sharing of electrons between the two atoms. Don't let the chemistry frighten you. We are merely showing this molecular arrangement so that you will have an understanding of the two types of fats heard about frequently in the media these days – saturated and unsaturated.

A fat is said to be saturated if there are no double bonds between the carbon atoms (in most cases the molecule picks up extra hydrogen atoms and this eliminates the double bonds).

Saturated fats are solid at room temperature. If there are double bonds present, the fat is said to be unsaturated. As the number of double bonds increases, the fat becomes more oily, and for this reason vegetable oils are termed polyunsaturated oils.

"The different combinations can make a fat/oil either desirable for health, performance and building muscle, or something to be avoided like the plague. As with everything in bodybuilding (supplements, drugs, equipment, etc.) there is also a wide range of differences in fats and oils that should be explored and understood by bodybuilders – or "normal" people for that matter – interested in improving their health and furthering development."

– Will Brink, regular *MuscleMag* columnist.

Ronnie
Coleman

These terms are important as there seems to be a connection between dietary fat types and heart disease. Animal fats tend to contain more saturated fatty acids than plant materials, and hence are potentially more dangerous down the road.

MEDIUM-CHAIN VERSUS LONG-CHAIN TRIGLYCERIDES

Besides the presence or absence of double bonds, fats may be classified by the number of carbon atoms contained in their chains. Fats containing eight to 12 carbon atoms in their chains are termed medium-chain triglycerides (MCTs). Fats containing more carbons have longer chains and are called long-chain triglycerides (LCTs).

LCTs are difficult to digest because of their complex structure. Although it varies, LCTs may take six to eight hours to digest and be absorbed. From a bodybuilding perspective, LCTs are counterproductive as any fat that is not burned as fuel (as fequently happens with LCTs) is stored as bodyfat.

OILS – WHAT WERE ONCE GOOD . . .

Foods that were once healthy for humans are now major contributors to heart disease and cancer because of modern processing techniques. To quote *MuscleMag* columnist Will Brink, "While the shelf-life of the product has been extended, the same cannot be said for extending human life." The typical vegetable oil has been bleached, bombarded with extremely high temperatures, mixed with chemicals, and subjected to the whole arsenal of food-processing abuse. In doing so, manufacturers have "created" a whole spectrum of toxic substances that were not originally present in food. Perhaps the most detrimental to health (this is not to say the other compounds are much safer) are what are known as "trans-fatty acids."

CIS AND TRANS – A WORLD OF DIFFERENCE

It would be nice and dandy if all oils were the same, but Mother Nature had other ideas. Some molecules contain carbon atoms joined together by double bonds, which may exist in two or more forms called isomers. This means they have the same type and number of atoms, but have structurally different shapes. The following is an example showing two isomers of dichloroethylene:

Cl Cl	Cl H
C = C	C = C
H H	H Cl
Cis-dichloroethylene	Trans-dichloroethylene

At first glance the two structures look the same, but a closer inspection reveals that the cis isomer contains both sets of like atoms on the same side of the carbon atoms, whereas the trans form has the atoms on opposite sides (there are more differences, but it's not necessary to go into detail).

Like the previous compound, fatty acids can exist in the cis or trans configuration. Cis forms are found in nature and human biochemistry has evolved to utilize such compounds (much the same as it has evolved to use "L" amino acids and not "D" forms). Unfortunately, the emergence of food processing techniques in the 1920s led to the manufacturing of trans forms of fatty acids (the processing procedures transformed the naturally occurring cis configuration into the trans form). As would be expected, these forms were not accepted too kindly by the human body and since their introduction 70 to 80 years ago, incidences of heart disease and stroke have taken a quantum leap forward.

PRACTICAL CONSIDERATIONS

For those concerned about long-term health (who isn't), the previous raises many important issues, especially when shopping at the supermarket. In general, all store-bought oils have undergone some degree of hydrogenation (extreme heat and processing). There are, however, a number of oils which are both healthy and essential, and bodybuilders should regularly include them in their diets. The following are among the more popular oils used by bodybuilders around the world.

MEDIUM-CHAIN TRIGLYCERIDE OIL (MCT)

Although a recent phenomenon in bodybuilding circles, MCTs have been used medically since the 1950s. Many individuals have trouble absorbing fat; therefore, biochemists went to work developing a class of fats that could be readily utilized by people suffering from fat-malabsorption diseases. In addition, MCT's ability to prevent muscle catabolism has made the oil valuable in the treatment of burn patients.

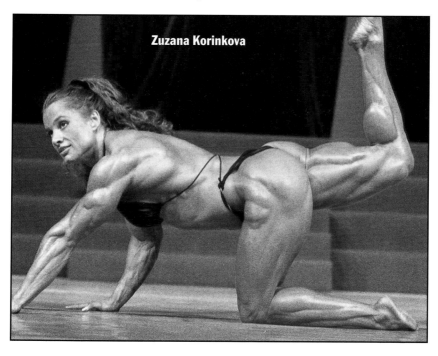

Zuzana Korinkova

Because of their shorter chain – usually six to 10 carbon atoms – and other unique molecular properties, MCTs bypass the long digestive processes that LCTs must go through, and are absorbed directly into the bloodstream. Also, unlike LCTs which go through the intestinal wall and are converted to fat and stored, MCTs go directly to the liver where they are rapidly oxidized.

Another difference between the two involves the amino acid L-carnitine. Most fatty acids require this amino acid to facilitate their ease into cell mitochondria (small organelles responsible for providing energy). MCT oils, however, are not dependant on L-carnitine and can go directly into the mitochondria.

One of MCTs biggest proponents is John Parrillo, regular *MuscleMag* columnist, and someone who is fast gaining a reputation as a trainer supreme. Parrillo markets MCT oil under the brand "CapTri." This product is an eight-carboned fatty acid made from refined coconut oil, but unlike raw forms doesn't contain any cholesterol. According to Parrillo, MCT oil has all of the good qualities of fat – such as energy supply – without the undesirable traits. He also adds that MCT acts like a carbohydrate (quick source of energy) without being stored as bodyfat.

Parrillo goes on, "You get almost as much energy as from pure fat – 8.8 calories per gram versus 9.0 calories per gram for fat – but CapTri gets into the bloodstream as fast as sugar. Best of all, CapTri or any other MCT oil can't be stored as bodyfat and must be burned as an energy source. It therefore speeds up your metabolism so you burn bodyfat faster and get more cut and muscular a lot quicker."

Among Parrillo's converts who are using or have used MCT oil are: Lenda Murray, Carla Dunlap, Penny Price, Ron Love, Mike Ashley, Henderson Thorne, and Rich Gaspari.

CapTri is a medium-chain triglyceride oil made from refined coconut oil.

> "This CapTri is fantastic stuff. I don't know what it is, but it really works. It's especially great the last six to eight weeks before a contest as it helps to maintain muscle mass while you diet down for a show. In the past I always lost too much size as I dieted down, but this time, using the CapTri, I was still able to train heavy right u p until the show, and in fact, I actually put size on while I was dieting down and losing fat. I never felt hungry. I never got that grouchy, irritable, low-carb feeling. I never felt better. I'm telling you this stuff is great."
> – Rita Boehm, 1990 overall Canadian bodybuilding champion commenting on CapTri, an MCT oil supplement.

WHAT DOES IT DO?

Bodybuilders who are hooked on MCT oil say it increases their energy, extends endurance, and lowers bodyfat. John Parrillo believes that by adding MCT to the diet, the body has a high-density energy source available. This means that glucose supplies are spared for longer, more intense workouts. Another benefit seems to be the effect MCT oils have on appetite. MCTs have been shown to increase the production of ketones – one of the by-products of fat metabolism – which can be used as a direct energy source. This suppresses the appetite, making it easier to stay on a diet, especially during the precontest season.

Also important is that ketones are burned by the body in preference to branched-chain amino acids – leaving these amino's available for muscle repair and growth.

From a health perspective, MCTs have been shown to reduce cholesterol absorption and lower overall cholesterol levels.

A DIFFERENT PERSPECTIVE?

Like most aspects of supplement use, there are differing opinions on MCT oils, and Dan Duchaine,

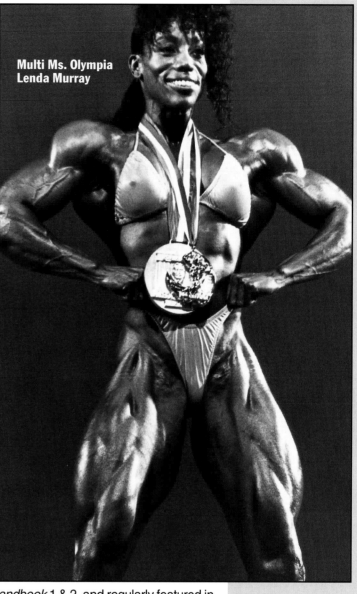

Multi Ms. Olympia Lenda Murray

author of the *Underground Steroid Handbook* 1 & 2, and regularly featured in *MuscleMag International*, takes some exception to Parrillo's views on MCT oils. Duchaine agrees with most of Parrillo's theory that MCTs are not stored as fat, but only in certain situations. He adds that not all MCTs are converted to ketones. This only happens when blood sugar is so low that insulin falls off enough to stimulate the pancreas to start releasing glucagon – the body's other glucose-regulating hormone. According to Duchaine, glucagon levels must be high for the body to start converting MCTs to ketones. Most athletes who have eaten even moderate amounts of carbohydrate will not have MCTs converted to ketones, but instead sent to the liver, reduced to smaller constituents, and ultimately stored as fat if not needed as fuel.

In defence of Parrillo, he does recommend reducing carbohydrate intake when using MCT oils, especially when preparing for a contest. This in turn backs up Duchaine's argument of keeping carbohydrate intake low and forcing the body to manufacture ketones instead of converting the MCTs to fat.

Milos Sarcev

HOW IT'S TAKEN

Like most supplements, MCT oil should not be taken in huge amounts during one sitting. John Parrillo suggests body-builders start at one-half tablespoon per meal for the first three days, and slowly increase the dosage. It should always be taken with food and never on an empty stomach.

Tolerance seems to improve over time and most pros who use MCT oil have worked up to as many as 20 tablespoons a day before their con-tests (at an average of 110 calories per tablespoon this works out to an extra 2200 calories a day!).

Although bodybuilders can bene-fit from MCT year-round, it plays a special role in the weeks leading up to a contest. By taking MCT oil, you can lose fat and still maintain high-energy levels. Further, by reducing carbohydrate intake, the body is forced into burning bodyfat for energy, while the MCT oil prevents the utilization of muscle tissue as fuel and keeps energy levels high.

Bodybuilders who go on crash diets see this all too well. As soon as caloric intake is reduced – especially carbohydrates – the body thinks it's in a state of starvation and begins to burn muscle tissue as fuel. Not only will such individuals feel chronically tired, but their hard-earned muscle size goes the way of the dodo bird.

By providing extra calories, MCT oil prevents the body from canni-balizing its muscle tissue for fuel. But unlike other fat sources it isn't stored. Not only will fat loss continue but muscle size will be maintained and on contest day you will feel healthy and full of energy.

SIDE EFFECTS

Although side effects from taking MCT oil are rarely reported, we would be remiss if we ignored the issue completely. There have been a few isolated studies suggesting MCT oil may reduce the absorption of the fat-soluble vitamins A, D, E, and K. This is of no concern to most bodybuilders as they frequently take vitamin supplements to prevent such deficiencies. One group that may want to avoid MCT oil are diabetics.

As mentioned earlier, MCT oil increases the body's production of ketones. As people with diabetes already have elevated ketone levels, MCT oil may aggrravate the problem producing the condition of acidoses – elevated body acidity, which can be fatal. Most of the common side effects reported are related to improper usage. Individuals who consume MCT oil on an empty stomach, or start out by taking multiple tablespoons, may experi-ence nausea, diarrhea, stomach cramps, and less frequently, vomiting.

"A good rule of thumb here is to try to derive 30 percent of your calories from MCT oil while limiting conventional fat to five percent of calories. You should see and feel a dramatic effect at these levels. Then make up the rest of your calories from unrefined, complex carbohydrates."

– John Parrillo, regular *MuscleMag* columnist offering his recommen-dations on the best way to add MCT oil to your diet.

For the most part, the previous can be avoided by following the procedures outlined earlier. Start out by taking a small amount and gradually work up to larger amounts. And no matter what the dosage, don't take MCT oil on an empty stomach (this goes for most supplements). Many bodybuilders start out fine by measuring the correct amount, but then throw caution to the wind and start adding MCT oil to just about everything consumed. Remember, take the extra time and condition your body.

PRIMROSE OIL

Although delegated to the fringe of the supplement spectrum, biochemists have recently begun taking a second look at primrose oil. The reason this supplement has been short shifted in the past is because of its association with massage or individuals using it to hold back the skin's aging process. Two respected endeavors to be sure, but unfortunately they overshadow many of the other important effects of primrose oil.

As the name would suggest, primrose oil is the name given to oils derived from the various species of primrose-related plants (the evening primrose, a large desert flower, being perhaps the most well-known). The ingredient that makes the product so important is gamma linoleic acid (GLA), which makes up about 10 percent of the oil's content. It was originally thought that gamma linoleic acid could be manufactured by everyone from existing linoleic supplies, but current thinking is that many individuals need to consume it in the diet.

The latest research suggests GLA levels may be deficient because of increased levels of "trans" forms of essential fatty acids. The body can manufacture GLA from "cis" linoleic acid but not the "trans" form. High levels of "trans" actually block GLA production.

With most diets being high in "trans" fatty acids, it's not surprising that many individuals have problems synthesizing adequate amounts of GLA. This in turn leads to GLA-related health problems.

WHAT DOES IT DO?

The advantage of primrose oil over other oils is its high concentrations of GLA and absence of "trans" form blocking agents. Primrose oil can affect the body in a number of ways, as seen in the following paragraphs.

Billy Smith

"Evening primrose oil helps to lower cholesterol levels and reduce acne, especially when those conditions have been induced by steroids. It also offers some protection to the liver of steroid users, and is recommended for general health and well-being."

– Greg Zulak, former *MuscleMag* editor commenting on the many benefits of evening primrose oil.

PROSTAGLANDINS

Prostaglandins are hormone-like substances which belong to a family (about 35 to 40 in all) of 20-carbon unsaturated fatty acid derivatives. They are manufactured from the fatty acids that make up the structural parts of plasma membranes – the specific type produced depending on which fatty acids are present.

Recent research suggests that there is a direct relationship between GLA and prostaglandin levels. A shortage of GLA means a reduction in prostaglandin synthesis. This can have serious implications as prostaglandins are believed to have a number of functions including: increasing or decreasing the level of cyclic AMP, raising or lowering blood presure, regulating digestion, inhibiting progesterone production by the corpus luteum, boosting the immune system, and regulating blood clotting. They also play a role in smooth-muscle contraction in the uterus and blood vessels.

Laura Binetti

ARTHRITIS

Arthritis can be defined as an inflammation of the tissues surrounding bone joints. There are two types of arthritis; osteoarthritis produced by the daily wear and tear on connective tissue; and rheumatoid arthritis caused by an inflammation of the joint-synovial membranes. Although primrose oil doesn't seem to benefit the former, it is very helpful for treating the latter.

Although the exact cause of rheumatoid arthritis is unknown, current research focuses on the body's immune system attacking the soft synovial tissue surrounding joints. There is also some evidence to suggest diet may play a role. In either case, 3 to 4 grams a day of primrose oil has been shown to reduce the pain often experienced by arthritis sufferers. The only drawback is that it generally takes a couple of months for the benefits to kick in.

FAT-BURNING PROPERTIES

Like beta-3 agonists, primrose oil has been linked to fat loss by stimulating brown adipose tissue. Although not fully understood, it is believed that high concentrations of gamma linoleic acid increases brown-fat mitochondrial activity. Studies by Dr. K.S. Vaddadi and Dr. David Horrobin found that primrose oil reduced bodyweight in over 50 percent of test subjects who were more than 10 percent overweight to begin with.[1]

IMPROVING BLOOD FLOW

Contrary to popular belief, heart disease is a 20th-century phenomenon. Prior to the 1920s, heart attacks were no more common than most other life-threatening ailments. Diseases caused by bacteria and viruses caused far more deaths. Starting in the 1920s, however, heart disease became rampant, and while such factors as reduced physical activity played a role, the primary culprit is believed to be changes in diet – especially the increased consumption of fats. As mentioned earlier, "trans" forms of fatty acids are harmful to the body, primarily because evolution made the "cis" forms the fat of choice. It can't be a coincidence that the increase in heart disease paralleled the introduction of man-made "trans" fatty acids into the food supply during the 1920s. One of the detrimental effects of such fats is to increase the "stickiness" of blood platelets leading to

Primrose oil is high in "cis" form fatty acids, which play a major role in keeping the blood clot free – making it an excellent supplement for those with a family history of heart disease.
– Tom Platz

clumping and internal blood clots. "Cis" form fatty acids, however, play a major role in keeping the blood slick and clot free. Primrose oil being high in "cis" linoleic acid is an excellent supplement for those with a family history of heart disease.

AND FOR STEROID USERS

Two of the negative side effects of anabolic steroids are increased levels of circulating fatty acids, and decreased levels of GLA. While such effects are transitory and will dissappear following cessation of drug use, those with a history of heart disease, or those remaining on steroids for extended periods of time (a practice we seriously suggest avoiding) should be cautious. Research has shown that primrose oil helps the body replace compounds that counteract some of the side effects of steroids. This is not to say taking primrose oil will allow you to use higher dosages of steroids for longer periods of time. But it will improve your odds of avoiding cardiovascular problems associated with steroids.

Gary Strydom, Francis Benfatto
and Mike Christian

ROUNDING OUT THE LIST

Rounding out the list of uses for primrose oil include treating menstrual and premenstrual problems, psoriasis and eczema, multiple sclerosis, acne (another common side effect of steroid use), scizophrenia, and hyperactivity.

SUPPLEMENTAL PRIMROSE OIL

The primary reasons for needing supplemental primrose oil are dietary deficiencies and fatty acid-metabolism impairment, but given its positive effects on overall health, everyone can benefit from primrose oil. There are numerous brands of primrose oil available, but many are misleading about the actual concentrations present. One product, however, called EFAMOL, is listed on page 467 of the *Canadian CPS*, and is therefore subject to federal regulations. Each capsule contains 500 milligrams of evening primrose oil with 13.6 IU of vitamin E. When used as a dietary supplement, the starting recommended dosage is 1 capsule three or four times per day, with meals. This can later be increased to 2 capsules three or four times per day. When used as a therapeutic agent (for eczema, chronic fatigue, premenstrual syndrome) the recommended dosage is 6 to 8 capsules daily.

SIDE EFFECTS

Although it's virtually impossible to overdose on primrose oil, the compound is not risk free. Reported side effects include headaches, diarrhea and nausea, though this is more likely if taken on an empty stomach or at a high dosage (20 capsules or more per day). Those who have experienced epileptic episodes while taking phenothiazine drugs should avoid primrose and related oils.

GRAPE SEED OIL

This oil was first produced in France as a substitute for olive oil. California is now the main supplier of grape seed oil. The grape seeds are washed, dried, ground and pressed. The resulting oil is odorless, tasteless, almost colorless, hypo-allergenic, cholesterol-free, and contains vitamin F. A similar oil is sunflower seed oil. This oil contains vitamin F, and is very similar to grape seed oil.

CLA – THE FUTURE OF SUPPLEMENT OILS?

As with protein, creatine, and fat-burning agents, the field of supplemental oil research is on the move. In the last ten years a new source of fatty acids – called conjugated linoleic acid (CLA) – was isolated from ground beef. And while preliminary, the research suggests CLA may hold great promise as a bodybuilding supplement in the not to distant future.

Without deluging the reader with complicated organic chemistry, the word "conjugated" means the molecule contains two double bonds separated by a single-bonded carbon atom. Although it seems trivial, such an arrangement has profound effects in biological organisms.

Romeo Villarino

CLA is found naturally in such foods as beef, dairy products, and turkey, but you would have to eat many pounds of one or more sources to get the four grams which seems to be the most beneficial dosage. As dairy products and beef are also high in fat, it makes more sense to get CLA from concentrated supplement sources rather than risk heart disease by consuming high amounts of fat.

BODYBUILDING APPLICATIONS

The old theory on fats and oils was that bodybuilders should consume as little as possible. But this view has changed in recent years thanks to such bodybuilding researcher/writers as Dan Duchaine and Dr. Mauro DiPasquale. Both of these highly acclaimed individuals have observed that bodybuilders who keep fat intake to a bare minimum make less progress than those who consume moderate amounts of certain fats including CLAs.

Although studies with humans are limited, the research on CLA use in animals is extensive. Numerous studies have demonstrated that animals fed diets high in CLA gain more muscular bodyweight and have reduced states of catabolism.[2,3] This last point is significant as most bodybuilding experts now feel anticatabolism is as important, if not more so, than anabolism (this concept serves as the basis for many of the high-tech supplements on the market – MET-Rx, RX-Fuel, and Phosphagain).

Other researchers suggest CLA increases the body's nitrogen-sparing abilities. As most readers know, positive nitrogen balance is essential for protein synthesis and hence muscular growth.

Finally, Dr. Barry Sears suggests CLA increases levels of eicosanoids – naturally occurring hormones which mediate the production of other hormones including testosterone and growth hormone.[4]

HOW MUCH?

Given the limited research available using human subjects, we have to rely on animal studies for guessing effective dosages for humans. In most studies, the best dosage seems to be around .01 to 2 percent of the animals weight. This works out to around 5 grams for a 200-pound bodybuilder. Assuming 1 gram from food sources, this leaves about 4 grams to be taken in supplement form. Like all ergogenic substances (both drugs and natural supplements), there will be individual differences.

THE PERFECT SUPPLEMENT?

Although too early to draw definite conclusions, it appears CLA holds great promise for bodybuilders. As of this writing, no side effects have been reported among animal or human subjects. Studies have suggested CLA may offer antioxidant properties including the ability to reduce the incidence of cancer.[5] This lack of toxicity means, unlike other supplements and drugs, there is no need to cycle the compound. Of course, you may want to experiment with cycling to avoid the tolerance factor which often develops with supplements.

If there is a disadvantage to CLA it's its availability. As of this writing, CLA supplements are not widely available in health-food stores. The good news is that there are no valid reasons for the FDA to stick its nose into pre-

Jay Cutler

Laura Creavalle

venting its wide distribution in the near future. And you can be sure that once the demand goes up, health-food stores and bodybuilding magazines will be flooded with advertisements for this most promising of ergogenic aids.

References

1) N. Jayde, "The Magic Bullet," *Flex*, 8:3 (May 1990).
2) S. Chin and others, "Conjugated Linoleic Acid is a Growth Factor for Rats as Shown by Enhanced Weight Gain and Improved Feed Efficiency," *Journal of Nutrition*, 124 (1994).
3) C.C. Miller and others, "Feeding Conjugated Linoleic Acid to Animals Partially Overcomes Catabolic Responses Due to Endotoxin Injection," *Biochemical and Biophysical Research Communication*, 198:3 (1994).
4) T.C. Luoma, "Can You Build Bigger Muscles With CLA?," *MuscleMedia 2000* (April 1996).
5) C. Ip and others, "Conjugated Linoleic Acid: A Powerful Anticarcinogen From Animal Food Sources," *Cancer*, 74 (1994).

CHAPTER TWENTY-TWO

Quick Energy Sources

A s most hard-training bodybuilders will admit, next to gaining muscle mass, the most difficult aspect to bodybuilding is finding enough energy to make it through a workout. Even during the off-season when caloric intake is high, there just doesn't seem to be adequate supplies of energy available. In many cases the problem is not so much the amount of calories, but what type. The accepted practice among athletes is to use carbohydrates as primary, and fats as secondary fuel sources. The problem, however, is that no matter what the energy source, it must first be metabolized by the body and stored in a usable form. And each of the steps involved in such metabolic processes can be a limiting variable. The ideal energy source therefore, is one that can be taken and either used immediately by the body for energy, or converted by one or two simple steps into a usable form.

Charles Clairmonte

To meet such demands, supplement researchers have come up with a host of products designed to provide athletes with a quick energy source. Many, such as glucose and other simple sugars, are well-known to readers (usually in the form of athletic drinks), but others like lactate and Coenzyme Q, while still in the preliminary stages of research, may hold promise for the future.

LACTATE

Given the negativity surrounding lactic acid, it's ironic that sports physiologists have suggested using its close cousin, lactate, as an energy source. Could this one-hydrogen-less compound be the ideal energy source for the next generation of bodybuilding superstars?

The late Andreas Munzer, Porter Cottrell and John Sherman.

Lactate is nothing more than the base version of the familiar acid lactic acid. The main difference between the two compounds is the presence or absence of one hydrogen atom. When lactic acid (or any other acid) loses a positively charged hydrogen atom it becomes a negatively charged base compound (the process is called disassociation). In biological systems most acids and bases switch back and forth trying to reach a state of equilibrium. Lactic acid/lactate equilibrium is no different, and varying degrees of both are found in the human body.

To seperate the two forms, chemists have devised a naming system where the acid form is called an "acid," and the base form receives the "ate" ending. The following table lists some common acids and their base counterparts:

ACID	BASE
Citric acid	Citrate
Acetic acid (vinegar)	Acetate
Glutamic acid	Glutamate
Lactic acid	Lactate

WHERE DOES IT COME FROM?

The primary energy source for most of the body's metabolic activities is adenosine triphosphate – ATP. There are two principal pathways by which the body can generate ATP. The aerobic (with oxygen) pathway involves the breakdown of a glucose molecule into two molecules of a compound called pyruvic acid. Pyruvic acid is itself broken down into carbon dioxide and water. The important factor in the last step is the presence of oxygen – aerobic respiration is oxygen dependant. As long as sufficient amounts of oxygen are present, the body will use the aerobic pathway for energy production. If the individual increases oxygen demands, the body compensates by increasing heart rate, lung rate, etc. A leisurely walk through the park or a round of golf will not overtax the body's ability to supply adequate amounts of oxygen, but if that slow walk becomes a fast run, or the round of golf is replaced by a two-hour bodybuilding workout, energy demands take a quantum leap and oxygen supplies become the limiting variable. Over the course of evolution, the mammalian body has developed a second pathway for supplying energy. Unlike the aerobic pathway, it does not require oxygen. Called anaerobic (without oxygen) respiration, it is the reason why your quadriceps burn after 15 to 20 reps of intense squats.

During strenuous exercise the amount of oxygen supplied to the muscles may not be adequate to completely break down pyruvic acid to carbon dioxide and water. Instead, pyruvic acid is reduced to lactic acid – the build up of which contributes to muscular aching and burning. Unlike the aerobic pathway which can last for long periods of time, anaerobic respiration only allows the muscles to keep working for a short duration. Most of the lactic acid is eventually removed back to the liver for conversion to glucose, but excess lactic acid may accumulate in the muscles and actually impair muscle contraction. A point is reached where the fatigue is so pronounced that further contraction is impossible.

Edgar Fletcher is feeling the burn – the result of anaerobic respiration.

POTENTIAL ROLES FOR LACTATE

Over the last twenty years many biochemists have changed their opinions regarding the usefulness of lactic acid and its derivative, lactate. Instead of being considered a waste product with no redeeming qualities, lactate is now thought to play a vital role in cellular respiration. Further, there is good evidence to suggest that many body tissues may actually prefer lactate as an energy source – more so than even glucose. Research hints that lactate may be the most superior fuel source for liver-glycogen synthesis.

David Dearth

Much of what we know concerning lactate is from the works of Dr. George Brooks, professor of physical education at the University of California. According to Dr. Brooks, lactic acid is quickly absorbed by various cells including the heart and other muscle tissues, and is used as an alternative energy source.[1]

Besides acting as an energy source, lactate may act as a blood buffer. As mentioned earlier in the text, increased blood acidity is detrimental to most metabolic processes. Lactate, which is negatively charged and consequently "seeks out" hydrogen-containing acids, may serve to neutralize excess acidity in muscles, promoting faster recovery. On the surface this sounds convincing, but lactate does not have the same buffering potential as other buffering agents like bicarbonates, phosphates, and even proteins. So while it may play a role in pH balance, it certainly doesn't have the same impact as other substances. (Keep this in mind when reading advertisers' claims about their lactate products.)

Research by Dr. Douglas Crist suggests the presence of lactic acid in the muscles during exercise may be the stimulus for growth hormone release. Theoretically, the consumption of lactate during a workout might produce an enhanced release of growth hormone.

Take caution, however, as the increase of natural growth hormone levels through diet may be a two-edged sword. GH will promote protein anabolism and increase fat oxidation, but it will also decrease the uptake of glucose by muscular tissues, causing a rise in blood-sugar levels. Thus, a diabetes-like situation is created. Many people are borderline diabetics but don't know it. Before taking such a supplement, speak to your physician, and get checked for diabetes just to be on the safe side.

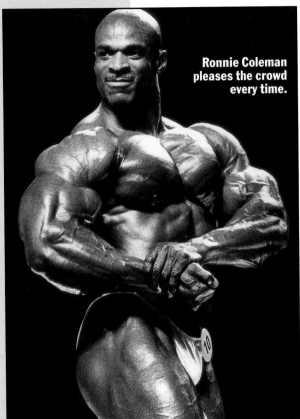

Ronnie Coleman pleases the crowd every time.

LACTATE AS A SUPPLEMENT?

With the evidence mounting, researchers began testing subjects to determine if lactate had ergogenic properties. One study conducted at California State University by Dr. Thomas Fahey used a form of lactate called polylactate combined with amino acids. The test subjects, all competitive cyclists, were divided into two groups. The control group recieved water containing aspartame, while the experimental group recieved a polylactate solution. Both groups rode a stationary cycle for three hours.

The results of the polylactate group included higher blood-sugar levels, more basic blood, and overall, less fatigue. The experimental group, despite consuming high concentrations of lactate also had blood-lactate levels comparable to resting values.[1] This means blood-lactate levels remained stationary throughout the experiment. Although not conclusive, evidence strongly suggests that the lactate was used as a fuel source.

BODYBUILDING APPLICATIONS

Given the nature of the exercise, it would seem that lactate supplements theoretically hold some promise for hard-training bodybuilders. Few forms of exercise change blood-pH balance like bodybuilding; and few place as great a demand on energy reserves. While carbohydrates are still king for muscle-glycogen synthesis, the evidence suggests that liver-glycogen synthesis may be increased through lactate supplementation.

The best energy supplement a bodybuilder could take would be one containing both lactate and carbohydrates. This would insure both glycogen pathways are stimulated (liver and muscle), leading to greater workout energy and stamina, and faster recovery between workouts.

We should add that despite the previous "scientific" evidence, the feedback from bodybuilders concerning lactate has been mixed. More bodybuilders say it didn't make a difference to their training as compared to those that said it did. We can only suggest you make your own evaluations by giving lactate a try. Don't be surprised if nothing dramatic happens.

SUCCINATES

Although succinates are among the most popular of bodybuilding supplements, their value is questionable. True, the theory behind succinates is sound – intermediate products of the citric acid or Kreb's cycle – but their practical application is less convincing.

According to advertisers, since succinates are part of the Kreb's cycle, (important for the production of ATP), supplementation (as with the supplement alpha-keto-gluterate, another intermediary of the Kreb's cycle) can boost ATP production. While promising in theory, there is little or no sound scientific evidence to back up these claims.

Other claims suggest succinates can decrease lactic-acid production (much of which is based on questionable Russian research), and increase creatine-phosphate levels. Such advertising may sound impressive, but in reality holds little biochemical merit. Succinates, while similar to the high-energy compounds creatine and ATP, are not utilized as much by the human body. Once again we have an example of advertisers cashing in on the "if some is good, more must be better" philosophy. Yes, the human body needs succinates (just as it needs protein, minerals, and vitamins), but there is little evidence to suggest it can serve as an ergogenic aid.

Perhaps the main problem with evaluating succinates is that they're often combined with other, more substantiated ergogenic nutrients. Most of these preparations (usually sold as "metabolic optimizers"), besides containing succinates, also contain branched-chain amino acids, carbohydrates, and a host of other beneficial compounds. The problem for the investigator is whether the positive results are due to the succinates, other nutrients, or a synergistic effect.

About all we can say concerning succinates is that while the evidence is sketchy, and they appear to be nontoxic, you might want to give them a try and see if they make any noticeable difference to your training. If they do, add them to your supplement arsenal. If not, put them on your "waste of money" list.

Jean-Pierre Fux

COENZYME Q (CoQ) – ENERGY FOR THE AGING BODYBUILDER

Although most of the research on this supplement is devoted to antiaging properties, CoQ holds great promise as an energy modulator for hard-training bodybuilders. And given the "aging" of our society (the average age of the population increasing because more and more people are living longer), CoQ may become one of the most impotant supplements for baby-boomer bodybuilders.

CoQ10, also known as ubiquinone, is a member of a group of biosubstances called coenzymes. As the name suggests, coenzymes help enzymes in regulating the body's various metabolic processes. Coenzymes are usually consumed in the diet, with vitamins being perhaps the most well-known coenzyme factors.

In recent years scientists have been looking at one coenzyme – CoQ10 – in more detail. Like many coenzymes, CoQ10 cannot be made by the body and must be consumed in the diet. Although widely aviaable in food, the body must first convert the precusor – CoQ – to a more usable form – in this case CoQ10. Scientists have determined that with age the rate of conversion declines, usually starting in the mid thirties. As we shall see, such deficiencies can have dire consequences.

WHAT DOES IT DO?

Given its importance for energy supply, CoQ is conveniently found in the mitochondrial membranes of body cells. These little storehouses of power spend virtually their entire lives generating energy for the body. They generate about 95 percent of the total energy extracted from the foods we eat. The chemical energy stored in food molecules is used by the mitochondria to pump protons across the mitochondrial membrane. Without CoQ10 you would not have enough energy to do even a few reps of a given exercise. Further, when CoQ10 levels decline most of the body's major organs are left in a state of energy deprival. The condition becomes worse if energy demands are increased by such factors as increased physical labor or exercise. For athletes, the first sign is chronic fatigue that is not releaved with extra rest.

In studies with mice, researchers have found that old mice given CoQ supplements remained vigorous and healthy as compared to the non-supplemented control group which died of factors related to old age. The researchers also found that CoQ-fed mice lived longer than would be expected – in some cases as much as 11 months longer.

Boyer Coe and Lou Ferrigno – posing to the max.

Besides increasing energy and vitality, CoQ seems to stimulate the body's immune system. Studies from the early 1970s showed that CoQ increased circulating levels of phagocytes – one of the body's primary defence scavengers. A decrease in CoQ levels, and hence decreased phagocytitic activity, is one of the theories why the immune response declines with age. One study which adds credence to this belief was conducted at the University of Texas at Austin. Experiments led by Dr. Karl Folkers showed that old mice who had lost most of their antibody-producing abilities regained their ability to develop the parasite-killing compounds when given a shot of CoQ.[2]

Research suggests CoQ can decrease free-radical damage, increase energy, and promote better heart functioning.
– Darrem Charles

A third benefit of CoQ concerns the heart. The highest concentrations of CoQ in the body are found within heart tissue. Studies with cardiac patients suggest that as we age CoQ levels decline. Studies form Japan show that CoQ supplements can reduce and in some cases reverse these declines. In fact, CoQ is available in Japan as a prescription medicine for heart disease.

A final benefit of CoQ supplementation is its ability to reduce free-radical damage. As discused earlier in the book, free radicals are substances produced by oxidation reactions, which over time can reach toxic levels, producing many of the effects which we call "aging." Research from Sweden suggests CoQ acts like vitamin E in its ability to reduce the harmful effects of free radicals produced by fat oxidation.

USE IN BODYBUILDING

With bodybuilding being one of the world's fastest growing sports (not so much the competitive as recreational forms), the proportion of "older" bodybuilders is increasing. Therefore, supplements which may reduce the effects of aging are in big demand. And while older bodybuilders may be in better shape than the general sedentary population, no one can stop the biological clock. With its ability to strengthen the heart and lower blood presure, CoQ10 is an excellent supplement for the "more senior" members of the sport.

There are also the anitoxidant abilities of CoQ10 to consider. As free-radical damage increases as we get older, it only follows that we should do everything in our power to slow the effects. CoQ10 has been shown to protect mitochondrial membranes from damage in the form of DNA loss.

The evidence regarding CoQ is not conclusive; nevertheless, it looks promising. Any substance that can increase energy, decrease free-radical damage, and promote better heart functioning is one to be seriously considered.

Jackie Paisley

SUPPLEMENTAL CoQ10

Although not a well-known supplement in North America, CoQ10 is very popular in Japan, and over 80 Japanese companies market the product in over 250 different forms including vitamins, minerals, and amino acids. Although the greatest concentrations of CoQ10 are in beef heart, the organ's lack of popularity in Japan has resulted in manufacturers producing CoQ10 through fermentation or synthetically.

While we will not go as far as to place CoQ10 in the "must use" catagory of supplements, there is evidence to suggest that hard-training athletes don't manufacture enough CoQ10 to meet their needs. Further, the anti-aging properties of the compound make it an excellent supplement for the "older" patrons of the sport.

Despite the sound research backing CoQ10, the FDA still refuses to sell the substance as a drug in the US. This is ironic as CoQ10 is really more of a vitamin than a drug. Like vitamins, but not drugs, CoQ10 is found in many foods and is really nothing more than a nutrient. And while concentrating the substance may produce limited "drug-like effects," the bottom line is that CoQ10 is not a dangerous pharmaceutical compound. Unfortunately, like many potentially beneficial substances, CoQ10 has become another causality of over-reactive drug-regulatory agencies.

DIMETHYLGLYCINE (DMG)

First isolated in the late 1940s from rice bran and apricot kernels, DMG is used by athletes to increase energy levels during exercise, and speed recovery between workouts. DMG is one of those borderline supplements which works for some but not for others. Like Smilax, DMG is primarily available as a sublingual liquid. To use, it's simply a matter of placing a few drops under the tongue.

DMG is believed to work by increasing the body's utilization of oxygen, which in turn leads to increased ATP production. More ATP means more energy and hence sustained power during intense exercise. There is also evidence to suggest DMG promotes the removal of lactic acid from muscles – once again increasing muscular recovery. We should add that the full benefits of DMG are not seen until complete, or near complete, muscular fatigue is reached. Therefore those bodybuilders following a "heavy duty" type of training schedule will probably benefit the most from DMG supplementation. Standard training techniques usually do not lead to complete exhaustion and therefore the full benefits of DMG will not be realized.

With regards to usage, the best effects are obtained by taking 2 or 3 drops every 30 minutes or so during intense exercise. Be warned. Given DMG's inconsistent results, don't be surprised if you're one of the ones who experiences little or no benefits from using the supplement. All we can say is give it a try and see what happens.

ENERGY BARS

Manufacturers create a number of supplements that take the bodybuilding world by storm. In the 1950s and 1960s it was protein powders; the 1970s and early 1980s introduced amino acids and glandulars; and now we have such crazes as creatine, HCA, and energy bars. While the first two individual supplements are backed by scientific data, the last product covers a broad spectrum of substances and relies more on hype and advertising than hard scientific evidence.

The term energy bar is in some respects misleading as many contain more protein than energy sources. In any case, such products are nothing more than candy-bar sized and shaped, containing everything from fats and carbohydrates to protein and minerals. Like most supplements, energy bars don't take the place of good nutrition, but if your lifestyle necessitates skipping meals, or you feel sluggish during your workouts, perhaps (and we say this guardedly) an energy bar would be ideal.

IT'S A WIDE, WIDE WORLD

It would be convenient if there were only one or two brands to choose from, but given the popularity of the product, it seems every supplement manufacturer out there has a particular version. This must be taken into account when choosing a sports bar as different sports have different nutritional requirements. For marathon runners, bars high in fat will probably not constitute the same problem as for a competitive bodybuilder ripping up for a contest. Generally speaking, bodybuilders should select a bar that is high in protein and carbohydrate, but low in fat.

Even with proper nutrition and adequate rest, many athletes "hit the wall" during their workouts. Low blood sugar is a frequent problem during such high-intensity events as cycling, swimming, and bodybuilding. On aver-

Choose wisely – there are so many energy bars to select from, but with vastly different carb/protein/fat ratios.

age, an individual has about 60 minutes of stored glycogen to use, and once blood sugar falls, you fatigue more quickly, motivation disappears, and in extreme cases, you feel disoriented and nauseous.

Although it varies, a hard-training athlete requires at least 50 calories per kilogram of bodyweight per day for a man, and at least 45 calories for a woman. This works out to 3400 calories for a 150-pound male and 2500 calories for a 120-pound female. According to researchers at Tufts University in Boston, 30 percent of male endurance athletes and 70 percent of male strength-sport athletes don't take in enough calories. The studies also found that the problem is worse with females, with the numbers being 88 percent and 100 percent respectively.

The obvious solution to the previous is to take in more food, but this has its limits. Most food sources have to be prepared, and this takes time. For hard-training athletes, time is often in short supply. What they need are calorie sources which require no preparation, taste great, and provide essential nutrients. As you probably guessed by now, energy bars are an ideal alternative.

WHAT THEY CONTAIN

The primary ingredients in energy bars are in the form of carbs, fats, and protein. Of the three, the body prefers carbohydrates as the main fuel source. Besides fueling the muscles, carbs supply the brain with most of its energy. Most energy bars use glucose as the main carb source, and the more popular bars supply upwards of 40 grams of carbohydrate each. The leader of the pack, Twin Lab's "Ultra Fuel," provides a wopping 100 grams of carbohydrate.

Another energy source is fat. If there are high levels circulating through your veins the evidence suggests it will be used as a fuel source before glycogen supplies. Some energy bars have up to 30 percent of their calories supplied in the form of fat. This sounds high (and it is) but it still falls below the 37 percent intake value for the typical North American whose diet is loaded with fat.

If you need to consume extra calories, the convenience of energy bars may be the solution.

If there is a disadvantage to using high-fat energy bars it's acclimation. One of the benefits of exercise – especially endurance training – is an improved ability to use fats as an energy source. Sedentary individuals usually store fat in adipose tissue, whereas highly conditioned athletes burn most, if not all of it for energy. This occurs because of the increased blood supply to fat stores which stimulates the release of fat-degrading enzymes. For athletes with such abilities, high-fat energy bars are a great source of fuel, while untrained individuals may want to avoid these versions. Although most bars only contain 2 to 4 grams of fat, one product, Champion Nutrition's "Super Heavyweight" bar contains 10 grams of fat.

The third energy source is amino acids, particularly the branched-chain aminos. At one time, biochemists assumed aminos were strictly limited to tissue repair, but the evidence now suggests they are used as an energy source as well. Some researchers claim that 70 percent of the fuel used by marathon runners is supplied by amino acids (one of the reasons why most are underweight and have a "stringy" appearance). Such popular brands as MET-Rx and Super Heavyweight provide 30 grams of protein per bar.

OTHER INGREDIENTS

To meet the demands of athletes (and to provide a basis for advertising) many manufacturers load their products with vitamins, minerals, chromium sources, and various herb-derived substances. The result is a nutritional snack which supplies most of the essential nutrients in a convenient manner. While the inclusion of vitamins and minerals makes sense, these substances are found in such low amounts that they won't provide much of an effect in the body. The only benefit of such substances is to allow manufacturers to claim their energy bars are complete, and hence, attract more buyers.

HOW TO SELECT AND USE ENERGY BARS

Perhaps the most basic guideline for choosing an energy bar is taste. Unlike many supplements, energy bars usually taste pretty good. Like candy bars though, there is much variation and you will have to make up your own mind. It doesn't make much sense to choose a bar which tastes awful and has to be forced down.

Denise Masino

Tom Platz

The next order of business is to select a bar which provides the calories and nutrients you want. If you are an endurance athlete, and your primary concern is energy, a bar high in calories will provide an extra source of energy. Such products as Champion Nutrition's Super Heavyweight bar and Twin Lab's Ultra Fuel contain nearly 500 calories per bar.

Bodybuilders on the other hand should keep fat levels low. In this case a bar high in carbohydrate and low in fat is recommended. Given the importance of amino acids – especially the branched-chain aminos – bars high in protein would benefit most athletes.

With regards to timing, it is recommended endurance athletes consume an energy bar a couple of hours before exercise, a few minutes before exercise, or during exercise. You can even take them after exercise to boost recovery. The worst time, however, would be about 45 to 60 minutes before exercising. This is because such a high level of carbohydrates will cause a rapid release of insulin which reduces blood-sugar levels, leading to sluggishness and drowsiness.

For bodybuilders and other athletes involved in strength sports, timing is not as crucial. The most popular times include 30 minutes before a workout or immediately after. In fact, taking them after working out probably makes the most sense as many individuals have trouble eating within the first 60 minutes following a workout. Not only will the carbohydrate replenish glycogen supplies but extra protein never goes astray – despite what some nutritionists would have you believe.

Whether bodybuilder or marathon runner, everyone who uses energy bars should take them with water. Energy bars are very concentrated and water is needed to help your digestive system break down and absorb the nutrients (one to two glasses is the recommended amount).

Don't fall into the trap of using energy bars as a replacement for good nutrition. Remember, energy bars are to be used as a supplement not a meal.

DO BODYBUILDERS NEED THEM?

Do bodybuilders need energy bars? Maybe not. While energy bars are simple to carry and use, they are also expensive. Adequate carbohydrate-rich substitutes that are cheaper include: low-fat granola bars (30 cents each), raisins (18 cents), bagels, fruit, yogurt, breakfast cereal, and bananas. Further, added vitamins and amino acids are not energy enhancers so much as price enhancers. If you are already using supplements, you don't need these extras, and certainly not at exorbitant prices. Our suggestion – buy a variety of low-fat granola bars at your local supermarket, and use the extra money for quality supplements.

COST

As supplements go, energy bars are moderately priced. A survey of numerous health-food stores and magazines reveals that prices generally range from about $1.49 to $2.49 US. If you consume one a day this works out to between $10.50 and $17.50 a week ($42 to $70 a month). As a suggestion, if you take a liking to energy bars and find you eat a couple every day, check with a distributor about purchasing in bulk. Instead of buying them individually, you may be able to purchase them in boxes of 10, 20, or more. Doing so will save you a lot of cash down the road.

Bagels provide a cheap and all-natural alternative to energy bars.

SIDE EFFECTS

The issue of side effects rarely applys to energy bars; nevertheless, like most food sources there are precautions to remember. If you suffer from diabetes, the high-sugar content of energy bars may seriously interfere with blood-sugar levels. If your diabetes is severe enough to warrant daily insulin injections, we strongly advise avoiding energy bars high in carbohydrates.

One side effect that ocassionally gets reported is diarrhea. This is probably due to the bar's high nutrient concentration. In most cases this can be avoided by drinking plenty of water. If this does not help, try experimenting with different brands. You might be allergic to an ingredient used by one manufacturer. If switching doesn't bring relief, we suggest skipping them altogether (of course, if you have problems with most supplements and even many foods, we advise you see a physician, as this may be indicitive of some underlying medical condition).

References
1) J. Brainum, *Muscle and Fitness*, 50:5 (1989).
2) M. Colgan, "Things Go Better With CoQ," *Muscle and Fitness*, 49:7 (1988).

BOOK SIX

Ergogenic Procedures and Techniques

"I have had no control over my god-given looks, but for the last few years I've been working really hard to build a better physique and to be recognized as a legitimate bodybuilder who happens to have a marketable appearance."

– Melissa Coates, IFBB Pro.

Melissa Coates

Garrett Downing

Surgery

The focus of this book is primarily on ergogenic aids; therefore, we thought it appropriate to include a section on what could be termed "ergogenic procedures."

Given the competitiveness of today's sports, and the "win at any cost" mentality, it should not come as a shock that many athletes go beyond the limits of nutrition and pharmacology. No matter how adequate the diet, or how broad the spectrum of drugs taken, there is a ceiling to human physical development and performance. All the protein in the world will not build 20-inch calves if an individual lacks the genetics to do so. And while, in many cases, the limiting factor is laziness a few unlucky bodybuilders were not blessed with "hugeness genetics" in some muscle groups.

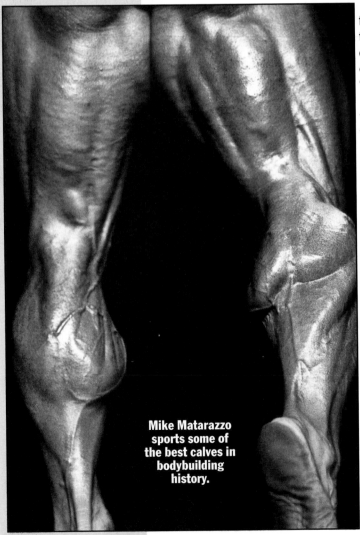

Mike Matarazzo sports some of the best calves in bodybuilding history.

The same holds true for bodyfat. There are unfortunate souls who through no fault of their own have great difficulty in losing bodyfat – irregardless of dieting techniques followed and "cutting" drugs used.

In the following chapters we will look at some of the controversial techniques utilized by bodybuilders to either maintain or surpass the physical appearance of their competitors. We should add that some of the procedures are banned by bodybuilding federations (muscle implants); others may be dangerous (liposuction); and a few are both potentially dangerous and limited in their effectiveness (electrostimulation).

Most people would agree that we live in a world based on physical appearance. All of our favorite TV and movie stars are "physically attractive," and for every plain-looking "character actor" there are thousands of others who are the embodiment of physical perfection. Many argue that taken to the extreme such a focus is unhealthy. Others contend that "ranking" individuals primarily on appearance is morally unjust. Perhaps they're right. But no matter what the argument there is no escaping the fact that those individuals with attrac-

Shawn Ray, Roland Cziurlok and the late Andreas Munzer.

tive facial features and outstanding physiques are "valued" more highly in modern society (the number of plastic surgeons in California alone can attest to this).

Such beliefs are so powerful that even children have been shown to associate intelligence with attractiveness. Psychologists have carried out experiments with preschoolers who were asked to "describe" their "new" teachers according to intelligence, friendliness, and appearance. Unbeknownst to the kids the new teachers were part of the experiment and were chosen to represent a wide cross section of physical attributes. As theorized, the most attractive female teachers were considered the most intelligent and friendly by the children. And while the children's attitudes are primarily learned, the results of the experiments are very persuasive.

Given the previous, is it any wonder that millions of individuals have resorted to surgery to make themselves more physically attractive? For athletes in sports where placement is based on judges' "opinions," the temptation is sometimes too great not to consider surgically altering the face or body. In such sports as gymnastics, figure skating, and bodybuilding, final placings are often so close that one wonders how the judges separated the contestants. And unfair as it may be, physical appearance plays a major role (in bodybuilding it is the deciding factor). Afterall, the judges are only human.

There are many forms of plastic surgery too numerous to list here. For the purposes of this book we shall look at the most common types and their implications for bodybuilders.

IMPLANTS

Perhaps the most contested ergogenic procedure in recent years has been the issue of implants. Numerous bodybuilders, who for years sported mediocre bodyparts, suddenly turn up onstage revealing appendages that bare little resemblance to their former selves.

"I never train my calves. My father has bigger calves than mine. One year I trained them up to 23 inches – they looked stupid – I couldn't get my pants over them. All I do is stretch my calves out because they cramp all the time."

– Mike Matarazzo, IFBB pro commenting on the "problems" he's had with his calves.

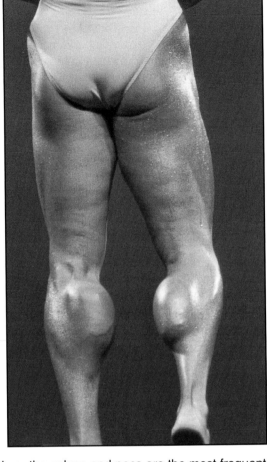

In rare cases, surgery does not have the intended outcome.

> "Although genetics plays a very large role in determining the size, shape and density of a muscle, genetics also control how easy it will be to obtain muscle growth. It sounds as if your family might have genetics to be lean, which is good, but you may find it harder to grow a muscle – say your calves – if nobody has them."
>
> – Marla Duncan, women's fitness champion and former *MuscleMag* columnist commenting on the role genetics plays in balancing muscular development.

For male bodybuilders, the calves and pecs are the most frequent targets for surgical alteration. For females, the breasts tend to recieve the most attention. As would be expected the procedures have sparked some heated debate in bodybuilding circles, and while IFBB officials have made calf and pec implants grounds for disqualification, breast implants are acceptable.

CALF IMPLANTS

Although most cases of weak calves are the result of inadequate or insufficient training, a few unlucky bodybuilders were born with what's popularly called "unfavourable genetics." This is a polite way of saying that no matter how hard the calves are trained, the little suckers won't respond. Regular readers of *MuscleMag International* and other bodybuilding magazines are no doubt familiar with the most famous cases of poor calf development. Bodybuilders such as Bill Grant, Dave Draper, and Robby Robinson spent thousands of hours blasting their calves from just about every conceivable angle, yet achieved only mediocrity for their efforts. Conversely, guys like Chris Dickerson, Mike Mentzer, and Mike Matarazzo sport some of the largest calves in bodybuilding history, while doing nothing out of the ordinary to get them.

In years gone by, being stuck with "stubborn calves" meant putting up with the condition, but today bodybuilders may opt for a different course of action. Taking a cue from their female counterparts, many male bodybuilders make an appointment with a plastic surgeon.

SURGICAL PROCEDURE

Although it displays the most dramatic results of any surgical procedure, implanting is one of the simpler to perform.

The old technique involved placing one large silicone implant just below the skin, on top of the underlying calf muscle. Unfortunately, incidents of slippage were common and in many cases the results looked artificial (the calf complex consists of numerous small muscles not one large one).

In recent years the procedure has evolved. It involves making a small, one- or two-inch incision behind the knee, and creating a hollow pocket under the fascia of the muscle (fibrous cover over the muscle). Although it varies, two or three, six- to eight-inch-long silicone prostheses are inserted into the pocket, between the underlying muscle and overlying fascia. Once securely in place, the incision is closed, bandaged, and given time to heal.

With regards to cost, the average price is $5000 to $10,000 US, depending on the extensiveness of the procedure. If carried out for reconstructive reasons (following a car- or job-related accident) most insurance policies will cover the cost, but check with your insurance company to be sure. Most policies don't cover the procedure if just for cosmetic reasons (enlarging the calves for bodybuilding).

RECOVERY

Recovery generally takes three to four weeks with the first week being the most difficult. Most report moderate degrees of pain following surgery which can be alleviated with strong over-the-counter painkillers like Tylenol and acetaminophen. Avoid aspirin though, as its anticoagulant properties may interfere with recovery.

It's generally recommended that patients stay in bed for the first week or so following surgery and limit walking. In fact, it will probably take a couple of weeks before you attain full walking ability; the length of time being determined by the size and number of prostheses inserted. After about a month, most, if not all the swelling will have subsided and normal walking can resume. There will probably be some tightness in the calf but this is to be expected as the skin stretches to accommodate the larger body underneath it.

Aaron Baker and Michael Francois

IMPLICATIONS FOR BODYBUILDERS

It has been frequently said that the three muscles that can't be hidden onstage are the abs, shoulders and calves. While the abs can be brought out with diet, and the shoulders "widened" to a degree with exercise, often times the same cannot be said for the calves. For someone who

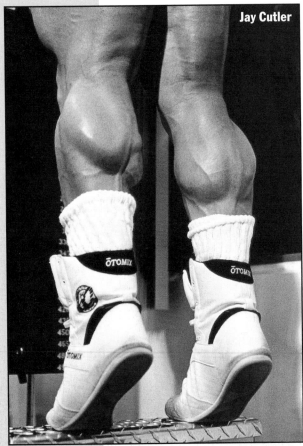

Jay Cutler

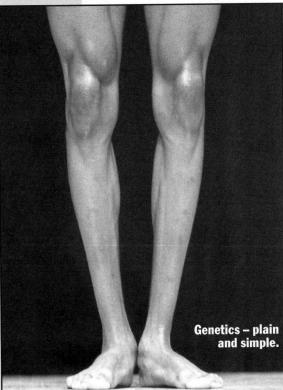

Genetics – plain and simple.

bodybuilds for recreation, a less than ideal set of calves is endurable. But for a competitive bodybuilder, lacklustre calves can mean hundreds of thousands of dollars in prize money. Given such pressure, and the ease and simplicity of surgical implants, it's not surprising that a few top pros have been accused of engaging in the procedure. Calf implants can increase the circumfrence of the calf muscle by one or two inches, a considerable advantage in today's highly competitive bodybuilding arena.

As of yet, no pro has come out and fessed up to the practice, but the results are hard to hide. Mediocre lower legs have been replaced by large, full, and vascular calves. In some cases the calves don't even look "natural" and have a balloon-like appearance. It's possible for beginners to totally transform their legs, as most make their best progress during the first few years of training; however, for a pro with ten, fifteen, or twenty years of experience, it's virtually impossible. Radical changes in diet, training, and even drugs, can only make so much difference.

Faced with such accusations most bodybuilding federations have banned the practice of calf implants, but it's more of a public-relations ploy than an enforceable one. The problem is detection. If the implant procedure was carried out by a reputable physician, it's virtually impossible to detect the incision. Granted, a few unlucky individuals with thin skin may reveal incision scars, but a bodybuilder who had the operation 10 to 12 months before a contest stands little chance of being caught. Even if it was possible to easily detect the implants, there is just no way competitors are going to line up for inspection like pieces of racing stock. The legal implications for the respective federations would be enormous. So while other competitors may scream "unfair," all we can say is that calf implants are going to be around for a while – at least until another procedure is perfected (fetal tissue perhaps?).

PEC IMPLANTS

Although not as popular with bodybuilders as calf implants, pec implants are becoming the rage with male models and actors. And like their female conuterparts who opt for breast implants, males see increasing their chest size as a way to land that big modeling contract or movie role.

While regular training will enlarge the pectorals of most, a few unlucky individuals are born with either a deficiency in chest muscle fibers, or in extreme cases, complete absence of one of the pectoral muscles. In the former case, exercise will bring some degree of enlargement. But as muscle growth is due to individual fibers expanding, not increasing in number, it stands to reason that a deficiency in fibers will hinder progress (recent evidence suggests that fibers may split in response to intense exercise, but this is a much contested issue). As for the latter case – no amount of training can increase the size of something that is not there. In fact, regular exercise will only enlarge other muscles making the deficiency more noticeable.

SURGICAL PROCEDURE

As with calf implants, the philosophy behind pec implants is to take something smaller and make it appear larger. The surgeon makes one or two incisions along the arm pit and pectoral region, and inserts two or three fusiform implants. These may be placed on top of the underlying muscle or under it, depending on how much muscle is there to begin with. If there is sufficient muscle, the implants are placed under it. If the muscle is totally absent or extremely shallow, the implants are placed on top. To simulate real pectoral

Pec-enlargement surgery is banned by most bodybuilding federations including the IFBB.

muscle, the implants are arranged longitudinally and fanned out to immitate the pectoral's various divisions. Although it varies, pec implants generally average about 15 centimeters in length, and about three to five centimeters in thickness.

Normally pec-enlargement surgery takes place in a physician's outpatient clinic, and requires one to two hours. If it's a one-side implant, it's relatively straightforward and uncomplicated. If, however, both pecs plus the sternum have to be built up, the surgery may require hospitalization. For women there is often the need for breast enlargement as well, so this may complicate matters.

After surgery the patient is often wrapped and secured to reduce chest contraction or movement. To prevent infection antibiotics are often prescribed. Full recovery generally takes four to six weeks, but once again, depends on the extent of the operation. There may be some initial numbness left over from surgery, but this is temporary and full sensation will return.

Breasts and a low-bodyfat level – an unbeatable combination for some women thanks to implants.

BREAST IMPLANTS

If calf implants are the most performed cosmetic procedure in males, by far the most performed female equivalent is breast implants. In fact, breast implants are the most popular form of cosmetic surgery for women, period – irregardless of sport or occupation.

A LONG HISTORY

North Americans have always held a fascination with large breasts, but the concept that women should have large bosoms recieved its greatest boost in the 1940s and 50s when such stars as Marilyn Monroe, Jane Mansfield, and Betty Grable paraded across cinema screens sporting the best that Mother Nature could offer. Granted, there followed periods of time where small breasts came into vogue – the Twiggy revolution of the 1960s – but the general idea that women are supposed to have large breasts has remained relatively constant over the centuries.

"Perhaps there might be some consideration of having seperate divisions of competition – one for the unblessed, unembellished and unabashed who would go unadorned, and another division for women with substantially sized breasts or inhibitions who would have covers on top."

– One *MuscleMag* reader responding to the state of affairs in womens' bodybuilding with regards to breast size and bodyfat percentage.

Given the vast spectrum in breast size across the female population it was only a matter of time before surgeons developed techniques to "help" women who were not endowed with large breasts. As techniques improved in effectiveness and safety, the number of women who opted for breast-enlargement surgery took a quantum leap. We should add that there are different attitudes on this issue across the globe, with North American women leading the way in implant surgery. Women in Europe don't seem to be as concerned about breast size and if their appearance changes over time, it doesn't seem to concern them as much. It will be interesting to see what trends develop as the world "shrinks" in response to the eletronic revolution. Will North American ideals be the new standard, or will European or Asian values of looking at the complete person take center stage.

HISTORY OF BREAST IMPLANTS

The skills demonstrated by a modern Beverly Hills plastic surgeon are the end product of nearly one hundred years of experimentation into breast enlargement. Early surgeons tried transplanting fat from other areas of the body into the breast region. Although it met with initial success, it had its drawbacks including scarring and the death of the fat tissue due to a decreased blood supply.

The next leap in enlargement techniques came about in the 1950s when surgeons tried implanting sponges into the breasts. Unfortunately, the sponges hardened with time and instead of larger, fuller breasts, patients were left with smaller, harder breasts that had an unnatural look to them.

Although the next form of enhancement held great promise, it met with serious consequences – the ramifications of which are still being experienced. Rarely a day goes by that some newspaper article or TV program doesn't mention the disastrous side effects of silicone implants. The procedure of injecting silicone directly into the breasts seemed to be the great technique surgeons were looking for as it was easy to perform and the results produced larger but still naturally looking breasts. Soon, however, the first side effects began surfacing. In small amounts, silicone is not that harmful to the body, but in the amounts used in breast implants, it sometimes migrated out of the breasts and into other tissues including the bloodstream. In many cases, the blood vessels became so clogged that blood flow to the breast tissue was impeded – the result of which was the death of the breast tissue, necessitating amputation. In other cases the implants were believed to have caused tumor development.

Although the procedure was in vogue for only ten years, millions of women had silicone implants, with thousands suffering horrendous side effects. Numerous law suits were filed on behalf of clients, and the legal ramifications continue to this day.

A SAFER ALTERNATIVE

About the only positive thing learned from silicone injections was that the breasts could be enlarged by putting something in there. The logical solution was to use a gel-filled bag that could be placed on top of the pectoral muscle. A number of materials were tried but surprisingly the ideal substance turned out to be silicone rubber called silastic gel. This choice initially met with resistance given the side effects associated with silicone implants, however, the vast differences between the two procedures was soon made clear, and today the technique is considered among the safest surgical procedures performed.

Today, breast-implant surgery is considered one of the safest surgical procedures performed.

HOW IT'S PERFORMED

Breast-enhancement surgery is considered relatively minor, even though anaesthetic is used and an incision is made. With the possible exception of accident victims, patients receiving breast implants are in excellent physical and psychological health. It may sound trivial, but physicians rank psychological well-being just as highly as physical health. In fact, even though it means losing thousands of dollars in business, most plastic surgeons will refuse a patient who holds inappropriate beliefs about breast enhancement. Thinking that larger breasts will save a relationship or catapult oneself to movie stardom are not considered valid reasons for breast enlargement by most surgeons.

The actual surgery is fairly straightforward with the gel-filled bag being placed on top of the pectoral muscle, under the mammary gland and adipose tissue. Another procedure involves placing the implant under the pectoral muscle, but contraction of the muscle tends to flatten and force the implant sideways so most surgeons only perform this version in extreme cases.

Early procedures involved making the incision at the base of the breast but this was found to leave a scar. Now most surgeons make a small cut next to the nipple, or along the side just under the armpit.

Like vasectomies, breast-enhancement surgery takes about an hour and can be performed in a physician's office under local anesthetic. Recovery time varies, but in most cases takes three or four weeks (with physiotherapy exercises commencing after about seven days and increasing accordingly).

Breast-enhancement surgery costs in the $5000 to $10,000 range – although specialized procedures may run well above this.

Lynea Brehm, Laura Binetti, Valerie Gangi, Inna Vit and Gayle Moher

APPLICATIONS TO BODYBUILDERS

It's ironic that a form of physical exercise designed to tone and increase the bustline may in fact decrease its size. But it's not the weight training that causes the size loss. Regular exercising will slightly increase bust size by enlarging the underlying pectoral muscles, as most women who take up weight training quickly discover. The problem occurs, however, when competitive female bodybuilders go on a precontest diet.

Inna Vit

"While agreeing that to have the bag (implant) slid under and not over the muscle is better, size is also an important consideration. The trouble comes when a pro bodybuilder is in the last stages of contest preparation. It's then, when her fat level is truly depleted, that the bigger implants look most obvious and at their worst. With fitness stars who never deplete to the same extent, muscle, fat levels and implant blend together so well that the round edge of the implant bag can hardly be seen. This is not so with physique stars. That's why smaller implants on a pro bodybuilder look much more attractive."

– Fitness contestant responding to an article in *MuscleMag* concerning implants for female bodybuilders and fitness contestants.

For those that don't know, the breasts are nothing more than fat tissue and mammary glands – and like most fat deposits will shrink when caloric intake is reduced. With bodybuilding standards for women having evolved to parallel those of men, it's not surprising that more and more women are striving to reduce their bodyfat percentage to two to four percent. This means sacrificing breast size, and here lies the problem. No matter how muscular or defined a female bodybuilder may become, most of the viewing public still expect females to have "ample breast size." And while onstage larger breasts may not make as big an impact as defined pectorals, offstage most women would prefer a larger bustline. For many female bodybuilders the logical solution is surgery.

Although we can't generalize and say "all," it's probably true that the vast majority of competitive female bodybuilders have had some sort of breast-enhancement surgery. This is obvious given the extremely low bodyfat pecentages which would not support the retainment of significant breast tissue.

Denise Masino

As of this writing, breast-enhancement surgery is accepted by most, if not all, bodybuilding federations. This means women are free to undertake the procedure without fear of penalization. Now muscles can be developed to the maximum, bodyfat levels lowered to the minimum, and perhaps most important, breast size can be increased to maintain the "curves" generally associated with the female form.

IMPLANT CONCLUSION

Perhaps the greatest risk for bodybuilders undergoing implants is not medical but political. As mentioned at the beginning of the chapter, muscle implants are banned by most bodybuilding federations including the IFBB. Conversely, breast implants are acceptable. The following rule has been adopted by the IFBB and applies to both amateur and professional bodybuilders.

> "The International Federation of Bodybuilders does not condone or accept muscle implants. Any artificial improvement of the "muscle" is in violation of the rules. Therefore any bodybuilder who aquires muscle implants for competitive purposes will face disqualification from the event in which he/she is competing and possible suspension for a period of time, which will be decided upon by an Executive Council Ad Hoc Committee.
>
> Breast implants are not considered to be against the rules because breasts are not considered muscles. For this reason, cosmetic surgery such as breast implants and facial alterations to enhance appearance are allowable. However, any artificial improvement of MUSCLE is strictly prohibited."

"Female competitors get breast implants for various reasons. Believe it or not, most get them more to improve their look in the off-season than onstage. Many times, because breasts are just fat, women athletes are left a little flat in this area, even in the off-season, because they've achieved a lower bodyfat level than the average women."

– Tonya Knight, pro bodybuilder commenting on the primary reasons female bodybuilders get breast implants.

OTHER SURGICAL TECHNIQUES

Besides implants, many bodybuilders have used other means to "improve" their physical appearance. After years of perfecting their bodies, many feel that a less than attractive face is holding back their progress. In most cases the feelings are unwarranted, but nevertheless the competitiveness of today's contests drives many to the surgeon's office. For others the ravages of father time have not been kind, and plastic surgery is a realistic and practical consideration. The following is but a sample of the many procedures that make up the plastic-surgery spectrum.

FACE LIFTS – RHYTIDECTOMY

Perhaps the most common form of cosmetic surgery is the face lift. At one time this procedure was only for the rich and famous of Beverly Hills, but not any more. Nowadays everyone from aspring actresses and models to athletes and the elderly are lining up at surgeons' offices.

In simple terms the face-lift procedure involves tightening the facial muscles and tissues of the face region. As a result, the overlying skin becomes less wrinkled and in a manner of speaking the face becomes "younger." For obese patients, surgeons may use liposuction to vacuum out excess adipose tissue (more on this technique later), and then remove any excess stretched skin. Although it varies, a complete face lift can take several hours to perform, but in many cases can be conducted in the doctor's office. This allows the individual to go home the same day. There is some initial swelling (as would be expected following surgery), but after a few days it subsides, allowing the skin to tighten and "hug" the face. The end result is a smoother, more youthful appearance.

NOSE JOB – RHINOPLASTY

For many individuals a complete face lift is neither necessary, nor desirable. Just one part of the face is bothersome, and in most cases this feature is the nose. Most of us know someone whose otherwise great facial features are offset by a nose that is proportionally too large. Most individuals ignore the trait and live life to the fullest. But for an actress seeking that big role or an athlete in a sport where facial appearance counts (bodybuilding, figure skating, etc.), that over-sized snoozer may need to be looked at.

To minimize the effect and reduce the likelihood of visible scars, most "nose jobs" are performed from the inside out. Afterwards the inside of the nose is packed with supportive material and the outside with a protective splint. After a few weeks the support braces are removed to allow any swelling or bruising to clear.

Like most implant and face-lift procedures, nose jobs can be conducted in the physician's clinic or office facilities. Bruising and pain is usually minimal and any swelling quickly disappears. Most nose jobs only involve slight modifications, although in cases of disease or accident, full reconstruction may be necessary.

HAIR CARE

This may seem like a contradiction in a sport where the absence of hair is emphasized, but many bodybuilders who prematurely lose their scalp hair opt for techniques to cover the "bald spot."

There are many reasons for the loss of scalp hair. In most cases it's genetic. Chances are, if other same-sex members of your family began losing their hair at an early age, the odds are you will too. Although it varies, most males who suffer male-pattern baldness begin losing scalp hair in their late 20s and early 30s.

Bodybuilders who use anabolic steroids are at special risk for hair loss due to the unique properties of androgenic drugs. Although the exact mechanism of action is not fully understood (one theory suggests steroids destroy hair follicles), it's accepted that most

Mauro Sarni

individuals who use anabolic steroids experience varying degrees of scalp hair loss. And it's not just the guys either. Many top female bodybuilders have creatively camouflaged their baldness with the aid of wigs.

Whatever the reason for hair loss, many bodybuilders are unhappy with the situation and seek remedies. Although wigs and toupees are options, in recent years science has provided two more realistic alternatives – Minoxidil and transplants.

MINOXIDIL

Up until the late 1970s individuals experiencing hair loss had few options to hide their baldness. Wigs and toupees were a partial solution. The biggest breakthrough came from the Upjohn pharmaceutical company. Upjohn was in the middle of tests on a new antihypertensive drug called Minoxidil, when a few of the test subjects noticed a peculiar side effect – scalp hair growth. Recognizing the potential of the new drug, Upjohn began testing a solution

> "In the past I had a couple of people in the industry tell me that I should get my nose done because it was, well, different. I always believed that you shouldn't change yourself just to please others, that if God gave you a dorky nose, you were meant to have a dorky nose. My husband changed that for me when he said, "If God hadn't wanted you to have the ability to get your dorky nose fixed, he wouldn't have made plastic surgery." If you dislike something about your body so much that it affects your life all the time, then sure, go ahead and make yourself feel better. Why not?"
>
> – Marla Duncan, former *MuscleMag* columnist commenting on her change in attitude towards plastic surgery.

Marla Duncan and Adrian Bathos

containing Minoxidil (one to three percent) that could be rubbed directly on the scalp.

To determine the effectiveness of the drug Upjohn conducted a one-year study in 27 centers across the United States. After one year, the researchers concluded that Minoxidil was effective in about 76 percent of the test subjects. While the amount of hair growth varied, from fine, sparse hair, to normal-sized fibers, the results showed great promise for sufferers of male-patterned baldness.[1]

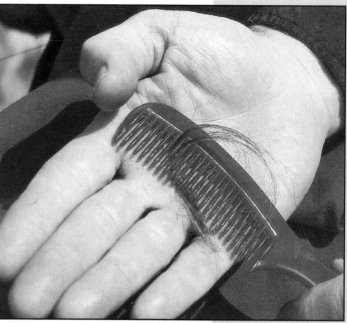

If the drug could be chastised for anything it was it's tendancy to promote "peach fuzz" type growth rather than mature hair fibers. During the Upjohn trials most researchers found that "real" hair growth varied between two and 23 percent. Further, the only men who showed potential for developing acceptable hair growth were those in their 20s and 30s, who still had a moderate degree of scalp hair.

Another finding was that Minoxidil had little effect on regenerating new hair growth on the front of the scalp, that is, it can't reverse the dreaded receeding hairline; although in a few cases it may slow it down.

Minoxidil's mechanism of action concerning hair growth is poorly understood. Some researchers suggest that it increases blood flow to the hair follicles, thus increasing the amount of nutrients available for hair growth. Others theorize the drug works by slowing down the rate of follicle degeneration, and reduces matrix aging – the cells which make up the hair fibers.

This last point has great significance for bodybuilders using steroids, as androgen-induced hair loss is believed to be related to follicle destruction and matrix degeneration.

SIDE EFFECTS

Side effects are usually related to misuse (the "if some is good, more is better," mentality); however, some individuals may be at special risk. Anyone with cardiovascular disease would be wise to avoid the drug given its potential to cause edema. And those with heart problems are at risk because of Minoxidil's stimulating effects on heart rate. Although not life threatening, some individuals report other side effects, including impotenence, dizziness, and skin rashes.

As a final comment, be warned that Minoxidil is not something to be used for a few months and then discarded (unless it doesn't work). It is a lifetime commitment, and any new growth will quickly fall out if the drug is discontinued.

While Minoxidil is not a cure for baldness, and from a statistical point of view has a low success rate (eight percent), for a few lucky individuals the drug is a godsend. Granted the cost is significant – $500 to $1000 a year for the rest of the individual's life – but for those who experience success, the results are worth the investment.

"In any case I would suspect that almost all anabolic steroids, regardless of structure, would increase male-pattern baldness if enough of the compound is used. There is no information on which anabolic steroids are safest at low to moderate levels."

– Dr. Mauro DiPasquale, best-selling author and regular *MuscleMag* columnist responding to a reader's question concerning the relationship between steroids and scalp-hair loss.

Lee Apperson

HAIR TRANSPLANTS

For the other 90 percent who have little success using Minoxidil, the only real solution to hair loss is a hair transplant. Hair transplants can take any number of forms. Perhaps the most common procedure is to take individual hair follicles from the lower part of the head and implant them in the bald area. Within four to six months the follicles take on a natural appearance. If done properly the transfered follicles keep on growing none the wiser, and in most cases last a lifetime.

Another procedure involves moving whole sections of scalp called flaps. Although a crude analogy, the technique is similar to transferring sods or strips of grass from one lawn to another. Like face lifts which often need to be performed in stages, hair transplanting usually requires a number of sessions to adequately complete the job. All procedures, however, are minor in nature and can be performed under local anaesthetic in the physician's clinic or office. Prices range from $1000 to $2000 to over $30,000, depend- ing on the amount of hair loss.

As a final note don't be afraid to "shop" around for a competent hair- transplant specialist. Like any popular cosmetic procedure there are skilled practitioners and others who should never have received their licence.

Skilled doctors will produce results that look natural. Conversely, those not familiar with their trade will leave you with the equivalent of a "picket fence" on your head. Likewise, giving a 45-year-old the hairline of a 18-year old doesn't make much sense (of course it's your money and if that is what you want, by all means go for it!).

HAIR RETARDANTS – THE LATEST FOR COMPETITIVE BODYBUILDERS

As would be expected, bodybuilders are more concerned with hair removal than hair loss – at least as it relates to body hair. Although a peculiarity to the general public, competitive bodybuilders are well aware of what's required on contest day – a large, ripped physique, totally absent of all body hair (except scalp hair). While shaving and electrolysis are still the most popular methods for doing so, chemical agents have made inroads in the hair-removal process. Women have long been familiar with such hair removal creams as "Nair," which disolve body hair after one application. They are simple to use and all it takes is one or two smears followed by a water rinse and the unwanted hair disappears.

Men have traditionally avoided such products for two chief reasons – the stigma of using a "women's product," and the amount of body hair involved. While the stigma question probably makes little sense, the biological aspect holds some merit. Men's body hair is much thicker than women's, and hence men would need to use enormous amounts of lotion to do an adequate job. In many cases it would take multiple applications to remove some of the coarser leg hair. For most men the cost and time seem unwarranted, so they reach for the razor.

In recent years researchers have taken a different approach to hair removal. Instead of removing hair that is already present, they have developed lotions that prevent or reduce the hair from growing in the first place. One such product is "Ultimate Hair-Away," a clear, organic-based liquid designed to allow women to reduce the time between shavings and waxings. While the product doesn't stop hair growth, it does allow users to greatly reduce the frequency of shaving or waxing. Once bodybuilders heard of this product, many had to give it a try. Anecdotal reports have been most encouraging, and males find it especially useful for reducing body hair in such hard to reach areas as the lower back.

There are other similar products on the market besides "Ultimate Hair-Away," but irregardless of the brand you use, the following points should be kept in mind. Never spread the lotion on without first trying it on a small area of the skin. In any given population there will be individuals who are allergic to a product's ingredients. It makes far more sense to test the product out on a small area of skin, rather than cover the whole body and develop an allergic reaction. Walking onstage with a rash covering most of your body is not the best way to impress the judges or spectators!

Another suggestion is to start your hair-removal treatment a few weeks before contest time. This gives you adequate time to do a decent job. If need be, you can touch up as contest day approaches. The extra time also allows you to test the product for effectiveness. Even the makers of such products admit that some individuals get nothing out of the lotions. If you fall into this catagory, you'll need the extra time for another hair-removal technique.

Shaving may be popular, but chemical agents have made inroads in the hair-removal process.

> **"Men who hate shaving have been using the product too, so that they don't have to shave as often. Some men using it have found they only need to shave once or twice a week instead of daily. Men with heavy facial hair, the type who get a 5 o'clock shadow by mid-day and who sometimes need to shave twice a day, are finding hair growth is lessened to the point where they need to shave just once and the 5 o'clock shadow doesn't appear until late in the evening.**
>
> – Greg Zulak, former *MuscleMag* editor and well-known bodybuilding writer commenting on the latest product for bodybuilders who wish to remove body hair by some other means than shaving.

LIPOSUCTION

Although a relatively new procedure, liposuction is fast becoming the technique of choice for removing fat from the face and body. And while it's usually reserved for cases of obesity, in recent years a number of bodybuilders have employed the procedure to get rid of pockets of stubborn adipose tissue.

The reason liposuction is so popular is because of what it removes. Stringent diet and exercise will reduce the size of fat cells, but liposuction goes one step further and removes the individual cells. Therefore, any weight gained will not be drawn to the liposucked spot. In effect, the storage cells for fat are no longer available and the body must look elsewhere.

SURGICAL PROCEDURE

Lee Haney

Just as the name indicates, liposuction involves the vacuuming or "sucking" out of adipose cells. A small incision is made over the desired fat deposit and a specialized "medical vacuum" connected to a small tube draws the fat cells out. In most cases only a few ounces of fat are removed but in circumstances of extreme obesity, many pounds may be eliminated.

Besides removing fat cells themselves, liposuction has another advantage – spot reduction. Contrary to popular belief there is little evidence to suggest that doing hundreds of situps will somehow "burn" fat off the midsection. As soon as the body experiences negative caloric intake, it begins to draw on fat deposits all over the body. As the midsection generally has the largest deposits, these are usually the hardest and last to eliminate. On the other hand, liposuction allows the surgeon to directly attack any fat deposit. If this happens to be the lower back or abdominal region, so much the better. Instead of many weeks or months of dieting, the midsection can be elinated with one treatment of liposuction.

AN IRONIC TWIST

Although considered a safe surgical procedure, there have been a few instances where patients have died from complications directly related to liposuction. In most cases the problems were related to the anaesthetic, or the individual contracted an infection. This raises an interesting point as liposuction is available to anyone who can afford it. In other words, it's perfectly legal. Anabolic steroids on the other hand are classified as illegal drugs in many countries, yet have never been listed as the direct cause of an individual's death – despite what some antisteroid groups proclaim. This raises the question as to why a surgical procedure that has been implicated in death is legal, when a class of drugs that has never been associated with such, is not.

SYNTHOL

Synthol is a German manufactured medical-grade MCT (medium-chain triglyceride) oil believed to contain a painkiller and other secret ingredients. Sold as a posing oil and topical analgesic, it is used by bodybuilders to swell the muscles. If you are to believe the hype, you can make two years of gains in three weeks! There is, however, no corresponding increase in strength. In fact, workouts are said to become painful after injection. The oil blends with the muscle fibers, which makes the entire muscle swell. Unlike Escilene, which blurs definition, Synthol increases both size and definition.

This product isn't cheap. Synthol sells for about $400 for one 100-millilitre tube. A similar (some say better) product is Muscle Sheen, which sells for $148.50 for one 100-millilitre tube. [2]

Because these products are sold as posing oils, they are not classified, which means they are not subject to legal or medical controls. How interested in hygiene do you think the manufacturers are when it comes to their products? Let's face it, there are vast differences in production techniques between products meant for injecting and those meant for topical application. The skin is the body's first line of defence against invading organisms. If you're going to bypass it with drugs and other chemicals you better be sure what you're injecting is pure (uncontaminated with germs). That bottle of posing oil you're injecting was not manufactured with internal use in mind.

JUST HOW FAR?

Like many drugs which originated for bodybuilding purposes, we can be sure Synthol will make it to the mainstream public. All of a sudden you don't have to work out or diet. Just wait until the plastic surgeons in Hollywood get hold of this one. Face lifts will be a thing of the past (sagging face muscles will suddenly get pumped up), breasts will bounce up, and penises will

"One of these days a top pro is going to burst onstage. Yet another oil slick to contend with. When will the madness stop?"

– Robert Kennedy, editor of *MuscleMag* giving his opinion on Synthol.

swell. That last part is scary because you know some idiot is going to inject every muscle down there! We don't know what happens to the injected muscle over the long term, or what happens if this stuff gets into the circulatory or lymphatic systems. And don't think you can get away with injecting regular MCT oil; we're talking medical grade, which has much higher standards of purity.

You can see where this is leading. It's bad enough that every Conan-wannabe will be inflating his body like a Good Year Tire, but how long before bodybuilders begin experimenting with various injectables, based on popular supplements? Creatine suspensions, vanadyl-sulfate solutions, and chromium mixtures will be brewed and injected into problem areas. The idea of people turning themselves into walking mosquito bites is scary. Until more scientific data is gathered, we strongly suggest you stay far away from this one.

MORAL CONSIDERATIONS OF ENHANCEMENT SURGERY

Although this may seem like a tangent on our part, the latest surgical-enhancement techniques have come under attack by some groups. In many cases the focus of assault centers on the issue of morality. Many argue that it's not right to change what "God" has given you. Further, our society places too much emphasis on physical appearance and such procedures as breast implants and face lifts are only adding to a person's vanity.

Francesca Petitjean

While there are a few individuals who will argue against any medical procedure in society, the contention against enhancement surgery is probably due to a combination of jealousy and ignorance. There are exceptions, but most vocal opponents of improving physical appearance tend to have little interest in exercise or physical fitness themselves, and as such have trouble understanding why anyone else would feel differently. Putting this aside, most of these same individuals would dearly love to be more attractive to others (this is not so much our opinion as a basic psychological trait of humans).

Another reason for "fighting" enhancement surgery lies with the newness of the techniques. Although some forms of surgery were tried 75 to 100 years ago, it's only in the last twenty years that the procedures have been perfected and classified as safe. Many of the most vocal

"There are women out there who have to get implants for their psychological well-being. Maybe they've had breast cancer or some medical problem with their breasts. In our society having breasts is part of being a women. Women who've had mastectomies can have a really hard time psychologically because men aren't always so understanding. It's so demoralizing for a women to lose that part of her femininity. I don't think it's fair for people to judge those who choose to have breast reconstruction or get breast implants. I don't know each girl's history. Sure, some do it for vanity, but it's their body and their choice. What right has anyone to condemn that choice?"

– Amy Fadhli, top fitness contestant voicing her opinions about those who criticize breast-enhancement surgery.

opponents still associate cosmetic surgery and implants with the horror stories of the 1950s and 1960s. They have trouble accepting that the days of silicone injections are over.

Perhaps the most outspoken critics are those whose beliefs are heavily influenced by religion. Many religions hold that vanity as it relates to physical appearance is a mortal sin. And those that seek to improve their "attractiveness" are destined for eternal damnation. In reality, there will always be someone who cannot accept cosmetic surgery, no matter what the circumstances.

THE OTHER SIDE OF THE COIN

We shouldn't leave this section without a few arguments in defence of cosmetic-enhancement surgery. If most people accept modern dentistry as a valid form of health, arguing against a "nose job" makes little sense. Is there really much of a difference between straightening teeth and correcting a crooked nose? What's the dissimilarity between spending $2000 for braces and $2000 for a hair transplant? You could argue that larger breasts and perfect teeth are bordering on counterfeit, but who cares if the end result is a more attractive person who feels more confident about himself or herself. Let's face it, millions of people invest thousands of hours in the gym every year trying to add a few inches to their chests and take away a few inches from their hips and waistlines. Are they all narcistic lost souls? Certainly not. And while there may be valid arguments against inflating a bodypart solely for the purpose of winning a bodybuilding contest, investing a few thousand dollars to improve one's facial features or reduce the midsection is no more a "crime" than lying in the sun to obtain a tan or running a few miles to keep the adipose tissue at bay. In our opinion, cosmetic surgery is just another means to improve both physical and psychological health, and modern medical science has brought us safe methods to do so.

Amy Fadhli and Richard Carlsson

References

1) L.L Bosley, "Addressing the Minoxidil Miracle," *Muscle and Fitness*, 50:1 (1989).
2) http://www.absl.demon.co.uk/page4.html

Blocking Agents and Procedures

"We test for everything through urine and blood samples. It's randomly scheduled every few weeks. It's not random in that some guys get tested and some guys don't – everyone gets tested. Dr. Mauro DiPasquale is in charge of it, and it far exceeds any testing in existence. As I mentioned earlier, other professional organizations attended our symposium to learn from our program. This will help all professional sports, not just bodybuilding."

– Jonathan Flora of the now defunct WBF bodybuilding federation commenting on the efforts made to remove steroids from professional bodybuilding.

One of the most interesting catagories of athletic pharmacology are masking or blocking agents. With the introduction of drug testing back in the early 70s, athletes began looking for ways to "beat" the various tests. The outcome of their search led to the development of a whole new area of sports pharmacology whose sole purpose was camouflaging the presence of other drugs. So precise has the "science" become that many compare the relationship between athletics and drug testing to terrorism and counterterrorism!

Using the athletic definition, blocking or masking agents are substances used by athletes to cover up or hide the presence of banned performance-enhancing drugs. Like most drugs, masking agents started their careers as legitimate medicines but once their "special concealment" properties became known, it wasn't long before athletes started adding them to their precontest stacks.

Porter Cottrell and Charles Clairmonte

Alq Gurley

Blocking procedures are techniques used by athletes to accomplish the same task as masking agents – pass a drug test. While the chemical forms are relatively safe, some of the procedural forms are radical and life threatening.

In the following chapter we will look at a few of the more popular blocking agents and procedures, and how athletes use them to "combat" modern drug-testing procedures.

MASKING AGENTS

Sulfonamides
Trade Names: Probecid, Benemid
Generic Name: probenecid
Tablet Size: 500 mg

Trade Names: Staticin, Caronamide
Generic Name: carinamide

One of the continuing goals of medical researchers is to increase the effectiveness of prescribed drugs. One way to do this is by prolonging the drug's circulation time in the body. For many popular drugs, like antibiotics, their metabolic lives may last no more than a few hours. To combat such short life spans researchers came up with a class of drugs called sulfonamides – two of the more popular being probenecid and carinamide.

Sulfonamides work by slowing down the movement of renal ions and hence decreasing the excretion rate of various drug compounds. Although primarily used for slowing the excretion rate of penicillin and related compounds, these drugs also reduce the amount of steroid metabolites in the urine – the by-products of steroid metabolism. Contrary to popular belief, most drug tests don't "detect" the parent drug compound, but instead look for the metabolite offspring. It's easy to see how a drug that reduces metabolite clearance became popular with athletes. Such was the case with sulfonamides, especially when it was found these drugs "block" the excretion rate of many testosterone compounds. We should add that since these agents reduce metabolite clearance, the term "masking" is not really appropriate as nothing is being masked (that is, covered up), but instead reduced.

HOW EFFECTIVE?

Once athletes learned of the blocking properties of various drugs they began using them in increasing numbers to escape detection at drug-tested events. The practice initially met with success as early drug tests were not capable of detecting the small amounts of metabolites present. But with the development of more sensitive tests, athletes who formally passed tests began getting caught.

Such positive tests came as a shock to many athletes as they assumed blocking agents stopped all excretion of drug metabolites. But such beliefs are misguided as sulfonamides only reduce drug clearance, not stop it entirely. This may have been adequate when drug tests were primitive,

"This 'Defend' stuff is supposed to mask the traces of metabolites that red-flag a urine sample at IOC-approved drug tests. Originally designed to beat tests used to sniff out recreational drug use, it was found, at least according to the company responsible, to work for steroids as well. Supposedly, the stuff works frighteningly well on the more frequently used and detected drugs, which have been the downfall of many a bodybuilder at a tested event."

– Steve Douglas, former *MuscleMag* columnist commenting on the masking agent "Defend," which was all the rage in the early 1990s.

Chris Cormier

but with increasing sophistication even the smallest traces of a drug are detectable.

While the increased sensitivity of drug tests reduced the amount of sulfonamide use by athletes, the IOC went a step further and elimnated them entirely by placing them on their list of banned substances. As most sulfon-amides are easily detectable in a drug test, a positive for any of them suggests that an athlete is trying to hide something and is hence penalized. In effect, a positive for a sulfon-amide carries just as much weight as a positive for clenbuterol or anabolic steroids – disqual-ification and banishment from the sport for a miniumum of two years (in many cases for life if this is the athlete's second offence).

SIDE EFFECTS

Most of the side effects associated with probenecid and related compounds are not life threatening, though if taken on an empty stom-ach they may produce nausea, vomiting, or diarrhea. Other side effects include sore gums, headache, and dizziness. Finally, some indi-viduals report a loss of appetitie during usage. For some bodybuilders, such effects are a help during the precontest season when weight loss is desirable. During the off-season however, most find the condition a hindrance.

THEIR BEST DAYS BEHIND THEM?

While some athletes will continue to use the drugs in sports where their use is not prohibited (though most major sports organizations follow the IOC lead), it's safe to say that the sulfonamide's best days are behind them.

DIURETICS

Although we discussed these drugs in detail earlier in the book, they deserve rementioning here given their use by athletes for passing drug tests.

As previously mentioned, diuretics work by interfering with the body's water-conserving mechanisms. The result is large quantities of very dilute urine. Many athletes use diuretics in the belief that dilute urine will somehow enable them to pass a drug test. Unfortunately, there are three reasons why such a strategy no longer works.

First, even dilute urine contains traces of drug metabolites, and any modern drug test will detect these. Second, sports federations have enacted legislation which requires urine samples to be of a certain concentration. Using a procedure called the specific gravity test (comparing a given volume of the substance with an equivalent volume of water), testers can determine if the urine has been diluted or not. And although determining what constitutes a "normal" specific gravity for urine (lets face it everyone is different), many sports federations require an athlete's urine to be a given concentration.

"The urine sample of Ben Johnson (Canada, 100 m) was found to contain metabolites of the drug stanazolol – an anabolic steroid."

– IOC official announcing to the world the most positive drug test in athletic history. Canadian sprinter Ben Johnson tested positive for stanazolol (Winstrol) following his victory in the 100-meter sprint at the 1988 summer Olympics.

The final reason for diuretics falling out of favor – at least as a method for passing a drug test – is that the IOC and most other federations have added them to the list of banned substances. Even if your urine is of an accepted concentration, and no traces of other banned substances are found, the presence of diuretics is enough to get you suspended. The rationale once again being that you are trying to hide something. It would be interesting to see how many bodybuilders – both pro and amateur – test positive for diuretics on the day of a contest!

EPITESTOSTERONE

One of the most effective drug tests developed since the early 1980s is what's called the testosterone to epitestosterone ratio. In simple terms, both hormones are naturally present in the human body at a ratio of about 1:1. In fact, epitestosterone is one of the breakdown metabolites of testosterone. When individuals take anabolic steroids or other testosterone compounds, their ratio swings towards the testosterone side of the equation. Once researchers established this, drug testers began measuring the athletes' ratios. If the ratio is "too far" towards the testosterone side, the athlete is given a positive test. As with diuretics, trying to get sports federations to give a precise definition of "too far" has met with little success. Given the variation among individuals with regards to body chemistry, there has no doubt been athletes who were wrongly convicted of having "unacceptable" ratios.

Irregardless of precise definitions, athletes were quick to develop an effective countermeasure to ratio testing. As Dan Duchaine, author of *The Underground Steroid Handbook*, pointed out, "anyone with half a creative brain could have figured it out." Since the test is based on detecting "too high" testosterone levels, athletes simply started injecting epitestosterone to bring the ratio back to the normal 1:1 ratio. According to reports athletes can inject epitestosterone as close as one hour before a drug test and produce a negative result.

Perhaps the most fascinating thing about epitestosterone is that it is not approved by the FDA, is not available by prescription, and has few if any legitimate medical uses. What this means is that it's only use appears to be for passing drug tests.

MASKING PROCEDURES

Besides using one drug to hide the presence of another drug, athletes often employ procedures to pass drug tests. Some of these are simple, slight-of-hand techniques, while others demonstrate just how far some athletes will go to avoid detection. The following are a few examples.

Edgar Fletcher

> **"In order to properly test for anabolic steroids, more sophisticated tests have to be done than are presently being done, and a lot more money spent. If they tried to detect anabolic steroids using the same techniques that they now use for the detection of cocaine etc., the results wouldn't stand up in a court of law."**
>
> – Dr. Mauro DiPasquale, regular *MuscleMag* columnist and best-selling author responding to a concerned reader's inquiry about testing in the workplace.

SUBSTITUTION

> "We all know that many professional bodybuilders use steroids. No one denies that and no one denies the fact that it is done to keep up with the competition. The issue of drugs was not the issue in this case. It was simply a situation where one athlete did not take her own drug test – period.
>
> – Jeff Everson, former *Muscle and Fitness* editor commenting on the suspension of Tonya Knight, after she had another female take her drug test.

At one time this was perhaps the simplest way to beat a drug test but it also happened to be one of the easiest ways to get caught! Many athletes, knowing they hadn't a snowball's chance in hell of passing a test, simply provided a urine sample that came from another individual. All it took was a concealed bottle of urine and the switch could easily be made in the collecting room.

Of course sports federations quickly caught on to the ruse and refined their procedures. Now instead of passing (or switching) the urine sample in private, a same-sex official from the sports federation accompanies the athlete into the urine-collecting booth. Many athletes complained of invasion of privacy, but for the most part the procedure has been accepted world wide by athletes.

Even with the tightening of sample-collecting procedures, many athletes found ways to cheat. One of the most effective but risky, is to send another individual to the drug-testing center to give the urine sample. This sounds like a far-fetched plan but is very simple as drug testers usually have no way of knowing the difference. Granted, large federations have picture IDs for their athletes, but at the local or even national level it comes down to a name tag and a few questions. Unless a given tester "knows" the athlete by face, the large number of athletes tested makes "getting caught" almost impossible.

Tonya Knight

The most famous bodybuilder to engage in such a practice was former Ms. International winner Tonya Knight, who used a surrogate to take her drug test shortly before the 1988 Ms. Olympia contest. After the "double" was turned in (with the apparent help from other competitors), Tonya was suspended from IFBB competition for two years.

Besides using doubles, many females use another method to switch urine samples (the male equivalent is described next).

> "The system is fair and can detect drug usage in the competitors, but it's no secret that most contestants get off the drugs a few weeks before the contest and easily come clean on the drug test. Even the most jaded yahoo isn't naive enough to believe that some of these competitors are drug free."
>
> – Tonya Knight, former *MuscleMag* columnist commenting on one of the many ways bodybuilders can use performance-enhancing drugs and still pass drug tests.

Numerous reports suggest that many females conceal a urine-filled condom in their vaginas. Once the urine sample is to be "passed," all it takes is a quick jab by a sharp fingernail and the condom breaks allowing the "clean" urine to flow into the sample bottle. Although close monitoring by officials greatly reduces the chances of such occurrences, with practice, many females have perfected this technique to an art form.

CATHETERIZATION

For those who think we have been biased towards females and their "anatomy advantage," let us show you the extreme to which some males go to in order to escape detection. During the 1988 to 1989 Dubbin Inquiry – the Canadian Government's investigation into drug use by athletes following Ben Johnson's positive test – stories were told of Canadian weightlifters using a radical form of substitution called catheterization.

Shawn Ray

The procedure involves using a long thin rubber hose (in medical terms called a catheter) which passes through the urethra into the person's bladder. When the individual is to be tested, he empties the bladder of his own urine and fills it with someone else's "clean" urine. Now you don't need to be a rocket scientist to see the risks involved in such madness. Besides the risk of infection from the rubber hose (no matter how sterile), there is also the risk of haemorrhaging. Further, do you know how much urine your bladder can hold? No, well most people don't either. The bladder is similar to a balloon that can only hold so much air. Overinflate and it bursts. Inject too much urine (no matter how "clean") and you run the risk of rupturing the bladder – leading to infection, severe blood loss, and even death.

And speaking of "clean," do you really think it's a good idea to be injecting someone elses urine into your bladder? In this day and age, what person is confident of another's sexual history? You may be receiving clean urine and hence pass a drug test, but you may also obtain a nasty little virus that kills you of AIDS down the road.

Perhaps the most ironic aspect to the whole catheter situation is that it may not work. After taking all the risks associated with implantation and operation, the athlete may still fail the drug test. When the athlete empties his bladder there is still enough urine adhering to the bladder walls to "contaminate" the injected "clean" urine. This small amount of urine may contain just enough drug metabolites to be detected by today's sensitive drug tests.

Besides residual urine, the individual's kidneys continue to filter urine and pass it on to the bladder. Once again, even small amounts of drug-containing urine may be enough to register positive on a sensitive drug test. At the Dubbin inquiry, Canadian weightlifter Jacques Demers (no relation to the former coach of the Montreal Canadians hockey team) still tested positive for steroids after his self-catheterization.

"I feel that we are damned if we do and damned if we don't. If they drug test the contest and you come in looking just good, the general public is not going to buy it. People come to see the best in the world."

– Shawn Ray, Mr. Olympia runner-up commenting on one of the problems faced by sports officials in removing performance-enhancing drugs from sports – the problem being once a standard has been set, the public will not accept anything less.

CHAPTER TWENTY-FIVE

Electrostimulation – Wired For Success

N o, this chapter is not a guide to the latest in psychedelic training. In fact the term "wired" is to be taken literally. It shouldn't come as a surprise that once scientists learned the body was heavily dependant on electrical energy, techniques would be developed to mimic such bio-energy. Two of these, ESM (electrical stimulation of muscles) and TENS (transcutaneous electrical nerve stimulation) have athletic potential, and while the debate continues as to their usefulness, many bodybuilders are first in line to find out for themselves – despite what the "experts" say. In the following chapter we take a look at the two in more detail, paying particular attention to their potential merits for bodybuilders.

ELECTRICAL MUSCLE STIMULATION – SHOCKING NEW GROWTH

Long-time readers of *MuscleMag International* will remember ads back in the early 1980s featuring Canadian bodybuilding champion John Cardillo promoting the benefits of electrical muscle stimulation. Although the machines never became as popular as expected, they have remained at the fringe of ergogenic procedures, and occasionally recieve a boost when some top bodybuilder mentions using them in his or her training. In recent years the technique's biggest promotor (and we mean "big" in many senses) has been Canadian colossus Paul Dillett. Issues of *MuscleMag International* feature ads showing massive Paul strapped with electrodes.

Electrical stimulation of muscles (ESM for short) first gained prominence back in the late '70s and early '80s, when reports of its use began coming out of the former Soviet Union.

> "There's no reason electrostimulation can't be applied to normal healthy muscles to complement a personal physical fitness program – passive electro-bodybuilding at home while reading or watching television."
>
> – Dr. Charles Godfrey, head of the rehabilitation department at Toronto's Wellesley Hospital.

Paul Dillett

Anticipating the rankings at the Ms. Olympia.

Unlike their Western counterparts who only used ESM for injury treatment, Soviet coaches and sports physicians were applying the technique to improve the performance of their top-rank athletes – including the hockey players who shocked everyone throughout the 1970s and early 1980s.

As the name suggests, two electrodes are placed at the ends of a given muscle and an electrical current is passed through the electrodes. The end result is what's called a tetanic contraction – similar to the strong muscle cramps usually associated with tetanus. All skeletal muscles are compatable with ESM, except the heart.

HOW IT WORKS

Although different techniques are used, the most common involve alternating the amplitude and frequency of the current waves to obtain different effects. One of the most common settings is 5000 HZ (hertz) which is close to the biological frequency of muscle and nerve functioning. Such settings not only promote muscular growth, but are believed to elevate the recovery abilities of an athlete.

Physiotherapists use the procedure to help treat injuries where regular strength training would be too intense. Perhaps the biggest advantage to EMS is its ability to stimulate muscle tissue without the stress usually associated with regular weight training. The virtual absence of skin irritation from the electrodes is also a big drawing point. Finally, unlike most fancy and expensive forms of weight-training equipment, ES machines can be bought for less than $200; and if money is no object, elaborate versions may be purchased for $1000 or more.

According to the manufacturers of such machines, ESM can accomplish better results than weightlifting in fewer minutes per day and over a shorter period of time. In a report released in the early 1980s by E-S distributor Siemens, twenty treatments over a six-week period resulted in a minimum 25 percent increase in strength and increase in girth of about 4.3 percent. And although the report's subjects were physiotherapy patients, the potential for strength training looks promising.

No procedure can take the place of hard and heavy training.
– Ronnie Coleman

Much of the basis of ESM treatment for rehabilitation lies with substitution. In patients with chronic tendon, ligament, or cartilage damage, regular ESM can strengthen the surrounding muscle tissue and allow it to take over much of the role of the damaged connective tissue. Strengthening the muscles with ESM places much less stress on the damaged connective tissue than regular free-weight or machine exercises.

USE IN BODYBUILDING

Athletes will get the most benefit from ESM when it takes the muscle cramp to the threshold of sharp pain. With regular use, tolerance increases to the point where individuals can accept up to 120 milliamps (thousandths of amperes) – enough to torture someone unfamiliar with the procedure. This is comparable to working up to a 300- to 400-pound bench press. You don't just walk into the gym and load up the bar. You must gradually accustom the muscle to heavier loads. The same holds true for ESM. Start with a low current and gradually increase.

The opposite holds true and underloading a muscle is next to useless. Only loading the muscle to its full capacity leads to maximum strength, and although the evidence for healthy athletes is limited, patients using ESM as a form of rehabilitation often experience weekly strength increases of 5 percent until 75 percent of the individual's previous strength level is reached. As would be expected, strength increases fall off as the 100 percent level is approached.

HOW MUCH AND HOW OFTEN

Most bodybuilders who use ESM recommend the procedure as a supplement to regular training, or as a method of strengthening muscles after injury. In other words, while a few jolts of ESM are better than doing nothing (that is, living a sedentary lifestyle), it doesn't take the place of regular exercise – especially the variety of muscle contractions and relaxations experienced during a typical bodybuilding workout.

The most frequent pattern of use involves "sets" of 10 "reps" – ten, 10-second charges separated with 50-second breaks. Most machines are controlled by a circular knob or button which operates like the dimmer switch on a light fixture. As you turn the knob the amperage increases.

Besides muscle stimulation, ESM also increases the respiratory and pulse rate – meaning the cardiovascular system receives a sort of workout. There is even evidence that ESM increases blood and lymph flow to and from the muscles. The effect is more reduced than regular weight training.

According to Dr. Charles Godfrey, head of the rehabilitaion department at Toronto's Wellesley Hospital, "Muscle use and development are the result of chemical changes and electrostimulation is merely a fast way of inducing and maximizing those changes." Finally, since the human body is about one-third muscle, stimulation of such muscles greatly enhances the body's capacity to transport oxygen. Not only does this enhance recovery between workouts, but it also promotes better metabolic efficiency.

Most bodybuilders who use ESM recommend the procedure as a supplement to regular training, or as a method of strengthening muscles after injury.

BUYING VERSUS CONSTRUCTING YOUR OWN

If you decide to try ESM, there are a number of options open to you. Like any new procedure, investing big bucks is unwise until you give it a trial run. If your gym has one, see if you can arrange a few sessions – either for free or a small fee. If not, check around to see if any gym friends have access. A friendly physiotherapist comes in handy in this regard.

If none of the previous are successful you probably have no choice but to invest a few hundred dollars and buy your own. Like most gadgets available, there is a broad spectrum of ESM machines available both in terms of price and complexity. Small two-pad versions can be bought for around $200. These are suited for shocking one muscle at a time and if you plan on "working" the whole body, make sure you budget out 45 to 60 minutes or more.

At the other end of the spectrum we find the large, multipad (20 or more) delux models. These machines allow you to train six to eight muscles or more at one sitting. And while the appearance resembles something from a Gestapo torture room, all it takes is 10 to 15 minutes to "shock" the whole body into supposedly new growth. Prices vary, but most can be bought for $600 to $800 US.

For those with the right connections, a less costly alternative is available. Most electricians have the know-how to build a simple ESM machine from parts available at electronic and hardware stores. All it takes is a few batteries (or device to convert AC to DC current), wires, and an assortment of cheap electronic components, and you have yourself a 60 to 80 milliampere ESM. And while it may not have the glamor of a comercially made job, it will get the job done at a fraction of the cost.

SAFETY CONSIDERATIONS

It may seem unwarranted on our part, but there are a few important safety considerations that must be highlighted.

The reason electricity is so popular with "torture experts" is because it is very effective – it hurts! Turn up the voltage high enough and it kills (we need only point you in the direction of the electric chair). While the voltage used in ESM machines is a fraction of that used for appliances, it still may pose a threat to some individuals. Those with heart problems or a history of heart conditions in their family should avoid ESM therapy. At the very least check with your physician beforehand (don't be surprised if he or she frowns on the idea; not so much out of safety but most physicians are against ESM as a form of "exercise").

Another consideration is the adjustment period. If your top squat is 350 pounds, what do you think will happen if you load the bar with 500 pounds and step back with it? You'll end up in traction, that's what. The same holds true for ESM. Don't think by "turning" up the juice you'll end up looking like Paul Dillett in two weeks. At the very least you'll be sore for a few days, but there's also the risk of producing such a violent contraction that the muscle rips away from the tendon. It sounds gruesome, looks worse, and requires surgery as well as many months of therapy to fix. Play it safe and slowly increase the intensity of the ESM sessions.

Ronnie Coleman and Flex Wheeler

TRANSCUTANEOUS ELECTRICAL NERVE STIMULATION (TENS)

Like many medical techniques, TENS is fast becoming popular as an athletic ergogenic procedure. Unlike ESM, however, the desired outcome is not increased muscle size and strength, but the alleviation of pain. The process involves passing a low-level electrical current through the skin to stimulate the nerves involved in painkilling. Used historically for medical therapy and surgery, TENS is fast gaining approval among sports physicians.

HOW IT WORKS

The medical literature is filled with scientific studies which indicate pain can be reduced if not elimnated by nerve stimulation. Although the exact mechanism of action is not fully understood, it is believed that a low-intensity current applied to areas of tissue damage can block pain impulses from reaching the brain. This is accomplished by stimulating fast-conducting A-beta nerve fibers which then prevent pain impulses traveling along A-delta and C fibers from reaching the areas of the brain where pain is perceived (pain is thought to be as much psychological as physiological in nature).

Besides stimulating specific pain-nullifying fibers, there is good evidence to suggest that electrical stimulation of nerves increases production of endorphins and enkephalins – the body's naturally occuring opiate painkillers.

TENS is an athletic ergogenic procedure known for its pain-relieving abilities. – Michael Francois

In addition to its painkilling abilities, TENS also speeds up the recovery process by reducing swelling and inflammation. Besides the physiological benefits, the practical applications allow athletes to resume training and competition sooner.

HOW IT'S ADMINISTERED

TENS therapy usually takes place in a health clinic under the direction of a physician or licensed technician. The equipment may be large and cumbersome – as most of the old models are – or small and portable. With the number of athletes using the procedure these days, and the emphasis on more home-based medical care, most machines fall under the latter description.

Dennis Newman and Debee Halo

No matter what the equipment size, the electrical current administered is usually in milliamperes, although good results are being obtained using microamperes. Most of the new machines, including the Alpha-Stim 2000, have built-in computers which measure the relative conductances of the body. This enables the physician to select the best points on the body for electrical stimulation. By an ironic twist of fate, these "best points" correspond to acupuncture points located thousands of years ago by Chinese healers.

A slight modification of TENS (in fact many of the latest machines incorporate the ability into them) is electrosleep. Using small clips that attach to the ear, it is possible to send a low ampere current into the brain. The current is not so much to stimulate sleep as to produce a calm, relaxed state in the individual. This state bears a strong resemblence to the alpha state manifested during hypnosis, daydreaming and meditation.

The usefulness of such states to athletes should be obvious. After a grueling two-hour workout or match, many athletes have difficulty calming down and relaxing. Many university coaches are finding that a 10-minute session of "electrosleep" is just the thing needed by athletes to achieve a state of tranquillity.

LIMITING FACTORS

It is fast becoming an important part of athletics, yet TENS is not without its drawbacks. Perhaps the most limiting element is availability. Unlike ESM machines which can be purchased directly through a magazine ad, TENS machines are much more restrictive in nature – usually only available to physiotherapists and physicians. Their high cost (thousands of dollars) also limits the number of individuals who have access to them.

Another practical concern is usage. It generally takes many hours of specialized practice to become proficient in the use of a TENS machine. You don't just attach the electrodes and "pump up the volume." As the procedure gains in popularity, no doubt the number of available practitioners will increase. It's possible that a few years down the road many weeks of painkillers will be replaced by a few sessions of electrical currents.

Chris Cormier and Lee Priest compare quad development.

BOOK SEVEN

Natural Ergogenesis

Marjo Selin

Jamo Nezzar

CHAPTER TWENTY-SIX

Herbs and Bodybuilding

Gunter Schlierkamp

"I'm concerned that some doctors take the attitude that if something is not taught in medical school, it doesn't exist."

– Dr. Lynn Marshall, University of Toronto researcher.[58]

Although used in Far East medicines for thousands of years, Western cultures have been reluctant to accept herbs as anything more than "food for the fringe element." Most physicians scoff at them, claiming any positive results can be explained by the placebo effect. It hasn't helped matters either that herbs have long been associated with hippie communes and others commited to the "back to the earth movement."

Ironically, it's because of this last point that herbs have gained popularity in recent years. With the daily news bombarding us with reports of the dangers of pesiticides and other drugs, many have decided to go back to basics and follow the advice of our ancestors (although as we shall see, many herb products may contain as many chemicals as their mainstream counterparts). On the surface this may seem nothing more than a fad response to a given problem, but this reaction is a valid one. Most of our modern medicines are derived from plants, and it's safe to say that many herbs contain useful ingredients that have yet to be isolated by science.

APPLICATIONS FOR BODYBUILDERS

While most bodybuilders laugh at the suggestion that herbs may have ergogenic potential – prefering instead to focus on synthetic drugs and high-tech supplements – the implications are enormous. At the forefront of herb research are sports scientists in the former Soviet Union who have taken "natural ergogenesis" to new heights. (see Chapter Twenty-Eight on "Soviet Supplements.") While we will be the first to admit that no herb can replace steroids as an anabolic agent, the fact remains that herbs contain ALL the nutrients needed by the body. Some herbs are great sources of vitamins and minerals, while others are loaded with protein. Then there's the unknown qualities to consider. Herbs are no doubt loaded with substances whose ergogenic potentials have yet to be realized.

The following chapter can be considered an introductory guide to herbs. By no means will we attempt to cover them all as there are thousands available. We will however, give a brief summary of some of the more popularly used herbs.

WHAT THEY ARE

Herbs are plants long valued for their aroma, taste or medicinal qualities.[1] Included in the vast spectrum of herbs are trees, schrubs, and small plants. The herb's ingredients may be obtained from the whole plant, or such parts as the stem, roots, and leaves. This has been proven in the past, as willow bark has provided us with aspirin and foxglove with digitalis.

> "Herbs may prove worthwhile in other capacities. Some, such as rosemary, have vitamin-like antioxidant qualities. Ordinary ginger has been used to treat nausea. And garlic is claimed to cure just about everything. Less mundane herbal substances like ginseng and gotu-kola may have benefits but one runs into the same problem of high cost for low return."
>
> – Stephen Brooke, *MuscleMag* contributor commenting on some of the lesser-known ergogenic aids – herbal preparations.

Andrew Pace, Gordon Lavelle and Kevin Christie in the thick of it.

Ronnie Coleman

One of the contended issues regarding herbs is that they are not put through special processing. A standard amount needed to produce a biological effect, so easily prepared with conventional medicine, is often hit-and-miss with herbs. This means herbs cannot be patented in their natural state. Drug companies are not interested in any plant unless the active component can be identified, synthesized and chemically altered just enough to make it different enough from the natural form, so as to make the new version patentable. Also, one herb might contain a multitude of chemicals that work together, or in spite of one another. Certain factors can affect the ingredient concentration or ratios and these include:

i) type of soil grown in
ii) climate during the season
iii) time of harvest
iv) manner of drying
v) contamination

Also important is the temperature produced during the cold-press – the process of squeezing the herbs between two wooden plates producing an extract. If the temperature exceeds 50-degrees centigrade, the desired plant oils and alkaloids could be damaged. It's easy to see how poor preparation techniques could result in one herbal supplement being effective, and a subsequent bottle useless.

LACK OF QUALITY CONTROL

There is no quality control regulation of the herbal industry in the United States. Pesticides and solvents used during extraction can leave residues in the final product.[1] Many herbs come from third-world countries where regulations, banning the use of carcinogenic chemicals, are ignored or non-existent. Therefore, many people who are using herbs to "escape" drugs and other dangerous chemicals may in fact be merely switching from one harm to another.

It is perhaps surprising to the reader (it was to the authors) that a $700 million dollar a year industry in the US is not required to submit products to the FDA! Hundreds of thousands of Americans are ingesting substances that are not regulated for product quality or safety. The only thing required is that the manufacturer list claims on the product which are supported by scientific testing. To get around this, suppliers include pamphlets (which are not covered by legislation) that list the many benefits of the herb being sold.[1]

Given the previous, we strongly advise readers to heed the following guidelines when using herbs:

i) Pregnant and nursing women should avoid using herbs. They can have harmful effects on the fetus or nursing infant.
ii) Children should not take herbs. Too little is known to justify the risk.
iii) Herbs can interact with precribed drugs. Always consult your doctor and your pharmacist before using a herb.
iv) Be wary of taking more than one herb at a time. Together, two herbs may produce undesired side effects which could be harmful.
v) Start with low doses as you might be allergic. Keep the label on the bottle. This information could prove useful to your doctor. Large doses could be dangerous, an example being licorice extract, which can affect heart rate.
vi) Look for "standardized extract" on the label; this is an international standard of quality.

The reader should not get the idea that the authors are opposed to herbs. Keep in mind that 30 percent of all modern drugs used today are derived from herbs.[1] We merely take the position that people should have adequate information before putting a substance into their bodies. While most people won't pick up a dirty needle and jab themselves with it, they don't think twice about using herbs that might be contaminated. Bottom line – consult your doctor and pharmacist, know your supplier, and find out all you can about how the herb is processed. What you don't know can kill you.

"We may extend our lives as a country; we may build battleships and navies and constitute great armies, but if the health of the people is to be undermined by these concoctions of fraudulant and bogus medicines, of what avail is it?"

– Senator Weldon B. Heyburn, in the US Senate, 1904.[2]

Anja Schreiner

BUYING HERBS

The first thing to know when purchasing any herb product is the difference between a whole herb and a herb extract. The strongest naturally occurring herbs might contain two to three percent of an active ingredient. This means 97 or 98 percent of the herb has no biological effect whatsoever. A product containing multiple herbs is virtually useless because each herb is only available in small amounts due to the small size of the capsule. It takes anywhere from 100 to 400 milligrams of an active ingredient to have any effect on the system. This means you either consume dozens (if not hundreds) of pills to recieve enough active ingredient, or take small amounts and waste your money. The solution to this is to buy products containing herb extracts. This boosts the concentration of the product and at the same time reduces the number of pills you need to take.

Unfortunately, many companies just add trace amounts to their product, allowing for great advertising but little biological effect. The reason they do this is cost. Herbal extracts cost a great deal more to produce than whole herbs. It takes far more resources and time to produce a product containing 20 times the active ingredient than the original herb. If you buy a product for $5 or $6 and the recommended dosage is five or six capsules, you can be pretty sure it won't do much for you.

For convenience we have divided herbs into five catagories: Diuretics, Muscle Building, Appearance, Stimulants and Tranquilizers.

What you are about to read is a list of herbs that could be used in bodybuilding. Some of this information comes from herbal use with animals, and others are extrapolations based on current knowledge. In other words, we are speculating about use in humans. Remember, herbs are natural drugs that have not been processed. This gives them an unknown quality that can be beneficial, dangerous, or both.

"The body and soul of both humans and animals are made so completely and wonderfully that they are capable of providing their own medicines, and therefore it is an insult to the Creator to force on the body unnatural substances of any kind."
– Quote from an Afghan Doctor, working in a US Military Hospital in Germany.[3]

Porter Cottrell enjoys a much-deserved win.

Laura Creavalle displaying the mass, symmetry and definition that makes her such a crowd pleaser.

THE HERB CATAGORIES

1) DIURETICS

Angelica (Angelica archangelica)
- This flowering plant obtains its name from its blooming date, May 8, which used to be celebrated as the day of Michael the Archangel.
- Besides its diuretic qualities, it is also known as a tonic and tranquilizer.
- Diabetics should avoid this herb, as it may cause flutuations in glucose levels.[4]

Buchu (Barosma betulina)
- A mountain plant, the leaves are consumed or brewed as a tea for their diuretic effect. No dosage is specified.[5]

Chueh Ming Tzu (Cassia tora)
- A mild diuretic, of which only the roots are used. Dosage can be specified by a Chinese pharmacist.[6]

Lily of the Valley (Convallaria majalis)
- This woodland plant can have a potent effect on heart rate, and should be handled with care.
- A very small amount of the flowers can be brewed in a cup of water, with a spoonful of honey added.
- It should only be taken while fasting, once in the morning and once at night.[3,4]
- For bodybuilders the best time to use this herb is the last week before a contest.

Chris Cormier and Kevin Levrone

Dandelion
- This common garden weed was introduced to North America by the Pilgrims, for making dandelion wine.
- The greens, flowers and root juices are consumed alone or in salads.
- This herb is a known diuretic, mild laxative, and claimed to be effective in restoring adrenal function.[7]

Pitcher Plant (Sarracenia)
- The roots of this bog-land plant can be consumed or used in a tea.
- No dosage is specified, but no toxic effects have ever been reported.[5]

2) MUSCLE BUILDING
Alfalfa (Medicago sativa)
- A well-known fodder crop, it is rich in vitamins and nitrates.
- It is known to increase speed in horses and greyhounds,[3] and has long been recognized as a muscle builder for people in the Arab world.
- It has such a good reputation that it was given the name "Al-Fal-Fa," which means "father of all foods."
- Alfalfa is also a diuretic and mild laxative. There is no recommended dose, but eating too much might cause gastrointestinal problems (because of the fiber content). Begin with small amounts.
- Alfalfa is known as a natural medicine for stomach ailments, inlcuding ulcers.
- An alternative method is to combine alfalfa with a mint-flavored herb and drink as a tea on a daily basis.[4]

Ashwaganda
- Made from the root of an Indian plant. It is used for treating low-sex drive, speeding recovery of overworked muscles, and encouraging tissue growth. It is therefore a muscle-building herb.
- No dose specified.[7]

Beech (Fagus sylvatica)

- A common deciduous tree. This herb (in the form of a tea brewed from the leaves and bark) is recommended for bodybuilders using HGH, insulin, or other preparations or diets which might create border-line diabetes.[3]

Birthwort (Aristolochia clematis)

- A flower commonly found growing amid the rubble of old buildings.
- It has a reputation as a female fertility herb.
- The plant must be well-dried and powdered, and then consumed in capsule form, or brewed and strained before serving.
- This plant is believed to increase strength in females (be warned, it is also claimed to increase your chances of getting pregnant!).
- The recommended dose is two tablespoons of the brewed herb, or two teaspoons of the dried herb.[3]

Blue Flag Iris (Iris versicolor)

- This is a waterside plant found in moist meadows.
- It has a general effect on the body as a whole, improving overall physical condition.
- The root is cut into thin transverse sections, and brewed, one tablespoon of root to one-half that of water or wine, producing an extract.
- The dose taken is one tablespoon of the brew, twice daily.[3]

Black Poplar (Populus nigra)

- This is a tree found on the edges of fields and meadows.
- It can be used as an appetite stimulant.
- The buds can be blended with wine or milk as a drink.[3]

Chris Cormier

Ch'ai Hu (Bupleurum falcatum)

- This herb is derived from the stalks of the plant.
- It has a reputation for strengthening the limbs, particularly the leg muscles.[6]

Ch'ai Hu Chia Lung Ku Mu Li T'sang

- This Chinese herbal tea (which is a combination of many herbs) is believed to be a powerful aphrodisiac. If true, one would expect that testosterone levels would increase, or that the tea would have a similar effect. This tea can be picked up at a Chinese pharmacy.[6]

Ch'e Chi'en Tsao (Plantago asiatica)

- This herb is made from the entire plant.
- If the seeds are used alone to make the herbal preparation, it is called Ch'e Chi'en Tzu.
- This herb is believed to increase sperm production and fertility; and if so would be expected to increase testosterone production.
- A Chinese pharmacy can recommend a specific dosage.[6]

Horse Chestnut (Aesculus hippocastanum)

- This is a parkland tree.
- The nuts are very nutritious and believed to strengthen the pulmonary system.
- The bitter flavor can be removed by soaking them in a solution of lime and water, and then washing thoroughly before eating.[3]
- It should be noted that only a few nuts might produce toxic symptoms in some individuals (nausea, dizziness, bleeding and vomiting).[5]
- Extreme caution should be exercised with this herb.

Aaron Baker

Paul Dillett,
Nasser El Sonbaty
and Vince Taylor

Bird Cherry (Prunus avium)
- This is a woodland tree.
- It is claimed to be high in "life-giving properties," and will thus increase physical strength.
- The bark or cherry fruit stalks may be boiled and the brew strained before drinking.[3]

Garlic
- This well-known herb can reduce cholesterol levels.
- One study found that one-half to one clove daily could lower cholesterol an average of nine percent.[8]
- Considering the heavy red-meat consumption of many bodybuilders, garlic would make an excellent addition to the diet.

Milk Thistle
- This herb is used to treat liver damage.
- This plant's small, hard fruits have been shown to protect the liver against a variety of toxins.
- The active ingredient is a concentrated extract called silymarin – a substance that apparantly prevents the membranes of undamaged liver cells from letting toxins enter.[8]
- Besides the increased production of metabolites and other waste products from exercise, this herb would be of benefit to bodybuilders using anabolic steroids.

Wood Betony (Stachys betonica)
- This is a woodland plant.
- It is claimed to be able to correct glandular deficiencies, and thus would be of benefit to bodybuilders coming off a steroid cycle.
- Two handfuls of the plant are added to one and one-half pints of water and one-quarter pound of brown sugar.
- The mixture is allowed to simmer until a syrup is formed.[3] The syrup can be consumed with porridge.

Rest-Harrow (Ononis arvensis)
- Follow directions as stated for the previous herb.
- One cup of the brew should be consumed in the morning, as well as one at night.
- It is claimed to relieve glandular deficiencies.[3] This would be of benefit to a bodybuilder coming off a steroid cycle.

Sarsaparilla (Smilax ornata)
- This Mexican plant has been a traditional cure for weakness, and used as an aphrodisiac.
- It contains an alkaloid that resembles testosterone.
- It may be taken as a tea,[4] but it should only be consumed for a short period of time.[5]

Strawberry (Fragaria vesca)
- This is a well-known cultivated fruit.
- It is believed to restore vitality, and thus would be of benefit for hard-training bodybuilders.
- Even if the claims about strawberries are untrue, they are an excellent source of vitamins.
- Bodybuilders should consume at least one cup of berries daily.[3]

Hop (Humulus lupulus)
- This is a climbing plant found growing in rich soil.
- The young spring shoots of hops have the same taste as asparagus.
- This herb is claimed to restore vitality and stimulate appetite.
- The recommended dose is five handfuls of hop flowers, eaten early in the morning.[3]

Achim Albrecht

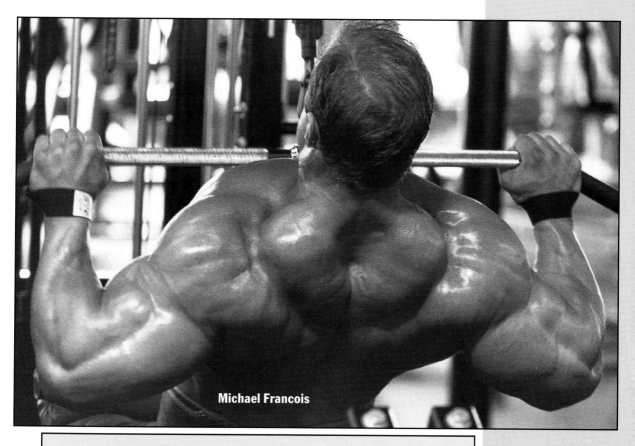

Michael Francois

Vanilla (Vanilla planifolia)
- This spice was considered to be an aphrodisiac in turn-of-the-century America.
- It is quite safe if taken in small amounts daily for a period of four weeks or less.
- Taking in the form of ice cream, however, will only make you fat!

Yohimbe
- Made from the bark of an African tree, this herb is sold as a men's aphrodisiac.
- Its active compound, yohimbine, is a prescription drug sometimes used to treat impotence.
- There is, however, no conclusive medical evidence to back up the claim that yohimbe-bark extracts can affect male sexual performance (only the synthetic derivatives of yohimbine in 10-milligram dosages seem to produce this effect). If true, it would be of benefit for bodybuilders because any improvement in sexual response might be linked to changes in hormone levels; thus the body would be in an anabolic state.
- Given the lack of credible evidence we doubt yohimbe holds much promise as an ergogenic aid.
- We should stress that an overdose of yohimbine can cause serious problems: weakness, nervous stimulation, paralysis, fatigue, stomach disorders and death. In the state of Georgia this herb is legally known as a dangerous drug and forbidden to be sold without a prescription.[8]

"Yohimbine is not, nor does it contain testosterone or any anabolic steroids; nor is testosterone required for the enhancement of sexual motivation by yohimbine."

– Dr. Mauro DiPasquale, best-selling author and regular *MuscleMag* columnist setting the record straight on the much hyped ergogenic aid, yohimbine.

3) APPEARANCE

Adder's Tongue (Ophioglossum vulgatum)
- This is a fern plant of fields and waste lands.
- It makes a supreme wound herb which can be used by bodybuilders to treat bruises caused by injections or dropped weights.
- French Gypsies make Adder's Tongue ointment, using equal parts of olive oil, nut fat and bees wax. Melt in a deep sauce pan at a low temperature, and add the ingredients until you have about one pint of liquid. Then add as much finely chopped Adder's Tongue as it will absorb. Pour into a container and seal. Use topically as needed.[3]

Alder (Alnus glutinosa)
- This is a tree commonly found along riverbanks.
- It is one of the most common shrubs in North America.
- The green leaves are astringent and cooling, and can be bound to injuries to reduce swelling.[3]

Yarrow (Achillea millefolium)
- This is a plant found in pastures.
- The flowers can be ground into a paste and spread on the scalp – supposedly as a cure for baldness.[3]
- If it works it holds enormous potential in bodybuilding, given the number of individuals suffering from steroid-induced baldness.

Rest-Harrow (Ononis arvensis)
- This is a plant found in dry places.
- A brew is made using two handfuls of the whole herb, or two well-sliced roots, brewed in one and one-half pints of water. Add one spoonful of castor oil, and massage into the scalp.[3]

Saw Palmetto
- This herb supposedly has the ability to reduce the androgenic effects of steroids and other testosterone derivatives.[8]
- This would be of value for female bodybuilders using steroids, in order to reduce masculinizing side effects.

Echinacea (Sampson Root)
- The root of this plant was used by the Sioux Indians to treat infected wounds and snakebites.
- It has the ability to reduce swelling and inflammation. Therefore, it may be of benefit for bodybuilders who have painful injection sites or who have used snake venom.[7]

4) STIMULANTS

A Chiao (Equus Asinus)
- This tonic isn't made from a herb, but from donkey skin.
- It can be picked up at a Chinese pharmacy.
- The pharmacist can specify the appropriate dosage.[6]

Barley-Honey Drink
- To one gallon of water add one-half pound of barley. Boil slowly until reduced to three-quarter gallon. Once tepid add one-half pound of honey.[3]

Bee Pollen
- A powder made up of the male gametes (sperm) produced by flowering plants.
- The pollen is picked up by bees and other insects, and carried to other flowers, allowing fertilization.
- Although claimed to be anabolic, the constituents and ratios of these pollens are suspect, and they can cause severe allergic reactions in some individuals.
- No safe dosage has been determined, but the pollen can be taken either as an injection or in capsule form.[5]

Blanche Water
- Wet four handfuls of bran with boiling water, and work it till it becomes clammy (the texture of porridge). Then add one quart of cold water. Strain, warm to tepid and stir in one-half pound of honey.[3]

Cayenne Pepper (Capsicum frutescens)
- A spice, it can be taken in powder or capsule form.
- No dosage is specified.[5]

Edgar Fletcher

Eucalyptus (Eucalyptus globulus)

- This herb is best known as being the favorite food of the Koala bear, an Auatralian Marsupial.
- The leaves produce an oil, which, when inhaled in the form of steam, can have a refreshing and stimulating effect.
- A solution of one teaspoon of oil to one cup of water can be poured on sauna rocks.[4]
- This is a great recovery system after a hard workout.

Chiang (Zingiber officinale)

- This Chinese herb is known in the west as ginger.
- It's a potent cardiac stimulant.[6]

Ma Huang

- Also called ephedra, this herb contains the stimulants pseudoephedrine and ephedrine.
- Promoted for weight control and found in energy-boosting formulas, the effects can be augmented by combining with aspirin and caffeine.
- On the negative side, ephedra can raise blood pressure and cause palpitations, nerve damage, muscle injury, psychosis, stroke and memory loss. (see Chapter Ten on "Ephedrine")

Lobelia

- Also called Indian tobacco, it is similar to nicotine in action, but less potent.
- Lobelia can both stimulate and depress the autonomic nervous system.
- In low doses (50 milligrams) Lobelia stimulates the lungs' bronchi and steps up breathing. Larger amounts could reduce breathing, drop blood pressure, induce sweating, rapid heart beat, coma and death.[8]

Peppermint (Mentha piperita)

- This herb is a popular flavoring added to many foods and confections.
- According to Greek mythology, the name "mint" comes from a beautiful nymph named Mintho. She was loved by the God of the Underworld, Pluto. His wife, Persephone, became jealous and changed Mintho into a fragrant plant, the mint. The aroma of mint alone is believed to strengthen the body.
- It may be consumed as a tea.[4]

Rose (Rosa canina)

- Both wild and domesticated roses have long been used in medicine.
- For the bodybuilder, a restorative tonic of four drops of oil to one cup of warm milk is recommended.[3]

5) TRANQUILIZERS

Chamomile (Anthemis nobilis)

- This ground-hugging herb derives its name from the Greek "kamai" (on the ground) and "melon" (apple), thus "ground apple."
- It may be taken as a tea, and is both a sedative and sleep inducer, both of which can be badly needed in the weeks leading up to a contest.[4]

Rock-Rose (Helianthemum canadense)
- A plant found in rocky places.
- This plant produces a calming effect, which is beneficial for a bodybuilder in the last stages of contest preparation.
- Daily dosage is a handful of the whole plant.[3]

Sharon Bruneau

References

1) S. M. Kleiner, "The True Nature of Herbs," *The Physician and Sports Medicine*, 23:10 (October 1995).
2) J.H. Young, *The Toadstool Millionaires – A Social History of Patent Medicine in America Before Federal Regulation*, (Princeton, New Jersey: Princeton University Press, 1961).
3) L.J. De Bairacli, *Herbal Handbook for Farm and Stable*, (Emmaus, Pennsylvania: Roedale Press Inc., 1976).
4) L.J. Dunne, *Nutrition Almanac*, 3d ed., (New York: McGraw Hill Publishing Co., 1990).
5) H.W. Griffith, *Complete Guide to Vitamins, Minerals, and Supplements*, (Tucson, Arizona: Fisher Books, 1988).
6) R. Hyatt, *Chinese Herbal Medicine – An Accepted Art and Modern Healing Science*, (New York: Thorsons Publishers Inc., 1984).
7) F. Hatfield, "Herbs, Plant Power for All Seasons," *Muscle and Fitness*, 51:9 (September 1990).
8) "Herbal Roulette," *Consumer Reports* (1996).
9) P. Chisolm and others, "Healers or Quacks?" Therapies Once Viewed As Fringe Are Becoming Mainstream," *Maclean's*, (September 1995).

CHAPTER TWENTY-SEVEN

Natural Anabolics, Anticatabolics and Hormone Boosters

With the crackdown on steroids and other anabolic drugs in the late 1980s and early 1990s, supplement manufacturers set out to fill the void (perhaps misleading as most anabolic drugs are still readily available) by promoting "natural" alternatives. In most cases the outlandish claims are just that – the promotion of inferior products using creative advertising. Often touted as "steroid replacers" and "testosterone boosters," most of these supplements are nothing more than glorified protein sources or a combination of vitamins, minerals, and other common food nutrients. The following are among the more popular supplements advertised as "natural" alternatives to performance-enhancing drugs. Some of them have a basis in science, while others are a complete waste of money and nothing more than advertising hype.

> **"I look upon sex as a natural and normal function, like eating and drinking. I feel the destructive thing about sex is worrying about it! So forget about it. It's a natural function."**
>
> – The late Vince Gironda, responding to a *MuscleMag* reader's question about whether or not sex could naturally increase testosterone levels.

GAMMA ORYZANOL

Although it still has its advocates, gamma-oryzanol usage seemed to peak in the mid to late 1980s, and in recent years has been replaced by such high-tech supplements as creatine, HCA, and carnitine. Since the supplement is obtained from the parenchymatous cells of various plants, it's bioactivity in humans is questionable.

What gave gamma oryzanol such great sales were manufacturers' claims that the substance had the positive attributes of anabolic steroids without the negative side effects. In this regard, gamma oryzanol supposedly increased lean muscle tissue, decreased bodyfat and improved cardiovascular endurance. Although the exact mechanism of action is not fully understood, it is believed gamma oryzanol exerts its effects by stimulating the hypothalamus gland.

Kevin Levrone

THE OLD FAMILIAR ARGUMENT

Hopefully after reading this far you see the problem with such claims. Any substance that can modify part of the brain and induce physiological changes is by definition a "drug." And as you know, most drugs – especially those that can do what gamma oryzanol is supposed to – are under tight regulatory control. If gamma oryzanol was such a powerful anabolic agent, you wouldn't be able to walk into a health-food store and buy as much as you wanted. It would only be available by prescription, but chances are it wouldn't even be obtainable this way.

SOURCES AND DOSAGE

For those who decide to try the supplement, here are a few tidbits of information. Most gamma-oryzanol preparations are derived from such plant oils as rice bran and wheat germ. After various manufacturing techniques – including dehydration – the substance appears in the form of a white powder. Most supplement preparations are combined with vitamin E (a popular choice given vitamin E's oil-based background), but you can also buy individual products. With regards to dosage, anecdotal reports suggest taking between 5 to 30 milligrams a day. Given such a broad range it's easy to see how personal preference plays a role. If you decide to use higher dosages (as most bodybuilders do) we recommend starting with low dosages (5 to 10 milligrams per day) and gradually increasing to 30 to 40 milligrams over a three- or four-week period. As with most supplements some individuals may have trouble tolerating high dosages.

Shawn Ray

YOHIMBINE

Yohimbine is a perfect example of what creative advertising and lack of knowledge can do for a mediocre supplement. The substance is derived from the dried bark of the Corynanthe Johimbe tree of the southern Cameroons and Congo region of Africa, and Quebracho of South America.

Yohimbine has been used for thousands of years as an aphrodisiac because of its effects on the human central nervous system. Being an alpha-sub-2-receptor antagonist, yohimbine blocks receptors in the brain leading to such physiological responses as increased heart rate and blood

Ian Harrison, Darrem Charles and Lee Priest

pressure, increased irritability, increased motor functioning, and vasodialation. Given such properties, yohimbine is sometimes used to treat impotence and counteract the effect of diabetes on the body's extremities (reduced blood flow in the legs is a frequent side effect of severe diabetes). There is also evidence to suggest that the substance increases the firing of noradrenaline cells, leading to heightened feelings of fear and anxiety.

The theory behind its use in sports is that since most aphrodisiacs are supposed to increase sexual prowess – possibly by increasing hormone levels – then such effects could be carried over into athletics. In other words more "testosterone" means greater muscle gains. While sounding great in theory, there are practical considerations which make the substance almost useless as an anabolic agent. First and foremost is the lack of credible evidence to suggest that it does increase natural hormone levels. Virtually all aphrodisiacs owe their success to the placebo effect – that is, if you believe it works, it will! From Spanish fly to seal penises, few accepted aphrodisiacs increase sexual powers by physiological means. Most are psychological in nature, and yohimbine, while possibly increasing blood flow to the genitalia, does not increase sexual prowess by increasing hormone levels.

A second major reason for dismissing yohimbine as an effective anabolic agent is its source – the bark of a plant. Although the latest Soviet research suggests that some plant hormones may have bioactivity in humans, plant substances generally have little or no effect on human physiology (their use as pharmaceuticals is an entirely different matter, but even then most need chemical modification). What yohimbine distributors have done is throw the word "sterol" around in an attempt to confuse the less informed, and judging by sales, they've done a pretty good job. But the fact remains that no plant "sterol" can act as an "anabolic steroid" in the human body.

We should add that some of the confusion surrounding yohimbine concerns the possible presence of methyltestosterone in a few supplement preparations. Some botanists suggest yohimbe bark contains methyltestosterone – one of the few forms of testosterone that is alleged to be bioactive in humans after being taken orally. But the research is divided on this issue as many studies suggest methyltestosterone is worthless for adults.

Jason Arntz

Besides possibly being present naturally, there are also stories about shady manufacturers adding methyltestosterone to their products in an attempt to boost sales and effectiveness. Not only is this practice illegal (and dangerous), but high levels of methyltestosterone can be toxic. Further, if you are competing in a drug-tested event, the methyltestosterone may register you a positive.

If you decide to use yohimbine, the recommended dose is 15 to 20 milligrams a day. These are figures for treating impotence and frigidity and no doubt bodybuilders are taking many times this amount. Tablet size varies from 1.5 to 5 milligrams, which makes calculating dosages rather easy.

In conclusion, yohimbine may hold some merit as an aphrodisiac because of its vasodilation effects, but as an anabolic agent it is virtually worthless. Some bodybuilders find it beneficial before a contest or before working out, claiming it produces a greater pump, so you might want to see if it produces the same effect for you. Finally, while the incidence of side effects from yohimbine is extremely low, and overdosing is not really an issue, play it safe and don't consume more than 10 to 15 milligrams at any one time.

If Smilax increased testosterone levels as much as distributors claimed, the FDA and Canadian equivalent would reclassify the substance as a drug.

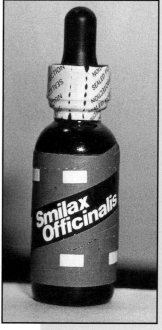

SMILAX

Like yohimbine, Smilax is a substance derived from a plant source, in this case the commonly available herb sarsaparilla. The full name of the substance is Smilax Officinalis, and while you can obtain the substance in natural form from the herb, supplement manufacturers have made available a much more potent concentrate version. To give the product a "drug like" appearance, manufacturers often package smilax in liquid form inside a "medicine like" bottle. To many in our drug-desensitized society, anything in such a bottle must produce wonderful effects, but as we shall see, appearance can be misleading.

HOW EFFECTIVE?

Distributers of Smilax claim that their product boosts natural production of testosterone, and cite studies carried out by Belgian researchers to back their claims. Few if any North American researchers have obtained the same results. Given the notority of former Eastern Bloc athletes for using anabolic steroids, we should be sceptical of such claims. Like yohimbine, Smilax sounds great in theory but has little or no scientific merit. And without sounding like a broken record, let us repeat that plant substances have little or no effect on human hormone biochemistry. As soon as plant sterols or related substances are consumed they are immediately degraded by the human digestive system into their component nutrients – protein, vitamins, and minerals.

We also must take into account the potential legalities of such claims. If Smilax increased testosterone levels as much as distributors claimed, the FDA and Canadian equivalent would reclassify the substance as a drug – and a very powerful one at that. Do you think soft-drink manufacturers would be allowed to use such a substance in their beverages? (Smilax is often used as a flavoring agent in root beer.)

Edgar Fletcher

In fact manufacturers are contradictory in their approach to marketing the substance. They claim increased testosterone levels without the risk of side effects. But even the most pro of steroid users will admit that all testosterone derivatives produce some degree of side effects (albeit not as severe as some would have us believe). How is it that high levels of natural testosterone (produced by Smilax of course) are "risk free," while exogenous sources are dangerous to an individual's health? See the problem. If Smilax was the powerful anabolic agent claimed, it would produce varying degrees of side effects and it would be banned by North American drug-regulatory agencies. The fact that neither are applicable gives some indication of the substance's effectiveness.

As a final comment, Smilax is relatively inexpensive as supplements go, with a one- or two-ounce bottle costing between $15 and $20. As most of the better supplements – the ones backed by credible research – cost many times this, you can bet that Smilax costs very little to produce. This is not to say price is the only factor in rating a supplement's quality, but the fact remains that to produce a quality, bioactive supplement, manufacturers must invest significant amounts of cash, which is then passed on to the consumer. And while there are expensive products that are overpriced and ineffective, the odds of a supplement being both potent and inexpensive (as smilax is supposed to be) is very remote.

Sharon Marvel

CHROMIUM

It is generally accepted that today's bodybuilder is far more knowledgable than his or her counterpart of thirty or forty years ago. This is not so much out of curiosity, as necessity. Every year sees a whole new generation of bodybuilders emerge from the national ranks to strut their stuff on the international scene. And with few exceptions, all are walking encyclopedias of nutritional know-how. Those that fail to keep up to date on the latest in ergogenic aids find themselves placing low on the competitive ladder.

Perhaps the biggest revolution in nutrition concerns the attention devoted to single-entity supplements. The multifaceted supplement drinks of years gone by have been delegated to second place by hundreds of supplements each devoted to a single objective. Besides ingesting the building blocks for muscular growth, bodybuilders now attempt to manipulate the rate at which the body turns these nutrients into coveted muscle tissue. In most cases their attempts fall short. This is because once the body has sufficient quantities of a given substance, taking an excess won't somehow increase a given metabolic rate. Still, having said that, many bodybuilders have turned to minerals and trace elements to achieve these goals, and one of them, chromium, is fast becoming one of the most popular.

While chromium is familiar to most as the shiny metal on cars, few realize that it plays a major role in metabolic functioning. The importance of chromium was ignored until the mid 1950s when animal experiments determined that chromium deficiency could seriously impair health. Before the results of these studies became available, it was believed that chromium was worthless to humans, and in some cases toxic.

From a biochemical aspect, chromium falls under the catagory of trace element. Unlike their more abundant mineral cousins such as sodium, calcium, and potassium, trace elements are only needed in small amounts by the body. But don't let the phrase "small amounts" mislead you. Chromium and such other trace elements as iodine, copper, and zinc are essential components of proper enzyme functioning.

Much of what we know about chromium is from the works of Dr. Walter Mertz, one of the pioneers of insulin/chromium research. In the late 1950s Dr. Mertz first isolated the biologically active form of chromium

Once the body has sufficient quantities of a given substance, taking an excess may do the body more harm than good.
– Chris Cormier

called GTF – Glucose Tolerance Factor. Later studies determined that GTF is an organic chromium complex which helps bind insulin to cell-membrane receptor sites. In the absence of chromium, insulin is hindered in its ability to affect glucose metabolism. Dr. Mertz also discovered that not all forms of chromium are biologically active and capable of affecting insulin. Only the form complexed with nicotinic acid and the four amino acids, glycine, cysteine, glutamic acid, and aspartic acid, is believed to be effective.

MECHANISM OF ACTION

From what scientists can deduce, the main function of chromium is to modulate blood-glucose levels. It does this by increasing the efficiency of insulin – the body's primary glucose-regulating hormone. Although the exact mechanism of action is not known, it is believed chromium increases the binding power of insulin to cellular receptors.

A second function of chromium is to reduce circulating cholesterol levels. Researchers at Mercy Hospital in San Diego gave 14 healthy adults 200 micro-grams of chromium a day (the form was chromium picolinate). The results showed total cholesterol levels dropped by 20 milli-grams/decilitre (a unit to measure blood volume), and LDL cholesterol levels dropped 10.5 percent. Although not conclu-sive, the results of this and other studies suggest chromium may hold potential for treating those with a predisposition to heart disease.

WHY TAKE CHROMIUM SUPPLEMENTS?

Given the prevalence of diabetes in North American society, it wasn't long before Dr. Mertz's findings were put to practical use. Starting in the 1960s, chromium supplements began to be used for treating those with insulin-related medical conditions.

It is well-documented that as we age our insulin efficiency drops. This may be due to any number of reasons: decreased insulin production, decreased receptor sensitivity, or even reduced numbers of insulin recep-tors. What ever the reason, giving chromium supplements to elderly people (or those experiencing similar problems) enhances blood-sugar control. Chromium supplements also recieved a boost when studies indicated that up to 80 percent of the chromium contained in food is removed during pro-cessing. Many Americans are recieving less than 20 percent of the RDA (50 to 200 micrograms per day).

Besides aging and dietary affects, athletes may be at special risk for chromium deficiency. Like most minerals and trace elements, chromium is excreted in the urine in greater amounts following intense training. It is also lost in sweat for similar reasons. Finally, high-carbohydrate diets are known to reduce chromium supplies.

All of the previous leads to the conclusion that chromium supplementation may be beneficial to certain individuals. But as with most supplements, chromium is not some magic pill that when taken in excess causes a profound increase in muscle growth. There is evidence to suggest that megadosing may lead to severe side effects.

THE EVOLUTION OF CHROMIUM SUPPLEMENTS

The first natural sources of chromium were Brewer's yeast tablets – made popular by the patrons of Muscle Beach back in the 1950s and 1960s. Although users swore to its benefits, Brewer's yeast is a poor source of chromium. Not only does it contain chromium in small amounts – about 2 micrograms/gram – but more important, less than half the chromium is in the biologically active GTF form.

The first chromium supplements made available were inorganic chromium salts of chloride, acetate, and oxide. Less than one percent of such forms are absorbed and utilized by the body. They are still popular and very inexpensive, but we warned, chromium supplements may be toxic to some individuals.

The next category of chromium supplements appeared in the early 1970s and consisted of chromium chelated (bound) to amino acids. Although safer and more easily absorbed, chelated forms of chromium are not capable of affecting insulin action to any degree.

The first step in the right direction occured in the 1980s when biochemists began to synthesize biologically active GTF. They did this by adding

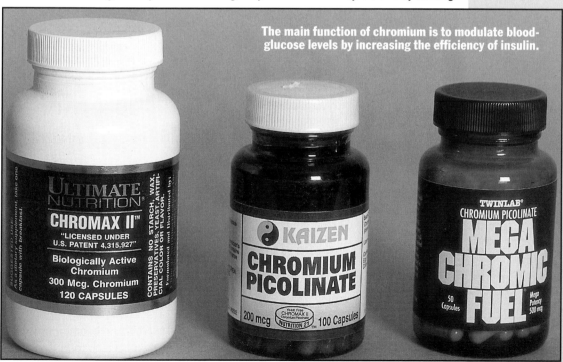

The main function of chromium is to modulate blood-glucose levels by increasing the efficiency of insulin.

inorganic chromium to live yeast cultures, which convert some of the chromium to GTF. If there was a drawback it was the limited supply of GTF produced – only 20 to 40 percent of the inorganic chormium was actually converted.

Throughout the late 1980s and early 1990s two forms of chromium supplements have come to dominate the market – chromium picolinate and chromium polynicotinate. While the latter is gaining acceptance as being legitimate, the former appears to be more hype than substance. Given the magazine attention both have recieved over the past five years, we are going to address each separately.

CHROMIUM PICOLINATE

Chromium picolinate is the complex form of chromium and picolinic acid – one of the metabolites of the amino acid tryptophan. It is structurally similar to the B-complex vitamin niacin, and recieved its greatest boost from Dr. Gary Evans of Bemidji State University, Minnesota, who claimed that test subjects taking chromium picolinate had reduced bodyfat levels, increased muscle mass, and lower cholesterol levels. On the surface such results sound convincing, but few other researchers have been able to duplicate the results of Dr. Evans' study. Further, the biochemistry behind chromium picolinate

doesn't seem to hold promise for insulin/chromium modulation. For example, studies cited by world-authority Dr. Walter Mertz suggest that chromium-picolinate complexes have little effect on insulin and are probably too tightly bound to be biologically active. In all probability the complex is excreted almost as fast as it's absorbed.

As a final comment, and the one that raises the most scepticism; the subjects in Dr. Evans' study were college football players who were not tested for performance-enhancing drugs including anabolic steroids. Given the prevalence of such drugs among football players, it's difficult to conclude whether the results obtained by Dr. Evans were due to some intrinsic properties of the chromium supplements or from anabolic steroids.

CHROMIUM POLYNICOTINATE

Given that the biologically active form of chromium is the form complexed with niacin, it only makes sense to use supplements that are as structurally similar to the organic form as possible.

Over the past five to six years such supplements have been developed. They usually go by any number of eye-catching trade names, but as long as the label reads "chromium polynicotinate" or "chromium nicotinate," you can be sure that it contains niacin-bound chromium.

Being niacin-based is not proof of bioactivity. Biochemists tell us that chromium can be bound to niacin in any number of different ways. And since no one is 100 percent sure what the molecular arrangement of GTF looks like, synthesizing GTF becomes a sort of supplement equivalent of Russian roulette.

Paul Dillett

HOW THEY ARE TAKEN

As with any form of mineral or trace-element supplement, chromium preparations should be taken with meals. This is because these substances catalyze and modulate the metabolism of other substances. For example, since insulin is released in response to sugar and carbohydrate ingestion, and since chromium potentiates the effects of insulin, it only makes sense to take chromium when insulin levels are highest.

There is one very important point we should add regarding dosage. When examining a supplement label, pay attention to the elemental values for the ingredients. Don't be misled into thinking a 100-microgram chromium tablet contains "100 micrograms of chromium." In all probability the tablet contains only a fraction of its weight in useable mineral. As an example, chromium picolinate supplements are approximately 12 percent chromium. The rest is made up of the picolinate portion of the compound. If the label says 200 micrograms on the bottle, you are only getting about 24 micrograms of the mineral chromium. If you wanted to get 400 micrograms of chromium (the minimum amount generally recommended for bodybuilders) you would need to consume about 3500 micrograms of chromium picolinate.

SIDE EFFECTS

Although rare, side effects from chromium use are occassionally reported. In most cases the form of chromium being used is to blame. Users of Brewer's yeast (and those that work out next to such individuals) often experience severe discomfort in the form of flatulence. And while not a life-threatening condition, it makes for some noxious moments at the squat rack. The yeast-produced chromium supplements can also produce allergic reactions.

Milos Sarcev and
Mauro Sarni

The chromium supplements with perhaps the most potential for side effects are chromium-picolinate preparations. According to Dr. Jerzy Meduski, a world-renowned biochemist and consultant for Weider Health and Fitness, chromium picolinate is a niacin antagonist, which means it competes with niacin for metabolic pathways in the body.[1] The implications of such are enormous and is one of the reasons why the FDA has not listed picolinate products as GRAS – Generally Recognized As Safe – for human consumption. It is recommended that bodybuilders use no more than 50 micrograms of this form of chromium daily.

Finally, while not conclusive, there is some evidence to suggest chromium picolinate may lead to chromosome damage. Of course, some researchers have dimissed these results saying chromium is no more dangerous than other trace elements and minerals. And the few studies that suggest chromium picolinate is dangerous were only conducted in the lab using dosages far above what could or would be found in the human body. Most substances can have adverse side effects if taken in high dosages. Aspirin, Gravol, and even vitamin E are considered "safe," but in high dosages can be life threatening. So the hysteria surrounding chromuim picolinate is for the most part unjustified. Given the disagreement within the scientific community, it's apparent that more research is needed before any definite conclusions can be drawn about the dangers of chromium-picolinate supplements.

With regards to chromium-polynicotinate products, few side effects have been reported as of this writing. Like most new supplements taken in high dosages, chromium polynicotinate may be linked to specific ailments down the road. Those with insulin problems – whether excess or insufficient production – should consult their physicians before taking any form of chromium.

DIBENCOZIDE

Dibencozide is one of a growing number of supplements that advertisers claim "works like steroids without the side effects." It first came into prominance in the early to mid 1980s when bodybuilding magazines began promoting the substance as the latest thing in supplementation. Like arginine and other "steroid replacers," dibencozide's merits were exaggerated by supplement manufacturers who misinterpreted, or worse, misrepresented studies that looked at the substance's effectiveness. In the following section we will look at both sides of the dibencozide debate, and afterwards you can make up your own mind as to whether or not to include it in your gym bag.

Dibencozide is the biologically active form of vitamin B12, also known as coenzyme B12 or adenosylcobalamin (throughout this chapter we will use the various names interchangeably). It received its first endorsements from Russian and European weightlifters and bodybuilders who regularly included it in their diets. To fully appreciate the difference between B12 and dibencozide we need to look at how each works in the body.

As most bodybuilders know, the B-complex vitamins, including B12, are essential to maintain proper health. They are liberated from animal sources by both cooking and digestion. Once in free form in the stomach, B12 is bound to substances called intrinsic factors to form a complex that is immune to futher breakdown in the stomach or the upper sections of the small intestine. Absorption only takes place at specialized receptor sites located in the ileum – the lower part of the small intestine which joins to the large intestine. One of the interesting things about absorption is that once the ileum has been exposed to high concentrations of B12 it blocks futher absorption of the vitamin for about four to five hours. During this interval the B12-intrinsic factor complex breaks down and B12 is transported to the bloodstream by a specialized carrier called transcobalamin II. Although it

Aaron Baker

"On which research did they back their claims? On a Polish study done back in the 1960s. A group of underweight children (not hard-training world-class athletes) suffering from anemia were divided into two groups. Half were given anabolic steroids, the other half dobencozide. Since dibencozide is very effective at curing anemia, it wasn't surprising that both groups gained bodyweight equally well. This was "proof" that dibencozide was as effective as steroids for adding bodyweight. But for a healthy athlete not suffering from anemia, it would have little effect on weight gain. For most bodybuilders and athletes it would do nothing because most take in lots of B12 from their vitamin supplements."

– Greg Zulak, former *MuscleMag* editor commenting on one of the ploys of many supplement manufacturers; that being misrepresentation of scientific research.

varies, peak concentrations of B12 do not appear in the bloodstream until 10 to 12 hours after consumption. Once in the bloodstream, B12 is carried to the liver where it is either stored or converted to coenzyme B12 as the need arises.

Coenzyme B12 is then released back into the bloodstream and absorbed by the body's various tissues. Absoprtion by tissues is dependant on B12 being converted to the bio-active version.

EARLY RESEARCH

Although a new supplement in bodybuilding circles, research into the workings of B12 has been ongoing since the late 1920s. Among the first studies were those in 1928 by Castle, who first coined the terms "extrinsic" – today known as vitamin B12 – and "intrinsic," which is still used. Don't let the terms frighten you as they are nothing more than the B12-intrinsic factor complex we just described.

In the late 1950s the bio-active form of B12 was isolated, and the rush was on to determine just what role it played in human biochemistry.

MECHANISM OF ACTION

Describing the various activities of B12 could take a whole book. For the purposes of this text we will outline the functions where B12 plays a major role.

"The result of a B12 deficiency can be serious nerve degeneration, causing great weakness, fatigue, and other symptoms. If these symptoms show signs of developing, the vegetarian should consult his or her family doctor immediately for B12 injections, the speediest way to prevent nerve degeneration, which can otherwise create a serious problem. Fortunately today there are sublingual B12 tablets in health-food stores which work very well at increasing the blood levels of this vitamin."

– The late Bruce Page, commenting on the importance of B12 supplementation for vegetarians.

Michael Francois

At the molecular level B12 is involved in the synthesis of the nucleic acids – DNA and RNA – and protein. Its mechansim of action is to assist in methylation, the process by which methyl groups (CH_3) are added to protein and nucleic acids. Deficiencies in B12 can lead to reductions in protein synthesis, cell maintenance, and ultimately overall body growth.

Another important function is the role B12 plays in fat oxidation. It does this by processing fats with odd-numbered carbon chains. This allows the maximum amount of energy to be utilized from fat sources. A deficiency in B12 can play havoc with a bodybuilder's contest preparation.

A final major function of B12 is helping to regulate the nervous system. Of particular importance is its role in maintaining the myelin sheath. The sheath acts like the plastic covering surrounding wire, and serves as a protective barrier which insulates the nerve from outside substances. This insures rapid nerve-impulse conduction. A deficiency in B12 can disrupt this delicate process resulting in poor muscular contraction and muscular weakness.

Rounding out the functions of B12 are its roles in blood-cell production and organ maintenance.

Laura Creavalle

THE ADVANTAGE OF B12 SUPPLEMENTS

The conversion of B12 that has been consumed in the diet to dibencozide and its use in the body has been explained. What happens, however, if you take dibencozide in capsule form? It will still form the vitamin-intrinsic-factor complex, but the complex is so tight that little of it becomes absorbed by the ileum. Manufacturers get around this by putting a coating on coenzyme B12 which prevents the intrinsic-factor complex from forming. This allows the vitamin to pass straight into the bloodstream where it acts on muscle, nerve, and other body cells. The advantage to taking B12 in this manner should be obvious. Instead of binding, unbinding, transporting to and from the liver, and liver metabolism, coenzyme B12 is transported to the cells much more quickly and efficiently.

One of the problems researchers have when working with dibencozide is that it decomposes in light (this is why manufacturers package the product in tinted bottles and darkened – usually brown – capsules). If these protective measures are not put in place, most of the dibencozide will decompose just by sitting on the shelf.

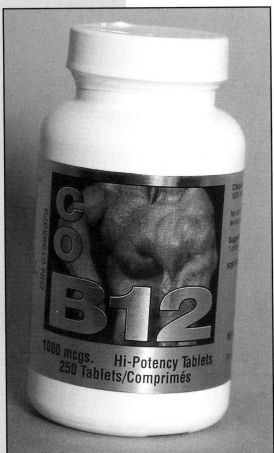

Dibencozide is nothing more than the bio-active form of coenzyme vitamin B12.

HOW EFFECTIVE?

Here we go again. Supplement manufacturers claim one thing, bodybuilders another, and scientific studies still another. What's an iron pumper to do!

Like just about every other new "steroid replacer" that comes on the market, dibencozide has its uses, but don't be easily mislead. Let us state that if dibencozide did what its manufacturers claimed, it would be classified as a drug and available only by prescription. Sound familiar?

No doubt many of you are countering with ads that state such claims as "safer than anabolic steroids" or "the most potent anabolic available" or how about "guaranteed to pass a drug test." On the surface these claims sound convincing but a closer look tells a different picture.

First of all, dibencozide should be safer than any anabolic steroid because it's not a drug but a vitamin that is needed on a daily basis by the human body. And because it's water-based the issue of toxicity is all but eliminated.

Second, as for being more potent than anabolic steroids, these claims are no doubt derived from a few European studies that showed how children and adolescents being treated with dibencozide gained more muscular bodyweight than subjects treated with Dianabol and Winstrol. Sounds convincing, right?

It may surprise you to learn that the subjects involved in the study were chronically ill children suffering from various growth maladies brought on, for the most part, by nutritional deficiencies. Further, the dosages of anabolic steroids given were far below those used by athletes. Given this, it only makes sense that the children taking B12 supplements under a laboratory setting would respond better than the steroid group. What these studies have to do with bodybuilders engaged in intense training and consuming high-protein diets is beyond us.

Finally, the issue of drug testing must be addressed. Those ads that claim dibencozide will not be detected in a drug test are really grasping at straws. As stated before, dibencozide is nothing more than the bio-active form of vitamin B12. Since when do sports organizations test for vitamins? Some less-informed individuals may think because of the medically sounding name – DIBENCOZIDE – they are taking a "drug" and therefore engaged in some sort of performance enhancement. But really, you can't fail a drug test because of vitamin supplementation.

All of the previous claims are used by supplement manufacturers to entice the uninformed to buy their products. While advertising a legitimate product is acceptable, exaggerating and misrepresenting studies for financial gain is not. While we do believe that biotech supplements are the future in bodybuilding, and may at some point duplicate the effects of steroids, the fact remains that no supplement currently available can achieve this on its own or in conjunction with other supplements. Yes, dibencozide has its place in modern bodybuilding – especially for vegetarians who may be deficient in

B12 (plant products are poor sources of B12) – but don't overestimate its abilities. Always try to keep things in perspective.

HOW TO USE DIBENCOZIDE

If you decide to use dibencozide, the first issue is choosing the right form. Most supplement manufacturers sell ordinary B12 – a fine vitamin as far as that goes, but certainly not in the same league as its coenzyme-B12 derivative. Only choose the bio-active form marketed as dibencozide or coenzyme B12. Also, take the capsule form as liquid versions are less stable and quickly deteriorate.

Although most biochemists recommend taking dibencozide about half an hour before working out, the bodybuilding scuttlebutt suggests taking it in the morning and in the evening. Most bodybuilders take 5,000 to 10,000 micrograms a day. For those not familiar with micrograms, this is equivilent to 5 to 10 milligrams. The reason we listed the dose in mircograms is because the more popular supplement manufacturers market dibencozide using these units. If you're more comfortable working in milligrams, simply divide micrograms by 1000 (for example, 10,000 micrograms/1000 = 10 milligrams).

**Always try to keep things in perspective. Don't overestimate a supplement's abilities.
– David Dearth**

Aaron Baker and
Van Smith

SIDE EFFECTS

Like all water-based vitamins, reports of side effects from B12 usage are
virtually unheard of. Some individuals may be sensitive to high dosages and
experience slight nausea, and in extreme cases there may be diarrhea, but
for the most part, B12 supplementation is relatively safe.

We should add that some B12 preparations may become toxic if
they decompose after sitting on the shelf for long periods of time, or are
exposed to light. This is because the element cobalt which is part of the B12
molecule is highly toxic when unbound from other atoms. This is an extreme
example but for ease of mind, use only those products that are well-pro-
tected from the light and haven't exceeded their expiry date.

BORON

Boron supplements are another example of how advertisers selectivly use
scientific data to make it sound as if their product is the greatest thing since
anabolic steroids. Unfortunately, many bodybuilders fall victim to the claims
and millions of dollars are being made without any benefits in return.

Boron is a trace mineral that seems to play a role in the metabolism
of magnesium, phosphorus and calcium. There is also some evidence to
suggest it may play a role in combating arthritis and osteoperosis.

WHAT IT SUPPOSEDLY DOES

Boron is like other minerals and trace elements in that the body needs a
certain amount for proper metabolic functioning. But advertisers would have
you believe that supplementary boron would increase the effects stated
above. To "back" their claims they cite studies that show how "individuals"

given boron had their levels of circulating testosterone boosted by 200 to 300 percent. Sounds impressive, doesn't it? What the advertisers failed to mention was that the "individuals" used as test subjects were post-menopausal women. And while there have been a few studies conducted on healthy male bodybuilders, none showed any difference between boron users and nonusers. Both groups showed slight increases in circulating testosterone, but this can easily be explained by hard training.[7] In short, a 20-year-old bodybuilder taking supplementary boron is really wasting his money.

VANADYL SULFATE

Like chromium, bodybuilders take vanadyl sulfate for its supposed insulin-like effects. The evidence is sketchy as to the effectiveness of such supplementation, but bodybuilders continue taking the substance even if it only provides the slightest ergogenic effect.

Vanadyl sulfate and its close cousin, vanadate, are derivatives of the trace element vanadium, which is needed by the body for proper nutrient regulation – particularly glucose and lipids. In its natural state, vanadium is toxic, but when combined with such other compounds as sulfate, it is not. Both vanadyl sulfate and vanadate cross the cell membrane and once inside are converted to the charged form of vanadyl (called ions).

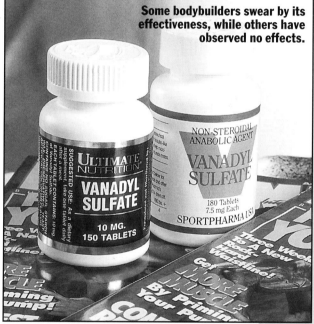

Some bodybuilders swear by its effectiveness, while others have observed no effects.

MECHANISM OF ACTION

Studies with mice have shown vanadate to be very effective at preserving glucose balance in animals with diabetes, obesity, and insulin resistance. Although not conclusive, the researchers concluded that vanadate produced its effects by promoting insulin-like effects in the liver and peripheral tissues.[2] Other studies with diabetic rats have produced similar results.[3] Besides its effects on glucose, vanadate seems to stimulate lipogenesis in animals with reduced insulin levels.[4] Other studies using diabetic animals showed vanadyl had the ability to preserve lipid, thyroid, and glucose levels despite decreased insulin levels.[5]

Perhaps the most significant finding of the studies was that vanadyl, while mimicking insulin's effects on glucose, had none of the hormone's anabolic effects. Studies with rats revealed that vanadyl-treated animals often lost bodyweight (of course this may be explained by decreased appetite and not some weight-decreasing property of vanadate). The anecdotal reports from bodybuilders suggest the supplement is another of those "you love it or hate it" types. There are bodybuilders who swear by its effectiveness, while others have observed no effect.

"Combined with proper anabolic nutrition, I defy anyone to come up with a better, safer performance-enhancement strategy. Vanadyl sulfate has replaced quite a handful of weapons in my arsenal of performance-enhancement tools, and I suspect it will emerge to be the most significant addition to modern-day performance enhancement."

– John Romano, *MuscleMag* contributor and one of the biggest proponents of the new bodybuilding supplement, vanadyl sulfate.

HOW MUCH?

Like most supplements, personal preference plays a role in determining the most effective dosage for vanadyl sulfate. As would be expected, many bodybuilders megadose and take 150 to 200 milligrams a day, but others get the same results using 40 to 50 milligrams a day. For those who decide to use large dosages (a practice we caution against), you might want to treat the supplement as a drug and cycle it. That is, use it for four to six weeks, and then take three or four weeks off. Not only will this decrease the chance of developing side effects, but it should increase the effectiveness as well, since most individuals develop tolerance to supplements with continued long-term use. At the first sign of serious problems, cease using the supplement.

SIDE EFFECTS

With regards to side effects, the issue of toxicity must not be overlooked. A few studies have suggested that high doses of vanadyl may produce negative effects on liver enzymes. Further, combining the compound with other agents known to cause liver toxicity (anabolic steroids being the best example) may lead to a negative synergistic effect.

Finally, given its effects on glucose levels, those with existing diabetic conditions (or worse, those who are borderline but don't realize it) would be wise to stay clear of any vanadyl-related compounds.

GAMMA HYDROXYBUTYRATE (GHB)

In the late 1980s and early 1990s, GHB became extremely popular with bodybuilders as a growth-hormone stimulating agent. Despite being advertised as otherwise, the substance is not a drug but a metabolite of the amino

Lee Apperson

John Caldarelli
hard at work.

acid GABA (see Chapter Fourteen on "Protein and Amino Acids") which according to some Japanese studies has significant effects on the pituitary hormones including HGH. Numerous theories have been put forward to explain GHB's mechanism of action. Some suggest GHB causes HGH release by directly stimulating the pituitary gland. Others theorize the metabolite influences such neurotransmitters as serotonin and dopamine. A third suggestion is based on synergism, with GHB acting in conjunction with numerous neurotransmitters to elevate HGH levels. Finally, a fourth hypothesis is more simplistic and suggests that GHB promotes deeper sleep, which, in turn, boosts HGH levels.

MECHANISM OF ACTION

No matter what the real metabolic pathway, bodybuilders quickly fell in love with GHB, and most swore that it improved anabolism and lipolysis (fat burning). Further, the tranquilizing effects were welcomed after a couple of strenuous hours in the gym. Some bodybuilders find the compound effective as a diuretic, although the exact mechanism of action for this is poorly understood. Unfortunately, once the FDA heard about the effects of the drug – particularly when combined with alcohol – it was banned.

POSSIBLY EFFECTIVE BUT . . .

GHB was banned after a few individuals combined it with alcohol, and had to be hospitalized. The condition produced was due to synergism, not some intrinsic property of GHB itself, nevertheless, the FDA in its "wisdom" banned

"Not good. Take too much vanadyl sulfate and you run the risk of having the excess accumulate in the kidneys, causing problems. Also, toxic quantities lower the levels of two very important enzymes which are largely responsible for energy production."

– Bill Starr, regular *MuscleMag* contributor commenting on the side effects of one of bodybuilding's most popular supplements, vanadyl sulfate.

Ericca Kern

the supplement (curiously alcohol, no doubt responsible for most of the side effects, is still available).

Despite the ban, GHB is still available on the black market, but as would be expected, sells for an enormous price. As with other black-market drugs, bodybuilders should practice caution if obtaining from an unreliable source. Besides the potential for being sold inert (useless) substances, how much quality control do you think basement labs practice? That fine powder you bought may harbor any number of microorganisms or industrial chemicals. Are the risks really worth it for a compound that has questionable benefits to begin with?

SIDE EFFECTS

Aside from the previous reactions with alcohol, there have been few serious side effects from GHB use. The most reported side effect is drowsiness, with most users reporting varying degrees of the condition (ironically the reason why some bodybuilders become "attached" to GHB).

There have been reports of bodybuilders becoming addicted to GHB, but such incidences are based on anecdotal reports and gym scuttlebutt, and not clinical diagnoses. As with most drugs and supplements, the potential for addiction is there and at the first sign of trouble (in most cases someone else will spot it before you recognize it in yourself) seek professional help.

GLANDULARS

These supplements are another perfect example of how creative advertising can reap millions of dollars without being true to manufacturers' claims. Although a fad at one time (and a popular one we might add), it is now generally accepted that glandular products are one of the poorest of supplements.

WHAT THEY ARE AND HOW THEY WORK

Glandular products are substances made from the extracts of animal glands and organs. The theory behind their functioning was that whatever gland the supplement was derived from, this is the gland that would be stimulated in the body. Such beliefs are not a product of the 20th century either. The ancient Greeks held that by slaying and eating the heart of a mighty warrior, somehow you added that person's strength to your own. Philosophers of the time suggested that by eating the brains of dead colleagues future geniuses could be created. And as recent as the last century, African tribesmen ate the hearts of lions to improve their courage.

Such beliefs have been refined and expanded upon by modern supplement manufacturers, and today just about every gland and organ imaginable has a corresponding supplement. For example, if you take pituitary extract, your pituitary is supposed to be stimulated to produce more growth hormone. Adrenal glandulars are supposed to boost your adrenal glands to produce more adrenaline which, in turn, leads to increased workout intensity and a better ability to combat stress. Taking heart glandulars increases blood flow. There are even claims that glandulars made from bull testes increase your testes to produce more testosterone. Sounds great in theory, but as we shall see, there are a number of reasons why glandulars don't live up to manufacturers' claims.

HOW INEFFECTIVE?

Perhaps the most basic reason to be sceptical of glandulars lies in their being readily available without prescription. Look at it this way, most glandulars are marketed to influence an individual's endocrine system. If such products could in fact boost hormone levels to any substantial degree, don't you think the FDA and other similar drug-regulatory agencies would classify these substances as "only available by prescription?"

Let's face it, any substance that can modify a person's endocrine system is a DRUG! And such drugs should only be taken on the advice and supervision of a physician. The fact that glandular supplements are available off the shelf in most health-food and drug stores should cause you to stop and question the outlandish claims made by advertisers.

A second reason for dismissing glandulars concerns their origins. All glandular products are made from the dried remains of animal sources. If you take pituitary extract, the odds are it came from sheep, pig, beef, or monkey sources. Although advertisers may claim otherwise, most animal

"If you took all the glandular tablets by the bottleful it wouldn't do the job for you. It might help a teeny bit, but you have to realize that if these supplements did a great deal for you they'd be under prescription like anabolic steroids and have to be bought through the FDA."

– Bill Pearl, former bodybuilding great commenting on the "effectiveness" of glandular supplements.

PLEASE RETURN DUMBELLS TO RACK

Craig Titus

hormones are biologically inactive in humans (unless biochemically modified). There are numerous reasons to account for this – chief of which are the differences in temperature and pH between humans and animals. A third reason for raising scepticism pertains to the cost of manufacturing glandular supplements. For every few ounces of biologically active hormone, hundreds, and in some cases thousands of pounds of animal glands and/or organs must be processed. You don't need to be a biochemist to deduce that this takes time and is costly. Yet glandular supplements are among the cheapest products available. A bottle of 100 tablets retails on average for $10 to $12. If such products contained any amount of real hormone there would be a quantum leap in price. The fact that drug insurance is such a big issue in Canada and the United States gives testament to the cost of drugs.

> "One of the more controversial types of supplements is glandulars. Whether they are useful or even usable substances to be found in properly prepared glands is open to debate; incon-clusive evidence suggests that some active com-ponents do enter the body. That does not mean they do any good there! The only thing one can say for sure about dried glandulars is that they are an excellent source of protein and, in the case of liver, a fairly cost -effective one."
>
> – Stephen Brooke, *MuscleMag* contribu-tor offering his views on glandulars, a popular supplement back in the 1980s, but one whose best days seem to have past.

A final reason for skipping glandulars involves how they're taken. Even though there is limited scientific evidence to suggest injected gland tissue (in actuality a few radioactive atoms) may make its way to target glands, all glandular products are taken orally. While convenient, most hormones are destroyed by the digestive system before they have a chance to reach the bloodstream. This is why most testosterone prepara-tions are taken by intramuscular injection, and why anabolic steroids have to be specifically modified if taken orally. So even if that pitui-tary or adrenal pill did contain bio-logically active ingedients, it would be deactivated by your digestive tract.

ARE THEY OF ANY USE?

About the only positive thing we can say about glandulars is that they will be treated by the body as just another form of protein, and broken down into its constituent amino acids. And while animal glands and organs are an excel-lent source of protein (although some are also high in fat), obtain-ing protein in tablet form is very expensive. For an equal amount of cash you could buy eight to 10 times the amount of another more usable protein. Our advice is to invest your money there.

Darrem Charles

Jackie Paisley

POTENTIAL DANGERS

This may seem like a contradiction given that we just described the biological inactivity of glandular products, but there is a hidden danger when
dealing with glandular products. The primary reason humans cook meat is
to kill any harmful microorganisms it may harbor. Eating raw meat is one
sure way to obtain a tape worm or salmonella poisoning. Although most
glandular products have been well-processed (the intense heat acting as a
sterilizing agent) – beware of any products that appear to be "basement
created" or advertised as "containing raw glandular tissue" (the claims may
for once be true, and could lead to serious side effects).

Just as there are bogus forms of steroids and growth hormone on
the market, so to do fake supplements occasionally turn up. In all likelihood
the manufacturers of such products do not have quality control on their
minds. Who knows what's contained in that pill or tablet. And if someone
offers to sell you injectable animal hormone – make an about face and report
him or her to the nearest law-enforcement agent. Animal hormone preparations contain some of the most deadly diseases known to man. The AIDS
virus initially came from rhesus monkeys. Do you really want to inject something into your thighs that may kill you six months down the road?

HYDROXY METHYLBUTYRATE (HMB)

Although the scientific evidence for this supplement is limited, the consensus among bodybuilders and researchers is that HMB holds great promise as one of the most effective "next generation" supplements.

HMB is a metabolite (breakdown product) of the amino acid leucine. The supplement form is manufactured by Metabolic Technologies (MTI) of Ames, Iowa. And while other supplement manufacturers have jumped on the bandwagon and released their own versions (most of which are fake by the way), MTI is the only legitimate supplier of the compound. MTI had to license the patents from the Iowa State University Research Foundation.

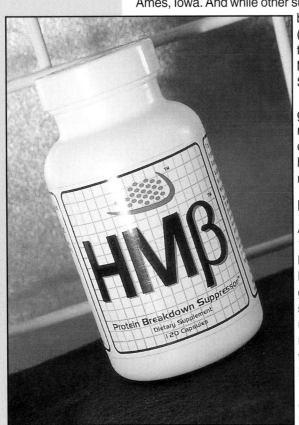

In the future other companies may be given permission to release their own legitimate form of HMB (including Bill Phillip's EAS company), however, as it stands, you would be taking a big risk buying a HMB product not manufactured by MTI.

HOW EFFECTIVE?

According to MTI, an abstract presented in 1995 at the American College of Sports Medicine Conference in Minneapolis, Minnesota, showed that individuals taking 3 grams of HMB gained up to 300 percent more strength and muscle mass than a control group using a placebo. They also demonstrated significant reductions in bodyfat. Another abstract with similar results is expected to be released in the near future.

While on the surface such abstracts do offer some evidence that HMB is a great bodybuilding supplement, we must point out that as of yet, no other documented scientific studies have been released to confirm the effectiveness of HMB. To quote one of MTI's competitors, "To date there are no original articles on HMB that have been published in peer-reviewed scientific journals." To add to the scepticism, the studies that "confirm" the effectiveness of HMB were funded by the very company that markets HMB – MTI.

Anecdotal reports on HMB are promising, but more documented scientific studies are needed to confirm the supplement's effectiveness.

The anecdotal reports from bodybuilders are for the most part very positive. Most users report rapid strength gains from using the compound, with increases in lean muscle tissue coming a bit slower. Finally, unlike creatine which seems to produce rapid weight gains, and then tapper off, the gains from HMB seem to be more sustained in nature.

MECHANISM OF ACTION

The producers of HMB are quick to point out that no one knows for sure just how HMB works. One theory suggests the compound prevents protein catabolism brought on by intense exercise. Another theory suggests it may modify signals between hormones and muscle cells. Finally, as a metabolite of leucine, it may work by increasing muscle-protein turnover (something leucine has been clinically determined to do).

HOW MUCH?

The newness of HMB means there is little anecdotal or scientific literature to rely on for accurately determining the best dosage. The few scientific studies suggest taking 3 grams a day, spread over three, 1-gram dosages. Dan Duchaine adds that since the compound has a short half-life (reported to be a few hours), it might make more sense to take 500 milligrams, six times daily.[6] This gives the same amount – 3 grams – but in a more gradual and sustained manner.

Being a metabolite of leucine, many readers may be tempted to obtain HMB in this manner. But studies suggest only about 5 percent of the amino acid is converted into HMB. To obtain 3 grams you would need to consume 60 grams of leucine! Not only is this expensive, but potentially dangerous.

Nikki Fuller

"When I started using HMB I put on four solid pounds the first month I was using it and noticed a significant increase in strength. The second month I was on HMB I gained another four pounds and continued to set new personal bests in lifts like the bench press and leg extension."

– Bill Phillips, *Muscle Media* publisher commenting on his personal experiences with HMB. Bill is quick to add that he is not aware if other users report similar gains.

With regards to timing, there doesn't seem to be any difference between taking on a full or empty stomach. Unlike many supplements taken on an empty stomach, HMB doesn't seem to cause stomach upset. This makes HMB a very convenient supplement as you can take it with or between meals.

DEHYDROEPIANDROSTERONE (DHEA)

The most talked about supplement since creatine is without a doubt DHEA. But to understand what it does, we need to do a quick review. As previously mentioned, the principal testicular hormone is testosterone, secreted by the Leydig or interstitial cells at a rate of about 7 milligrams per day. But the testes (and the adrenal cortex) also secrete small amounts of testosterone precursors; a delta4-androstenidione and DHEA. Both can be converted to testosterone by other tissues, hence they would be expected to indirectly contribute a small amount of androgen activity. In females, the adrenal cortex produces DHEA and DHEA-S (DHEA-sulfate), which are precursors of estrogens E1, E2, E3 and E4, and progesterone.[8] Again, a small amount of testosterone is produced (via chemical conversion of DHEA and the estrogens). Therefore, for bodybuilders, we can best describe DHEA as a proto-hormone (a hormone that is taken because it is converted into a desired hormone). DHEA is the most abundant adrenocorticoid steroid, with serum levels 20 times higher than that of any other adrenal hormone. The concentration of the sulfated form, DHEA-S, is 300 to 500 times that of DHEA.[9] Commercially available DHEA may be made from yams (totally useless and unabsorbable), or from human urine.[10]

> **"The thing that I've noticed is a return of morning erections."**
>
> – Dr. William Regelson, 70 year-old medical oncologist and DHEA advocate.

What can science tell us about the possible applications for DHEA? In clinical use, an uncontrolled trial in AIDS patients found that taking DHEA was associated with reductions in viral load.[11] Open, uncontrolled trials in patients with multiple schlerosis found that DHEA increased subjective feelings of strength, stamina and well-being, but did not improve disability.[12] A study with 28 patients with systemic lupus found that 200 milligrams of DHEA daily for three months produced improvement in the disease.[13] A six-month trial comparing 50 milligrams of DHEA daily with a placebo in thirteen men and seventeen women, 40 to 70 years old, found the drug restored serum levels of the hormone to those found in young adults. Also found were increased serum levels of insulin-like growth factor in both sexes. Those treated with the hormone reported an increase in physical and psychological well-being.[14] In another study, a majority of patients treated with DHEA also reported an increase in physical and psychological well-being. Similar results were obtained in a 12-month trial with 100 milligrams of DHEA daily in eight women and eight men aged 50 to 65.[15]

What do DHEA advocates say? Basically, that it's the best thing since sliced bread. Even though DHEA was first identified in 1934, it is only now becoming fashionable.

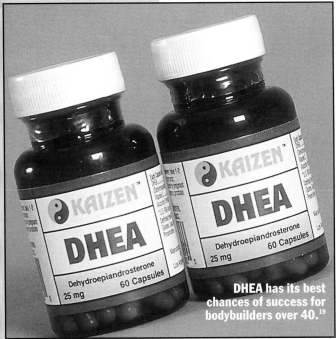

DHEA has its best chances of success for bodybuilders over 40.[19]

Paul DeMayo

The following is a list of alleged benefits (but remember, hard scientific evidence for these claims is lacking).

– Living longer. DHEA levels rise sharply during puberty, and decrease for the rest of our lives. The suggestion is that by raising levels of DHEA, many age-related conditions can be alleviated, or even prevented.
– Fat-burning. DHEA is believed to increase metabolic rate.
– Boosted energy levels. Users report they feel mentally and physically better. This could also be a by-product of improved sleep, as is commonly reported.
– Best bang since the big one! Men and women report better sexual performance and more satisfaction.
– For bodybuilders, the most important is its alleged anabolic effect.[16]

If these claims are true, why should bodybuilders use DHEA? Let's put all the pieces of the picture together. One of the major obstacles facing bodybuilders is fat loss without any associated muscle loss. During the precontest phase a strict diet and aerobics are put into place to strip away the thin layer of fat that covers hard-gained muscles. Unfortunately, in doing so, muscle is oftern lost along with fat.

In animal studies, DHEA appears to act as a thermogenic drug. When animals were given DHEA in their diet, it did not affect their appetite. It did affect the synthesis of fatty acids and overall amounts of bodyfat. The effect was so profound that, if given to starved animals that were later fed food rich in fat, the DHEA blocked fat synthesis and the animals remained thin. To better understand how this drug works, scientists looked at the energy-producing centers found in cells. At first they thought DHEA restricted the amount of energy available for fat synthesis. To their surprise, after 21 days of DHEA treatments, there was a 20 percent increase in oxygen use by the body. Although this demonstrated that energy restriction was not what blocked fat synthesis, it did show that DHEA was causing the burning of excess fat. Part of the energy produced was utilized in the synthesis and deposition of protein, both of which require large amounts of energy. In fact, it takes more energy to make protein than it does to make fat.[17]

Weighing the pros and cons of a drug or supplement is essential if you want to be the best athlete you can be – mentally and physically.
– Mauro Sarni

A brief cell-biology discussion is needed to help explain what is happening at the cellular level. Among the organelles found in cells are membrane-bound bodies called lysosomes. All lysosomes are related, directly or indirectly, to intracellular digestion. The material to be digested may be of extracellular or intracellular origin. Lysosomes contain enzymes known collectively as acid hydrolases. These enzymes can quickly dissolve all of the major molecules that comprise the cell, and would do so if they were not confined in structures surrounded by membranes.

One function of lysosomes is to accomplish the self-destruction of injured cells or cells that have outlived their usefulness; this is why lysosomes are sometimes referred to as "suicide sacks." Lysosomes also destroy certain organelles (membrane-bound structures that have specific functions in cellular physiology) that are no longer useful. In addition, lysosomes are involved in the digestion of materials taken into the cell in membranous vacuoles (sacks). Lysosomes fuse with the membrane of the vacuole, discharging their hydrolytic enzymes into the vacuole to digest the material. Lysosomes also play a part in the breakdown of normal cellular waste products, and in the turnover of cellular constituents.

Similar to the lysosomes are a number of vesicles (sacks) called microbodies, which contain enzymes. Among these microbodies are the peroxisomes, which contain a collection of oxidative enzymes that play a role in the decomposition of certain compounds.[18]

Now back to our previously mentioned animal studies. The sites of oxygen consumption and fat breakdown are in the peroxisomes, found in the liver cells. The excess of DHEA causes the peroxisomes to proliferate and work overtime. The peroxisomes use oxygen to break down fats, which are then used as a source of energy. This is all stimulated by the inactivation of

DHEA. The liver senses that the body does not need excess amounts of this substance floating around in the blood, so it activates its drug-metabolizing enzymes contained in the peroxisomes. The beauty of this phenomenon is that it is an energy-wasting process that does not trap the energy in high-energy compounds, such as ATP (the body's main source of stored energy at the cellular level). All this energy is released as heat, the essence of thermogenesis.

DHEA may allow one to burn away excess bodyfat without having to go on a calorie-restricted diet. This would virtually eliminate the cuts cycle and allow mass-building to continue until contest time. And just when it appears that things couldn't get any better, much of the energy used in burning fat is then utilized to build protein and lean muscle! In addition, because DHEA can be converted to testosterone, there is an additional anabolic effect.[17]

Rounding out the positive effects of DHEA are its effects on the thyroid system. There is evidence that DHEA may also affect the production of thyroxine (thyroid hormone). Thyroxine can stimulate protein synthesis, fat breakdown and oxygen consumption. It is known that people who produce excess thyroxin are lean, while those who produce too little are obese.

Sound too good to be true? What do the studies say? The problem is that there hasn't been a great deal of controlled scientific studies carried out. The few that exist report a positive effect, but they are generally not conclusive. Whether DHEA has any effect on body composition, fat distribution, serum lipid levels or insulin sensitivity is unclear.[13]

Is DHEA safe? Provided DHEA is used responsibly (avoided by individuals with prostate hypertrophy or high blood pressure) and only after clearance from a physician, there are no known serious side effects besides androgenic ones (acne, hair loss, hirsutism, and deepening of the voice) in women.[19] But there is a potential downside. DHEA can aromatize to estrogen and thus lead to elevated levels of serum estrogen. This process is not conducive to achieving the type of muscle mass and low bodyfat levels bodybuilders desire. Research has shown that DHEA can act as an estrogenic compound in men.[9] Scientists have also suggested that as a weak

Jitka Harazimova

androgen, DHEA could occupy the receptor site for testosterone. Obviously, for bodybuilding applications, it is not beneficial to have a weak androgen occupying a receptor that could have a stronger androgen such as testosterone in its place. The net effect would be estrogenic. DHEA could actually decrease the output of testosterone by inhibiting the release of luteinizing hormone (LH) and follicle-stimulating hormone (FSH), in turn suppressing the hypothalamic-pituitary-testicular axis (HPTA).[20] And in one animal study done at Northwestern University Medical School, 14 out of 16 rats fed DHEA for 84 weeks developed liver cancer.[21]

The Canadian government has made DHEA a controlled substance, which means it cannot be prescribed for performance-enhancement purposes and is in the same drug classification as amphetamines and anabolic steroids. If you're a Canadian, you can't have it in your possession without a prescription, can't bring it in from the US, and if you're dumb enough to sell some to your buddies, you're looking at serious jail time. The logic behind this decision by Health and Welfare Canada (the federal agency responsible for drug classification) is that because this drug is in fact a hormone, and a hormone may have a multitude of effects on the body, the drug should only be used, if at all, for specific medical conditions. The other reason was the questionable quality of the DHEA being sold. Officials felt that Canadian consumers were being ripped off. American readers should familiarize themselves with what supplements they can and cannot bring into Canada.

**Whether DHEA has any effect on body composition, fat distribution, serum lipid levels or insulin sensitivity is unclear.[13]
– Dave Fisher**

In the US, you can walk into any health-food store or pharmacy and buy your favorite brand without a prescription. The only problem is the perennial supplement issue, quality. Anything derived from yams is generally dismissed as being useless. Experts advise that you only buy pharmaceutical-grade DHEA (98.8 to 99 percent pure DHEA). How long this will last is anyone's guess, as the Food and Drug Administration (FDA) consider DHEA a drug. Under the Federal Food, Drug and Cosmetic Act, a substance that is offered for a nonfood purpose and that is intended or advertised to affect the body's normal functioning is classified as a drug. All new drugs require pre-market approval.[10]

Edgar Fletcher

Economics and research will determine future availability of DHEA. Because DHEA cannot be patented, drug companies are testing synthetic analogues that lack the natural hormone's known side effects. Drug testing takes time. DHEA may be approved for specific illnesses, such as lupus,[21] but it is unlikely in the present political climate that doctors will be able to prescribe DHEA as a performance-enhancing drug.

If you decide to try DHEA, what dosage should you use? Dosages vary, depending on which experts you wish to cite. DHEA is taken orally. A dose of 1.6 grams of DHEA daily over four weeks, taken by men of normal weight, resulted in weight loss. Overweight men under the same conditions did not lose weight. The explanation for the difference was that the overweight men might not have received a sufficient amount of DHEA to elicit a physiological response. The leaner men probably had more DHEA to start with, and thus supplementation did the trick. Also, a single dose is probably not the appropriate way to administer DHEA.

In animal studies DHEA was administered according to bodyweight. Logically, one would expect a person who weighs more to need a larger dose than a person who weighs less. It would also help to know what the initial blood levels of DHEA were. This information would allow the dosage to be given based on a person's individual need, since no two people are alike.

The other problem in calculating a dosage is that the speed of DHEA metabolism is still unknown. Several daily doses may be needed to maintain effective levels for a longer period of time.[10] Bill Phillips – executive editor of *MuscleMedia* – recommends 100 to 200 milligrams per day for men, taken in two evenly divided doses in the morning and before bed. For women he suggests a maximum of 25 milligrams per day, though positive results may be obtained with as little as 5 milligrams per day. In his opinion, if you don't have results with 200 milligrams per day, than megadosing (1000 milligrams or more per day) is a waste of time. This drug has its best chances of success for bodybuilders over 40.[19]

ANDROSTENEDIONE

Androstenedione is a testosterone metabolite that has recently become a "hot" supplement. It is commercially derived from the pollen of Scotch Pine trees[19] or from "tall oil," a waste by-product of the pulp and paper industry.[22] Because this drug is a steroid hormone, it is in the same drug classification as anabolic steroids in Canada, and thus is not legally available for body-building purposes. It is legal in the US, and available without a prescription. It is believed to boost blood levels of testosterone. According to the German patent for androstenedione, 50 milligrams given orally to men raised plasma testosterone levels from 140 to 183 percent above baseline, while 100 milligrams of oral androstenedione raised levels from 211 to 237 percent above baseline. Blood levels start rising about 15 minutes after oral administration of androstenedione and stay elevated for around three hours. A maximum peak in blood-testosterone levels is seen around one to one and one-half hours after ingestion.

It is further claimed that if androstenedione is taken as directed, once a day prior to physical activity, the positive benefits can be had without any significant negative feedback response to natural testosterone production. The explanation given is that because the elevation only lasts for a few hours, there is not enough time for the pituitary gland to respond. And because levels are raised during exercise, a time when blood flow to muscles is optimized and catabolic functions prevail, the body's utilization of testosterone is maximized.[23]

As the drug has a harsh effect on nasal membranes, bodybuilders prefer to take it orally. Bill Phillips suggests a dosage of 50 to 100 milligrams in the morning, possibly to be repeated in the evening. He recommends a single dose before exercise as a strength booster.[19]

TRIBULUS TERRESTRIS

This plant is taken because it is believed to have a synergistic effect when taken with DHEA. Also known as Puncturevine, Goathead or the Cross of Malta, it is a member of the Calthrop family and is an annual that reproduces by seeds. It is a prostrate, matforming plant with trailing stems. The leaves are opposite, pinnate, one to two inches long with four to eight pairs of leaflets.

> "By nasal intake of androstenedione, the testosterone/ epitestosterone ratio increases and returns to normal within one day. However, even though the ratio returns to normal, the serum testosterone level remains elevated."
>
> – Michael Oettel, pharmacologist who worked at the East German Research Institute for Body Culture and Sport, in Leipzig. East German athletes competing at the 1988 Olympics in Seoul, South Korea used this nasal spray. It was taken because it was believed to improve athletic performance, and was not believed to have any significant anabolic effect.[19]

Kim Chizevsky

The yellow flowers are one-quarter to one-half inches wide with five petals. The fruit is a hard, spiny bud that breaks into five tack-like sections at maturity. This plant grows in pastures, cultivated fields and waste places.[24]

This herb has a long history in Eastern medicine. For 5,000 years it has been used in China and India to boost hormone production in men and women, and treat urinary tract problems, itchy skin and blood purification.[25]

Popular brands of Tribulus include Tribestan, Triboxin, and Immortale. According to Dr. Jim Wright, Tribestan is standardized on the basis of the predominating compound Sopharma, referred to as protodioscin. He cites a study in which men aged 28 to 45 took 250-milligram tablets three times a day for five days, resulting in a 30 percent increase in circulating testosterone levels. His explanation for this is that Tribestan stimulates the secretion of leutinizing hormone (LH), a gonad-stimulating hormone produced by the pituitary gland. In some cases, an increase in the level of estradiol also occurred. Thus while this herb could enhance growth-hormone secretion and overall mass increases, this could bode poorly for those who are highly susceptible to gynecomastia or insulin resistance. In women, follicle-stimulating hormone, but not leutinizing hormone, and estradiol, but not testosterone were increased. This differential allows Tribestan to be effectively used by both sexes to stimulate reproductive function.[26]

Michael Francois

Bodybuilders are taking Tribulus terrestris as part of a "steroid like" stack suggested by Bill Phillips. He recommends 750 to 1250 milligrams per day of Tribulus terrestris in divided doses with meals, and stacking it with DHEA (100 milligrams per day) and androstenedione (100 milligrams per day).[19]

GROWING TESTOSTERONE RECEPTORS THROUGH DIET?

For a change of pace we're concluding the chapter with an alternative method of natural ergogenesis. Besides taking substances to help boost natural testosterone levels, there is evidence to suggest that the number of testosterone receptors may be increased by diet. During research into anabolic steroids, the authors of "Black Market Roids," *MuscleMag International*, (February 1993) encountered individuals stacking five to seven different anabolic steroids who were just as big as those using low doses of only one anabolic steroid. Why? The answer concerns both diet and genetics. Going on the juice will not compensate for poor diet or a lack of testosterone receptors. Some people are naturally muscular because they have been blessed, not with higher testosterone levels, but with more receptors with which their testosterone can interact with. The latest research has been directed at manipulating endogenous hormones through diet. A simpler approach would be to increase the number of receptors. There is limited evidence to suggest this can be done using soya and licorice (not the candy, but the herbal root called Glycyrrhiza glabra).

Both soya and licorice possess compounds resembling estrogen which can survive the digestive process to exert an estrogenic effect. Estrogen has the remarkable property of inducing the production of testosterone receptors. By including these two foods in your daily diet, you may experience an enhanced anabolic effect from your own natural testosterone.

Before you start consuming vast quantities of licorice, please be warned that excessive amounts can cause hypertension and cardiac dysfunction. Check with your doctor before you add licorice to your daily diet. Only consume small amounts and do not use licorice on a daily basis for an extended period of time (more than four weeks). If you suddenly experience headaches, nausea, weakness or irregular heartbeat, discontinue and seek immediate medical attention.

Besides taking substances to help boost natural testosterone levels, there is evidence to suggest that the number of testosterone receptors you have may be increased through your diet.

References

1) F. Hatfield, "Chromium Wars," *Muscle and Fitness*, 51:1 (January 1990).

2) S.M. Brichard and others, "Marked Improvement of Glucose Homeostasis in Diabetic Mice Given Oral Vanadate," *Diabetes*, 39:11 (1990).

3) S.M. Brichard and others, "Long-Term Improvement of Glucose Homeostasis By Vanadate Treatment in Diabetic Rats," *Endocrinology*, 123:4 (1988).

4) I.G. Fantus and others, "Vanadate Augments Insulin Stimulated Insulin Receptor Kinase Activity and Prolongs Insulin Action in Rat Adipocytes: Evidence for Transduction of Amplitude of Signalling Into Duration of Response," *Diabetes*, 43:3 (1994).

5) S. Ramanadham and others, "Oral Vanadate in Treatment of Diabetes Mellitus in Rats," *American Journal of Physiology*, 257:3 (1989).

6) B. Philips, "Uncensored Q and A," *Muscle Media 2000* (May 1996).

7) J. Brainum, "Advanced Nutrition," *Flex*, 14:3 (May 1996).

8) G. Ross, *Essentials of Human Physiology*, 2d ed., (Chicago: Year Book Medical Publishers Inc., 1982).

9) P. Ebeling and V.A Kolvisto, "Physiological Importance of Dehydroepiandrosterone," *The Lancet*, 343 (1994), 1479-1481.

10) Drugdex Editorial Staff, DHEA and Weight Loss, Drug Consult from Drugdex, 1995.

11) P. Salvato and others, Intl. Conf. AIDS, July 7-12, 1996.

12) M. Kalimi and W. Regelson, eds., T*he Biological Role of Dehydroepiandrosterone*, (New York: Walter de Gruyter, 1990), 81.

13) "Dehydroepiandrosterone (DHEA)," *The Medial Letter On Drugs and Therapeutics*, 38:985 (October 11, 1996).

14) A.J. Morales and others, *Journal of Clinical Endocrinology and Metabolism*, 78:1360 (1994).

15) J.E. Nestler, "Current Opinion," *Endocrinol. Diabetes*, 3:202 (1996).

16) J. O'Brien, *Why Everyone's Talking About DHEA!*, (Boca Raton: Globe Communications Corp.,1997).

17) D. Sparkman, "DHEA," *MuscleMag International* (October 1997).

18) M. Fogiel, *The Biology Problem Solver*, (505 Eighth Ave., New York: 1984) Research and Education Association.

19) B. Phillips, *3rd Sports Supplement Review*, (Golden, Colorado: Mile High Publishing, 1997).

20) D. Cloutare and W. Brink, "DHEA – Yea or Nay?," *MuscleMag International* (February 1997), 202-207.

21) B. Bilger, "Forever Young," *The Sciences*, (September/October 1995).

22) Forbes Medi-Tech, "Androstenedione Progress Report," http://www.cdn-news.com/database/main/1996/9/30/FM0930.html

23) http://www.mesomorphosis.com/androsteneFAQ.htm, 09/04/97

24) Puncture Vine, http://www.fortnet.org/CWMA/puncture.html

25) L&S Natural Inc., "Puncturevine," http://home.earthlink.net/~lsnatural/Puncturevine.html

26) J. Wright, "Sex, A Natural Wonder, Increased Sex Drive and Higher Levels of Testosterone, All From an Herbal Preparation," *Muscle and Fitness*, http://www.muscle-fitness.com/sex/tribulus.html

Jay Cutler

Soviet Supplements

With the collapse of the former Soviet Union, Western bodybuilders have seen a barrage of substances marketed as the "latest in Soviet sports nutrition." Just about every issue of the more popular bodybuilding magazines introduces another Soviet supplement that is considered to be the end all to athletic supplementation. Like their Western counterparts, Soviet manufactuers are producing a broad spectrum of ergogenic aids. Therefore, ascertaining which ones hold promise and which are totally useless is no easy task.

Kevin Levrone

WHAT THEY ARE

One of the best ways to determine if a given supplement is of any benefit is to see if it is used by top Soviet national team members. All sports supplements used by former Soviet athletes must be of high biological value. This means that once the substance enters the body it is capable of change within the body. The Soviets have distinguished between two types of ergogenic supplements – endogenous and exogenous. Endogenous forms are those substances taken separately in chemical form and include basic elements (sodium, potassium, nitrogen, etc.). They include regulators like creatine phosphate, and high-molecular-weight substances like DNA and amino acids.

Exogenous substances are those substances that enter the body in food, including the main nutrient categories such as protein, minerals, vitamins, fats, and carbohydrates, as well as special nutritional compounds such as adaptogens and biochemical cycle intermediates.

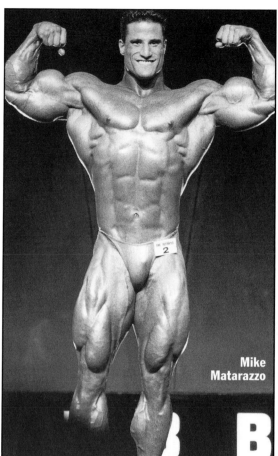

Mike Matarazzo

HOW THEY ARE USED

In most cases the substance is taken for at least 20 to 30 days. This is because it takes time for the active ingredient to gradually build up the body's adaptive systems, including anabolic functions both during and after training. The Soviets also suggest not to stay on one substance for any longer than 40 days. This is because like most pharmacological agents, the body can build tolerance and become desensitized to a given supplement. For this reason Soviet coaches have their athletes follow a 30-day cycle with two or three weeks of abstinence from a particular supplement. This shouldn't sound too earth shattering as many North American nutrition experts suggest the same thing.

In the following section we will look at the broad catagories of Soviet supplements. To conclude we will look at a few of the more popular substances in detail. Many will be familiar to Western athletes, but others (like Mumie and Retibol) are considered state of the art in former Soviet countries, and have only come to the attention of Western athletes in the past five years or so.

No longer can one all-encompassing term be used to describe "Soviet" athletes since the collapse of the Soviet Union. As much of the research for this section was written both before and after the collapse we interchanged various terms to describe Soviet athletes and researchers. Among the most frequently used precollapse terms will be "Soviet," "Russian," and "Eastern Bloc." Conversely, we will use the previous terms with the prefix "former" if the information is relevant to after the collapse.

THE BROAD CATAGORIES OF SOVIET SUPPLEMENTS

ADAPTOGENS

Adaptogens are substances extracted from plant and animal sources, with their primary function being to increase the body's nonspecific resistance to stress. They are used by all elite athletes from the former Soviet Union. Among their actions are energizing the nervous system, balancing metabolism, and boosting the body's immune response to outside stressors. All of these are important to athletes undergoing intense training.

The most popular Soviet adaptogens are Eleutherococcus, rantarin, Mumie, pantocrine, saparal, sterguliae, and araliae. They are usually administered for three or four weeks during an athlete's heavy phase of the training cycle.

"Our recent research using biologically important compounds from plants to elevate the anabolic and restorative potentials of the well-trained athlete will be of interest to dedicated bodybuilders. The goal of this long-term research, conducted at three laboratories in Russia, has been to isolate compounds from plants which act as analogs to human anabolics and to include them at full potency within crude extracts. These extracts are then given to athletes at specific times in the training cycle for maximum anabolic, restorative and protective effects."

– Dr. Moris Silber and Dr. Boris Feldkoren, former researchers at the Research Institute of Physical Culture, St. Petersburg, Russia.

Geir Borgan Paulsen

ANTIOXIDATIVE

Studies carried out by Soviet researchers have shown that specific substances call antioxidants help reduce stress on muscle tissue. Their maximum benefit appears to be in times of high-endurance exercise rather than heavy training. This is because during periods of increased aerobic work, the body is producing more free radicals. Free radicals are the by-products of cellular metabolism, and are believed to play a role in speeding up the aging process. They also slow muscle recovery and metabolic efficiency. The Soviets are firm believers in using antioxidants such as vitamins C and E, selenium, and the amino acid glutathione, to reduce cellular inflammation, improve immunity, and increase endurance capacity. The recommendations for bodybuilders are to use them during periods of increased aerobic training (the precontest season) when losing bodyfat is a priority.

ANABOLIC AGENTS

The Soviets have classified a number of natural substances as anabolics. These include special amino acid preparations, inosine and Mumie. Unlike their Western counterparts, Soviet athletes are not big users of protein powders because such preparations are not believed to have biological activity. On the other hand such amino acids as arginine for growth-hormone release, and branched-chain amino acids for muscle synthesis are extensively used. Mumie being both an anabolic/adaptogenic substance is used to stimulate muscle growth and boost metabolism.

ENERGETIC

Not to be forgotton are those substances that supply the body with fuel for metabolism. Many preparations in this catagory are also used by Western athletes. Supplements such as glucose polymers are effective at resupplying working muscles with carbohydrates for energy, at creating an insulin response for anabolism, and providing sufficient calories for fast recovery from intense exercise. The Soviets use metabolic-optimizer formulas containing anywhere from 50 to 90 percent glucose polymers.

Another popular carbohydrate source is fructose which is used to replenish liver-glycogen and blood-glucose levels to improve metabolism and eliminate drops in blood sugar.

Other popular energizers are metabolic intermediates such as lactate, pyruvate, and succinate. Such compounds feed into various biochemical cycles – including the Kreb's or citric acid cycle (see Appendix 3) – to produce ATP from the catabolism of glucose. Other compounds popular with Soviet athletes include L-carnitine, the amino acid alanine, and creatine phosphate.

BUFFERING AGENTS

To fully understand the role of buffering agents a brief introduction to the pH scale is needed. Most biochemical solutions contain a mixture of hydrogen (H^+) and hydroxyl (OH^-) ions disolved in them. If the solution has a higher percentage of H^+ ions it is termed acidic. If the OH^- ions predominate, the solution is termed basic. To compare solutions chemists have devised what's called the pH scale. It ranges from 1 to 14 with 1 being the most acidic and 14 being the most basic. If a solution contains equal amounts of H^+ and OH^- ions it is termed neutral and rates a 7 on the pH scale.

Melissa Coates

Human blood is slightly basic and falls around 7.4 on the pH scale. Because it is so sensitive to pH changes, the body has developed biological substances over the course of evolution called buffers, which help offset changes in pH. If an acidic substance is suddenly introduced into the body, basic buffers (above 7 on the pH scale) will be released to keep the blood's pH near the desired 7.4 value. Likewise, basic chemicals will cause a release of acidic buffers.

During periods of intense exercise, one of the products given off by the fatiguing muscles is lactic acid. Like all acids, lactic acid causes the pH of the intracellular fluid to fall towards the acid range. As most body tissues were not designed to withstand acidic levels for extended periods of time, the high levels of lactic acid cause an increase in muscular fatigue and a decrease in muscular efficiency. The intense burning you feel toward the final reps of a set of bicep curls or squats is primarily due to a build-up of lactic acid.

The Soviets have found that such buffering agents as bicarbonate and lactate (the basic form of lactic acid that contains an extra hydrogen atom) are very effective at reducing acidity levels and improving performance during anaerobic training. Tests on top-ranked wrestlers carried out at the Moscow Physical Culture center concluded that lactate is an ideal acid buffer and efficient energy source as a gloconeogenic precursor for the liver. If there is a disadvantage to using buffers its the precision that is needed for effective acid/base control. Too low a dosage is usually ineffective, while too high a dosage often causes stomach upset.

SPECIFIC SOVIET SUPPLEMENTS

RETIBOL – NATURAL STEROID ALTERNATIVE

Over the past few years bodybuilders have seen a proliferation in products whose manufacturers claim they provide the benefits of anabolic steroids without the potential side effects. Most claims are not based on scientific evidence, so many individuals are probably wasting good money on products that are nothing more than jazzed-up vitamin, mineral and protein sources. Every now and then, however, a product comes along that, while not conclusive, is backed by scientific evidence suggesting it may hold beneficial properties for athletes. One such substance is Retibol, and bodybuilders can thank the collapse of the former Soviet Union for its emergance on the Western sports scene.

Retibol is the name given to a supplement first manufactured by Soviet sports researchers, and it forms the cornerstone of a new generation of natural supplements used by elite Russian athletes. Although the name suggests otherwise, Retibol is in fact a combination of various plant sterols. Studies carried out by major labs in Russia "suggest" that Retibol has 45 to 50 percent the anabolic action of some commonly used anabolic steroids. Further, it doesn't appear to produce any of the androgenic effects that are sometimes seen in anabolic steroid users. And unlike steroids which are believed to work by modifying transcription of ribosomal RNA, Retibol is shown to stimulate biosynthesis at the cellular level. Let's take a closer look at this promising Soviet muscle-building agent.

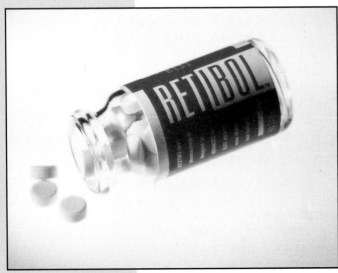

PLANT STEROLS AND THE ROAD TO RETIBOL

At one time plant hormones were dismissed as secondary plant products, but they are now beginning to receive the attention they deserve. The reason for the delayed interest concerns the results of early studies which looked at the effects of animal hormones on plants. Certain animal steroids were injected into plants in the hope that they would make the plants flower. As would be expected, the results were negative, and this led researchers to conclude that the reverse was also true – plant

Ronnie Coleman

hormones have no biological use in animals. This attitude remained until the late 1960s, when two reseachers (Okui and Otaka) found otherwise.

Like their animal counterparts, many plant hormones are steroid in nature and have very complex molecular arrangements based on carbon rings. Research carried out over the last 25 years has led many to suggest that a few plant sterols may be biologically active in humans.

WHERE DOES IT COME FROM?

Like most drugs derived from plants, Retibol is manufactured by combining numerous extracts from the leaves and roots of three primary plants: Pfaffia paniculata, Rhaponticum and Leuzea carthemoides, and Ajuga turkestancia. Over the past ten years, Japanese and Russian researchers have determined that when such extracts are combined they accelerate protein synthesis in humans (in a similar manner to testosterone). Further research indicated, however, that Retibol had a different mechanism of action. Instead of influencing nucleic transcription as do anabolic steroids and other testosterone derivatives, Retibol is believed to stimulate protein synthesis by modifying ribosomal translation. One of the best pieces of evidence to support separate pathways is that when anabolic steroids are used in conjunction with Retibol, there are additive effects – more so than if both drugs had the same metabolic pathway.

ITS USE IN SPORTS

In the past, Soviet coaches gave Retibol to athletes after an anabolic steroid cycle to prolong the effects of the steroids. The main reason for such cycling was to maintain muscle size and strength, yet still pass a drug test. Russian coaches who have worked for five years with athletes taking Retibol claim

Mike Matarazzo

that the anabolic effect is between 45 and 55 percent of anabolic steroids. Certain rules, however, must be followed, and these include:

1) Training must be of high intensity and volume.
2) The user must be on a building cycle, not a maintenance or cutting cycle.
3) The athlete should be at an advanced level of training.
4) Protein must be consumed to at least one gram per pound of bodyweight.
5) A high-calorie diet must be followed to stimulate the muscle-building process.

Russian researchers have found that even by following the previous recommendations, about 10 percent of athletes receive little benefit from Retibol. The theories for this occurance range from individual genetic makeup to reduced receptor sites capable of interecting with Retibol.

HOW TO TAKE RETIBOL

A typical dosage is two tablets twice daily for smaller (170 pounds) athletes, and three tablets twice daily for larger athletes. A typical cycle is 10 to 14 days on, five off, then another 10 to 14 on. According to Rick Brunner, director for Atletika – the American agent for Retibol marketing, bodybuilders can effectively use the compound for a 20- to 30-day cycle, taking it two hours before a workout and two hours after. He also reccomends stopping the use three to five days before competition as some athletes report slight muscle tightness.

SIDE EFFECTS

According to the latest Russian research, all the sterols available in Retibol were assayed for both androgenic and estrogenic activity. None of the compounds analyzed showed any trace of hormonal activity and consequently related side effects. Additional studies have determined that Retibol does not bind to androgenic receptors no matter what the dosage used.

We must add that like many of the new supplements coming on stream, Retibol has only been used by athletes since the late 1980s. And for the most part these athletes were former Soviet athletes under constant medical supervision. It will be interesting to see what surprises are in store now that Retibol has a US agent distributing the product. Given the attitude of many North American athletes to consume dosages far beyond those recommended (and no doubt far above their Soviet counterparts), it's quite possible that side effects will begin to surface in the next few years.

ELEUTHROCOCCUS – PLANT-BASED RECOVERY AID

Although more commonly called Siberian ginseng, the botanists among you will recognize it as Eleuthrococcus senticosus (hence forth known as EC). The EC plant is a four to seven foot high spiny shrub that grows in the wooded regions of Eastern Siberia. Given the plant's large range of growth – over 25 million acres – it is easily collected and processed for commercial use.

The discovery of EC came about during a search for cheaper versions of Panax ginseng – the commonly used herbal tonic. Under the direction of Dr. Israel Brekhman, Soviet plant researchers began screening numerous plant and animal substances which showed potential as adaptogenic aids. Before we go further it should be pointed out that the Soviets classify a substance as an adaptogen if it meets the following criteria:

1) The substance must not cause any negative disruptions to the body's normal physiological workings.
2) The substance should be nonspecific and should reduce adverse effects from physical, chemical, and biological factors.
3) The substance should produce a normalizing action irrespective of the direction of the pathological changes.

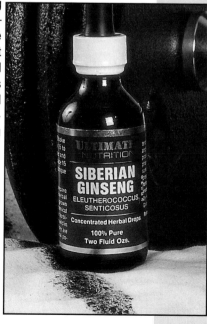

> "Ginseng helps reduce stress by improving the overall function of the adrenal glands. It helps protect us from radiation, enables our restorative processes to recover faster after intense physical activity and reduces the incidence of sickness from flu and other respiratory diseases."
>
> – Bill Starr, regular *MuscleMag* contributor adding his own voice to the potential benefits of ginseng to hard-training bodybuilders.

From their research the Soviet team concluded the one single plant-based adaptogen that came closest to meeting the previous was EC. Investigations show the active ingredients in EC include glycosides, aralin, alkaloids, and oils that play a role in the regulation of neurotransmission. Among EC's positive effects are increases in performance, energy metabolism, memory, and cardiovascular functioning.

ITS MANY USES

It didn't take long for Soviet researchers to deduce that EC was a benefit to anyone experiencing a great deal of stress. It's first uses were in the treatment of post-traumatic stress, but later began to be applied to those experiencing physical (injury, heavy work, sport), chemical (toxic, drug), or biological (bacteria, virus, hormonal) stress.

In Russia EC is commonly used by miners, heavy machine operators, and others who are under job stress and require something to bring them back into balance and improve their productivity. According to Dr.

Vince Taylor

Brekhman, the majority of the adaptogenic effects become apparent only when the body's resistance is diminished or when it is taxed by very stressful requirements. In short, the greater the stress the larger the benefits from EC. This is the main reason why individuals not undergoing great stress will not recieve much benefit from such substances. Athletes experiencing both the stress of day-to-day living and intense exercise are one group who would greatly benefit from EC supplementation.

Besides the previous, active substances of EC are known to have antiradical and antioxidant abilities (substances produced by body metabolism which are believed to build up over time and produce the side effects commonly known as aging). This makes the substance especially useful for treating the elderly, cancer patients, or those with wasting diseases.

USE IN BODYBUILDING

Although bodybuilding has not enjoyed the popularity in the former Soviet Union as other countries, through the actions of the IFBB and other bodybuilding federations, the sport is fast gaining acceptance.

The use of EC in sport is well-documented, and Soviet research literature is flooded with both anecdotal and scientific reports. Suffice to say that Eastern Bloc athletes have been using EC for several years and it is a staple supplement within the pharmacological plans of athletes on national teams. In one study young athletes given EC supplements while under intense training showed a 23.3 percent increase in total work, compared to a group given an inert placebo pill.[1]

The major benefit of EC to bodybuilders will be the increases in training volume and intensity, and the consequent recovery from such training loads. The Soviets have found that the best results are obtained when EC is taken during the last two to three weeks of hard training, and during the recovery week of a five-week cycle (four intense training weeks followed by one week of recovery). Studies indicate that EC can stimulate training intensity and volume by as much as 12 percent.

HOW AND WHEN TO USE

Both Russian and American researchers suggest EC is most beneficial for intermediate and advanced bodybuilders who need an extra boost in their training. Because EC affects the energetic, restorative, and anabolic effects of the body, it can be used with promising effect by any athlete training at a high-stress level. Once again the harder the training the greater the benefit.

The dosages recommended are 400 milligrams, two or three times daily, if used as a recovery aid, and 1200 to 1600 milligrams (three or four tablets) just before a workout if used as a biostimulant. Many Russian athletes using EC as a stimulant double this amount before a competition, but we caution against overusing EC from day one. Like most supplements you will need to experiment with different dosages to see how it affects your individual body chemistry.

WHERE TO FIND IT

EC (Siberian ginseng) is not new to North America. It can be found in most health-food stores. But there are a few things to consider before you start whipping bottles from store shelves. The supplement comes in many forms, from powders and tinctures, to tablets and capsules. It ranges in potency from raw material to high-quality standardized extract. For best results the Russians recommend using extracts ranging from 8:1 to 10:1.

We emphasize the last point because no doubt many bodybuilders have tried EC supplements and received little or no results. This may be the result of poor quality, or how it was used. Since EC is from a plant it is important to only use products that are high in bioactive substances. Improper picking, transport, excretion, or processing can degrade or eliminate most of EC's bioactivity. Most North American preparations are so low in active ingredients that they are virtually useless as an athletic supplement. It is advised that bodybuilders buy only those extracts that are standardized for some of the various eleutherosides (the active ingredients found in EC preparations) which consist of eleutheroside A, B, B1, C, G, and E.

Athletes experiencing both the stress of day-to-day living and intense exercise are one group who would greatly benefit from EC supplementation. – Alq̇ Gurley

Michael Francois and Denise Paglia

One of the most potent forms of EC is manufactured by Atletika – a joint US/Russian corporation which distributes Russian-designed food supplements. Their product called Atletika EC is available in tablet form in potent 10:1 extract concentrations standardized for both eleutheroside B and E. The address for Atletika can be obtained from any recent copy of *MuscleMag International*.

SCHIZANDRA CHINENSIS

This plant, a member of the magnolia family, contains berries which have adaptogenic properties. When taken as a tincture (1:5) for 20 to 30 drops, two or three times daily or in a complex with other adaptogens, Schizandra berries are known to increase working capacity, improve muscular co-ordination, and promote sleep. Anecdotal reports suggest that the best therapeutic course consists of 20 to 30 days on followed by one or two weeks off.

PANTOCRINE

Pantocrine is made from the antlers of male spotted axis deer which are found in the far eastern sections of the former Soviet Union. Biochemists have isolated over 20 elements in pantocrine and among the active ingredients are the amino acids alanine, leucine, and proline, as well as various glycosides. Research from the early 1940s indicates that pantocrine increases working capacity of fatigued muscles, accelerates recovery from training, and improves mental capacity. As pantocrine is in such demand, suppliers have trouble meeting manufacturers' quotas. Because of the limited number of deer, the annual output of antlers does not exceed 20 tons – a figure that satisfies only about 10 to 15 percent of the demand. Fortunately, Soviet researchers foresaw this and began looking for alternatives. One such compound is called Rangicrin, and the evidence suggests that it may be even more effective than its pantocrine cousins.

RANGICRIN

Rangicrin is a supplement derived from the inner part of A-grade antlers of male reindeer. Like most deer, reindeer shed their antlers once each year. Collectors gather the horns which are then powdered to make supplement tablets. Although any antler will do, biochemists have determined that horns from male reindeer, seven to eight years old, contain the highest concentrations of active substances. And unlike the declining axis deer herds which limit pantocrine supplies, there are over two million domesticated and 600,000 wild reindeer in Russia (this does not include another 1.4 million in other countries of the former Soviet Union).

> **"It is shown to be a powerful biostimulant and anticatabolic supplement for use during intense training cycles and during competitions, as well as a gonadotropic to 'jump start' the sexual organs of anabolic steroid abusers and reduce or prevent testes and prostate dysfunction."**
>
> – Dr. Moris Silber, Russian researcher commenting on the athletic benefits to the natural supplement, Rangicrin.

To make Rangicrin extract the antlers are dried in special drying chambers for several days under low heat to maintain full bioactivity. Repercolation of the antlers yields a 1:1 liquid extract which is then vacuum evaporated to produce tablets containing approximately 300 milligrams of bioactive Rangicrin.

What gives reindeer antlers the nod over axis deer antlers is their composition. Although both contain varying amounts of lipids, nitrogen fractions and minerals, reindeer antlers are much higher in carbohydrates (about twice as much), and contain superior levels of proteins.

Greg Reid

MECHANISM OF ACTION

Rangicrin belongs to the generation of Soviet supplements known as adaptogens since it produces effects similar to ginseng, Mumie, and Schizandra. Perhaps Rangicrin's most important characteristic however, is its gonadotropic abilities. Studies with animals have shown that the substance increases the weights of various gonad organs by as much as one third. Further, unlike other adaptogens which exert their influence only on immature animals, Rangicrin reduces atrophy of the prostate and seminal vesicles after castration of mature animals.

In humans, Rangicrin is used to treat elderly subjects suffering from age-related, sex-gland dysfunction. Although not conclusive, the evidence suggests that the low sex drive often associated with old age can be treated, and in some cases reversed with regular Rangicrin therapy.

A COUNTER TO THE NEGATIVE EFFECTS OF STEROIDS?

Once its effects on sex drive became knowm researchers turned their attention to using the substance as a form of therapy for anabolic steroid users. As most readers know, heavy use of testosterone, or its steroid derivitives, suppresses the body's own natural levels. When users go "off the juice," it may take months or even a year for their natural hormone levels to "kick"

Rory Leidelmeyer

back in. Russian researchers have discovered that using Rangicrin during and after a steroid cycle greatly reduces these negative side effects. Athletes report that decreases in sex drive which normally accompany steroid cessation are less pronounced when using Rangicrin.

DOSAGES

Given its high biological strength and anticatabolic actions, Rangicrin is given in lower dosages than other Soviet supplements. Used as an adaptogen, the average dosage for Rangicrin is 600 milligrams, two or three times daily during the competitive season. Many strength athletes use the product as a stimulant and take 900 to 1500 milligrams, 20 to 40 minutes before competition. Although it varies, the stimulating effects usually last two to three hours. Russian research seems to back this as numerous studies have shown that subjects given Rangicrin increased their endurance by as much as 33 percent.

When used as a counter to steroid-related side effects, Soviet athletes take 600 to 900 milligrams of Rangicrin starting about 15 days before a steroid cycle, and continue through the cycle. As soon as steroid use is stopped, the athletes increase Rangicrin dosage to 1800 to 2000 milligrams a day for 10 days.

ALCES-V

Like Rangicrin and Pantocrine, Alces-V is made from the antlers of a member of the deer family – this time bull elk. The active compound is obtained from the soft, nutrient-rich covering called velvet, which covers the antlers during the short growth phase in the spring. After extraction the compound is further refined to yield numerous biologically important substances.

The reason Alces-V is so powerful lies in the elks' diet – a combination of nutrient-rich grasses supplemented with feed concentrates. Although it varies, the antlers are harvested in the velvet stage about 45 days into maturity. While the anabolic effects of Alces-V are similar to Rangicrin, the substance appears to offer greater potential for speeding recovery time and elevating the athlete's moods. This is especially noticable in athletes following long training cycles.

WHAT DOES IT CONTAIN?

Alces-V contains both organic and inorganic compounds, and this includes mono- and disaccharides, nitrogen fractions, proteins, polypeptide hormones, nucleic acids, sterols, and lipids. Of these, the sterols and peptide hormones probably account for Alces-V's antcatabolic properties. The compound also contains high amounts of vanadium, which might explain Alces-V's fat-burning abilities, especially during periods of high-intensity exercise. Evidence for this comes from studies involving vanadium-deprived animals which gained considerable bodyfat. Although not fully understood, it is believed the deprivation of vanadium interferes with proper thyroid functioning – the result of which is a slower metabolism.

Jeff Poulin

MECHANSIM OF ACTION

Besides the previously mentioned fat-burning properties, Alces-V also has adaptogenic properties. Like Mumie, pantocrine, and Rangicrin, Alces-V increases the body's resistance to internal and external stressors. It is believed to accomplish this by increasing the brain's sensitivity to feedback control hormones. As a general rule, hypothalmic sensitivity to such feedback hormones as cortisol, testosterone, and thyroid declines in individuals experiencing such stressors as disease, work, or intense exercise. Studies with Russian athletes have shown that Alces-V acts as a defensive buffer against such homeostatic declines.

HOW TO TAKE ALCES-V

Soviet research suggests that Alces-V works most efficiently when taken at night. This is because it contains various pineal compounds known to work in sync with the body's circadian rhythms.

One of the most expensive Far East supplements, Mumie is derived from plants which have been decaying for hundreds of years in the Tajikistan republic of middle Asia.

One of the most popular stacking routines is to take another adaptogen like Rangicrin during the day and Alces-V later in the evening. For example, Soviet athletes often take three to five tablets of Rangicrin during the day and three or four tablets of Alces-V at night.

In most cases Alces-V is taken in cycles of ten days followed by three to five days of abstinence. Further, Soviet coaches often have athletes pyramid dosages from low (one tablet) to high (four tablets) and back to low (one tablet) again. The pyramid itself is broken down into three phases of three days increasing dosage, four days maximum dosage, and three days decreasing dosage.

SAPARAL

Isolated from aralia roots, this substance is popularly used by former Eastern Bloc athletes as both a stimulant and weak anabolic agent. The glycosides in saparal are known to increase protein synthesis, including increased activity of enzymes involved in carbohydrate and fat metabolism. Although it varies, most athletes take saparal after meals in dosages of 50 milligrams for 20 to 30 days. As with pantocrine, saparal use is stopped for about two weeks between cycles.

MUMIE

Studied by the Soviets for over 80 years, Mumie is one of the most popular substances used by former Eastern Bloc athletes. In fact hundreds of research papers and numerous books have been written on Mumie in the former Soviet Union. Even though athletes used mumie before anabolic steroids became available, it is still popular as an ergogenic aid.

Mumie is black in color, has the texture of putty, and has a unique taste and aroma. Unlike most Soviet adaptogens which are obtained from living trees, Mumie is derived from plants which have been decaying for hundreds of years in the Tajikistan republic of middle Asia.

Biochemists have analyzed Mumie and found that among its active ingredients are glycosides, saponins, chlorophyl, essential oils, keratin, flavanoids, benzoic acid, minerals, amino acids, and various plant sterols. Given such an assortment, it isn't any wonder that Mumie has ergogenic properties.

Besides its biostimulating effects, Mumie promotes the movement of important mineral substances into muscle and bone. Soviet athletes use Mumie to increase lean bodyweight, increase cardiac output, stimulate the immune system, and reduce recovery time between workouts.

Another use for Mumie is treating age and sport-related degenerative disorders. Scientists speculate that high concentrations of dicarbonic acids such as succinic, glutamic and aspartic acid indicate Mumie has outstanding anti-inflammatory and healing effects. Such products are the result of oxidative deamination of amino acids and are indicative of Mumie's ability to reduce joint soreness in the knees, shoulders, and elbows. This is a godsend for both arthritis sufferers and athletes involved in strength sports.

Due to its alleged effectiveness and hence high demand, Mumie is one of the most expensive Far East supplements. And like most supplements which are in high demand, there are various forms of Mumie available – some of which are of low quality. The best form is available in 200 milligrams tablets and is certified as being a genuine extract. As Mumie is soft at room temperature, it is recommended that the tablets be frozen and released from their package in the hard form. They can then be swallowed with water or some other liquid.

Porter Cottrell

For bodybuilders wanting to maximize Mumie's effects, recommended use is 300 to 600 milligrams daily for seven to 10 days. The best period for use would be during the last week of heavy training and for about a week into recovery. A two- to three-week break between cycles is also recommended (a common practice for supplement use in Russia).

Like most supplements derived in the former Soviet Union, Mumie is only available from the joint Soviet/American company Atletika. Although beginner bodybuilders will benefit from using Mumie, intermediates and advanced trainers will probably recieve the greatest advantage from the substance. Given Mumie's positive effects on joint pain, arthritis sufferers or athletes with connective-tissue injuries might want to give the substance a try.

ADAPTOZOL

Adaptozol is not one substance but a whole complex of adaptogenic agents. The mixture contains EC, Schizandra, suma, astragulus, and licorice. Besides its slight anabolic effects, Adaptozol is found to improve overall metabolism and energy transfer. Like most Soviet adaptogens, Adaptozol is taken two or three times a day for 20 to 30 days, followed by two or three weeks of abstinence. Soviet research suggests that Adaptozol's benefits are facilitated when combined with amino acids.

TONEDRIN

This substance was intitially developed to combat the effects of jet lag, but in recent years Tonedrin has become popular with athletes. It is a relatively new product developed from Soviet and Chinese sources and is taken in conjunction with inosine and amino acids which seem to improve its anabolic effects. Although popular with other athletes, Tonedrin is especially prevalent among weightlifters and bodybuilders who use it during their heavy phase of training. Once again the accepted dosage is two or three tablets daily for three or four weeks, followed by two weeks of cessation.

SOVIET SECRETS – CONCLUSION

The previous are just a sample of the ergogenic substances that have helped former Soviet and Eastern Bloc athletes dominate the international amateur sports arena. One of the reasons the Soviets are leading the way in natural supplements is the change in attitude towards performance-enhancing drugs. Contrary to popular Western beliefs, Soviet athletes are relying less and less on steroids and other drugs. The reasons for such a change include a much more open society and the introduction of year-round random testing by various Soviet sports federations.

Where previously the bulk of research went into designing new drugs and procedures for beating drug tests, the Soviets are now investing heavily in plant extracts that promote the same effects without side effects.

Western researchers who have extensively studied Soviet supplements (including regular *MuscleMag International* contributor Rick Brunner) have detected a number of differences between Soviet and Western philosophies towards supplementation.

The first concerns how supplements are tested. For the most part, Soviet ergogenic substances are tested on hard-training athletes. In the west most nutritional products tend to be tried on sedentary subjects. Granted newer supplement manufacturers like MET-Rx, L&S Research, and Twinlab have begun to follow the Soviet lead, but for the most part, Western supplements receive less testing with fewer athletic test subjects.

Alq Gurley

J.J. Marsh

Another difference is the role of coaches in former Soviet countries. Unlike most Western athletes who are often left to their own devices when it comes to supplements, Soviet coaches are an intergral part of a Soviet athlete's training – and this includes monitoring and designing supplement programs.

We should add that a number of bodybuilding trainers follow the Soviet style of intergrated coaching. Such supertrainers as John Parrillo and Scott Abel make supplementation as much a part of a bodybuilder's program as training – and the late Vince Gironda was probably 50 years ahead of his contemporaries in this regard.

A third difference could be called "target specificity." Soviet supplements are selectively aimed at one specific biological function, whereas their Western counterparts tend to be more general in nature. It's not surprising that in the last ten years Western supplement manufacturers have begun to market more and more one-ingredient supplements. In fact, two of the more popular, inosine and dibencozide, received their first boost from Soviet athletes.

Closely related to the previous is the issue of dosage. Where Western practices primarily center on providing enough of a substance to allow the body to carry out specific tasks adequately, Soviet research is heavily geared towards using larger dosages to increase specific biological tasks.

Another difference is the Soviet philosophy on cycling supplements. Unlike Western athletes who tend to take supplements in megadosages in one super combination, Soviet athletes have refined supplement usage to an art form. At certain times it's approprate to take amino acids, while at others, adaptogens are heavily used. The Soviets also endorse the cycling of supplements so that athletes have periods when no supplements are used. Not only does this prevent tolerance, but it also lets the body revert back to its presupplement state.

A final difference concerns advertising. Soviet athletes rarely if ever are confronted by full-color, glossy ads proclaiming the benefits of one supplement over another. This is because supplementation is taken more seriously and supplements are only administered by coaches and team doctors. It will be interesting to see if Western marketing strategies take hold now that the Soviet Union has collapsed and democracy has gained a foothold.

Reference

1) K. Asano and others, *Planta Medico*, 3 (1986).

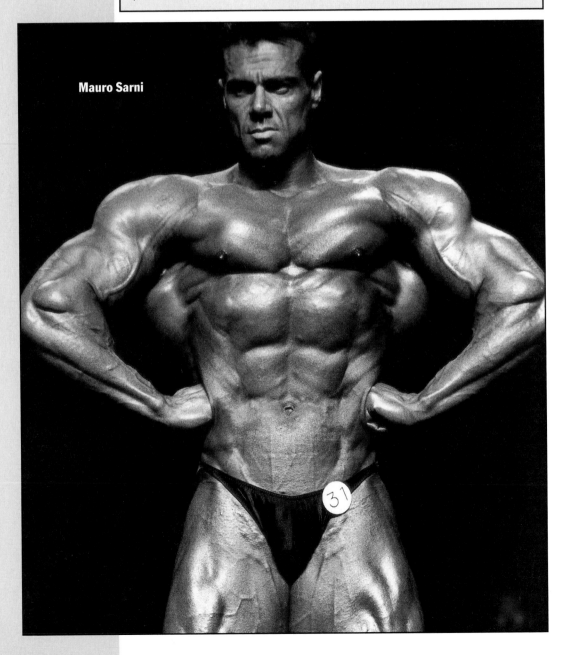

Mauro Sarni

Milos Sarcev

Peptide Growth Factors – The Wave of the Future?

> **"Most growth factors act as regulators of local processes such as wound healing, tissue repair, regeneration, or ordinary replacement of aged cells, but some are found in circulation and may function as true hormones. IGF-1 is especially important in this regard in mediating many of the actions of GH."**
>
> – John Parrillo, *MuscleMag* columnist commenting on one of the newest rages to hit the bodybuilding world – peptide growth factors.

n the last ten years medical science has taken a quantum leap in terms of treatment techniques. Drugs and practices that would astound Pasteur and Banting are now routine in hospitals and clinics, and at the forefront of such medical science is bioengineering.

Once scientists unraveled the mysteries of DNA and cracked the genetic code, it was only a short leap to practical applications. From synthetic growth hormone to enzyme-producing bacteria, biotechnology has changed the way we live.

From a bodybuilding standpoint it's the advances in nutrition that have played the greatest role in producing today's physiques. Granted the "antidrug advocates" will argue that much of the improvement in present-day bodybuilders is due to the latest drugs – and maybe they have a point – but only at the upper levels. The fact remains that most individuals who work out at the local gym are in much better shape than their counterparts of twenty or thirty years ago. Are we to suggest that they're all using drugs – certainly not! If there is one factor that has revolutionized modern bodybuilding, it is the leaps made in nutrition. And at the center of this new wave are peptide growth factors.

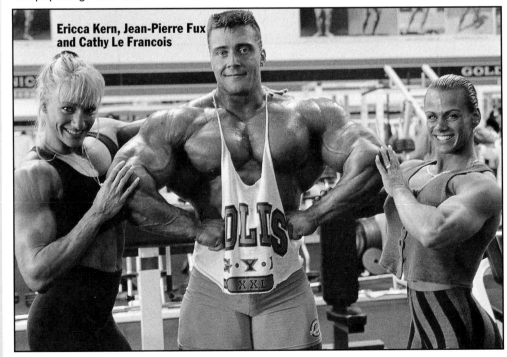

Ericca Kern, Jean-Pierre Fux and Cathy Le Francois

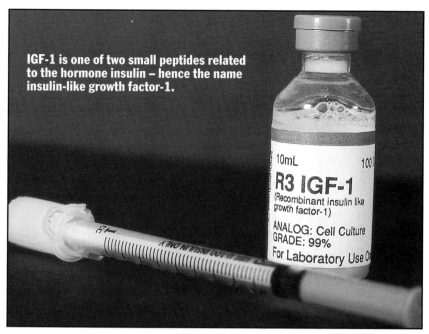

IGF-1 is one of two small peptides related to the hormone insulin – hence the name insulin-like growth factor-1.

Peptide growth factors are protein-based molecules which regulate such important biological activities as blood-cell formation, nerve repair, bone mending, skin growth, muscle development, and cartilage maintenance. For the purposes of this chapter we will only look at a few – including insulin-like growth factor (IGF) – and discuss their implications for creating the super bodybuilder of the future.

INSULIN-LIKE GROWTH FACTOR-1 (IGF-1)

In their never-ending quest to unlock the secrets of the human body, scientists have made great strides in their understanding of how growth factors work over the last ten years. One of them, IGF-1, not only promotes muscle growth, but speeds repair in other tissues as well. And while the agent has limited ability when used alone, when combined with such other anabolic compounds as steroids and HGH, the effects on muscle tissue and bodyfat are tremendous.

IGF-1 is one of two small peptides related to the hormone insulin – hence the name insulin-like growth factor-1 (the biochemists among you might like to know the IGF-1 peptide chain is 67 amino acids long, and resembles proinsulin – the form of insulin stored in the pancreas). IGF-1 is produced in many tissues and released systematically by the liver usually in response to meals. IGF-1 is an effector molecule which operates within a family of extremely powerful signaling enzymes called "tyrosine-kinases." Over the last five years kinases have become the focus of much research, particularly as they relate to growth. Although still inconclusive, the evidence seems to suggest that IGF-1 has more anabolic potential than any other known compound – including anabolic steroids.

This is because steroids do not necessarily direct new muscle protein synthesis or differentiation the way IGF-1 does. They merely force the muscle cells to become more efficient at retaining such building blocks as amino acids. Perhaps the most overlooked fact about IGF-1 is that it is heavily influenced by HGH. HGH tells cells to make new IGF-1, rather than

"Similar to growth hormone, IGF-1 is a potent anabolic hormone which also stimulates protein build-up in muscle and other tissues. However, IGF-1 production is dependent upon growth hormone, the master regulator of body growth. That is, an increase in growth hormone levels stimulates the liver and other tissues to increase production of IGF-1. Thus, when IGF-1 levels increase, it means that growth hormone levels are also increased; whereas when IGF-1 levels are low, growth hormone levels are also low. Simultaneous increases in these two potent growth factors combine to produce a dramatic increase in the growth potential of the body."

– Dr. Douglas M. Crist, *MuscleMag* contributor commenting on the interrelationship between growth hormone and the latest fad in bodybuilding – IGF-1.

Ed Corney

to rely on localized IGF-1.[1] Once synthesized, IGF-1 increases nutrient uptake and expansion. In a manner of speaking, IGF-1 is the intermediary between HGH and muscular anabolism. Without IGF-1, HGH would be much less significant as a growth enhancer.

Besides its anabolic effects, IGF-1 has anticatabolic properties. Bodybuilders are well aware that one of the real problems with achieving extreme muscular development lies not just with promoting anabolism but decreasing catabolism. This is an important point as studies indicate that IGF-1 helps prevent weight loss in the elderly and during periods of starvation.[2]

WHERE IT COMES FROM AND HOW IT'S CONTROLLED

Although IGF-1 is manufactured in a number of places including the kidneys, muscles, colostrum (a thin milky fluid secreted by the female mammary glands just before milk is released), intestinal tract, and pituitary gland, it is the liver which produces most of the body's circulating IGF-1. Once synthesized, IGF-1 binds to plasma proteins not surprisingly called IGF-1 binding proteins (IGFBPs). This step is important as it prolongs the life of IGF-1 from 30 minutes to 12 to 16 hours. It also means that unlike HGH, which is released in bursts (peak time is during sleep), IGF-1 is released constantly throughout the day. Age also seems to play a role in IGF-1 release; with small amounts being released in childhood, large amounts during the teenage years, and reduced amounts after the age of 50.

There is evidence to suggest IGF-1 can be controlled by diet. Studies have shown those who eat high-calorie diets – particularly those high in protein – have increased IGF-1 levels. Conversely, eating too few calories for prolonged periods of time shuts down IGF-1 production. One of the best pieces of evidence to confirm this are AIDS patients who usually show drastic reductions in IGF-1 production. Other studies done on fasting indicate IGF-1 levels start to decline after about 24 hours of fasting. This last point is important for bodybuilders in the weeks leading up to a contest. Drastically reducing caloric intake to shed bodyfat may also shut down IGF-1 levels, leading to the dreaded state of catabolism and muscle loss. Hence we have another reason for keeping bodyfat relatively low throughout the year.

The latest research suggests high levels of individual amino acids may increase IGF-1 levels. Subjects given up to 30 grams a day of arginine aspartate showed significant increases in IGF-1 levels. Before injesting huge amounts of arginine, however, we must point out that as of yet, such studies have only been conducted on elderly patients whose natural IGF-1 levels have no doubt declined with age. No studies exist to verify the same results in healthy young bodybuilders. And even if it was true, taking 30 grams of

"You know, IGF is so new that it's like a shot in the dark. Most of the talk is still speculation and guesswork."

– Will Brink, regular *MuscleMag* columnist commenting on the unknown aspect of IGF-1.

arginine is not simply a matter of popping a few pills. With an average tablet/capsule being 500 milligrams in size, you would need to consume 60 of them to get the required dosage! Our advice is to hold off on megadosing with aminos until more is known about the release mechanisms of IGF-1.

MECHANISM OF ACTION – A MIXED BAG OF EFFECTS?

IGF-1 is unique in that it acts like both insulin and HGH in its effects on skeletal muscles. It does this by increasing protein synthesis and decreasing protein deterioration. For bodybuilders, IGF-1's ability to stimulate DNA and cell multiplication should be music to the ears.

Studies have suggested that IGF-1 exerts its effects by mediating both IGF-1 receptors and insulin receptors. Studies with rats showed that when injected, IGF-1 produced effects virtually identical to insulin.[3] However, unlike insulin, it doesn't seem to be involved in glucose homeostasis. Theoretically, this means the drug is "safer" than insulin as numerous bodybuilders have ended up in diabetic comas from insulin abuse (we say "theoretically" because as we shall see later, IGF-1 has other side effects).

One of the surprising characteristics of IGF-1 is that it is heavily interdependant on other hormone levels. If taken alone, it may be counterproductive – not only reducing anabolic effects but actually decreasing insulin and HGH secretion. Further, while high doses of IGF-1 may increase nitrogen retention (one of the primary states necessary for anabolism), blood-sugar levels may be drastically reduced.

A lesser-known property of IGF-1 is its effects on the production of red-blood cells. Like the hormone erythropoietin, IGF-1 has been shown (at least in the lab) to boost production of red-blood cells.[3] No doubt, some endurance athletes

Roland Cziurlok

will add IGF-1 to their arsenal of drugs used to up their red-blood-cell counts (part of the banned practice of "blood doping").

Probably the most important aspect to understanding how IGF-1 works can be found in the latest research suggesting IGF-1 is moderated by a protein called IGF-1 binding protein – IGFBP-3. IGFBP-3 controls IGF-1's circulation in the body and the anabolic effects of IGF-1 quickly dissappear when IGFBP-3 levels drop.[4] This effect has been demonstrated in studies with AIDS patients using IGF-1 to combat the muscle-wasting properties of the virus. For the first six to eight weeks IGF-1 has great anabolic actions, but by 10 to 12 weeks, a plateau is reached. Blood work indicates that while IGF-1 levels are high, IGFBP-3 levels have decreased dramatically. Without the binding protein to carry it, IGF-1 is basically useless.

Although not fully understood, it seems continued use of IGF-1 causes the body to initiate a feedback loop which shuts down IGFBP-3 production. The latest research is focusing on ways to bypass this feedback loop – with the use of such hormones as insulin and HGH taking center stage. Insulin is especially promising as it seems to bypass the feedback loop and keep IGFBP-3 production high, thus allowing any circulating IGF-1 to have a longer life span in the body.

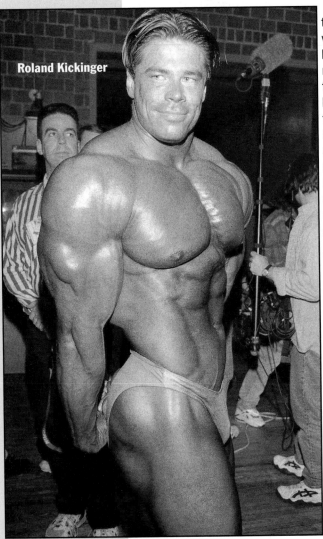

Roland Kickinger

While researchers are using such techniques to improve treatment in those with AIDS and other patients, bodybuilders seemed to have stumbled on the routine by a combination of accident and tradition. It's safe to assume that most bodybuilders don't know about such things as IGFBP-3 and IGF-1 feedback loops, but virtually all know that by stacking different kinds of drugs, they can magnify the drugs' effects. So while researchers have taken the scientific approach, bodybuilders have followed custom and simply added IGF-1 to their already full drug combo.

THE RESEARCH – HOW EFFECTIVE?

As with HGH, clenbuterol, and anabolic steroids, the effectiveness of exogenous IGF-1 is debated by the scientific community. Some studies have shown no increase in protein synthesis or reduction in catabolism, while others have demonstrated significant anabolic effects. In one study reported in *The Journal Of Clinical Endocrinology and Metabolism*, researchers divided subjects into three groups; group one received IGF-1 alone; group two received IGF-1 plus the catabolic hormone prednisone; and group three received prednisone alone. After trials using 100 milligrams of IGF-1, given twice

Thomas Burianek, Thomas Zechmeister and Thomas Omar Farag, the "Good" the "Bad" and the "Ugly."

daily, the researchers concluded that IGF-1 promotes protein anabolism, while at the same time decreasing catabolism.[4]

THERAPEUTIC APPLICATIONS

Like steroids, growth hormone, and other drugs used by bodybuilders, IGF-1 was initially developed for medical purposes (something conveniently omitted by antidrug groups). The latest research is looking at using IGF-1 for the treatment of such life-threatening diseases as multiple sclerosis, diabetes, and Lou Gehrig's disease. Further research is investigating the role of IGF-1 in haulting the muscle loss that accompanies such wasting diseases as cancer and AIDS. Finally, a study reported in *Clinical Endocrinology* found that IGF-1 may hold promise in fighting heart disease due to its ability to lower circulating blood-cholesterol and fat levels.[5]

USE BY BODYBUILDERS

As would be expected, any substance that can be described with the words "anabolic," "anticatabolic," "muscle building," or "HGH promoting," will be used by bodybuilders – irregardless of the potential side effects or cost. And as would be expected, most bodybuilders who use IGF-1 are stacking the drug with other anabolic agents such as steroids, clenbuterol, insulin, and HGH. While most bodybuilders are probably stacking out of habit (the old "shot gun" approach – take as many and as much as you can), there is some evidence to suggest this practice makes pharmacological sense (ignoring the potential side effects of such drug combinations).

Endocrinologists and biochemists have discovered that two drugs taken together often produce a combined effect that is greater than the added effects of the drugs taken separately. Called the "synergistic effect," it helps explain why bodybuilders who use multiple drugs gain much more muscle mass than those who only use one or two drugs.

Studies involving IGF-1 and HGH indicate that when taken together, they produce a marked increase in nitrogen retention – much more so than if either were taken seperately. In addition, taking HGH helps eleviate the hypoglycemia often produced when IGF-1 is taken alone.[6,7]

Such effects are not limited to IGF-1 and HGH. Other studies show the same synergism when insulin is combined with IGF-1, HGH is combined with insulin, or when IGF-1 is combined with testosterone preparations. The latter example is interesting as studies using testosterone enanthate and nandrolone decanoate (but no IGF-1) showed increases in serum IGF-1 in the order of 21 percent and 9 percent respectively.[8] Such data has led many researchers to suggest that one of the ways anabolic steroids work is by increasing IGF-1 levels.

Besides the body's natural supply of IGF-1, it is found in small amounts in the colostrum of pregnant women.

What all of the previous means is that a bodybuilder stacking three or four of these preparations is maximizing his or her anabolic and anticatabolic abilities. It's quite normal for a pro bodybuilder these days to be stacking steroids, insulin, HGH, and IGF-1 all at once. Then come contest time such drugs as thyroid medications and diuretics are added to the cocktail. Without close medical supervision, such polypharmacology is potentially dangerous, but few can argue that today's bodybuilders are not a quantum leap ahead of their counterparts ten or twenty years ago.

SOURCES, COST, AND OTHER TIDBITS

Besides the body's natural supply of IGF-1, the growth factor is found in small amounts in colostrum – the milky white fluid produced by the mammary glands of pregnant women. You can buy colostrum at most health-food stores, but one major practical consideration makes this a poor way of obtaining IGF-1. Like many supplements, IGF-1 is a peptide-based molecule (that is, it's made up of chains of amino acids). Your digestive system will treat IGF-1 like any other peptide molecule and break it into individual amino acids (the same way it cleaves other protein sources). What you end up with is another source of protein that bears no resemblance to the original IGF-1 molecule.

The most abundant source of IGF-1 is through gene-manipulated bacteria. Based on recombinant DNA techniques (with Genentech leading the way), this method allows for an almost unlimited supply of IGF-1. In appearance, IGF-1 comes as a freeze-dried white powder which requires refrigeration and an absence of light (like most synthetic preparations, IGF-1 decomposes when exposed to light – something else to keep in mind when buying from the black market). When used, the powder must be mixed with sterile water to produce 50 cc.

Like many synthesized drugs, IGF-1 is very expensive to obtain on the black market, and there are reports of a month's supply costing $5000 to $10,000 (other reports tell of 50-milliliter bottles selling for $800 to $1,000 on the street.)[9] And since the drug is not approved by the FDA (as of this writing it's only used in research), the black market will probably remain the main source for bodybuilders for the next couple of years.

This means IGF-1 is probably going to remain a drug only for those that can afford it. Most "Joe averages" are not capable of plunking down $10,000 to $20,000 every couple of weeks for a few IGF-1 shots. Perhaps a few elite bodybuilders will make the investment – especially if they feel their competition is doing so – but for members at the local gym, IGF-1 will probably remain just something to talk about.

SIDE EFFECTS

Given that most forms of IGF-1 on the black market have been manufactured for experimental use only, bodybuilders who use the drugs may be setting themselves up for injury down the road. It's not that experimental drugs are unsafe, but they have not gone through the rigorous tests that a drug destined for human use would have. This means impurities may sneak in, and while a rat with a super immune system may experience no side effects (remember these little critters can live their entire lives in sewer tunnels), the consequences for humans could be tragic.

Kevin Levrone

"I think we need to look at this whole IGF-1 thing a little bit more before we call it a miracle. I remember they all thought HGH was the balls, and by itself it did zip. Then there was clenbuterol . . . two weeks after you use it, it stops working. We need a healthy dose of skepticism here. And we really don't know what we are dealing with nor how much we need to use."

– Dan Duchaine, author of the *Underground Steroid Handbook*, commenting on the unknown properties of IGF-1.

Besides impurities, IGF-1 is similar to HGH in that it's manufactured in different forms. The most popular is called "long-acting" because it's life in cell cultures has been extended by adding 8, 10 or 15 extra amino acids. As with research-grade HGH, this form of IGF-1 was not designed for human injection. But because it's much cheaper than standard forms, it's the most popular with bodybuilders. Unfortunately, the long-term implications of such usage are unknown. One suggestion is that you run the risk of developing antibodies against your IGF-1. If this happens – good-bye muscle gains, and perhaps good-bye immune system.

Another important issue is the relative newness of IGF-1 and related drugs. As of yet few comprehensive studies involving IGF-1 use in humans have been conducted (none have been conducted on bodybuilders). Further, anecdotal information – like that obtained from 50 years of anabolic steroid use – has not been developed yet for IGF-1. The few bodybuilders taking the drug are the first generation of users. What these individuals learn by trial and error will no doubt make its way around the gym grapevine, but until then, each new user is more or less left to his or her own devices.

A third cause for concern is the manner in which IGF-1 is used by bodybuilders. Although we eluded to this earlier, the stacking and "cocktailing" regimes that many bodybuilders follow (what Dr. Mauro DiPasquale calls "polypharmacology") has for the most part not been duplicated in the laboratory (for obvious legal and moral reasons). While combining various drugs may produce an incredible synergistic effect, it may also open up a Pandora's box of unknown side effects. When you add the potential for tainted and bogus black-market drugs to enter the equation, the results could be devastating.

Jeff Poulin

In conclusion, we stress that no one really knows what the long-term side effects of IGF-1 are. Even short-term use is poorly understood. True, there is good animal data available, and the file on human use is growing, but the pool of knowledge out there on IGF-1 use for ergogenesis is very small indeed. It's quite possible that the limited information may serve nothing more than to encourage use without outlining the risks. Our advice is to avoid IGF-1 until more is known.

FINAL COMMENTS

For those who doubt the effectiveness of such peptide-based growth factors, just look at how much a baby grows in the first few months of life. From an average of seven pounds to twenty or thirty pounds, a baby is doubling or even tripling in weight. A 200-pound bodybuilder is not going to weigh 400 pounds after three months of growth-factor therapy, but the potential is there to add many pounds of muscular bodyweight.

There is only one major drawback to obtaining IGF-1 and other growth factors – they are, as of yet, not FDA approved for over-the-counter sale. Neither are most of the other commonly used performance-enhancing drugs. However, this hasn't cut down on their use.

If and when growth factors become commerically available, it's possible that future bodybuilders will be as far ahead of today's

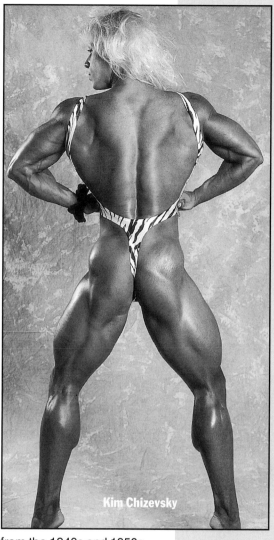

Kim Chizevsky

competitors as they are ahead of bodybuilders from the 1940s and 1950s.

References

1) J. Isgaard and others, "Growth Hormone Regulates the Level of Insulin-Like Growth Factor-1 in Rats Skeletal Muscle," *Journal of Endocrinology*, 120 (1989).

2) M. Poll and P.C. Bates, "Manipulation of Growth and Muscle Protein Metabolism By Exogenous Insulin-like Growth Factor-1 and Growth Hormone," *Acta Paediatr Scand*, 367 (1990).

3) Zapf, "Insulin-Like Growth Factor-1, Somatmedins, Structure, Secretion, Biological Actions, and Physiological Role," *Hormone Research*, 24 (1986).

4) N. Mauras and B. Beaufrere, "Recombinant Human Insulin-Like Growth Factor-1," *Journal of Clinical Endocrin Metabolism*, 80:3 (1995).

5) T.C. Luoma, "T.C. Talks," *Muscle Media 2000* (April 1996).

6) S.R. Kupfer and others "Enhancement of Anabolic Effects of Growth Hormone and Insulin-Like Growth Factor-1 By Use of Both Agents Simultaneously," *Journal of Clinical Investigation*, 91:2 (1993).

7) D.R. Clemmons, "Use of Growth Hormone and Insuline-Like Growth Factor-1 in Catabolism That is Induced By Negative Energy Balance," *Hormone Research*, 40:1-3 (1993).

8) Hobbes and others, *Journal of Clinical Endocrin Metabolism*, 77:3 (1993).

9) T.C. Luoma, "IGF-1, Possibly the Most Potent Bodybuilding Drug Ever," *Muscle Media 2000*, (January 1996).

BOOK EIGHT

Future
Ergogenesis

Cathy Le Francois

Roland Cziurlok

Antioxidants

Dorian Yates and
Kevin Levrone

Antioxidants have slowly made their way onto the pages of the more popular bodybuilding magazines. It has taken a long time, however, because antioxidants have been overshadowed by other popular supplements such as amino acids, dibencozide, inosine, and creatine phosphate. But research in the last ten years has indicated that it takes more than just raw materials to maintain health, it also requires substances to combat the waste products produced by the most basic aspect of existence – cellular respiration. And chief among these waste products are free radicals.

OXIDATION AND FREE RADICALS

It's ironic that one of the most important metabolic processes – oxidation – is also potentially one of the most detrimental in terms of health. To fully understand this mechanism we need to look at what goes on at the cellular level.

Cells are not loosely scattered throughout the body but arranged into highly organized tissues – each with specific structures and functions. On another level, cells can be thought of as distinct, individual life forms. This is because each is contained within a soft yet highly protective barrier called a cell membrane (plant cells have a stiffer outer "shell" called a cell wall). Membranes are very selective in what they allow to cross into and out of the cell. They allow useful substances to pass freely in both directions, but only allow harmful waste products to pass outwards. If this unique property of the membrane is hindered in any way, cell damage or even death may occur. Over the past ten years researchers have made great strides in determining that oxidation is one such "enemy" of cell membranes; and not only can it lead to cell damage but it may also be a contributing factor in overall body aging.

Without going into too much biochemistry, oxidation is a process that involves the loss of electrons from atoms or molecules, the primary benefit of which is to release energy in the form of an electron tranfer. In most cases this energy is used constructively as with fat and carbohydrate oxidation (burning). But if the energy is not focused properly it has the potential to be destructive.

Oxygen is controlled by the body as long as it remains in the dioxygen or O_2 form. If however, it gains an electron and becomes negatively charged it becomes highly reactive. This means it will combine (react) with any other unstable atom or molecule it comes in contact with. Given the potential danger of negatively charged oxygen, the body has evolved defence mechanisms which convert the unstable form of oxygen back to the stable O_2 form. The chief neutralizing agents are enzymes, which if for any reason become defective, lead to toxic levels of cell-destroying oxygen.

Negatively charged oxygen is just one example of what biochemists call "free radicals." The term is applied to any molecule which contains a single unpaired electron. As chemists say, electrons don't like to be left alone, and continiously "search" for partners to pair up with. And they are not selective in their search either. As soon as they encounter another atom with a similar electronic arrangement, you can be sure that a reaction will take place – irregardless of its effects on the body.

By far the most numerous free radicals in the human body are waste products left over from the reaction of fat with oxygen (it's a similar process to what happens when fat is left out in the open and reacts with air and water, and although we give the name "rancid" to the discoloration and aroma produced, it's a form of oxidation). Metabolic activity in mitochondria produce superoxide radicals. These are negatively charged oxygen molecules which are normally converted into hydrogen peroxide by a specific enzyme. The peroxide is itself neutralized by another enzyme in the peroxisomes of the cell and converted into the harmless form of oxygen and water.

Besides the previous, free radicals can form from exposure to radiation, pesticides and herbicides in food and water, smog, cigarette smoke, and the breakdown of such chemicals as peroxides and drugs. Finally, and here's the important point for athletes, excessive exercise has been shown to increase free-radical production in the human body. But please don't stop exercising on account of this. Physical activity also increases the destruction of free radicals and following a well-balanced diet (as most athletes do) also increases free-radical neutralization.

ATTACK AND COUNTERMEASURES

Once free radicals are formed, they can follow four primary pathways to neutralization. First, they may react with other highly unstable free radicals and cause little or no damage to the body's tissues. An example where two "wrongs" do in fact make a "right."

Second, they can combine with normal biological components leading to severe tissue and cell destruction. One of the most serious forms of free-radical damage pertains to heart disease. Scientists have theorized that low-density lipoprotein becomes oxidized and then damages the lining of arteries. This damage gives cholesterol a place to grab on to.

A third pathway involves the destruction of free radicals by special defense enzymes such as glutathione peroxidase and superoxide dismutase. In these cases the free radicals are broken down and metabolized before they get a chance to inflict damage on the body.

The fourth pathway consists of free-radical neutralization by scavengers appropriately called antioxidants. These last two pathways are important as both are interelated with antioxidants, facilitating the action of free-radical killing enzymes.

ANTIOXIDANTS

Antioxidants are nutrients which counteract the actions of free radicals within the body. They are especially important in neutralizing the harmful effects of oxygen and peroxide.

There are three broad catagories of antioxidants available to fight free radicals.

Excessive exercise has been shown to increase free-radical production in the human body. – Sue Price

1) Water-soluble forms (such as vitamin C and glutathione)
2) Fat-soluble forms (such as vitamins A and E)
3) Forms bound to large molecules called biopolymers.

Mike Matarazzo

All three forms offer free radicals an alternative substance to react with rather than body tissues and cells.

Besides combining with free radicals to neutralize them, antioxidants have preventive properties. They can inhibit the production of free radicals by inactivating key metal elements (such as copper and iron) which promote their formation. In most cases inactivation takes the form of binding with the trace element.

One of the most promising areas of research involves the role antioxidants play in reducing the risk of developing cancer. More than ten years of research has produced over 150 studies that suggest eating diets high in naturally occuring antioxidants greatly reduces the chances of acquiring certain types of cancer. So although antioxidants are often talked about in the same manner as "home remedies," there is a substantial amount of research to support their significance.

REASONS FOR SUPPLEMENTATION

Although most of the known antioxidants are supplied in a well-balanced diet, there are situations where supplementation may be necessary. And although we are not saying that individuals should definitely supplement, the evidence is building in favour of it.

Individuals who may want to supplement are those who live in large, polluted cities. Although not conclusive, the available evidence suggests that city residents are at special risk for free-radical damage. This is not surprising given their exposure to an assortment of harmful chemicals.

The next group of individuals are those who eat a large percentage of refined foods. Few things can destroy and leach out substances with antioxidant properties as much as the intense heat used in food manufacturing. Vitamins are especially vulnerable. Another group who should supplement are the elderly. Besides eating less than younger populations (studies consistently show that elderly subjects are at greater risk for malnutrition), elderly people have reduced metabolisms – an unavoidable part of aging. Among the consequences are an increase in free-radical production, and a reduced ability to fight such degeneration.

Eddie Moyzan

Last but not least, athletes may want to supplement their diet with antioxidants. Studies have shown that many athletes who have curtailed their fat intake have diets deficient in vitamin E. This puts them at risk for cell damage, especially those who train outdoors in large, polluted cities. Ironic as it may seem, the best sources of vitamin E are seeds, nuts, wheat germ, and foods rich in vegetable oils. While we are not suggesting that people should increase their fat intake just for the vitamin-E content, athletes on low-fat diets should be extra cautious.

WHAT TO TAKE

The following are some of the more common substances that have known antioxidant properties. We strongly suggest you include both water- and fat-soluable forms in your diet. This is because free-radical formation and damage occurs in both water-based mediums and in fatty tissue. By taking both forms of antioxidants you will cover all the bases.

VITAMIN A

This fat-based vitamin can be stored in the body so increased supplementation is not recommended. For those that smoke, vitamin A is a must as cigarette smoke is detrimental to lung tissue. Regular supplementation helps maintain lung tissue, albeit not as much as if you were to quit smoking.

VITAMIN C

There have been entire books devoted to this vitamin, and while perhaps not the "wonder" substance of some of its more vocal proponents, many in the biochemistry and nutrition fields agree that vitamin C is one of the most beneficial vitamins. Research indicates that the need for vitamin C goes up with increased exposure to stress, pollution, and infection; and since it's a water-based vitamin it must be taken throughout the day as the body does not store it.

     As a word of advice, instead of buying large-dose tablets (500 milligrams or more), get the smaller size (50 to 100 milligrams). This is because the body can only use 30 to 50 milligrams at any given time. The remainder is excreted in the urine. Most individuals who megadose with vitamin C report excreting highly colorful (sharp orange and yellow) urine. What they are looking at is money wasted. For every 500-milligram tablet you take, about 450 milligrams goes down the drain.

VITAMIN E

As mentioned earlier, the best sources of vitamin E are vegetable oils. As athletes and others following low-fat diets may be deficient in vitamin E, we suggest taking at least 100 milligrams a day. Since it's a fat-based vitamin and therefore storable by the body, there is the risk of reaching toxic levels. We should add that there have been few reported cases of vitamin-E

Melissa Coates

"Selenium is an excellent antioxidant, but only when taken in conjunction with vitamin E. They work together in protecting the cell walls from oxidation, in antagonizing mercury and cadmium, in encouraging the cells' fight to combat invading bacteria and they help to fortify the capacity of macrophages to destroy tumors."

– Bill Starr, regular *MuscleMag* contributor commenting on the antioxidant abilities of selenium when taken in conjunction with vitamin E.

overdosing. In most situations the individuals in question were either mega-dosing (5,000 to 10,000 milligrams per day) or suffering from some sort of metabolic condition.

Among vitamin E's greatest attributes is its ability to prevent cell membranes from oxidation. Although often touted as a "cure" for infertility and impotence, there is little medical evidence to back up these claims. It is possible that a deficiency in vitamin E will interfere with fertility and sexual functioning, but to suggest that extra amounts of the vitamin will "boost" sexual prowess is misleading.

GLUTATHIONE

This substance is a tripeptide made from the amino acids glutamic acid, glycine, and cystine. Among its functions are the destruction of free radicals formed from peroxides. There is also promising research to suggest that glutathione can increase liver detoxification in recovering alcoholics.

Debbie Kruck

SELENIUM

Selenium is a trace element that works with vitamin E to fight free-radical damage – especially plasma membranes. Although not fully understood, it is believed that selenium increases the efficiency of enzymes which break down free radicals.

PYCNOGENOL

Pycnogenol is the trade name of a new antioxidant that's extracted from the bark of a species of pine trees which grow in France. The active ingredients are brightly colored pigments called bioflavonoids. The makers of Pycnogenol claim their product reinforces vitamin-C function in capillary walls and helps strengthen collagen (the substance that gives capillary walls both elasticity and strength). The product also supposedly hunts down free radicals and prevents peroxidation.

Besides its biochemical properties, Pycnogenol is reported to dissolve in minutes and be active in the body for three days. Tests conducted at both the Pasteur Institute and Huntington Institute suggest that Pycnogenol promotes a higher level of physical ability while at the same time protecting the body from bruises and strains. Evidence also suggests that once such damage has occurred, Pycnogenol can help speed up the rate of repair.

The massive
Jean-Pierre Fux.

Genetic Engineering – The Future of Bodybuilding

So far we have been focusing on procedures and substances that have the potential to maximize muscular bodyweight. But in all cases the limiting factor is an individual's genetics. From the moment of conception a person's characteristic traits have been set. For most, no amount of food, training, or rest will produce a muscular 20-inch arm. Others build outstanding physiques except for perhaps one bodypart, which in many cases are the calves. And while laziness or inadequate training is sometimes at fault, it is, for the most part, genetics that decide the fate of your physique. But now that genetic engineering has arrived, it seems a biological equalizer is just around the corner.

"I knew I had genetics for bodybuilding after a few months of training, because no matter what I did – and I knew next to nothing about training – my muscles kept growing and growing."

– Dave Hawk, former pro bodybuilder and teenage champion commenting on the role genetics played in his career.

A BRIEF INTRODUCTION TO GENETICS

Although theorized for hundreds of years, it was the works of Austrian monk Gregor Mendel, in the mid to late 1800s, that layed the foundation for contemporary genetics. Mendel is often referred to as the "father" of modern genetics. The next big breakthrough came in 1869 when Johann Miescher, a Swiss physician, isolated a series of large molecules which he named nucleic acids because of their location (the nucleus of the cell) and pH (acid). Two types of nucleic acids were isolated: deoxyribonucleic acid (DNA), and ribonucleic acid (RNA). Although this was the first major step in deterimining the secrets to human variation it was not until the early 1950s that the pieces finally came together.

Dave Hawk

During the early 20th century, gene research gradually shifted from the cellular to the molecular level. While different strategies and theories accounted for some of the deviation, the primary reason was the advancement in technology, allowing scientists to make more detailed studies at the molecular level.

The greatest breakthrough in genetics came in the 1950s, first from the works of Linus Pauling, and later from the Nobel prize-winning team of Watson and Crick. Pauling's contribution came in the early 1950s when he suggested the structure of protein molecules. He proposed that protein molecules had the shape of either left- or right-hand helixes. Pauling's suggestion was so powerful that in 1953 James Watson and Frances Crick, two enterprising researchers, proposed that DNA was also double helical in shape and resembled a twisted or winding staircase. So important was this discovery that Watson and Crick were jointly awarded the Nobel prize for their efforts.

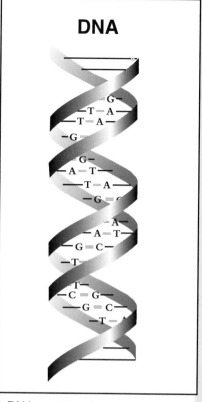

DNA

Further research determined that DNA contains four nitrogenous bases – the double-ringed purines (adenine and guanine) and the single-ringed pyrimidines (thymine and cytosine). For convenience geneticists abbreviate the four as A, G, T, and C. RNA is similar, except instead of thymine (T) it contains the base uracil (U). In double-stranded DNA (it "unwinds" to form single strands during replication) the two strands are held together by hydrogen bonds which connect pairs of nitrogenous bases.

It wasn't long after Watson and Crick discovered the structure of DNA that scientists began postulating medical applications. Further research led scientists to discover that DNA is not one entity, but rather composed of individual segments called genes.

Genes can be called the "instructors" or "determiners" of the organism, as they direct and control all cellular functions. They serve as a blueprint for the organism's development. Genes control everything from eye and hair color to height and body metabolism. Besides normal characteristics (called traits), genes are also responsible for many genetic diseases.

Information is passed from cell to cell, and from generation to generation, by the nucleic acids which are contained in thread-like structures called chromosomes, found in the nucleus of the cell.

Each species of organism has a specific number of chromosomes. Humans contain forty-six. During reproduction the sperm or egg contains half the number of chromosomes (twenty-three each) so that when they fuse the total number is once again doubled to forty-six. This mechanism of action is so precise that if something goes wrong, an incorrect number of chromosomes can be passed to the offspring. Any number of genetic diseases may then be produced – with Down's syndrome being perhaps the most well-known.

Terry Mitsos

WHAT IS GENETIC ENGINEERING?

Once geneticists had a firm grasp on how genes, DNA, and chromosomes interrelate to control individual variation, it wasn't long before the first suggestions of manipulation were made. Hollywood was first out of the gate with their series of B-movies in the 1950s which featured all sorts of genetic mutants. On a more down-to-earth level, the first serious attempts at gene manipulation didn't take place until the late 1960s, and even then the results were far from wonderous.

Gene manipulation or genetic engineering, as it's fast becoming known, involves the alteration or rearrangement of genes to change an organism's normal pattern of growth. So powerful have the techniques become that many research philosophers compare the field to "playing God." The following examples are presented to give an indication of just how much potential genetic engineering holds.

FROM PLANTMEN TO SUPERSENSORY WOMEN

The advent of genetic engineering has done more than allow scientists to treat genetic diseases, it has opened up a whole spectrum of possibilities that 20 years ago were unheard of. In the book *Who Should Play God*, authors

Ted Howard and Jeremy Rifkin suggest that ongoing research is looking at the possibility of designing humans with digestive systems capable of digesting hay and other grasses (humans have poor digestive abilities for plant material and the little that is broken down is by bacteria). If this doesn't grab your attention, how about inserting plant genes into humans to produce photosynthesizing skin? Instead of having to ingest carbohydrates humans could produce their own from carbon and water by merely lying in the sun (the way green plants do).

One area of research that is rapidly advancing is in the field of fetal-tissue implants. Presently, fetal brain cells are being implanted into the brain tissue of adults suffering from Parkinson's disease. The theory is that the young cells will take the place of the patient's dead and dying brain cells – leading to a partial resurgence of lost cognitive abilities. The results are remarkable and such patients show marked improvements in such cognitive operations as memory, thought, and reasoning (only the controversy over the source of the cells – aborted fetuses – has prevented the treatment from gaining widespread acceptance).

How long will it be before such technology is applied to bodybuilders? Have weak calves? Try a few fetal cells. Your back not measuring up to Dorian Yates'? See you at the lab on Monday morning. It sounds farfetched but we've gone from bloodletting to open-heart surgery in less than 100 years.

For those who enjoyed Arnold Schwarzenegger's movie *Junior*, the plot may not be that farfetched. A few noted researchers go as far as to suggest that in the near future it may be possible to implant female uteri in males. A combination of artificial fertilization and mammary gland stimulation, and the first child born to a male may become a distinct possibility.

Your back not measuring up to Dorian Yates' or Nasser El Sonbaty's? The future of genetic engineering may provide a solution.

Perhaps the most important field of research in recent years involves "gene mapping" – the pinpointing on chromosomes of individual genes responsible for individual traits or characteristics. Although a few years away, it's only a matter of time before "reprogramming" genes will allow parents to select their child's height, hair colour or eye colour.

BUILDING THE SUPER BODYBUILDER

The implications of genetic engineering to athletics are enormous. At the most basic level we have cloning. Cloning is the technique whereby an identical organism can be "grown" from a single cell of a parent cell. No courting, dating, or sex required! Just take a hair or skin sample and in a short period of time a whole new organism, genetically identical to the donor parent, is produced (check out the great movie *The Boys From Brazil*).

Can you imagine five Dorian Yates' trading poses with five Nasser El Sonbatys'? How about ten Paul Dilletts crunching down into a series of most musculars. For those that view such images with skepticism, remember that mice have already been cloned, and only strict laws (called biological moratoriums) have prevented such experiments with humans. Many well-respected geneticists suggest that cloning humans is already possible, and not a figment of some writer's imagination.

If cloning has its limits it's that the offspring are identical to the parents. Any imperfections will be passed on. As would be expected, science can get around this by embryo fusion and gene splicing.

Embryo fusion involves combining two eggs or early embryos to give the resulting child the benefit of four variations of genetics – two parents per embryo. What this means is that a child could be "tailor made" to possess the traits of four different humans. Combine embryo fusion with gene splicing (the insertion of individual genes into an egg, sperm, or embryo) and the bodybuilder of the 21st century is created. Now let's see what he would look like.

"So how big is Greg Kovacs? If your average untrained man on the street is a dingy, and your typical champion bodybuilder is the equivalent of a large yacht, huge bodybuilders like Dorian Yates, Nasser El Sonbaty, and Paul Dillett, who all weigh over 300 pounds in the off-season, would have to be considered big ships – maybe even ocean liners. But what would you call the Paul Bunyan-like Mr. Kovacs, who stands 6'2" and weighs 360 pounds in quite hard muscular condition? A supertanker? A battleship? An aircraft carrier?"

– Greg Zulak, former *MuscleMag* editor and well-known writer trying to put some perspective on the size of Canadian bodybuilder, Greg Kovacs, who quite possibly represents the next generation of bodybuilders.

Thomas Burianek, Thomas Omar Farag and Thomas Zechmeister

The first trait desired would be a large frame with room to add slabs of muscle on. Frames belonging to Paul Dillet, Lou Ferrigno, Arnold Schwarzenegger, or Rolf Moeller would serve nicely in this regard. The next order of business would be a metabolism capable of building large amounts of muscle tissue without depositing any degree of fat. First to come to mind are Sergio Oliva and Franco Columbu – both of whom were famous for their muscle density, low bodyfat levels, and ability to follow less than perfect diets.

Although not a prerequisite, our superbodybuilder should be designed with above-average strength levels. It's pretty much accepted that the largest, thickest bodybuilders are those who also happen to be the strongest. The genes of such superstars as Chris Cormier, Mike Francois, Greg Kovacs, or Dorian Yates would suffice in this regard.

Rounding out the list of characteristics would be a dark-skin complexion, fast recovery abilities between workouts, unlimited energy reserves, and a gift for designing and choreographing posing routines.

Finally, given the success that our genetically engineered bodybuilder would probably enjoy, a strong business sense would be warranted. For this, he or she would need above-average intelligence. This is not out of science's reach. Rats given appropriate amounts of growth hormone at the right time can have their brain sizes increased 70 to 80 percent. Further, such rats show an equivalent increase in learning ability.

Greg Kovacs

MORAL CONSIDERATIONS

As would be expected, the previous techniques are not without their distracters. Let's face it, "creating" a new human hybrid is a quantum leap above grafting a new flower. And while the techniques for doing so may be remotely similar, the end products have virtually nothing in common.

The first implication that will arise is the question of ownership. If a superhuman is created, does it legally belong to the lab that manufactured it, the donors who supplied the various DNA components, or is the new being a distinct entity which posseses all the rights and freedoms of everyone else in society? Answering such questions will challenge the greatest legal minds for years to come.

"Mayo Clinic researchers have isolated a gene that causes specific cells to attack joints and are developing a technique to suppress only the problem-causing cells."

– The late Bruce Page, commenting on one of the many benefits of genetic engineering, despite criticism from some groups.

Another concern is the control of such technology. Most "inventions," whether inanimate or organic in nature have military applications. In fact much of the research for new technology is conducted or funded by defence money. A "race" of superstrong, superintelligent soldiers, which can be cloned in unlimited numbers is now just the stuff of science-fiction movies, but what about 50 or 100 years down the road? Just think what the outcome would be if another Stalin or Hitler had access to such progeny.

Dorian Yates

From an athletic viewpoint, we have the issue of raised standards to think about. Bodybuilding has already reached the stage where drug use is an absolute must at the upper echelon of competition. No mere "natural" can hope to compete against 250-pound, ripped behemoths. If such standards exsist now, think about the physiques genetic engineering could conjure up. How does a bodybuilder with the frame of Paul Dillett, chest and arms of Arnold Schwarzenegger, legs of Tom Platz, back of Dorian Yates, shoulders of Sergio Oliva, and abs of Serge Nubret grab you! And we are not talking about one individual here, but every competitor that steps onstage. These would be the new

Spectators attend bodybuilding competitions to witness "freaky mass," but they also go to see the individual variations of each physique.

standards. Is this what competitive sport is all about? Congratulations and can I have your geneticists autograph!

Closely related to the previous is the question of acceptance. Part of the appeal of bodybuilding is the distinctness of individual physiques. Take a look at the differences between Shawn Ray, Dorian Yates, and Vince Taylor. All have advantages and disadvantages, but each has managed to get the most out of his individual genetics. Where would the competition be if all competitors had perfect bodyparts? How would judges choose winners in such genetically crafted contests? Further, wouldn't audiences quickly tire of such monotony? As it stands now, most audience members have their favorites and such preference is usually based on physique variation. In many cases people identify with the pro whose physique resembles their own – albeit on a larger scale. There is no way an average "natural" viewer could identify with some 300-pound genetically manufactured entity. Sure it may satisfy the "freakiness craving" found in many, but as for using such standards to compare one's self – forget it. It's just as well you put the latest comic book hero on your wall.

While the techniques discussed in the previous chapter are still a few years down the road, remember many roads are not as long as they look and others have short cuts. Look at the leaps in computer technology over the past five years. We've gone from Commodore 64s to a world-wide Internet. Individuals can live their whole lives sitting at their computer keyboard. Everything from TV and stereos to video phones and games are now made possible by one piece of equipment – the home-based personal computer system.

Jitka Harazimova

Genetic engineering is progressing along similar lines. We now have bacteria capable of manufacturing chemicals that some humans are deficient in. There is even talk of using bacteria to perform the functions of diseased or removed organs. Fetal-tissue implants mean new hope for Parkinson's sufferers, and such technology is just around the corner for bodybuilders with weak bodyparts. And while there are those that argue against such applications, try telling that to an athlete who stands to make millions of dollars in endorsement fees (the main reason why drug use is so rampant in athletics). There's an old saying that you can't stop progress, and while the exact definition of "progress" is sometimes blurred, we can be sure that the last word on genetic engineering has yet to be written.

CHAPTER THIRTY-TWO

Metabolic Optimizers

Bodybuilding is similar to other sports in that it's not too difficult to predict future trends. Given the strides made by nutritional scientists, we firmly believe that the future of bodybuilding will be dominated by naturally derived supplements. Many of the newer compounds show promise for bodybuilders wanting to maximize their muscle gains without tempting the steroid genie. Of course, one could argue that if a "natural" compound produces drug-like effects, by definition it is a drug. If so, perhaps down the road pharmacologists might consider changing their definition of "drug." This would allow natural supplement drugs, with few if any side effects, to be treated separately from other drugs that have harmful side effects.

As it stands now any new supplement that produces drug-like effects is quickly banned in Canada and the United States. Political pressure often leads to the banishment of substances that have few effects of any kind.

Every week some new supplement product hits the market, and unlike its protein-powder ancestors, was designed, manufactured, and tested using the most up-to-date scientific research methods. Everything from double-blind studies to trials using animals and humans have been conducted on these products. Further, with few exceptions, most of the companies marketing these products don't promote them as an alternative to HGH or anabolic steroids. In short, they keep things in perspective.

The main reason for the increased quality of today's supplements is that good old American equalizer – marketplace competition. Given the annual value of the supple-

Tom Prince

Lenda Murray and
Kim Chizevsky

ment business (estimated to be in the billions), it's not surprising that there
has been a proliferation in the number of corporations producing food supplements. With so many to choose from, consumers can afford to shop around
and get the best value for their dollar. No longer can fly-by-night supplement
manufacturers pop up out of nowhere and make outlandish claims about
their product. They must deliver a quality product, backed up by university
studies, or they'll quickly find themselves out in the ergogenic-aid graveyard.

Over the last ten years such companies and products as
Phosphagain, MET-RX, TwinLab, Cybergenics, Strength Systems USA, and
MuscleTech have developed reputations for bringing food supplements into
the 21st century. In the following chapter we'll look at some of these in more
detail and their role in creating the bodybuilder of the next century.

OPTIMIZING YOUR METABOLISM

Although often called other names, they are most commonly known as metabolic optimizers. The term was first coined back in the late 1980s by
Champion Nutrition to promote their various products, including the ground-
breaking Metabolol. Although they were the first major company to develop
multi-ingredient ergogenic supplements, it wasn't long before other supplement manufacturers jumped on the bandwagon. The promotional campaigns
bordered on war, with the new "upstarts" featuring ads showing Champion
Nutrition's products being "crushed" by the supposedly new breed of optimizers. And although Champion Nutrition's original product has been over-
taken in popularity by new products from such manufacturers as MET-Rx,
TwinLab, and GNC, the term "metabolic optimizer" has now become the all-
encompassing term to describe products containing wide assortments of
supposedly ergogenic compounds.

> "The last group of
> supplements I
> recommend for
> enhancing pump
> during training are
> the metabolic
> optimizers. These
> products take a
> "shotgun" approach
> to nutrition,
> basically containing
> any supplement
> thought to have
> some nutritional and
> or muscle-building,
> fat-burning, energy-
> promoting quality."
>
> – Greg Zulak, former
> *MuscleMag* editor
> commenting on the
> latest bodybuilding
> supplements –
> metabolic optimizers.

WHAT THEY CAN AND CAN'T DO

Metabolic optimizers were developed to take advantage of the advances in ergogenic supplements. With research showing that some natural substances

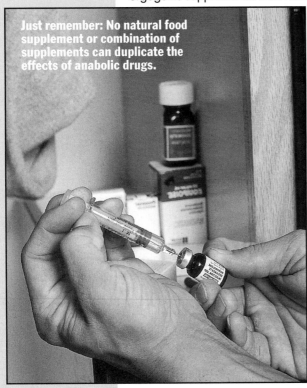

Just remember: No natural food supplement or combination of supplements can duplicate the effects of anabolic drugs.

do in fact have limited ergogenic abilities, it was only a matter of time before manufacturers started combining them into one "super" supplement. Although the actual ingredients vary from product to product, all are alike in that they contain substances that have both anabolic and anticatabolic properties. And while some companies emphasize the anabolic aspect and others focus on anticatabolism, all can be grouped under the heading of optimizers. Now before you get carried away with excitement, there is one major point that needs some additional clarifying.

Although many of the metabolic-optimizer products are promoted as being "'steroid replacers" or "anabolic promoters," none produce the same degree of effects of anabolic steroids or other powerful anabolic agents. As of yet there is no way they can. Such advertising is misleading and don't think by spending hundreds of dollars you are obtaining a "natural alternative" or "equivalent" to anabolic drugs.

This is not to say metabolic optimizers don't have a place in modern bodybuilding. They do. With advances in biochemistry, the odds are they will come close to, if not equal, the effects of performance-enhancing drugs. But as it stands right now, while perhaps being the leading edge of ergogenic aids, they will not promote the same muscle gains as anabolic steroids. Yes, individuals deficient in nutrients will benefit from metabolic optimizers, and yes there is even some evidence to suggest that those following good diets will obtain additional benefits from them as well. The catch is, no natural food supplement or combination of supplements can duplicate the effects of anabolic drugs.

FIRST ORIGINS

Although the term metabolic optimizer was coined for bodybuilding purposes, the general concept goes back over thirty years to the early days of the space program. As would be expected there are numerous requirements for "space nutrition." First and foremost, the food must be nutritious. Second, given the small confines of a space capsule, keeping waste products to a minimum is an absolute necessity, because the less waste the less resources needed for dealing with it.

Using these variables as a guideline, Nasa developed food products which, while small in size, provided the astronauts with the wide spectrum of nutrients needed to both maintain high-energy levels and counteract the negative aspects of zero gravity. These space-aged supplements could be called "meal replacers," and in fact many supplement manufacturers currently include such terminology in their brochures.

There is no way we can cover all the metabolic-optimizer products on the market. However, to give the reader a better understanding of the scope of products available, we will look at a few of the more popular brands. We must caution that most of the information is obtained from the manufacturers themselves. Consequently, to say it's a tad biased is an understatement. As with any supplement, we suggest keeping a bit of scepticism at arm's reach when listening to the claims of the advertisers. Not so much to dismiss the declarations outright, but to maintain an atmosphere of realism. If every supplement did what the manufacturers claimed, the planet would be full of Dorian Yates', Flex Wheelers, and Nasser El Sonbatys. The fact that it isn't should give you an idea of where things stand.

MET-Rx

MET-Rx is the name given to perhaps the most popular metabolic optimizer currently available, and is the brainchild of Dr. Scott Connelly of Southern California. The product grew out of Dr. Connelly's research into supporting critically ill patients suffering from life-threatening catabolic states. By studying such patients and the nature of their conditions, Dr. Connelly discovered a wide variety of compounds, that when administered consistently and in the right combinations, had profound abilities for reversing catabolism.

True muscle-building intensity as displayed by Jean-Pierre Fux.

THE THEORY BEHIND ANTICATABOLISM

Although perhaps old news to many, a brief discussion on catabolism is needed. The sum total of all the reactions in the body is called metabolism. This itself can be broken down into anabolism and catabolism. Muscle growth is the result of new tissue being synthesized from amino acids in response to damage or exercise stimulation. This "building up" is called anabolism and although it sounds straightforward, is really only one part of a circular mechanism. You see, if the stressors that started the anabolic reactions are reduced, or if the stressors become too great – as with overtraining – the body begins tearing down the muscle tissue. This process is known as catabolism, and such factors as increased catabolic hormones (one example being cortisol), decreased nutrient intake, or increased energy demands, all serve to remove amino acids from muscle protein and thus reduce muscle size.

Given the previous we see that there are two primary ways to increase muscle size – increase anabolism, or decrease catabolism (another way of saying increase anticatabolism). While steroids are touted as being "anabolic" in nature, the most recent research suggests they produce most of their effects by anticatabolism. Apparently steroids compete with cortisol receptors and prevent the catabolic hormone from breaking down hard-earned muscle tissue. So while past research centered on promoting anabolism, the new trend is toward reducing catabolism.

MET-Rx – THE ULTIMATE ANTICATABOLIC AGENT?

We raised these last points because the basis to MET-Rx's success lies with anticatabolism. According to Dr. Connelly, the product produces a number of positive effects on health and body-composition alterations. And one of these is to block the cortisol elevations that occur secondary to trauma, injury, or surgical procedures, thus preventing the unwanted catabolic reactions in already critically ill patients. By now you should begin to see the connection to bodybuilding. While exercise stimulates the

Paul DeMayo

release of testosterone and growth hormone, it also stimulates the release of cortisol and other catabolic hormones. The ratio of the various hormones determines if the individual will gain or lose muscle tissue.

THE RESEARCH

To test the effects of his new supplement array, Dr. Connelly set up an experiment involving 32 healthy male subjects. For validity he chose participants similar in size, weight, height, and age. The group was then split into two fractions, with one group recieving MET-Rx and the other group serving as the control.

Dr. Connelly then had the two groups follow an identical exercise programs for 56 days. For comparison purposes, cortisol levels were measured in both groups before and after the trial program. The results showed the MET-Rx group gained, on average, about 500 percent more lean muscle tissue than the control group. The Met-Rx group also showed no changes in cortisol levels, while the control group had levels increased by almost 20 percent.

Other studies carried out by a Colorado-based research team (under licence from Dr. Connelly) have shown similar results, with two experimental groups having success rates of 86 percent and 88 percent. According to the research team, of the more than 100 muscle-building agents studied, none produced the same results as MET-Rx. They have never seen athletes respond with the same level of praise for a previous product.

HOW IT IS USED

Although initially designed for clinical settings, MET-Rx has been upgraded for athletic use. MET-Rx comes in powder form and must be mixed with a beverage – usually milk, water, or juice. Although it can be mixed freehand, for best results use a blender. Unlike many protein powders, MET-Rx rarily causes stomach upset or bloating, except in cases of allergy or extreme sensitivity to one of the product's constituents.

A serving of MET-Rx contains 260 calories, 37 grams of protein, 23 grams of carbohydrate, and only 2 grams of fat. It is loaded with minerals and vitamins – essential catalysts for adequate utilization of the main food constituents.

Perhaps MET-Rx's greatest ingredient is Dr. Connelly's own compound called Metamyosyn. This ingredient is really a blend of over 50 different protein isolates including high-grade whey and caseinate milk proteins (those with lactose intolerance will be happy to know that MET-Rx is 99 percent lactose free). Although Dr. Connelly will not admit to the exact

Aaron Baker

makeup of the rest of MET-Rx ingredients, all are, as he says, "derived from foods that are FDA approved."

Like many supplements, Dr. Connelly recommends taking MET-Rx according to bodyweight. For those weighing around 150 pounds, he suggests two servings daily. Those in the 150- to 200-pound range should take the product three times daily. Finally, the larger members of the sport – 200 pounds or more – will obtain the best results by taking MET-Rx four times daily.

Dr. Connelly also suggests consuming the product at regular intervals with or between meals or as a meal replacement. No matter what schedule you follow, try to include a period 90 minutes after your workout. This is the time period when the body is specifically craving muscle-building nutrients.

HOW TO OBTAIN MET-Rx

Like most bodybuilding supplements, MET-Rx is available in virtually all health-food stores. In addition, the distributers of MET-Rx have broken new ground by having most major drug stores and discount stores carry their product. To help beginners they have produced a special introductory kit which cobtains 12 individual serving packets. Costing around $37.80 US, the kit not only provides three or four days' worth of MET-Rx, but also an "Owner's Manual," a one-year subscription to an update newsletter, and a video featuring Dr. Connelly explaing the philosophy behind MET-Rx supplementation. Although it varies, regular users of the product will spend an average of $120 to $150 for a month's supply. On the surface this sounds expensive, but if you had to buy all the known ingredients separately (not to mention the unknown substances), you would have to pay hundreds of dollars.

IS IT A STEROID REPLACER?

The answer to this question is an unequivocal no! Even Dr. Connelly will admit that MET-Rx does not produce the same degree of effects of anabolic steroids. But the key word here is "degree." While MET-Rx is not as powerful as a performance-enhancing drug, it does maximize the potential of natural bodybuilders. And perhaps most important, doesn't produce any of the side effects sometimes associated with bodybuilding drugs.

BEWARE OF IMITATORS!

Given the success of MET-Rx, it's not surprising that there has been an explosion of such products on the market, some of which make reference to MET-Rx in their advertising (albeit in a negative manner). Many of them go a step further and try to include part of the MET-Rx trade name in their own names – MET-Ex-Rx, Bio-Rx, and RX Fuel. While the lawyers for all concerned will no doubt argue for years (Dr. Connelly has filed lawsuits against a number of these imitators), the supplement market has been flooded in recent years. Some of the products are cheap copycats, others have been designed to beat MET-Rx in quality. In most cases it's left to the reader to sift through the claims and sort superiority from inferiority.

DEFINITION

Although not as popular as MET-Rx, a new product called Definition is fast gaining aceptance as a legitimate contender to MET-Rx's crown. Definition is produced by the Infinity company of Mesa, Arizona, USA. Infinity realized that to be competitive with MET-Rx they would have to design a product that was superior in quality but cost less; and according to their advertising brochures, they feel they've succeeded.

To promote their product, Infinity places a great emphasis on direct nutrient comparison with MET-Rx. They also claim their product is more readily absorbed than MET-Rx. The following is Infinity's comparison of their product "Definition" with Dr. Connelly's MET-Rx. For convenience we have broken the nutrients down into the familiar nutrient catagories. Please keep in mind that with any comparison there will be biases depending on who is doing the comparing. As most of the following is from Infinity, you can guess which way the pendulum swings.

Debbie Kruck

NUTRIENT CATAGORY COMPARISON:

PROTEIN

The protein in Definition is a blended form of whey protein and egg albumin with an absorption ratio of 3.9, which means it is highly absorbable. According to Infinity their product provides the perfect blend of amino acids necessary for homeostasis. Their whey source has also been processed using cold-filtration techniques, insuring little or no denaturing of the protein. Not content to leave it at that, Infinity adds that MET-Rx's whey protein is "the least expensive form of whey." Further, the caseinate in MET-Rx is an inexpensive form of protein with poor absorption properties.

Laura Binetti

CARBOHYDRATE

While admitting that the carbohydrate in MET-Rx is a good source – maltodextrin – Infinity points out that nothing is included to make sure those carbohydrates are broken down and delivered to the body. Therefore they have added the enzyme amylase to their product to speed the rate at which carbohydrates are broken down by the body.

FATS

This is the one catagory where Infinity feels their product is far superior to MET-Rx. According to Infinity, the fat used in MET-Rx is from partially hydrogenated coconut oil which according to most biochemists is one of the worst sources available. It raises cholesterol and LDL, and is one of the greatest contributors to cardiovascular disease.

Another of Infinity's contentious issues is the method of preparation of MET-Rx's fatty oils. According to Infinity, MET-Rx uses hydrogenation techniques which convert "cis" forms into "trans" forms. (see Chapter Twenty-One on "Oils") As the body evolved to use the naturally occuring "cis" forms, the introduction of large amounts of "trans" forms can play havoc with long-term health.

To avoid the previous, Definition uses lecithin as its fat source – one of the few fats that keeps cholesterol levels low and soluble (that is, less likely to form sticky, plaque deposits). In terms of amount, MET-Rx provides two grams of fat per serving while Definition contains less than one gram.

VITAMINS

Besides the previous nutrients, Infinity feels its product has the edge in vitamin quality too. Their contention with MET-Rx is source. MET-Rx supposedly uses synthetic vitamins which are only a fraction of the whole food-vitamin complex. Your body must come up with the other components on its own. The vitamins in Definition are from whole food sources and according to Infinity contain the whole vitamin complex, not just segments.

MINERALS

Although both MET-Rx and Definition provide a good source of minerals, Infinity feels their product is better given the binding process. In order for minerals to be absorbed and utilized properly by the body, they must first be bound to something. The minerals in MET-Rx are bound to phosphates, chlorides, citrates, oxides, sulfates, and carbonates. According to Infinity – and backed up by other biochemical research – such substances produce bonding that makes for poor mineral absorption. With the average range being two to four percent, you would have to consume 50 milligrams to absorb one to two milligrams of the mineral (this leads to the question,

Mark Erpelding

What happens to the other 48 milligrams?). Infinity says it has solved the absorption problem by using amino acid-bound minerals. This is the state in which the minerals exist naturally so absorption is "guaranteed'" to be in the 95 to 100 percent range.

As an example to show the "superiority" of their product, Infinity compares the sources of chromium between Definition and MET-Rx. As discussed earlier, chromium is one of the most essential minerals in the body and is involved in such metabolic processes as fat burning and insulin regulation. Definition contains a unique, patented form of chromium called Chromium Chelavite, while MET-Rx uses chromium picolinate. According to Infinity their product has the ability to reduce cortisol levels, and they use research results to back up these claims. Chromium picolinate, however, is one of the poorest sources of chromium available and in some cases may be toxic to the liver.

Paul Dillett and Flex Wheeler reflect on the competition at hand.

HERBS

It is easy to compare this catagory as MET-RX contains no herbal products. Definition on the other hand contains ten whole food herbs. Infinity included these in their product to address the unknown factor. No credible biochemist would suggest that science has identified all the substances needed by the body for proper functioning. No doubt there are hundreds of compounds in food that are just as essential to life as the more well-known nutrients of protein, vitamins, and minerals. Infinity has choosen herbs known for their nutrient composition, thus insuring the body is getting the maximum amount of nutrients possible.

SWEETENERS, ENZYMES, AND COST

Like herbs, Infinity has added numerous enzymes to its product to aid digestion, while MET-Rx has not. Included in these are protease, lipase, amylase, and cellulase. Infinity adds that they have provided all the enzymes necessary to break down all the included nutrients.

 With regards to sweeteners, Infinity uses low-glycemic fructose and raw honey in its product, while MET-Rx uses aspartame – a compound that Infinity quickly adds has been linked to side effects such as dizziness, nausea, headaches, and in rare cases visual disturbances.

 The final comparison catagory is cost. Infinity raises the question of why MET-Rx costs more per serving – $3.16 versus $1.49 – when they supposedly use inferior and cheaper ingredients. Infinity points out that for a little under half the price, Definition provides much more in the way of nutrition.

IS IT BETTER?

As with any supplement, there are going to be varying opinions on this issue. MET-Rx is still the most popular metabolic optimizer available, although they did have a head start. Definition on the other hand is the new kid on the block, and as such must establish credibilty. They are to be admired for their advertising strategy which directly compares the two products. If Infinity's claims are true on paper, their product is superior. But there are a number of points to keep in mind. First, Infinity had the benefit of taking MET-Rx's label of ingredients and improving on it, adding more compounds of supposedly better quality. Second, quality on paper doesn't always translate into practical results. There are probably just as many bodybuilders who achieve great results from MET-Rx as Definition. Third, Infinity based their comparisons on the original MET-Rx product. As would be expected, MET-Rx is being upgraded to combat the new upstarts challenging their position at the top. In doing so they are no doubt fielding a product that is, according to their ads, "only one step in a continuing evolution in nutritional therapy for optimizing human metabolism."

EAS PRODUCTS

EAS – Experimental and Applied Sciences – is the brainchild of Bill Phillips – familar to most readers as the writer of the *Anabolic Reference Guide* and updates, and the series of *Supplement Review* books produced by his company Mile High Publications. Bill's contribution to the sport of bodybuilding is enormous, especially since the introduction of the ground-breaking magazine, *Muscle Media*. EAS was set up to produce and market the best supplements possible, with out the hype that usually accompanies such products. Being an avid bodybuilder himself, Bill was tired of outrageous claims by supplement manufacturers that promised so much but offered so

little. Not wanting to join such a fraternity, Bill used his resources to launch EAS – a scientifically based supplement research company, devoted soley to producing the very best bodybuilding supplements. Unlike many supplements, EAS products are backed by credible scientific research – one of the underlying philosophies of EAS/*Muscle Media*. Although they have other products, the following are two of their most recent and best selling. In fact, EAS is giving the sport's leader, MET-Rx, a run for its money.

PHOSPHAGAIN

Although marketed by EAS, Phosphagain was initially developed from research carried out by Dr. Richard Krieder of Memphis University. Dr. Krieder decided to investigate the effectiveness of numerous supplements on gaining lean body mass. He chose 28 bodybuilders, each of whom had about six years of training under their belts. Before starting the experiment Dr. Krieder measured the subjects' fat and muscle content. The experiment consisted of dividing the subjects into three groups. One group received a commercially available weight-gain supplement; a second group was given a carbohydrate supplement containing maltodextrin; while the third received the newly designed Phosphagain product.

The 28 bodybuilders followed an identical training routine and diet for 28 days and then had their bodyfat and muscle levels measured. The first two groups gained about 1.47 pounds of lean muscle tissue, but group one also gained about 1.56 pounds of fat. Group two – the carbohydrate group – appeared to lose .11 pounds of fat.

The most amazing results were demonstrated by the Phosphagain group which after 28 days gained 4.44 pounds of muscle tissue while losing .26 pounds of fat. What this means is that the Phosphagain group gained 302 percent more muscle while ingesting far fewer calories.

WHAT IT CONTAINS

The researchers who designed Phosphagain set out to develop a product that could stimulate lean muscle tissue without supplying huge amounts of calories. Although many in the bodybuilding game feel bodybuilders need to consume thousands of calories a day to grow, keep in mind many of the most popular bodybuilding drugs (clenbuterol, testosterone, insulin, etc.) work even if food intake is low in calories. Using this as a guide, Anthony Almada and colleagues developed Phosphagain – a "low-calorie lean-mass stimulator."

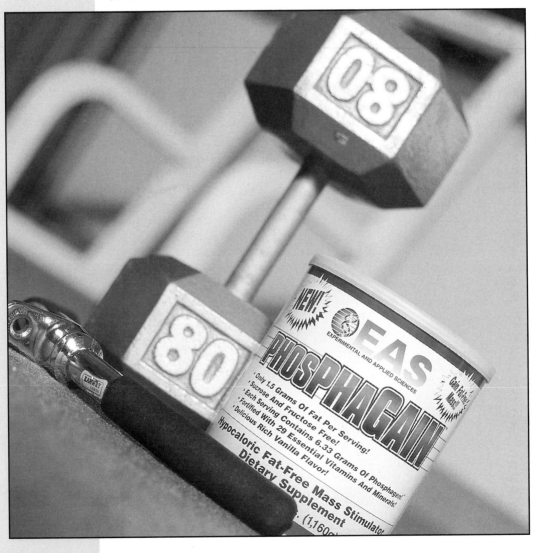

Laura Bass

On the surface, Phosphagain compares well with other popular optimizers, supplying 20 grams of protein, 19 grams of carbs, and 50 percent of all RDA vitamins and minerals per serving. Where Phosphagain comes out ahead is in fat and calorie content. Unlike similar products which contain 2 grams of fat per serving (one notable exception being RX-Fuel which is supposedly fat free), Phosphagain contains only 1.5 grams of fat. But perhaps the biggest difference is in calories supplied – 180 per serving versus 250 to 260.

The backbone to Phosphagain's effectiveness is a patented mixture called Nitrogenin. This formula developed by Experimental and Applied Sciences contains a select mixture of soy-free, high-quality protein with reduced lactose content. Also included is a simple/complex carbohydrate mix, and vitamins and minerals. And if this was not enough, EAS added creatine in the form of pure creatine monohydrate to Phosphogain.

This last point led to some critics suggesting that Phosphagain's benefits were due to the creatine alone. To test this, EAS compared the results of creatine-alone users with Phosphagain users. As expected, creatine's effects appeared to be amplified by the other constituents of Phosphagain.

Rounding out the ingredients of Phosphagain are the amino acids glutamine and taurine (we should add taurine is a "contested" amino acid and while some biochemists accept it as an amino, others only go as far as to say it has amino-like properties). The importance of glutamine was discussed earlier. Suffice to say, it is crucial to muscle growth and development, playing a major role in DNA and RNA synthesis.

Taurine is thought by many to be a nonessential amino acid, which means it can be synthesized in the body from other amino acids – specifically cysteine and methionine. Recent research suggests taurine is an important part of many physiological mechanisms. It functions as an antioxidant. Tissues that produce high amounts of oxidants also contain increased levels of taurine. For example, the retinas of the eyes contain high concentrations of taurine, and animals with taurine-synthesizing deficiencies often

go blind. There is even evidence to suggest newborn infants who are not breast-fed may be at increased risk for developing taurine deficiencies.

Related to the previous is the ability of taurine to possibly counteract the negative effects of clenbuterol – one of which is to decrease taurine levels. Rats given clenbuterol showed a marked increase in taurine excretion, and while the reasons are not fully understood, it is believed clen-buterol removed the necessary precursor amino acids from the liver and concentrated them in the muscles (taurine is primarily synthesized in the liver).

Another function of taurine is to instigate insulin-like effects. Although not conclusive, the evidence suggests taurine may be able to stimulate insulin receptors found on the outside of the cell. Once stimulated these receptors signal the cell to increase carbohydrate and amino acid transport – both of which contribute to increased muscle synthesis. Given all of the previous it's easy to see why a bodybuilder might want to take Phosphogain, if for no other reason than to keep taurine levels high.

MYOPLEX

After Dr. Connelly developed MET-Rx, his next step was distributing it to the bodybuilding market. With a huge distribution network already in place from running Mile High Productions, it was inevitable that Bill Phillips would become involved in distributing MET-Rx; and most agree that Bill played a major role in MET-Rx's early success. Eventually, however, a point was reached where the popularity of MET-Rx outgrew even Bill's abilities to supply the mass-market appeal the product had obtained. Eventually all parties concerned agreed to allow a California-based company to take over MET-Rx's distribution. Not wanting to be left out of the high-tech supplement business, Bill turned his attention to creating MYOPLEX PLUS – his own rival to MET-Rx.

As with all EAS products, MYOPLEX PLUS contains only those ingredients that have been scientifically proven to have some ergogenic potential. Using MET-Rx as a guide, EAS produced a product that is in many respects superior to the original MET-Rx product.

WHAT IT CONTAINS

The chief ingredient of MYOPLEX PLUS is ion-exchange whey protein (42 grams per serving) – considered by most experts to be the best protein source for bodybuilders (this is 2 to 5 grams per serving higher than similar products). In addition, the product contains such ergogenic ingredients as alpha-ketogluterate, taurine, arginine, borage oil, and HCA (none of which were included in the original MET-Rx product). Other selling points of MYOPLEX PLUS are its taste, easy mixing ability, and mildness on the stomach. Further, MYOPLEX PLUS is moderately priced compared to many other high-tech optimizers. In terms of fat and carbohydrates, MYOPLEX PLUS contains the same amounts per serving – 2 grams and 24 grams respectively.

EAS – LEADING THE WAY

Given the success of *Muscle Media*, and the "telling it like it is" reputation of Bill Phillips, it's not surprising that EAS has fast become a major player on the supplement scene. No doubt the future will see EAS release other great products that will provide bodybuilders with the latest in state-of-the-art supplements.

MUSCLETECH

If the rumors coming out of the labs of this new company are true, MuscleTech may be the most important supplement manufacturer of the next century.

MuscleTech is a new Canadian company whose main goal is to test the limits of state-of-the-art food supplements. Over the last couple of years they have been conducting studies using top professional and amateur bodybuilders – including the monstrous 350-pound Greg Kovacs. The data coming out of their labs suggests that their products are among the most effective ever produced. We know this sounds like more supplement hype, but two of those convinced of the findings are former *MuscleMag International* editor, Greg Zulak, and Dr. Mauro DiPasquale, one of the world's leading experts on ergogenic aids.

MuscleTech is headed by an individual who like many, had been bodybuilding for 10 years and felt ripped off by the claims of most supplement manufacturers. Rather than get depressed and drop the whole matter, he took the bull by the horns, so to speak, and vowed to do something about it. Instead of using hype as his guide, he undertook a massive review of the scientific literature, attempting to separate the biochemical fact from myth.

"After perusing the material I have to say that, if it's true, these may be the most powerful and effective supplements ever concocted."

– Greg Zulak, former *MuscleMag* editor and noted bodybuilding writer commenting on the potential of MuscleTech's products.

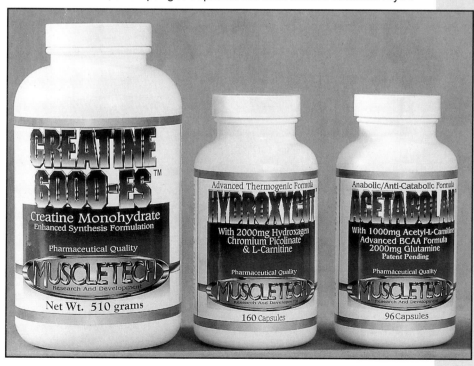

One of his first findings was that most supplements had drawbacks – usually in the form of lacklustre quality or improper dosage. After thousands of hours of research and experimentation, MuscleTech feels that they have developed the most potent and effective supplements ever created.

Convinced that certain food supplements did have ergogenic potential, they set out to determine which these were and in what dosages. Instead of following the old school of thought – starting with low dosages and working up – the company went for broke at the very beginning, and gave test subjects the maximum dosages possible.

Another contention that MuscleTech has with most current supplements is their lack of "synergistic nutrients." As discussed earlier, synergism is the term used to describe the increased effect of two or more substances combined together – much more so than the effects produced separately. The expert staff at MuscleTech are strong believers in supplement synergism, but unlike many, believes the opposite can also occur – supplements taken in the wrong dosages or combinations can be rendered ineffective.

Greg Kovacs

THE SUPPLEMENTS

To give you some idea of the ground MuscleTech is breaking, let's take a look at three of their new products – Acetabolan, Hydroxycut, and Creatine 6000 ES.

ACETABOLAN

Acetabolan is MuscleTech's trade name for the substance acetylcarnitine (ACL). The product also contains glutamine, OKG, and branched-chain amino acids. Unlike the false claims made about Smilax, boron, and yohimbine, studies have shown that ACL can actually increase serum testosterone levels brought on by various forms of stress. As exercise is one form of stress, Acetabolan may be an ideal supplement for a hard-training bodybuilder. What's more, ACL doesn't appear to have any of the side effects often associated with anabolic steroids or other testosterone-based compounds. According to Greg Zulak, besides the previous positive attributes, coming off ACL doesn't produce depression, gynecomastia, or increased estrogen levels. If this is not enough to convince you, many bodybuilders in the studies, who previously used steroids, report that ACL's effects are as good, and in some cases better than the anabolics.

Research suggests ACL is a very powerful anticatabolic agent.

Besides ACL's anabolic effects and apparent lack of side effects, the research suggests that the substance is a very powerful anticatabolic agent. As many informed bodybuilders know, one of the biggest detriments to muscle growth is superintense training. This is because intense exercise causes the body to release increased amounts of catabolic hormones like cortisol. Such agents immediately begin to remove amino acids from muscle tissue, leading to protein degeneration – the end result being muscle wasting. Exercise also raises testosterone levels and the two "fight it out" in determining whether the individual grows, remains the same, or heaven forbid, loses muscular bodyweight. The last scenario is called overtraining and is caused by too much exercise, as well as not allowing the body sufficient time to recover between workouts. Here's where ACL comes into play.

If individuals push too hard (as many do these days in trying to imitate their favorite bodybuilding stars), instead of increasing their testosterone levels they may cause serum concentrations to drop. Studies using ACL show that it has the ability to prevent such hormone decreases, allowing the body to remain in a net anabolic state in much the same manner as that produced by anabolic steroids (the main reason why many suggest renaming anabolic steroids to anticatabolic steroids).

We should add that the benefits of ACL are not limited to bodybuilders as the medical community has shown great interest in acetylcarnitine. Although the evidence is preliminary, ACL appears to lessen the effects of aging, as well as reduce cholesterol levels. It also seems to increase reflex action and stimulate memory and other cognitive operations – decreases of which are common to most eldely people. There is even evidence to suggest that ACL slows the deteriorative effects of Alzheimer's disease.

Finally, perhaps the most desired effects of ACL are those concerning sex drive. Unlike steroids and other testosterone derivatives, which cause flutuations in sex drive, ACL only increases sex drive by increasing natural testosterone levels. Not only is this a benefit to bodybuilders, but elderly males will find the product helpful in battling age-related declines in sex drive.

Dorian Yates

HYDROXYCUT

Hydroxycut is MuscleTech's name for their product containing hydroxycitric acid (HCA). Numerous studies have shown this compound to be a very powerful fat-burning agent. It does this by reducing the conversion of carbohydrate to fat. It also increases the storage of carbohydrate as glycogen – leading to better muscle pumps and more energy during workouts.

Besides 1000 milligrams of HCA, MuscleTech's product also contains ephedrine and caffeine – both of which are well-known to bodybuilders as fat-burning agents. By combining the three, MuscleTech has created what they believe to be the most potent fat-burning supplement available.

CREATINE 6000ES

By far the most popular supplement to come along in recent years is creatine monohydrate. But unlike previous fads, creatine is backed up by both scientific research and the great results experienced by virtually all users. MuscleTech has developed what they feel is the most potent creatine product available – Creatine 6000ES.

Creatine 6000ES is named because of the amount of creatine per serving – 6000 milligrams! But MuscleTech hasn't stopped there. Research carried out over the last few years indicates creatine is best absorbed and synthesized by the body when the amino acids glycine, arginine, and methionine are present in high concentrations. To meet these demands, MuscleTech has produced the only creatine supplement containing these important aminos.

THE RESEARCH

To compare their products with other well-known supplements, MuscleTech began a series of studies involving 12 test subjects. To keep the studies as accurate as possible, the subjects chosen were all advanced bodybuilders. Not only do advanced trainers know their bodies, but more important, make far less gains than a typical beginner who may put on 10 to 20 pounds in a few short months. Another requirement was that the subjects were in a continious state of training. This helps rule out the phenomenom of muscle memory where bodybuilders gain back lost muscle tissue at a faster rate than gaining for the first time.

Kim Chizevsky

To standardize the tests, the subjects were put on similar training programs, had their muscle size and bodyfat percentage measured, and were requested to keep their diets the same as before. Additionally, each swore not to use other supplements or performance-enhancing drugs.

The study was then divided into three phases – each lasting 30 days. During the first month all subjects received a high-quality whey protein supplement providing 60 extra grams of protein a day. The next month saw the whey protein being replaced by a high-calorie weight-gain powder (2000 extra calories). Finally the subjects received a stack of MuscleTech's three previously described supplements during the last month of the test.

At the end of the three-month period the results were tabulated and comparisons made. For simplicity we have listed the results in the following table.

SUPPLEMENT	MUSCLE GAIN	FAT GAIN OR LOSS
Whey Protein	1.7 lb	1.6 lb loss
High Calorie	1.1 lb	4.8 lb gain
MuscleTech	8.9 lb	4.1 lb loss

Jean-Pierre Fux

To say the results were impressive is an understatement. The MuscleTech trial showed gains of 500 percent more muscle tissue and losses of 250 percent more bodyfat than either of the other supplement trials. As Greg Zulak stated after hearing the results, "MuscleTech subjects experienced greater gains than those I've read of in some steroid-use studies."

SIDE EFFECTS

As of yet no side effects have been reported in any of the MuscleTech test subjects. This is surprising given the dosages used and results obtained. It is possible that the short duration of MuscleTech's research has played a role in this. It generally takes a couple of years (not counting allergic reactions of course) to "feel out" a particular drug or supplement.

Having said that, maybe we should give MuscleTech the benefit of the doubt. Perhaps they have created the perfect supplements – as powerful as anabolic steroids, without the associated side effects. Only time will tell what the future holds for this exciting new supplement manufacturer from Canada.

Robert Kennedy's Formula One Elite Supplement Series is sold exclusively through MuscleMag International retail stores.

MUSCLEMAG INTERNATIONAL – NOW IN THE RUNNING

Robert Kennedy, known to most of you as the founder and publisher of *MuscleMag International* (one of the leading hardcore bodybuilding magazines) and *Oxygen* (a phenomenal female fitness magazine), has finally come out with his own supplement line, Formula One Elite Supplement Series. No doubt about it, Formula One is truly in the running with the BIG BOYS! Formula One Elite Supplement Series is sold exclusively through MuscleMag International retail stores, and although this state-of-the-art line is relatively new, the bodybuilding community is already raving about the physical improvements resulting from its regular use. The Formula One Elite Supplement Series includes Pure L-Glutamine, Ion-Exchange Whey Protein, Creatine Pre-Load, and Egg Albumen. MuscleMag plans on continuing it's renowned reputation by producing an ultra high-quality supplement line for bodybuilders and general sports enthusiasts at an affordable price.

BOOK NINE

Putting It
All Together

Melissa Coates

Flex Wheeler

Timing Your Supplement Intake

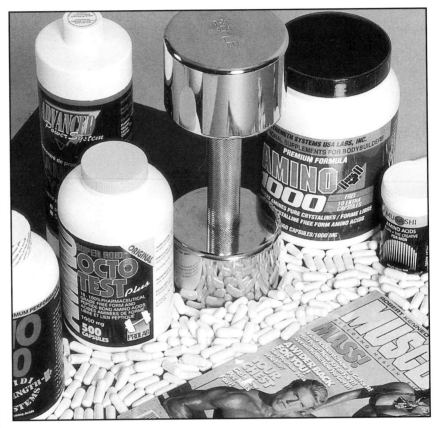

"Vince has determined that his students make satisfactory progress when they alternate using supplements for three days and then lay off for three days. There is no reason to doubt him, and you will avoid overloading your body if you follow this method. Take all your supplements for three days and then set them aside for days four, five, and six."

– Norman Zale, regular *MuscleMag* contributor offering advice on long-term supplementation.

Throughout this book we have provided a broad introduction to the many catagories of ergogenic supplements and procedures. It's now up to you to give them a try and choose your favorites. For obvious reasons we can't recommend the substances that are illegal – no matter how effective they might be. If you decide to try some of these, remember, the authorities are always looking for scapegoats. And the media is quickly tiring of covering the arrests of dealers and users of such street drugs as cocaine, heroine, and LSD. But a bodybuilder arrested for steroid possession – now that's glamorous and entertaining! All it takes is a few bottles of Winstrol and you're the star of *Hard Copy* and facing hard time in a penitentiary. Our advice is to avoid steroids, growth hormone, and other illegal performance-enhancing drugs – no matter how tempting.

Having said that, most of the substances and procedures described in this book are legal and readily available. Of course this does not rule out side effects, and where applicable, heed the dangers we have presented.

Just because something is for over-the-counter sale does not mean it's "safe." There isn't a substance in existence that won't produce side effects in a certain percentage of a given population. To some, vitamins are toxic, to others high concentrations of protein produce digestive problems. And given the newness of many of the more popular supplements, we can expect reports of side effects to increase as time goes on.

THE PERFECT SUPPLEMENT ROUTINE?

Like training, we can honestly say there is no "right" way to supplement – but there are definitely "wrong" ways. And like exercising, devising the best supplement routine is a matter of personal experimentation. Only you can decide what supplements work best for you. We can give general advice, but nothing specific. True, if you are lucky enough to have access to a knowledgable personal trainer like John Parrillo, Greg Zulak, or Scott Abel, specific advice can be obtained, but for the most part you'll have to work things out on your own.

CHRONOBIOLOGY – IS IT ALL IN THE TIMING?

No other species is as rigid in conforming to "time" as human beings. On average we work 9-to-5 jobs; eat around 7 am, 12 pm, and 6 pm; and go to bed between 11 pm and 12 am. Our whole lives are so programmed around time that we have invented a piece of machinery to measure it – affectionately

Like exercising, devising the best supplement routine is a matter of personal experimentation.
– Dave Fisher and Sue Price

"Sport supplements are often used without considering what point the individual bodybuilder is at within his training cycle, or how he is performing physically. In other words, supplementation is often used in a shotgun manner without any scientific basis. Furthermore, supplements are often taken without determining exactly which supplements are needed at any particular time in the bodybuilder's training cycle."

– Jay Schroeder, regular *MuscleMag* contributor commenting on the haphazard approach taken by many bodybuilders with regards to supplementation.

known as the clock. But for those who feel time is a man-made entity, controlled by the good people at Timex, let us be the first to point out that time was around a long time (no pun intended) before we were.

Humans have adjusted to time by evolving daily cycles called circadian rhythms. The word circadian comes from the Latin "about a day" and forms the basis of the science of studying biological time called chronobiology. Scientists in this field have discovered that humans are under the influence of many factors – both internal and external – which control how we measure and perceive time. Some, like the monthly lunar cycle and daily tides, are precise and can be measured. Others, like the amount of light, temperature, and even social contacts, are less consistent and produce wide variation among individuals.

Mike Quinn

As researchers are discovering, the human body has its own "clock," called a biological clock, which conforms more or less to the 24-hour day – the amount of time it takes the earth to spin 360 degrees on its axis. In this age of *Star Trek* and *The X-Files*, we could assume that aliens from another planet with a different rotational period have different rhythms.

Those who are regular, long-distance jet travelers are very familiar with their biological clocks. If you are used to sleeping at 11 pm, traveling three or four "time zones" will shift your biological clock off by many hours. Take a trip half way round the world and nighttime for you is daytime for the local residents. This effect is called jet lag, and it generally takes one day per time zone crossed to fully readjust to the new sleep and wake periods.

APPLICATIONS TO BODYBUILDING

What's all this to do with supplements? Well, the study of chronobiology has allowed physicians to get the maximum benefit out of drug therapy. Just as energy levels and moods flutuate during the day, so too does body chemistry heavily depend on circadian rhythms. As an example, heart attacks occur most frequently in the early morning hours, due to the greatest concentration of clotting factors occuring at this time. But conveniently, aspirin – one of the best anticlotting drugs – is also absorbed most effectively at this time. Conversely, other anticlotting drugs like heparin are absorbed best at night. Such factors are taken into account by physicians to insure patients are getting the best care possible.

Another use for chronobiology is to design your supplement schedule. Given the body's "peaks" and "valleys" for certain nutrients, you can consume supplements to match the body's fluctuations in hormones, water balance, and energy demands. Given the limited data available on the lesser-known supplements, we will limit our chronobiology discussion to four major nutrients: protein, carbohydrates, vitamins, and minerals.

As a final comment we must point out that chronobiology is not an exact science. The following is a general discussion on arranging supplements according to biorhythms. As with most aspects of bodybuilding, supplement timing is often a matter of individual variation.

PROTEIN TIMING

Given that protein is a nutrient mainly used for tissue synthesis, not energy, it doesn't make much sense to consume it before or during a workout. A large protein meal before a workout can not only give you a bloated feeling, but the extra food in your stomach will divert much blood away from the muscle cells. Further, research suggests protein synthesis shuts down during exercise, and the body diverts most of its metabolic processes to energy production. The one possible exception to the previous is the intake of amino acids – especially the branched-chain aminos.

For the first 60 to 90 minutes of exercise, the body primarily uses stored glycogen as its fuel source. If, however, the workout lasts longer than 90 minutes, glycogen supplies run out, forcing the body to start using another fuel source; and as is often the case the alternative source is protein – specifically amino acids.

After exercise ceases, the body continues to stockpile aminos, reaching a peak about 90 minutes after the workout. Satisfied that high amounts of energy are no longer needed, the body begins to repair muscle damage sustained during exercise. It seems logical then to consume aminos before a workout or immediately after, and to limit heavy protein intake to postworkout time periods.

You may want to consider matching your protein intake with your training schedule for maximum benefit. – Chris Cormier

Besides matching protein intake to exercise, there is evidence to suggest that the body also absorbs protein and aminos at different rates throughout the day. Studies with army subjects show that when liver is eaten at 8 am there immediately follows an increase in blood-plasma levels, while eating the same liver at 8 pm shows decreases in circulating amino acid levels. In addition, increasing the amount of protein consumed had no effect on the previous results.[1] The researchers theorized that protein control was under the influence of such hormones as HGH and thyroid hormone, produced in the greatest amounts during sleep. Further, it appears protein utilization was not so much dependant on amount as timing.

CARBOHYDRATE TIMING

Although the consensus is to take simple carbohydrates during or close to your workout to provide energy for exercise and speed recovery afterwards, there is good evidence to suggest eating your complex carbohydrates at different times during the day.

As soon as sleep sets in, the body begins drawing on glycogen reserves to get it through the night. Look at it this way, an average person doesn't consume any food for approximately six to eight hours. As these hours are the body's primary repair periods, it must rely soley on stored energy sources. Most biochemists suggest that liver-glycogen stores are used up by 4 to 6 am. This means when you get up in the morning, the last thing you should do is skip breakfast (the name should indicate the importance of the meal – breakfast – "breaking" the "fast" of the previous night). It follows that your first priority is to get some good carbohydrates into your system. While simple sugars will do, by far the best sources are complex in nature. Many pro bodybuilders start their day with a bowl of rice or some pasta-based food. Another favourite is oatmeal. Not only does this replenish glycogen stores lost during the night, but it also fills the muscles for future exercise – which for most is later in the day.

The other time to eat carbohydrates is before bedtime. This not only increases liver-glycogen levels, but also facilitates the release of the serotonin precusor, tryptophan, into the brain. As discused earlier, serotonin is one of the neurotransmitters responsible for initiating sleep. Of course there is a possible disadvantage to such a practice. Although not conclusive, the evidence suggests HGH release is reduced when blood-sugar levels are high. So it all comes downs to priorities – increasing glycogen supplies or increasing HGH release.

VITAMIN AND MINERAL TIMING

Vitamin chronobiology is usually a factor of vitamin type. Water-based vitamins (B and C) are not stored by the body, and as such are rapidly excreted

> **"Supplements should never be used continiously since the body adapts to them and may shut down or alter some of the normal pathways. The end result may be that the body needs the supplement to function normally. This is a type of addiction although not to be compared to the addiction seen with illicit drugs. Intermittent use of supplements, especially if you feel they help, should not be a problem."**
>
> – Dr. Mauro DiPasquale, regular *MuscleMag* columnist.

Flex Wheeler and Nasser El Sonbaty on wash day.

through the kidneys. This means for maximum benefit you should take them in small amounts periodically throughout the day – about every three to four hours.

The fat-based vitamins are stored by the body and don't need to be consumed daily – although most bodybuilders do. There are some who argue that vitamin E is not stored and is excreted in 12 to 20 hours. But as this is a contentious issue we don't suggest daily megadoses of the vitamin. Instead take small amounts daily or every second day.

Mineral timing is another matter. Research suggests calcium excretion is highest during the sleep hours and most physicians recommend taking calcium supplements right before bed. With regards to potassium, the data reveals that for most people, potassium levels peak between 7 and 8 pm. This is due to the potassium-excreting effects of cortisol earlier in the day. Given that potassium levels are lowest in morning and mid afternoon, it follows that such potassium-rich foods as bananas be consumed during this time period.

> Spread your supplements out over all your meals – including snacks. This insures adequate nutrients are continuously fusing into your system.
> – Sue Price and Dave Fisher

SUPPLEMENTATION FOR MAXIMUM GROWTH!

As a way of concluding the book, we thought we would tie things together by giving a hypothetical daily supplement schedule. Please don't take this as gospel. It is merely a way to show how supplements can be spread over a typical day to benefit your training in the most effective manner possible. If you decide to follow it word for word, fine. But at the first sign of trouble (that is, MCT oil makes you nauseous, vitamins produce diarrhea, HCA produces sore joints, etc.), either omit the given supplement or switch to a different brand.

We have divided the schedule into seven catagories, and for simplicity we discuss each in their daily sequence. All the supplements mentioned are available at better health-food and drug stores.

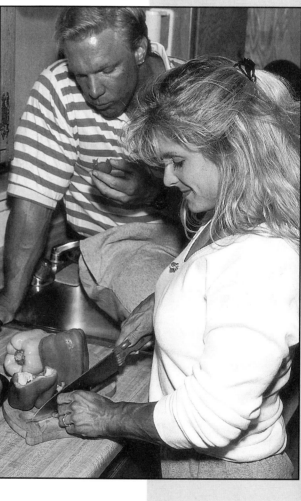

BEFORE BREAKFAST

The best supplements to take immediately upon waking are amino acid combinations designed to promote growth-hormone release. From a scientific standpoint, the best are arginine and lysine preparations, but there is some evidence to suggest orthinine also works.

WITH MEALS

It's amazing how many bodybuilders consume dozens of supplement pills on an empty stomach, not realizing that most supplements need to be combined with food to be effective. And don't assume that taking them all with one meal is going to speed things up either. For maximum benefit, spread the supplements out over all your meals – including snacks. This insures adequate nutrients are continuously fusing into your system. Although it varies, you should take the following supplements with meals: vitamins,

Astrid Falconi

minerals, liver tablets, free-form amino acids, branched-chain amino acids, fat-burning supplements like choline, inositol, carnitine, and HCA as well as medium-chain triglyceride oil.

BEFORE YOUR WORKOUT

The main goal of a preworkout snack is to boost energy reserves, and leading the way in this regard are creatine supplements. Try "loading" 20 to 30 grams a day for 7 to 10 days, followed by a maintenance schedule of 5 to 10 grams a day. Virtually every bodybuilder who uses the stuff swears by it for increasing stamina and boosting recovery between workouts.

Other preworkout supplements are carbohydrate preparations, inosine, and electrolyte drinks. A word of advice on carbohydrates: Don't load up on simple sugars only to cause a massive release of insulin 30 minutes later. Instead of energy to spare, you may become drowsy halfway through your workout.

DURING YOUR WORKOUT

For obvious reasons you don't want to place much of a demand on the digestive system while working out. Instead, limit your consumption to sipping drinks containing carbohydrates and electrolytes. The former will keep energy levels high, while the latter replaces electrolytes lost through sweating.

IMMEDIATELY AFTER WORKING OUT

Although a few bodybuilders like to consume a large meal immediately after working out, most individuals cannot handle heavy amounts of food in the first 60 minutes after exercise. Therefore, we recommend taking some sort of carbohydrate beverage to replace glycogen levels lost during the workout.

To meet the muscles' requirements, we suggest taking a good protein supplement as well. Supplements such as desiccated liver and amino acids serve nicely in this regard. If you have trouble gaining weight, try a nutrient-packed energy bar. Many of these products are loaded with most of the main food constituents. If it's contest time though, avoid the bars containing high levels of fat.

SNACKS

Although frowned upon by many in the general population, snacks are a must for a bodybuilder trying to gain lean muscle tissue. Snacks often form the extra two or three meals eaten by bodybuilders to obtain those badly needed calories.

Snacks can consist of just about every type of supplement out there. The most common, however, are protein shakes. We suggest a good milk and egg protein, or one of the latest whey supplements. For those vegetarian bodybuilders reading, there are numerous plant proteins available, but make sure you choose one that contains all the amino acids. Most plant products are deficient in one or more amino acids – especially the essential aminos – so it's up to you to choose a product that has been engineered to meet specific requirements.

Although it's tempting to combine a dozen pills or tablets together to form a snack, we strongly suggest avoiding this practice. As stated earlier, most nutrients – especially vitamins and minerals – are required for digestion and absorption of other food substances. Taking them on an empty stomach is, for the most part, a waste of money. Protein tablets and amino acids are the exception. Most of these products are designed to be taken on their own. Many bodybuilders find washing them down with a glass of milk makes an ideal snack.

In recent years protein shakes have been given a run for their money by the latest high-tech metabolic optimizers. Products such as MET-Rx, Cybergenics, and Phospogain are fast becoming the snack of choice by hard-training bodybuilders. And although they're on the pricy side, they nevertheless hold the advantage of supplying most of the known food nutrients in one serving. If you have the extra cash we suggest giving one of these products a try. It may be just the thing needed to kick start your system into new growth.

"We could reach those levels of performances in 10 years with nonsteroidal anabolics and anticatabolics. In fact, I believe we can go beyond where we are now."

– Dan Duchaine, steroid guru, and best-selling author commenting on the potential of natural ergogenic aids.

Bruce Patterson pushes past the pain barrier for a greater muscle pump.

BEFORE BED

Although we don't recommend eating before bed, there are a few supplements that can be taken to make "dreamland" more productive. To maximize HGH levels during sleep, take your amino-acid growth-hormone releasers once again. As discussed earlier in the book, HGH levels are at their maximum during the sleeping hours.

If getting to sleep is a problem try a few capsules of tryptophan. This amino works great as a natural sleep aid. Frank Zane, three-time Mr. Olympia, swears by its effectiveness.

Given the long stretch (an average of six to eight hours) without eating, we suggest consuming a small amount of carbohydrates before bed. Nothing heavy, just enough to reduce the amount removed from muscles during the overnight sleep period.

CONCLUSION

There you have it, a super supplement guide for maximizing your progress. The skeptics among you will no doubt argue that most of these are a waste of money. In a few cases, yes. But understand that ALL the top bodybuilders in the world, both amateur and professional, make supplementation an important part of their lives. It can be argued that the sport's "older" members never used the variety of supplements presently being taken by today's patrons. True, but then again most of the supplements available today didn't exist forty or fifty years ago. If they did, we can be sure the "guys from Muscle Beach" would have used them – they used everything else.

There's also the matter of physique quality to think about. Today's bodybuilders are much larger, stronger, and more ripped than their counterparts of forty years ago. And while some of it is due to advances in pharmacology – especially HGH – the fact remains that many of the patrons of Venice Beach (forty years ago) also used performance-enhancing drugs, yet their physiques don't measure up to today's standards. (This is a much debated point given today's emphasis on mass at any cost, versus the emphasis on symmetry and proportions thirty or forty years ago.)

It's all but impossible not to conclude that supplements enhance performance. And while some of them are almost totally worthless in their benefits, others like creatine, HCA, and the latest metabolic optimizers are backed by solid scientific evidence.

Jason Arntz

Reference
1) J. Brainum, "Chronobiology," *Muscle and Fitness*, 51:7 (1990).

Dennis Newman

Questions and Answers

Jean-Pierre Fux

Throughout MuscleMag's twenty-five years of history, we have received literally thousands of questions concerning ergogenic aids. While we do our best to answer most of them, logistically we can't answer them all due to the huge numbers. For this reason the most popular questions are passed on to our regular columnists like Greg Zulak, Dr. Mauro DiPasquale, and Robert Kennedy. Each month the answers are printed in *MuscleMag International*. The following are just a sample of the questions received over the years.

ANOTHER DRUG BANNED

Q. Could you please let me know your opinion about a supplement called cyclofenil? I have heard a lot about it lately, that it works like a drug, so much so the FDA is pulling it off the market. Is cyclofenil any good and how safe is it?

A. Cyclofenil is a drug that has properties similar to HCG and clomid. It stimulates the testicles to produce more testosterone and thus increases the level of serum testosterone. Cyclofenil, once sold as an over-the-counter drug, must now be prescribed by a physician.

INSULIN INSENSITIVITY

Q. I have been hearing so much recently about "insulin sensitivity" and "insulin management" as the ultimate way to grow muscle. How do I improve my insulin sensitivity?

A. I am of the opinion, as are many researchers, that most people are somewhat insulin insensitive, which means your cells do not take in glucose as readily as they should. This leads to fat accumulation and a host of other problems. Before I tell you how to improve your insulin sensitivity, you should know what can cause insulin insensitivity. Diets that are high in saturated fat, the use of steroids or growth hormone, lack of exercise, high-carbohydrate or high-sugar diets, low-fiber intake, and many other factors can lead to insulin insensitivity. Nutrients that have been found to improve insulin sensitivity are chromium, vanadyl sulfate, vitamin E, vitamin C, magnesium, fiber, and omega-3 fatty acids.

LOWERING CORTISOL?

Q. A guy in my gym says he has this great new supplement called Cytadren. He claims it will lower cortisol and save muscle. Should I use this supplement? How much should I take?

A. Wow, hold the presses! Cytadren is not a supplement, but a drug used to treat Cushing's syndrome, which is a disease characterized by the overproduction of the muscle-wasting hormone cortisol. Since this is a supplement column, and not a drug column I am not going to spend a lot of time on this. Cytadren will certainly lower cortisol levels, but it has possible side effects such as joint pain and lower androgen output. Unless you have access to a lab that will monitor all your hormones on a weekly basis, I recommend you stay away from Cytadren.

THE BEST SUPPLEMENT?

Q. How about the much-advertised MET-Rx? Some of my friends from Seattle tell me they've gotten amazing results with this product.

A. Just like your friends, I have started taking the product MET-Rx. During his recent trip to Maui, Lee Labrada introduced me to it, and I have now taken it for three weeks, and have relied on it as a major source of protein. I must say that MET-Rx is the first protein supplement that doesn't give me any indigestion whatsoever, and my strength seems to be going up, plus I have more energy throughout the day. I also like MET-Rx because it tastes so good.

Roland Cziurlok strikes a pose.

THE TRUTH ABOUT STEROIDS

Q. I write to you because I seek the truth. Are steroids as bad as people would have me believe they are (I am not talking about megadoses of them) or is that the answer the government feeds us because they have yet to figure out a way to make a profit by selling them?

A. *You're right of course. Steroids aren't as bad for you as the media, bureaucrats, government and most physicians would have you believe. In fact, anabolic steroids are just like any other medication. If taken properly under a doctor's supervision they are perfectly safe – or at least as safe as, say, birth control pills.*

Bruce Patterson is in fine form.

BEWARE OF OUTLANDISH CLAIMS!

Q. I'd like to ask you something about supplements. There are so many on the market and they all make such wonderful claims. How do you know what is real and what is not? Should I spend my money on any of them? I'm very confused about this and I hope you can help me out.

A. *You're right. They all do make such wonderful claims, don't they? I don't know what's real and what's not. How do you know? One rule I go by is this: "If it sounds too good to be true, it probably is." But when it comes to comparing one vitamin to the next, who can tell? I just go for the most potent one. If I may say so, I do like Twinlab stuff. They seem to have some good honest products (and no I'm not on the Twinlab payroll).*

WHAT DO YOU TAKE?

Q. Can you tell me how you eat before and after training? Do you take supplements? Do you use protein powder?

A. *I do take supplements. I take a vitamin megapak with my breakfast in the morning. It's best to take vitamins with food or you may get an upset stomach. I train in the morning, so I get up about two hours before I plan to arrive at the gym. My breakfast is a very important meal and consists of mostly carbohydrates. I usually eat 2 ounces of oatmeal, 6 ounces of baked yam, and 6 egg whites. My training takes about one and a half to two hours. By then it's about time for lunch. My lunch usually consists of chicken or fish and a large green salad. My dinner is somewhat the same. I do not use protein powders because I enjoy eating protein rather than drinking it.*

BLOOD BOOSTERS?

Q. Can you tell me about the new drug EPO? I understand it is almost impossible to detect and will give an athlete a huge advantage.

A. In tests in Stockholm, Sweden, 15 average athletes were given EPO injections. According to Bjorn Ekblam (professor of physiology at Karolinska Institute, Stockholm) EPO (erythroporetin) can improve an athlete's performance amazingly. This does not mean that it would necessarily make a bodybuilder bigger or better. Its main effect is to increase aerobic efficiency. No side effects were noticed on the 15 test subjects as it is a natural hormone, but EPO proponents agree that an overdose could prove fatal. EPO is prescribed to treat anemia in chronic kidney failure patients on dialysis, as well as to treat severe anemia related to AZT therapy in HIV-infected patients (so as to decrease the need for transfusions). Yes, EPO is extremely difficult to detect in testing procedures.

YOHIMBE BARK

Q. Several months ago I purchased two products from a mail-order company – cyclofenil and yohimbe bark. I took the yohimbe bark for about one month with no results. I have been taking the cyclofenil for two months and have gained seven pounds, my lifts have gone up and I have noticed an unusual amount of acne on my back and arms. Could you tell me about these two products and if you recommend them as ergogenic agents? Are these products for real or are they just another placebo rip off like those described in your books?

Alq Gurley

A. Yohimbine is essentially useless as an ergogenic aid while cyclofenil has properties similar to HCG and clomid – it stimulates the testicles to produce more testosterone. This increased testosterone has resulted in your weight and strength gains, and in the acne. Cyclofenil must now be prescribed by a physician.

AMINO POWER!

Q. My question is about amino acids. I live in Canada and seeing how you're from Canada I thought you might know of a good product line that I can purchase here. There are so many different types of amino acids that I don't know which one to get.

A. Ordinarily I'm not in the habit of promoting or endorsing specific products, but I'll make an exception just this one time. A friend of mine in Canada has a brand-new line of top-grade amino acids. I've only used them for a short time because they're new, but they seem to be good quality and I'll continue to use them. I called my friend Brian in Canada to get the technical data on his aminos so I could relay it on to you. Here it is: It's the Amino 600 capsule produced by SportPharma Canada. It is a profiled blend of di- and tri-peptide-bonded pharmaceutical-grade amino acids derived from enzymatic digest of lactalbumin.

Sonny Schmidt

RALGRO - INTO THE UNKNOWN

Q. What's Ralgro? I have read that it is a protein/ anabolic agent. The *Merck Index* lists it as an anabolic (veterinary). What is its mechanism of action, and what are its side effects? Can it be used safely by humans?

A. No one really knows how Ralgro works although I've given a few possible mechanisms in some of the books that I've written. Several years ago I contacted the company that distributes Ralgro in Canada. I couldn't get a satisfactory answer from them as to Ralgro's mechanism of action. They don't know either. Since it's targeted for cattle and not people, there's no active research going on which is likely to give us an answer as to its safety and effectiveness in humans. I would not consider Ralgro any more dangerous than other drugs used by athletes. Still, it's not a drug I would recommend you use because I'm not sure just how it works and what the long-term effects are. There is some evidence to show that Ralgro, in some people, has significant estrogenic effects.

ONLY IN MODERATION

Q. Do you drink any alcohol? Is it okay to drink beer and wine occasionally? Does alcohol make it impossible to lose fat?

A. I have a glass of red or white wine two or three times a week. Based on everything I've read on alcohol consumption it seems that a moderate amount of wine is actually good for us. I don't know about beer, though. By cutting their consumption, some of my clients have lost pounds in just a couple of weeks and achieved a new trimmer midsection! A cup of dry wine has 204 calories, and a cup of 4.5 percent beer has 101 calories. Drinking wine or beer too often and in large quantities would certainly give you plenty of extra calories you don't need.

MORE ON "ROIDS"

Q. My question is about steroids. I'd like to know which ones are the best and where I can get them. Do you have any extras and if so, can you send them to me?

A. Oh boy, I know that a couple of issues ago I said something about all the pro bodybuilders being on drugs. And yes, drugs are very much used in our sport (all sports!). That's the way it is. But it's still a subject that is very touchy with a lot of people. It's not something that can be freely talked about without catching a lot of flack. Hell, if I told you what to take and where to get it, I'd probably be in court getting sued by someone fast. Hey, you're on your own on this one.

THE MYSTERY OF MINERALS

Q. What exactly is a mineral and why do humans need to have them?

A. Carbohydrates, proteins, lipids, and vitamins are all organic substances. This means they are all compounds of the chemical element carbon. We require, in addition to these nutrients, certain chemical elements in their inorganic forms, that is, not bound to carbon. These elements are classified as dietary minerals. Now that you have me sounding like my science teachers, let's name a few: calcium, potassium, sulfur, and chlorine. There are minerals that are required by the human body in amounts much smaller than the above-mentioned elements, and they are called "trace minerals." This catagory includes iron, iodine, copper, and zinc. All of these nutrients participate in many biochemical processes necessary for the maintenance of health.

GYNECOMASTIA

Q. I was wondering why there seems to be less gynecomastia among the pros and top amateurs seen in the magazines lately. Bitch tits used to be as common as dirt among leading bodybuilders. Is it just that less drugs are used these days or have the champs gotten smarter and learned how to avoid getting bitch tits?

A. Maybe a little of both. Actually, the champs of today probably don't use less drugs than the champs of six or seven years ago, when bitch tits were really prevalent. They use more of the drugs like growth hormone and clenbuterol which do not cause gynecomastia, and less of the highly androgenic drugs which do. Also, Nolvadex is now commonly used to combat the aromatization process that causes bitch tits. Don't forget, many champs have had surgery to have their bitch tits removed.

Incredible muscle separation as displayed by Flex Wheeler.

WHICH SUPLEMENTS?

Q. I see a lot of ads in the muscle magazines for supplements like Smilax, vanadyl sulfate, GABA, creatine, and amino acids. Do they help you to gain weight? I have limited funds so I'm wondering if I should put my money into food or buy the supplements?

A. *No question about it Chris, you should put your money into good food. Supplements are always secondary to food. Supplements are just that, a supplement to your diet. If you're eating donuts and coffee for breakfast, hot dogs and Coke for lunch, and Kraft Dinner and Coke for supper, you'll never make good gains no matter how hard you train or how many supplements (or drugs for that matter) you take. The only food supplements I would recommend for you at this stage of your career are a good vitamin-mineral supplement to cover all your nutritional bases and a high-quality protein powder for extra protein and calories.*

VEGETARIAN PROTEIN

Q. I've been training with weights for just a few months. I know I need to eat a lot of protein to make my muscles bigger, but I really don't like red meat and very rarely eat chicken or turkey either. If possible, I'd like to be a vegetarian bodybuilder. Do you think I can get more muscular without eating a lot of animal proteins?

A. *Yes, you can get bigger even if you don't eat animal proteins. For instance, combine lentils with rice, corn, or wheat and you get an amino acid combination that is the same as in animal foods. How about egg whites? Or nonfat plain yogurt? I think that a lacto-ovo-vegetarian diet is a definite option for a bodybuilder who wishes to exclude animal proteins from his or her diet. And egg protein powders can be used too.*

Mike Quinn

STEROID SIDE EFFECTS

Q. I've been on and off steroids for quite a few years. To tell you the truth I've suffered no ill effects except some stiffness in the joints, but now I'm looking in the mirror and I find I'm losing hair rapidly and the wrinkles and lines in my face are awesome. Could this be due to steroids?

A. *Quite frankly you are lucky not to have suffered more serious effects. Habitual, heavy steroid users almost always suffer physical damage. According to Caleb Finch, a professor in neurobiology of aging at the University of Southern California, steroid use can trigger certain aging mechanisms. Overzealous bodybuilders who use steroids to extend their training potential may be* *subjecting themselves to neuro-logical disorders and senile dementia. Hair loss, and deep facial lines are definitely two side effects of heavy steroid use.*

CREATINE

Q. I enjoyed your article on fat-burning products and trust your opinion on supplements and nutrition. What do you think of creatine? Should I take this supplement? What exactly is creatine?

A. Creatine is responsible for replenishing the high-energy com-pound in the body known as ATP. ATP is the universal energy mole-cule of the body. Your ability to sustain a contraction is directly related to your levels of ATP. When your stores of ATP are used up during the last few reps of a set,

creatine phosphate donates a phosphate to replenish your ATP stores. Plain and simple, creatine phosphate can donate a phosphate to ADP to make ATP. If you increase your intracellular CP pool by taking a creatine supplement, you make more CP available to muscles. The status of intra-cellular CP is also related to muscle catabolism, cell volume, and is essential for protein synthesis. So my answer to you would have to be, "Yes! You should definitely try creatine."

SHOULD I BUY . . .

Q. I recently purchased a product that contains plant sterols, wild yam and boron. The label says it will help with building muscle and losing fat. Should I take it?

A. No, you should not use the product. It is a total scam. Junk foods like that really burn my butt. Before you go off and buy some piece of dirt pro-duct like that start with a good multivitamin, a high-quality protein powder, and a solid diet of good food. Once you have done that you can think about adding additional supplements.

STEROID TESTING

Q. I am a 21-year-old bodybuilder who will be graduating from college in May. I am currently being interviewed by many companies which require a drug test before hiring. Do these tests detect steroids? Could steroids cause a positive result? I have been taking Anavar.

A. Companies don't normally test for anabolic steroids as they are usually concerned with illicit drugs. However, if they wished they could have a urine sample analyzed for anabolic steroids, but I've yet to hear of a company in North America that's doing this. Anabolic steroids will not interfere with the testing of other compounds.

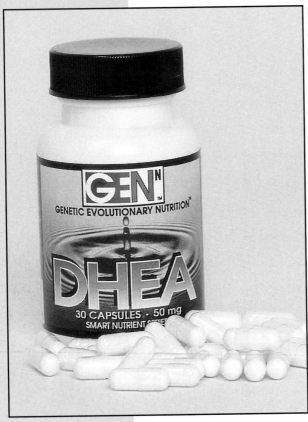

DHEA

Q. I am writing you about a new drug called dehydroepiandrosterone or DHEA. I understand that this is not an anabolic steroid, although as a supplement it is supposed to have an anabolic effect. I was wondering if you have heard of this supplement. Could it be considered anabolic?

A. *DHEA is a natural hormone produced mainly in the adrenal glands and found in both males and females. It has endocrinological activity per se and also acts as a steroid precursor for both gonadal and peripheral estrogen and testosterone production. Although DHEA is actually a weak androgen, it has been invested with almost cult status and is wrongly believed to be a wonder drug against cancer, aging, and obesity, and as an ergogenic compound. It is not an anabolic.*

SLOWING DOWN NATURALLY!?

Q. How can one slow down one's metabolism naturally without using drugs?

A. *You have a serious problem. Why in hell would you want to slow down your metabolism? I know you think it will help you put on weight. It sure will – pounds and pounds of blubber! Trust me, you don't want to slow what most are trying to speed up through countless hours of aerobics. Make the most of this natural advantage: Eat your face off, boy.*

If you are dead set on slowing your metabolism, however, there are a few things you can do. Try plunking down on a couch and not moving for any reason, eating very little protein, and not getting excited about anything. Sure enough, in a few months your metabolism should slow down to a snail's pace. Now every little celery stick you eat will turn to fat! Why do you idiots keep wasting my time?

UPSET STOMACH

Q. Every time I take vitamins I get an upset stomach. I think I'm weird . . . help!

A. *The reason could be the brand of vitamins, the time of day they're taken, or whether or not you've eaten. Experiment with all of these variables, and I'm sure you'll find a plan that works. If not, you might want to see your doctor, especially if you have allergies or are taking prescription medicine.*

TOO MUCH PROTEIN?

Q. I follow a high-protein diet, trying for 50 grams of protein, six times daily. My doctor tells me this is too much and puts too much strain on my liver. How can I get the protein I need without putting a strain on my liver?

A. Try free-form amino acids which bypass the liver and go directly into the bloodstream. This places no strain on the liver and you get all the protein you need.

CONFUSED!

Q. I am entering my first competition in two months and I am confused about my diet. Some people at the gym say that I should keep up my carbs and drop my protein as I get closer to the contest, while others insist that I should do the opposite – drop my carbs and up my protein. The latter group say that increasing my protein will help me maintain my muscle mass as I diet down for the show. How do you do it?

A. I'm from the second group, John. As I diet down for my shows, I raise my protein intake and drop my carbs. I agree that doing so helps to maintain muscle mass as I burn fat. If I reduce my protein, my muscle mass suffers.

First invest your money in good food, then supplement your diet with a multivitamin and a good protein powder.

SHOTGUNNING SUPPLEMENTS

Q. I am especially interested in OKG. If you have any information on this substance, I would be very grateful to receive it, thanks.

A. You should be aware that although compounds such as OKG (ornithine alphaketoglutarate), glutamine, and the branched-chain amino acids, either alone or in combination, can be useful as both anabolic and anticatabolic compounds, the results they produce are not comparable to the effects obtained through the use of drugs such as anabolic steroids. It would be helpful to consider the use of these compounds and the vast majority of other supplements, such as creatine and MET-Rx as aids to maximizing your natural athletic potential rather than ways to chemically alter your basic makeup.

BORON – LESS THAN ADVERTISED

Q. I am a 17-year-old bodybuilder who has been lifting for about two years. I have two questions regarding boron. Does it work? If so, should I keep training like a natural bodybuilder or like a steroid user? Thanks for any info you can send my way.

A. The supplement boron is nowhere near comparable to anabolic steroids. In fact, there are no supplements available that mimic the powerful muscle-building effects of the "juice." Mind you, boron won't kill you as quickly. Steroids are synthetic reproductions of the male hormone testosterone, whereas most supplements are just higher dosages of what's already found in food naturally.

Your body produces steroid hormones all the time. Unfortunately a large percentage of these are inactive. Boron is a trace mineral supplement companies claim helps to double or triple the amount of "active" hormone. Most athletes who have tried boron report no dramatic increases in size and strength. Buy a good protein powder instead.

WHAT'S THAT COLOR?

Q. Why is it that when I use a B-complex tablet, no matter what brand, my urine changes to a bright yellow? Is it a filler in the tablets or am I excreting what I cannot digest?

A. *There shouldn't be anything to worry about. Riboflavin (vitamin B2), which comprises a large part of the B-complex, has a naturally bright, yellow color, which, in some people, spills over into the urine. There is no need to be concerned.*

CALF IMPLANTS

Q. I'm thinking of having calf implants because I cannot build my lower legs. What are your thoughts on this?

Tony Pearson

A. *Numerous bodybuilders have had calf implants including Tony Pearson and Alfred Neugebauer. The IFBB has now banned calf implants, although breast implants are allowed based on the fact that the breasts are glands and not muscles.*

My thoughts on implants are that they look more like balloons than muscles. The worst scenario of course is that your surgeon gives you odd-sized implants. Keep with the calf raises Michael. All lower legs can be improved.

CHOLINE AND INOSITOL

Q. I want to know if choline and inositol work in helping the body lose fat. Also I have heard that regular doses of cider vinegar, lecithin and kelp can also help definition. What is the truth?

A. *This is a difficult question. The medical profession tend to frown on the usefulness of any of these ingredients as fat mobilizers. However, many bodybuilders swear by some, or all of the above, especially when taken in conjunction with a low-calorie diet. The difficulty is in knowing which, if any, of the supplements work, and whether or not increased definition (fat loss) is due to the supplements or to the calorie-reduced diet, or to both. The answer, of course, would be more definite if some unbiased authority would arrange some strict, controlled tests on practicing bodybuilders.*

TOO MANY CARBS

Q. I know a bodybuilder needs carbs, but when I eat carbs, I get real puffy, so much so that I find it hard to get my pants on. I eat mostly low-fat protein (chicken, fish, turkey), with just a little red meat, occasionally. For carbs I eat fruit, potatoes, yams, dates, etc. What is my problem and is there anything on the market I can buy to substitute for the carbs?

A. I don't think the problem is carbs, David. I think it is the type of carbs you eat and the amounts. First of all, you must distinguish between complex carbohydrates and simple carbohydrates. There is a big difference. You want and need lots of complex carbs in your diet – baked potatoes, yams, rice, raw vegetables, oatmeal, and pasta, for example – but you do not want simple carbohydrates or simple sugars in your diet – fruit juices, dates, too much fruit, candy, honey, etc. In short, anything that is sugar. Complex carbs promote muscle gain, and are better for replenishing glycogen stores in the muscles. I think you're eating too many simple carbs. Stick to the complex carbs I recommended above – an occasional piece of fruit is alright – and the fat and the bloat you have been experiencing should lessen.

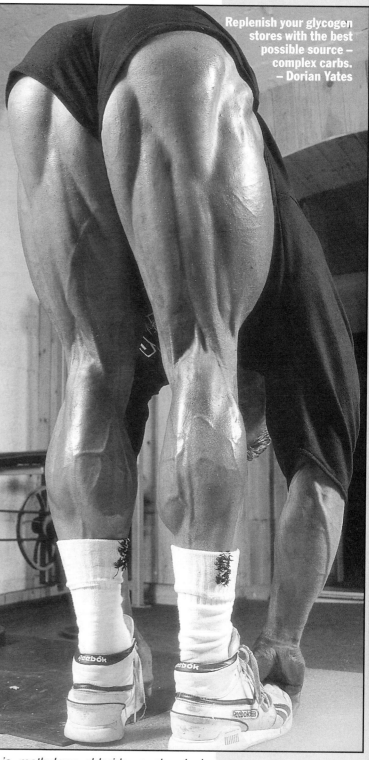

Replenish your glycogen stores with the best possible source – complex carbs.
– Dorian Yates

UTILIZATION

Q. Give me the facts on protein assimilation. I take a protein supplement but I sometimes wonder if I am utilizing it 100 percent. Please help me with this problem.

A. Every food element, protein included, requires certain conditions before it can be properly utilized. One important requirement is hydrochloric acid. No matter how much protein you eat you will not utilize it fully if you do not have enough. Hydrochloric acid may be purchased at your local health-food store.

NOT ANY SAFER?

Q. What's this I hear about decaffeinated coffee being bad for you? Is nothing sacred?

A. Apparently the solvent used to extract caffeine from coffee beans is methylene chloride, a chemical suspected of causing cancer. Nothing is entirely safe. Latest statistics show that farmers are more likely to get certain types of cancer than others. The reason being that they are subjected to more animal viruses, farm chemicals, and dust from hay and stored corn.

Supplements should never be seen as "steroid replacements." – Dave Fisher

DO THEY WORK?

Q. Do supplements work? I've seen so many ads in various bodybuilding magazines, including yours, that claim steroid-level results. Is this possible? I want to get as big as I can but I don't want to spend ungodly amounts of money on garbage. I'm very confused and would appreciate any help and advice you can give. Thanks.

A. Don't fall for these claims you speak of. The truth of the matter is that supplements are nothing more than that – supplements. They provide nutrients, vitamins, minerals, and so forth, that are already found naturally in food, but usually not in such high concentrations. For this reason they do have their place in a trainer's program, but should never be seen as "steroid replacements."

AND MORE STEROIDS . . .

Q. Bob, how much do anabolic steroids help in creating a bodybuilding champion?

A. Steroids help some bodybuilders immensely and others just a lot. Success in our sport really comes down to several factors: discipline, persistence, guts, and yes, genetics. After all these attributes are taken into account, one must remember that everyone responds differently to hormone therapy. Some see a metamorphosis with anabolic chemicals, while others simply "respond." Steroids do work – and work big! One last detail . . . in case you've forgotten, steroids are illegal!

MCTs

Q. What are medium-chain triglycerides?

A. Medium-chain triglycerides (MCTs) are special dietary nutrients derived from coconut oil. MCTs have been used for over thirty years in hospital nutrition. They contain over twice the energy of carbohydrates, and are still absorbed and metabolized as easily as carbohydrates. Your red muscles prefer MCT as an energy source during exercise. MCTs have been shown to reduce bodyfat, improve the metabolism of carbohydrates and proteins and enhance the absorption of essential elements like calcium and potassium. MCTs will give you extra energy during hard workouts and allow you to recover quicker.

BEE POLLEN

Q. Just a quick nutrition question: What does bee pollen do, and is it beneficial to bodybuilders? Thanks.

A. Thank you for your question. Some of the benefits of bee pollen are said to be an increase in energy, both strength and endurance; therefore, bee pollen can be beneficial to a hard-training bodybuilder. Bee pollen contains many vitamins and minerals plus all the necessary amino acids. Bee pollen also helps improve the immune system, and it is good for the skin.

TAMOXIFEN

Q. In *Drug Use & Detection in Amateur Sports* (pg 78), Dr. DiPasquale states tamoxifen is being used to increase endogenous testosterone production. However in *Anabolic Steroid Side Effects* he states (pg 29) that "tamoxifen may be counterproductive in that it has been shown to decrease testicular steroidogenesis, and that tamoxifen reduced the synthesis of testosterone." My question is: If used soley by itself, will tamoxifen increase endogenous testosterone production?

A. The overall effect of tamoxifen in most males is an increase in serum LH and testosterone. The effect of tamoxifen on the hypothalmus pituitary axis seems to overshadow any effect tamoxifen has on the testicles. In order to find out just how it works with you, have a serum LH and testosterone done before you begin taking it and then after using it for a few weeks. If you go this route, be sure and let me know how you respond.

Astrid Falconi

ANABOLIC COMBINATION?

Q. I have heard that alfalfa and desiccated liver, when eaten together, have the same effect on the body as anabolic steroids. Is this true?

A. From time to time we hear stories about "miracle" foods or food combinations but there really are no such things. Everyone in the weight game is familiar with the outstanding qualities of desiccated liver but alfalfa is just begining to gain popularity. A prerequisite to planning a nutritionally balanced, muscle-building diet is to include food or food supplements which will aid the body in the elimination of the daily ingestion and/or build-up of toxins which could otherwise slow down the activites of the body. The assay of alfalfa points out that there is no other known food which contains the variety, quantity and quality of nutrients as does this legume. For example, alfalfa contains amino acids, trace minerals and vitamins; it is also the best-known source of vitamin K. The only disadvantage of alfalfa is that its nutrients are bound up in its tough cellulose cell wall, making it impossible for us to digest because we lack the necessary enzymes. The only way to overcome this problem is by using an alfalfa supplement where the cell walls have already been broken down for you.

Flex Wheeler

VITAMIN E

Q. I want to know about vitamin E. I have heard about supplemental vitamin E giving rats extra energy in controlled tests. I also believe Olympic athletes use vitamin E to give them extra energy for their events. Can vitamin E help me in my bodybuilding?

A. Vitamin E is a necessary nutrient, but if you are eating normally it is impossible not to get adequate amounts. Taking large dosages will not improve your stamina.

DIBENCOZIDE

Q. I have recently seen ads in various magazines claiming that dibencozide is comparable to steroids in its anabolic affects. Does this stuff really work? The ads show graphs of various popular steroids and dibencozide and say dibencozide is actually more effective than steroids for promoting muscle growth. Is this true?

A. Save your money, Brian. In studies I have just completed, dibencozide didn't do any better than a placebo (sugar pill). Those studies mentioned in the ads you've seen are not scientifically valid and the results are taken out of context. Malnourished children in Poland were given dibencozide and steroids. These children were anemic and since dibencozide is just coenzyme B12, the children naturally gained weight as fast as healthy people given steroids. The ads are very misleading.

HOW MUCH PROTEIN?

Q. How much protein should I eat each day and what are the best types of protein to eat?

A. I recommend you eat about one gram of protein per pound of bodyweight. You should eat only low-fat protein – egg whites, white meat from chicken and turkey, very lean red meat, but no whole milk, cheese, pork or lamb, and not to many whole eggs.

EXPIRY DATES

Q. I'm writing to you regarding steroids. Would testosterone which has expired in 1988 still be any good now? Does it retain its full potency, or is some lost? I have used testosterone after four months from the expiry date, but what about three years?

A. Most medications are good for a few years after the expiration date;

Jeff Poulin

however, they're usually not as potent, losing on average 10 percent per year. I think that all the testosterone expiration dates you mentioned in your letter are still good, since they are all oil-based medications with added preservatives. The 1988 one might be somewhat less potent than the others. Some medications do deteriorate more rapidly, with a small number actually becoming toxic. In the case of the oil-based testosterones or other anabolic steroids, there might be problems if the oil has gone rancid. In these cases the oil looks murky and the drug shouldn't be used. Its been my experience that water-based products, depending on the product and type of preservative used, tend to deteriorate faster than their oil-based contemporaries.

CHAPTER THIRTY-FIVE

Who's Who in Ergogenesis

L ike any topic relating to the sport of bodybuilding, ergogenic research is not limited to one individual. Since the first true ergogenic aids – anabolic steroids – made their debut in sports over fifty years ago, numerous individuals have contributed their expertise in understanding the phenomenom of performance enhancement. The following are a few of the more famous individuals or research organizations that have become household names in bodybuilding gyms around the world. We apologize to any person or organization that we may have erroneously overlooked.

Flex Wheeler

Will Brink – One of the newest members in the field of ergogenesis, Will has his own column in *MuscleMag International* called "Intake Update." Will is currently completing a science degree at Harvard University and has authored numerous articles on drug and supplement ergogenesis. His latest work is *Priming The Anabolic Environment: A Practical And Scientific Guide to the Art and Science of Building Muscle.*

Cambridge Ergogenic Institute – Throughout the late 1980s and early 1990s, this company's ads were frequently seen in *MuscleMag International.* Their books include *Ultimate Steroid Manual,* and *Steroid Protection: The Facts!* With the crackdown on advertising for such books, little has been heard from this company in recent years.

Dr. Michael Colgan – Dr. Colgan is a regular contributor to the bodybuilding magazine *Muscle Media.* His regular feature, "State of the Art," covers the latest drugs and supplements making their rounds on the sports scene.

Dr. Scott Connelly – Dr. Connelly is the creator of the highly successful MET-Rx anticatabolic bodybuilding supplement. As of this writing, MET-Rx is the most popular natural bodybuilding product in the world. Dr. Connelly developed MET-Rx to combat various muscle-wasting conditions in hospital patients. Tests with bodybuilders showed it to be among the most effective natural muscle builders available. MET-Rx is marketed by Myosystems, Inc. of Golden, Colorado, USA.

Cybergenics – This "supplement" is marketed by L&S Research of New Jersey. We emphasize the word "supplement" because Cybergenics is not so much a supplement as a total way of "natural ergogenesis." The philosophy behind Cybergenics is to take every natural supplement that has ever been remotely linked to offering ergogenic potential. In addition, the marketers of Cybergenics include a detailed exercise program to maximize the benefits supposedly offered by the supplement. Many critics of Cybergenics argue that it's probably the exercise program that contributes the most to the success of the Cybergenics system. Whether this is true or not, L&S Research made millions in the early 1990s promoting Cybergenics as a "natural alternative" to anabolic steroids (although such advertising has since been toned down) before other more popular supplements like MET-Rx and Twinlab became available.

Dorian Yates

Dr. Mauro DiPasquale – Considered the leading authority on drug use in sports, Dr. DiPasquale has written numerous best-selling books on the subject including *Beyond Anabolic Steroids; Anabolic Steroid Side Effects – Fact, Fiction and Treatment;* and *Drug Use and Detection in Amateur Sports.* Besides these works, Dr. DiPasquale has his own monthly column in *MuscleMag International* called "Doctor's Corner." Unlike most in the medical field who subscribe to the propaganda spread by sports organizations and law-enforcement agencies, Dr. DiPasquale bases his opinions and writings on hard scientific fact. This approach has led him to be highly respected by bodybuilders the world over.

Dan Duchaine – Often called "the steroid guru," Dan has become perhaps the most famous name in ergogenesis. Although many criticize him for his liberal views on performance-enhancing drugs, he has garnered legions of fans who admire him for his "telling it like it is" approach. His books *The Underground Steroid Handbooks* 1 & 2, have become bodybuilding's best sellers, and Dan has been featured on numerous TV and radio shows. After serving time for steroid dealing, Dan is now one of the chief writers for *Muscle Media.*

Phil Embleton and Gerard Thorne – Authors of this book and *MuscleMag International's Encyclopedia of Bodybuilding*, Phil and Gerard started their writing careers with *Steroid Myths – The Responsible Use Of Anabolic Steroids.* Rather than focus on the actual use of anabolic steroids, the authors tried to present steroids as an academic subject to be studied rather than criticized. Besides these books, the authors carried out an extensive study of the black market in anabolic steroids in Atlantic Canada, published in *MuscleMag International* (February 1993).

P. Grunding and M. Bachmann – Two of the newest authors to come onto the bodybuilding scene, their latest book, *World Anabolic Review 1996*, is by far the largest book ever written on anabolic steroids. It contains over

Roland Cziurlok shows awesome
mass – even when relaxed.

400 pages and over 500 photographs, all devoted to making the reader an expert on the subject. It is available from MB Muscle Books, Houston, Texas, USA.

Mick Hart – One of the latest contributors to *MuscleMag International*, Mick is well-known to British bodybuilders as the publisher of the very informative bodybuilding magazine, *No Bull Collection*. Like Dan Duchaine, Mick has developed a reputation for "telling it like it is," and his "earthy" British sense of humour has endeared him to thousands of bodybuilders around the world.

Dr. Fred Hatfield – Dr. Hatfield is a former powerlifting champion and one of the senior writer/editors with *Muscle and Fitness* magazine. Besides his regular magazine contributions, Dr. Hatfield has written numerous books including *Anabolic Steroids – What Kind and How Many*, and *Bodybuilding, A Scientific Approach*. Like Dr. DiPasquale, Dr. Hatfield realizes that some athletes will use drugs no matter what the cost, so he takes a practical rather than paranoid approach to their use.

L&S Research – This New Jersey-based company first came to prominence with their series of steroid-related books, back in the mid to late 1980s. Among the most successful of the series were *Anabolic Steroids and Bodybuilding*, *In Quest Of Size*, and *Human Growth Hormone*. With the crackdown on steroids and other bodybuilding drugs, L&S Research developed the Cybergenics system of natural ergogenesis.

MET-Rx – Currently the most popular of bodybuilding supplements, MET-Rx is the brainchild of Dr. Scott Connelly of California. Dr. Connelly initially developed the product to treat medical patients suffering from an array of muscle-wasting conditions. As the active ingredients are powerful anticatabolic agents, he theorized they may have great potential in bodybuilding. After a series of studies reported great muscle gains in bodybuilders, Dr. Connelly arranged for a Colorado company to market the product. Virtually all users of the product report significant muscle gains and fat loss. A combination of great advertising plus word of mouth have made MET-Rx the number-one bodybuilding supplement available.

Mile High Publishing – Perhaps the leading organization in terms of ergogenesis reasearch, Mile High made a name for itself back in the late 1980s and early 1990s, with their highly successful *Anabolic Reference Guide* and updates. Their multipage ads in *MuscleMag International* were a staple for years until political pressure forced the magazine to abandon such advertising. Run by Bill Phillips, Mile High was probably the first major company devoted to analyzing the various drugs and supplements used by bodybuilders. Their policy of trying to remain unbiased is a welcome breath of fresh air for bodybuilders trying to run the gauntlet of supplement advertising. In recent years Mile High has become better known as the publishers of the very successful magazine *Muscle Media*.

Muscle Media – *Muscle Media* has carved a niche for itself by catering to the "ergogenic seekers" of the sport. Recognizing that most supplement advertising is overhyped, the publishers of *Muscle Media* – Mile High Publishing of Colorado – have set out to examine the merits of every ergogenic supplement or drug that is available. Their frank approach has attracted a loyal following, but as would be expected such openness has also brought condemnation from the more conservative members of the bodybuilding fraternity. In defence of *Muscle Media*, they do not promote drug use by athletes, but instead offer information and advice to those that do. In addition, their writing staff is highly qualified and includes such respected individuals as Dan Duchaine, Bill Phillips, and Dr. Robert Price.

MuscleTech – This Canadian company's primary goal was to develop a line of natural supplements that produce steroid-like muscle gains without the risk of side effects. If the series of articles by regular *MuscleMag* writer Greg Zulak are any indication, they may have succeeded. Reports indicate that most users of their products (including the monstrous 350-plus pound Greg Kovacs) have achieved gains comparable to other more dangerous anabolic drugs.

Lee Priest

John Parrillo – Although John writes very little on ergogenic drugs, his knowledge on ergogenic supplements and nutrition is second to none. His regular feature in *MuscleMag* called "Parrillo Performance" is considered state of the art for bodybuilders trying to maximize their potential. Besides his writings, John has established himself as one of the best trainers in the business and numerous champion bodybuilders can thank John for their competitive success.

Jean-Pierre Fux

Bill Phillips – One of the most respected writers in the field of ergogenesis, Bill is owner of Mile High Publishing and senior editor of *Muscle Media* magazine. In addition, he has written the very successful *Natural Supplement Review* and *Anabolic Reference Guide* plus updates. Like Dr. Mauro DiPasquale, Dan Duchaine and others, Bill tries to take an unbiased approach to ergogenic aids, and if he feels a particular supplement is worthless, he will say so. In fact most of the supplements in his *Natural Supplement Review* received only poor to moderate endorsements.

Dr. Robert Price – Dr. Price is one of the regular contributors to *Muscle Media* and is fast gaining acceptance as one of the leading authorities on ergogenic aids. His regular column "Ergogenic Review" is considered on of the most informative on the subject of performance-enhancing drugs.

Dr. John Ziegler – Not counting Soviet research, Dr. Ziegler was probably the first North American to examine the effects of anabolic steroids in bodybuilders. Influenced by reports of Russian sports doctors doping their weightlifters, Dr. Ziegler conducted numerous experiments using the anabolic steroid Dianabol during the late 1950s. Dr. Ziegler terminated his studies after realizing most of the bodybuilders in his test group were taking dosages far beyond what he instructed. Although the amount of data collected was limited, many consider Dr. Ziegler the "father" of steroid research in the United States.

Lee Priest in the midst of muscle growth.

Greg Zulak – Although more of an author of training articles than ergogenic-aid articles, Greg began captivating regular readers of *MuscleMag International* in 1996 with his series of articles on MuscleTech. So informative were Greg's articles that many were left asking why the former editor of *MuscleMag* didn't spend more time on the subject.

Description of Anabolic Steroids

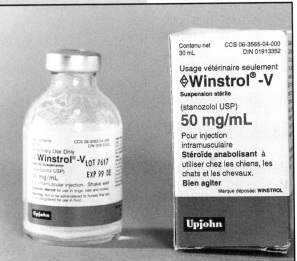

Trade Name: Winstrol, Winstrol-V
Generic Name: stanazolol
Tablet Size: 2 mg
Suspension: 50 mg/cc
Therapeutic Dose: 6 mg/day
Gym Dose: 50 to 700 percent

Most athletes consider Winstrol a weak steroid. Many athletes such as sprinters avoid Winstrol because of its tendency to make the muscles stiff. Although slightly toxic to the liver, most of the side effects are related to the oral form. In dosages of 16 milligrams per day orally and 150 to 200 milligrams per week injectable most of the side effects associated with anabolic steroids (acne, water retention, conversion to estrogen, etc.) are eliminated. Winstrol rarely produces psychological (behavioral) side effects when used in low to moderate dosages.

Trade Name: Maxibolin
Generic Name: ethylestrenol
Tablet Size: 2 mg
Therapeutic Dose: 4 to 8 mg/day
Gym Dose: 150 to 400 percent

Maxibolin is a progesterone-based steroid. Thus, while it produces androgenic/anabolic effects, it is in fact a female hormone.

Trade Name: Dianabol
Generic Name: methandrostenolone
Tablet Size: 2.5 and 5 mg
Therapeutic Dose: 5 mg/day
Gym Dose: 50 to 800 percent

Formally one of the most used anabolic steroids, this drug is no longer manufactured under the trade name Dianabol, but a new version has recently turned up on the black market under the name of Noposim. The reason methandrostenolone is still popular on the black market is economics. It is one of the easiest and cheapest steroids to manufacture, and such characteristics make it ideal for counterfeiters – low investment and high returns.

Most users report great weight gains while using the drug, although much of the weight is in the form of fluid retention. Nevertheless, its instant gratification properties has led Dianabol to be affectionately called the "beginner's steroid." There have been a few studies written up in the medical literature that tie Dianabol to psychotic episodes. But we should add that the individuals in question were using extremely high dosages for extended periods of time. In addition, the subjects were using other steroids as well. As for side effects, Dianabol has never been considered "safe," and side effects such as gynecomastia, liver-enzyme imbalances, and excessive acne are frequently reported.

For the competitive athletes among you, methandrostenelone is only detectable back to about three weeks before a drug test. If the dosages are small, an athlete can use it as close as four or five days before the drug test. Such quick clearance times are why athletes switch from injectables to orals in the weeks leading up to a drug test. Not only will the orals help maintain performance gains, but the risk of getting caught in a drug test is greatly reduced.

> Trade Name: Nilivar
> Generic Name: norethandrolone
> Therapeutic Dose: 10 mg/day
> Gym Dose: 300 percent

Originally marketed by Searle, it was later replaced by Anavar which reportably has fewer androgenic side effects.

> Trade Name: Anavar, Oxandrin
> Generic Name: oxandrolone
> Tablet Size: 2.5 and 20 mg
> Therapeutic Dose: 50 to 80 mg/day for AIDS treatment
> Gym Dose: 250 to 350 percent

Considered by athletes to be one of the best strength-producing steroids, this drug is no longer manufactured under the trade name Anavar. In dosages of 15 to 20 milligrams per day, Anavar produces excellent strength gains with few side effects. The drug is popular with women athletes as it produces few androgenic side effects. In recent years Anavar has become one of the more commonly faked steroids on the black market.

Oxandrolone has been in the news quite a bit recently as there is a growing movement to use the drug to treat AIDS patients. Clinical trials have been so successful that Biotechnology General is releasing a 20-milligram tablet of oxandrolone under the trade name of Oxandrin. One of the biggest changes is in the dosages prescribed by physicians. Unlike the 5- to 10-milligram dosages used years ago, physicians are now using dosages comparable to those taken by body-builders – 50 to 80 milligrams per day.

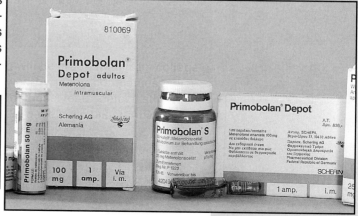

> Trade Name: Primobolan
> Generic Name: methenolone
> Tablet Size: 5, 25 and 50 mg
> Therapeutic Dose: 10 to 20 mg/day
> Gym Dose: 50 to 400 percent

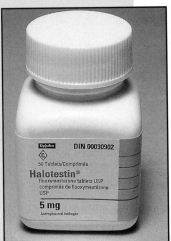

Primobolan is considered to be one of the safest of all anabolic steroids. As it has only 1/100th the androgenicity of testosterone, it is very popular with female athletes. Bodybuilders find that Primobolan has excellent muscle-sparing properties while on a precontest diet.

> Trade Name: Halotestin
> Generic Name: fluoxymesterone
> Tablet Size: 2, 5 and 10 mg
> Therapeutic Dose: 2 to 30 mg/day
> Gym Dose: 100 to 175 percent

Although this drug has very good anabolic properties, it is also one of the more androgenic steroids and should be avoided by female athletes. Halotestin is so androgenic in fact that medical texts often list the drug as an androgenic rather than an anabolic.

> Trade Name: Anadrol-50, Androyd
> Generic Name: oxymetholone
> Tablet Size: 5,10 and 50 mg
> Therapeutic Dose: 5 mg/day
> Gym Dose: 500 to 1000 percent

With the crackdown on anabolic steroid distribution, many of the most commonly used anabolic steroids such as Dianabol and Anavar are no longer available. The result has been a switch to drugs that are available – irregardless of the risks. Anadrol-50 is one such drug and has filled in the void left by the absence of other drugs. Anadrol-50 is perhaps the most potent of all steroids. Virtually all users report fast strength and muscle gains after only a few months on this steroid. The gains, however, are short-lived, and quickly dissappear following cessation of drug use. Besides its powerful anabolic properties, Anadrol-50 is highly androgenic (at least as far as anabolic steroids go) and such side effects as acne, hair loss, and gynecomastia are common. Although the medical literature is sketchy, most of the cases of peliosis hepatitis associated with anabolic steroids have involved Anadrol-50. Athletes should be extremely wary of using this steroid, and if they do, constant monitoring by a physician is an absolute must.

> Trade Name: Metandren
> Generic Name: methyltesterone
> Tablet Size: 5, 10 and 25 mg
> Therapeutic Dose: 50 mg/day
> Gym Dose: 150 percent

This drug is taken sublingually and since it has both high androgenic and anabolic properties, it should be avoided by female athletes. Many athletes report a motivational boost from the drug due to its effects on aggression levels.

> Trade Name: Esiclene
> Generic Name: formebolone
> Tablet Size: 5 mg
> Vial Size: 2 ccs
> Gym Dose: 30 to 120 ccs per contest

Esiclene is manufactured by IPB Pharmaceuticals of Milan, Italy. This drug is unique in that it's primarily used for one of its side effects. Unlike other steroids which are used to speed recovery and reverse catabolism, Esiclene's desired effects are localized. Injected directly into a muscle, the drug causes a temporary but pronounced swelling of the muscle. Although it varies, Esiclene may cause an increase of one inch or more to a specific muscle group. Since the drug is painful to inject, preparations are mixed with Lidocain (an anesthetic) to numb the sensation.

Bodybuilders use Esiclene to bring up such lagging bodyparts as the calves, but like most steroids, Esiclene gets abused and stories circulate of top pros injecting every muscle group before a major contest. Most body-builders inject a few hours before the show as injecting earlier (a week or more) can give the muscles a soft puffy look.

As with most drugs on the black market, the price of Esiclene is greatly marked up from the manufacturers cost. A box of 6 vials (12 cc) costs $6 US in Italy but may cost $100 or more on the Canadian and US black markets.

Trade Name: Deca-Durabolin
Generic Name: nandrolone decanoate
Vial Size: 2 mL at 100 mg/cc
Therapeutic Dose: 50 to 100 mg every 3 or 4 weeks
Gym Dose: 300 to 600 percent (200 to 300 mg/week)

Prior to advances in drug-testing procedures, Deca-Durabolin was one of the more popularly used steroids. The reason for its decline is it's ability to be traced back 18 months or more in a drug test. In terms of toxicity, Deca-Durabolin is one of the safest steroids and users report few side effects when used in low to moderate doses.

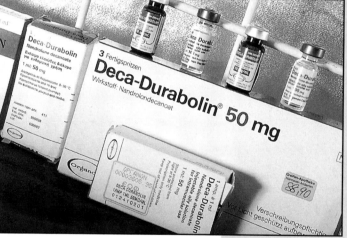

After injection, it generally takes Deca-Durabolin about three weeks to release. Deca-Durabolin has a useful time period of about two weeks, but it's breakdown metabolites may linger for one or two years. This is why it's fast losing its appeal with drug-tested athletes. Even after deciding to compete "clean" they may test positive for the drug.

In recent years Deca-Durabolin has been used successfully to treat AIDS patients. This is because Deca has a positive effect on boosting the immune system – the complete opposite of what the AIDS virus is doing. While the steroid is not a "cure" for AIDS, it does help a savaged immune system.

Trade Name: Android
Generic Name: testosterone
Therapeutic Dose: 50 mg, 3 times per week
Gym Dose: 50 to 400 percent

Trade Name: Oreton, Perandren
Generic Name: testosterone propionate
Therapeutic Dose: 25 mg, 2 to 4 times per week
Gym Dose: 50 to 400 percent

Trade Name: Depo-Testosterone
Generic Name: testosterone cypionate
Therapeutic Dose: 100 to 400 mg every 2 to 4 weeks
Gym Dose: 50 to 400 percent

Trade Name: Delatestryl
Generic Name: testosterone enanthate
Therapeutic Dose: 100 to 400 mg every 2 to 4 weeks
Gym Dose: 50 to 400 percent

All of these testosterone derivatives are highly anabolic – producing some of the quickest gains seen among anabolic agents – but they also rate very high for androgenic effects. Among the side effects often associated with testosterone derivatives are acne, hair loss, insomnia, aggression, elevated blood pressure, and impotence.

Although prices flutuate, these drugs are among the cheapest to buy on the black market and hence are widely used in high doses. Teenagers are at special risk for these drugs as they often convert to estrogen and produce gynecomastia. Given their high androgenic effects females should never use these drugs.

Trade Names: Andriol, Pantestone
Generic Name: testosterone undecanoate
Tablet Size: 40-mg capsules
Therapeutic Dose: 1 to 2 capsules daily
Gym Dose: 3 to 5 capsules/day

This relatively new steroid has to be taken in high dosages as it has a very short active life in the body. Unlike most other testosterone derivatives, Andriol does not convert to estrogen in significant amounts – thus greatly reducing the risk of gynecomastia. In addition, side effects such as liver abnormalities and sex-drive changes are rarely reported. Frequent side effects include acne, hair loss, and increased aggression levels.

Trade Name: Durabolin
Generic Name: nandrolone phenoprionate
Therapeutic Dose: 50 to 100 mg/week
Gym Dose: 100 to 200 percent

This drug is very similar in action to Deca-Durabolin, but has a shorter life. As with most nandrolone derivatives, Durabolin is one of the easiest drugs to detect in a drug test.

Trade Name: Equipose
Generic Name: boldenone undecyclenate
Therapeutic Dose: Not applicable
Gym Dose: Varies

As the name implies, this steroid was developed to treat debilitated animals, particularly race horses. Dosages of up to 200 milligrams per week produce good size and strength gains with little risk of side effects such as acne, water retention, and liver abnormalities. On the negative side, this drug quickly converts to estrogen and may produce gynecomastia. Behavioral side effects are rarely associated with Equipose use.

Trade Name: Parabolan
Generic Name: trenbolone
Tablet Size: 76-mg ampoule
Therapeutic Dose: 1 ampoule every 2 weeks
Gym Dose: 200 to 400 percent

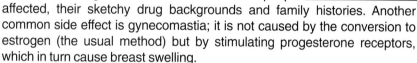

Parabolin is one of the most effective anabolic steroids, but many users report severe side effects including nightmares, insomnia and severe mood swings. In rare cases paronia has been experienced, but the evidence is inconclusive given the small numbers of people affected, their sketchy drug backgrounds and family histories. Another common side effect is gynecomastia; it is not caused by the conversion to estrogen (the usual method) but by stimulating progesterone receptors, which in turn cause breast swelling.

Trade Name: Finajet
Generic Name: trenbolone
Therapeutic Dose: 50 mg/mL shot every second day
Gym Dose: 200 to 400 percent

Finajet is a veterinary drug that was developed to treat debilitated animals. As it was never intended for human use, it's acetate form means most individuals have trouble using it. There have been documented cases of athletes on Finajet suffering severe side effects such as chronic hepatitis and temporary insanity. This is one steroid athletes should definitely avoid.

SNAKE VENOMS

Although not an anabolic steroid, we thought it would be interesting to show the extremes that some bodybuilders go to just to obtain a slight competitive advantage. At least one bodybuilder has stated publicly (on an American TV talkshow) that he used snake venom to increase the size of his muscles. As most people are aware, snake bites cause tremendous swelling at the site of injection. This has the effect of causing the muscles to appear more developed than they really are, a potent advantage during a contest.

Snake venom is produced by the poison glands, and injected through the fangs when a snake bites its prey. In some snakes the venom has two functions: It immobilizes the prey by paralyzing it so it can be swallowed; and it begins digesting the animal's flesh. Venom contains hemotoxins, cardiotoxins, and neurotoxins. Most snake venoms contain all three toxins, as well as many other components, but some generalities exist. Pit viper venom is more likely to cause serious tissue damage because this venom contains components which start the digestive process. With high dosages of venom, cardiotoxic and neurotoxic symptoms can develop. Coral snake venom rarely results in local tissue damage, and the venom's effects are primarily neurotoxic and cardiotoxic. Mojave snake venom can cause significant neurological problems with few local symptoms. Copperhead venom is mild and not life threatening for a healthy adult. Finally, such snakes as cobras and tiger snakes contain some of the most toxic venoms known to man. A single bite from a cobra or tiger snake can kill a full-grown elephant.

Moderate swelling lasting from one to several hours can even be expected with a small dose of venom or noxious saliva from a nonvenomous snake. The injection site can be quite painful, and can be treated with acetaminophen, ibuprophen, and heat or ice. Inadvertently injecting directly into an artery can result in coma and/or death.

The previous is one of the most obscure, and hopefully least used of contest-enhancement procedures, though some individuals will try just about anything. Remember, snakes use venom for one purpose – to kill! Is that local bodybuilding contest really so important that you want to mess around with venoms which in small doses can kill an adult elephant? For obvious reasons, we highly recommend avoiding such ergogenic aids and leave venom to those who know how to use it best – snakes.

Lee Priest

Representative Steroid Stacks

The following are examples of the more commonly used steroid stacks. At first we hesitated to include them given the controversy surrounding steroid use, nevertheless, we realized that some readers will use steroids no matter what the risks. The following are stacks designed to maximize muscle gains and minimize health risks. We are by no means encouraging those who are not presently using steroids to start. In countries where steroid use is illegal you should not involve yourself with them in any way. This is especially true for our teenage readers. There is good evidence to suggest that anabolic steroids pose a serious health risk to this age group. As for older readers, if you decide to follow one or more of the following, only do so under medical supervision. The black market is flooded with fake and potentially harmful drugs. You never know what you're getting. We stress again that many countries are cracking down on steroid use. This is especially true for our American readers, and if you get caught you'll probably do hard prison time. Be warned.

OFF-SEASON STACKS

1) Winstrol orals, Maxibolin orals, and Primobolan injectable: This is a six- to eight-week stack that produces good size, good strength, and fair recuperative effects. Increase dosages with the oral Winstrol and Maxibolan until you've reached a maximun of 5 tablets a day of each. Take one 100-milligram shot of Primobolan once a week. To keep estrogenic activity minimized take one Nolvadex tablet a day as well. It is also reccomended that men take 50 milligrams of Drolban (a steroid used to treat impotence) a week to sustain sex drive.

2) Testosterone undecanoate orals, Dura Proviron orals, and Deca-Durabolin injectable: This is an eight-week stack that starts with two weeks of 100 milligrams per week of Deca-Durabolin before starting the orals. You then take the orals for six weeks and continue with the Deca-Durabolin at 100 milligrams per week. Proviron is administered at 2 tablets per day and testosterone undecanoate at three 40-milligram capsules per day. This is another good strength, size, and recuperative stack.

3) Anavar orals, Primobolan orals, and Parabolan injectable: Suggested dosages are 3 tablets for every 100 pounds of bodyweight with the Anavar, one 50-milligram tablet of Primobolan a day, and one shot of Parabolan every eight days. Considered to be one of the best strength stacks and fair for increasing size and recuperation.

4) Sustanon 250 injectable, Proviron orals, and Nolvedex: A six-week stack that yields excellent strength, size, and recuperative abilities with a slight degree of water retention. One shot of Sustanon 250 per week, one Proviron, and one Nolvadex a day.

PRECONTEST STACKS

With the emphasis on appearing ripped for contests, bodybuilders use pre-contest stacks that minimize water retention.

1) Primobolan acetate injectable, Winstrol V injectable, Anavar orals, and Halotestin: The Primobolan acetate is taken in one shot every other day, the Winstrol V at one cc every other day, one 10-milligram tablet of Halotestin and 8 tablets of Anavar are suggested daily. One Nolvadex a day will also help keep estrogenic activity to a minimum.

2) Permastril/Masteron injectable, Primobolan acetate orals, and Winstrol V: Permastril and Masteron are trade names for dromostanolone propionate, a non-aromatizing compound that has a reputation for creating fullness and hardness. One 2-milliliter vial should be taken every 4 days, along with two Primobolan 50-milligram tablets and one cc of Winstrol V every other day. Take one Nolvadex as well. This stack is followed for five weeks.

3) Primobolan acetate injectable, Anavar orals, Halotestin orals, and Winstrol orals: the Primobolan is taken every other day, while 6 to 10 tablets of Anavar are taken per day. Start taking Halotestin two weeks out from the contest at 2 tablets a day, and the Winstrol is kept at 4 tablets a day. One Nolvadex a day is also recommended.

4) Equipose injectable, Anavar orals, and Primobolan orals: Equipose is taken at one shot of 100 milligrams every week, the Anavar is again between 6 to 10 tablets a day, and Primobolan is kept at 2 tablets per day at 50 milligrams per tablet. As before this is a five-week stack that should include one Nolvadex tablet a day.

Joe Spinello

Citric Acid (Kreb's) Cycle

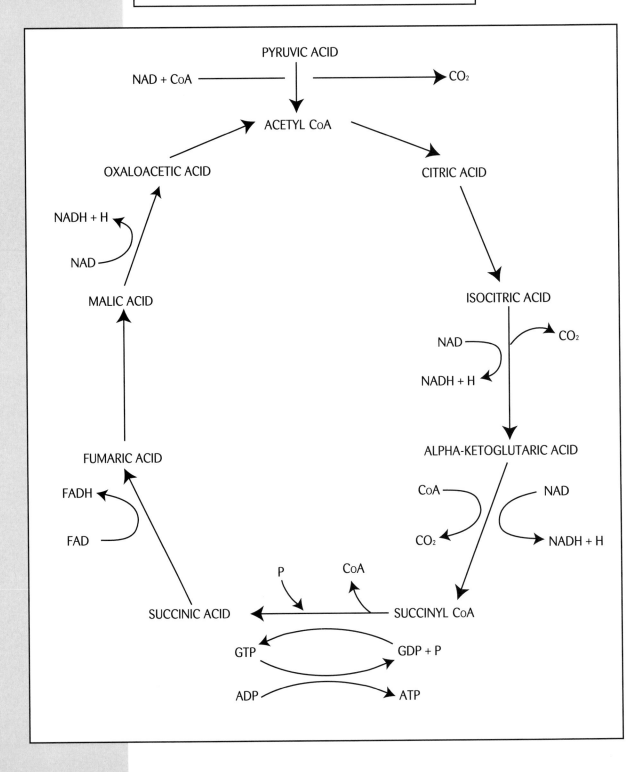

GUIDE TO THE CITRIC ACID CYCLE

1) Pyruvic acid, the end product of glycolysis, is converted to acetyl CoA by the enzyme pyruvate dehydrogenase complex. In the process, NADH, H, and CO_2 are given off.

2) Acetyl CoA combines with oxaloacetic acid to form citric acid. The enzyme involved is citrate synthase.

3) Citric acid is geometrically rearranged by the enzyme aconitase to form isocitric acid.

4) Isocitric acid is converted into alpha-ketoglutaric acid by the enzyme isocitrate dehydrogenase. In the process CO_2 and hydrogen are given off.

5) Alpha-ketoglutaric acid loses two H and CO_2 to form succinyl CoA. The enzyme involved is alpha-ketoglutarate dehydrogenase.

6) Succinyl CoA is broken down by succinyl CoA synthetase to form succinic acid, in the process generating one molecule of ATP.

7) Succinic acid is converted to fumaric acid by the enzyme succinate dehydrogenase and the loss of two H.

Bruce Patterson

8) Fumaric acid is rearranged by the enzyme fumarase to form malic acid.

9) Malic acid loses two H, producing oxaloacetic acid, which is then used to start the cycle once more. The enzyme involved is malate dehydrogenase.

NET RESULT OF THE CITRIC ACID CYCLE

At the completion of the citric acid cycle, one glucose molecule has yielded four new molecules of ATP – two from glycolysis and two from two turns of the cycle. Additional energy is released by the electron-transport system in which electrons are transferred from molecules of NADH + H and FADH to molecules of oxygen. In the process, some of the chemical energy is used to synthesize ATP, and the rest is given off as heat. Most of the energy produced by the citric acid cycle is produced by this method with 32 molecules of ATP being liberated. The total number of ATP molecules produced by the cycle is 36: two from glycolysis, two from two turns of the cycle, and 32 from the electron-transport system.

APPENDIX 4

Glycogenesis

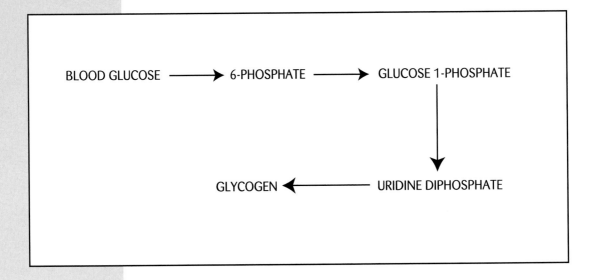

BLOOD GLUCOSE ──────→ 6-PHOSPHATE ──────→ GLUCOSE 1-PHOSPHATE

GLYCOGEN ←────── URIDINE DIPHOSPHATE

APPENDIX 5

Glycogenolysis

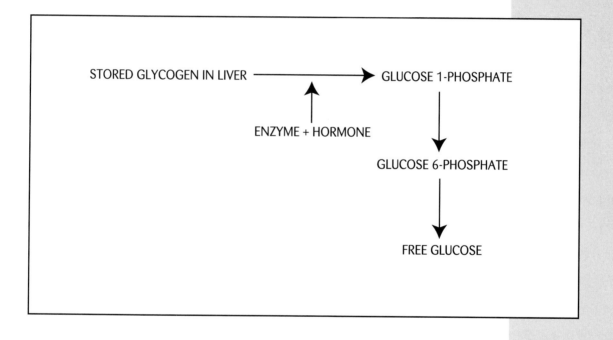

Common Sugars

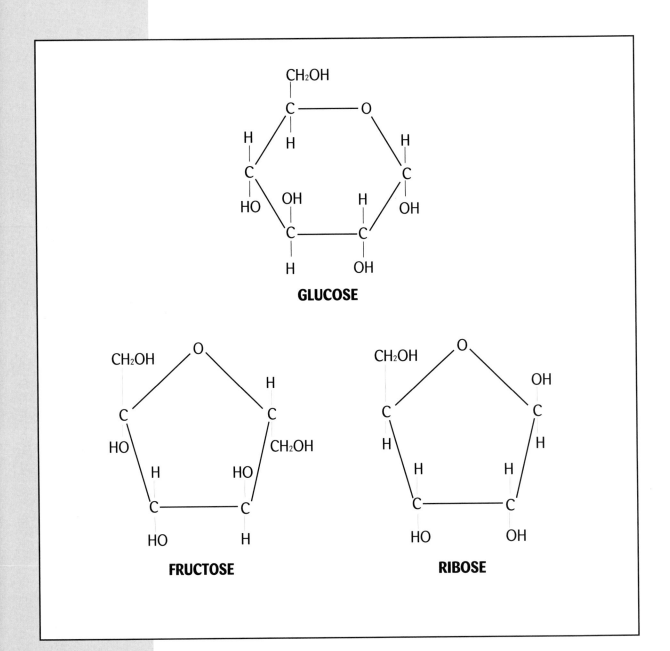

GLUCOSE

FRUCTOSE

RIBOSE

Bruce Patterson and Jeff Poulin

Well-Known Ergogenic-Aid Books

We would be confident authors indeed if we claimed our book was the "end all" to the given topic; and while we are certain that this manual is as up to date as the next one, there are still numerous others out there that are highly informative. Some can be classified as "how to" manuals, designed primarily for users. Others take a medical approach and offer advice on how to avoid unwanted side effects – particulary as they apply to ergogenic drugs. Still others are designed to "frighten" users and as such rely on carefully selected studies to further spread antisteroid propaganda. Finally, and this tends to be the trend these days, there are books that cover the whole spectrum of ergogenesis both legal and illegal.

Many of the following books are no longer in print but may occassionally turn up at flea markets and used bookstores. The newer ones can be obtained at most better bookstores and through ads featured in the various muscle magazines including *MuscleMag International*. We are not going to rate them, but instead give a brief summary of each books' characteristics.

***Death In The Locker Room*; Robert Goldman, MD** – One of the first books of its kind, *Death In the Locker Room* was released in the mid 1980s. While comprehensive in its scope, the book is biased in that the author relies heavily on animal studies and case studies with humans suffering from various medical problems. This, combined with the author's obvious dislike of steroids, results in a slanted view that anabolic steroids are extremely dangerous. While the book satisfies the antisteroid element, and has sold extremely well, it is not really applicable for healthy athletes who want unbiased information on anabolic steroids.

***The Underground Steroid Handbook* I & 2; Dan Duchaine** – Considered by many to be the bibles of anabolic steroid use, Dan Duchaine was probably the first serious user/dealer of steroids to actually sit down and write how things "really stand" with bodybuilders and steroids. These two books were not written to "please" antisteroid advocates. Instead, Dan set out to provide users with a guide that would make using steroids "relatively safe." Virtually every steroid or related drug is covered in these two desktop published books, and Dan even outlines various drug combinations for cycling steroids. If one word could summarize these books it's "practicality."

***Ultimate Muscle Mass*; Dan Duchaine** – A follow-up to his earlier *Underground Steroid Handbooks*, this text branches out to include such topics as growth hormone, new supplements, and training strategies. In many ways this smaller book is a prelude to his much larger work, the newly released *Body Opus*.

***Underground Body Opus*; Dan Duchaine** – This is the latest release from steroid "guru" Dan Duchaine. *Body Opus* explores the cutting edge of ergogenic aids and gaining muscular bodyweight. Unlike his previous books which primarily centered on steroids and related drugs, Dan uses *Body Opus* to examine the full spectrum of bodybuilding agents. At an advertised 354 pages, it is one of the most thorough books ever written on the subject, and makes a welcome addition to any bodybuilder's library.

***Steroid Myths*; Gerard Thorne and Phil Embleton** – *Steroid Myths* was the first book written by the authors of this text. Unlike a number of previous books which were either for or against steroids, the authors tried to take an unbiased stance concerning steroid use by athletes. Based on over 200 references, most of them from medical journals, *Steroid Myths* explores the many facets of drug use by athletes. If there is one theme permeating throughout the book it is that steroids are not the "cancer-causing, psychotic-inducing chemicals" that some people make them out to be. Although no longer in print, copies can still be obtained from *MuscleMag International's* book ordering department.

***Anabolic Side Effects – Fact, Fiction and Treatment*; Dr. Mauro DiPasquale** – Written by a medical doctor and former powerlifting champion, this book is praised for its unbiased approach to anabolic steroid use. Although he doesn't advocate the use of steroids, Dr. DiPasquale nevertheless realizes that many individuals will use steroids no matter how much negative preaching. Rather than let such individuals stumble about in ignorance, Dr. DiPasquale provides good, solid medical advice on how to avoid unwanted side effects.

***Beyond Anabolic Steroids*; Dr. Mauro DiPasquale** – This book is a follow up to the previous book, and explores the many substances used by athletes to replace or enhance the effects of anabolic steroids. With his unique style, Dr. DiPasquale covers the whole spectrum of drug use, with a special emphasis on minimizing or avoiding side effects.

***Drug Use And Detection In Amateur Sports*; Dr. Mauro DiPasquale** – This book is part of a package which also includes regular yearly updates. Primarily aimed at amateur athletes, the book and updates are also popular with those who run sporting events. Although it varies, the newsletters focus on the latest drugs used by athletes, and the detection of such by sporting organizations. In short, Dr. DiPasquale covers both sides of the athletic fence.

***Priming The Anabolic Environment*; Will Brink** – This book is a collection of essays and articles written over the years by regular *MuscleMag* columnist Will Brink. Like Duchaine's *Body Opus*, Will covers the full spectrum of procedures and techniques that will maximize a bodybuilder's potential for gaining muscular body mass. Although he covers steroids and other drugs, Will's primary emphasis is on the latest legal supplements that offer potential for ergogenesis. The book is currently available from *MuscleMag International's* book order department.

***World Anabolic Review 1996*; P. Grunding and M. Bachmann** – Probably the largest, most thorough anabolic steroid reference guide, the *World Anabolic Review 1996* contains over 400 pages and 500 photographs pertaining to steroid use in athletics. Like most of the recent books on steroids, this one tries to cover both sides of the issue rather than frighten users with misleading propaganda. It can be ordered through ads seen in *MuscleMag International.*

***Anabolic Reference Guide*; Bill Phillips** – One of the most thorough guides ever written on anabolic steroids, this book is written by Bill Phillips, publisher of the ground-breaking bodybuilding magazine *Muscle Media*. Like Dan Duchaine before him (who incidently is a major contributor to *Muscle Media*), Bill set out to provide the bodybuilder with the most practical information available regarding anabolic steroid use. Earlier in its production run, individuals who ordered the book also received regular updates that covered the latest in ergogenesis. The updates became so popular that Bill turned them into the previously mentioned *Muscle Media* magazine. The book itself has been updated frequently throughout the years and the latest, *Anabolic Reference Guide 1996* is available from Bill's company, Mile High Publishing.

***The Steroid Bible*; Bell International, Santa Barbara California** – This limited-run book was designed primarily for users of ergogenic drugs, although it also covers information on legal supplements. The book is not believed to be currently in production and its limited success was probably due to competition from other authors like Bill Phillips, Dan Duchaine, and Dr. Mauro DiPasquale.

***Ultimate Steroid Manual* and *Steroid Protection: The Facts!*; Cambridge Ergogenic Institute, Cambridge, MA** – Both these books were frequently advertised in the pages of *MuscleMag International* in the early 1990s. Like many similar "how to" books, pressure from antisteroid groups led to the cancellation of their advertising in the mid 1990s. Although primarily designed for the user, these little books contain a wealth of information concerning anabolic steroids and related drugs.

***Gray Market Supplement Guide* and *Muscle Pharmaceuticals*; Cambridge Ergogenic Institute, Cambridge, MA** – These books are Cambridge Institute's latest works. Not wanting to be left behind in the ergogenic-aid revolution, Cambridge Institute upgraded their previous publications, focusing less on "how to" and more on hardcore scientific information. Of course to satisfy the user element, they also provide the latest drugs and drug cycles. Finally, they explore the latest in legal ergogenesis, with a special emphasis on legal supplements that have what they call a "grey" area.

***Anabolic Steroids: What Kind and How Many*; Fred Hatfield** – Written by well-known bodybuilding writer, Fred Hatfield, PhD, this small book was one of the first to provide users with practical advice on using anabolic steroids in a safe manner. Like Dr. Mauro DiPasquale, Dr. Hatfield doesn't condone steroid use, but realizes that some individuals are going to use them irregardless of the attempts made to persuade otherwise. With his powerlifting background and extensive involvement in the weightlifting field, Dr. Hatfield offers insights into steroid use that many others can't. For this reason his book is popular with competitive athletes.

***Anabolic Steroids and Sports, Volumes I and II*; James E. Wright, PhD** – One of the first books to treat steroids as a legitimate scientific subject, Dr. Wright has written extensively on drug use in sports. Besides bodybuilding publications, Dr. Wright's articles have appeared in numerous medical journals. Unlike Dr. Goldman's *Death In The Locker Room* which appeared around the same time, *Anabolic Steroids and Sports* takes an unbiased look at steroids and presents the medical evidence in a relatively frank manner.

***Anabolic Steroids and the Athlete* and *Hormonal Manipulation*; William N. Taylor, MD** – It is a pity these books aren't receiving the coverage of some of the other books we've reviewed, as both contain a wealth of information. Besides being a medical doctor, Will Taylor is an avid bodybuilder, and as such can easily relate to athletes using performance-enhancing drugs. Like Dr. Wright, Dr. Taylor based much of his writing on medical fact not propaganda.

***Anabolic Steroids and Bodybuilding, In Quest of Size* and *Human Growth Hormone*; L & S Research** – All three of these books were frequently seen advertised in the pages of *Muscle and Fitness* back in the mid to late 1980s. The first book, *Anabolic Steroids and Bodybuilding*, was similar to works by Dr. James Wright and Dr. Will Taylor, in that it relied heavily on medical references to objectively examine the phenomenom of anabolic steroid use. The second book, *In Quest Of Size*, is 100 pages long, and explores the various steroid drugs and their effects. Although useful as a general reference guide, the book was aimed primarily at users. The third, *Human Growth Hormone*, was one of the first books available to look at HGH use in bodybuilding.

***Anabolic Steroids and Drug-Free, Scientific Natural Alternatives*; Dr. Thomas Fahey** – This is one of the latest releases on ergogenesis. In a manner similar to Will Brink, Dr. Fahey touches on steroids and other illegal drugs, but, for the most part, the text explores natural means to boost athletic performance.

***Competitive Bodybuilding*; Joe Weider** – Although this book primarily focuses on training strategies for advanced bodybuilders, we mention it because it is one of the few books of its kind to include a chapter which takes an objective look at anabolic steroid use in bodybuilding. Following the, "You shouldn't use them, but if you do here's some tips" approach, Weider is to be commended for his honesty. Most bodybuilding instruction books either tell you steroids don't work or that they'll kill you in short order.

***MuscleMag International's Encyclopedia of Bodybuilding*; Phil Embleton and Gerard Thorne** – Like Weider's *Competitive Bodybuilding*, this work is primarily devoted to bodybuilding instruction. But since it contains two large chapters on steroids, nutrition, and supplements, we highly recommend it.

Beyond Training; **Dr. Melvin Williams** – This 216-page book takes an objective look at how athletes use performance-enhancing drugs. Unlike most books on steroids, this one is not aimed at bodybuilders but sports in general. In addition it focuses more on "what they are" rather than "how do I use them." For these reasons the text is also applicable to coaches, instructors, and anyone wishing to know more about performance-enhancing drugs.

Unethical Dieter's Handbook and ***Anabolic/Pharmaceutical Athlete's Handbook***; **A.V.I. Publishing, Monrovia, California** – These handbooks were advertised in the pages of *MuscleMag International* back in the mid 1990s. The *Unethical Dieter's Handbook* is a guide to supplements and drugs used by bodybuilders to achieve the "ripped" condition on contest day. The *Pharmaceutical Athlete's Handbook* is a traditional "how to" book on performance-enhancing drugs. While coaches and those with a general interest in drugs will find the book useful, it is primarily aimed at those who actually use the drugs.

RECOMMENDED BODYBUILDING MAGAZINES

Given the ever-changing world of bodybuilding magazines, there's no way we can present all the publications as the list changes almost every month. The following are the ones that have, for the most part, stood the test of time. While some are devoted almost entirely to ergogenesis all contain information on the latest state-of-the-art supplements.

Muscle and Fitness – Published by Joe Weider, this top-selling bodybuilding magazine was formerly called *Muscle Builder/Power*. Since Joe introduced *Flex* magazine back in the mid 1980s, *Muscle and Fitness* now caters more to those who use bodybuilding as a form of fitness rather than those with competitive aspirations.

Flex – The "hardcore" younger brother of *Muscle and Fitness* magazine, *Flex* was developed to satisfy the competitive element among the bodybuilding public. Besides the regular articles on ergogenic supplements, *Flex* contains a section called "Drug World" which discusses the latest research concerning bodybuilding drugs. This segment is so successful because all the articles are based on medical studies which are fully referenced.

Ironman – Published by well-known bodybuilding writer John Balik, *Ironman* is one of bodybuilding's oldest publications. Like *MuscleMag International*, *Ironman* caters to all sectors of the bodybuilding spectrum – from general fitness to hardcore training. One of *Ironman's* biggest selling points is the regular features that explore the latest in ergogenic aids.

Muscle Media– Published by Bill Phillips of Mile High Publishing, *Muscle Media* grew out of Bill's *Anabolic Reference Guide* updates, and has established itself as the source for the latest in ergogenesis. With steroid "guru" Dan Duchaine as a major contributor, *Muscle Media* has carved out a significant niche for itself in the bodybuilding world. One of the magazine's biggest selling points is its approach to dealing with bodybuilding drugs and supplements. In short, if the supplement has few merits, the staff at *Muscle*

Media pull no punches in saying so. Although containing no contest coverage and few training "secrets" of the sport's major stars, *Muscle Media* has shaken up the bodybuilding world like few others. Most of the other bodybuilding publications have followed *Muscle Media's* lead and added extra columns and articles on ergogenesis.

Muscular Development – Published by Advanced Research Press, *Muscular Development* is another magazine primarily aimed at the hardcore bodybuilder. Like *Ironman* and *MuscleMag*, *Muscular Development* carries a mixture of training articles, contest coverage, and the latest in bodybuilding supplements and drugs. To their credit, *Muscular Development,* for the most part, references all scientific articles.

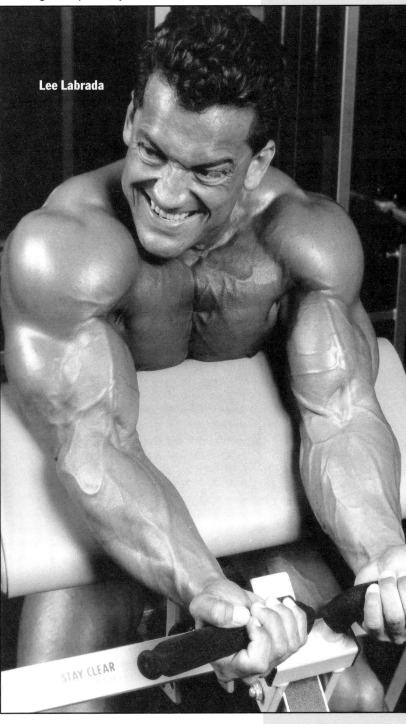

Lee Labrada

MuscleMag International – Created and published by Robert Kennedy, *MuscleMag* has risen from relative obscurity to become one of the most dominant bodybuilding publications in the world. Besides carrying the latest contest coverage and training articles, *MuscleMag* was one of the first publications to take an unbiased stance on drug use in bodybuilding. Others either ignored it or preached propaganda. *MuscleMag* was also one of the few (and probably the last) bodybuilding magazines to carry ads for books on the how-to-use illegal ergogenic aids. Each month such writers as Dr. Mauro DiPasquale, Will Brink, John Parrillo, and Mick Hart convey the latest information on egogenesis to readers. It was a combination of responses to such information and feedback from *MuscleMag International's Encyclopedia of Bodybuilding* that led to the publication of this book.

Glossary

Acromegaly – one of the side effects attributed to excessive amounts of growth hormone. The condition is characterized by a thickening of the ends of the bones, particularly in the forehead and elbows.

Adaptogens – group of substances reputed to offer the body varying degrees of protection against internal and external stressors. Although slow to catch on in North America, athletes in the former Soviet Union have being using them for years.

Addiction – condition where the body becomes so accustomed to a given drug that it can no longer function properly without it. Addiction may be physical or psychological in nature, and breaking the addiction usually involves a short period of withdrawal where the body readjusts to its predrug state.

Adenosine triphosphate (ATP) – the body's chief energy source during cellular respiration. During periods of increased energy requirements, ATP is broken down into adenosine diphosphate (ADP) and phosphate (P).

Agonist – pharmacological term used to describe a drug that stimulates receptors to produce a given biochemical response.

Amino acids – often called the "building blocks of life," amino acids are subunits that join together in sequences to form protein. Amino acids are named as such because they contain both an acid and an amine chemical side unit.

Anabolic – chemical reaction in the body where smaller subunits are combined to form larger units. As an example, amino acids are joined together to form long polypeptide chains which in turn join to form strands of protein.

Anabolic steroids – name given to the group of drugs developed to mimic the anabolic effects of the naturally occurring hormone testosterone. Anabolic steroids are by far the most popular performance-enhancing drugs.

Androgenic – term used to describe one of the two primary catagories of effects produced by such agents as anabolic steroids and testosterone. Androgenic effects include acne, increased facial hair, and the development of secondary sex characteristics.

Antagonist – pharmacological term used to describe a drug that blocks or shuts down a receptor, thus reducing or terminating a given biochemical response.

Anticatabolic drugs – class of drugs that halt or slow down the wasting effects of catabolic hormones such as cortisol.

Antidiuretic hormone (ADH) – hormone produced by the posterior pituitary responsible for fluid and mineral conservation in the mammalian body. Bodybuilders often take ADH blockers to promote water loss in the days leading up to a bodybuilding contest.

Antioxidants – group of substances reputed to neutralize harmful free radicals produced during cellular respiration.

Arthritis – an inflammation of the tissues surrounding the bone joints. There are two types of arthritis; osteoarthritis produced by the daily wear and tear on connective tissue; and rheumatoid arthritis caused by an inflammation of the joint-synovial membranes.

Beta agonists – class of drugs that stimulate the beta adrenoreceptors. Beta agonists are popularly used by bodybuilders to promote fat loss.

Biological value (BV) – scale of measurement used to determine what percentage of a given nutrient source is utilized by the body. The scale is most frequently applied to protein sources, particularly whey protein.

Blocking agents – general term used by athletes to describe any class of drugs or substances that prevent a banned substance from being detected in a drug test. In recent years such agents have declined in popularity since most sports federations have added them to their list of banned substances.

BMR (short for Basil Metabolic Rate) – the speed at which the resting body consumes energy (calories).

Buffering agents – any group of substances used to reduce the acidity caused by the build-up of lactic acid during intense exercise.

Carbohydrate – a molecule composed of carbon, hydrogen, and oxygen. It serves as the body's primary short-term fuel source.

Catabolic – chemical reactions in the body where larger units are broken down into smaller subunits. As an example, muscle tissue may be broken down into protein strands which, in turn, may be cleaved into individual amino acids.

Catheterization – an extreme method of passing a drug test whereby the athlete – usually male – injects "clean" urine into his bladder by way of a long thin hose called a catheter.

Circadian rhythm – daily cycles of bodily function, commonly called the biological clock.

Cocktailing – slang term used by athletes to refer to the practice of taking as many different performance-enhancing drugs as possible.

Corticosteroids – class of hormones that are catabolic in nature. Corticosteroids like adrenalin and cortisol are released in response to internal and external stressors, one of which is exercise.

Cycling – the practice of alternating periods of drug use with periods of abstinence. Cycling is believed to allow the body to readjust to its predrug state, thus reducing the risk of developing severe side effects.

Dehydration – biological state where the body has insufficient water levels for proper functioning. As the human body is over 90 percent water, athletes must continuously replenish the water lost during intense exercise.

Delivery method – the route of administration of a given drug or supplement. The most common delivery methods are oral (mouth) and injection (needle).

Depressants – class of drugs that slow down the central nervous system. Although not technically performance-enhancing drugs, many athletes use depressants to relax between competitions and training.

Diuretics – class of drugs used by athletes to decrease water conservation. Body-builders use diuretics to increase muscular definition and separation. Unfortunately, besides fluid loss, diuretics also flush life-sustaining electrolytes from the body.

Electrolytes – charged atoms called ions which help regulate the body's various metabolic systems. Athletes regularly consume drinks enriched with electrolytes such as potassium, calcium, and sodium to replace those lost in sweat.

Electrostimulation – muscle-stimulation technique involving the use of a low-voltage electric current. Although of limited use in physiotherapy, the technique's merits as an ergogenic aid are questionable.

Epinephrine (also called adrenaline) – this hormone, produced by the adrenal medulla, initiates the "flight or fight" response, preparing the body to deal with a stressful event. Athletes often use the hormone as a thermogenic drug because one of the side effects is fat mobilization.

Ergogenic aids – all-encompassing term used to describe any substance that enhances athletic performance. It comes from the Greek *ergo* to work, and *genesis* the beginning.

Essential amino acids – the nine amino acids that cannot be manufactured by the body and must be consumed in the diet.

Estrogen – one of the two primary sex hormones of the female body – the other being progesterone. In males excess testosterone is converted to estrogen often leading to the condition of gynecomastia.

Fat – a high-energy molecule which provides the body with long-term fuel reserves. Fat also serves as a precursor for many hormones and offers the body varying degrees of insulation and cushioning.

Feedback control – process by which the body's hormonal systems monitor their own levels of circulating hormones.

Free radicals – electrically charged particles produced during cellular respiration. Although not fully understood, it is believed a build-up of free radicals leads to a gradual decline in health (known as aging).

Genetic engineering – the science of manipulating an organism's predetermined genetic code at the DNA level. Genetic engineering allows for variations that otherwise would not be possible by natural reproductive means.

Glandulars – group of supplements derived from the dehydration of animal organs and glands. They are reputed to work by stimulating the corresponding organ or gland in humans. As a group, glandulars are among the most worthless of supplements.

Glycogenesis – the biochemical process by which glucose is converted into glycogen.

Glycogenolysis – the biochemical process by which the liver converts stored glycogen back into glucose for use as a fuel.

Growth hormone – peptide hormone secreted by the pituitary gland responsible for the repair and growth of tissues such as bones, muscles, and organs. In recent years growth hormone has become one of the most popular agents used by professional bodybuilders.

Gynecomastia – condition in males caused by an excess of testosterone or an excess of a testosterone-derived agent. When it becomes converted (aromatized) to estrogen the excess estrogen stimulates receptors in the nipple area leading to a swelling which resembles female breasts. The condition is commonly called "bitch tits." The condition is often severe enough to warrant surgical removal.

Hormone – chemical messenger released by an endocrine gland that travels to a target organ and produces a given response. Hormones may be steroid or peptide in nature.

Hormonal manipulation – the practice of altering the body's hormonal systems to increase or decrease a given physiological effect. Such alterations allow athletes to achieve performance levels far beyond those possible by normal means.

Implants – the use of artificial prosthetics – usually silicone – to increase the size of a given bodypart. In males the calves and chest are the most frequent targets of implants while in females the breasts are the usual site.

Insulin – hormone produced by the pancreas which controls the blood's level of glucose and amino acids.

Kreb's cycle (also called the citric acid cycle) – this complex biochemical pathway is the body's primary method for producing ATP.

Lactic Acid – a product given off during aerobic respiration. Lactic acid was once thought to be strictly a waste product, however recent evidence suggests that a version of lactic acid called lactate is used by the liver to replenish glycogen supplies.

Liposuction – surgical technique where fat cells are removed by vacuuming. Originally limited to extremely obese individuals, the procedure has become popular with the mainstream population.

Masculinization – general term used to describe the host of side effects experienced by female users of anabolic steroids. Common effects include deepening of the voice, facial hair growth, and clitoral enlargement.

Medium – term used to describe the substance that a given injectable drug is disolved or suspended in. Most anabolic drugs are suspended in either an oil-based or water-based solution.

Megadosing – the practice of taking athletic drugs and supplements in dosages far beyond those needed to obtain a desired effect.

Metabolic optimizer – general term used to describe any supplement that boosts an athlete's recovery system. Most metabolic optimizers contain a substance that is reputed to offer some degree of performance enhancement.

Metabolism – the sum total of all biochemical reactions that take place in the human body. Metabolism can be divided into anabolism and catabolism, the sum total of which determines whether an individual gains or loses weight.

Mineral – a naturally occurring inorganic element used for the regulation of metabolism.

Neurotransmitters – chemicals released into the clefts between nerve cells in order to carry nerve signals within the brain.

Nostrum – ancient term used to describe any blend or concoction made by the person who recommends it. Despite the term's age, it is applicable to modern supplement advertising.

Painkillers – class of drugs used to nullify the sensation of pain. Painkillers range from mild forms (aspirin), to powerful agents (morphine).

Peptide – term used to describe any substance which is protein in nature and composed of sequences of amino acids. Polypeptide chains join together to form protein strands.

Peptide growth factors – peptide-derived hormone-like substances that promote growth and tissue repair. In athletic circles, a peptide growth factor called insulin-like growth factor-1 (IGF-1) has become one of the most popular agents added to drug stacks.

Placebo effect – pharmacological term used to describe the effects produced by an inert (inactive) substance. Often called "mind over matter," the placebo effect is used to explain the positive actions of many supplements which are in many cases nothing more than nutrients.

Polypharmacology – term first coined by Dr. Mauro DiPasquale to describe the bodybuilding practice of simultaneously stacking numerous performance-enhancing drugs.

Positive nitrogen balance – biochemical state where nitrogen levels are sufficiently high enough to allow protein synthesis to occur. Positive nitrogen balance is one of the conditions accelerated by anabolic steroids.

Prostaglandins – hormone-like substances made from fatty acids in plasma membranes which control such processes as digestion and cardiovascular functioning.

Protein – general term used to describe molecules that are composed of specific sequences of amino acids. Protein is the body's primary building material and while small amounts can be manufactured, most must be consumed in the diet.

Receptor – point or location on a target cell that serves as the attachment point for a given drug. Receptors are generally specific for only one class of drugs.

Roid rage – popular name given to the uncontrollable outburst of anger and violence exhibited by anabolic steroid users. Despite never being proven by the medical community, the term is continuously exaggerated by the mainstream media.

Saturated fatty acids – fat molecules that do not have double bonds between their carbon atoms and are usually solid at room temperature. Saturated fats are considered to play a major role in the development of cardiovascular disease.

Shotgunning – another term used to describe the practice of consuming megadoses of multiathletic drugs. For many athletes the limiting factor on drug use is cost.

Snake oil – This is a general term used to describe any supplement or concoction that doesn't give the same degree of results as claimed by its advertisers. It originated with traveling carnivals back in the 1800s.

Stacking – the practice of taking two or more performance-enhancing drugs at one time. The actual drugs, combinations, and dosages are known as a stack.

Steroid – biochemical term used to denote a molecule having three, 6 carbon-containing rings, and one, 5 carbon-containing ring. Steroid molecules form the nucleus of many of the body's hormones.

Steroid replacer – general term used to describe any naturally occurring substance that supposedly duplicates the effects of anabolic steroids. As of yet no "steroid replacer" is as effective as any anabolic drug.

Stimulants – class of drugs that increase or excite the central nervous system. Stimulants may be mild (ephedrine), or powerful (amphetamines).

Supplement – any substance that is taken above and beyond the nutrients obtained in the daily diet. Most supplements are nothing more than nutrients, but a few do enhance physical performance.

Synergism – the biochemical phenomenom where two or more drugs interact to produce an effect that is greater than the effects of the individual drugs. In bodybuilding terms, growth hormone and IGF-1 taken seperately produce limited results, but when taken together produce dramatic increases in size and strength.

Testosterone – the primary male sex hormone. Females also have testosterone, though in low concentrations, which has led it to being termed a "male" hormone. Most anabolic steroids are derivatives of testosterone.

Thermogenesis – process by which stored fat is liberated and mobilized so that it can be burned as a fuel source. The most popular bodybuilding thermogenic agents are ephedrine and caffeine.

Thyroid gland – small gland located in the neck that controls the body's level of calcium and overall metabolic rate. Bodybuilders often add thyroid drugs to their precontest drug stacks to increase their body's metabolic rate and increase the rate of fat loss.

Unsaturated fatty acids – fat molecules which have double bonds between their carbon atoms and are usually liquid at room temperature. Generally speaking, as the number of double bonds increase, the fat becomes more oily in nature.

Vitamin – organic compound used by the body to regulate metabolism. Vitamins may be water-based or fat-based.

Index

Photo Index

Contributing Photographers

Josef Adlt, Jim Amentler, Alex Ardenti, Doris Barrilleaux, Garry Bartlett,
John A. Butler, Paula Crane, Ralph DeHaan, Bill Dobbins, Irvin Gelb,
Kevin Horton, Robert Kennedy, Jason Mathas, Mitsuru Okabe,
Rick Schaff, Art Zeller